THE COLLECTED WORKS
OF W. B. YEATS

VOLUME III

THE COLLECTED WORKS OF W. B. YEATS

Richard J. Finneran and George Mills Harper, *General Editors*

W. B. YEATS

Autobiographies

EDITORS

William H. O'Donnell
and
Douglas N. Archibald

ASSISTANT EDITORS

J. Fraser Cocks III and Gretchen Schwenker

Designed by Jennifer Dossin
Set in Sabon

Printed and bound in Great Britain by
Antony Rowe Ltd, Chippenham and Eastbourne

Library of Congress Cataloging-in-Publication Data is available.

ISBN 0-333-99046-3
Outside North America

CONTENTS

EDITORS' PREFACE

In 1938, Mrs. Yeats told her husband, '"AE was the nearest to a saint you or I will ever meet. You are a better poet but no saint. I suppose one has to choose"' (L 838). It is a distinction Yeats seems to have already endorsed in these lines from 'The Choice', written in 1931:

> The intellect of man is forced to choose
> Perfection of the life, or of the work,
> And if it take the second must refuse
> A heavenly mansion, raging in the dark. (P 246)

But Yeats rarely makes simple choices, presenting us instead with a career of vacillations, of attempts—always willful, sometimes heroic—to have it both ways. No less than Keats, he thought that the poet leads a life of allegory and that his works are comments on it. Before comment, and as part of the process of perfection, comes transformation. He explained, in the 'First Principles' section of his 'Introduction' to his works, written in 1937:

> A poet writes always of his personal life, in his finest work out of its tragedies, whatever it be, remorse, lost love, or mere loneliness; he never speaks directly as to someone at the breakfast table, there is always a phantasmagoria. Dante and Milton had mythologies, Shakespeare the characters of English history, or of traditional romance; even when the poet seems most himself, when he is Raleigh and gives potentates the lie, or Shelley 'a nerve o'er which do creep the else unfelt oppressions of mankind', or Byron when 'the soul wears out the breast as the sword wears out the sheath', he is never the bundle of accident and incoherence that sits down to breakfast; he has been re-born as an idea, something intended, complete. (LE 204)

Autobiographies invites us to attend to that rebirth, to the process by which accident and incoherence become complete, by which life, passing through phantasmagoria, becomes meaning, and experience becomes myth. It is that great Romantic achievement: a vision of personal history as art, and *Autobiographies* is the essential companion to the poems and plays. It shows Yeats at work—summoning his people, realizing his places, making a world—and so continues to dramatize and fulfill his belief that the act of writing entails a complex creation of a self. He had made the point in that bold youthful quatrain about revisions:

> The friends that have it I do wrong
> When ever I remake a song,
> Should know what issue is at stake:
> It is myself that I remake. (P 551)

Autobiographies is an allusive and illusive book. Yeats is not careful about details, dates, and references. It is difficult to escape the impression that he is wholly dependable about what is happening to and in his imagination, and how exciting it is, and not fully dependable about anything else. We are convinced that Yeats knew what he was about; like Stephen Dedalus in *Ulysses,* he knew that this wonderful, shrewd, intimate book would ultimately reside 'in all the great libraries of the world, including Alexandria'; both writers enjoyed the sense that they were creating projects for future generations of scholars. This is the first edition to take up that challenge by providing a full set of explanatory notes. The 1,003 notes are marked in the text by superscript numbers; the notes are printed on pages 419–527. Those notes selectively include particularly interesting excerpts from earlier versions of revised passages.

Explanatory notes are not used for simple, straightforward mentions of the name of a person, place, organization, or historical event, or of the title of a book, play, poem, or story. Instead, those names and titles are described with 1,500 augmented entries in the index. Those augmented entries provide a person's name, birth and death dates, nationality, and profession; for books or other texts, the augmented entries identify the author, genre, and date. The page references in the index will lead the reader to any other occurrences in the text or notes.

The eighteen notes written by Yeats are printed among the explanatory notes, flagged with the heading 'WBY'S NOTE'. If the note was added later or was revised or omitted in any printing, that is mentioned. Explanatory notes to Yeats's notes are marked by superscript letters and are printed immediately following his note.

In *Estrangement* and *The Death of Synge,* each of the ninety-six sections is headed with a brief statement of its dating in the manuscript and a cross-reference to the manuscript transcription in *Memoirs.* For abbreviations of names and titles, see the List of Abbreviations, pages 33–36 below.

Background Notes on Writers, pages 531–539 below, provides a concise introduction to twenty writers who were important to Yeats but who receive only comparatively brief mention in *Autobiographies.*

DA WHO

TEXTUAL INTRODUCTION

Yeats assembled *Autobiographies* from a half-dozen separately published works, so an editor's first task is to establish the contents, sequence, and titles to be used. Here we can turn to direct evidence from WBY, Mrs. Yeats, and Thomas Mark (1890–1963), the Macmillan editor in London on whom WBY relied and who worked with WBY's books from the 1920s through the 1950s, coming back from semi-retirement to work on *Autobiographies* (1955). Yeats, Mrs. Yeats, and Thomas Mark all worked on the 1932/1936 corrected page proofs of the Macmillan 'Edition de Luxe', volume VI, *Autobiographies* (NLI Ms. 30,140), which is the last complete text of *Autobiographies* approved by the author. *Autobiographies* (1955) used the same contents, sequence, and titles as the 1932/1936 proofs, as does the present edition.

If the Macmillan Edition de Luxe had reached publication, it would have been the obvious choice as the copy-text for this edition, since it was the latest version approved by the author. The only portion of *Autobiographies* that was not in the 12 July 1932 corrected page proofs was *Dramatis Personae* (1936), and for that the same set of Edition de Luxe volume VI materials (NLI Ms. 30,140) contains corrected page proofs of *Dramatis Personae* (1936) that WBY did not himself see, but which he and Mrs. Yeats authorized Thomas Mark to correct on his behalf.

The editor's task is to bring those Edition de Luxe proofs to final publishable form. Those proofs were first marked in 1932 and, in part, in 1936. The same set of proofs may have been worked on again in 1939, and certainly was used in the 1950s to prepare *Auto-biographies* (1955). The extant documentary evidence is not suffi-cient to allow confident determination of which markings were made, and by whom, in the 1950s. The Macmillan, London, office files for the 1950s are not extant, and reportedly were destroyed. That difficulty is mitigated to a considerable extent by the knowl-edge that the changes made in the 1950s were supervised by

Thomas Mark, who still had at least some access to Mrs. Yeats. The editorial changes introduced in *Autobiographies* (1955) thus can be regarded as a continuation of the correction process evident on the 1932/1936 proofs for volume VI of the Edition de Luxe. But we cannot ignore the significance of one capricious verbal revision during the somewhat similar production of Macmillan's *Essays and Introductions* (1961), where the word 'important' in its 1959 page proofs was replaced by 'famous' to shorten a line and avoid hyphenation (see LE xi). Thus it is not possible to state that if WBY had come back from the grave in 1955 he would have approved all of the 1950s editorial changes. It is clear, however, that those revisions were supervised by a very highly qualified editor and were, in the main, made to bring the 1932/1936 Edition de Luxe volume VI proofs to a smooth, publishable form. *Autobiographies* (1955) thus is the best available basis for a text of *Autobiographies*.

The practical result has been that this edition uses the text of *Autobiographies* (1955), with only thirteen emendations to the 156,000 words of text and three emendations to WBY's notes. Those sixteen changes, which are listed on page 528 below, consist of four corrections of printer's errors, the addition of one apostrophe, nine instances of hyphenation or word-division, and two trivial changes of format. The copy-text's errors of names, dates, and quotations have been left standing, but are pointed out in the notes. Similarly, two errors by the typist who transcribed the manuscript are mentioned in notes (5 and 7, p. 481) but are not corrected in the text because WBY let them stand in all printings.

Instances where the copy-text uses old spelling such as 'subtil' (note 57, p. 475 below) for 'subtle' or usage such as 'my Catholic acquaintance adapt their ancient rules' have been left unemended, as are wordings in which the sense is retrievable, though perhaps with some effort, as 'and all that he may get their ears' (p. 229, l. 5–6 below) where the meaning is 'and all [so] that he may get their ears'. The reader is invited to be patient and recall Aubrey Beardsley's remark quoted by WBY: 'Yes, yes; but beauty is so difficult' (p. 255, l. 27 below).

All ellipses in the text are authorial. All hyphens that occur within a line in this edition are authorial. No hyphens at line divisions in this edition are authorial, except for seventy-three instances in which an authorial hyphen happens to occur ambiguously at a line division in this edition; those are identified, for convenience, in the appended 'End-of Line Word-Division', which also gives a list of the sixty-six instances of end-of-line word-division in the copy-text that could possibly affect hyphenation.

In the headings of diary entries in *Estrangement* and *The Death of Synge,* when the copy-text provides a heading with place and/or date, those are printed at the left margin, set in italics in upper- and lower-case letters, and end without punctuation.

The following typographical and format conventions are silently adopted in each prose volume of *The Collected Edition of W. B. Yeats:*

1 The presentation of headings is standardized. In this volume, the main headings are set in full capitals (capitals and small capitals for subtitles), and include brief details of date and source (for fuller bibliographical information, see the Textual Introduction and List of Abbreviations). Section numbers, except in the diary entries in *Estrangement* and *The Death of Synge,* are in roman capitals. All headings are centered and have no concluding full point.

2 The opening line of each paragraph is indented, except following a displayed heading or section break.

3 British single quotation mark conventions are used in the text and in WBY's notes.

4 A colon that introduces a quotation is not followed by a dash.

5 Except in headings, the titles of stories and poems are placed within quotation marks; titles of books, plays, long poems, periodicals, operas, statues, paintings, and drawings are set in italics.

6 Abbreviations such as 'i.e.' are set in roman type.

7 A dash—regardless of its length in the copy-text—is set as a spaced em rule when used as punctuation. When a dash indicates an omission, as in 'J——', a two-em rule is used.

8. Ampersands are expanded to 'and'.

9. Each signature of the author is indented from the left margin, set in upper- and lower-case letters, and ends without punctuation; when present, the place and date are indented from the left margin, set in italics in upper- and lower-case letters, and end without punctuation.

*   *   *

The remainder of this introduction is an account of the history of the composition and printing of the constituent parts of *Autobiographies*, treated in the order they were written, rather than by their sequence in *Autobiographies*. Curtis Bradford's early study of some of these materials remains useful (*Yeats at Work*, pages 337–77), as is Conrad Balliet's *W. B. Yeats: A Census of the Manuscripts* (New York: Garland, 1990) with the supplement in *Yeats: An Annual of Critical and Textual Studies,* 13 (1995), 125–200. J. Fraser Cock's long series of collations for the present edition has been invaluable.

The earliest writing incorporated in *Autobiographies* is from WBY's journal from 1909, plus a few passages from 1911–14, although they were written as journal entries and were not selected and adapted for publication until nearly two decades later in *Estrangement* (1926) and *The Death of Synge* (1928).

The beginning of *Autobiographies* comes, as might be expected, with *Reveries over Childhood and Youth*, written as *Memory Harbour* and published in 1916. In a letter to his sister Lily Yeats, 28 July (1914), WBY explained, 'I have all but finished the first draft of a book called *Memory Harbour* after a picture of Jack's'—a small watercolor painted in 1900 by their younger brother, Jack Yeats, who presented it to WBY after it had been exhibited in Dublin in 1900 and London in 1901; for a description see page 72 and note 109, p. 427. The letter continues, 'It is about my life up to twenty & most of it is about Sligo. . . . It is not autobiography in the ordinary sense, but reveries about the past' (transcription John Kelly). The book was listed by the Cuala Press as *Memory Harbour: A Revery on my Childhood and Youth,* but by February 1915 its title had changed because, as a Cuala Press advertisement in that month explained, the 'title has been used before, so Mr. Yeats has altered the title to "Reveries over Childhood and Youth"' (laid in *A Broadside*). For the title change and Filson Young's *Memory Har-*

bour (London: Grant Richards, 1909), see Warwick Gould, 'Titles of Yeats's *Autobiographies'*, *Yeats Annual*, 11 (1995), 205–18. A complete manuscript titled 'Biography' and dated 'Xmas 1914' is at Colby College, Waterville, Maine; it has some typescript inserts and some manuscript inserts dictated to Ezra Pound at Stone Cottage (NLI Ms. 30,868). Three other typescripts (one ribbon copy and two carbons), each with light corrections are extant (HRC Texas, University of Tulsa, and Houghton Library, Harvard). The proposed title 'Memory Harbour' is not used in the manuscript or in the corrected complete typescript, which is titled with a singular form, *A Reverie over Childhood and Youth,* from which *Reveries* Cuala 1916 was set. The singular title is printed on the first page of the Cuala Press book (Wade no. 111). But by the time the compositor had reached the colophon, the title had shifted to the plural form used on the front cover, title page, and colophon. That plural title, *Reveries over Childhood and Youth,* has continued in all subsequent printings. The Cuala Press book was finished October 1915 and published 20 March 1916, with a portfolio of illustrations featuring a color plate of *Memory Harbour.* The Macmillan, London, edition followed in October 1916, with Jack Yeats's painting as a color frontispiece (Wade no. 113 and New York, no. 112).

In late 1915, WBY told his father, 'I am going on with the book', picking up the narrative in 1887, where *Reveries* had left off. But, he added, 'the rest shall be for my eye alone' (L 603). Bradford, who in 1954–55 studied the manuscript of 168, incompletely paginated, loose-leaf sheets, now in the Burns Library, Boston College, has convincingly dated its composition as 1915–16. The manuscript is titled 'Autobiography', but is now better known by the description that WBY wrote in March 1921 on its envelope: 'Private. A first rough draft of Memoirs made in 1916–17 and containing much that is not for publication now, if ever. Memoirs down to 1896 or thereabouts.' A smooth transcription by Denis Donoghue was published, with useful notes, as *Memoirs* in 1972; that edition also gives the full text of the journal from which WBY selected the excerpts he published in 1926 as *Estrangement* and in 1928 as *The Death of Synge.* The 'First Draft' manuscript is a franker and more personal treatment of parts of *The Trembling of the Veil,* written 1920–22 and a portion of *Dramatis Personae,* written much later, in 1934. Bradford in 1954–55 tried to sort the loose sheets by their four slightly different types of paper and concluded that WBY probably first wrote an account of his relations with Maud Gonne, whom he had met 30 January 1889, and then added the other, interspersed parts. The 'First Draft' resembles *Reveries* in being a loosely unified, chronological narrative that offers little commentary on the actions.

We cannot know WBY's motivation for writing the 'First Draft', but he was only willing to invest enough effort to produce an unpolished text. He then set it aside for four years until, on 26 November (1920) he wrote to Lady Gregory, 'I have begun again work on my "Memoirs" for publication in I hope "The Dial". I shall do now 1887 to [say] 1897. It will be a study of my own generation more or less & I will stop before I get to "The Theatre" ' (Berg NYPL). In 1920, the American critical and literary journal *The Dial*, recently relocated from Chicago to New York, had set a bold new course to publish the highest quality work of both established and new writers and artists. In March 1920, its new editor began paying Ezra Pound $750 a year to find suitable works as their European agent; see Nicholas Joost, *Scofield Thayer and The Dial: An Illustrated History* (Carbondale and Edwardsville: Southern Illinois University Press, 1964), page 166. The next month, WBY's first contribution was published in the *Dial*, followed by eleven poems in November 1920. The first version of 'Four Years, 1887–1891', Book I of *The Trembling of the Veil*, exists in two successive complete manuscripts and associated stray pages (NLI Ms. 30,471, 30,472, 30,536), as well as the corrected typescripts for the *London Mercury* (Bodleian Library, Oxford, Ms. Don.C.187, fols. 42–114) and for the *Dial* (partial, Bienecke Library, Yale, Za Dial). It was published in three installments in the June, July, and August issues of the *London Mercury* and simultaneously in the *Dial*. Bradford (*Yeats at Work*, pages 350–56) suggests that when WBY wrote 'Four Years, 1887–1891', he began by reviewing the 'First Draft', but that except for one section on Maud Gonne, which he later deleted in the second manuscript of 'Four Years, 1887–1891', did not work directly from the 'First Draft' and that he was not rewriting the corresponding parts of the 'First Draft': 'The order of incidents is entirely different, much new material has been added, and there are few verbal echoes of the earlier work' (page 351). 'Four Years, 1887–1891', though less personally revealing, is considerably expanded in its treatment and, importantly, its ambitions now are less concerned with chronological narration than with commentary, analysis, and judgment. *The Trembling of the Veil* highlights recurring motifs such as his opposition to the dominance of science and realistic art. He is impelled to analyze and categorize persons and events in terms of his recently developed 'system' and its associated doctrines such as 'Unity of Being' and 'Unity of Culture'; see note 126, page 456.

WBY wrote to Lady Gregory on 10 June (1921) to tell her of an offer of £500 from T. Werner Laurie to publish a subscription edition of a volume of memoirs, of which 'Four Years 1887–1891' would constitute the opening one-third. WBY mentioned that he was receiving praise from readers of the magazine installments, and he reaffirmed that he planned to continue the memoirs 'down to the start of the theatre probably' (L 670). The terms of the contract for *The Trembling of the Veil* 1922 called for payment of £250 on delivery of the manuscript by June 1922, publication of the thousand copies within six months, and an exclusion of other editions for three years (L 669–70). And, in fact, WBY submitted the manuscript at the end of May 1922 (L 685), the book was published in October 1922 (Wade no. 133), and the Macmillan *Autobiographies* (Wade no. 151) was published more than four years later, on 5 November 1926.

In a letter to George Russell (AE), 1 July (1921), WBY described 'Four Years, 1887–1891' as a 20,000-word section 'of what will be a 60,000 word book'; he added that he doubted if he 'would have faced the whole book with a good heart, but for starting with the lesser task' (L 670). WBY was sensitive to the difficulty of writing frankly about living persons, but he also believed that 'the life of a man of genius because of his greater sincerity is often an experiment that needs analysis and record. At least my generation so valued personality that it thought so', as he explained in the preface, dated May 1922, to *The Trembling of the Veil* (page 111 below). In that letter, WBY promised to show Russell the as yet unwritten description of him and the mystics around him at the Ely Place house in Dublin (pages 194–202 below, in 'Ireland after Parnell'), and WBY assured him that he would 'publish nothing that you dislike' (L 670). On the other hand, the preface to *The Trembling of the Veil* ends: 'I have said all the good and all the evil: I have kept nothing back necessary to understanding' (page 111 below; WBY added the last three words when he read the page proofs). Similarly, a year after the letter to Russell, WBY gently prevaricated when he was worried that his friend Olivia Shakespear might be upset by his portrayal of her cousin Lionel Johnson in 'Ireland after Parnell' (pages 184–86 below), in the current issue of the *London Mercury* (June 1922, 144–46). He sought to excuse himself by mentioning that the magazine 'had had to shorten everything, to leave out everything mystical or startling to their readers for they only have space for 16,000 words of the 30,000 I sent them, so do not judge the memoirs as a whole till you get the book. It needs the wild mystical part to lift it out of gossip, and that mystical part will not be as clear as it should be for lack of diagrams and the like. Lady Gregory is in great enthusiasm over the book and it has already brought in much money' (L 685). In fact, there had been no cuts in the section on Lionel Johnson, though what WBY told her about the magazine abridgment was accurate.

WBY worked steadily on the next three parts of *The Trembling of the Veil*: 'Ireland after Parnell', 'Hodos Chameliontos', and 'The Tragic Generation'. He finished a description of Lionel Johnson (page 184), midway through 'Ireland after Parnell', on 1 August 1921 (L 671). A month earlier, in a letter to George Russell, WBY had announced the tentative title for the volume: 'I may call the book *The Trembling of the Veil* (Mallarmé said "The whole age is full of the trembling of the veil of the temple") but some better may occur.' That 1 July 1921 letter to Russell continued with a description of his current plans: 'You may perhaps have seen what the *London Mercury* has published [of 'Four Years, 1887–1891']. I shall insert [a] fresh chapter in that and lead up to the later part and my object will be to suggest, indirectly, things descriptive of characters and events in the main, and only here and there to directly state certain simple philosophical ideas about Ireland, and about human nature in general' (L 671). In the 1 August 1921 letter to Olivia Shakespear, WBY said more about his labors on 'Ireland after Parnell' and the benefits to be gained:

> I am mired in my propaganda in Ireland 1891-2-3-4, the years just before you and I met, and it is difficult as so much that is essential has to be left out. I am characterizing

Hyde, AE [George Russell], O'Grady, Lionel [Johnson]; and characterizing, without naming, my especial enemies, the Tower and wolf-dog, harp and shamrock, verdigris-green sectaries who wrecked my movement for the time. *Then I shall take up* London again, Wilde's collapse, *Savoy* etc, and pray that some imp of abundance brings all without strain up to the needed 60,000 words (20,000 have appeared in the *London Mercury*—though part a little cut down and despoiled of my best Blavatsky tale). I find this memoir writing makes me feel clean, as if I had bathed and put on clean linen. It rids me of something and I shall return to poetry with a renewed simplicity. Have you been reading me in the *Mercury?* I am afraid Ezra [Pound] will not forgive me for publishing there: he had recommended the *English Review* but I have just as fierce a quarrel with that periodical as he has with the *Mercury,* so what could I do? (L 672)

His deleted 'best Blavatsky tale' might simply be her jibe at her vegetarian disciples, 'My children, have you had any vegetarian babies?', which WBY himself had omitted from the second holograph manuscript of 'Four Years, 1887–1891' (Bradford, *Yeats at Work,* page 355). In December 1921, the Cuala Press republished the magazine version as *Four Years* (Wade no. 131), with two extended additions (page 146, line 30–page 147, line 13 and page 156, line 1–page 157, line 2, below), and occasional local revisions. When WBY sent a copy to Olivia Shakespear, 22 December 1921, he commented that this was the first third of 'the complete memoirs. As they go on they will grow less personal, or at least less adequate as personal representation, for the most vehement part of youth must be left out, the only part that one well remembers and lives over again in memory when one is in old age, the paramount part. I think this will give all the more sense of inadequateness from the fact that I study every man I meet at some moment of crisis—I alone have no crisis' (L 675).

Curtis Bradford gives a detailed reconstruction of the composition of the remaining sections of *The Trembling of the Veil:* 'Ireland after Parnell' (titled 'Ireland after the Fall of Parnell' only in *Trembling* 1922), 'Hodos Chameliontos' (titled 'Hodos Camelionis' only in *Trembling* 1922), 'The Tragic Generation,' and 'The Stirring of the Bones.'

As WBY mentioned to Olivia Shakespear in the letter quoted above, the periodical publication of these new materials as 'More Memories' in the *London Mercury* (May–August 1922) and the *Dial* in New York (May–October 1922) was an excerpt. It was complete for 'Ireland after Parnell' through what is now section XI, and was heavily cut from the middle of section XII on through 'Hodos Chameliontos' and 'The Tragic Generation,' ending with what is now its section X. In the periodical version, the section numbering is consecutive and no titles are used except 'More Memories'.

In the last week of May 1922, WBY finished and sent to the publisher, T. Werner Laurie, *The Trembling of the Veil*, which he described in a letter to John Quinn, to whom the volume is dedicated, as 'my book of memoirs'; WBY expected to receive the proofs by July 1922 (L 682). After the publication of *Trembling* 1922 (Wade no. 133) in October 1922, WBY published additional materials for 'The Stirring of the Bones', section VI, on 'The Vision of the Archer', in the *Criterion* (London) and the *Dial* (New York) in July 1923. Bradford (page 372) has pointed out two likely errors by the typist who transcribed WBY's manuscript of 'The Stirring of the Bones'; for the manuscript readings, which were never restored, see notes 5 and 7, page 481 below.

At the end of 1923, when WBY was awarded the Nobel Prize, he delivered a lecture titled 'The Irish Dramatic Movement', to the Royal Swedish Academy in Stockholm on 13 December 1923. The Nobel committee publishes laureates' lectures, and WBY, who claims to have spoken extemporaneously—although more probably from lecture notes as was often his practice—wrote out a version from memory after he returned to Dublin. That was published in 1924 in *Les Prix Nobel en 1923* (Wade no. 316), with four notes, and was also issued separately the same year, as *Les Prix Nobel en 1923: The Irish Dramatic Movement* (Wade no. 144). The lecture was reprinted, with two additional notes, the last of which is dated 15 June 1924, in the Cuala Press volume *The Bounty of Sweden: A Meditation, and a Lecture* (Wade no. 146) in July 1925. The lecture has been included in all subsequent editions of *Autobiographies* that contain *The Bounty of Sweden*, except the Macmillan, New

York, volume *The Autobiography of William Butler Yeats,* published 30 August 1938 (Wade no. 198) and its re-issue in 1953 (Wade no. 211G).

The main part of *The Bounty of Sweden* is what the book's title calls a 'meditation'. When WBY was writing it during January 1924, he described it as 'a sort of "bread and butter letter" to Sweden', and he explicitly made it 'at last a part of my autobiography' (L 701, 703). It is titled 'Stockholm: A Meditation' in the manuscript and revised typescript (NLI Ms. 30,288), which otherwise correspond closely to the Cuala printing, *The Bounty of Sweden,* which has a preface dated 15 June 1924 but was not published until July 1925. In the interim, it was published in the *London Mercury* and the *Dial* (New York) in September 1924. The Cuala edition incorporated some local revisions to the periodical text.

The three-year exclusive period for *The Trembling of the Veil* would expire October 1925, and prior to that the preparations began for the Macmillan *Autobiographies* (Wade no. 151), which would collect *Reveries over Childhood and Youth* and *The Trembling of the Veil.* On 29 April 1925, Macmillan, London, wrote to WBY's agent, A. P. Watt, asking about a possible sixth volume in their collected edition that had begun in November 1922 with *Later Poems* (Wade no. 134/135) and *Plays in Prose and Verse* (Wade no. 136/137), followed by *Plays and Controversies* (Wade no. 139/140) in November 1923, *Essays* (Wade no. 141/142) in May 1924, and *Early Poems and Stories* (Wade no. 147/148) in September 1925. The letter asks, 'Will you kindly let me know whether this volume is likely to mature, or whether Mr. Yeats has given up the idea of writing it? We should very much like to publish it as the sixth volume and include it in the series' (BL Add. Ms. 55618, fol. 211).

Macmillan received WBY's revised copy on 8 February 1926 (BL Add. Ms. 55631, fol. 148) and, after some delays from a general strike, sent him revised proofs in September 1926 (BL Add. Ms. 55641, fol. 309). When WBY returned the proofs on 30 September 1926, he suggested a revision to the title by inserting '*Autobiographies:*' before the proof's title *Reveries over Childhood and Youth. The Trembling of the Veil,* arguing persuasively, 'I think that it is a mistake to give the book no title except that of the two volumes contained in it, especially as you will have to call it for short by the name of the first which happens to be the least successful. I have therefore called the book *"Autobiographies"* and put the names of the two volumes as sub-title.' (BL Add. Ms. 55003, fol. 93).

Autobiographies was published 5 November 1926 in London; the New York edition (Wade no. 152) was published 25 January 1927 in a limited edition, followed two weeks later by the regular edition. *Autobiographies* incorporated the July 1923 addition of 'The Vision of the Archer' (pages 279–82 below), as well as three footnotes and a large number of local revisions throughout the book. Notable among those is a very slightly more dignified portrayal of MacGregor Mathers, who had died in 1918 and whose widow had objected to the 1922 version (see WBY's note 117, pages 453–55 below). After the mention of Mathers's drinking, WBY now added: 'It was in some measure a Scottish pose and whether he carried it into later life like his Jacobite opinions I do not know' (page 257 below). He replaced, with the text that now begins at page 258, line 5, a paragraph that had mentioned Mathers's skill at chess, his melancholia, and his insanity:

> War was to bring, or be brought by, anarchy, but that would be a passing stage, he declared, for his dreams were all Napoleonic. He certainly foresaw some great role that he could play, had made himself an acknowledged master of the war-game, and for a time taught it to French officers for his living. He was to die of melancholia, and was perhaps already mad at certain moments or upon certain topics, though he did not make upon me that impression in those early days, being generous, gay, and affable. (*Trembling* 1922, page 212)

The next step in the textual history of *Autobiographies* comes in 1932, as the projected volume VI of the never-published Macmillan 'Edition de Luxe'. In the interim, the Cuala Press had published three volumes that were to become part of *Autobiographies: The Bounty of Sweden* in 1925 and two adaptations of early diaries, *Estrangement* in 1926 and *The Death of Synge* in 1928, already discussed above. WBY had sent copy to Macmillan before mid-September 1931 and Macmillan had at one time planned to publish the seven-volume Edition de Luxe in spring 1932. *Autobiographies,* as volume VI of the Edition de Luxe, advanced to page proofs, date-stamped 12 July 1932 (NLI Ms. 30,140), that were set from *Autobiographies* 1926 and those three Cuala Press volumes. Macmillan sent WBY on 23 August 1932 'the complete proofs of Volume VI "*Autobiographies*", together with the copy from which it is set up, including the Cuala Press volumes of the two Diaries and "The Bounty of Sweden" ' (BL Add. Ms. 55371, fol. 569). WBY and, presumably, Mrs. Yeats read the proofs, but the Edition de Luxe then languished for a few years, victim of the economic and literary postponements that would eventually end it.

The last section of *Autobiographies* to be written was *Dramatis Personae,* first titled *Lady Gregory,* as WBY told Olivia Shakespear, 27 February (1934):

> I have come out of my reveries to write to you. I do nothing all day long but think of the drama I am building up in my *Lady Gregory.* I have drawn [Edward] Martyn and his house, Lady Gregory and hers, have brought George Moore upon the scene, finished a long analysis of him, which pictures for the first time this preposterous person. These first chapters are sensations and exciting and will bring George [Mrs. Yeats] much household money when she sends them out to English and American magazines. I am just beginning on Woburn Buildings, building up the scene there—alas the most significant image of those years [WBY's love affair with Olivia Shakespear] must be left out. This first part will probably be made up of extracts from letters to Lady Gregory and my comments. My first fifty pages—probably to be published before the rest—will bring me to about 1900. It is curious how one's life falls into definite sections—in 1897 a new scene was set, new actors appeared. (L 820)

Much of *Dramatis Personae* is a weaving together of his correspondence with Lady Gregory; the description of WBY's rooms at 18 Woburn Buildings comes in section IX. Whatever the plan was for early publication of an excerpt, it did not happen. The Cuala Press *Dramatis Personae* was set from an extensively revised typescript (NLI Ms. 30,601) that Bradford suggests (page 373) was dictated from a manuscript in the Houghton Library, Harvard. The Cuala Press volume was finished in the second week of October 1935 (an earlier proof of its colophon had read 'the last week of September 1935' NLI Ms. 30,029); it was published 9 December 1935 (Wade no. 183).

Even before the Cuala Press volume was officially published, WBY proposed a new volume to Harold Macmillan, London, who replied 14 October 1935, 'I am delighted to hear that you have some new autobiographical papers for us, and I shall look forward with great interest to seeing the MS' (BL Add. Ms. 55772, fol. 323–33). Periodical publication came first in the *London Mercury* (November and December 1935); American periodical publication was in the *New Republic* (26 February, 11 and 25 March, and 8 and 22 April 1936). WBY instructed Macmillan to use the Cuala text rather than that of the *London Mercury* because, as he explained, in a letter that his agent quoted to Macmillan: 'The London Mercury is incorrect; they were sent final proofs to print from but partially used instead a typed copy which was originally sent them by you and on which Mr. Yeats worked on after you had received it. Not only is the London Mercury incorrect but for some reason or other they made "cuts" ' (BL Add. Ms. 54902, fol. 225).

The Macmillan page proofs of *Dramatis Personae*, date-stamped 4 February 1936, served a dual function. They were prepared both for the separate *Dramatis Personae*, which includes *Estrangement, The Death of Synge,* and *The Bounty of Sweden,* without the Cuala Press preface or notes, and for an up-dated volume in the Edition de Luxe. The portion of the *Dramatis Personae* proofs that contains *Estrangement, The Death of Synge,* and *The Bounty of Sweden* is descended from the Edition de Luxe 12 July 1932 proofs and incorporates the corrections of compositor's errors that are marked in those earlier proofs. WBY had sailed for Majorca at the end of November 1935, while Mrs. Yeats remained in Dublin. In late January 1936, WBY suffered a dangerous collapse from heart and kidney illnesses. At the doctor's urgent summons, Mrs. Yeats flew to Majorca on 2 February 1936 and cabled Watt: 'Tell Macmillan impossible Yeats correct proofs Stop Ask Mr. Marks [*sic*] pass them for press Yeats.' Macmillan replied to Watt, 12 February 1936: 'Mr. Mark will read "Dramatis Personae" for press, as requested in your telegram from Mrs. Yeats' (BL Add. Ms. 57777, fol. 111).

The Macmillan, London, *Dramatis Personae* (Wade no. 187) was published 15 May 1936, three days after the New York edition (Wade no. 186), which because it had been set from proofs sent from London is of only secondary textual interest. Similarly, *The Autobiography of William Butler Yeats* (Wade no. 198), published 30 August 1938 only in New York and which omitted the Nobel lecture 'The Irish Dramatic Movement,' carries no special textual authority.

Another New York project has a similarly limited, derivative role in the textual history of *Autobiographies*. The Scribners 'Dublin Edition,' a limited, subscription, collected edition that was to parallel approximately the Macmillan, London, Edition de Luxe, had been agreed to by WBY on 3 December 1935 (Callan, *Yeats on Yeats,* pages 90–92, letters 1 and 2). Macmillan, London, and Scribners reached an agreement on arrangements for the Scribners edition, which was to be in 'seven or eight' volumes, on 8 October 1936 (*Yeats on Yeats,* pages 92–93, letter 3). On a typewritten, eight-page list of contents, with queries, for the Edition de Luxe, sent to WBY on 27 October 1936, Thomas Mark asked about the Nobel lecture in *The Bounty of Sweden,* which, he noted, 'was struck out on the [12 July 1932] proofs of Vol VI by the author, but it is included in the "Dramatis Personae" volume [and which is not struck out on the 4 February 1936 proofs]. Should it, after all, be retained for this edition?' Yeats replied, 'Yes' (NLI Ms. 30,248).

WBY sent Scribners, on 14 June 1937, the copy-text for *Autobiographies,* consisting of pages from *Autobiographies* (1926) and *Dramatis Personae* (1936) (including the Nobel lecture), with a list of corrections (HRC Texas, Scribners Archive, 'Miscellaneous' Case). WBY's insistence that Scribners follow the London text and arrangement for the *Autobiographies* volume is reconfirmed in another detailed list of contents sent by Mrs. Yeats to Hansard Watt, 22 June 1937, and forwarded to Scribners (Princeton, Scribners Archive, Author files I, box 147, folder Yeats 1).

Then for a while very little work was done on the *Autobiographies* volumes in the Macmillan and the Scribners collected editions apart from arranging for illustrations and, at Scribners, counting the number of words. Late in 1938, Macmillan made tentative plans to append the *On the Boiler* essays to *Autobiographies.* WBY's death in January 1939 re-ignited both publishers' interest in their collected editions, and the plans for the Macmillan edition expanded to eleven volumes (BL Add. Ms. 55890, fol. 1). A printed 'Preliminary Notice' of the Macmillan Edition de Luxe listed *Autobiographies* as volumes VI and VII, with contents the same as they would eventually be in the Macmillan, London, 1955 *Autobiographies* and in this edition, but in a two-volume format that divided *The Trembling of the Veil* between 'Hodos Chameliontos' and 'The Tragic Generation,' and with notes at the end of each volume. The Nobel lecture, 'The Irish Dramatic Movement', was specifically included. (Princeton, Scribners Archive, Author Files I, box 174, folder Yeats 2 [2 copies]).

In April 1939, Mrs. Yeats suggested to Harold Macmillan that *On the Boiler,* which still had not yet been published, be assigned to an additional volume 'to be added to this edition at a later date', and which would be called *Essays and Autobiographical Fragments.* She proposed including the uncollected essays 'If I were Four-and-Twenty' (published 23 and 30 August 1919 and eventually collected in the Cuala Press *If I were Four-and-Twenty* in 1940) and 'Ireland, 1921–1931' (published 30 January 1932 and in *Spectator's Gallery: Essays, Sketches, Short Stories & Prose from the Spectator 1932,* edited by Peter Fleming and Derek Verschoyle, London: Cape, 1933) (BL Add. Mss. 54904, fol. 171 and 55822, fols. 342–44). By 19 June 1939, Macmillan had decided not to add *On the Boiler* to the two volumes of *Autobiographies,* and on 21 June, Thomas Mark sent Mrs. Yeats 'the complete marked proofs of Volumes VI and VII "Autobiographies" with the original marked proofs' (BL Add. Mss. 55824, fols. 501–2 and 55825, fol. 554). On 20 June, he had sent her the proofs of volumes III and IV (*Plays*) and on 26 June, he sent proofs of volumes VIII (*Mythologies*), IX (*Discoveries*), and X (*Essays*). She returned the proofs of volumes III and IV (*Plays*) before 1 July, and on 5 July 1939 she returned the proofs of volumes VI and VII (*Autobiographies*) (BL Add. Ms. 55826, fol. 196; Mrs. Yeats letter to Thomas Mark, 5 July 1939, Macmillan Archives, Basingstoke). Thomas Mark acknowledged receipt of the *Autobiographies* proofs on 7 July (BL Add. Ms. 55826, fol. 374). Those proofs are not extant.

Britain declared war on 3 September 1939 and the Macmillan Edition de Luxe, also known as the 'Coole Edition', soon ground to a stop, awaiting, as Thomas Mark told Mrs. Yeats, 'better times'

(19 October 1939, BL Add. Ms. 55830, fol. 334). Concurrently in New York the plans for Scribners's 'Dublin Edition' had expanded to eleven volumes. A handwritten list of contents in 1939 shows volumes VI and VII as ' "*Autobiographies*" (including pages from On the Boiler)' (HRC Texas, Scribners Archive, Case X). But then it too was postponed indefinitely.

Because the Macmillan, London, office files for the 1950s are not extant, we are left with only sketchy evidence for reconstructing the preparation of the Macmillan, London, *Autobiographies,* published 11 March 1955 (Wade no. 211L), except that it used the Edition de Luxe volume VI page proofs (NLI Ms. 30,140) that are comprised of the 12 July 1932 page proofs marked by Thomas Mark and WBY, which include *Estrangement, The Death of Synge,* and *The Bounty of Sweden* (with the Nobel lecture, 'The Irish Dramatic Movement', cancelled by WBY), plus a subsequent set of page proofs of *Dramatis Personae* (1936) with the printed page numbers associated with that edition rather than the volume VI page numbers printed in the 12 July 1932 proofs. The reprintings of *Autobiographies* (1955) from the 1970s onwards are marred by the fairly frequent vignetting of part of a letter at a page margin; earlier issues are free of those production problems.

Macmillan, New York, re-issued its 1938 volume *The Autobiography of William Butler Yeats* in 1953 and then in 1958 published a reset paperback edition, still titled *The Autobiography of William Butler Yeats,* but with the Nobel lecture, 'The Irish Dramatic Movement', restored.

WHO

ACKNOWLEDGMENTS

The editors are pleased to acknowledge the generous assistance of Jonathan Allison, David R. Clark, Richard Finneran, Mary FitzGerald, John Flynn, Adrian Frazier, Warwick Gould, George Harper, John Kelly, Christine Mahoney, William M. Murphy, Dan Olsen, Ronald Schuchard, Michael J. Sidnell, Deirdre Toomey, the Yeats Society of Sligo, and the library staffs of Boston College, the British Library, University of California Los Angeles William Andrews Clark Library, University of Chicago, Colby College, University College Cork, Cornell University, Emory University, Harvard University, University of Texas Humanities Research Center, the Library of Congress, the Macmillan Archive, University of Memphis, National Library of Ireland, State University of New York at Stony Brook Yeats Archive, New York Public Library, Princeton University, Washington University in St. Louis, and Yale University. Research travel was funded in part by an American Philosophical Society grant-in-aid to William O'Donnell, and the editors have received support from Colby College and the University of Memphis.

LIST OF ABBREVIATIONS

1932/1936 page proofs   Marked page proofs of *Autobiographies* for the never-published London: Macmillan 'Edition de Luxe', date-stamped 12 July 1932, 4 Feb 1936 (NLI Ms. 30,140)

Autobiographies (1926)   *Autobiographies: Reveries over Childhood and Youth and The Trembling of the Veil* (London: Macmillan, 1926) (Wade no. 151); also (New York: Macmillan, 1927) (Wade no. 152)

Autobiographies (1955)   *Autobiographies* (London: Macmillan, 1955) (Wade no. 211L)

Autobiographies (New York 1938)   *The Autobiography of William Butler Yeats consisting of Reveries over Childhood and Youth / The Trembling of the Veil and Dramatis Personae* (New York: Macmillan, 1938) (Wade no. 198); re-issued 1953 (Wade no. 211G)

Autobiographies (New York 1958)   *The Autobiography of William Butler Yeats consisting of Reveries over Childhood and Youth / The Trembling of the Veil and Dramatis Personae,* Doubleday Anchor Books paperback (Garden City, New York: Doubleday, 1958) (Wade no. 211O)

Berg NYPL   Henry W. and Albert A. Berg Collection, New York Public Library, Astor, Lenox and Tilden Foundations

BL   British Library

Bounty of Sweden (Cuala 1925)   *The Bounty of Sweden: A Meditation, and a Lecture Delivered before the Royal Swedish Academy and Certain Notes by William Butler Yeats* (Dublin: Cuala Press, 1925) (Wade no. 146)

Bradford, *Yeats at Work* (Carbondale and Edwardsville: Southern Illinois University Press, 1965)

Brophy   Brigid Brophy, *Beardsley and his World* (London: Thames and Hudson, 1976)

Callan, *Yeats on Yeats*   Edward Callan, *Yeats on Yeats: The Last Introductions and the 'Dublin' Edition* New Yeats Papers XX (Mountrath, Portlaoise: Dolmen Press, 1981)

Castiglione   Baldassare Castiglione (1478–1529), *The Book of the Courtier* (Il *Cortegiano* [1527]), trans. Sir Thomas Hoby (in 1561), The Tudor Translations series. (London: Nutt, 1900) (O'Shea no. 351)

CL1   *The Collected Letters of W. B. Yeats, I: 1865–1895,* ed. John Kelly, associate ed. Eric Domville (Oxford: Clarendon Press; New York: Oxford University Press, 1986)

CL2   *The Collected Letters of W. B. Yeats, II: 1896–1900,* eds. Warwick Gould, John Kelly, and Deirdre Toomey (Oxford: Clarendon Press; New York: Oxford University Press, 1997)

CL3   *The Collected Letters of W. B. Yeats, III: 1901–1904,* eds. John Kelly and Ronald Schuchard (Oxford: Clarendon Press; New York: Oxford University Press, 1994)

CPlays   W. B. Yeats, *Collected Plays* (London: Macmillan, 1952)

Cuchulain of Muirthemne   Lady Gregory, *Cuchulain of Muirthemne: The Story of the Men of the Red Branch of Ulster* (London: Murray, 1902) (O'Shea no. 792)

Death of Synge   (1928) *The Death of Synge, and Other Passages from an Old Diary* (Dublin: Cuala Press, 1928) (Wade no. 162)

Dictionary of Art   The Dictionary of Art, ed. Jane Turner (London: Macmillan; New York: Grove's Dictionaries, 1996)

Dramatis Personae   (1936) *Dramatis Personae 1896–1902. Estrangement. The Death of Synge. The Bounty of Sweden* (London: Macmillan, 1936) (Wade no. 187); also (New York: Macmillan, 1936) (Wade no. 186)

E&I   W. B. Yeats, *Essays and Introductions* (London and New York: Macmillan, 1961)

Ex   W. B. Yeats, *Explorations,* selected by Mrs. W. B. Yeats (London: Macmillan, 1962; New York: Macmillan, 1963)

FFT   W. B. Yeats, *Fairy and Folk Tales of the Irish Peasantry,* ed. W. B. Yeats, Camelot Classics series, no. 32 (London: Scott, 1888)

Foster 1   Roy F. Foster, *W. B. Yeats: A Life, I: The Apprentice Mage 1865–1914* (Oxford and New York: Oxford University Press, 1997)

Gods and Fighting Men   Lady Gregory, *Gods and Fighting Men: The Story of the Tuatha de Danaan and of the Fianna of Ireland* (London: Murray, 1904), (O'Shea no. 795); reprint. (Gerrards Cross, Bucks.: Colin Smythe, 1970)

Hail and Farewell! I: Ave   George Moore, *Hail and Farewell! I: Ave* (London: Heinemann, 1911), (O'Shea no. 1353)

Harper, Making of A Vision   George M. Harper, *The Making of Yeats's A Vision: A Study of the Automatic Script,* 2 vols. (London: Macmillan, 1987)

Harper, Yeats's Golden Dawn   George M. Harper, *Yeats's Golden Dawn* (London: Macmillan, 1974)

Hone, JBY Letters   *Letters to His Son W. B. Yeats and Others, 1869–1922,* ed. Joseph Hone (London: Faber and Faber, 1944; New York: E. P. Dutton, 1946)

Hone, Yeats   Joseph Hone, *W. B. Yeats 1865–1939* (London: Macmillan, 1942)

HRC Texas   Harry Ransom Humanities Research Center, University of Texas at Austin

Images of a Poet   *W. B. Yeats: Images of a Poet,* ed. D. J. Gordon (Manchester: Manchester University Press, 1961)

JBY John Butler Yeats (1839–1922)

Keynes *The Complete Writings of William Blake with Variant Readings,* ed. Geoffrey Keynes (London: Oxford University Press, 1966)

L *The Letters of W. B. Yeats,* ed. Allan Wade (London: Hart-Davis, 1954; New York: Macmillan, 1955)

LE W. B. Yeats, *Later Essays,* ed. W. H. O'Donnell (New York: Scribner, 1994; London: Macmillan)

LM *The London Mercury*

LY note Lily Yeats marginalia, in 1936, in a copy of *Reveries over Childhood and Youth* (New York: Macmillan, 1916) (Wade no. 112; O'Shea no. 2414), Collection of ABY

LY scrapbook Lily Yeats's scrapbooks (collection of Michael Yeats); quoted in William M. Murphy, *Prodigal Father: The Life of John Butler Yeats (1839–1922)* (Ithaca: Cornell University Press, 1978) and in William M. Murphy, *The Yeats Family and the Pollexfens of Sligo* (Dublin: Dolmen Press, 1971)

MBY Collection of Michael Yeats, Dalkey, Co. Dublin

McGarry James P. McGarry, *Place names in the Writings of William Butler Yeats,* ed. Edward Malins (Gerrards Cross, Bucks.: Colin Smythe, 1976)

Mem W. B. Yeats, *Memoirs,* ed. Denis Donoghue (London: Macmillan, 1972; New York: Macmillan, 1973)

Murphy, Family Secrets William M. Murphy, *Family Secrets: William Butler Yeats and His Relatives* (Syracuse: Syracuse University Press, 1995)

Murphy, Prodigal Father William M. Murphy, *Prodigal Father: The Life of John Butler Yeats (1839–1922)* (Ithaca: Cornell University Press, 1978)

Murphy, Yeats Family William M. Murphy, *The Yeats Family and the Pollexfens of Sligo* (Dublin: Dolmen Press, 1971)

Myth W. B. Yeats, *Mythologies* (London and New York: Macmillan, 1959)

NLI National Library of Ireland

O'Shea Edward O'Shea, *A Descriptive Catalog of W. B. Yeats's Library* (New York: Garland, 1985) and 'The 1920s Catalogue of W. B. Yeats's Library', *Yeats Annual No. 4,* ed. Warwick Gould (London: Macmillan, 1986), pp. 279–90

P W. B. Yeats, *The Poems,* revised edition, ed. Richard J. Finneran (New York: Macmillan, 1989; London: Macmillan, 1991)

P&I W. B. Yeats, *Prefaces and Introductions: Uncollected Prefaces and Introductions by Yeats to Works of Other Authors and to Anthologies Edited by Yeats,* ed. W. H. O'Donnell (London: Macmillan, 1989; New York: Macmillan, 1990)

Poets and Dreamers Lady Gregory, *Poets and Dreamers: Studies and Translations from the Irish* (Dublin: Hodges, Figges; London: John Murray, 1903)

Prix Nobel en 1923   (Wade no. 316) *Les Prix Nobel en 1923* (Stockholm: Nordstet & Söner, 1924) (Wade no. 316)

Prix Nobel en 1923: The Irish Dramatic Movement   Stockholm 1924 (Wade no. 144) *Les Prix Nobel en 1923. The Irish Dramatic Movement* (Stockholm: Norstedt & Fils, 1924) (Wade no. 144)

Reade   Brian Reade, *Beardsley* (London: Studio Vista, 1967)

Reveries 1916   *Reveries over Childhood and Youth* (London: Macmillan, 1916) (Wade no. 113) and (New York: Macmillan, 1916) (Wade no. 112)

Reveries Cuala 1916   *Reveries over Childhood and Youth* (Churchtown, Dundrum: Cuala Press, 1915) (Wade no. 111)

SB   W. B. Yeats, *The Speckled Bird,* ed. W. H. O'Donnell (Toronto: McClelland and Stewart, title page 1976 [1977])

SIU   Special Collections, Morris Library, Southern Illinois University at Carbondale

Trembling (1922)   *The Trembling of the Veil* (London: T. Werner Laurie, 1922) (Wade no. 133)

UP1   *Uncollected Prose by W. B. Yeats,* vol. 1, ed. John P. Frayne (New York: Columbia University Press; London: Macmillan, 1970)

UP2   *Uncollected Prose by W. B. Yeats,* vol. 2, eds. John P. Frayne and Colton Johnson (London: Macmillan, 1975; New York: Columbia University Press, 1976)

V(1925)   W. B. Yeats, *A Vision* (London: Werner Laurie, title page 1925 [January 1926])

V   W. B. Yeats, *A Vision,* 2nd ed. (London: Macmillan, 1937)

V(1925)CE   *A Critical Edition of Yeats's* A Vision (1925), eds. George Mills Harper and Walter Kelly Hood (London: Macmillan, 1978)

VP   *The Variorum Edition of the Poems of W. B. Yeats,* eds. Peter Allt and Russell K. Alspach (New York: Macmillan, 1957; cited from the corrected 3rd printing, 1966, or later printings)

VPlays   *The Variorum Edition of the Plays of W. B. Yeats,* ed. Russell K. Alspach (London and New York: Macmillan, 1966; cited from the corrected 2nd printing, 1966, or later printings)

Wade   Allan Wade, *A Bibliography of the Writings of W. B. Yeats,* 3rd ed., rev. Russell K. Alspach (London: Hart-Davis, 1968)

WBY   William Butler Yeats (1865–1939)

Weintraub   Stanley Weintraub, *Aubrey Beardsley: Imp of the Perverse* (University Park: Pennsylvania State University Press, 1976)

WWB   *The Works of William Blake: Poetic, Symbolic, and Critical,* eds. Edwin J. Ellis and W. B. Yeats, 3 vols. (London: Quaritch, 1893)

Yeats the European   *Yeats the European,* ed. A. Norman Jeffares, Princess Grace Irish Library series 3 (Gerrards Cross, Bucks.: Colin Smythe, 1989)

REVERIES OVER CHILDHOOD AND YOUTH

TO

THOSE FEW PEOPLE

MAINLY PERSONAL FRIENDS

WHO HAVE READ

ALL THAT I HAVE WRITTEN

PREFACE

Sometimes when I remember a relative that I have been fond of, or a strange incident of the past, I wander here and there till I have somebody to talk to. Presently I notice that my listener is bored; but now that I have written it out, I may even begin to forget it all. In any case, because one can always close a book, my friend need not be bored.

I have changed nothing to my knowledge; and yet it must be that I have changed many things without my knowledge; for I am writing after many years and have consulted neither friend, nor letter, nor old newspaper, and describe what comes oftenest into my memory.

I say this fearing that some surviving friend of my youth may remember something in a different shape and be offended with my book.

W. B. YEATS
Christmas Day, 1914

REVERIES OVER
CHILDHOOD AND YOUTH

My first memories are fragmentary and isolated and contemporaneous, as though one remembered some first moments of the Seven Days. It seems as if time had not yet been created, for all thoughts are connected with emotion and place without sequence.

I remember sitting upon somebody's knee, looking out of an Irish window at a wall covered with cracked and falling plaster, but what wall I do not remember, and being told that some relation once lived there. I am looking out of a window in London. It is in Fitzroy Road.[1] Some boys are playing in the road and among them a boy in uniform, a telegraph-boy perhaps. When I ask who the boy is, a servant tells me that he is going to blow the town up, and I go to sleep in terror.

After that come memories of Sligo, where I live with my grandparents.[2] I am sitting on the ground looking at a mastless toy boat with the paint rubbed and scratched, and I say to myself in great melancholy, 'It is further away than it used to be', and while I am saying it I am looking at a long scratch in the stern, for it is especially the scratch which is further away. Then one day at dinner my great-uncle, William Middleton,[3] says, 'We should not make light of the troubles of children. They are worse than ours, because we can see the end of our trouble and they can never see any end', and I feel grateful, for I know that I am very unhappy and have often said to myself, 'When you grow up, never talk as grown-up people do of the happiness of childhood'. I may have already had the night of misery when, having prayed for several days that I might die, I began to be afraid that I was dying and prayed that I might live. There was no reason for my unhappiness. Nobody was unkind, and my grandmother has still after so many years my gratitude and my reverence. The house was so big that there was always a room to hide in, and I had a red pony and a garden where I could wander, and there were two dogs to follow at my heels, one white with some black spots on his head and the other with long black hair all over him. I used to think about God and fancy that I was very wicked, and one day when I threw a stone and hit a duck in the yard by mischance and broke its wing, I was full of wonder when I was told that the duck would be cooked for dinner and that I should not be punished.

Some of my misery was loneliness and some of it fear of old William Pollexfen, my grandfather.[4] He was never unkind, and I cannot remember that he ever spoke harshly to me, but it was the custom to fear and admire him. He had won the freedom of some Spanish city, for saving life perhaps, but was so silent that his wife never knew it till he was near eighty, and then from the chance visit of an old sailor. She asked him if it was true and he said it was true, but she knew him too well to question and his old shipmate had left the town. She too had the habit of fear. We knew that he had been in many parts of the world, for there was a great scar on his hand made by a whaling-hook, and in the dining-room was a cabinet with bits of coral in it and a jar of water from the Jordan for the baptizing of his children and Chinese pictures upon rice-paper and an ivory walking-stick from India that came to me after his death. He had great physical strength and had the reputation of never ordering a man to do anything he would not do himself. He owned many sailing-ships and once, when a captain just come to anchor at Rosses Point reported something wrong with the rudder, had sent a messenger to say, 'Send a man down to find out what's wrong'. 'The crew all refuse' was the answer, and to that my grandfather answered, 'Go down yourself', and not being obeyed, he dived from the main deck, all the neighbourhood lined along the pebbles of the shore. He came up with his skin torn but well informed about the rudder. He had a violent temper and kept a hatchet at his bedside for burglars and would knock a man down instead of going to law, and I once saw him hunt a party of men with a horsewhip. He had no relation, for he was an only child, and, being solitary and silent, he had few friends. He corresponded with Campbell of Islay who had befriended him and his crew after a shipwreck, and Captain Webb, the first man who had swum the Channel and who was drowned swimming the Niagara Rapids, had been a mate in his employ and a close friend. That is all the friends I can remember, and yet he was so looked up to and admired that when he returned from taking the waters of Bath his men would light bonfires along the railway line for miles; while his partner, William Middleton, whose father[5] after the great famine[6] had attended the sick for weeks, and taken cholera from a man he carried in his arms into his own house and died of it, and was himself civil to everybody and a cleverer man than my grandfather, came and went without notice. I think I confused my grandfather with God, for I remember in one of my attacks of melancholy praying that he might punish me for my sins, and I was shocked and astonished when a daring little girl—a cousin, I think—having waited under a group of trees in the avenue, where she knew he would pass near four o'clock on the way to his dinner, said to him, 'If I were you and you were a little girl, I would give you a doll'.

Yet for all my admiration and alarm, neither I nor any one else thought it wrong to outwit his violence or his rigour; and his lack of suspicion and something helpless about him made that easy while it stirred our affection. When I must have been still a very little boy, seven or eight years old perhaps, an uncle[7] called me out of bed one night, to ride the five or six miles to Rosses Point to borrow a railway-pass from a cousin.[8] My grandfather had one, but thought it dishonest to let another use it, but the cousin was not so particular. I was let out through a gate that opened upon a little lane beside the garden away from earshot of the house, and rode delighted through the moonlight, and awoke my cousin in the small hours by tapping on his window with a whip. I was home again by two or three in the morning and found the coachman waiting in the little lane. My grandfather would not have thought such an adventure possible, for every night at eight he believed that the stable-yard was locked, and he knew that he was brought the key. Some servant had once got into trouble at night and so he had arranged that they should all be locked in. He never knew, what everybody else in the house knew, that for all the ceremonious bringing of the key the gate was never locked.

Even to-day when I read *King Lear* his image is always before me, and I often wonder if the delight in passionate men in my plays and in my poetry is more than his memory. He must have been ignorant, though I could not judge him in my childhood, for he had run away to sea when a boy, 'gone to sea through the hawse-hole' as he phrased it, and I can but remember him with two books—his

Bible and Falconer's *Shipwreck,* a little green-covered book that lay always upon his table; he belonged to some younger branch of an old Cornish family.[9] His father had been in the Army,[10] had retired to become an owner of sailing-ships, and an engraving of some old family place[11] my grandfather thought should have been his hung next a painted coat of arms in the little back parlour. His mother had been a Wexford woman,[12] and there was a tradition that his family had been linked with Ireland for generations and once had their share in the old Spanish trade with Galway. He had a good deal of pride and disliked his neighbours, whereas his wife, a Middleton,[13] was gentle and patient and did many charities in the little back parlour among frieze coats and shawled heads, and every night when she saw him asleep went the round of the house alone with a candle to make certain there was no burglar in danger of the hatchet. She was a true lover of her garden, and before the care of her house had grown upon her, would choose some favourite among her flowers and copy it upon rice-paper. I saw some of her handiwork the other day and I wondered at the delicacy of form and colour and at a handling that may have needed a magnifying-glass it was so minute. I can remember no other pictures but the Chinese paintings, and some coloured prints of battles in the Crimea upon the wall of a passage, and the painting of a ship at the passage end darkened by time.

My grown-up uncles and aunts, my grandfather's many sons and daughters, came and went, and almost all they said or did has faded from my memory, except a few harsh words that convince me by a vividness out of proportion to their harshness that all were habitually kind and considerate. The youngest of my uncles[14] was stout and humorous and had a tongue of leather over the keyhole of his door to keep the draught out, and another whose bedroom was at the end of a long stone passage had a model turret-ship in a glass case. He was a clever man[15] and had designed the Sligo quays, but was now going mad and inventing a vessel of war that could not be sunk, his pamphlet explained, because of a hull of solid wood. Only six months ago my sister[16] awoke dreaming that she held a wingless sea-bird in her arms and presently she heard that he had died in his madhouse, for a sea-bird is the omen that announces the death or danger of a Pollexfen. An uncle, George Pollexfen,[17] afterwards astrologer and mystic, and my dear friend, came but seldom from

Ballina, once to a race-meeting with two postilions dressed in green; and there was that younger uncle[18] who had sent me for the railway-pass. He was my grandmother's favourite, and had, the servants told me, been sent away from school for taking a crowbar to a bully.

I can only remember my grandmother punishing me once. I was playing in the kitchen and a servant in horseplay pulled my shirt out of my trousers in front just as my grandmother came in, and I, accused of I knew not what childish indecency, was given my dinner in a room by myself. But I was always afraid of my uncles and aunts, and once the uncle who had taken the crowbar to the bully found me eating lunch which my grandmother had given me and reproved me for it and made me ashamed. We breakfasted at nine and dined at four and it was considered self-indulgent to eat anything between meals; and once an aunt told me that I had reined in my pony and struck it at the same moment that I might show it off as I rode through the town, and I, because I had been accused of what I thought a very dark crime, had a night of misery. Indeed I remember little of childhood but its pain. I have grown happier with every year of life as though gradually conquering something in myself, for certainly my miseries were not made by others but were a part of my own mind.

II

One day some one spoke to me of the voice of the conscience, and as I brooded over the phrase I came to think that my soul, because I did not hear an articulate voice, was lost. I had some wretched days until being alone with one of my aunts[19] I heard a whisper in my ear, 'What a tease you are!' At first I thought my aunt must have spoken, but when I found she had not, I concluded it was the voice of my conscience and was happy again. From that day the voice has come to me at moments of crisis, but now it is a voice in my head that is sudden and startling. It does not tell me what to do, but often reproves me. It will say perhaps, 'That is unjust' of some thought; and once when I complained that a prayer had not been heard, it said, 'You have been helped'. I had a little flagstaff in front of the house and a red flag with the Union Jack in the corner. Every night I pulled my flag down and folded it up and laid it on a shelf in my bedroom, and one morning before breakfast I found it, though I knew I had folded it up the night before, knotted round the bottom of the flagstaff so that it was touching the grass. I must have heard the servants talking of the faeries, for I concluded at once that a faery had tied those four knots and from that on believed that one had whispered in my ear. I have been told, though I do not remember it myself, that I saw, whether once or many times I do not know, a supernatural bird in the corner of the room. Once, too, I was driving with my grandmother a little after dark close to the Channel that runs for some five miles from Sligo to the sea, and my grandmother showed me the red light of an outward-bound steamer and told me that my grandfather was on board, and that night in my sleep I screamed out and described the steamer's wreck. The next morning my grandfather arrived on a blind horse found for him by grateful passengers. He had, as I remember the story, been asleep when the captain aroused him to say they were going on the rocks. He said, 'Have you tried sail on her?' and judging from some answer that the captain was demoralized took over the command and, when the ship could not be saved, got the crew and passengers into the boats. His own boat was upset and he saved himself and some others by swimming; some women had drifted ashore, buoyed up by their crinolines. 'I was not so much afraid of the sea as of that terrible man with his oar', was the comment of a schoolmaster who was among the survivors. Eight men, were, however, drowned and my grandfather suffered from that memory at intervals all his life, and if asked to read family prayers never read anything but the shipwreck of Saint Paul.[20]

I remember the dogs more clearly than any one except my grandfather and grandmother. The black hairy one had no tail because it had been sliced off, if I was told the truth, by a railway train. I think I followed at their heels more than they did at mine, and that their journeys ended at a rabbit-warren behind the garden; and sometimes they had savage fights, the black hairy dog, being well protected by its hair, suffering least. I can remember one so savage that the white dog would not take his teeth out of the black dog's hair till the coachman hung them over the side of a water-butt, one outside and one in the water. My grandmother once told the coachman to cut the hair like a lion's hair and, after a long consultation with the stable-boy,[21] he cut it all over the head and shoulders and left it

on the lower part of the body. The dog disappeared for a few days
and I did not doubt that its heart was broken.

There was a large garden behind the house full of apple-trees,
with flower-beds and grass-plots in the centre, and two figure-heads
of ships, one among the strawberry plants under a wall covered
with fruit-trees and one among the flowers. The one among the
flowers was a white lady in flowing robes, while the other, a stalwart man in uniform, had been taken from a three-masted ship of
my grandfather's called the *Russia,* and there was a belief among
the servants that the stalwart man represented the Tsar and had
been presented by the Tsar himself. The avenue, or as they say in
England the drive, that went from the hall door through a clump of
big trees to an insignificant gate and a road bordered by broken and
dirty cottages, was but two or three hundred yards, and I often
thought it should have been made to wind more, for I judged people's social importance mainly by the length of their avenues. This
idea may have come from the stable-boy, for he was my principal
friend. He had a book of Orange rhymes,[22] and the days when we
read them together in the hayloft gave me the pleasure of rhyme for
the first time. Later on I can remember being told, when there was
a rumour of a Fenian[23] rising, that rifles had been served out to the
Orangemen; and presently, when I had begun to dream of my future
life, I thought I would like to die fighting the Fenians. I was to build
a very fast and beautiful ship and to have under my command a
company of young men who were always to be in training like athletes and so become as brave and handsome as the young men in the
story-books, and there was to be a big battle on the sea-shore near
Rosses and I was to be killed. I collected little pieces of wood and
piled them up in a corner of the yard, and there was an old rotten
log in a distant field I often went to look at because I thought it
would go a long way in the making of the ship. All my dreams were
of ships; and one day a sea-captain who had come to dine with my
grandfather put a hand on each side of my head and lifted me up to
show me Africa, and another day a sea-captain pointed to the
smoke from the pern-mill on the quays[24] rising up beyond the trees
of the lawn, as though it came from the mountain, and asked me if
Ben Bulben[25] was a burning mountain.

Once every few months I used to go to Rosses Point or Ballisodare to see another little boy, who had a piebald pony that had once

been in a circus and sometimes forgot where it was and went round and round. He was George Middleton,[26] son of my great-uncle William Middleton. Old Middleton had bought land, then believed a safe investment, at Ballisodare and at Rosses, and spent the winter at Ballisodare and the summer at Rosses. The Middleton and Pollexfen flour mills were at Ballisodare, and a great salmon weir, rapids, and a waterfall, but it was more often at Rosses that I saw my cousin. We rowed in the river-mouth or were taken sailing in a heavy slow schooner yacht or in a big ship's boat that had been rigged and decked. There were great cellars under the house, for it had been a smuggler's house a hundred years before, and sometimes three loud raps would come upon the drawing-room window at sundown, setting all the dogs barking: some dead smuggler giving his accustomed signal. One night I heard them very distinctly and my cousins often heard them, and later on my sister.[27] A pilot had told me that, after dreaming three times of a treasure buried in my uncle's garden, he had climbed the wall in the middle of the night and begun to dig but grew disheartened 'because there was so much earth'. I told somebody what he had said and was told that it was well he did not find it, for it was guarded by a spirit that looked like a flat-iron. At Ballisodare there was a cleft among the rocks that I passed with terror because I believed that a murderous monster lived there that made a buzzing sound like a bee.

It was through the Middletons perhaps that I got my interest in country stories, and certainly the first faery-stories that I heard were in the cottages about their houses. The Middletons took the nearest for friends and were always in and out of the cottages of pilots and of tenants. They were practical, always doing something with their hands, making boats, feeding chickens, and without ambition. One of them[28] had designed a steamer many years before my birth and, long after I had grown to manhood, one could hear it—it had some sort of obsolete engine—many miles off wheezing in the Channel like an asthmatic person. It had been built on the lake and dragged through the town by many horses, stopping before the windows where my mother[29] was learning her lessons, and plunging the whole school into candlelight for five days, and was still patched and repatched mainly because it was believed to be a bringer of good luck. It had been called after the betrothed of its builder *Janet,* long corrupted into the more familiar *Jennet,* and the betrothed died in my youth having passed her eightieth year and been her husband's plague because of the violence of her temper. Another Middleton[30] who was but a year or two older than myself used to shock me by running after hens to know by their feel if they were on the point of dropping an egg. They let their houses decay and the glass fall from the windows of their greenhouses, but one among them at any rate had the second sight.[31] They were liked but had not the pride and reserve, the sense of decorum and order, the instinctive playing before themselves that belongs to those who strike the popular imagination.

Sometimes my grandmother would bring me to see some old Sligo gentlewoman whose garden ran down to the river, ending there in a low wall full of wallflowers, and I would sit up upon my chair, very bored, while my elders ate their seed-cake and drank their sherry. My walks with the servants were more interesting; sometimes we would pass a little fat girl, and a servant persuaded me to write her a love-letter, and the next time she passed she put her tongue out. But it was the servants' stories that interested me. At such-and-such a corner a man had got a shilling from a recruiting sergeant by standing in a barrel and had then rolled out of it and shown his crippled legs. And in such-and-such a house an old woman had hid herself under the bed of her guests, an officer and his wife, and on hearing them abuse her beaten them with a broomstick. All the well-known families had their grotesque or tragic or romantic legends, and I often said to myself how terrible it would be to go away and die where nobody would know my story. Years afterwards, when I was ten or twelve years old and in London, I would remember Sligo with tears, and when I began to write, it was there I hoped to find my audience. Next to Merville where I lived was another tree-surrounded house where I sometimes went to see a little boy who stayed there occasionally with his grandmother, whose name I forget and who seemed to me kind and friendly, though when I went to see her in my thirteenth or fourteenth year I discovered that she only cared for very little boys. When the visitors called I hid in the hay-loft and lay hidden behind the great heap of hay while a servant was calling my name in the yard.

I do not know how old I was (for all these events seem at the same distance) when I was made drunk. I had been out yachting with an uncle and my cousins and it had come on very rough. I had lain on deck between the mast and the bowsprit and a wave had burst over me and I had seen green water over my head. I was very proud and very wet. When we got into Rosses again, I was dressed up in an older boy's clothes so that the trousers came down below my boots, and a pilot gave me a little raw whiskey. I drove home on an outside car and was so pleased with the strange state in which I found myself that for all my uncle could do I cried to every passer-by that I was drunk, and went on crying it through the town and everywhere until I was put to bed by my grandmother and given something to drink that tasted of blackcurrants and so fell asleep.

III

Some six miles off towards Ben Bulben and beyond the Channel, as we call the tidal river between Sligo and the Rosses, and on top of a hill there was a little square two-storeyed house covered with creepers and looking out upon a garden where the box borders were larger than any I had ever seen, and where I saw for the first time the crimson streak of the gladiolus and awaited its blossom with excitement. Under one gable a dark thicket of small trees made a shut-in mysterious place, where one played and believed that something was going to happen. My great-aunt Micky lived there. Micky was not her right name, for she was Mary Yeats,[32] and her father had been my great-grandfather, John Yeats,[33] who had been Rector of Drumcliff, a few miles further off, and died in 1847. She was a spare, high-coloured, elderly woman and had the oldest-looking cat I had ever seen, for its hair had grown into matted locks of yellowy white. She farmed and had one old man-servant, but could not have farmed at all, had not neighbouring farmers helped to gather in the crops, in return for the loan of her farm implements and 'out of respect for the family', for as Johnny MacGurk, the Sligo barber, said to me, 'The Yeats's were always very respectable'. She was full of family history; all her dinner-knives were pointed like daggers through much cleaning, and there was a little James I. cream-jug with the Yeats motto and crest, and on her dining-room mantelpiece a beautiful silver cup that had belonged to my great-great-grandfather,[34] who had married a certain Mary Butler.[35] It had upon it the Butler crest and had been already old at the date 1534, when the initials of some bride and bridegroom were engraved under the lip. All its history for generations was rolled up inside it upon a piece of paper yellow with age, until some caller took the paper to light his pipe.

Another family[36] of Yeats, a widow and her two children on whom I called sometimes with my grandmother, lived near in a long low cottage, and owned a very fierce turkey-cock that did battle with their visitors; and some miles away lived the secretary to the Grand Jury and land agent, my great-uncle, Mat Yeats,[37] and his big family of boys and girls; but I think it was only in later years that I came to know them well. I do not think any of these liked the Pollexfens, who were well off and seemed to them purse-proud, whereas they themselves had come down in the world. I remember them as very well-bred and very religious in the Evangelical way and thinking a good deal of Aunt Micky's old histories. There had been among our ancestors a King's County soldier,[38] one of Marlborough's generals, and when his nephew[39] came to dine he gave him boiled pork, and when the nephew said he disliked boiled pork he had asked him to dine again and promised him something he would like better. However, he gave him boiled pork again and the nephew took the hint in silence. The other day as I was coming home from America,[40] I met one of his descendants whose family has not another discoverable link with ours, and he too knew the boiled pork story and nothing else. We have the General's portrait,[41] and he looks very fine in his armour and his long curly wig, and underneath it, after his name, are many honours that have left no tradition among us. Were we countrypeople, we could have summarized his life in a legend. Other ancestors or great-uncles bore a part in Irish history; one saved the life of Sarsfield[42] at the battle of Sedgemoor; another, taken prisoner[43] by King James's army, owed his to Sarsfield's gratitude;[44] another, a century later,[45] roused the gentlemen of Meath against some local Jacquerie,[46] and was shot dead upon a county road, and yet another[47] 'chased the United Irishmen[48] for a fortnight, fell into their hands and was hanged'. The notorious Major Sirr, who arrested Lord Edward Fitzgerald and gave him the bullet-wound he died of in the jail, was godfather to several of my great-great-grandfather's children; while, to make a balance, my great-grandfather had been Robert Emmet's friend[49] and was suspected and imprisoned though but for a few hours. One great-uncle[50] fell at New Orleans in 1813, while another, who became Governor of Penang,[51] led the forlorn hope at the taking of Rangoon, and even in the last generation of all there had been lives of some power and pleasure. An old man[52] who had entertained many famous people in his eighteenth-century house, where battlement and tower showed the influence of Horace Walpole,[53] had but lately, after losing all his money, drowned himself, first taking off his rings and chain and watch as became a collector of many beautiful things; and once, to remind us of more passionate life, a gunboat put into Rosses, commanded by the illegitimate son[54] of some great-uncle or other. Now that I can look at their miniatures, turning them over to find the name of soldier, or lawyer, or Castle[55] official, and wondering if they cared for good books or good music, I am delighted with all that joins my life to those who had power in Ireland or with those anywhere that were good servants and poor bargainers, but I cared nothing as a child for Micky's tales. I could see my grandfather's ships come up the bay or the river, and his sailors treated me with deference, and a ship's carpenter made and mended my toy boats and I thought that nobody could be so important as my grandfather. Perhaps, too, it is only now that I can value those more gentle natures so unlike his passion and violence. An old Sligo priest has told me how my great-grandfather, John Yeats, always went into his kitchen rattling the keys, so much did he fear finding some one doing wrong, and of a speech of his when the agent of the great landowner of his parish brought him from cottage to cottage to bid the women send their children to the Protestant school. All promised till they came to one who cried, 'Child of mine will never darken your door'. 'Thank you, my woman', he said, 'you are the first honest woman I have met to-day.' My uncle, Mat Yeats,[56] the land agent, had once waited up every night for a week to catch some boys who stole his apples and when he caught them had given them sixpence and told them not to do it again. Perhaps it is only fancy or the softening touch of the miniaturist that makes me discover in their faces some courtesy and much gentleness. Two eighteenth-century faces[57] interest me the most, one that of a great-great-grandfather,[58] for both have under their powdered curling wigs a half-feminine charm, and as I look at them I discover a something clumsy and heavy in myself. Yet it was a Yeats who spoke the only eulogy that turns my head: 'We have ideas and no passions, but by marriage with a Pollexfen we have given a tongue to the sea cliffs'.[59]

Among the miniatures there is a larger picture, an admirable drawing by I know not what master, that is too harsh and merry for its company. He was a connection and close friend of my great-grandmother Corbet, and though we spoke of him as 'Uncle Beattie'[60] in our childhood, no blood relation. My great-grandmother who died at ninety-three had many memories of him. He was the friend of Goldsmith[61] and was accustomed to boast, clergyman though he was, that he belonged to a hunt-club of which every member but himself had been hanged or transported for treason, and that it was not possible to ask him a question he could not reply to with a perfectly appropriate blasphemy or indecency.

IV

Because I had found it hard to attend to anything less interesting than my thoughts, I was difficult to teach. Several of my uncles and aunts had tried to teach me to read, and because they could not, and because I was much older than children who read easily, had come to think, as I have learnt since, that I had not all my faculties.[62] But for an accident they might have thought it for a long time. My father[63] was staying in the house and never went to church, and that gave me the courage to refuse to set out one Sunday morning. I was often devout, my eyes filling with tears at the thought of God and of my own sins, but I hated church. My grandmother tried to teach me to put my toes first to the ground because I suppose I stumped on my heels, and that took my pleasure out of the way there. Later on when I had learnt to read I took pleasure in the words of the hymn, but never understood why the choir took three times as long as I did in getting to the end; and the part of the service I liked, the sermon and passages of the Apocalypse and Ecclesiastes, were no compensation for all the repetitions and for the fatigue of so much standing. My father said if I would not go to church he would teach me to read. I think now that he wanted to make me go for my grandmother's sake and could think of no other way. He was an angry and impatient teacher[64] and flung the reading-book at my head, and next Sunday I decided to go to church. My father had, however, got interested in teaching me, and only shifted the lesson to a week-day till he had conquered my wandering mind. My first clear image of him was fixed on my imagination,

I believe, but a few days before the first lesson. He had just arrived
from London and was walking up and down the nursery floor. He
had a very black beard and hair, and one cheek bulged out with a
fig that was there to draw the pain out of a bad tooth. One of the
nurses (a nurse had come from London with my brothers and sisters) said to the other that a live frog, she had heard, was best of all.
Then I was sent to a dame-school kept by an old woman[65] who
stood us in rows and had a long stick like a billiard cue to get at the
back rows. My father was still at Sligo when I came back from my
first lesson and asked me what I had been taught. I said I had been
taught to sing, and he said, 'Sing then', and I sang—

> Little drops of water,
> Little grains of sand,
> Make the mighty ocean
> And the pleasant land

high up in my head. So my father wrote to the old woman that I
was never to be taught to sing again, and afterwards other teachers
were told the same thing. Presently my elder sister[66] came on a long
visit and she and I went to a little two-storeyed house in a poor
street where an old gentle taught us spelling and grammar. When
we had learned our lesson well, we were allowed to look at a sword
presented to her father who had led troops in India or China and to
spell out a long complimentary inscription on the silver scabbard.
As we walked to her house or home again we held a large umbrella
before us, both gripping the handle and guiding ourselves by looking out of a round hole gnawed in the cover by a mouse. When I
had got beyond books of one syllable, I began to spend my time in
a room called the library, though there were no books in it that I
can remember except some old novels I never opened and a many-
volumed encyclopaedia[67] published towards the end of the eighteenth century. I read this encyclopaedia a great deal and can
remember a long passage considering whether fossil wood despite
its appearance might not be only a curiously shaped stone.

My father's unbelief had set me thinking about the evidences of
religion and I weighed the matter perpetually with great anxiety,
for I did not think I could live without religion. All my religious
emotions were, I think, connected with clouds and cloudy glimpses
of luminous sky, perhaps because of some Bible picture of God's

speaking to Abraham or the like. At least I can remember the sight moving me to tears. One day I got a decisive argument for belief. A cow was about to calve, and I went to the field where the cow was with some farm-hands who carried a lantern, and next day I heard that the cow had calved in the early morning. I asked everybody how calves were born, and because nobody would tell me, made up my mind that nobody knew. They were the gift of God, that much was certain, but it was plain that nobody had ever dared to see them come, and children must come in the same way. I made up my mind that when I was a man I would wait up till calf or child had come. I was certain there would be a cloud and a burst of light and God would bring the calf in the cloud out of the light. That thought made me content until a boy of twelve or thirteen, who had come on a visit for the day, sat beside me in a hay-loft and explained all the mechanism of sex. He had learnt all about it from an elder boy whose pathic[68] he was (to use a term he would not have understood) and his description, given, as I can see now, as if he were telling of any other fact of physical life, made me miserable for weeks. After the first impression wore off, I began to doubt if he had spoken truth, but one day I discovered a passage in the encyclopaedia that, though I only partly understood its long words, confirmed what he had said. I did not know enough to be shocked at his relation to the elder boy, but it was the first breaking of the dream of childhood.

My realization of death came when my father and mother and my two brothers and my two sisters were on a visit. I was in the library when I heard feet running past and heard somebody say in the passage that my younger brother, Robert,[69] had died. He had been ill for some days. A little later my sister and I sat at the table, very happy, drawing ships with their flags half-mast high. We must have heard or seen that the ships in the harbour had their flags at half-mast. Next day at breakfast I heard people telling how my mother and the servant had heard the banshee[70] crying the night before he died. It must have been after this that I told my grandmother I did not want to go with her when she went to see old bedridden people because they would soon die.

V

At length when I was eight or nine an aunt[71] said to me, 'You are going to London. Here you are somebody. There you will be nobody at all.' I knew at the time that her words were a blow at my father, not at me, but it was some years before I knew her reason. She thought so able a man as my father could have found out some way of painting more popular pictures if he had set his mind to it and that it was wrong of him 'to spend every evening at his club'. She had mistaken, for what she would have considered a place of wantonness, Heatherley's Art School.

My mother and brother and sister were at Sligo perhaps when I was sent to England, for my father and I and a group of landscape-painters lodged at Burnham Beeches with an old Mr. and Mrs. Earle.[72] My father was painting the first big pond you come to if you have driven from Slough through Farnham Royal. He began it in spring and painted all through the year, the picture changing with the seasons, and gave it up unfinished when he had painted the snow upon the heath-covered banks. He is never satisfied and can never make himself say that any picture is finished. In the evening he heard me my lessons or read me some novel of Fenimore Cooper's. I found delightful adventures in the woods—one day a blindworm and an adder fighting in a green hollow—and some-times Mrs. Earle would be afraid to tidy the room because I had put a bottle full of newts on the mantelpiece. Now and then a boy from a farm on the other side of the road threw a pebble at my window at daybreak, and he and I went fishing in the big second pond. Now and then another farmer's boy and I shot sparrows with an old pep-per-box revolver and the boy would roast them on a string. There was an old horse one of the painters called The Scaffolding, and sometimes a son of old Earle's drove with me to Slough and once to Windsor, and at Windsor we made our lunch of cold sausages bought from a public-house. I did not know what it was to be alone, for I could wander in pleasant alarm through the enclosed parts of the Beeches, then very large, or round some pond imagin-ing ships going in and out among the reeds and thinking of Sligo or of strange seafaring adventures in the fine ship I should launch when I grew up. I had always a lesson to learn before night and that was a continual misery, for I could very rarely, with so much to remember, set my thoughts upon it and then only in fear. One day my father told me that a painter had said I was very thick-skinned and did not mind what was said to me, and I could not understand how anybody could be so unjust. It made me wretched to be idle, but one could not help it. I was once surprised and shocked. All but my father and myself had been to London, and Kennedy and Farrar and Page, I remember the names vaguely, arrived laughing and talking. One of them had carried off a card of texts from the waiting-room of the station and hung it up on the wall. I thought, 'He has stolen it', but my father and all made it a theme of merry conversation.

Then I returned to Sligo for a few weeks as I was to do once or twice in every year for years, and after that we settled in London. Perhaps my mother and the other children had been there all the time, for I remember my father now and again going to London. The first house we lived in was close to Burne-Jones's house at North End,[73] but we moved after a year or two to Bedford Park.[74] At North End we had a pear-tree in the garden and plenty of pears, but the pears used to be full of maggots, and almost opposite lived a schoolmaster called O'Neill, and when a little boy told me that the schoolmaster's great-grandfather had been a king I did not doubt it. I was sitting against the hedge and iron railing of some villa-garden there, when I heard one boy say to another it was something wrong with my liver that gave me such a dark complexion and that I could not live more than a year. I said to myself, 'A year is a very long time, one can do such a lot of things in a year', and put it out of my head. When my father gave me a holiday and later when I had a holiday from school I took my schooner boat to the Round Pond, sailing it very commonly against the two cutter yachts of an old naval officer. He would sometimes look at the ducks and say, 'I would like to take that fellow home for my dinner', and he sang me a sailor's song about a 'coffin ship'[75] which left Sligo after the great famine, that made me feel very important. The servants at Sligo had told me the story. When she was moved from the berth she had lain in, an unknown dead man's body had floated up, a very evil omen; and my grandfather, who was Lloyd's agent,[76] had condemned her, but she slipped out in the night. The pond had its own legends; and a boy who had seen a certain model steamer 'burned to the water's edge' was greatly valued as a friend. There

was a little boy I was kind to because I knew his father had done
something disgraceful though I did not know what. It was years
before I discovered that his father was but the maker of certain popular statues, many of which are now in public places. I had heard
my father's friends speak of him. Sometimes my sister[77] came with
me, and we would look into all the sweet-shops and toy-shops on
our way home, especially into one opposite Holland House because
there was a cutter yacht made of sugar in the window, and we
drank at all the fountains. Once a stranger spoke to us and bought
us sweets and came with us almost to our door. We asked him to
come in and told him our father's name. He would not come in, but
laughed and said, 'O, that is the painter who scrapes out every day
what he painted the day before'. A poignant memory came upon
me the other day while I was passing the drinking-fountain near
Holland Park, for there I and my sister had spoken together of our
longing for Sligo and our hatred of London. I know we were both
very close to tears and remember with wonder, for I had never
known any one that cared for such mementoes, that I longed for a
sod of earth from some field I knew, something of Sligo to hold in
my hand. It was some old race instinct like that of a savage, for we
had been brought up to laugh at all display of emotion. Yet it was
our mother, who would have thought its display a vulgarity, who
kept alive that love. She would spend hours listening to stories or
telling stories of the pilots and fishing-people of Rosses Point, or of
her own Sligo girlhood, and it was always assumed between her
and us that Sligo was more beautiful than other places. I can see
now that she had great depth of feeling, that she was her father's
daughter. My memory of what she was like in those days has grown
very dim, but I think her sense of personality, her desire of any life
of her own, had disappeared in her care for us and in much anxiety
about money. I always see her sewing or knitting in spectacles and
wearing some plain dress. Yet ten years ago when I was in San Francisco,[78] an old cripple came to see me who had left Sligo before her
marriage; he came to tell me, he said, that my mother 'had been the
most beautiful girl in Sligo'.

The only lessons I had ever learned were those my father taught
me, for he terrified me by descriptions of my moral degradation and
he humiliated me by my likeness to disagreeable people; but
presently I was sent to school at Hammersmith.[79] It was a Gothic

building of yellow brick: a large hall full of desks, some small class-
rooms, and a separate house for boarders, all built perhaps in 1860
or 1870. I thought it an ancient building and that it had belonged
to the founder of the school, Lord Godolphin, who was romantic to
me because there was a novel about him. I never read the novel,[80]
but I thought only romantic people were put in books. On one side,
there was a piano factory of yellow brick, upon two sides half-fin-
ished rows of little shops and villas all yellow brick, and on the
fourth side, outside the wall of our playing-field, a brick-field of cin-
ders and piles of half-burned yellow bricks. All the names and faces
of my schoolfellows have faded from me except one name without
a face and the face and name of one friend, mainly no doubt
because it was all so long ago, but partly because I only seem to
remember things dramatic in themselves or that are somehow associated with unforgettable places.

For some days, as I walked homeward along the Hammersmith
Road, I told myself that whatever I most cared for had been taken
away. I had found a small, green-covered book given to my father
by a Dublin man of science; it gave an account of the strange sea
creatures the man of science had discovered among the rocks at
Howth or dredged out of Dublin Bay. It had long been my favourite
book;[81] and when I read it I believed that I was growing very wise,
but now I should have no time for it nor for my own thoughts.
Every moment would be taken up learning or saying lessons, or in
walking between school and home four times a day, for I came
home in the middle of the day for dinner. But presently I forgot my
trouble, absorbed in two things I had never known, companionship
and enmity. After my first day's lesson, a circle of boys had got
around me in a playing-field and asked me questions, 'Who's your
father?' 'What does he do?' 'How much money has he?' Presently a
boy said something insulting. I had never struck anybody or been
struck, and now all in a minute, without any intention upon my
side, but as if I had been a doll moved by a string, I was hitting at
the boys within reach and being hit. After that I was called names
for being Irish, and had many fights and never, for years, got the
better in any one of them; for I was delicate and had no muscles.
Sometimes, however, I found means of retaliation, even of aggres-
sion. There was a boy with a big stride, much feared by little boys,
and finding him alone in the playing-field, I went up to him and

said, 'Rise upon Sugaun and sink upon Gad'. 'What does that mean?' he said. 'Rise upon hay-leg and sink upon straw', I answered, and told him that in Ireland the sergeant tied straw and hay to the ankles of a stupid recruit to show him the difference between his legs. My ears were boxed, and when I complained to my friends, they said I had brought it upon myself; and that I deserved all I got. I probably dared myself to other feats of a like sort, for I did not think English people intelligent or well-behaved unless they were artists. Every one I knew well in Sligo despised Nationalists and Catholics, but all disliked England with a prejudice that had come down perhaps from the days of the Irish Parliament.[82] I knew stories to the discredit of England, and took them all seriously. My mother had met some English who did not like Dublin because the legs of the men were too straight, and at Sligo, as everybody knew, an Englishman had once said to a car-driver, 'If you people were not so lazy, you would pull down the mountain and spread it out over the sand and that would give you acres of good fields'. At Sligo there is a wide river-mouth and at ebb tide most of it is dry sand, but all Sligo knew that in some way I cannot remember it was the spreading of the tide over the sand that left the narrow Channel fit for shipping. At any rate the carman had gone chuckling all over Sligo with his tale. People would tell it to prove that Englishmen were always grumbling. 'They grumble about their dinners and everything—there was an Englishman who wanted to pull down Knocknarea', and so on. My mother had shown them to me kissing at railway stations, and taught me to feel disgust at their lack of reserve, and my father told how my grandfather, William Yeats,[83] who had died before I was born, when he came home to his Rectory in County Down from an English visit, spoke of some man he had met on a coach road who 'Englishman-like' told him all his affairs. My father explained that an Englishman generally believed that his private affairs did him credit, while an Irishman, being poor and probably in debt, had no such confidence. I, however, did not believe in this explanation. My Sligo nurses, who had in all likelihood the Irish Catholic political hatred, had never spoken well of any Englishman. Once when walking in the town of Sligo I had turned to look after an English man and woman whose clothes attracted me. The man, I remember, had grey clothes and knee-breeches and the woman a grey dress, and my nurse had said contemptuously, 'Tow-rows'—perhaps, before my time, there had been some English song with the burden 'tow row row'[84]—and everybody had told me that English people ate skate and even dog-fish, and I myself had only just arrived in England when I saw an old man put marmalade in his porridge.

I was divided from all those boys, not merely by the anecdotes that are everywhere perhaps a chief expression of the distrust of races, but because our mental images were different. I read their boys' books and they excited me, but if I read of some English victory, I did not believe that I read of my own people. They thought of Cressy and Agincourt[85] and the Union Jack and were all very patriotic, and I, without those memories of Limerick[86] and the Yellow Ford[87] that would have strengthened an Irish Catholic, thought of mountain and lake, of my grandfather and of ships. Anti-Irish feeling was running high, for the Land League[88] had been founded and landlords had been shot, and I, who had no politics, was yet full of pride, for it is romantic to live in a dangerous country.

I daresay I thought the rough manners of a cheap school, as my grandfather Yeats had those of a chance companion, typical of all England. At any rate I had a harassed life and got many a black eye and had many outbursts of grief and rage. Once a boy, the son of a great Bohemian glass-maker, who was older than the rest of us, and had been sent out of his country because of a love affair, beat a boy for me because we were 'both foreigners'. And a boy who grew to be the school athlete and my chief friend[89] beat a great many. His are the face and name that I remember—his name was of Huguenot origin and his face like his gaunt and lithe body had something of the American Indian in colour and lineament.

I was very much afraid of the other boys, and that made me doubt myself for the first time. When I had gathered pieces of wood in the corner for my great ship, I was confident that I could keep calm among the storms and die fighting when the great battle came. But now I was ashamed of my lack of courage; for I wanted to be like my grandfather, who thought so little of danger that he had jumped overboard in the Bay of Biscay after an old hat. I was very much afraid of physical pain, and one day when I had made some noise in class, my friend the athlete was accused and I allowed him to get two strokes of the cane before I gave myself up. He had held out his hands without flinching and had not rubbed them on his sides afterwards. I was not caned, but was made to stand up for the rest of the lesson. I suffered very much afterwards when the thought came to me, but he did not reproach me.

I had been some years at school before I had my last fight. My friend, the athlete, had given me many months of peace, but at last refused to beat any more and said I must learn to box, and not go near the other boys till I knew how. I went home with him every day and boxed in his room, and the bouts had always the same ending. My excitability gave me an advantage at first and I would drive him across the room, and then he would drive me across and it would end very commonly with my nose bleeding. One day his father, an elderly banker, brought us out into the garden and tried to make us box in a cold-blooded, courteous way, but it was no use. At last he said I might go near the boys again and I was no sooner inside the gate of the playing-field than a boy flung a handful of mud and cried out, 'Mad Irishman'. I hit him several times on the face without being hit, till the boys round said we should make friends. I held out my hand in fear, for I knew if we went on I should be beaten, and he took it sullenly. I had so poor a reputation as a fighter that it was a great disgrace to him, and even the masters made fun of his swollen face; and though some little boys came in a deputation to ask me to lick a boy they named, I had never another fight with a school-fellow. We had a great many fights with the street boys and the boys of a neighbouring charity school. We had always the better because we were not allowed to fling stones, and that compelled us to close or do our best to close. The monitors had been told to report any boy who fought in the street, but they only reported those who flung stones. I always ran at the athlete's heels, but I never hit any one. My father considered these fights absurd, and even that they were an English absurdity, and so I could not get angry enough to like hitting and being hit; and then, too, my friend drove the enemy before him. He had no doubts or speculations to lighten his fist upon an enemy that, being of low behaviour, should be beaten as often as possible, and there were real wrongs to avenge: one of our boys had been killed by the blow of a stone hid in a snowball. Sometimes we on our side got into trouble with the parents of boys. There was a quarrel between the athlete and an old German who had a barber's shop we passed every day on our way home, and one day he spat through the window and hit the German on his bald head—the monitors had not forbidden spitting. The German ran after us, but when the athlete squared up he went away. Now, though I knew it was not right to spit at people, my admiration for my friend arose to a great height. I spread his fame over the school, and next day there was a fine stir when somebody saw the old German going up the gravel walk to the headmaster's room. Presently there was such a noise in the passage that even the master had to listen. It was the headmaster's red-haired brother turning the old German out and shouting to the man-servant, 'See that he doesn't steal the top-coats'. We heard afterwards that he had asked the names of the two boys who passed his window every day and been told the names of the two head boys who passed also but were notoriously gentlemanly in their manners. Yet my friend was timid also and that restored my confidence in myself. He would often ask me to buy the sweets or the ginger-beer because he was afraid sometimes when speaking to a stranger.

I had one reputation that I valued. At first when I went to the Hammersmith swimming-baths with the other boys, I was afraid to plunge in until I had gone so far down the ladder that the water came up to my thighs; but one day when I was alone I fell from the spring-board which was five or six feet above the water. After that I would dive from a greater height than the others and I practised swimming under water and pretending not to be out of breath when I came up. And then, if I ran a race, I took care not to pant or show any sign of strain. And in this I had an advantage even over the athlete, for though he could run faster and was harder to tire than anybody else he grew very pale; and I was often paid compliments. I used to run with my friend when he was training to keep him in company. He would give me a long start and soon overtake me.

I followed the career of a certain professional runner for months, buying papers that would tell me if he had won or lost. I had seen him described as 'the bright particular star of American athletics', and the wonderful phrase had thrown enchantment over him. Had he been called the particular bright star, I should have cared nothing for him. I did not understand the symptom for years after. I was nursing my own dream, my form of the common schoolboy dream, though I was no longer gathering the little pieces of broken and rotting wood. Often, instead of learning my lesson, I covered the white squares of the chessboard on my little table with pen-and-ink pictures of myself doing all kinds of courageous things. One day my father said, 'There was a man in Nelson's ship at the battle of Trafalgar, a ship's purser, whose hair turned white; what a sensitive temperament! that man should have achieved something!' I was vexed and bewildered, and am still bewildered and still vexed, finding it a poor and crazy thing that we who have imagined so many noble persons cannot bring our flesh to heel.

VI

The headmaster[90] was a clergyman, a good-humoured, easy-going man, as temperate, one had no doubt, in his religious life as in all else, and if he ever lost sleep on our account, it was from a very proper anxiety as to our gentility. I was in disgrace once because I went to school in some brilliant blue homespun serge my mother had bought in Devonshire, and I was told I must never wear it again. He had tried several times, though he must have known it was hopeless, to persuade our parents to put us into Eton clothes,[91] and on certain days we were compelled to wear gloves. After my first year, we were forbidden to play marbles because it was a form of gambling and was played by nasty little boys, and a few months later told not to cross our legs in class. It was a school for the sons of professional men who had failed or were at the outset of their career, and the boys held an indignation meeting when they discovered that a new boy was an apothecary's son (I think at first I was his only friend), and we all pretended that our parents were richer than they were. I told a little boy who had often seen my mother knitting or mending my clothes that she only mended or knitted because she liked it, though I knew it was necessity.

It was like, I suppose, most schools of its type, an obscene, bullying place, where a big boy would hit a small boy in the wind to see him double up, and where certain boys, too young for any emotion of sex, would sing the dirty songs of the street, but I daresay it suited me better than a better school. I have heard the headmaster say, 'How has So-and-so done in his Greek?' and the class-master reply, 'Very badly, but he is doing well in his cricket', and the headmaster reply to that, 'O, leave him alone'. I was unfitted for school work, and though I would often work well for weeks together, I had to give the whole evening to one lesson if I was to know it. My thoughts were a great excitement, but when I tried to do anything with them, it was like trying to pack a balloon into a shed in a high wind. I was always near the bottom of my class, and always making excuses that but added to my timidity; but no master was rough with me. I was known to collect moths and butterflies and to get into no worse mischief than hiding now and again an old tailless white rat in my coat-pocket or my desk.

There was but one interruption of our quiet habits, the brief engagement of an Irish master,[92] a fine Greek scholar and vehement teacher, but of fantastic speech. He would open the class by saying, 'There he goes, there he goes', or some like words as the headmaster passed by at the end of the hall. 'Of course this school is no good. How could it be with a clergyman for headmaster?' And then perhaps his eye would light on me, and he would make me stand up and tell me it was a scandal I was so idle when all the world knew that any Irish boy was cleverer than a whole class-room of English boys, a description I had to pay for afterwards. Sometimes he would call up a little boy who had a girl's face and kiss him upon both cheeks and talk of taking him to Greece in the holidays, and presently we heard he had written to the boy's parents about it, but long before the holidays he was dismissed.

VII

Two pictures come into my memory. I have climbed to the top of a tree by the edge of the playing-field, and am looking at my schoolfellows and am as proud of myself as a March cock when it crows to its first sunrise. I am saying to myself, 'If when I grow up I am as clever among grown-up men as I am among these boys, I shall be a famous man'. I remind myself how they think all the same things and cover the school walls at election times with the opinions their fathers find in the newspapers. I remind myself that I am an artist's son and must take some work as the whole end of life and not think as the others do of becoming well off and living pleasantly. The other picture is of a hotel sitting-room in the Strand, where a man is hunched up over the fire. He is a cousin[93] who has speculated with another cousin's money and has fled from Ireland in danger of arrest. My father has brought us to spend the evening with him, to distract him from the remorse that he must be suffering.

VIII

For years Bedford Park was a romantic excitement. At North End my father had announced at breakfast that our glass chandelier was absurd and was to be taken down, and a little later he described the village Norman Shaw was building. I had thought he said, 'There is to be a wall round and no newspapers to be allowed in'. And when I had told him how put out I was at finding neither wall nor gate, he explained that he had merely described what ought to be. We were to see De Morgan tiles, peacock-blue doors and the pomegranate pattern and the tulip pattern of Morris, and to discover that we had always hated doors painted with imitation grain, the roses of mid-Victoria, and tiles covered with geometrical patterns that seemed to have been shaken out of a muddy kaleidoscope. We went to live in a house like those we had seen in pictures and even met people dressed like people in the story-books. The streets were not straight and dull as at North End, but wound about where there was a big tree or for the mere pleasure of winding, and there were wood palings instead of iron railings. The newness of everything, the empty houses where we played at hide-and-seek, and the strangeness of it all, made us feel that we were living among toys. We could imagine people living happy lives as we thought people did long ago when the poor were picturesque and the master of a house could tell of strange adventures over the sea. Only the better houses had been built. The commercial builder had not begun to copy and to cheapen, and besides we only knew the most beautiful houses, the houses of artists. My two sisters and my brother and myself had dancing lessons in a low, red-brick and tiled house that drove away dreams, long cherished, of some day living in a house made exactly like a ship's cabin. The dining-room table, where Sindbad the sailor might have sat, was painted peacock-blue, and the woodwork was all peacock-blue and upstairs a window niche was so big and high up that there was a flight of steps to go up and down by and a table in the niche. The two sisters of the master of the house,[94] a well-known Pre-Raphaelite painter,[95] were our teachers, and they and their old mother were dressed in peacock-blue and in dresses so simply cut that they seemed a part of every story. Once when I had been looking with delight at the old woman, my father, who had begun to be influenced by French art, muttered, 'Imagine dressing up your old mother like that'.

My father's friends were painters who had been influenced by the Pre-Raphaelite[96] movement but had lost their confidence. Wilson, Page, Nettleship, Potter are the names I remember, and at North End I remember them most clearly. I often heard one and another say that Rossetti had never mastered his materials, and though Nettleship had already turned lion-painter, my father talked constantly of the designs of his youth, especially of *God creating Evil,* which Rossetti praised in a letter my father had seen 'as the most sublime conception in ancient or modern art'.[97] In those early days, that he might not be tempted from his work by society, he had made a rent in the tail of his coat; and I have heard my mother tell how she had once sewn it up, but before he came again he had pulled out all the stitches. Potter's exquisite *Dormouse,*[98] now in the Tate Gallery, hung in our house for years. His dearest friend was a pretty model[99] who was, when my memory begins, working for some position in a Board School. I can remember her sitting at the side of the throne in the North End studio, a book in her hand, and my father hearing her say a Latin lesson. Her face was the typical mild, oval face of the painting of that time, and may indeed have helped in the moulding of an ideal of beauty. I found it the other day drawn in pencil on a blank leaf[100] of a volume of *The Earthly Paradise.* It was at Bedford Park a few years later that I was to hear Farrar, whom I had first known at Burnham Beeches, tell of Potter's death and burial. Potter had been very poor and had died from the effects of semi-starvation. He had lived so long on bread and tea that his stomach had withered—I am sure that was the word used—and when his relations found out and gave him good food, it was too late. Farrar had been at the funeral and had stood behind some well-to-do people who were close about the grave and saw one point to the model, who had followed the hearse on foot and was now crying at a distance, and say, 'That is the woman who had all his money'. She had often begged him to allow her to pay his debts, but he would not have it. Probably his rich friends blamed his poor friends, and they the rich, and I daresay nobody had known enough to help him. Besides, he had a strange form of dissipation, I have heard some one say; he was devoted to children, and would become interested in some child— his *Dormouse* is a portrait of a child—and spend his money on its education. My sister remembers seeing him paint with a dark glove on his right hand, and his saying that he had used so much varnish the reflection of the hand would have teased him but for the glove. 'I will soon have to paint my face some dark colour', he added. I have no memory, however, but of noticing that he sat at the easel, whereas my father always stands and walks up and down, and that there was dark blue, a colour that always affects me, in the background of his picture. There is a public gallery of Wilson's work[101] in his native Aberdeen and my sisters have a number of his landscapes—wood-scenes for the most part—painted with phlegm and melancholy, the romantic movement drawing to its latest phase.

IX

My father read out poetry, for the first time, when I was eight or nine years old. Between Sligo and Rosses Point, there is a tongue of land covered with coarse grass that runs out into the sea or the mud according to the state of the tide. It is the place where dead horses are buried. Sitting there, my father read me the *Lays of Ancient Rome*. It was the first poetry that had moved me after the stable-boy's Orange rhymes. Later on he read me *Ivanhoe* and *The Lay of the Last Minstrel,* and they are still vivid in the memory. I re-read *Ivanhoe* the other day, but it has all vanished except Gurth, the swineherd, at the outset and Friar Tuck and his venison pasty, the two scenes[102] that laid hold of me in childhood. *The Lay of the Last Minstrel* gave me a wish to turn magician that competed for years with the dream of being killed upon the sea-shore. When I first went to school, he tried to keep me from reading boys' papers, because a paper, by its very nature, as he explained to me, had to be made for the average boy or man and so could not but thwart one's growth. He took away my paper and I had not courage to say that I was but reading and delighting in a prose retelling of the *Iliad.* But after a few months, my father said he had been too anxious and became less urgent about my lessons and less violent if I had learnt them badly, and he ceased to notice what I read. From that on I shared the excitement which ran through all my fellows on Wednesday afternoons when the boys' papers were published, and I read endless stories I have forgotten as I have forgotten *Grimm's Fairy-Tales* that I read at Sligo, and all of Hans Andersen except *The Ugly*

Duckling which my mother had read to me and to my sisters. I remember vaguely that I liked Hans Andersen better than Grimm because he was less homely, but even he never gave me the knights and dragons and beautiful ladies that I longed for. I have remembered nothing that I read, but only those things that I heard or saw. When I was ten or twelve my father took me to see Irving play Hamlet, and did not understand why I preferred Irving to Ellen Terry, who was, I can now see, the idol of himself and his friends. I could not think of her, as I could of Irving's Hamlet, as but myself, and I was not old enough to care for feminine charm and beauty. For many years Hamlet was an image of heroic self-possession for the poses of youth and childhood to copy, a combatant of the battle within myself. My father had read me the story of the little boy murdered by the Jews in Chaucer[103] and the tale of Sir Thopas, explaining the hard words, and though both excited me, I had liked Sir Thopas best and been disappointed that it left off in the middle. As I grew older, he would tell me plots of Balzac's novels, using incident or character as an illustration for some profound criticism of life. Now that I have read all the *Comédie Humaine,* certain pages have an unnatural emphasis, straining and overbalancing the outline, and I remember how, in some suburban street, he told me of Lucien de Rubempré's duel after the betrayal of his master, and how the wounded Lucien hearing some one say that he was not dead had muttered, 'So much the worse'.[104]

I now can but share with a friend my thoughts and my emotions, and there is a continual discovery of difference, but in those days, before I had found myself, we could share adventures. When friends plan and do together, their minds become one mind and the last secret disappears. I was useless at games. I cannot remember that I ever kicked a goal or made a run, but I was a mine of knowledge when I and the athlete and those two notoriously gentlemanly boys—theirs was the name that I remember without a face—set out for Richmond Park, or Coombe Wood or Twyford Abbey to look for butterflies and moths and beetles. Sometimes to-day I meet people at lunch or dinner whose address sounds familiar and I remember of a sudden that a gamekeeper chased me from the plantation behind their house, or that I turned over the cow-dung in their paddock in the search for some rare beetle believed to haunt the spot. The athlete was our watchman and our safety. He would suggest, should we meet a carriage on the drive, that we take off our hats and walk on as though about to pay a call. And once when we were sighted by a gamekeeper at Coombe Wood, he persuaded the elder of the brothers to pretend to be a schoolmaster taking his boys for a walk, and the keeper, instead of swearing and threatening the law, was sad and argumentative. No matter how charming the place (and there is a little stream in a hollow where Wimbledon Common flows into Coombe Wood that is pleasant in the memory), I knew that those other boys saw something I did not see. I was a stranger there. There was something in their way of saying the names of places that made me feel this.

X

When I arrived at the Clarence Basin, Liverpool (the dock Clarence Mangan had his first name from), on my way to Sligo for my holidays I was among Sligo people. When I was a little boy, an old woman who had come to Liverpool with crates of fowl made me miserable by throwing her arms around me, the moment I had alighted from my cab, and telling the sailor who carried my luggage that she had held me in her arms when I was a baby. The sailor may have known me almost as well, for I was often at Sligo quay to sail my boat; and I came and went once or twice in every year upon the s.s. *Sligo* or the s.s. *Liverpool* which belonged to a company that had for directors my grandfather and his partner William Middleton. I was always pleased if it was the *Liverpool*, for she had been built to run the blockade during the war of North and South.

I waited for this voyage always with excitement and boasted to other boys about it, and when I was a little boy had walked with my feet apart as I had seen sailors walk. I used to be sea-sick, but I must have hidden this from the other boys and partly even from myself; for, as I look back, I remember very little about it, while I remember stories I was told by the captain or by his first mate, and the look of the great cliffs of Donegal, and Tory Island men coming alongside with lobsters, talking Irish and, if it was night, blowing on a burning sod to draw our attention. The captain,[105] an old man with square shoulders and a fringe of grey hair round his face, would tell his first mate, a very admiring man, of fights he had had on shore at Liverpool; and perhaps it was of him I was thinking when I was very small and asked my grandmother if God was as strong as sailors. Once, at any rate, he had been nearly wrecked; the *Liverpool* had been all but blown upon the Mull of Galloway with her shaft broken, and the captain had said to his mate, 'Mind and jump when she strikes, for we don't want to be killed by the falling spars'; and when the mate answered, 'My God, I cannot swim', he had said, 'Who could keep afloat for five minutes in a sea like that?' He would often say his mate was the most timid of men and that 'a girl along the quays could laugh him out of anything'. My grandfather had more than once given him a ship of his own, but he had always thrown up his berth to sail with his old captain where he felt safe. Once he had been put in charge of a ship in a dry dock in Liverpool, but a boy was drowned in Sligo, and before the news could have reached him he wired to his wife, 'Ghost, come at once, or I will throw up berth'. He had been wrecked a number of times, and maybe that had broken his nerve or maybe he had a sensitiveness that would in another class have given him taste and culture. I once forgot a copy of *Count Robert of Paris* on a deck-seat, and when I found it again, it was all covered with the prints of his dirty thumb. He had once seen the coach-a-baur or death coach.[106] It came along the road, he said, till it was hidden by a cottage and it never came out on the other side of the cottage.

Once I smelled new-mown hay when we were quite a long way from land, and once when I was watching the sea-parrots (as the sailors call the puffin) I noticed they had different ways of tucking their heads under their wings, or I fancied it, and said to the captain, 'They have different characters'. Sometimes my father came too, and the sailors when they saw him coming would say, 'There is John Yeats and we shall have a storm', for he was considered unlucky.

I no longer cared for little shut-in places, for a coppice against the stable-yard at Merville where my grandfather lived or against the gable at Seaview[107] where Aunt Micky lived, and I began to climb the mountains, sometimes with the stable-boy for companion, and to look up their stories in the county history. I fished for trout with a worm in the mountain streams and went out herring-fishing at night; and because my grandfather had said the English were in the right to eat skate, I carried a large skate all the six miles or so from Rosses Point, but my grandfather did not eat it.

One night, just as the equinoctial gales were coming, when I was sailing home in the coastguard's boat, a boy told me a beetle of solid gold, strayed maybe from Poe's 'Gold Bug', had been seen by somebody in Scotland and I do not think that either of us doubted his news. Indeed, so many stories did I hear from sailors along the wharf, or round the fo'castle fire of the little steamer that ran between Sligo and Rosses, or from boys out fishing that the world seemed full of monsters and marvels. The foreign sailors wearing earrings did not tell me stories, but like the fishing-boys I gazed at them in wonder and admiration.

When I look at my brother's[108] picture, *Memory Harbour*[109]— houses and anchored ship and distant lighthouse all set close together as in some old map—I recognize in the blue-coated man with the mass of white shirt the pilot[110] I went fishing with, and I am full of disquiet and of excitement, and I am melancholy because I have not made more and better verses. I have walked on Sindbad's yellow shore and never shall another's hit my fancy.

I had still my red pony, and once my father came with me riding too, and was very exacting. He was indignant and threatening because he did not think I rode well. 'You must do everything well,' he said, 'that the Pollexfens respect, though you must do other things also.' He used to say the same about my lessons, and tell me to be good at mathematics. I can see now that he had a sense of inferiority among those energetic, successful people. He himself, some Pollexfen told me, though he rode very badly, would go hunting upon anything and take any ditch. His father, the County Down Rector,[111] though a courtly man and a scholar, had been so dandified a horseman that I had heard of his splitting three riding-breeches before he had settled into his saddle for a day's hunting, and of his first Rector exclaiming, 'I had hoped for a curate but they have sent me a jockey'.[112]

Left to myself, I rode without ambition, though getting many falls, and more often to Rathbroughan, where my great-uncle Mat lived, than to any place else. His children and I used to sail our toy boats in the river before his house, arming them with toy cannon, touch-paper at all the touch-holes, always hoping but always in vain that they would not twist about in the eddies but fire their cannon at one another. I must have gone to Sligo sometimes in the Christmas holidays, for I can remember riding my red pony to a hunt. He balked at the first jump, to my relief, and when a crowd of boys began to beat him, I would not allow it. They all jeered at me for being afraid. I found a gap and when alone tried another ditch, but the pony would not jump that either; so I tied him to a tree and lay down among the ferns and looked up into the sky. On my way home I met the hunt again and noticed that everybody avoided the dogs, and to find out why they did so rode to where the dogs had gathered in the middle of the lane and stood my pony amongst them, and everybody began to shout at me.

Sometimes I would ride to Castle Dargan, where lived a brawling squireen, married to one of my Middleton cousins,[113] and once I went thither on a visit with my cousin, George Middleton. It was, I daresay, the last household where I could have found the reckless Ireland of a hundred years ago in final degradation. But I liked the place for the romance of its two ruined castles facing one another across a little lake, Castle Dargan and Castle Fury.[114] The squireen lived in a small house his family had moved to from their castle some time in the eighteenth century, and two old Miss Furys, who let lodgings in Sligo, were the last remnants of the breed of the other ruin. Once in every year he drove to Sligo for the two old women, that they might look upon the ancestral stones and remember their gentility, and he would put his wildest horses into the shafts to enjoy their terror.

He himself, with a reeling imagination, knew not where to find a spur for the heavy hours. The first day I came there he gave my cousin a revolver (we were upon the high road), and to show it off, or his own shooting, he shot a passing chicken; and half an hour later, at the lake's edge under his castle, now but the broken corner of a tower with a winding stair,[115] he fired at or over an old countryman walking on the far edge of the lake. The next day I heard him settling the matter with the old countryman over a bottle of whiskey, and both were in good humour. Once he had asked a timid aunt of mine if she would like to see his last new pet, and thereupon had marched a racehorse in through the hall door and round the dining-room table. And once she came down to a bare table because he had thought it a good joke to open the window and let his harriers eat the breakfast. There was a current story, too, of his shooting, in the pride of his marksmanship, at his own door with a Martini-Henry rifle[116] till he had shot the knocker off. At last he quarrelled with my great-uncle, William Middleton, and to avenge himself gathered a rabble of wild country lads, mounted them and himself upon the most broken-down rascally horses he could lay hands on and marched them through Sligo under a Land League[117] banner. After that, having now neither friends nor money, he made off to Australia or to Canada.

I fished for pike at Castle Dargan and shot at birds with a muzzle-loading pistol until somebody shot a rabbit and I heard it squeal. From that on I would kill nothing but the dumb fish.

XI

We left Bedford Park for a long thatched house[118] at Howth, County Dublin. The land war was now at its height and our Kildare land,[119] that had been in the family for many generations, was slipping from us. Rents had fallen more and more, we had to sell to pay some charge or mortgage, but my father and his tenants parted without ill-will. During the worst times, an old tenant[120] had under his roof my father's shooting-dog and gave it better care than the annual payment earned. He had set apart for its comfort the best place at the fire; and if some man were in the place when the dog walked into the house, the man must needs make room for the dog. And a good while after the sale, I can remember my father being called upon to settle some dispute between this old man and his sons.

I was now fifteen; and as he did not want to leave his painting my father told me to go to Harcourt Street[121] and put myself to school. I found a bleak eighteenth-century house, a small playing-field full of mud and pebbles, fenced by an iron railing, and opposite a long hoarding and a squalid, ornamental railway station. Here, as I soon found, nobody gave a thought to decorum. We worked in a din of voices. We began the morning with prayers, but when class began the headmaster, if he was in the humour, would laugh at Church and Clergy. 'Let them say what they like', he would say, 'but the earth does go round the sun.' On the other hand there was no bullying and I had not thought it possible that boys could work so hard. Cricket and football, the collecting of moths and butterflies, though not forbidden, were discouraged. They were for idle boys. I did not know, as I used to, the mass of my school-fellows; for we had little life in common outside the class-rooms. I had begun to think of my school work as an interruption of my natural-history studies, but even had I never opened a book not in the school course, I could not have learned a quarter of my night's work. I had always done Euclid easily, making the problems out while the other boys were blundering at the blackboard, and it had often carried me from the bottom to the top of my class; but these boys had the same natural gift and instead of being in the fourth or fifth book were in the modern books at the end of the primer; and in place of a dozen lines of Virgil with a dictionary, I was expected to learn with the help of a crib a hundred and fifty lines. The other boys were able to learn the translation off, and to remember what words of Latin and English corresponded with one another, but I, who, it may be, had tried to find out what happened in the parts we had not read, made ridiculous mistakes; and what could I, who never worked when I was not interested, do with a history lesson that was but a column of seventy dates? I was worst of all at literature, for we read Shakespeare for his grammar exclusively.

One day I had a lucky thought. A great many lessons were run through in the last hour of the day, things we had learnt or should have learnt by heart overnight, and not having known one of them for weeks, I cut off that hour without anybody's leave. I asked the mathematical master to give me a sum to work and nobody said a word. My father often interfered, and always with disaster, to teach me my Latin lesson. 'But I have also my geography', I would say. 'Geography', he would reply, 'should never be taught. It is not a training for the mind. You will pick up all that you need, in your general reading.' And if it was a history lesson, he would say just the same, and 'Euclid', he would say, 'is too easy. It comes naturally to the literary imagination. The old idea, that it is a good training for the mind, was long ago refuted.' I would know my Latin lesson so that it was a nine days' wonder, and for weeks after would be told it was scandalous to be so clever and so idle. No one knew that I had learnt it in the terror that alone could check my wandering mind. I must have told on him at some time or other, for I remember the headmaster saying, 'I am going to give you an imposition because I cannot get at your father to give him one'. Sometimes we had essays to write; and though I never got a prize, for the essays were judged by handwriting and spelling, I caused a measure of scandal. I would be called up before some master and asked if I really believed such things, and that would make me angry, for I had written what I had believed all my life, what my father had told me, or a memory of the conversation of his friends. I was asked to write an essay on 'Men may rise on stepping-stones of their dead selves to higher things'. My father read the subject to my mother who had no interest in such matters. 'That is the way', he said, 'boys are made insincere and false to themselves. Ideals make the blood thin, and take the human nature out of people.' He walked up and down the room in eloquent indignation, and told me not to write on such a subject at all, but upon Shakespeare's lines,[122] 'To thine own self be true, and it must follow, as the night the day, thou canst not then be false to any man'. At another time, he would denounce the idea of duty: 'Imagine', he would say, 'how the right sort of woman would despise a dutiful husband'; and he would tell us how much my mother would scorn such a thing. Maybe there were people among whom such ideas were natural, but they were the people with whom one does not dine. All he said was, I now believe, right, but he should have taken me away from school. He would have taught me nothing but Greek and Latin, and I would now be a properly educated man, and would not have to look in useless longing at books that have been, through the poor mechanism of translation, the builders of my soul, nor face authority with the timidity born of excuse and evasion. Evasion and excuse were in the event as wise as the house-building instinct of the beaver.

XII

My London school-fellow,[123] the athlete, spent a summer with us, but the friendship of boyhood, founded upon action and adventure, was drawing to an end. He was still my superior in all physical activity and climbed to places among the rocks that even now are uncomfortable memories, but I had begun to criticize him. One morning I proposed a journey to Lambay Island, and was contemptuous because he said we should miss our mid-day meal. We hoisted a sail on our small boat and ran quickly over the nine miles and saw on the shore a tame sea-gull, while a couple of boys, the sons of a coastguard, ran into the water in their clothes to pull us to land, as we had read of savage people doing. We spent an hour upon the sunny shore and I said, 'I would like to live here always, and perhaps some day I will'. I was always discovering places where I would like to spend my whole life. We started to row home, and when dinner-time had passed for about an hour, the athlete lay down on the bottom of the boat doubled up with the gripes. I mocked at him and at his fellow-countrymen whose stomachs struck the hour as if they were clocks.

Our natural history, too, began to pull us apart. I planned some day to write a book about the changes through a twelvemonth among the creatures of some hole in the rock, and had some theory of my own, which I cannot remember, as to the colour of sea-anemones: and after much hesitation, trouble and bewilderment, was hot for argument in refutation of Adam and Noah and the Seven Days. I had read Darwin and Wallace, Huxley and Haeckel, and would spend hours on a holiday plaguing a pious geologist,[124] who, when not at some job in Guinness's brewery, came with a hammer to look for fossils in the Howth Cliffs. 'You know', I would say, 'that such-and-such human remains cannot be less, because of the strata they were found in, than fifty thousand years old.' 'O!' he would answer, 'they are an isolated instance.' And once when I pressed hard my case against Ussher's chronology,[125] he begged me not to speak of the subject again. 'If I believed what you do', he said, 'I could not live a moral life.' But I could not even argue with the athlete, who still collected his butterflies for the adventure's sake, and with no curiosity but for their names. I began to judge his intelligence, and to tell him that his natural history had as little to do with science as his collection of postage stamps. Even during my schooldays in London, influenced perhaps by my father, I had looked down upon the postage stamps.

XIII

Our house for the first year or so was on the top of a cliff, so that in stormy weather the spray would soak my bed at night, for I had taken the glass out of the window, sash and all. A literary passion for the open air was to last me for a few years. Then for another year or two we had a house overlooking the harbour[126] where the one great sight was the going and coming of the fishing fleet. We had one regular servant, a fisherman's wife, and the occasional help of a big, red-faced girl who ate a whole pot of jam while my mother was at church and accused me of it. Some such arrangement lasted until long after the time I write of, and until my father going into the kitchen by chance found a girl, engaged during a passing need, in tears at the thought of leaving our other servant, and promised that they should never be parted. I have no doubt that we lived at the harbour for my mother's sake. She had, when we were children, refused to take us to a seaside place because she heard it possessed a bathing-box,[127] but she loved the activities of a fishing village. When I think of her, I almost always see her talking over a cup of tea in the kitchen with our servant, the fisherman's wife, on the only themes outside our house that seemed of interest—the fishing-people of Howth, or the pilots and fishing-people of Rosses Point. She read no books, but she and the fisherman's wife would tell each other stories that Homer might have told, pleased with any moment of sudden intensity and laughing together over any point of satire. There is an essay called 'Village Ghosts'[128] in my *Celtic Twilight* which is but a record of one such afternoon, and many a fine tale has been lost because it had not occurred to me soon enough to keep notes. My father was always praising her to my sisters and to me, because she pretended to nothing she did not feel. She would write him letters telling of her delight in the tumbling clouds, but she did not care for pictures, and never went to an exhibition even to see a picture of his, nor to his studio to see the day's work, neither now nor when they were first married. I remember all this very clearly and little after it until her mind had gone in a stroke of paralysis and she had found, liberated at last from financial worry, perfect happiness feeding the birds at a London window. She had always, my father would say, intensity, and that was his chief word of praise; and once he added to the praise, 'No spendthrift ever had a poet for a son, though a miser might'.

XIV

The great event of a boy's life is the awakening of sex.[129] He will bathe many times a day, or get up at dawn and having stripped leap to and fro over a stick laid upon two chairs, and hardly know, and never admit, that he had begun to take pleasure in his own nakedness, nor will he understand the change until some dream discovers it. He may never understand at all the greater change in his mind.

It all came upon me when I was close upon seventeen like the bursting of a shell. Somnambulistic country girls, when it is upon them, throw plates about or pull them with long hairs in simulation of the poltergeist,[130] or become mediums for some genuine spirit-mischief, surrendering to their desire of the marvellous. As I look backward, I seem to discover that my passions, my loves and my despairs, instead of being my enemies, a disturbance and an attack, became so beautiful that I had to be constantly alone to give them my whole attention. I notice that now, for the first time, what I saw when alone is more vivid in my memory than what I did or saw in company.

A herd had shown me a cave some hundred and fifty feet below the cliff path and a couple of hundred above the sea, and told me that an evicted tenant called Macrom, dead some fifteen years, had lived there many years, and shown me a rusty nail in the rock which had served perhaps to hold up some wooden protection from wind and weather. Here I stored a tin of cocoa and some biscuits, and instead of going to my bed, would slip out on warm nights and sleep in the cave on the excuse of catching moths. One had to pass over a rocky ledge, safe enough for any one with a fair head, yet seeming, if looked at from above, narrow and sloping; and a remonstrance from a stranger who had seen me climbing along it doubled my delight in the adventure. When, however, upon a bank holiday, I found lovers in my cave, I was not content with it again till I heard that the ghost of Macrom had been seen a little before the dawn, stooping over his fire in the cave-mouth. I had been trying to cook eggs, as I had read in some book, by burying them in the earth under a fire of sticks.

At other times, I would sleep among the rhododendrons and rocks in the wilder part of the grounds of Howth Castle. After a while my father said I must stay indoors half the night, meaning that I should get some sleep in my bed; but I, knowing that I would be too sleepy and comfortable to get up again, used to sit over the kitchen fire till half the night was gone. Exaggerated accounts spread through the school, and sometimes when I did not know a lesson some master would banter me about the way my nights were spent. My interest in science began to fade, and presently I said to myself, 'It has all been a misunderstanding'. I remembered how soon I tired of my specimens, and how little I knew after all my years of collecting, and I came to believe that I had gone through so much labour because of a text, heard for the first time in Saint John's Church in Sligo, and copied Solomon, who had knowledge of hyssop and of tree,[131] that I might be certain of my own wisdom. I still carried my green net, but I began to play at being a sage, a magician or a poet. I had many idols, and as I climbed along the narrow ledge I was now Manfred on his glacier, and now Prince Athanase with his solitary lamp, but I soon chose Alastor for my chief of men and longed to share his melancholy, and maybe at last to disappear from everybody's sight as he disappeared drifting in a boat along some slow-moving river between great trees.[132] When I thought of women they were modelled on those in my favourite poets and loved in brief tragedy, or like the girl in *The Revolt of Islam*,[133] accompanied their lovers through all manner of wild places, lawless women without homes and without children.

XV

My father's influence upon my thoughts was at its height. We went to Dublin by train every morning, breakfasting in his studio.[134] He had taken a large room with a beautiful eighteenth-century mantelpiece in a York Street tenement-house, and at breakfast he read passages from the poets, and always from the play or poem at its most passionate moment. He never read me a passage because of its speculative interest, and indeed did not care at all for poetry where there was generalization or abstraction however impassioned. He would read out the first speeches of the *Prometheus Unbound,* but never the ecstatic lyricism of that famous fourth act; and another day the scene where Coriolanus[135] comes to the house of Aufidius and tells the impudent servants that his home is under the canopy. I have seen *Coriolanus* played a number of times since then, and read it more than once, but that scene is more vivid than the rest, and it is my father's voice that I hear and not Irving's or Benson's. He did not care even for a fine lyric passage unless he felt some actual man behind its elaboration of beauty, and he was always looking for the lineaments of some desirable, familiar life. When the spirits sang their scorn of Manfred, and Manfred answered, 'O sweet and melancholy voices',[136] I was told that they could not, even in anger, put off their spiritual sweetness. He thought Keats a greater poet than Shelley,[137] because less abstract, but did not read him, caring little, I think, for any of that most beautiful poetry which has come in modern times from the influence of painting. All must be an idealization of speech, and at some moment of passionate action or somnambulistic reverie. I remember his saying that all contemplative men were in a conspiracy to overrate their state of life, and that all writers were of them, excepting the great poets. Looking backwards, it seems to me that I saw his mind in fragments, which had always hidden connections I only now begin to discover. He disliked the Victorian poetry of ideas, and Wordsworth but for certain passages or whole poems. He said one morning over his breakfast that he had discovered in the shape of the head of a Wordsworthian scholar,[138] an old and greatly respected clergyman whose portrait he was painting, all the animal instincts of a prize-fighter. He despised the formal beauty of Raphael, that calm which is not an ordered passion but an hypocrisy, and attacked Raphael's life for its love of pleasure and its self-indulgence. In literature he was always Pre-Raphaelite, and carried into literature principles that, while the Academy was still unbroken,[139] had made the first attack upon academic form.

He no longer read me anything for its story, and all our discussion was of style.

XVI

I began to make blunders when I paid calls or visits, and a woman I had known and liked as a child told me I had changed for the worse. I wanted to be wise and eloquent, an essay on the younger Ampère had helped me to this ambition, and when I was alone I exaggerated my blunders and was miserable. I had begun to write poetry in imitation of Shelley and of Edmund Spenser,[140] play after play—for my father exalted dramatic poetry above all other kinds—and I invented fantastic and incoherent plots.[141] My lines but seldom scanned, for I could not understand the prosody in the books, although there were many lines that taken by themselves had music. I spoke them slowly as I wrote and only discovered when I read them to somebody else that there was no common music, no prosody. There were, however, moments of observation; for, even when I caught moths no longer, I still noticed all that passed; how the little moths came out at sunset, and how after that there were only a few big moths till dawn brought little moths again; and what birds cried out at night as if in their sleep.

XVII

At Sligo, where I still went for my holidays, I stayed with my uncle, George Pollexfen,[142] who had come from Ballina to fill the place of my grandfather, who had retired. My grandfather had no longer his big house, his partner William Middleton was dead, and there had been legal trouble. He was no longer the rich man he had been, and his sons and daughters were married and scattered. He had a tall, bare house[143] overlooking the harbour, and had nothing to do but work himself into a rage if he saw a mud-lighter mismanaged or judged from the smoke of a steamer that she was burning cheap coal, and to superintend the making of his tomb. There was a Middleton tomb and a long list of Middletons on the wall, and an almost empty space for Pollexfen names, but he had said, because there was a Middleton there he did not like, 'I am not going to lie with those old bones'; and already one saw his name in large gilt letters on the stone fence of the new tomb. He ended his walk at Saint John's[144] churchyard almost daily, for he liked everything neat and compendious as upon shipboard, and if he had not looked after the tomb himself the builder might have added some useless ornament. He had, however, all his old skill and nerve. I was going to Rosses Point on the little trading steamer and saw him take the wheel from the helmsman and steer her through a gap in the Channel wall, and across the sand, an unheard-of course, and at the journey's end bring her alongside her wharf at Rosses without the accustomed zigzagging or pulling on a rope but in a single movement. He took snuff when he had a cold, but had never smoked nor taken alcohol; and when in his eightieth year his doctor advised a stimulant, he replied, 'No, no, I am not going to form a bad habit'.

My brother had partly taken my place in my grandmother's affections. He had lived permanently in her house for some years now, and went to a Sligo school where he was always bottom of his class. My grandmother did not mind that, for she said, 'He is too kindhearted to pass the other boys'. He spent his free hours going here and there with crowds of little boys, sons of pilots and sailors,

as their well-liked leader, arranging donkey races or driving don-
keys tandem, an occupation which requires all one's intellect
because of their obstinacy. Besides he had begun to amuse everybody with his drawings; and in half the pictures he paints to-day I
recognize faces that I have met at Rosses or the Sligo quays. It is
long since he has lived there, but his memory seems as accurate as
the sight of the eye.

George Pollexfen was as patient as his father was impetuous,
and did all by habit. A well-to-do, elderly man, he lived with no
more comfort than when he had set out as a young man. He had a
little house and one old general servant and a man to look after his
horse, and every year he gave up some activity and found that there
was one more food that disagreed with him. A hypochondriac, he
passed from winter to summer through a series of woollens that
had always to be weighed; for in April or May, or whatever the date
was, he had to be sure he carried the exact number of ounces he had
carried upon that date since boyhood. He lived in despondency,
finding in the most cheerful news reasons of discouragement, and
sighing every twenty-second of June over the shortening of the
days. Once in later years, when I met him in Dublin sweating in a
midsummer noon, I brought him into the hall of the Kildare Street
Library,[145] a cool and shady place, without lightening his spirits; for
he but said in a melancholy voice, 'How very cold this place must
be in winter-time'. Sometimes when I had pitted my cheerfulness
against his gloom over the breakfast-table, maintaining that neither
his talent nor his memory nor his health were running to the dregs,
he would rout me with the sentence, 'How very old I shall be in
twenty years'. Yet this inactive man, in whom the sap of life seemed
to be dried away, had a mind full of pictures. Nothing had ever happened to him except a love affair, not, I think, very passionate, that
had gone wrong, and a voyage when a young man. My grandfather
had sent him in a schooner to a port in Spain where the shipping
agents were two Spaniards called O'Neill, descendants of Hugh
O'Neill, Earl of Tyrone, who had fled from Ireland in the reign of
James I.; and their Irish trade was a last remnant of the Spanish
trade that had once made Galway wealthy. For some years he and
they had corresponded, for they cherished the memory of their origin. In some Connacht burying-ground, he had chanced upon the
funeral of a child with but one mourner, a distinguished foreign-

looking man. It was an Austrian Count[146] burying the last of an Irish family, long nobles of Austria, who were always carried to that half-ruined burying-ground.

My uncle had almost given up hunting and was soon to give it up altogether, and he had once ridden steeplechases and been, his horse-trainer said, the best rider in Connacht.[147] He had certainly great knowledge of horses, for I have been told, several counties away, that at Ballina he cured horses by conjuring. He had, however, merely great skill in diagnosis, for the day was still far off when he was to give his nights to astrology and ceremonial magic. His servant, Mary Battle, who had been with him since he was a young man, had the second sight and that, maybe, inclined him to strange studies. One morning she was about to bring him a clean shirt, but stopped, saying there was blood on the shirt-front and that she must bring him another. On his way to his office he fell, crossing over a little wall, and cut himself and bled on to the linen where she had seen the blood. In the evening, she told him that the shirt she had thought bloody was quite clean. She could neither read nor write and her mind, which answered his gloom with its merriment, was rammed with every sort of old history and strange belief. Much of my *Celtic Twilight* is but her daily speech.

My uncle had the respect of the common people as few Sligo men have had it; he would have thought a stronger emotion an intrusion on his privacy. He gave to all men the respect due to their station or their worth with an added measure of ceremony, and kept among his workmen a discipline that had about it something of a regiment or a ship, knowing nothing of any but personal authority. If a carter, let us say, was in fault, he would not dismiss him, but send for him and take his whip away and hang it upon the wall; and having reduced the offender, as it were, to the ranks for certain months, would restore him to his post and his whip. This man of diligence and of method, who had no enterprise but in contemplation, and claimed that his wealth, considerable for Ireland, came from a brother's or partner's talent, was the confidant of my boyish freaks and reveries. When I said to him, echoing some book I had read, that one never knew a countryside till one knew it at night he was pleased (though nothing would have kept him from his bed a moment beyond the hour); for he loved natural things and had learnt two cries of the lapwing, one that drew them to where he stood and one that made them fly away. And he approved, and arranged my meals conveniently, when I told him I was going to walk round Lough Gill and sleep in a wood. I did not tell him all my object, for I was nursing a new ambition. My father had read to me some passage out of *Walden,* and I planned to live some day in a cottage on a little island called Innisfree, and Innisfree was opposite Slish Wood where I meant to sleep.

I thought that having conquered bodily desire and the inclination of my mind towards women and love, I should live, as Thoreau lived, seeking wisdom. There was a story in the county history[148] of a tree that had once grown upon that island guarded by some terrible monster and borne the food of the gods. A young girl pined for the fruit and told her lover to kill the monster and carry the fruit away. He did as he had been told, but tasted the fruit; and when he reached the mainland where she had waited for him, he was dying of its powerful virtue. And from sorrow and from remorse she too ate of it and died. I do not remember whether I chose the island because of its beauty or for the story's sake, but I was twenty-two or three before I gave up the dream.

I set out from Sligo about six in the evening, walking slowly, for it was an evening of great beauty; but though I was well into Slish Wood by bedtime, I could not sleep, not from the discomfort of the dry rock I had chosen for my bed, but from my fear of the wood-ranger. Somebody had told me, though I do not think it could have been true, that he went his round at some unknown hour. I kept going over what I should say if found and could not think of anything he would believe. However, I could watch my island in the early dawn and notice the order of the cries of the birds.

I came home next day unimaginably tired and sleepy, having walked some thirty miles partly over rough and boggy ground. For months afterwards, if I alluded to my walk, my uncle's general servant[149] (not Mary Battle, who was slowly recovering from an illness and would not have taken the liberty) would go into fits of laughter. She believed I had spent the night in a different fashion and had invented the excuse to deceive my uncle, and would say to my great embarrassment, for I was as prudish as an old maid, 'And you had a good right to be fatigued'.

Once when staying with my uncle at Rosses Point, where he went for certain months of the year, I called upon a cousin[150] towards midnight and asked him to get his yacht out, for I wanted to find what sea-birds began to stir before dawn. He was indignant and refused; but his elder sister had overheard me and came to the head of the stairs and forbade him to stir, and that so vexed him that he shouted to the kitchen for his sea-boots. He came with me in great gloom, for he had people's respect, he declared, and nobody so far said that he was mad, as they said I was, and we got a very sleepy boy out of his bed in the village and set up sail. We put a trawl out, as he thought it would restore his character if he caught some fish, but the wind fell and we were becalmed. I rolled myself in the mainsail and went to sleep, for I could sleep anywhere in those days. I was awakened towards dawn to see my cousin and the boy turning out their pockets for money and had to rummage in my own pockets. A boat was rowing in from Roughley with fish and they wanted to buy some and pretend they had caught it, but all our pockets were empty. I had wanted the birds' cries for the poem that became fifteen years afterwards *The Shadowy Waters*, and it had been full of observation had I been able to write it when I first planned it. I had found again the windy light that moved me when a child. I persuaded myself that I had a passion for the dawn, and this passion, though mainly histrionic like a child's play, an ambitious game, had moments of sincerity. Years afterwards when I had finished *The Wanderings of Oisin*, dissatisfied with its yellow and its dull green, with all that overcharged colour inherited from the romantic movement, I deliberately reshaped my style, deliberately sought out an impression as of cold light and tumbling clouds. I cast off traditional metaphors and loosened my rhythm, and recognizing that all the criticism of life known to me was alien and English, became as emotional as possible but with an emotion which I described to myself as cold. It is a natural conviction for a painter's son to believe that there may be a landscape that is symbolical of some spiritual condition and awakens a hunger such as cats feel for valerian.

XVIII

I was writing a long play[151] on a fable suggested by one of my father's early designs. A king's daughter loves a god seen in the luminous sky above her garden in childhood, and to be worthy of him and put away mortality, becomes without pity and commits crimes, and at last, having made her way to the throne by murder, awaits his coming among her courtiers. One by one they become chilly and drop dead, for, unseen by all but her, her god is in the hall. At last he is at her throne's foot and she, her mind in the garden once again, dies babbling like a child.

XIX

Once when I was sailing with my cousin, the boy who was our crew talked of a music-hall at a neighbouring seaport,[152] and how the girls there gave themselves to men, and his language was as extravagant as though he praised that courtesan after whom they named a city or the Queen of Sheba herself. Another day he wanted my cousin to sail some fifty miles along the coast and put in near some cottages where he had heard there were girls 'and we would have a great welcome before us'. He pleaded with excitement (I imagine that his eyes shone) but hardly hoped to persuade us, and perhaps but played with fabulous images of life and of sex. A young jockey and horse-trainer, who had trained some horses for my uncle, once talked to me of wicked England while we cooked a turkey for our Christmas dinner, making it twist about on a string in front of his harness-room fire. He had met two lords in England where he had gone racing, who 'always exchanged wives when they went to the Continent for a holiday'. He himself had once been led into temptation and was going home with a woman, but having touched his scapular by chance, saw in a moment an angel waving white wings in the air. Presently I was to meet him no more and my uncle said he had done something disgraceful about a horse.

XX

I was climbing up a hill at Howth when I heard wheels behind me and a pony-carriage drew up beside me. A pretty girl[153] was driving alone and without a hat. She told me her name and said we had friends in common and asked me to ride beside her. After that I saw a great deal of her and was soon in love. I did not tell her I was in love, however, because she was engaged. She had chosen me for her confidant and I learned all about her quarrels with her lover. Several times he broke the engagement off, and she fell ill, and friends had to make peace. Sometimes she would write to him three times a day, but she could not do without a confidant. She was a wild creature, a fine mimic, and given to bursts of religion. I had known her to weep at a sermon, call herself a sinful woman, and mimic it after. I wrote her some bad poems and had more than one sleepless night through anger with her betrothed.

XXI

At Ballisodare an event happened that brought me back to the superstitions of my childhood. I do not know when it was, for the events of this period have as little sequence as those of childhood. I was staying with cousins at Avena House, a young man a few years older, and a girl of my own age and perhaps her sister who was a good deal older. My girl cousin[154] had often told me of strange sights she had seen at Ballisodare or Rosses. An old woman three or four feet in height and leaning on a stick had once come to the window and looked in at her, and sometimes she would meet people on the road who would say, 'How is So-and-so?', naming some member of her family, and she would know, though she could not explain how, that they were not people of this world. Once she had lost her way in a familiar field, and when she found it again the silver mounting on a walking-stick belonging to her brother which she carried had vanished. An old woman in the village said afterwards, 'You have good friends amongst them, and the silver was taken instead of you'.[155]

Though it was all years ago, what I am going to tell now must be accurate, for no great while ago she wrote out her unprompted memory of it all and it was the same as mine. She was sitting under an old-fashioned mirror reading and I was reading in another part of the room. Suddenly I heard a sound as if somebody was throwing a shower of peas at the mirror. I got her to go into the next room and rap with her knuckles on the other side of the wall to see if the sound could come from there, and while I was alone a great thump came close to my head upon the wainscot and on a different wall of the room. Later in the day a servant heard a heavy footstep going through the empty house, and that night, when I and my two cousins went for a walk, she saw the ground under some trees all in a blaze of light. I saw nothing, but presently we crossed the river and went along its edge where, they say, there was a village destroyed, I think in the wars of the seventeenth century, and near an old graveyard. Suddenly we all saw a light moving over the river where there is a great rush of waters. It was like a very brilliant torch. A moment later the girl saw a man coming towards us who disappeared in the water. I kept asking myself if I could be deceived. Perhaps after all, though it seemed impossible, somebody was walking in the water with a torch. But we could see a small light low down on Knocknarea seven miles off, and it began to move upward over the mountain slope. I timed it on my watch and in five minutes it reached the summit, and I, who had often climbed the mountain, knew that no human footstep was so speedy.

From that on I wandered about raths and faery hills[156] and questioned old women and old men and, when I was tired out or unhappy, began to long for some such end as True Thomas[157] found. I did not believe with my intellect that you could be carried away body and soul, but I believed with my emotions and the belief of the countrypeople made that easy. Once when I had crawled into the stone passage[158] in some rath of the third Rosses, the pilot who had come with me called down the passage: 'Are you all right, sir?'

And one night as I came near the village of Rosses on the road from Sligo, a fire blazed up on a green bank at my right side seven or eight feet above me, and another fire suddenly answered from Knocknarea. I hurried on doubting, and yet hardly doubting in my heart that I saw again the fires that I had seen by the river at Ballisodare. I began occasionally telling people that one should believe whatever had been believed in all countries and periods, and only reject any part of it after much evidence, instead of starting all over afresh and only believing what one could prove. But I was always ready to deny or turn into a joke what was for all that my secret fanaticism. When I had read Darwin and Huxley and believed as they did, I had wanted, because an established authority was upon my side, to argue with everybody.

XXII

I no longer went to the Harcourt Street school and we had moved from Howth to Rathgar.[159] I was at the art schools in Kildare Street,[160] but my father, who came to the school now and then, was my teacher. The masters left me alone, for they liked a very smooth surface and a very neat outline, and indeed understood nothing but neatness and smoothness. A drawing of the Discobolus, after my father had touched it, making the shoulder stand out with swift and broken lines, had no meaning for them; and for the most part I exaggerated all that my father did. Sometimes indeed, out of rivalry to some student near, I too would try to be smooth and neat. One day I helped the student next me, who certainly had no artistic gifts, to make a drawing of some plaster fruit. In his gratitude he told me his history. 'I don't care for art', he said. 'I am a good billiard player, one of the best in Dublin; but my guardian said I must take a profession, so I asked my friends to tell me what I could do without passing an examination, and here I am.' It may be that I myself was there for no better reason. My father had wanted me to go to Trinity College[161] and, when I would not, had said, 'My father and grandfather and great-grandfather have been there'. I did not tell him that neither my classics nor my mathematics were good enough for any examination.

I had for fellow-student an unhappy 'village genius',[162] sent to Dublin by some charitable Connacht landlord. He painted religious pictures upon sheets nailed to the wall of his bedroom, a *Last Judgment* among the rest. Then there was a wild young man[163] who would come to school of a morning with a daisy-chain hung round his neck; and George Russell, 'A.E.', the poet and mystic. He did not paint the model as we tried to, for some other image rose always before his eyes (a Saint John in the Desert I remember), and already he spoke to us of his visions. One day he announced that he was leaving the art schools because his will was weak and the arts or any other emotional pursuit could but weaken it further.

Presently I went to the modelling class to be with certain elder students who had authority among us. Among these were John Hughes and Oliver Sheppard, well known now as Irish sculptors. The day I first went into the studio where they worked, I stood still upon the threshold in amazement. A pretty gentle-looking girl was modelling in the middle of the room, and all the men were swearing at her for getting in their light with the most violent and fantastic oaths, and calling her every sort of name, and through it all she worked in undisturbed diligence. Presently the man nearest me saw my face and called out, 'She is stone deaf, so we always swear at her and call her names when she gets in our light'. In reality I soon found that every one was kind to her, carrying her drawing-boards and the like, and putting her into the tram at the day's end.

We had no scholarship, no critical knowledge of the history of painting, and no settled standards. A student would show his fellows some French illustrated paper that we might all admire now some statue by Rodin or Dalou and now some declamatory Parisian monument, and if I did not happen to have discussed the matter with my father I would admire with no more discrimination than the rest. That pretentious monument to Gambetta[164] made a great stir among us. No influence touched us but that of France, where one or two of the older students had been already and all hoped to go. Of England I alone knew anything. Our ablest student had learnt Italian to read Dante, but had never heard of Tennyson or Browning, and it was I who carried into the school some knowledge of English poetry, especially of Browning, who had begun to move me by his air of wisdom. I do not believe that I worked well, for I wrote a great deal and that tired me, and the work I was set to bored me. When alone and uninfluenced, I longed for pattern, for Pre-Raphaelitism, for an art allied to poetry, and returned again and again to our National Gallery to gaze at Turner's *Golden Bough*.[165] Yet I was too timid, had I known how, to break away from my father's style and the style of those about me. I was always hoping that my father would return to the style of his youth, and make pictures out of certain designs now lost, that one could still find in his portfolios. There was one of an old hunchback in vague mediaeval dress, going through some underground place where there are beds with people in the beds; a girl half rising from one has seized his hand and is kissing it. I have forgotten its story, but the strange old man and the intensity in the girl's figure are vivid as in my childhood.[166] There is some passage, I believe in the Bible, about a man who saved a city and went away and was never heard of again, and here he was in another design,[167] an old ragged beggar in the market-place laughing at his own statue. But my father would say, 'I must paint what I see in front of me. Of course I shall really paint something different because my nature will come in unconsciously.' Sometimes I would try to argue with him, for I had come to think the philosophy of his fellow-artists and himself a misunderstanding created by Victorian science, and science I had grown to hate with a monkish hate; but no good came of it, and in a moment I would unsay what I had said and pretend that I did not really believe it. My father was painting many fine portraits,[168] Dublin leaders of the bar, college notabilities, or chance comers whom he would paint for nothing if he liked their heads; but all displeased me. In my heart I thought that only beautiful things should be painted, and that only ancient things and the stuff of dreams were beautiful. And I almost quarrelled with my father when he made a large water-colour, one of his finest pictures and now lost, of a consumptive beggar-girl.[169] And a picture at the Hibernian Academy of cocottes with yellow faces sitting before a café by some follower of Manet's made me miserable for days,[170] but I was happy when partly through my father's planning some Whistlers were brought over and exhibited, and did not agree when my father said, 'Imagine making your old mother an arrangement in grey!'[171] I did not care for mere reality and believed that creation should be deliberate, and yet I could only imitate my father. I could not compose anything but a portrait and even to-day I constantly see people as a portrait-painter, posing them in the mind's eye before such-and-such a background. Meanwhile I was still very much of a child, sometimes drawing with an elaborate frenzy, simulating what I believed of inspiration, and sometimes walking with an artificial stride in memory of Hamlet[172] and stopping at shop-windows to look at my tie gathered into a loose sailor-knot and to regret that it could not be always blown out by the wind like Byron's tie in the picture.[173] I had as many ideas as I have now, only I did not know how to choose from among them those that belonged to my life.

XXIII

We lived in a villa[174] where the red bricks were made pretentious and vulgar with streaks of slate colour, and there seemed to be enemies everywhere. At one side indeed there was a friendly architect, but on the other some stupid stout woman and her family. I had a study with a window opposite some window of hers, and one night when I was writing I heard voices full of derision and saw the stout woman and her family standing in the window. I have a way of acting what I write and speaking it aloud without knowing what I am doing. Perhaps I was on my hands and knees, or looking down over the back of a chair talking into what I imagined an abyss. Another day a woman asked me to direct her on her way and while I was hesitating, being so suddenly called out of my thought, a woman from some neighbouring house came by. She said I was a poet and my questioner turned away contemptuously. Upon the other hand, the policeman and tramway conductor thought my absence of mind sufficiently explained when our servant told them I was a poet. 'O, well,' said the policeman, who had been asking why I went indifferently through clean and muddy places, 'if it is only the poetry that is working in his head!' I imagine I looked gaunt and emaciated, for the little boys at the neighbouring cross-road used to say when I passed by: 'O, here is King Death again'. One morning when my father was on the way to his studio, he met his landlord[175] and they had this conversation: 'Do you think now that Tennyson should have been given that peerage?' 'One's only doubt is if he should have accepted it: it was a finer thing to be Alfred Tennyson.' There was a silence, and then: 'Well, all the people I know think he should not have got it.' Then, spitefully: 'What's the good of poetry?' 'O, it gives our minds a great deal of pleasure.' 'But wouldn't it have given your mind more pleasure if he had written an improving book?' 'O, in that case I should not have read it.' My father returned in the evening delighted with his story, but I could not understand how he could take such opinions lightly and not have seriously argued with the man.

None of these people had ever seen any poet but an old white-haired man who had written volumes of easy, too-honeyed verse, and run through his money and gone clean out of his mind. He was a common figure in the streets and lived in some shabby neighbourhood of tenement houses where there were hens and chickens among the cobble-stones. Every morning he carried home a loaf and gave half of it to the hens and chickens, the birds, or to some dog or starving cat. He was known to live in one room with a nail in the middle of the ceiling from which innumerable cords were stretched to other nails in the walls. In this way he kept up the illusion that he was living under canvas in some Arabian desert. I could not escape like this old man from house and neighbourhood, but hated both, hearing every whisper, noticing every passing glance.

When my grandfather came for a few days to see a doctor, I was shocked to see him in our house. My father read out to him in the evening Clark Russell's *Wreck of the 'Grosvenor'*; but the doctor forbade it, for my grandfather got up in the middle of the night and acted through the mutiny, as I acted my verse, saying the while, 'Yes, yes, that is the way it would all happen'.

XXIV

From our first arrival in Dublin, my father had brought me from time to time to see Edward Dowden.[176] He and my father had been college friends and were trying, perhaps, to take up again their old friendship. Sometimes we were asked to breakfast, and afterwards my father would tell me to read out one of my poems. Dowden was wise in his encouragement, never overpraising and never unsympathetic, and he would sometimes lend me books. The orderly, prosperous house where all was in good taste, where poetry was rightly valued, made Dublin tolerable for a while, and for perhaps a couple of years he was an image of romance. My father would not share my enthusiasm and soon, I noticed, grew impatient at these meetings. He would sometimes say that he had wanted Dowden when they were young to give himself to creative art, and would talk of what he considered Dowden's failure in life. I know now that he was finding in his friend what he himself had been saved from by the conversation of the Pre-Raphaelites. 'He will not trust his nature', he would say, or 'He is too much influenced by his inferiors', or he would praise 'Renunciants',[177] one of Dowden's poems, to prove what Dowden might have written. I was not influenced, for I had imagined a past worthy of that dark, romantic face. I took literally his verses, touched here and there with Swinburnian rhetoric, and believed that he had loved, unhappily and illicitly; and when through the practice of my art I discovered that certain images about the love of woman were the properties of a school, I but changed my fancy and thought of him as very wise.

I was constantly troubled about philosophic questions. I would say to my fellow-students at the art schools, 'Poetry and sculpture exist to keep our passions alive'; and somebody would say, 'We would be much better without our passions'. Or I would have a week's anxiety over the problem: do the arts make us happier, or more sensitive and therefore more unhappy? And I would say to Hughes or Sheppard, 'If I cannot be certain they make us happier I will never write again'. If I spoke of these things to Dowden he would put the question away with good-humoured irony: he seemed to condescend to everybody and everything and was now my sage. I was about to learn that if a man is to write lyric poetry he must be shaped by nature and art to some one out of half a dozen traditional poses, and be lover or saint, sage or sensualist, or mere mocker of all life; and that none but that stroke of luckless luck can open before him the accumulated expression of the world. And this thought before it could be knowledge was an instinct.

I was vexed when my father called Dowden's irony timidity, but after many years his impression has not changed, for he wrote to me but a few months ago, 'It was like talking to a priest. One had to be careful not to remind him of his sacrifice.'[178] Once after breakfast Dowden read us some chapters of the unpublished *Life of Shelley*, and I who had made the *Prometheus Unbound* my sacred book was delighted with all he read. I was chilled, however, when he explained that he had lost his liking for Shelley and would not have written it but for an old promise to the Shelley family. When it was published, Matthew Arnold made sport of certain conventionalities and extravagances[179] that were, my father and I had come to see, the violence or clumsiness of a conscientious man hiding from himself a lack of sympathy.[180]

Though my faith was shaken, it was only when he urged me to read George Eliot that I became angry and disillusioned and worked myself into a quarrel or half-quarrel. I had read all Victor Hugo's romances and a couple of Balzac's and was in no mind to like her. She seemed to have a distrust or a distaste for all in life that gives one a springing foot. Then, too, she knew so well how to enforce her distaste by the authority of her mid-Victorian science or by some habit of mind of its breeding, that I, who had not escaped the fascination of what I loathed, doubted while the book lay open whatsoever my instinct knew of splendour. She disturbed me and alarmed me, but when I spoke of her to my father, he threw her aside with a phrase, 'O, she was an ugly woman who hated handsome men and handsome women'; and he began to praise *Wuthering Heights*.

Only the other day, when I got a volume of Dowden's letters,[181] did I discover that the friendship between Dowden and my father had long been an antagonism. My father had written from Fitzroy

Road in the 'sixties that the brotherhood, by which he meant the poet Edwin Ellis, Nettleship and himself, 'abhorred Wordsworth'; and Dowden, not remembering that another week would bring a different mood and abhorrence, had written a pained and solemn letter. My father had answered that Dowden believed too much in the intellect, that all valuable education was but a stirring up of the emotions and that this did not mean excitability. 'In the completely emotional man', he wrote, 'the least awakening of feeling is a harmony in which every chord of every feeling vibrates. Excitement is the feature of an insufficiently emotional nature, the harsh vibrating discourse of but one or two chords.' Living in a free world accustomed to the gay exaggeration of the talk of equals, of men who talk and write to discover truth and not for popular instruction, he had already, when both men were in their twenties, decided, it is plain, that Dowden was a provincial.[182]

XXV

It was only when I began to study psychical research and mystical philosophy that I broke away from my father's influence. He had been a follower of John Stuart Mill and so had never shared Rossetti's conviction that it mattered to nobody whether the sun went round the earth or the earth round the sun. But through this new research, this reaction from popular science, I had begun to feel that I had allies for my secret thought.

Once when I was in Dowden's drawing-room a servant announced my late headmaster.[183] I must have got pale or red, for Dowden with some ironical, friendly remark brought me into another room and there I stayed until the visitor was gone. A few months later, when I met the headmaster again, I had more courage. We chanced upon one another in the street and he said, 'I want you to use your influence with So-and-so, for he is giving all his time to some sort of mysticism and he will fail in his examination'. I was in great alarm, but I managed to say something about the children of this world being wiser than the children of light. He went off with a brusque 'Good morning'. I do not think that even at that age I would have been so grandiloquent but for my alarm. He had, however, aroused all my indignation. My new allies and my old had alike sustained me. 'Intermediate examinations', which I had always refused, meant money for pupil and for teacher, and that alone. My father had brought me up never when at school to think of the future or of any practical result. I have even known him to say, 'When I was young, the definition of a gentleman was a man not wholly occupied in getting on'. And yet this master wanted to withdraw my friend from the pursuit of the most important of all the truths. My friend,[184] now in his last year at school, was a 'show boy', and had beaten all Ireland again and again, but now he and I were reading Baron Reichenbach on Odic Force[185] and manuals published by the Theosophical Society.[186] We spent a good deal of time in the Kildare Street Museum passing our hands over the glass cases, feeling or believing we felt the Odic Force flowing from the big crystals. We also found pins blindfolded and read papers on our discoveries to the Hermetic Society[187] that met near the roof in York Street. I had, when we first made our Society, proposed for our consideration that whatever the great poets had affirmed in their finest moments was the nearest we could come to an authoritative religion, and that their mythology, their spirits of water and wind, were but literal truth. I had read *Prometheus Unbound* with this thought in mind and wanted help to carry my study through all literature. I was soon to vex my father by defining truth as 'the dramatically appropriate utterance of the highest man'. And if I had been asked to define the 'highest man', I would have said perhaps, 'We can but find him as Homer found Odysseus when he was looking for a theme'.

My friend had written to some missionary society to send him to the South Seas, when I offered him Renan's *Life of Christ*[188] and a copy of *Esoteric Buddhism*. He refused both, but a few days later while reading for an examination in Kildare Street Library, he asked in an idle moment for *Esoteric Buddhism* and came out an esoteric Buddhist. He wrote to the missionaries withdrawing his letter and offered himself to the Theosophical Society as a *chela*. He was vexed now at my lack of zeal, for I had stayed somewhere between the books, held there perhaps by my father's scepticism. I said, and he thought it was a great joke though I was serious, that even if I were certain in my own mind, I did not know 'a single person with a talent for conviction'. For a time he made me ashamed of my world and its lack of zeal, and I wondered if his world (his father[189] was a notorious Orange leader) where everything was a matter of belief was not better than mine. He himself proposed the immediate

conversion of the other 'show boy', a clever little fellow, now a
Dublin mathematician[190] and still under five feet. I found him a day
later in much depression. I said, 'Did he refuse to listen to you?'
'Not at all,' was the answer, 'for I had only been talking for a quarter of an hour when he said he believed.' Certainly those minds,
parched by many examinations, were thirsty.

Sometimes a Professor of Oriental Languages[191] at Trinity College, a Persian, came to our Society and talked of the magicians of
the East. When he was a little boy, he had seen a vision in a pool of
ink, a multitude of spirits singing in Arabic, 'Woe unto those that
do not believe in us'. And we persuaded a Brahmin philosopher[192] to
come from London and stay for a few days with the only one
among us who had rooms of his own. It was my first meeting with
a philosophy that confirmed my vague speculations and seemed at
once logical and boundless. Consciousness, he taught, does not
merely spread out its surface but has, in vision and in contemplation, another motion and can change in height and in depth. A
handsome young man with the typical face of Christ, he chaffed me
good-humouredly because he said I came at breakfast and began
some question that was interrupted by the first caller, waited in
silence till ten or eleven at night when the last caller had gone, and
finished my question.

XXVI

I thought a great deal about the system of education from which I
had suffered, and believing that everybody had a philosophical
defence for all that he did, I desired greatly to meet some schoolmaster that I might question him. For a moment it seemed as if I
should have my desire. I had been invited to read out a poem called
'The Island of Statues', an Arcadian play in imitation of Edmund
Spenser, to a gathering of critics who were to decide whether it was
worthy of publication in the College magazine. The magazine had
already published a lyric[193] of mine, the first ever printed, and people began to know my name. We met in the rooms of Mr. C. H.
Oldham, now Professor of Political Economy at our new University; and though Professor Bury, then a very young man, was to be
the deciding voice, Mr. Oldham had asked quite a large audience.
When the reading was over and the poem had been approved I was

left alone, why I cannot remember, with a young man who was, I had been told, a schoolmaster. I was silent, gathering my courage, and he also was silent; and presently I said without anything to lead up to it, 'I know you will defend the ordinary system of education by saying that it strengthens the will, but I am convinced that it only seems to do so because it weakens the impulses'. Then I stopped, overtaken by shyness. He made no answer but smiled and looked surprised as though I had said, 'You will say they are Persian attire; but let them be changed'.

XXVII

I had begun to frequent a club[194] founded by Mr. Oldham, and not from natural liking, but from a secret ambition. I wished to become self-possessed, to be able to play with hostile minds as Hamlet played, to look in the lion's face, as it were, with unquivering eyelash. In Ireland harsh argument which had gone out of fashion in England was still the manner of our conversation, and at this club Unionist and Nationalist[195] could interrupt one another and insult one another without the formal and traditional restraint of public speech. Sometimes they would change the subject and discuss Socialism, or a philosophical question, merely to discover their old passions under a new shape. I spoke easily and, I thought, well till some one was rude and then I would become silent or exaggerate my opinion to absurdity, or hesitate and grow confused, or be carried away myself by some party passion. I would spend hours afterwards going over my words and putting the wrong ones right. Discovering that I was only self-possessed with people I knew intimately, I would often go to a strange house where I knew I would spend a wretched hour for schooling's sake. I did not discover that Hamlet had his self-possession from no schooling but from indifference and passion-conquering sweetness, and that less heroic minds can but hope it from old age.

XXVIII

I had very little money and one day the toll-taker at the metal bridge over the Liffey and a gossip of his laughed when I refused the halfpenny and said, 'No, I will go round by O'Connell

Bridge'.[196] When I called for the first time at a house in Leinster Road several middle-aged women were playing cards and suggested my taking a hand and gave me a glass of sherry. The sherry went to my head and I was impoverished for days by the loss of sixpence. My hostess was Ellen O'Leary, who kept house for her brother John O'Leary,[197] the Fenian, the handsomest old man I had ever seen. He had been condemned to twenty years' penal servitude but had been set free after five on condition that he did not return to Ireland for fifteen years. He had said to the Government, 'I will not return if Germany makes war on you, but I will return if France does'. He and his old sister lived exactly opposite the Orange leader, for whom he had a great respect. His sister stirred my affection at first for no better reason than her likeness of face and figure to the matron of my London school, a friendly person, but when I came to know her I found sister and brother alike were of Plutarch's people.[198] She told me of her brother's life, of the foundation of the Fenian movement, and of the arrests that followed (I believe that her own sweetheart had somehow fallen among the wreckage), of sentences of death pronounced upon false evidence amid a public panic, and told it all without bitterness. No fanaticism could thrive amid such gentleness. She never found it hard to believe that an opponent had as high a motive as her own, and needed upon her difficult road no spur of hate.

Her brother seemed very unlike on a first hearing, for he had some violent oaths, 'Good God in Heaven' being one of them; and if he disliked anything one said or did, he spoke all his thought, but in a little one heard his justice match her charity. 'Never has there been a cause so bad', he would say, 'that it has not been defended by good men for good reasons.' Nor would he overvalue any man because they shared opinions; and when he lent me the poems of Davis and the Young Irelanders,[199] of whom I had known nothing, he did not, although the poems of Davis had made him a patriot, claim that they were very good poetry.[200]

He had the moral genius that moves all young people and moves them the more if they are repelled by those who have strict opinions and yet have lived commonplace lives. I had begun, as would any other of my training, to say violent and paradoxical things to shock provincial sobriety, and Dowden's ironical calm had come to seem but a professional pose. But here was something as spontaneous as the life of an artist. Sometimes he would say things that would have sounded well in some heroic Elizabethan play. It became my delight to rouse him to these outbursts, for I was the poet in the presence of his theme. Once when I was defending an Irish politician who had made a great outcry because he was treated as a common felon, by showing that he did it for the cause's sake, he said, 'There are things that a man must not do to save a nation'. He would speak a sentence like that in ignorance of its passionate value, and would forget it the moment after.

I met at his house friends of later life, Katharine Tynan,[201] who still lived upon her father's farm, and Dr. Hyde,[202] still a college student who took snuff like those Mayo countrypeople whose stories and songs he was writing down. One constant caller looked at me with much hostility—jealous of my favour in O'Leary's eyes perhaps, though later on he found solider reason for hostility—John F. Taylor,[203] an obscure great orator. The other day in Dublin I overheard a man murmuring to another one of his speeches as I might some Elizabethan lyric that is in my very bones. It was delivered at some Dublin debate, some College society perhaps. The Lord Chancellor[204] had spoken with balanced unemotional sentences, now self-complacent, now derisive. Taylor began, hesitating and stopping for words, but after speaking very badly for a little, straightened his figure and spoke as out of a dream: 'I am carried to another age, a nobler society, and another Lord Chancellor is speaking. I am at the Court of the first Pharaoh.' Thereupon he put into the mouth of that Egyptian all his audience had listened to, but now it was spoken to the children of Israel. 'If you have any spirituality as you boast, why not use our great empire to spread it through the world, why still cling to that beggarly nationality of yours? What are its history and its works weighed with those of Egypt?' Then his voice changed and sank: 'I see a man at the edge of the crowd; he is standing listening there, but he will not obey'; and then with his voice rising to a cry, 'had he obeyed he would never have come down the mountain carrying in his arms the Tables of the Law in the language of the outlaw'.[205]

I braved Taylor again and again as one might a savage animal as a test of courage, but always found him worse than my expectation. I would say, quoting Mill, 'Oratory is heard, poetry is overheard'.[206] And he would answer, his voice full of contempt, that there was always an audience; and yet, in his moments of lofty speech, he himself was alone no matter what the crowd.

At other times his science or his Catholic orthodoxy, I never could discover which, would become enraged with my supernaturalism. I can but once remember escaping him unabashed and unconquered. I said with deliberate exaggeration at some evening party at O'Leary's, 'Five out of every six people have seen a ghost'; and Taylor fell into my net with, 'Well, I will ask everybody here'. I managed that the first answer should come from a man who had heard a voice he believed to be that of his dead brother, and the second from a doctor's wife who had lived in a haunted house and met a man with his throat cut, whose throat as he drifted along the garden-walk 'had opened and closed like the mouth of a fish'. Taylor threw up his head like an angry horse, but asked no further question, and did not return to the subject that evening. If he had gone on he would have heard from everybody some like story though not all at first hand, and Miss O'Leary would have told him what happened at the death of one of the MacManus brothers,[207] well known in the politics of Young Ireland.[208] One brother was watching by the bed where the other lay dying and saw a strange hawk-like bird fly through the open window and alight upon the breast of the dying man. He did not dare to drive it away and it remained there, as it seemed, looking into his brother's eyes until death came, and then it flew out of the window. I think, though I am not sure, that she had the story from the watcher himself.

With O'Leary Taylor was always, even when they differed, as they often did, gentle and deferential, but once only, and that was years afterwards, did I think that he was about to include me among his friends. We met by chance in a London street and he stopped me with an abrupt movement: 'Yeats,' he said, 'I have been thinking. If you and . . .' (naming another aversion) 'were born in a small Italian principality in the Middle Ages, he would have friends at Court and you would be in exile with a price on your head.' He went off without another word, and the next time we met he was no less offensive than before. He, imprisoned in himself, and not the always unperturbed O'Leary comes before me as the tragic figure of my youth. The same passion for all moral and physical splendour that drew him to O'Leary would make him beg leave to wear, for some few days, a friend's ring or pin, and gave him a heart that every pretty woman set on fire. I doubt if he was happy in his loves; for those his powerful intellect had fascinated were, I believe, repelled by his coarse red hair, his gaunt ungainly body, his stiff movements as of a Dutch doll, his badly rolled, shabby umbrella. And yet with women, as with O'Leary, he was gentle, deferential, almost diffident.

A Young Ireland Society[209] met in the lecture-hall of a workmen's club in York Street with O'Leary for president, and there four or five university students and myself and occasionally Taylor spoke on Irish history or literature. When Taylor spoke, it was a great event, and his delivery in the course of a speech or lecture of some political verse by Thomas Davis gave me a conviction of how great might be the effect of verse, spoken by a man almost rhythm-drunk, at some moment of intensity, the apex of long-mounting thought. Verses that seemed when one saw them upon the page flat and empty caught from that voice, whose beauty was half in its harsh strangeness, nobility and style. My father had always read verse with an equal intensity and a greater subtlety, but this art was public and his private, and it is Taylor's voice that has rung in my ears and awakens my longing when I have heard some player speak lines, 'so naturally', as a famous player said to me, 'that nobody can find out that it is verse at all'. I made a good many speeches, more, I believe, as a training for self-possession than from desire of speech.

Once our debates roused a passion that came to the newspapers and the streets. There was an excitable man[210] who had fought for the Pope against the Italian patriots and who always rode a white horse in our Nationalist processions. He got on badly with O'Leary, who had told him that 'attempting to oppress others was a poor preparation for liberating your own country'. O'Leary had written some letter to the Press condemning the 'Irish-American Dynamite Party',[211] as it was called, and defining the limits of 'honourable warfare'. At the next meeting, the papal soldier rose in the middle of the discussion on some other matter and moved a vote of censure on O'Leary. 'I myself', he said, 'do not approve of bombs, but I do not think that any Irishman should be discouraged.' O'Leary ruled him out of order. He refused to obey and remained standing. Those round him began to threaten. He swung the chair he had been sitting on round his head and defied everybody. However, he was seized from all sides and thrown out, and a special meeting called to expel him. He wrote letters to the papers and addressed a crowd somewhere. 'No Young Ireland Society', he protested, 'could expel a man whose grandfather[212] had been hanged in 1798.' When the night of the special meeting came his expulsion was moved, but before the vote could be taken an excited man announced that there was a crowd in the street, that the papal soldier was making a speech, that in a moment we should be attacked. Three or four of us ran and put our backs to the door while others carried on the debate. It was an inner door with narrow glass windows at each side and through these we could see the street-door and the crowd in the street. Presently a man asked us through the crack in the door if we would as a favour 'leave the crowd to the workmen's club upstairs'. In a couple of minutes there was a great noise of sticks and broken glass, and after that our landlord came to find out who was to pay for the hall-lamp.

XXIX

From these debates, from O'Leary's conversation, and from the Irish books he lent or gave me has come all I have set my hand to since. I had begun to know a great deal about the Irish poets who had written in English. I read with excitement books I should find unreadable to-day, and found romance in lives that had neither wit nor adventure. I did not deceive myself; I knew how often they wrote a cold and abstract language, and yet I who had never wanted to see the houses where Keats and Shelley lived would ask everybody what sort of place Inchedony[213] was, because Callanan had named after it a bad poem in the manner of *Childe Harold*. Walking home from a debate, I remember saying to some college student, 'Ireland cannot put from her the habits learned from her old military civilization and from a Church that prays in Latin. Those popular poets have not touched her heart, her poetry when it comes will be distinguished and lonely.' O'Leary had once said to me, 'Neither Ireland nor England knows the good from the bad in any art, but Ireland unlike England does not hate the good when it is pointed out to her'. I began to plot and scheme how one might seal with the right image the soft wax before it began to harden. I had noticed that Irish Catholics among whom had been born so many political martyrs had not the good taste, the household courtesy and decency of the Protestant Ireland I had known, yet Protestant Ireland seemed to think of nothing but getting on in the world. I thought we might bring the halves together if we had a national literature that made Ireland beautiful in the memory, and yet had been freed from provincialism by an exacting criticism, a European pose.[214]

XXX

Some one at the Young Ireland Society gave me a newspaper that I might read some article or letter. I began idly reading verses describing the shore of Ireland as seen by a returning, dying emigrant. My eyes filled with tears and yet I knew the verses were badly written—vague, abstract words such as one finds in a newspaper. I looked at the end and saw the name of some political exile[215] who had died but a few days after his return to Ireland. They had moved me because they contained the actual thoughts of a man at a passionate moment of life, and when I met my father I was full of the discovery. We should write out our own thoughts in as nearly as possible the language we thought them in, as though in a letter to an intimate friend. We should not disguise them in any way; for our lives give them force as the lives of people in plays give force to their words. Personal utterance, which had almost ceased in English literature, could be as fine an escape from rhetoric and abstraction as drama itself. But my father would hear of nothing but drama;[216] personal utterance was only egotism. I knew it was not, but as yet did not know how to explain the difference. I tried from that on to write out of my emotions exactly as they came to me in life, not changing them to make them more beautiful. 'If I can be sincere and make my language natural, and without becoming discursive, like a novelist, and so indiscreet and prosaic,' I said to myself, 'I shall, if good luck or bad luck make my life interesting, be a great poet; for it will be no longer a matter of literature at all.' Yet when I re-read those early poems which gave me so much trouble, I find little but romantic convention, unconscious drama. It is so many years before one can believe enough in what one feels even to know what the feeling is.

XXXI

Perhaps a year before we returned to London, a Catholic friend[217] brought me to a spiritualistic séance at the house of a young man lately arrested under a suspicion of Fenianism, but released for lack of evidence. He and his friends had been sitting weekly about a table in the hope of spiritual manifestation and one had developed mediumship. A drawer full of books had leaped out of the table when no one was touching it, a picture had moved upon the wall. There were some half-dozen of us, and our host began by making passes until the medium fell asleep sitting upright in his chair. Then the lights were turned out, and we sat waiting in the dim light of a fire. Presently my shoulders began to twitch and my hands. I could easily have stopped them, but I had never heard of such a thing and I was curious. After a few minutes the movement became violent and I stopped it. I sat motionless for a while and then my whole body moved like a suddenly unrolled watch-spring, and I was thrown backward on the wall. I again stilled the movement and sat at the table. Everybody began to say I was a medium, and that if I would not resist some wonderful thing would happen. I remembered that Balzac had once desired to take opium for the experience' sake, but would not because he dreaded the surrender of his will. We were now holding each other's hands and presently my right hand banged the knuckles of the woman next to me upon the table. She laughed, and the medium, speaking for the first time, and with difficulty, out of his mesmeric sleep, said, 'Tell her there is great danger'. He stood up and began walking round me making movements with his hands as though he were pushing something away. I was now struggling vainly with this force which compelled me to movements I had not willed, and my movements became so violent that the table was broken. I tried to pray, and because I could not remember a prayer, repeated in a loud voice—

> 'Of Man's first disobedience and the fruit
> Of that forbidden tree whose mortal taste
> Brought death into the world, and all our woe . . .
> Sing, Heavenly Muse.'[218]

My Catholic friend had left the table and was saying a Paternoster and Ave Maria in the corner. Presently all became still and so dark that I could not see anybody. I described it to somebody next day as like going out of a noisy political meeting on to a quiet country road. I said to myself, 'I am now in a trance but I no longer have any desire to resist'. But when I turned my eyes to the fireplace I could see a faint gleam of light, so I thought, 'No, I am not in a trance'. Then I saw shapes faintly appearing in the darkness and thought, 'They are spirits'; but they were only the spiritualists and my friend at her prayers. The medium said in a faint voice, 'We are through the bad spirits'. I said, 'Will they ever come again do you think?' and he said, 'No, never again, I think', and in my boyish vanity I thought it was I who had banished them.

For years afterwards I would not go to a séance or turn a table and would often ask myself what was that violent impulse that had run through my nerves. Was it a part of myself—something always to be a danger perhaps; or had it come from without, as it seemed?

XXXII

I had published my first book of poems by subscription, O'Leary finding many subscribers, and a book of stories,[219] when I heard that my grandmother was dead and went to Sligo for the funeral. She had asked to see me, but by some mistake I was not sent for. She had heard that I was much about with a beautiful, admired woman[220] and feared that I did not speak of marriage because I was poor, and wanted to say to me, 'Women care nothing about money'. My grandfather was dying also and only survived her a few weeks. I went to see him and wondered at his handsome face now sickness had refined it, and noticed that he foretold the changes in the weather by indications of the light and of the temperature that would have meant nothing to another. As I sat there my old childish fear returned and I was glad to get away. I stayed with my uncle whose house was opposite where my grandfather lived, and walking home one day we met the doctor. The doctor said there was no hope and that my grandfather should be told, but my uncle would not allow it. He said, 'It would make a man mad to know he was dying'. In vain the doctor pleaded that he had never known a man not made calmer by the knowledge. I listened sad and angry, but my uncle always took a low view of human nature, his very tolerance which was exceedingly great came from his hoping nothing of anybody. Before he had given way my grandfather lifted up his arms and cried out, 'There she is',[221] and fell backward dead. Before he was dead, old servants of that house where there had never been noise or disorder began their small pilferings, and after his death there was a quarrel over the disposition of certain mantelpiece ornaments of no value.

XXXIII

For some months now I have lived with my own youth and childhood, not always writing indeed but thinking of it almost every day, and I am sorrowful and disturbed. It is not that I have accomplished too few of my plans, for I am not ambitious; but when I think of all the books I have read, and of the wise words I have heard spoken, and of the anxiety I have given to parents and grandparents, and of the hopes that I have had, all life weighed in the scales of my own life seems to me a preparation for something that never happens.

THE END

THE TREMBLING
OF THE VEIL

PREFACE

I have found in an old diary a saying from Stéphane Mallarmé, that his epoch was troubled by the trembling of the veil[1] of the Temple. As those words were still true, during the years of my life described in this book, I have chosen *The Trembling of the Veil* for its title.

Except in one or two trivial details, where I have the warrant of old friendship, I have not, without permission, quoted conversation or described occurrence from the private life of named or recognizable living persons. I have not felt my freedom abated, for most of the friends of my youth are dead and over the dead I have an historian's rights. They were artists and writers and certain among them men of genius, and the life of a man of genius, because of his greater sincerity, is often an experiment that needs analysis and record. At least my generation so valued personality that it thought so. I have said all the good I know and all the evil: I have kept nothing back necessary to understanding.

W. B. YEATS
Thoor Ballylee,[2]
May 1922

BOOK I

FOUR YEARS: 1887–1891

I

At the end of the 'eighties my father and mother, my brother and sisters and myself, all newly arrived from Dublin, were settled in Bedford Park[3] in a red-brick house with several mantelpieces of wood, copied from marble mantelpieces designed by the brothers Adam, a balcony and a little garden shadowed by a great horse-chestnut tree. Years before we had lived there, when the crooked ostentatiously picturesque streets with great trees casting great shadows had been a new enthusiasm: the Pre-Raphaelite movement at last affecting life. But now exaggerated criticism had taken the place of enthusiasm, the tiled roofs, the first in modern London, were said to leak, which they did not, and the drains to be bad, though that was no longer true; and I imagine that houses were cheap. I remember feeling disappointed because the co-operative stores, with their little seventeenth-century panes, had lost the romance I saw there when I passed them still unfinished on my way to school; and because the public-house, called The Tabard after Chaucer's Inn, was so plainly a common public-house; and because the great sign of a trumpeter designed by Rooke, the Pre-Raphaelite artist, had been freshened by some inferior hand. The big red-brick church[4] had never pleased me, and I was accustomed, when I saw the wooden balustrade that ran along the slanting edge of the roof where nobody ever walked or could walk, to remember the opinion of some architect friend of my father's, that it had been put there to keep the birds from falling off. Still, however, it had some village characters and helped us to feel not wholly lost in the metropolis. I no longer went to church as a regular habit, but go I sometimes did, for one Sunday morning I saw these words painted on a board in the porch: 'The congregation are requested to kneel during prayers; the kneelers are afterwards to be hung upon pegs provided for the purpose'. In front of every seat hung a little cushion and these cush-

ions were called 'kneelers'. Presently the joke ran through the community, where there were many artists who considered religion at
best an unimportant accessory to good architecture and who disliked that particular church.

II

I could not understand where the charm had gone that I had felt,
when as a schoolboy of twelve or thirteen I had played among the
unfinished houses, once leaving the marks of my two hands,
blacked by a fall among some paint, upon a white balustrade.

Yet I was in all things Pre-Raphaelite. When I was fifteen or sixteen my father had told me about Rossetti and Blake and given me
their poetry to read; and once at Liverpool on my way to Sligo I
had seen *Dante's Dream*[5] in the gallery there, a picture painted
when Rossetti had lost his dramatic power and to-day not very
pleasing to me, and its colour, its people, its romantic architecture
had blotted all other pictures away. It was a perpetual bewilderment that when my father,[6] moved perhaps by some memory of his
youth, chose some theme from poetic tradition, he would soon
weary and leave it unfinished. I had seen the change coming bit by
bit and its defence elaborated by young men fresh from the Paris
art schools. 'We must paint what is in front of us', or 'A man must
be of his own time', they would say, and if I spoke of Blake or Rossetti they would point out his bad drawing and tell me to admire
Carolus Duran and Bastien-Lepage.[7] Then, too, they were very
ignorant men; they read nothing, for nothing mattered but 'knowing how to paint', being in reaction against a generation that
seemed to have wasted its time upon so many things. I thought
myself alone in hating these young men, their contempt for the
past, their monopoly of the future, but in a few months I was to
discover others of my own age who thought as I did, for it is not
true that youth looks before it with the mechanical gaze of a well-
drilled soldier. Its quarrel is not with the past, but with the present,
where its elders are so obviously powerful and no cause seems lost
if it seem to threaten that power. Does cultivated youth ever really
love the future, where the eye can discover no persecuted Royalty
hidden among oak leaves, though from it certainly does come so
much proletarian rhetoric?

I was unlike others of my generation in one thing only. I am very religious, and deprived by Huxley and Tyndall,[8] whom I detested, of the simple-minded religion of my childhood, I had made a new religion, almost an infallible Church of poetic tradition, of a fardel of stories, and of personages, and of emotions, inseparable from their first expression, passed on from generation to generation by poets and painters with some help from philosophers and theologians. I wished for a world where I could discover this tradition perpetually, and not in pictures and in poems only, but in tiles round the chimney-piece and in the hangings that kept out the draught. I had even created a dogma: 'Because those imaginary people are created out of the deepest instinct of man, to be his measure and his norm, whatever I can imagine those mouths speaking may be the nearest I can go to truth'. When I listened they seemed always to speak of one thing only: they, their loves, every incident of their lives, were steeped in the supernatural. Could even Titian's *Ariosto*[9] that I loved beyond other portraits have its grave look, as if waiting for some perfect final event, if the painters before Titian had not learned portraiture while painting into the corner of compositions full of saints and Madonnas their kneeling patrons? At seventeen years old I was already an old-fashioned brass cannon full of shot, and nothing had kept me from going off but a doubt as to my capacity to shoot straight.

III

I was not an industrious student and knew only what I had found by accident and I found nothing I cared for after Titian, and Titian I knew from an imitation of his *Supper of Emmaus* in Dublin,[10] till Blake and the Pre-Raphaelites; and among my father's friends were no Pre-Raphaelites. Some indeed had come to Bedford Park in the enthusiasm of the first building and others to be near those that had. There was Todhunter,[11] a well-off man who had bought my father's pictures while my father was still Pre-Raphaelite; once a Dublin doctor he was now a poet and a writer of poetical plays; a tall, sallow, lank, melancholy man, a good scholar and a good intellect; and with him my father carried on a warm exasperated friendship, fed, I think, by old memories and wasted by quarrels over matters of opinion. Of all the survivors he was the most dejected and the least estranged, and I remember encouraging him, with a sense of worship shared, to buy a very expensive carpet designed by Morris. He displayed it without strong liking and would have agreed had there been any to find fault. If he had liked anything strongly he might have been a famous man, for a few years later he was to write, under some casual patriotic impulse, certain excellent verses now in all Irish anthologies; but with him every book was a new planting, and not a new bud on an old bough. He had, I think, no peace in himself. But my father's chief friend was York Powell,[12] a famous Oxford Professor of History, a broad-built, broad-headed, brown-bearded man clothed in heavy blue cloth and looking, but for his glasses and the dim sight of a student, like some captain in the Merchant Service. One often passed with pleasure from Todhunter's company to that of one who was almost ostentatiously at peace. He cared nothing for philosophy, nothing for economics, nothing for the policy of nations; for history, as he saw it, was a memory of men who were amusing or exciting to think about. He impressed all who met him, seemed to some a man of genius, but had not enough ambition to shape his thought, nor enough conviction to give rhythm to his style and remained always a poor writer. I was too full of unfinished speculations and premature convictions to value rightly his conversation, informed by a vast erudition, which would give itself to every casual association of speech and company, precisely because he had neither cause nor design. My father, however, found Powell's concrete narrative manner in talk a necessary completion of his own, and when I asked him in a letter many years later where he got his philosophy replied, 'From York Powell', and thereon added, no doubt remembering that Powell was without ideas, 'by looking at him'. Then there was a good listener,[13] a painter in whose hall hung a big picture painted in his student days of Ulysses sailing home from the Phaeacian court, an orange and a skin of wine at his side, blue mountains towering behind; but who lived by drawing domestic scenes and lovers' meetings for a weekly magazine that had an immense circulation among the imperfectly educated. To escape the boredom of work, which he never turned to but under pressure of necessity and usually late at night, with the publisher's messenger in the hall, he had half filled his studio with mechanical toys of his own invention, and perpetually increased their number. A model railway train at intervals puffed its way along the walls, passing several railway stations and signal-boxes; and on the floor lay a camp with attacking and defending soldiers and a fortification that blew up when the attackers fired a pea through a certain window; while a large model of a Thames barge hung from the ceiling. Opposite our house lived an old artist who worked also for the illustrated papers for a living, but painted landscapes for his pleasure, and of him I remember nothing except that he had outlived ambition, was a good listener, and that my father explained his gaunt appearance by his descent from Pocahontas. If all these men were a little like becalmed ships, there was certainly one man whose sails were full. Three or four doors off on our side of the road lived a decorative artist[14] in all the naïve confidence of popular ideals and the public approval. He was our daily comedy. 'I myself and Sir Frederick Leighton are the greatest decorative artists of the age', was among his sayings, and to show that he at any rate knew nothing of discouragement a great lych-gate, bought from some country churchyard, reared its thatched roof, meant to shelter bearers and coffin, above the entrance to his front garden. In this fairly numerous company— there were others though no other face rises before me—my father and York Powell found listeners for a conversation that had no special loyalties, or antagonisms; while I could only talk upon set topics, being in the heat of my youth, and the topics that filled me with excitement were never spoken of.

IV

Bedford Park had a red-brick clubhouse[15] with a little theatre that began to stir my imagination. I persuaded Todhunter to write a pastoral play and have it performed there.

A couple of years before, while we were still in Dublin, he had given at Hengler's Circus, remodelled as a Greek Theatre, a most expensive performance of his *Helena of Troas,* an oratorical Swinburnian play which I had thought as unactable as it was unreadable. Since I was seventeen I had constantly tested my own ambition with Keats's praise[16] of him who left 'great verse unto a little clan', so it was but natural that I should persuade him for the moment that we had nothing to do with the great public, that it should be a point of honour to be content with our own little public, that he should write of shepherds and shepherdesses because people would expect them to talk poetry and move without melodrama. He wrote his *Sicilian Idyll,* which I have not looked at for thirty years, and never rated very high as poetry, and had the one unmistakable success of his life. The little theatre was full for twice the number of performances intended, for artists, men of letters and students had come from all over London.

I made through these performances a close friend and a discovery that was to influence my life. Todhunter had engaged several professional actors with a little reputation, but had given the chief woman's part to Florence Farr, who had qualities no contemporary professional practice could have increased, the chief man's part to an amateur, Heron Allen, solicitor, fiddler and popular writer on palmistry. Heron Allen and Florence Farr read poetry for their pleasure. While they were upon the stage no one else could hold an eye or an ear. Their speech was music, the poetry acquired a nobility, a passionate austerity that made it akin for certain moments to the great poetry of the world. Heron Allen, who had never spoken in public before except to lecture upon the violin, had the wisdom to reduce his acting to a series of poses, to be the stately shepherd with not more gesture than was needed to 'twitch his mantle blue'[17] and to let his grace be foil to Florence Farr's more impassioned delivery. When they closed their mouths, and some other player opened his, breaking up the verse to make it conversational, jerking his body or his arms that he might seem no austere poetical image but very man, I listened in raging hatred. I kept my seat with difficulty, I searched my memory for insulting phrases, I even muttered them to myself that the people about might hear. I had discovered for the first time that in the performance of all drama that depends for its effect upon beauty of language, poetical culture may be more important than professional experience.

Florence Farr[18] lived in lodgings some twenty minutes' walk away at Brook Green, and I was soon a constant caller, talking over plays that I would some day write her. She had three great gifts, a tranquil beauty like that of Demeter's image near the British Museum Reading-Room door,[19] and an incomparable sense of rhythm and a beautiful voice, the seeming natural expression of the image. And yet there was scarce another gift that she did not value above those three. We all have our simplifying image, our genius, and such hard burden does it lay upon us that, but for the praise of others, we would deride it and hunt it away. She could only express hers through an unfashionable art, an art that has scarce existed since the seventeenth century, and so could only earn unimportant occasional praise. She would dress without care or calculation as if to hide her beauty and seem contemptuous of its power. If a man fell in love with her she would notice that she had seen just that movement upon the stage or had heard just that intonation and all seemed unreal. If she read out some poem in English or in French all was passion, all a traditional splendour, but she spoke of actual things with a cold wit or under the strain of paradox. Wit and paradox alike sought to pull down whatever had tradition or passion and she was soon to spend her days in the British Museum Reading-Room and become erudite in many heterogeneous studies, moved by an insatiable, destroying curiosity. I formed with her an enduring friendship that was an enduring exasperation—'Why do you play the part with a bent back and a squeak in the voice? How can you be a character actor, you who hate all our life, you who belong to a life that is a vision?' But argument was no use, and some Nurse in Euripides must be played with all an old woman's infirmities and not as I would have it, with all a Sibyl's majesty, because 'it is no use doing what nobody wants', or because she would show that she 'could do what the others did'.

I used in my rage to compare her thoughts, when her worst mood was upon her, to a game called Spillikins which I had seen played in my childhood with little pieces of bone that you had to draw out with a hook from a bundle of like pieces. A bundle of bones instead of Demeter's golden sheaf! Her sitting-room at the Brook Green lodging-house was soon a reflection of her mind, the walls covered with musical instruments, pieces of Oriental drapery, and Egyptian gods and goddesses painted by herself in the British Museum.

V

Presently a hansom drove up to our door at Bedford Park with Miss Maud Gonne,[20] who brought an introduction to my father from old John O'Leary, the Fenian leader. She vexed my father by praise of war, wars for its own sake, not as the creator of certain virtues but as if there were some virtue in excitement itself. I supported her against my father, which vexed him the more, though he might have understood that, apart from the fact that Carolus Duran and Bastien-Lepage were somehow involved, a man young as I could not have differed from a woman so beautiful and so young. To-day, with her great height and the unchangeable lineaments of her form, she looks the Sibyl I would have had played by Florence Farr, but in that day she seemed a classical impersonation of the Spring, the Virgilian commendation 'She walks like a goddess'[21] made for her alone. Her complexion was luminous, like that of apple-blossom through which the light falls, and I remember her standing that first day by a great heap of such blossoms in the window. In the next few years I saw her always when she passed to and fro between Dublin and Paris, surrounded, no matter how rapid her journey and how brief her stay at either end of it, by cages full of birds, canaries, finches of all kinds, dogs, a parrot, and once a full-grown hawk from Donegal. Once when I saw her to her railway carriage I noticed how the cages obstructed racks and cushions and wondered what her fellow-travellers would say, but the carriage remained empty. It was years before I could see into the mind that lay hidden under so much beauty and so much energy.[22]

VI

Some quarter of an hour's walk from Bedford Park, out on the high road to Richmond, lived W. E. Henley,[23] and I, like many others, began under him my education. His portrait, a lithograph by Rothenstein, hangs over my mantelpiece among portraits of other friends. He is drawn standing, but because doubtless of his crippled legs he leans forward, resting his elbows upon some slightly suggested object—a table or a window-sill. His heavy figure and powerful head, the disordered hair standing upright, his short irregular beard and moustache, his lined and wrinkled face, his eyes steadily fixed upon some object in complete confidence and self-possession, and yet as in half-broken reverie, all are there exactly as I remember him. I have seen other portraits and they too show him exactly as I remember him, as though he had but one appearance and that seen fully at the first glance and by all alike. He was most human— human, I used to say, like one of Shakespeare's characters—and yet pressed and pummelled, as it were, into a single attitude, almost into a gesture and a speech as by some overwhelming situation. I disagreed with him about everything, but I admired him beyond words. With the exception of some early poems founded upon old French models[24] I disliked his poetry, mainly because he wrote in *vers libre,* which I associated with Tyndall and Huxley, and Bastien-Lepage's clownish peasant staring with vacant eyes at her great boots;[25] and filled it with unimpassioned description of a hospital ward where his leg had been amputated.[26] I wanted the strongest passions, passions that had nothing to do with observation, and metrical forms that seemed old enough to have been sung by men half asleep or riding upon a journey. Furthermore, Pre-Raphaelitism affected him as some people are affected by a cat in the room, and though he professed himself at our first meeting without political interests or convictions, he soon grew into a violent Unionist and Imperialist. I used to say when I spoke of his poems, 'He is like a great actor with a bad part; yet who would look at Hamlet in the grave scene if Salvini[27] played the grave-digger?' and I might so have explained much that he said and did. I meant that he was like a great actor of passion—character-acting meant nothing to me for many years—and an actor of passion will display some one quality of soul, personified again and again, just as a great poetical painter, Titian, Botticelli, Rossetti, may depend for his greatness upon a type of beauty which presently we call by his name. Irving, the last of the sort on the English stage, and in modern England and France it is the rarest sort, never moved me but in the expression of intellectual pride, and though I saw Salvini but once I am convinced that his genius was a kind of animal nobility. Henley, half inarticulate—'I am very costive', he would say—beset with personal quarrels, built up an image of power and magnanimity till it became, at moments, when seen as it were by lightning, his true self. Half his opinions were the contrivance of a subconsciousness that sought always to bring life to the dramatic crisis and expression to that point of artifice where the true self could find its tongue. Without opponents there had been no drama, and in his youth Ruskinism[28] and Pre-Raphaelitism, for he was of my father's generation, were the only possible opponents. How could one resent his prejudice when, that he himself might play a worthy part, he must find beyond the common rout, whom he derided and flouted daily, opponents he could imagine moulded like himself? Once he said to

me in the height of his Imperial propaganda, 'Tell those young men
in Ireland that this great thing must go on. They say Ireland is not
fit for self-government, but that is nonsense. It is as fit as any other
European country, but we cannot grant it.' And then he spoke of his
desire to found and edit a Dublin newspaper. It would have
expounded the Gaelic propaganda then beginning, though Dr.
Hyde had, as yet, no League,[29] our old stories, our modern literature—everything that did not demand any shred or patch of government. He dreamed of a tyranny, but it was that of Cosimo de'
Medici.

VII

We gathered on Sunday evenings[30] in two rooms, with folding doors
between, and hung, I think, with photographs from Dutch masters,
and in one room there was always, I think, a table with cold meat. I
can recall but one elderly man—Dunn[31] his name was—rather silent
and full of good sense, an old friend of Henley's. We were young men,
none as yet established in his own or in the world's opinion, and Henley was our leader and our confidant. One evening, I found him alone
amused and exasperated. 'Young A—— ', he cried, 'has just been
round to ask my advice. Would I think it a wise thing if he bolted with
Mrs. B——? "Have you quite determined to do it?" I asked him.
"Quite." "Well," I said, "in that case I refuse to give you any
advice".' Mrs. B—— was a beautiful talented woman, who, as the
Welsh Triad[32] said of Guinevere, 'was much given to being carried off'.
I think we listened to him, and often obeyed him, partly because he
was quite plainly not upon the side of our parents. We might have a
different ground of quarrel, but the result seemed more important
than the ground, and his confident manner and speech made us
believe, perhaps for the first time, in victory. And besides, if he did
denounce, and in my case he certainly did, what we held in secret reverence, he never failed to associate it with things or persons that did
not move us to reverence. Once I found him just returned from
some art congress[33] in Liverpool or in Manchester. 'The Salvation
Armyism of art', he called it, and gave a grotesque description of some
city councillor he had found admiring Turner. He, who hated all that
Ruskin praised, thereupon had derided Turner, and finding the city
councillor the next day on the other side of the gallery, admiring some

Pre-Raphaelite there, derided that Pre-Raphaelite. The third day
Henley discovered the poor man on a chair in the middle of the room
staring disconsolately upon the floor. He terrified us also and certainly
I did not dare, and I think none of us dared, to speak our admira-
tion for book or picture he condemned, but he made us feel always
our importance, and no man among us could do good work, or show
the promise of it, and lack his praise. I can remember meeting of a
Sunday night Charles Whibley, Kenneth Grahame, author of *The
Golden Age,* Barry Pain, now a well-known novelist, R. A. M.
Stevenson, art critic and a famous talker, George Wyndham, later on
a Cabinet Minister and Irish Chief Secretary, and now or later
Oscar Wilde, who was some ten years older than the rest of us. But
faces and names are vague to me, and while faces that I met but once
may rise clearly before me, a face met on many a Sunday has perhaps
vanished. Kipling came sometimes, I think, but I never met him; and
Stepniak, the Nihilist, whom I knew well elsewhere but not there,
said, 'I cannot go more than once a year, it is too exhausting'. Henley got the best out of us all, because he had made us accept him as
our judge and we knew that his judgment could neither sleep, nor be
softened, nor changed, nor turned aside. When I think of him, the
antithesis that is the foundation of human nature being ever in my
sight, I see his crippled legs as though he were some Vulcan perpetually forging swords for other men to use; and certainly I always
thought of C——,[34] a fine classical scholar, a pale and seemingly gentle man, as our chief swordsman and bravo. When Henley founded
his weekly newspaper, first the *Scots,* afterwards the *National
Observer,*[35] this young man wrote articles and reviews notorious for
savage wit; and years afterwards when the *National Observer* was
dead, Henley dying, and our cavern of outlaws empty, I met him in
Paris very sad and, I think, very poor. 'Nobody will employ me
now', he said. 'Your master is gone', I answered, 'and you are like
the spear in an old Irish story that had to be kept dipped in poppy-
juice that it might not go about killing people on its own account.' I
wrote my first good lyrics and tolerable essays[36] for the *National
Observer,* and as I always signed my work could go my own road in
some measure. Henley often revised my lyrics, crossing out a line or
a stanza and writing in one of his own, and I was comforted by my
belief that he also rewrote Kipling,[37] then in the first flood of popularity. At first, indeed, I was ashamed of being rewritten and

thought that others were not, and only began investigation when the editorial characteristics—epigrams, archaisms, and all—appeared in the article upon Paris fashions and in that upon opium by an Egyptian Pasha. I was not compelled to full conformity, for verse is plainly stubborn; and in prose, that I might avoid unacceptable opinions, I wrote nothing but ghost or faery stories, picked up from my mother or some pilot at Rosses Point, and Henley saw that I must needs mix a palette fitted to my subject-matter. But if he had changed every 'has' into 'hath' I would have let him, for had not we sunned ourselves in his generosity? 'My young men outdo me and they write better than I', he wrote in some letter praising Charles Whibley's work, and to another friend with a copy of my 'Man Who Dreamed of Faeryland': 'See what a fine thing has been written by one of my lads'.

VIII

My first meeting with Oscar Wilde[38] was an astonishment. I never before heard a man talking with perfect sentences, as if he had written them all overnight with labour and yet all spontaneous. There was present that night at Henley's, by right of propinquity or of accident, a man full of the secret spite of dullness, who interrupted from time to time, and always to check or disorder thought; and I noticed with what mastery he was foiled and thrown. I noticed, too, that the impression of artificiality that I think all Wilde's listeners have recorded came from the perfect rounding of the sentences and from the deliberation that made it possible. That very impression helped him, as the effect of metre, or of the antithetical prose of the seventeenth century, which is itself a true metre, helped its writers, for he could pass without incongruity from some unforeseen, swift stroke of wit to elaborate reverie. I heard him say a few nights later: 'Give me *The Winter's Tale*, "Daffodils that come before the swallow dares", but not *King Lear*. What is *King Lear* but poor life staggering in the fog?' and the slow, carefully modulated cadence sounded natural to my ears. That first night he praised Walter Pater's[39] *Studies in the History of the Renaissance:* 'It is my golden book; I never travel anywhere without it; but it is the very flower of decadence: the last trumpet should have sounded the moment it was written.' 'But', said the dull man, 'would you not have given us time to read it?' 'O no,' was the retort, 'there would have been plenty of time afterwards—in either world.' I think he seemed to us, baffled as we were by youth, or by infirmity, a triumphant figure, and to some of us a figure from another age, an audacious Italian fifteenth-century figure. A few weeks before I had heard one of my father's friends, an official in a publishing firm[40] that had employed both Wilde and Henley as editors, blaming Henley, who was 'no use except under control', and praising Wilde, 'so indolent but such a genius'; and now the firm became the topic of our talk. 'How often do you go to the office?' said Henley. 'I used to go three times a week', said Wilde, 'for an hour a day, but I have since struck off one of the days.' 'My God,' said Henley, 'I went five times a week for five hours a day and when I wanted to strike off a day they had a special committee meeting.' 'Furthermore,' was Wilde's answer, 'I never answered their letters. I have known men come to London full of bright prospects and seen them complete wrecks in a few months through a habit of answering letters.' He too knew how to keep our elders in their place, and his method was plainly the more successful, for Henley had been dismissed. 'No, he is not an aesthete', Henley commented later, being somewhat embarrassed by Wilde's Pre-Raphaelite entanglement; 'one soon finds that he is a scholar and a gentleman.' And when I dined with Wilde a few days afterwards he began at once, 'I had to strain every nerve to equal that man at all'; and I was too loyal to speak my thought: 'You and not he said all the brilliant things'. He, like the rest of us, had felt the strain of an intensity that seemed to hold life at the point of drama. He had said on that first meeting, 'The basis of literary friendship is mixing the poisoned bowl'; and for a few weeks Henley and he became close friends till, the astonishment of their meeting over, diversity of character and ambition pushed them apart, and, with half the cavern helping, Henley began mixing the poisoned bowl for Wilde. Yet Henley never wholly lost that first admiration, for after Wilde's downfall he said to me: 'Why did he do it? I told my lads to attack him and yet we might have fought under his banner.'

IX

It became the custom, both at Henley's and at Bedford Park, to say that R. A. M. Stevenson, who frequented both circles, was the bet-

ter talker. Wilde had been trussed up like a turkey by undergradu-
ates, dragged up and down a hill, his champagne emptied into the
ice-tub, hooted in the streets of various towns, and, I think, stoned,
and no newspaper named him but in scorn; his manner had hard-
ened to meet opposition and at times he allowed one to see an
unpardonable insolence. His charm was acquired and systematized,
a mask which he wore only when it pleased him, while the charm of
Stevenson belonged to him like the colour of his hair. If Stevenson's
talk became monologue we did not know it, because our one object
was to show by our attention that he need never leave off. If
thought failed him we would not combat what he had said, or start
some new theme, but would encourage him with a question; and
one felt that it had been always so from childhood up. His mind
was full of fantasy for fantasy's sake and he gave as good entertain-
ment in monologue as his cousin Robert Louis in poem or story. He
was always 'supposing'; 'Suppose you had two millions, what
would you do with it?' and 'Suppose you were in Spain and in love,
how would you propose?' I recall him one afternoon at our house
at Bedford Park, surrounded by my brother and sisters and a little
group of my father's friends, describing proposals in half a dozen
countries. There your father did it, dressed in such-and-such a way
with such-and-such words, and there a friend must wait for the lady
outside the chapel door, sprinkle her with holy water and say, 'My
friend Jones is dying for love of you'. But when it was over, those
quaint descriptions, so full of laughter and sympathy, faded or
remained in the memory as something alien from one's own life,
like a dance I once saw in a great house, where beautifully dressed
children wound a long ribbon in and out as they danced. I was not
of Stevenson's party, mainly, I think, because he had written a book
in praise of Velasquez,[41] praise at that time universal wherever Pre-
Raphaelitism was accurst, and to my mind, that had to pick its symbols where its ignorance permitted, Velasquez seemed the first
bored celebrant of boredom. I was convinced from some obscure
meditation that Stevenson's conversational method had joined him
to my elders and to the indifferent world, as though it were right for
old men, and unambitious men and all women, to be content with
charm and humour. It was the prerogative of youth to take sides
and when Wilde said, 'Mr. Bernard Shaw has no enemies but is
intensely disliked by all his friends', I knew it to be a phrase I should

never forget, and felt revenged upon a notorious hater of romance, whose generosity and courage I could not fathom.

X

I saw a good deal of Wilde at that time—was it 1887 or 1888?—I have no way of fixing the date except that I had published my first book, *The Wanderings of Oisin,* and that Wilde had not yet published his 'Decay of Lying'. He had, before our first meeting, reviewed my book[42] and despite its vagueness of intention, and the inexactness of its speech, praised without qualification; and what was worth more than any review, he had talked about it; and now he asked me to eat my Christmas dinner with him, believing, I imagine, that I was alone in London. He had just renounced his velveteen, and even those cuffs turned backward over the sleeves, and had begun to dress very carefully in the fashion of the moment. He lived in a little house at Chelsea that the architect Godwin had decorated with an elegance that owed something to Whistler. There was nothing mediaeval nor Pre-Raphaelite, no cupboard door with figures upon flat gold, no peacock-blue, no dark background. I remember vaguely a white drawing-room with Whistler etchings, 'let into' white panels, and a dining-room all white, chairs, walls, mantelpiece, carpet, except for a diamond-shaped piece of red cloth in the middle of the table under a terracotta statuette, and, I think, a red-shaded lamp hanging from the ceiling to a little above the statuette. It was perhaps too perfect in its unity, his past of a few years before had gone too completely, and I remember thinking that the perfect harmony of his life there, with his beautiful wife and his two young children, suggested some deliberate artistic composition.

He commended and dispraised himself during dinner by attributing characteristics like his own to his country: 'We Irish are too poetical to be poets; we are a nation of brilliant failures, but we are the greatest talkers since the Greeks'. When dinner was over he read to me from the proofs of 'The Decay of Lying' and when he came to the sentence, 'Schopenhauer has analysed the pessimism that characterises modern thought, but Hamlet invented it. The world has become sad because a puppet was once melancholy',[43] I said, 'Why do you change "sad" to "melancholy"?' He replied that he wanted a full sound at the close of his sentence, and I thought it no excuse and an example of the vague impressiveness that spoilt his writing for me. Only when he spoke, or when his writing was the mirror of his speech, or in some simple faery-tale, had he words exact enough to hold a subtle ear. He alarmed me, though not as Henley did, for I never left his house thinking myself fool or dunce. He flattered the intellect of every man he liked; he made me tell him long Irish stories and compared my art of story-telling to Homer's; and once when he had described himself as writing in the census paper 'age 19, profession genius, infirmity talent' the other guest, a young journalist fresh from Oxford or Cambridge, said, 'What should I have written?' and was told that it should have been 'profession talent, infirmity genius'. When, however, I called, wearing shoes a little too yellow—unblackened leather had just become fashionable—I realized their extravagance when I saw his eyes fixed upon them; and another day Wilde asked me to tell his little boy a faery-story, and I had but got as far as 'Once upon a time there was a giant' when the little boy screamed and ran out of the room. Wilde looked grave and I was plunged into the shame of clumsiness that afflicts the young. And when I asked for some literary gossip for some provincial newspaper,[44] that paid me a few shillings a month, I was told that writing literary gossip was no job for a gentleman.

Though to be compared to Homer passed the time pleasantly, I had not been greatly perturbed had he stopped me with 'Is it a long story?' as Henley would certainly have done. I was abashed before him as wit and man of the world alone. I remember that he deprecated the very general belief in his success or his efficiency, and, I think, with sincerity. One form of success had gone: he was no more the lion of the season and he had not discovered his gift for writing comedy, yet I think I knew him at the happiest moment of his life. No scandal had touched his name, his fame as a talker was growing among his equals, and he seemed to live in the enjoyment of his own spontaneity. One day he began, 'I have been inventing a Christian heresy', and he told a detailed story, in the style of some early Father, of how Christ recovered after the Crucifixion, and escaping from the tomb, lived on for many years, the one man upon earth who knew the falsehood of Christianity. Once Saint Paul visited his town and he alone in the carpenters' quarter did not go to hear him preach. Henceforth the other carpenters noticed that, for some unknown reason, he kept his hands covered. A few days afterwards

I found Wilde with smock frocks in various colours spread out upon the floor in front of him, while a missionary explained that he did not object to the heathen going naked upon week-days, but insisted upon clothes in church. He had brought the smock frocks in a cab that the only art-critic whose fame had reached Central Africa might select a colour; so Wilde sat there weighing all with a conscious ecclesiastic solemnity.

XI

Of late years I have often explained Wilde to myself by his family history. His father was a friend or acquaintance of my father's father and among my family traditions there is an old Dublin riddle: 'Why are Sir William Wilde's[45] nails so black?' Answer: 'Because he has scratched himself'. And there is an old story still current in Dublin of Lady Wilde[46] saying to a servant, 'Why do you put the plates on the coal-scuttle? What are the chairs meant for?' They were famous people and there are many like stories; and even a horrible folk-story, the invention of some Connacht peasant, that tells how Sir William Wilde took out the eyes of some man, who had come to consult him as an oculist, and laid them upon a plate, intending to replace them in a moment, and how the eyes were eaten by a cat. As a certain friend of mine, who has made a prolonged study of the nature of cats, said when he first heard the tale, 'Cats love eyes'. The Wilde family was clearly of the sort that fed the imagination of Charles Lever, dirty, untidy, daring, and what Charles Lever, who loved more normal activities, might not have valued so highly, very imaginative and learned. Lady Wilde, who when I knew her received her friends with blinds drawn and shutters closed that none might see her withered face, longed always perhaps, though certainly amid much self-mockery, for some impossible splendour of character and circumstance. She lived near her son in level Chelsea, but I have heard her say, 'I want to live on some high place, Primrose Hill or Highgate, because I was an eagle in my youth'. I think her son lived with no self-mockery at all an imaginary life; perpetually performed a play which was in all things the opposite of all that he had known in childhood and early youth; never put off completely his wonder at opening his eyes every morning on his own beautiful house, and in remembering that he had dined yesterday with a duchess, and that he delighted in Flaubert and Pater, read Homer in the original and not as a schoolmaster reads him for the grammar. I think, too, that because of all that half-civilized blood in his veins he could not endure the sedentary toil of creative art and so remained a man of action, exaggerating, for the sake of immediate effect, every trick learned from his masters, turning their easel painting into painted scenes. He was a parvenu, but a parvenu whose whole bearing proved that if he did dedicate every story in *A House of Pomegranates*[47] to a lady of title, it was but to show that he was Jack and the social ladder his pantomime beanstalk. 'Did you ever hear him say "Marquess of Dimmesdale"?' a friend of his once asked me. 'He does not say "the Duke of York" with any pleasure.'

He told me once that he had been offered a safe seat in Parliament and, had he accepted, he might have had a career like that of Beaconsfield, whose early style resembles his, being meant for crowds, for excitement, for hurried decisions, for immediate triumphs. Such men get their sincerity, if at all, from the contact of events; the dinner-table was Wilde's event and made him the greatest talker of his time, and his plays and dialogues have what merit they possess from being now an imitation, now a record, of his talk. Even in those days I would often defend him by saying that his very admiration for his predecessors in poetry, for Browning, for Swinburne and Rossetti, in their first vogue while he was a very young man, made any success seem impossible that could satisfy his immense ambition: never but once before had the artist seemed so great, never had the work of art seemed so difficult. I would then compare him with Benvenuto Cellini who, coming after Michael Angelo, found nothing left to do so satisfactory as to turn bravo and quarrel with the man who broke Michael Angelo's[48] nose.

XII

I cannot remember who first brought me to the old stable beside Kelmscott House, William Morris's[49] house at Hammersmith, and to the debates held there upon Sunday evenings by the Socialist League. I was soon of the little group who had supper with Morris afterwards. I met at these suppers very constantly Walter Crane, Emery Walker, in association with Cobden-Sanderson, the printer

of many fine books, and less constantly Bernard Shaw and Cock-
erell, now of the Fitzwilliam Museum, Cambridge, and perhaps but
once or twice Hyndman the Socialist and the Anarchist Prince
Kropotkin. There, too, one always met certain more or less educated workmen, rough of speech and manner, with a conviction to
meet every turn. I was told by one of them, on a night when I had
done perhaps more than my share of the talking, that I had talked
more nonsense in one evening than he had heard in the whole
course of his past life. I had merely preferred Parnell, then at the
height of his career, to Michael Davitt, who had wrecked his Irish
influence by international politics. We sat round a long unpolished
and unpainted trestle table of new wood in a room where hung
Rossetti's *Pomegranate,* a portrait of Mrs. Morris,[50] and where one
wall and part of the ceiling were covered by a great Persian carpet.
Morris had said somewhere or other that carpets were meant for
people who took their shoes off when they entered a house and
were most in place upon a tent floor. I was a little disappointed in
the house, for Morris was an ageing man content at last to gather
beautiful things rather than to arrange a beautiful house. I saw the
drawing-room once or twice, and there alone all my sense of decoration, founded upon the background of Rossetti's pictures, was
satisfied by a big cupboard painted with a scene from Chaucer by
Burne-Jones; but even there were objects, perhaps a chair or a little
table, that seemed accidental, bought hurriedly perhaps and with
little thought, to make wife or daughter comfortable. I had read as
a boy, in books belonging to my father, the third volume of *The
Earthly Paradise,* and *The Defence of Guenevere,* which pleased me
less, but had not opened either for a long time. *The Man Who
Never Laughed Again* had seemed the most wonderful of tales till
my father had accused me of preferring Morris to Keats, got angry
about it, and put me altogether out of countenance. He had spoiled
my pleasure, for now I questioned while I read and at last ceased to
read; nor had Morris written as yet those prose romances that
became after his death so great a joy that they were the only books
I was ever to read slowly that I might not come too quickly to the
end. It was now Morris himself that stirred my interest, and I took
to him first because of some little tricks of speech and body that
reminded me of my old grandfather[51] in Sligo, but soon discovered
his spontaneity and joy and made him my chief of men. To-day I do

not set his poetry very high, but for an odd altogether wonderful line, or thought; and yet, if some angel offered me the choice, I would choose to live his life, poetry and all, rather than my own or any other man's. A reproduction of his portrait by Watts[52] hangs over my mantelpiece with Henley's, and those of other friends. Its grave wide-open eyes, like the eyes of some dreaming beast, remind me of the open eyes of Titian's *Ariosto,* while the broad vigorous body suggests a mind that has no need of the intellect to remain sane, though it give itself to every fantasy: the dreamer of the Middle Ages. It is 'the fool of Faery[53] . . . wide and wild as a hill', the resolute European image that yet half remembers Buddha's motionless meditation, and has no trait in common with the wavering, lean image of hungry speculation, that cannot but because of certain famous Hamlets of our stage fill the mind's eye. Shakespeare himself foreshadowed a symbolic change, that is, a change in the whole temperament of the world, for though he called his Hamlet 'fat' and even 'scant of breath',[54] he thrust between his fingers agile rapier and dagger.

The dream world of Morris was as much the antithesis of daily life as with other men of genius, but he was never conscious of the antithesis and so knew nothing of intellectual suffering. His intellect, unexhausted by speculation or casuistry, was wholly at the service of hand and eye, and whatever he pleased he did with an unheard-of ease and simplicity, and if style and vocabulary were at times monotonous, he could not have made them otherwise without ceasing to be himself. Instead of the language of Chaucer and Shakespeare, its warp fresh from field and market—if the woof were learned—his age offered him a speech, exhausted from abstraction, that only returned to its full vitality when written learnedly and slowly.

The roots of his antithetical dream were visible enough: a never idle man of great physical strength and extremely irascible—did he not fling a badly baked plum-pudding through the window upon Christmas Day?—a man more joyous than any intellectual man of our world, he called himself 'the idle singer of an empty day',[55] created new forms of melancholy, and faint persons, like the knights and ladies of Burne-Jones, who are never, no, not once in forty volumes, put out of temper. A blunderer who had said to the only unconverted man at a Socialist picnic in Dublin, to prove that equality came easy, 'I was brought up a gentleman and now as you can see associate with all sorts', and left wounds thereby that rankled after twenty years, a man of whom I have heard it said, 'He is always afraid that he is doing something wrong and generally is', he wrote long stories with apparently no other object than that his persons might show to one another, through situations of poignant difficulty, the most exquisite tact.

He did not project, like Henley or like Wilde, an image of himself, because having all his imagination set upon making and doing he had little self-knowledge. He imagined instead new conditions of making and doing; and in the teeth of those scientific generalizations that cowed my boyhood, I can see some like imagining in every great change, and believe that the first flying-fish first leaped, not because it sought 'adaptation' to the air, but out of horror of the sea.

XIII

Soon after I began to attend the lectures a French class was started in the old coach-house for certain young Socialists who planned a tour in France, and I joined it, and was for a time a model student constantly encouraged by the compliments of the old French mistress. I told my father of the class, and he asked me to get my sisters admitted. I made difficulties and put off speaking of the matter, for I knew that the new and admirable self I was making would turn, under family eyes, into plain rag-doll. How could I pretend to be industrious, and even carry dramatization to the point of learning my lessons, when my sisters were there and knew that I was nothing of the kind? But I had no argument I could use, and my sisters were admitted. They said nothing unkind, so far as I can remember, but in a week or two I was my old procrastinating idle self and had soon left the class altogether. My elder sister stayed on and became an embroideress under Miss May Morris,[56] and the hangings round Morris's big bed at Kelmscott House, Oxfordshire, with their verses about lying happily in bed when 'all birds sing in the town of the tree', were from her needle, though not from her design. She worked for the first few months at Kelmscott House, Hammersmith, and in my imagination I cannot always separate what I saw and heard from her report, or indeed from the report of that tribe

or guild who looked up to Morris as to some worshipped mediaeval king. He had no need for other people. I doubt if their marriage
or death made him sad or glad, and yet no man I have known was
so well loved; you saw him producing everywhere organization and
beauty, seeming, almost in the same instant, helpless and triumphant; and people loved him as children are loved. People much
in his neighbourhood became gradually occupied with him or
about his affairs, and without any wish on his part, as simple people become occupied with children. I remember a man who was
proud and pleased because he had distracted Morris's thoughts
from an attack of gout by leading the conversation delicately to the
hated name of Milton. He began at Swinburne: 'O, Swinburne',
said Morris, 'is a rhetorician; my masters have been Keats and
Chaucer, for they make pictures.' 'Does not Milton make pictures?'
asked my informant. 'No,' was the answer, 'Dante makes pictures,
but Milton, though he had a great earnest mind, expressed himself
as a rhetorician.' 'Great earnest mind' sounded strange to me, and I
doubt not that were his questioner not a simple man Morris had
been more emphatic. Another day the same man started by praising
Chaucer, but the gout was worse, and Morris cursed Chaucer for
destroying the English language with foreign words.

He had few detachable phrases, and I can remember little of his
speech, which many thought the best of all good talk, except that it
matched his burly body and seemed within definite boundaries
inexhaustible in fact and expression. He alone of all the men I have
known seemed guided by some beast-like instinct and never ate
strange meat. 'Balzac! Balzac!' he said to me once, 'O, that was the
man the French bourgeoisie read so much a few years ago.' I can
remember him at supper praising wine: 'Why do people say it is
prosaic to be inspired by wine? Has it not been made by the sunlight and the sap?' and his dispraising houses decorated by himself:
'Do you suppose I like that kind of house? I would like a house like
a big barn, where one ate in one corner, cooked in another corner,
slept in the third corner, and in the fourth received one's friends';
and his complaining of Ruskin's objection to the underground railway: 'If you must have a railway the best thing you can do with it
is to put it in a tube with a cork at each end'. I remember, too, that
when I asked what led up to his movement, he replied: 'O, Ruskin
and Carlyle, but somebody should have been beside Carlyle and

punched his head every five minutes'. Though I remember little, I do not doubt that, had I continued going there on Sunday evenings, I should have caught fire from his words and turned my hand to some mediaeval work or other.

Just before I had ceased to go there I had sent my *Wanderings of Oisin* to his daughter, hoping of course that it might meet his eyes, and soon after sending it I came upon him by chance in Holborn. 'You write my sort of poetry', he said, and began to praise me and to promise to send his praise to the *Commonweal*,[57] the League organ, and he would have said more had he not caught sight of a new ornamental cast-iron lamp-post and got very heated upon that subject.

I did not read economics, having turned Socialist because of Morris's lectures and pamphlets, and I think it unlikely that Morris himself could read economics. That old dogma of mine seemed germane to the matter. If the men and women imagined by the poets were the norm, and if Morris had, in let us say *News from Nowhere*, then running through the *Commonweal*, described such men and women, living under their natural conditions, or as they would desire to live, then those conditions themselves must be the norm and could we but get rid of certain institutions the world would turn from eccentricity. Perhaps Morris himself justified himself in his own heart by as simple an argument, and was, as the Socialist D——[58] said to me one night, walking home after some lecture, 'an Anarchist without knowing it'. Certainly I and all about me, including D—— himself, were for chopping up the old king for Medea's pot. Morris had told us to have nothing to do with the parliamentary Socialists, represented for men in general by the Fabian Society and Hyndman's Social Democratic Federation and for us in particular by D——. During the period of transition mistakes must be made, and the discredit of these mistakes must be left to 'the bourgeoisie'; and besides, when you begin to talk of this measure, or that other, you lose sight of the goal, and see, to reverse Swinburne's description of Tiresias,[59] 'Light on the way but darkness on the goal'. By mistakes Morris meant vexatious restrictions and compromises—'If any man puts me into a labour squad, I will lie on my back and kick'. That phrase very much expresses our idea of revolutionary tactics: we all intended to lie upon our backs and kick. D——, pale and sedentary, did not dislike labour squads and we all hated him with the left side of our heads, while admiring him immensely with the right side. He alone was invited to entertain Mrs. Morris, having many tales of his Irish uncles, more especially of one particular uncle who had tried to commit suicide by shutting his head into a carpet-bag.[60] At that time he was an obscure man, known only for a witty speaker at street corners and in Park demonstrations. He had, with an assumed truculence and fury, cold logic, an invariable gentleness, an unruffled courtesy, and yet could never close a speech without being denounced by a journeyman hatter,[61] with an Italian name. Converted to Socialism by D——, and to Anarchism by himself, with swinging arm and uplifted voice, this man put, and perhaps exaggerated, our scruple about Parliament. 'I lack', said D——, 'the bump of reverence'; whereon the wild man shouted, 'You 'ave a 'ole'. There are moments when looking back I somewhat confuse my own figure with that of the hatter, image of our hysteria, for I too became violent with the violent solemnity of a religious devotee. I can even remember sitting behind D—— and saying some rude thing or other over his shoulder.

I don't remember why I gave it up but I did quite suddenly and the push may have come from a young workman[62] who was educating himself between Morris and Karl Marx. He had planned a history of the Navy, and when I had spoken of the battleships of Nelson's day had said, 'O, that was the decadence of the battleship', but if his naval interests were mediaeval, his ideas about religion were pure Karl Marx, and we were soon in perpetual argument. Then gradually the attitude towards religion of almost everybody but Morris, who avoided the subject altogether, got upon my nerves, for I broke out after some lecture or other with all the arrogance of raging youth. They attacked religion, I said, or some such words, and yet there must be a change of heart and only religion could make it. What was the use of talking about some new revolution putting all things right, when the change must come, if come it did, with astronomical slowness, like the cooling of the sun, or it may have been like the drying of the moon? Morris rang his chairman's bell, but I was too angry to listen, and he had to ring it a second time before I sat down. He said that night at supper, 'Of course I know there must be a change of heart, but it will not come as slowly as all that. I rang my bell because you were not being understood.' He did not show any vexation, but I never returned after that night; and yet I did not always believe what I had said, and only gradually gave up thinking of and planning for some near sudden change for the better.

XIV

I spent my days at the British Museum[63] and must, I think, have been delicate, for I remember often putting off hour after hour consulting some necessary book because I shrank from lifting the heavy volumes of the catalogue; and yet to save money for my afternoon coffee and roll I often walked the whole way home to Bedford Park. I was compiling, for a series of shilling books, an anthology of Irish faery-stories,[64] and, for an American publisher, a two-volume selection from the Irish novelists[65] that would be somewhat dearer. I was not well paid, for each book cost me more than three months' reading; and I was paid for the first some twelve pounds ('O, Mr. E.,'[66] said publisher to editor, 'you must never again pay so much!') and for the second twenty, but I did not think myself badly paid, for I had chosen the work for my own purposes.

Though I went to Sligo every summer, I was compelled to live out of Ireland the greater part of every year, and was but keeping my mind upon what I knew must be the subject-matter of my poetry. I believed that if Morris had set his stories amid the scenery of his own Wales, for I knew him to be of Welsh extraction and supposed wrongly that he had spent his childhood there, that if Shelley had nailed his Prometheus, or some equal symbol, upon some Welsh or Scottish rock, their art would have entered more intimately, more microscopically, as it were, into our thought and given perhaps to modern poetry a breadth and stability like that of ancient poetry. The statues of Mausolus and Artemisia[67] at the British Museum, private, half-animal, half-divine figures, all unlike the Grecian athletes and Egyptian kings in their near neighbourhood, that stand in the middle of the crowd's applause, or sit above measuring it out unpersuadable justice, became to me, now or later, images of an unpremeditated joyous energy, that neither I nor any other man, racked by doubt and inquiry, can achieve; and that yet, if once achieved, might seem to men and women of Connemara or of Galway their very soul. In our study of that ruined tomb raised by a queen to her dead lover, and finished by the unpaid labour of great sculptors, after her death from grief, or so runs the tale, we cannot distinguish the handiwork of Scopas from that of Praxiteles; and I wanted to create once more an art where the artist's handiwork would hide as under those half-anonymous chisels, or as we find it in some old Scots ballads, or in some twelfth- or thirteenth-century Arthurian romance. That handiwork assured, I had martyred no man for modelling his own image upon Pallas Athene's buckler; for I took great pleasure in certain allusions to the singer's life one finds in old romances and ballads, and thought his presence there all the more poignant because we discover it half lost, like portly Chaucer, behind his own maunciple and pardoner upon the Canterbury roads. Wolfram von Eschenbach, singing his German Parsifal,[68] broke off some description of a famished city to remember that in his own house at home the very mice lacked food, and what old ballad-singer[69] was it who claimed to have fought by day in the very battle he sang by night? So masterful indeed was that instinct that when the minstrel knew not who his poet was, he must needs make up a man: 'When any stranger asks who is the sweetest of singers, answer with one voice: "A blind man; he dwells upon rocky Chios;[70] his songs shall be the most beautiful for ever".' Elaborate modern psychology sounds egotistical, I thought, when it speaks in the first person, but not those simple emotions which resemble the more, the more powerful they are, everybody's emotion, and I was soon to write many poems where an always personal emotion was woven into a general pattern of myth and symbol. When the Fenian poet[71] says that his heart has grown cold and callous—'For thy hapless fate, dear Ireland, and sorrows of my own'—he but follows tradition, and if he does not move us deeply, it is because he has no sensuous musical vocabulary that comes at need, without compelling him to sedentary toil and so driving him out from his fellows. I thought to create that sensuous, musical vocabulary, and not for myself only, but that I might leave it to later Irish poets, much as a mediaeval Japanese painter left his style as an inheritance to his family, and I was careful to use a traditional manner and matter, yet changed by that toil, impelled by my share in Cain's curse,[72] by all that sterile modern complication, by my 'originality', as the newspapers call it, did something altogether different. Morris set out to make a revolution that the persons of his *Well at the World's End*[73] or his *Water of the Wondrous Isles*, always, to my mind, in the likeness of Artemisia and her man, might walk his native scenery; and I, that my native scenery might find imaginary inhabitants, half planned a new method and a new culture. My mind began drifting vaguely towards that doctrine of 'the mask' which has convinced me that every passionate man (I have nothing to do with mechanist, or philanthropist, or man whose eyes have no preference) is, as it were, linked with another age, historical or imaginary, where alone he finds images that rouse his energy. Napoleon was never of his own time, as the naturalistic writers and painters bid all men be, but had some Roman emperor's image in his head and some condottiere's[74] blood in his heart; and when he crowned that head with his own hands he had covered, as may be seen from David's painting,[75] his hesitation with that emperor's old suit.

XV

I had various women friends on whom I would call towards five o'clock mainly to discuss my thoughts that I could not bring to a man without meeting some competing thought, but partly because their tea and toast saved my pennies for the 'bus-ride home; but with women, apart from their intimate exchanges of thought, I was timid and abashed. I was sitting on a seat in front of the British Museum feeding pigeons when a couple of girls sat near and began enticing my pigeons away, laughing and whispering to one another, and I looked straight in front of me, very indignant, and presently went into the Museum without turning my head towards them. Since then I have often wondered if they were pretty or merely very young. Sometimes I told myself very adventurous love-stories with myself for hero, and at other times I planned out a life of lonely austerity, and at other times mixed the ideals and planned a life of lonely austerity mitigated by periodical lapses. I had still the ambition, formed in Sligo in my teens, of living in imitation of Thoreau on Innisfree, a little island in Lough Gill, and when walking through Fleet Street very homesick I heard a little tinkle of water and saw a fountain in a shop-window which balanced a little ball upon its jet, and began to remember lake water. From the sudden remembrance came my poem 'Innisfree',[76] my first lyric with anything in its rhythm of my own music. I had begun to loosen rhythm as an escape from rhetoric and from that emotion of the crowd that rhetoric brings, but I only understood vaguely and occasionally that I must for my special purpose use nothing but the common syntax. A couple of years later I would not have written that first line with its conventional archaism—'Arise and go'—nor the inversion in the last stanza. Passing another day by the new Law Courts,[77] a building that I admired because it was Gothic—'It is not very good', Morris had said, 'but it is better than anything else they have got and so they hate it'—I grew suddenly oppressed by the great weight of stone, and thought, 'There are miles and miles of stone and brick all round me', and presently added, 'If John the Baptist or his like were to come again and had his mind set upon it, he could make all these people go out into some wilderness leaving their buildings empty', and that thought, which does not seem very valuable now, so enlightened the day that it is still vivid in the memory. I spent a few days at Oxford copying out a seventeenth-century translation of Poggio's *Liber Facetiarum* or the *Hypnerotomachia* of Poliphilo for a publisher[78]—I forget which, for I copied both—and returned very pale to my troubled family. I had lived upon bread and tea because I thought that if antiquity found locust and wild honey nutritive, my soul was strong enough to need no better. I was always planning some great gesture, putting the whole world into one scale of the balance and my soul into the other and imagining that the whole world somehow kicked the beam. More than thirty years have passed and I have seen no forcible young man of letters brave the metropolis without some like stimulant; and all after two or three, or twelve or fifteen years, according to obstinacy, have understood that we achieve, if we do achieve, in little sedentary stitches as though we were making lace. I had one unmeasured advantage from my stimulant: I could ink my socks, that they might not show through my shoes, with a most haughty mind, imagining myself, and my torn tackle, somewhere else, in some far place 'under the canopy . . . i' the city of kites and crows'.[79]

In London I saw nothing good and constantly remembered that Ruskin had said to some friend of my father's, 'As I go to my work at the British Museum I see the faces of the people become daily more corrupt'. I convinced myself for a time that on the same journey I saw but what he saw. Certain old women's faces filled me with horror, faces that are no longer there, or if they are pass before me unnoticed: the fat blotched faces, rising above double chins, of women who have drunk too much beer and eaten much meat. In Dublin, I had often seen old women walking with erect heads and gaunt bodies, talking to themselves with loud voices, mad with drink and poverty, but they were different, they belonged to romance. Da Vinci had drawn women who looked so, and so carried their bodies.

XVI

I attempted to restore one old friend of my father's to the practice of his youth, but failed, though he, unlike my father, had not changed his belief. My father brought me to dine at Wigmore Street with Jack Nettleship,[80] once inventor of imaginative designs and now a painter of melodramatic lions. At dinner I had talked a great deal—too much, I imagine, for so young a man, or maybe for any man—and on the way home my father, who had been plainly anxious that I should make a good impression, was very angry. He said I had talked for effect and that talking for effect was precisely what one must never do; he had always hated rhetoric and emphasis and had made me hate it; and his anger plunged me into great dejection. I called at Nettleship's studio the next day to apologize, and Nettleship opened the door himself and received me with enthusiasm. He had explained to some woman guest that I would probably talk well, being an Irishman, but the reality had surpassed, etc., etc. I was not flattered, though relieved at not having to apologize, for I soon discovered that what he really admired was my volubility, for he himself was very silent. He seemed about sixty, had a bald head, a grey beard, and a nose, as one of my father's friends used to say, like an opera-glass, and sipped cocoa all the afternoon and evening from an enormous tea-cup that must have been designed for him alone, not caring how cold the cocoa grew. Years before he had been thrown from his horse, while hunting, and broke his arm, and because it had been badly set suffered great pain for a long time. A little whiskey would always stop the pain, and soon a little became a great deal and he found himself a drunkard, but having signed his liberty away for certain months he was completely cured. He had acquired, however, the need of some liquid which he could sip constantly. I brought him an admiration settled in early boyhood, for my father had always said, 'George Wilson was our born

painter, but Nettleship our genius', and even had he shown me nothing I could care for, I had admired him still because my admiration
was in my bones. He showed me his early designs, and they, though
often badly drawn, fulfilled my hopes. Something of Blake they certainly did show, but had in place of Blake's joyous, intellectual
energy a Saturnian passion and melancholy. God Creating Evil, the
deathlike head with a woman and a tiger coming from the forehead,
which Rossetti—or was it Browning?—had described as 'the most sublime conception[81] of ancient or modern art', had been lost, but there
was another version of the same thought, and other designs never published or exhibited. They rise before me even now in meditation, especially a blind Titan-like ghost floating with groping hands above the
tree-tops. I wrote a criticism,[82] and arranged for reproductions with
the editor of an art magazine, but after it was written and accepted
the proprietor, lifting what I considered an obsequious caw in the Huxley, Tyndall, Carolus Duran, Bastien-Lepage rookery,[83] insisted
upon its rejection. Nettleship did not mind its rejection, saying,
'Who cares for such things now? Not ten people', but he did mind
my refusal to show him what I had written. Though what I had written was all eulogy, I dreaded his judgment, for it was my first art criticism. I hated his big lion pictures, where he attempted an art too much
concerned with the sense of touch, with the softness or roughness, the
minutely observed irregularity of surfaces, for his genius; and I think
he knew it. 'Rossetti used to call my pictures pot-boilers', he said, 'but
they are all—all'—and he waved his arm to the canvases—'symbols'.
When I wanted him to design gods, and angels, and lost spirits once
more, he always came back to the point: 'Nobody would be
pleased'. 'Everybody should have a raison d'être'[84] was one of his
phrases. 'Mrs.——'s articles are not good but they are her raison d'être.'
I had but little knowledge of art, for there was little scholarship in
the Dublin art schools, so I overrated the quality of anything that could
be connected with my general beliefs about the world. If I had been
able to give angelical or diabolical names to his lions I might have liked
them also and I think that Nettleship himself would have liked them
better and liking them better have become a better painter. We had
the same kind of religious feeling, but I could give a crude philosophical
expression to mine while he could only express his in action or with
brush and pencil. He often told me of certain ascetic ambitions, very
much like my own, for he had kept all the moral ambition of youth,

as for instance—'Yeats, the other night I was arrested by a policeman—was walking round Regent's Park barefooted to keep the flesh under—good sort of thing to do. I was carrying my boots in my hand and he thought I was a burglar and even when I explained and gave him half-a-crown, he would not let me go till I had promised to put on my boots before I met the next policeman.'

He was very proud and shy and I could not imagine anybody asking him questions and so I was content to take these stories as they came: confirmations of what I had heard of him in boyhood. One story heard in boyhood had stirred my imagination particularly, for, ashamed all my boyhood of my lack of physical courage, I admired what was beyond my imitation. He thought that any weakness, even a weakness of body, had the character of sin, and while at breakfast with his brother, with whom he shared a room on the third floor of a corner house, he said that his nerves were out of order. Presently he left the table, and got out through the window and on to a stone ledge that ran along the wall under the window-sills. He sidled along the ledge, and turning the corner with it, got in at a different window and returned to the table. 'My nerves', he said, 'are better than I thought.'

Nettleship said to me, 'Has Edwin Ellis[85] ever said anything about the effect of drink upon my genius?' 'No', I answered. 'I ask', he said, 'because I have always thought that Ellis has some strange medical insight.' Though I had answered 'No', Ellis had only a few days before used these words: 'Nettleship drank his genius away'. Ellis, but lately returned from Perugia where he had lived many years, was another old friend of my father's but some years younger than Nettleship or my father. Nettleship had found his simplifying image, but in his painting had turned away from it, while Ellis, the son of Alexander Ellis,[86] a once famous man of science, who was perhaps the last man in England to run the circle of the sciences without superficiality, had never found that image at all. He was a painter and poet, but his painting, which did not interest me, showed no influence but that of Leighton. He had started perhaps a couple of years too late for Pre-Raphaelite influence, for no great Pre-Raphaelite picture was painted after 1870, and left England too soon for that of the French painters. He was, however, sometimes moving as a poet and still more often an astonishment. I have known him cast something just said into a dozen lines of musical verse, without apparently ceasing to talk; but the work once done he could not or would not amend it, and my father thought he lacked all ambition. Yet he had at times nobility of rhythm—an instinct for grandeur, and after thirty years I still repeat to myself his address to Mother Earth:

> O mother of the hills, forgive our towers,
> O mother of the clouds, forgive our dreams.[87]

And there are certain whole poems that I read from time to time or try to make others read. There is that poem where the manner is unworthy of the matter, being loose and facile, describing Adam and Eve fleeing from Paradise.[88] Adam asks Eve what she carries so carefully, and Eve replies that it is a little of the apple-core kept for their children. There is that vision concerning 'Christ the Less',[89] a too hurriedly written ballad, where the half of Christ sacrificed to the divine half 'that fled to seek felicity' wanders wailing through Golgotha, and there is 'The Saint and the Youth', in which I can discover no fault at all. He loved complexities—'Seven silences like candles round her face' is a line of his—and whether he wrote well or ill had always a manner which I would have known from that of any other poet. He would say to me, 'I am a mathematician with the mathematics left out'—his father was a great mathematician— or 'A woman once said to me, "Mr. Ellis, why are your poems like sums?" ' And certainly he loved symbols and abstractions. He said once, when I had asked him not to mention something or other, 'Surely you have discovered by this time that I know of no means whereby I can mention a fact in conversation'.

He had a passion for Blake, picked up in Pre-Raphaelite studios, and early in our acquaintance put into my hands a scrap of notepaper on which he had written some years before an interpretation of the poem that begins—

> The fields from Islington to Marybone,
>   To Primrose Hill and Saint John's Wood,
> Were builded over with pillars of gold,
>   And there Jerusalem's pillars stood.[90]

The four quarters of London represented Blake's four great mythological personages, the Zoas, and also the four elements. These few sentences were the foundation of all study of the philosophy of William Blake that requires an exact knowledge for its pursuit and that traces the connection between his system and that of Swedenborg[91] or of Boehme. I recognized certain attributions, from what is sometimes called the Christian Cabbala, of which Ellis had never heard, and with this proof that his interpretation was more than fantasy he and I began our four years' work upon the 'Prophetic Books' of William Blake. We took it as almost a sign of Blake's personal help when we discovered that the spring of 1889, when we first joined our knowledge, was one hundred years from the publication of *The Book of Thel,* the first published of the 'Prophetic Books', as though it were firmly established that the dead delight in anniversaries. After months of discussion and reading we made a concordance of all Blake's mystical terms, and there was much copying to be done in the Museum and at Redhill, where the descendants of Blake's friend and patron, the landscape-painter, John Linnell, had many manuscripts. The Linnells were narrow in their religious ideas and doubtful of Blake's orthodoxy, whom they held, however, in great honour, and I remember a timid old lady who had known Blake when a child saying, 'He had very wrong ideas, he did not believe in the historical Jesus'. One old man[92] sat always beside us, ostensibly to sharpen our pencils but perhaps really to see that we did not steal the manuscripts, and they gave us very old port at lunch, and I have upon my dining-room walls their present of Blake's Dante engravings.[93] Going thither and returning, Ellis would entertain me by philosophical discussion varied with improvised stories, at first folk-tales which he professed to have picked up in Scotland, and, though I had read and collected many folk-tales, I did not see through the deceit. I have a partial memory of two more elaborate tales, one of an Italian conspirator flying barefoot, from I forget what adventure through I forget what Italian city, in the early morning. Fearing to be recognized by his bare feet, he slipped past the sleepy porter at an hotel, calling out 'Number So-and-so' as if he were some belated guest. Then passing from bedroom door to door he tried on the boots, and just as he got a pair to fit, a voice cried from the room, 'Who is that?' 'Merely me, sir,' he called back, 'taking your boots.' The other was of a martyr's Bible, round which the cardinal virtues had taken personal form—this a fragment of Blake's philosophy. It was in the possession of an old clergyman when a certain jockey called upon him, and the cardinal virtues, confused between jockey and clergyman, devoted themselves to the jockey.[94] As whenever he sinned a cardinal virtue interfered and turned him back to virtue, he lived in great credit, and made, but for one sentence, a very holy death. As his wife and family knelt round in admiration and grief he suddenly said 'Damn'. 'O, my dear,' said his wife, 'what a dreadful expression!' He answered, 'I am going to Heaven', and straightway died. It was a long tale, for there were all the jockey's vain attempts to sin, as well as all the adventures of the clergyman, who became very sinful indeed, but it ended happily, for when the jockey died the cardinal virtues returned to the clergyman. I think he would talk to any audience that offered, one audience being the same as another in his eyes, and it may have been for this reason that my father called him unambitious. When he was a young man he had befriended a reformed thief and had asked the grateful thief to take him round the thieves' quarters of London. The thief, however, hurried him away from the worst saying, 'Another minute and they would have found you out. If they were not the stupidest of men in London, they had done so already.' Ellis had gone through a detailed, romantic and witty account of all the houses he had robbed and all the throats he had cut in one short life.

His conversation would often pass out of my comprehension, or indeed, I think, of any man's, into a labyrinth of abstraction and subtlety and then suddenly return with some verbal conceit or turn of wit. The mind is known to attain in certain conditions of trance a quickness so extraordinary that we are compelled at times to imagine a condition of unendurable intellectual intensity from which we are saved by the merciful stupidity of the body, and I think that the mind of Edwin Ellis was constantly upon the edge of trance. Once we were discussing the symbolism of sex in the philosophy of Blake and had been in disagreement all the afternoon. I began talking with a new sense of conviction and after a moment Ellis, who was at his easel, threw down his brush and said that he had just seen the same explanation in a series of symbolic visions. 'In another moment', he said, 'I should have been off.' We went into the open air and walked up and down to get rid of that feeling, but presently we came in again and I began again my explanation, Ellis lying upon the sofa. I had been talking some time when Mrs. Ellis came into the room and said, 'Why are you sitting in the dark?' Ellis answered, 'But we are not', and then added in a voice of wonder, 'I thought the lamp was lit, and that I was sitting up, and now I find that I am lying down and that we are in darkness.' I had seen a flicker of light over the ceiling but thought it a reflection from some light outside the house.

XVII

I had already met most of the poets of my generation. I had said, soon after the publication of *The Wanderings of Oisin,* to the editor of a series of shilling reprints, who had set me to compile tales of the Irish faeries, 'I am growing jealous of other poets and we will all grow jealous of each other unless we know each other and so feel a share in each other's triumph'. He was a Welshman, lately a mining engineer, Ernest Rhys, a writer of Welsh translations and original poems, that have often moved me greatly though I can think of no one else who has read them. He was perhaps a dozen years older than myself and through his work as editor knew everybody who would compile a book for seven or eight pounds. Between us we founded The Rhymers' Club,[95] which for some years was to meet every night in an upper room with a sanded floor in an ancient eating-house in Fleet Street called the Cheshire Cheese. Lionel Johnson, Ernest Dowson, Victor Plarr, Ernest Radford, John Davidson, Richard Le Gallienne, T. W. Rolleston, Selwyn Image, Edwin Ellis, and John Todhunter came constantly for a time, Arthur Symons and Herbert Horne, less constantly, while William Watson joined but never came and Francis Thompson came once but never joined; and sometimes if we met in a private house, which we did occasionally, Oscar Wilde came. It had been useless to invite him to the Cheshire Cheese, for he hated Bohemia. 'Olive Schreiner', he said once to me, 'is staying in the East End because that is the only place where people do not wear masks upon their faces, but I have told her that I live in the West End because nothing in life interests me but the mask.'

We read our poems to one another and talked criticism and drank a little wine. I sometimes say when I speak of the club, 'We had such-and-such ideas, such-and-such a quarrel with the great

Victorians, we set before us such-and-such aims', as though we had many philosophical ideas. I say this because I am ashamed to admit that I had these ideas and that whenever I began to talk of them a gloomy silence fell upon the room. A young Irish poet,[96] who wrote excellently but had the worst manners, was to say a few years later, 'You do not talk like a poet, you talk like a man of letters', and if all the Rhymers had not been polite, if most of them had not been to Oxford or Cambridge, the greater number would have said the same thing. I was full of thought, often very abstract thought, longing all the while to be full of images, because I had gone to the art schools instead of a university. Yet even if I had gone to a university, and learned all the classical foundations of English literature and English culture, all that great erudition which once accepted frees the mind from restlessness, I should have had to give up my Irish subject-matter, or attempt to found a new tradition. Lacking sufficient recognized precedent, I must needs find out some reason for all I did. I knew almost from the start that to overflow with reasons was to be not quite well-born; and when I could I hid them, as men hide a disagreeable ancestry; and that there was no help for it seeing that my country was not born at all. I was of those doomed to imperfect achievement, and under a curse, as it were, like some race of birds compelled to spend the time needed for the making of the nest in argument as to the convenience of moss and twig and lichen. Le Gallienne and Davidson, and even Symons, were provincial at their setting out, but their provincialism was curable, mine incurable; while the one conviction shared by all the younger men, but principally by Johnson and Horne, who imposed their personalities upon us, was an opposition to all ideas, all generalizations that can be explained and debated. Symons fresh from Paris would sometimes say, 'We are concerned with nothing but impressions', but that itself was a generalization and met but stony silence. Conversation constantly dwindled into 'Do you like So-and-so's last book?' 'No, I prefer the book before it', and I think that but for its Irish members, who said whatever came into their heads, the club would not have survived its first difficult months. I saw—now ashamed that I saw 'like a man of letters', now exasperated at the indifference of these poets to the fashion of their own river-bed—that Swinburne in one way, Browning in another, and Tennyson in a third, had filled their work with what I called 'impurities', curiosities about politics, about science, about history, about religion; and that we must create once more the pure work.

Our clothes were for the most part unadventurous like our conversation, though I indeed wore a brown velveteen coat, a loose tie, and a very old Inverness cape, discarded by my father twenty years before and preserved by my Sligo-born mother whose actions were unreasoning and habitual like the seasons. But no other member of the club, except Le Gallienne, who wore a loose tie, and Symons, who had an Inverness cape that was quite new and almost fashionable, would have shown himself for the world in any costume but 'that of an English gentleman'. 'One should be quite unnoticeable', Johnson explained to me. Those who conformed most carefully to the fashion in their clothes generally departed furthest from it in their handwriting, which was small, neat, and studied, one poet—which, I forget—having founded his upon the handwriting of George Herbert. Dowson and Symons I was to know better in later years when Symons became a very dear friend, and I never got behind John Davidson's Scottish roughness and exasperation, though I saw much of him, but from the first I devoted myself to Lionel Johnson. He and Horne and Image and one or two others shared a man-servant and an old house in Charlotte Street, Fitzroy Square,[97] typical figures of transition, doing as an achievement of learning and of exquisite taste what their predecessors did in careless abundance. All were Pre-Raphaelite, and sometimes one might meet in the rooms of one or other a ragged figure, as of some fallen dynasty, Simeon Solomon, the Pre-Raphaelite painter, once the friend of Rossetti and of Swinburne, but fresh now from some low public-house. Condemned to a long term of imprisonment for a criminal offence, he had sunk into drunkenness and misery. Introduced one night, however, to some man who mistook him, in the dim candlelight, for another Solomon, a successful academic painter and R.A., he started to his feet in a rage with, 'Sir, do you dare to mistake me for that mountebank?' Though not one had hearkened to the feeblest caw, or been spattered by the smallest dropping from any Huxley, Tyndall, Carolus Duran, Bastien-Lepage bundle of old twigs I began by suspecting them of lukewarmness, and even backsliding, and I owe it to that suspicion that I never became intimate with Horne, who lived to become the greatest English authority upon Italian life in the fifteenth century and to write the one standard work on Botticelli.[98] Connoisseur in several arts, he had designed a little church in the manner of Inigo Jones for a burial-ground near the Marble Arch. Though I now think his little church a masterpiece, its style was more than a century too late to hit my fancy, at two- or three-and-twenty; and I accused him of leaning towards that eighteenth century—

> That taught a school
> Of dolts to smooth, inlay, and clip, and fit
> Till, like the certain wands of Jacob's wit,
> Their verses tallied.[99]

Another fanaticism delayed my friendship with two men, who are now my friends and in certain matters my chief instructors. Somebody, probably Lionel Johnson, brought me to the studio of Charles Ricketts and Charles Shannon, certainly heirs of the great generation, and the first thing I saw was a Shannon picture of a lady and child, arrayed in lace, silk and satin, suggesting that hated century. My eyes were full of some more mythological mother and child and I would have none of it and I told Shannon that he had not painted a mother and child, but elegant people expecting visitors, and I thought that a great reproach. Somebody writing in the *Germ* had said that a picture of a pheasant and an apple was merely a picture of something to eat, and I was so angry with the indifference to subject, which was the commonplace of all art criticism since Bastien-Lepage, that I could at times see nothing else but subject. I thought that, though it might not matter to the man himself whether he loved a white woman or a black, a female pickpocket or a regular communicant of the Church of England, if only he loved strongly, it certainly did matter to his relations and even under some circumstances to his whole neighbourhood. Sometimes indeed, like some father in Molière, I ignored the lover's feelings altogether and even refused to admit that a trace of the devil, perhaps a trace of colour, may lend piquancy, especially if the connection be not permanent.

Among these men, of whom so many of the greatest talents were to live such passionate lives and die such tragic deaths, one serene man, T. W. Rolleston, seemed always out of place; it was I who brought him there, intending to set him to some work in Ireland later on. I have known young Dublin working-men slip out of their workshop to see the second Thomas Davis passing by, and can even remember a conspiracy, by some three or four, to make him 'the leader of the Irish race at home and abroad', and all because he had regular features; and when all is said Alexander the Great and Alcibiades were personable men, and the Founder of the Christian religion was the only man who was neither a little too tall nor a little too short, but exactly six feet high. We in Ireland thought as do the plays and ballads, not understanding that, from the first moment wherein Nature foresaw the birth of Bastien-Lepage, she has only granted great creative power to men whose faces are contorted with extravagance or curiosity, or dulled with some protecting stupidity.[100]

I had now met all those who were to make the nineties of the last century tragic in the history of literature, but as yet we were all seemingly equal, whether in talent or in luck, and scarce even personalities to one another. I remember saying one night at the Cheshire Cheese, when more poets than usual had come, 'None of us can say who will succeed, or even who has or has not talent. The only thing certain about us is that we are too many.'

XVIII

I have described what image—always opposite to the natural self or the natural world—Wilde, Henley, Morris copied or tried to copy, but I have not said if I found an image for myself. I know very little about myself and much less of that anti-self:[101] probably the woman who cooks my dinner or the woman who sweeps out my study knows more than I. It is perhaps because Nature made me a gregarious man, going hither and thither looking for conversation, and ready to deny from fear or favour his dearest conviction, that I love proud and lonely things. When I was a child and went daily to the sexton's daughter for writing lessons, I found one poem in her School Reader that delighted me beyond all others: a fragment of some metrical translation from Aristophanes wherein the birds sing scorn upon mankind.[102] In later years my mind gave itself to gregarious Shelley's dream[103] of a young man, his hair blanched with sorrow, studying philosophy in some lonely tower, or of his old man, master of all human knowledge, hidden from human sight in some shell-strewn cavern on the Mediterranean shore. One passage above all ran perpetually in my ears:

Some feign that he is Enoch: others dream
He was pre-Adamite, and has survived
Cycles of generation and of ruin.
The sage, in truth, by dreadful abstinence,
And conquering penance of the mutinous flesh,
Deep contemplation and unwearied study,
In years outstretched beyond the date of man,
May have attained to sovereignty and science
Over those strong and secret things and thoughts
Which others fear and know not.

MAHMUD

                              I would talk
With this old Jew.

HASSAN

                    Thy will is even now
Made known to him where he dwells in a sea-cavern
'Mid the Demonesi, less accessible
Than thou or God! He who would question him
Must sail alone at sunset, where the stream
Of Ocean sleeps around those foamless isles,
When the young moon is westering as now,
And evening airs wander upon the wave;
And, when the pines of that bee-pasturing isle,
Green Erebinthus, quench the fiery shadow
Of his gilt prow within the sapphire water,
Then must the lonely helmsman cry aloud
'Ahasuerus!' and the caverns round
Will answer 'Ahasuerus!' If his prayer
Be granted, a faint meteor will arise,
Lighting him over Marmora; and a wind
Will rush out of the sighing pine-forest,
And with the wind a storm of harmony
Unutterably sweet, and pilot him
Through the soft twilight to the Bosphorus:
Thence, at the hour and place and circumstance
Fit for the matter of their conference,

The Jew appears. Few dare, and few who dare
Win the desired communion.[104]

Already in Dublin, I had been attracted to the Theosophists
because they had affirmed the real existence of the Jew, or of his
like, and, apart from whatever might have been imagined by Huxley, Tyndall, Carolus Duran and Bastien-Lepage, I saw nothing
against his reality. Presently having heard that Madame Blavatsky[105]
had arrived from France, or from India, I thought it time to look the
matter up. Certainly if wisdom existed anywhere in the world it
must be in some lonely mind admitting no duty to us, communing
with God only, conceding nothing from fear or favour. Have not all
peoples, while bound together in a single mind and taste, believed
that such men existed and paid them that honour, or paid it to their
mere shadow, which they have refused to philanthropists and to
men of learning?

XIX

I found Madame Blavatsky in a little house at Norwood, with but,
as she said, three followers left—the Society of Psychical Research[106]
had just reported on her Indian phenomena—and as one of the
three followers sat in an outer room to keep out undesirable visitors, I was kept a long time kicking my heels. Presently I was admitted and found an old woman in a plain loose dark dress: a sort of
old Irish peasant woman with an air of humour and audacious
power. I was still kept waiting, for she was deep in conversation
with a woman visitor. I strayed through folding doors into the next
room and stood, in sheer idleness of mind, looking at a cuckoo
clock. It was certainly stopped, for the weights were off and lying
upon the ground, and yet, as I stood there, the cuckoo came out and
cuckooed at me. I interrupted Madame Blavatsky to say, 'Your
clock has hooted me'. 'It often hoots at a stranger', she replied. 'Is
there a spirit in it?' I said. 'I do not know', she said; 'I should have
to be alone to know what is in it.' I went back to the clock and
began examining it and heard her say, 'Do not break my clock'. I
wondered if there was some hidden mechanism and I should have
been put out, I suppose, had I found any, though Henley had said
to me, 'Of course she gets up fraudulent miracles, but a person of
genius has to do something; Sarah Bernhardt sleeps in her coffin'.

Presently the visitor went away and Madame Blavatsky explained that she was a propagandist for women's rights who had called to find out 'why men were so bad'. 'What explanation did you give her?' I said. 'That men were born bad, but women made themselves so', and then she explained that I had been kept waiting because she had mistaken me for some man whose name resembled mine and who wanted to persuade her of the flatness of the earth.

When I next saw her she had moved into a house at Holland Park, and some time must have passed—probably I had been in Sligo where I returned constantly for long visits—for she was surrounded by followers. She sat nightly before a little table covered with green baize and on this green baize she scribbled constantly with a piece of white chalk. She would scribble symbols, sometimes humorously explainable, and sometimes unintelligible figures, but the chalk was intended to mark down her score when she played patience. One saw in the next room a large table where every night her followers and guests, often a great number, sat down to their vegetable meal, while she encouraged or mocked through the folding doors. A great passionate nature, a sort of female Dr. Johnson, impressive, I think, to every man or woman who had themselves any richness, she seemed impatient of the formalism and the shrill abstract idealism of those about her, and this impatience broke out in railing and many nicknames: 'O, you are a flapdoodle, but then you are a Theosophist and a brother'. The most devout and learned of all her followers said to me, 'H. P. B. has just told me that there is another globe stuck on to this at the North Pole, so that the earth has really a shape something like a dumb-bell'. I said, for I knew that her imagination contained all the folk-lore of the world, 'That must be some piece of Eastern mythology'. 'O no, it is not,' he said, 'of that I am certain, and there must be something in it or she would not have said it.' Her mockery was not kept for her followers alone, and her voice would become harsh, and her mockery lose fantasy and humour, when she spoke of what seemed to her scientific materialism. Once I saw this antagonism, guided by some kind of telepathic divination. I brought a very able Dublin woman[107] to see her and this woman had a brother, a physiologist whose reputation, though known to specialists alone, was European, and because of this brother a family pride in everything scientific and modern. The Dublin woman scarcely opened her mouth the whole evening and

her name was certainly unknown to Madame Blavatsky, yet I saw
at once in that wrinkled old face bent over the cards, and the only
time I ever saw it there, a personal hostility, the dislike of one
woman for another. Madame Blavatsky seemed to bundle herself
up, becoming all primaeval peasant, and began complaining of her
ailments, more especially of her bad leg. But of late her Master—
her 'old Jew', her 'Ahasuerus'—cured it, or set it on the way to be
cured. 'I was sitting here in my chair', said she, 'when the Master
came in and brought something with him which he put over my
knee, something warm which enclosed my knee—it was a live dog
which he had cut open.' I recognized a cure used sometimes in
mediaeval medicine. I did not and I do not doubt that she described
an actual vision, but its use at that moment and in that company
was a masterpiece of fantastic brutality. She had two Masters, and
their portraits, ideal Indian heads, painted by some most incompe-
tent artist, stood upon either side of the folding doors. One night
when talk was impersonal and general, I sat gazing through the
folding doors into the dimly lighted dining-room beyond. I noticed
a curious red light shining upon a picture and got up to see where
the red light came from. It was the picture of an Indian and as I
came near it slowly vanished. When I returned to my seat, Madame
Blavatsky said, 'What did you see?' 'A picture', I said. 'Tell it to go
away.' 'It is already gone.' 'So much the better', she said; 'I was
afraid it was mediumship. But it is only clairvoyance.' 'What is the
difference?' 'If it had been mediumship, it would have stayed in
spite of you. Beware of mediumship; it is a kind of madness; I know,
for I have been through it.'

I found her almost always full of gaiety that, unlike the occasional joking of those about her, was illogical and incalculable and
yet always kindly and tolerant. I had called one evening to find her
absent but expected every moment. She had been somewhere at the
seaside for her health and arrived with a little suite of followers. She
sat down at once in her big chair, and began unfolding a brown-
paper parcel while all looked on full of curiosity. It contained a
large family Bible. 'This is a present for my maid', she said. 'What,
a Bible and not even annotated!' said some shocked voice. 'Well,
my children,' was the answer, 'what is the good of giving lemons to
those who want oranges?' When I first began to frequent her house,
as I soon did very constantly, I noticed a handsome clever woman

of the world[108] there, who seemed certainly very much out of place, penitent though she thought herself. Presently there was much scandal and gossip, for the penitent was plainly entangled with two young men who were expected to grow into ascetic sages. The scandal was so great that Madame Blavatsky had to call the penitent before her and to speak after this fashion: 'We think that it is necessary to crush the animal nature; you should live in chastity in act and thought. Initiation is granted only to those who are entirely chaste'; but after some minutes in that vehement style, the penitent standing crushed and shamed before her, she had wound up, 'I cannot permit you more than one'. She was quite sincere but thought that nothing mattered but what happened in the mind, and that if we could not master the mind our actions were of little importance. One young man[109] filled her with exasperation, for she thought that his settled gloom came from his chastity. I had known him in Dublin where he had been accustomed to interrupt long periods of asceticism, in which he would eat vegetables and drink water, with brief outbreaks of what he considered the Devil. After an outbreak he would for a few hours dazzle the imagination of the members of the local theosophical society with poetical rhapsodies about harlots and street-lamps, and then sink into weeks of melancholy. A fellow-theosophist once found him hanging from the window-pole, but cut him down in the nick of time. I said to the man who cut him down, 'What did you say to each other?' He said, 'We spent the night telling comic stories and laughing a great deal'. This man, torn between sensuality and visionary ambition, was now the most devout of all, and told me that in the middle of the night he could often hear the ringing of the little 'astral bell' whereby Madame Blavatsky's Master called her attention, and that, although it was a silvery low tone, it made the whole house shake. Another night I found him waiting in the hall to show in those who had right of entrance, on some night when the discussion was private, and as I passed he whispered into my ear, 'Madame Blavatsky is perhaps not a real woman at all. They say that her dead body was found many years ago upon some Italian battle-field.' She had two dominant moods, both of extreme activity, one calm and philosophic, and this was the mood always on that night in the week when she answered questions upon her system, and as I look back after thirty years I often ask myself 'Was her speech automatic? Was she a trance medium, or in some similar state, one night in every week?' In the other mood she was full of fantasy and inconsequent raillery. 'That is the Greek Church, a triangle like all true religion', I recall her saying, as she chalked out a triangle on the green baize, and then as she made it disappear in meaningless scribbles, 'It spread out and became a bramble-bush like the Church of Rome'. Then rubbing it all out except one straight line, 'Now they have lopped off the branches and turned it into a broomstick and that is Protestantism'. And so it was night after night, always varied and unforeseen. I have observed a like sudden extreme change in others, half whose thought was supernatural; and Laurence Oliphant records somewhere or other like observations. I can remember only once finding her in a mood of reverie; something had happened to damp her spirits, some attack upon her movement, or upon herself. She spoke of Balzac, whom she had seen but once, of Alfred de Musset, whom she had known well enough to dislike for his morbidity, and George Sand, whom she had known so well that they had dabbled in magic together of which 'neither knew anything at all' in those days; and she ran on, as if there was nobody there to overhear her, 'I used to wonder at and pity the people who sell their souls to the Devil, but now I only pity them. They do it to have somebody on their side', and added to that, after some words I have forgotten, 'I write, write, write as the Wandering Jew[110] walks, walks, walks'.

Besides the devotees, who came to listen and to turn every doctrine into a new sanction for the puritanical convictions of their Victorian childhood, cranks came from half Europe and from all America, and they came that they might talk. One American said to me, 'She has become the most famous woman in the world by sitting in a big chair and permitting us to talk'. They talked and she played patience, and totted up her score on the green baize, and generally seemed to listen, but sometimes she would listen no more. There was a woman who talked perpetually of 'the divine spark' within her, until Madame Blavatsky stopped her with, 'Yes, my dear, you have a divine spark within you and if you are not very careful you will hear it snore'. A certain Salvation Army captain probably pleased her, for, if vociferous and loud of voice, he had much animation. He had known hardship and spoke of his visions while starving in the streets and he was still perhaps a little light in the head. I wondered what he could preach to ignorant men, his

head ablaze with wild mysticism, till I met a man who had heard
him near Covent Garden. 'My friends,' he was saying, 'you have the
kingdom of Heaven within you and it would take a pretty big pill
to get that out.'

Meanwhile I had got no nearer to proving that the sage Ahasuerus[111] 'dwells in a sea-cavern 'mid the Demonesi', nor did I learn
any more of those 'Masters' whose representative Madame
Blavatsky claimed to be. All there seemed to feel their presence,
and all spoke of them as if they were more important than any visible inhabitant of the house. When Madame Blavatsky was more
silent, less vivid than usual, it was 'because her Masters were
angry'; they had rebuked her because of some error, and she professed constant error. Once I seemed in their presence, or that of
some messenger of theirs. It was about nine at night, and half a
dozen of us sat round her big table-cloth, when the room filled
with the odour of incense. Somebody came from upstairs, but
could smell nothing—had been outside the influence, it seems—but
to myself and the others it was very strong. Madame Blavatsky
said it was a common Indian incense, and that some pupil of her
Master's was present; she seemed anxious to make light of the matter and turned the conversation to something else. Certainly it was
a romantic house, and I did not separate myself from it by my own
will. I had learned from Blake to hate all abstraction, and, irritated
by the abstraction of what were called 'esoteric teachings', I began
a series of experiments. Some book or magazine published by the
Society had quoted from an essay upon magic by some seventeenth-century writer.[112] If you burnt a flower to ashes and put the
ashes under, I think, the receiver of an air-pump, and stood the
receiver in the moonlight for so many nights, the ghost of the
flower would appear hovering over its ashes. I got together a committee which performed this experiment without results. The 'esoteric teachings' had declared that a certain very pure kind of indigo
was the symbol of one of the seven principles into which they
divided human nature. I got with some difficulty a little of this pure
indigo, and gave portions of it to members of the committee, and
asked them to put it under their pillows at night and record their
dreams. I argued that all natural scenery must be divided into
seven types according to these principles, and by their study we
could rid the mind of abstraction. Presently a secretary, a friendly,

intelligent man, asked me to come and see him, and, when I did, complained that I was causing discussion and disturbance.[113] A certain fanatical hungry face had been noticed red and tearful, and it was quite plain that I was not in agreement with their methods or their philosophy. 'We have certain definite ideas', he said, 'and we have but one duty, to spread them through the world. I know that all these people become dogmatic, that they believe what they can never prove, that their withdrawal from family life is for them a great misfortune, but what are we to do? We have been told that all spiritual influx into the Society will come to an end in 1897 for exactly one hundred years; before that date our fundamental ideas must be spread in all countries.' I knew the doctrine, and it made me wonder why that old woman, or the 'Masters' from whom, whatever they were or were not, her genius had come, insisted upon it; for influx of some kind there must always be. Did they dread heresy, or had they no purpose but the greatest possible immediate effect?

XX

At the British Museum Reading-Room I often saw a man of thirty-six, or thirty-seven, in a brown velveteen coat, with a gaunt resolute face, and an athletic body, who seemed, before I heard his name, or knew the nature of his studies, a figure of romance. Presently I was introduced, where or by what man or woman I do not remember. He was called Liddell Mathers, but would soon, under the touch of 'The Celtic Movement',[114] become MacGregor Mathers, and then plain MacGregor.[115] He was the author of *The Kabbala Unveiled*,[116] and his studies were two only—magic and the theory of war, for he believed himself a born commander and all but equal in wisdom and in power to that old Jew. He had copied many manuscripts on magic ceremonial and doctrine in the British Museum, and was to copy many more in Continental libraries, and it was through him mainly that I began certain studies and experiences, that were to convince me that images well up before the mind's eye from a deeper source than conscious or subconscious memory. I believe that his mind in those early days did not belie his face and body—though in later years it became unhinged, as Don Quixote's was unhinged—for he kept a proud head amid great poverty. One that boxed with him nightly has told me that for many weeks he could knock him down, though Mathers was the stronger man, and only knew long after that during those weeks Mathers starved. He had spoken to me, I think at our first introduction, of a society which sometimes called itself—it had a different name among its members—'The Hermetic Students',[117] and in May or June 1887 I was initiated into that society in a Charlotte Street studio, and being at a most receptive age, shaped and isolated. Mathers was its governing mind, a born teacher and organizer. One of those who incite—less by spoken word than by what they are—imaginative action. We paid some small annual subscription, a few shillings for rent and stationery, but no poor man paid even that and all found him generous of time and thought. With Mathers I met an old white-haired Oxfordshire clergyman,[118] the most panic-stricken person I have ever known, though Mathers' introduction had been, 'He unites us to the great adepts of antiquity'. This old man took me aside that he might say, 'I hope you never invoke spirits—that is a very dangerous thing to do. I am told that even the planetary spirits turn upon us in the end.' I said, 'Have you ever seen an apparition?' 'O yes, once,' he said. 'I have my alchemical laboratory in a cellar under my house where the Bishop cannot see it. One day I was walking up and down there when I heard another footstep walking up and down beside me. I turned and saw a girl I had been in love with when I was a young man, but she died long ago. She wanted me to kiss her. O no, I would not do that.' 'Why not?' I said. 'O, she might have got power over me.' 'Has your alchemical research had any success?' I said. 'Yes, I once made the elixir of life. A French alchemist said it had the right smell and the right colour' (the alchemist may have been Eliphas Levi, who visited England in the 'sixties, and would have said anything), 'but the first effect of the elixir is that your nails fall out and your hair falls off. I was afraid that I might have made a mistake and that nothing else might happen, so I put it away on a shelf. I meant to drink it when I was an old man, but when I got it down the other day it had all dried up.'

Soon after my first meeting with Mathers he emerged into brief prosperity, becoming for two or three years Curator of a private museum at Forest Hill, and marrying a young and beautiful wife, the sister of the philosopher, Henri Bergson. His house at Forest Hill was soon a romantic place to a little group, Florence Farr—she too had been initiated—myself, and some dozen fellow-students. I think that it was she, her curiosity being insatiable, who first brought a tale of marvel and that she brought it in mockery and in wonder. Mathers had taken her for a walk through a field of sheep and had said, 'Look at the sheep. I am going to imagine myself a ram', and at once all the sheep ran after him; another day he had tried to quell a thunderstorm by making symbols in the air with a Masonic sword, but the storm had not been quelled; and then came the crowning wonder. He had given her a piece of cardboard on which was a coloured geometrical symbol and had told her to hold it to her forehead and she had found herself walking upon a cliff above the sea, seagulls shrieking overhead. I did not think the ram story impossible, and even tried half a dozen times to excite a cat by imagining a mouse in front of its nose, but still some chance movement of the flock might have deceived her. But what could have deceived her in that final marvel? Then another brought a like report, and presently my own turn came. He gave me a cardboard symbol and I closed my eyes. Sight came slowly, there was not that sudden miracle as if the darkness had been cut with a knife, for that miracle is mostly a woman's privilege, but there rose before me mental images that I could not control: a desert and a black Titan raising himself up by his two hands from the middle of a heap of ancient ruins. Mathers explained that I had seen a being of the order of Salamanders[119] because he had shown me their symbol, but it was not necessary even to show the symbol, it would have been sufficient that he imagined it. I had already written in my diary, under some date in 1887, that Madame Blavatsky's 'Masters' were 'trance personalities',[120] and I must have meant such beings as my black Titan, only more lasting and more powerful. I had found when a boy in Dublin on a table in the Royal Irish Academy[121] a pamphlet on Japanese art and read there of an animal painter[122] so remarkable that horses he had painted upon a temple wall had slipped down after dark and trampled the neighbours' fields of rice. Somebody had come into the temple in the early morning, had been startled by a shower of water-drops, had looked up and seen painted horses still wet from the dew-covered fields, but now 'trembling into stillness'.

I had soon mastered Mathers' symbolic system, and discovered that for a considerable minority—whom I could select by certain unanalysable characteristics—the visible world would completely vanish, and that world summoned by the symbol take its place. One day when alone in a third-class carriage, in the very middle of the railway bridge that crosses the Thames near Victoria, I smelt incense. I was on my way to Forest Hill; might it not come from some spirit Mathers had called up? I had wondered when I smelt it at Madame Blavatsky's if there might be some contrivance, some secret censer, but that explanation was no longer possible. I believed that Salamander of his but an image, and presently I found analogies between smell and image. That smell must be thought-created, but what certainty had I that what had taken me by surprise could be from my own thought, and if a thought could affect the sense of smell, why not the sense of touch? Then I discovered among that group of students that surrounded Mathers a man who had fought a cat in his dreams and awaked to find his breast covered with scratches. Was there an impassable barrier between those scratches and the trampled fields of rice? It would seem so, and yet all was uncertainty. What fixed law would our experiments leave to our imagination?

Mathers had much learning but little scholarship, much imagination and imperfect taste, but if he made some absurd statement, some incredible claim, some hackneyed joke, we would half-consciously change claim, statement or joke, as though he were a figure in a play of our composition. He was a necessary extravagance, and he had carried further than any one else a claim implicit in the romantic movement from the time of Shelley and of Goethe; and in body and in voice at least he was perfect; so might Faust[123] have looked in his changeless aged youth. In the credulity of our youth we secretly wondered if he had not met with, perhaps even been taught by, some old man who had found the elixir. Nor did he undeceive us. 'If you find the elixir', he was accustomed to say, 'you always look a few years younger than the age at which you found it. If you find it at sixty you will look fifty for a hundred years.' None of us would have admitted that we believed in stone or elixir, the old Oxfordshire clergyman excited no belief, yet one among us certainly laboured with crucible or athanor. Ten years ago I called upon an elderly solicitor, on some business, but at his private house, and I remembered whose pupil he had been when I found among the ashes of the hearth a little earthen pot. He pretended that he studied alchemy that he might some day write its history, and I found, when I questioned others, that for twenty years there had been just such a little pot among the ashes.

XXI

I generalized a great deal and was ashamed of it. I thought it was my business in life to be an artist and a poet, and that there could be no business comparable to that. I refused to read books and even to meet people who excited me to generalization, all to no purpose. I said my prayers much as in childhood, though without the old regularity of hour and place, and I began to pray that my imagination might somehow be rescued from abstraction and become as preoccupied with life as had been the imagination of Chaucer. For ten or twelve years more I suffered continual remorse, and only became content when my abstractions had composed themselves into picture and dramatization. My very remorse helped to spoil my early poetry, giving it an element of sentimentality through my refusal to permit it any share of an intellect which I considered impure. Even in practical life I only very gradually began to use generalizations, that have since become the foundation of all I have done, or shall do, in Ireland. For all I know all men may have been so timid, for I am persuaded that our intellects at twenty contain all the truths we shall ever find, but as yet we do not know truths that belong to us from opinions caught up in casual irritation or momentary fantasy. As life goes on we discover that certain thoughts sustain us in defeat, or give us victory, whether over ourselves or others, and it is these thoughts, tested by passion, that we call convictions. Among subjective men (in all those, that is, who must spin a web out of their own bowels) the victory is an intellectual daily re-creation of all that exterior fate snatches away, and so that fate's antithesis; while what I have called 'the Mask'[124] is an emotional antithesis to all that comes out of their internal nature. We begin to live when we have conceived life as tragedy.

XXII

A conviction that the world was now but a bundle of fragments possessed me without ceasing. I had tried this conviction on the

Rhymers, thereby plunging into greater silence an already too-silent evening. 'Johnson,' I was accustomed to say, 'you are the only man I know whose silence has beak and claw.' I had lectured on it to some London Irish society, and I was to lecture upon it later on in Dublin, but I never found but one interested man, an official of the Primrose League,[125] who was also an active member of the Fenian Brotherhood. 'I am an extreme conservative apart from Ireland', I have heard him explain; and I have no doubt that personal experience made him share the sight of any eye that saw the world in fragments. I had been put into a rage by the followers of Huxley, Tyndall, Carolus Duran, and Bastien-Lepage, who not only asserted the unimportance of subject whether in art or literature, but the independence of the arts from one another. Upon the other hand, I delighted in every age where poet and artist confined themselves gladly to some inherited subject-matter known to the whole people, for I thought that in man and race alike there is something called 'Unity of Being',[126] using that term as Dante used it when he compared beauty in the *Convito* to a perfectly proportioned human body. My father, from whom I had learned the term, preferred a comparison to a musical instrument so strung that if we touch a string all the strings murmur faintly. There is not more desire, he had said, in lust than in true love, but in true love desire awakens pity, hope, affection, admiration, and, given appropriate circumstance, every emotion possible to men. When I began, however, to apply this thought to the State and to argue for a law-made balance among trades and occupations my father displayed at once the violent Free Trader and propagandist of liberty. I thought that the enemy of this unity was abstraction, meaning by abstraction not the distinction but the isolation of occupation, or class or faculty:

> Call down the hawk from the air,
> Let him be hooded or caged
> Till the yellow eye has grown mild,
> For larder and spit are bare,
> The old cook enraged,
> The scullion gone wild.[127]

I knew no mediaeval cathedral, and Westminster, being a part of abhorred London, did not interest me, but I thought constantly of

Homer and Dante, and the tombs of Mausolus and Artemisia,[128] the great figures of King and Queen and the lesser figures of Greek and Amazon, Centaur and Greek. I thought that all art should be a Centaur finding in the popular lore its back and its strong legs. I got great pleasure, too, from remembering that Homer was sung,[129] and from that tale of Dante hearing a common man sing some stanza from the *Divine Comedy,* and from Don Quixote's meeting with some common man that sang Ariosto. Morris had never seemed to care greatly for any poet later than Chaucer and though I preferred Shakespeare to Chaucer I begrudged my own preference. Had not Europe shared one mind and heart, until both mind and heart began to break into fragments a little before Shakespeare's birth? Music and verse began to fall apart when Chaucer robbed verse of its speed that he might give it greater meditation, though for another generation or so minstrels were to sing his lengthy elaborated *Troilus and Criseyde;* painting parted from religion in the later Renaissance that it might study effects of tangibility undisturbed; while, that it might characterize, where it had once personified, it renounced, in our own age, all that inherited subject-matter which we have named poetry. Presently I was indeed to number character itself among the abstractions, encouraged by Congreve's saying that 'passions are too powerful in the fair sex to let humour', or, as we say, character, 'have its course'.[130] Nor have we fared better under the common daylight, for pure reason has notoriously made but light of practical reason, and has been made light of in its turn from that morning when Descartes discovered that he could think better in his bed than out of it; nor needed I original thought to discover, being so late of the school of Morris, that machinery had not separated from handicraft wholly for the world's good, nor to notice that the distinction of classes had become their isolation. If the London merchants of our day competed together in writing lyrics they would not, like the Tudor merchants, dance in the open street before the house of the victor; nor do the great ladies of London finish their balls on the pavement before their doors as did the great Venetian ladies, even in the eighteenth century, conscious of an all-enfolding sympathy. Doubtless because fragments broke into ever smaller fragments we saw one another in a light of bitter comedy, and in the arts, where now one technical element reigned and now another, generation hated generation, and accomplished beauty was snatched away when it had most engaged our affections. One thing I did not foresee, not having the courage of my own thought: the growing murderousness of the world.

> Turning and turning in the widening gyre
> The falcon cannot hear the falconer;
> Things fall apart; the centre cannot hold;
> Mere anarchy is loosed upon the world,
> The blood-dimmed tide is loosed, and everywhere
> The ceremony of innocence is drowned;
> The best lack all conviction, while the worst
> Are full of passionate intensity.[131]

XXIII

If abstraction had reached, or all but reached its climax, escape might be possible for many, and if it had not, individual men might still escape. If Chaucer's personages had disengaged themselves from Chaucer's crowd, forgot their common goal and shrine, and after sundry magnifications became each in turn the centre of some Elizabethan play, and had after split into their elements and so given birth to romantic poetry, must I reverse the cinematograph? I thought that the general movement of literature must be such a reversal, men being there displayed in casual, temporary, contact as at the Tabard door. I had lately read Tolstoy's *Anna Karenina* and thought that where his theoretical capacity had not awakened there was such a turning back: but a nation or an individual with great emotional intensity might follow the pilgrims, as it were, to some unknown shrine, and give to all those separated elements, and to all that abstract love and melancholy, a symbolical, a mytho-logical coherence. Not Chaucer's rough-tongued riders, but rather an ended pilgrimage, a procession of the Gods! Arthur Symons brought back from Paris stories of Verhaeren and Maeterlinck, and so brought me confirmation, as I thought, and I began to announce a poetry like that of the Sufis. I could not endure, how-ever, an international art, picking stories and symbols where it pleased. Might I not, with health and good luck to aid me, create some new *Prometheus Unbound;* Patrick or Columcille, Oisin or

Finn, in Prometheus' stead; and, instead of Caucasus, Cro-Patrick
or Ben Bulben? Have not all races had their first unity from a
mythology that marries them to rock and hill? We had in Ireland
imaginative stories, which the uneducated classes knew and even
sang, and might we not make those stories current among the educated classes, rediscovering for the work's sake what I have called
'the applied arts of literature', the association of literature, that is,
with music, speech, and dance; and at last, it might be, so deepen
the political passion of the nation that all, artist and poet, craftsman and day-labourer would accept a common design? Perhaps
even these images, once created and associated with river and
mountain, might move of themselves and with some powerful, even
turbulent life, like those painted horses that trampled the rice-fields
of Japan.

XXIV

I used to tell the few friends to whom I could speak these secret
thoughts that I would make the attempt in Ireland but fail, for our
civilization, its elements multiplying by division like certain low
forms of life, was all-powerful; but in reality I had the wildest
hopes. To-day I add to that first conviction, to that first desire for
unity, this other conviction, long a mere opinion vaguely or inter-
mittently apprehended: nations, races, and individual men are unified by an image, or bundle of related images, symbolical or
evocative of the state of mind which is, of all states of mind not
impossible, the most difficult to that man, race, or nation; because
only the greatest obstacle that can be contemplated without despair
rouses the will to full intensity.

A powerful class by terror, rhetoric, and organized sentimentality may drive their people to war, but the day draws near when they
cannot keep them there; and how shall they face the pure nations of
the East when the day comes to do it with but equal arms? I had
seen Ireland in my own time turn from the bragging rhetoric and
gregarious humour of O'Connell's generation and school, and offer
herself to the solitary and proud Parnell as to her anti-self, buskin
followed hard on sock, and I had begun to hope, or to half hope,
that we might be the first in Europe to seek unity as deliberately as
it had been sought by theologian, poet, sculptor, architect, from the

eleventh to the thirteenth century. Doubtless we must seek it differently, no longer considering it convenient to epitomize all human knowledge, but find it we well might could we first find philosophy and a little passion.

BOOK II

IRELAND AFTER PARNELL[1]

I

A couple of years before the death of Parnell, I had wound up my introduction to those selections from the Irish novelists with the prophecy[2] of an intellectual movement at the first lull in politics, and now I wished to fulfil my prophecy. I did not put it in that way, for I preferred to think that the sudden emotion that now came to me, the sudden certainty that Ireland was to be like soft wax[3] for years to come, was a moment of supernatural insight. How could I tell, how can I tell even now?

There was a little Irish society of young people, clerks, shop-boys, and shop-girls, called 'The Southwark Irish Literary Society', and it had ceased to meet because the girls got the giggles when any member of the Committee got up to speak. Every member of it had said all he had to say many times over. I had given them a lecture about the falling asunder of the human mind, as an opening flower falls asunder, and all had professed admiration because I had made such a long speech without quotation or narrative; and now I invited the Committee to my father's house at Bedford Park, and there proposed a new organization, 'The Irish Literary Society'.[4] T. W. Rolleston came to that first meeting, and it was because he had much tact, and a knowledge of the technical business of commit-tees, that a society was founded which was joined by every London-Irish author and journalist. In a few months somebody had written its history, and published that history, illustrated by our portraits, at a shilling.[5] When it was published I was in Dublin, founding a society there called 'The National Literary Society',[6] and affiliating it with certain Young Ireland Societies in country towns which seemed anxious to accept its leadership. I had definite plans; I wanted to create an Irish Theatre; I was finishing my *Countess Cathleen* in its first meagre version, and thought of a travelling company to visit our country branches; but before that there must be a popular imaginative literature. I arranged with Mr. Fisher Unwin[7] and his reader, Mr. Edward Garnett—a personal friend of mine—that when our organization was complete Mr. Fisher Unwin was to publish for it a series of books at a shilling each. I told only one man[8] of this arrangement, for after I had made my plans I heard an alarming rumour. Old Sir Charles Gavan Duffy was coming from Australia to start an Irish publishing-house, and publish a series of books, and I did not expect to agree with him, but knew that I must not seek a quarrel. The two societies were necessary because their lectures must take the place of an educated popular Press, which we had not, and have not now, and create a standard of criticism. Irish literature had fallen into contempt; no educated man ever bought an Irish book; in Dublin Professor Dowden, the one man of letters with an international influence, was accustomed to say that he knew an Irish book by its smell, because he had once seen some books whose binding had been fastened together by rotten glue; and Standish O'Grady's last book[9] upon ancient Irish history—a book rather wild, rather too speculative, but forestalling later research—had not been reviewed by any periodical or newspaper in England or in Ireland.

At first I had great success, for I brought with me a list of names written down by some member of the Southwark Irish Literary Society, and for six weeks went hither and thither appealing and persuading. My first conversation was over a butter-tub in some Dublin back street, and the man agreed with me at once; everybody agreed with me; all felt that something must be done, but nobody knew what. Perhaps they did not understand me, perhaps I kept back my full thoughts, perhaps they only seemed to listen; it was enough that I had a plan, and was determined about it. When I went to lecture in a provincial town, a workman's wife, who wrote patriotic stories in some weekly newspaper, invited me to her house, and I found all her children in their Sunday best. She made a little speech, very formal and very simple, in which she said that what she wrote had no merit, but that it paid for her children's schooling; and she finished her speech by telling her children never to forget that they had seen me. One man compared me to Thomas Davis, another said I could organize like Davitt,[10] and I thought to succeed as they did, and as rapidly. I did not examine this applause, nor the true thoughts of those I met, nor the general condition of the country, but I examined myself a great deal, and was puzzled at myself. I knew that I was shy and timid, that I would often leave some business undone, or purchase unmade, because I shrank from facing a strange office or a shop a little grander than usual, and yet here was I delightedly talking to strange people every day. It was many years before I understood that I had surrendered myself to the chief temptation of the artist, creation without toil. Metrical composition is always very difficult to me, nothing is done upon the first day, not one rhyme is in its place; and when at last the rhymes begin to come, the first rough draft of a six-line stanza takes the whole day. At that time I had not formed a style, and sometimes a six-line stanza would take several days, and not seem finished even then; and I had not learnt, as I have now, to put it all out of my head before night, and so the last night was generally sleepless, and the last day a day of nervous strain. But now I had found the happiness that Shelley found when he tied a pamphlet to a fire balloon.[11]

II

At first I asked no help from prominent persons, and when some clerk or shop-assistant would say, 'Dr. So-and-so or Professor So-and-so will have nothing to do with us', I would answer, 'When we prove we can gather sheep shepherds will come'. Presently, come they did, old, middle-aged, or but little older than myself, but all with some authority in their town: John O'Leary, John F. Taylor, Douglas Hyde, and Standish O'Grady, and of these much presently; Dr. Sigerson, learned, artificial, unscholarly, a typical provincial celebrity, but a friendly man;[12] Count Plunkett, Sinn Feiner of late and Minister of Dáil Eireann; Dr. Coffey, now head of the National University; George Coffey, later on Curator of the Irish Antiquities at the Museum of the Royal Dublin Society; Patrick J. McCall, poet and publican of Patrick Street, and later member of the Corporation; Richard Ashe King, novelist and correspondent of *Truth,* a gentle, intelligent person, in nothing typical of the Dublin of that time; and others, known or unknown. We were now important, had our Committee-room in the Mansion House, and I remember that the old Mansion House butler recognized our importance so fully that he took us into his confidence once in every week, while we sat waiting for a quorum. He had seen many Lord Mayors, and remembered those very superior Lord Mayors who lived before the extension of the municipal franchise,[13] and spoke of his present masters with contempt. Among our persons of authority, and among the friends and followers they had brought, there were many who at that time found it hard to refuse if anybody offered for sale a pepper-pot shaped to suggest a round tower with a wolf-dog at its foot, who would have felt it inappropriate to publish an Irish book that had not harp and shamrock and green cover, so completely did their minds move amid Young Ireland images and metaphors, and I thought with alarm of the coming of Sir Charles Gavan Duffy; while here and there I noticed that smooth, smiling face that we discover for the first time in certain pictures by Velasquez; the hungry, mediaeval speculation vanished that had worn the faces of El Greco,[14] and in its place a self-complacent certainty that all had been arranged, all provided for, all set out in clear type, in manual of devotion or of doctrine. These, however, were no true disciples of Young Ireland, for Young Ireland had sought a nation unified by political doctrine alone, a subservient art and letters aiding and abetting. The movement of thought which had, in the 'fifties and 'forties in Paris and London and Boston, filled literature, and especially poetical literature, with curiosities about science, about history, about politics, with moral purpose and educational fervour—abstractions all—had created a new instrument for Irish politics, a method of writing that took its poetical style from Campbell, Scott, Macaulay, and Béranger, with certain elements from Gaelic, its prose style—in John Mitchel, the only Young Ireland prose-writer who had a style at all—from Carlyle. To recommend this method of writing as literature without much reservation and discrimination, I contended, was to be deceived or to practise deception. If one examined some country love-song, one discovered that it was not written by a man in love, but by a patriot who wanted to prove that we did indeed possess, in the words of Daniel O'Connell, 'the finest peasantry upon earth'. Yet one well-known anthology was introduced by the assertion that such love-poetry was superior to 'affected and artificial' English love-songs like 'Drink to me only with thine eyes'[15]—'affected and artificial', the very words used by English Victorians who wrote for the newspapers to discourage capricious, personal writing. Yet the greater number—even of those who thought our famous anthology, *The*

Spirit of the Nation,[16] except for three or four songs, but good election rhyme—looked upon such poetry as certain enlightened believers look upon the story of Adam and Eve and the apple, or that of Jonah and the whale, which they do not question publicly, because such stories are an integral part of religion to simple men and women. I, upon the other hand, being in the intemperance of my youth, denied, as publicly as possible, merit to all but a few ballads translated from Gaelic writers, or written out of a personal and generally tragic experience.

III

The greater number of those who joined my Society had come under the seal of Young Ireland at that age when we are all mere wax; the more ambitious had gone daily to some public library to read the bound volumes of Thomas Davis's old newspaper,[17] and tried to see the world as Davis saw it. No philosophic speculation, no economic question of the day disturbed an orthodoxy which, unlike that of religion, had no philosophic history, and the religious bigot was glad that it should be so. Some few of the younger men were impatient, and it was these younger men, more numerous in the London than in the Dublin society, who gave me support; and we had been joined by a few older men—some personal friends of my own or my father's—who had only historical interest in Thomas Davis and his school. Young Ireland's prose had been as much occupied with Irish virtue as its poetry, and more with the invader's vices, and we were soon mired and sunk into such problems as to whether Cromwell was altogether black, the heads of the old Irish clans altogether white, the Danes[18] mere robbers and church-burners (they tell me at Rosses Point that the Danes keep to this day the maps of the Rosses fields they were driven out of in the ninth century, and plot their return) and as to whether we were or were not once the greatest orators in the world. All the past had been turned into a melodrama with Ireland for blameless hero and poet; novelist and historian had but one object, that we should hiss the villain, and only a minority doubted that the greater the talent the greater the hiss. It was all the harder to substitute for that melodrama a nobler form of art, because there really had been, however different in their form, villain and victim; yet fight that rancour I must, and if I had not made some head against it in 1892 and 1893 it might have silenced in 1907 John Synge, the greatest dramatic genius of Ireland. I am writing of disputes that happened many years ago, that led in later years to much bitterness, and I may exaggerate their immediate importance and violence, but I think I am right in saying that disputes about the merits of Young Ireland so often interrupted our discussion of rules, or of the merit of this or that lecturer, and were so aggravated and crossed by the current wrangle between Parnellite and anti-Parnellite that they delayed our public appearance for a year. Other excited persons, doubtless, seeing that we are of a race intemperate of speech, had looked up from their rancours to the dead Lord Mayors upon the wall, superior men whose like we shall not see again, but never, I think, from rancours so seemingly academic. I was preparing the way without knowing it for a great satirist and master of irony,[19] for master-works stir vaguely in many before they grow definite in one man's mind, and to help me I had already flitting through my head, jostling other ideas and so not yet established there, a conviction that we should satirize rather than praise, that original virtue arises from the discovery of evil. If we were, as I had dreaded, declamatory, loose, and bragging, we were but the better fitted—that declared and measured—to create unyielding personality, manner at once cold and passionate, daring long-premeditated act; and if bitter beyond all the people of the world, we might yet lie—that too declared and measured—nearest the honeyed comb:[20]

> Like the clangour of a bell
> Sweet and harsh, harsh and sweet,
> That is how he learnt so well
> To take the roses for his meat.[21]

IV

There were others with followers of their own, and too old or indifferent to join our Society. Old men who had never accepted Young Ireland, or middle-aged men kept by some family tradition to the school of thought before it arose, to the Ireland of Daniel O'Connell and of Lever and of Thomas Moore, convivial Ireland with the traditional tear and smile. They sang Moore's *Melodies,*[22] admitted no poetry but his, and resented Young Ireland's political objections to it as much as my generation's objection to its artificial and easy rhythm; one, an old commercial traveller, a Gaelic scholar who kept an erect head and the animal vigour of youth, frequented the houses of our leading men, and would say in a loud voice, 'Thomas Moore, sir, is the greatest heroic poet of ancient or modern times'. I think it was the Fire-Worshippers in *Lalla Rookh*[23] that he preferred to Homer; or, jealous for the music of the *Melodies,* he would denounce Wagner, then at the top of his vogue; 'I would run ten miles through a bog to escape him', he would cry. Then there was a maker of tombstones of whom we had heard much but had seen little, an elderly fighting man, lately imprisoned for beating a wine-merchant. A young member of the London society, afterwards librarian to the National University, D. J. O'Donohue, who had published a dictionary of the Irish poets,[24] containing, I think, two thousand names, had come to Dublin and settled there in a fit of patriotism. He had been born in London, and spoke the most Cockney dialect imaginable, and had picked up—probably from London critics—a dislike for the poetry of Thomas Moore. The tombstone-maker invited him to tea, and he arrived with a bundle of books, which he laid beside him upon the table. During tea he began expounding that dislike of his; his host was silent, but he went on, for he was an obstinate little man. Presently the tombstone-maker rose, and having said solemnly, 'I have never permitted that great poet to be slandered in my presence', seized his guest by the back of the collar, and flung him out into the street, and after that flung out the books one after another. Meanwhile the guest—as he himself told the tale—stood in the middle of the street, repeating, 'Nice way to treat a man in your own 'ouse'.

V

I shared a lodging[25] full of old books and magazines, covered with dirt and dust, with the head of the Fenian Brotherhood, John O'Leary. 'In this country', he had said to me, 'a man must have upon his side the Church or the Fenians, and you will never have the Church.' He had been converted to Nationalism by the poems of Davis, and he wished for some analogous movement to that of Davis, but he had known men of letters, had been the friend of

Whistler, and knew the faults of the old literature. We had made him the President of our Society,[26] and without him I could do nothing, for his long imprisonment and longer exile, his magnificent appearance, and, above all, the fact that he alone had personality, a point of view not made for the crowd's sake, but for self-expression, made him magnetic to my generation. He and I had long been friends, he had stayed with us at Bedford Park, and my father had painted his portrait,[27] but if I had not shared his lodging he would have opposed me. He was an old man, and my point of view was not that of his youth, and it often took me half the day to make him understand—so suspicious he was of all innovation—some simple thing that he would presently support with ardour. He had grown up in a European movement when the revolutionist thought that he, above all men, must appeal to the highest motive, be guided by some ideal principle, be a little like Cato or like Brutus,[28] and he had lived to see the change Dostoievsky examined in *The Possessed*.[29] Men who had been of his party—and oftener their sons—preached assassination and the bomb; and, worst of all, the majority of his countrymen followed after constitutional politicians who practised opportunism, and had, as he believed, such low morals that they would lie, or publish private correspondence, if it might advance their cause. He would split every practical project into its constituent elements, like a clerical casuist, to find if it might not lead into some moral error; but, were the project revolutionary, he would sometimes temper condemnation with pity. Though he would cast off his oldest acquaintance did he suspect him of rubbing shoulders with some carrier of bombs, I have heard him say of a man who blew himself up in an attempt to blow up Westminster Bridge, 'He was not a bad man, but he had too great a moral nature for his intellect, not that he lacked intellect'. He did not explain, but he meant, I suppose, that the spectacle of injustice might madden a good man more quickly than some common man. Such men were of his own sort, though gone astray, but the constitutional politicians he had been fighting all his life, and all they did displeased him. It was not that he thought their aim wrong, or that they could not achieve it; he had accepted Gladstone's Home Rule Bill;[30] but that in his eyes they degraded manhood. 'If England has been brought to do us justice by such men', he would say, 'that is not because of our strength, but because of her weakness.' He had a particular hatred

for the rush of emotion that followed the announcement of Gladstone's conversion, for what was called 'The Union of Hearts', and
derided its sentimentality. 'Nations may respect one another,' he
would say, 'they cannot love.' His ancestors had probably kept little shops, or managed little farms in County Tipperary, yet he hated
democracy, though he never used the word either for praise or
blame, with more than feudal hatred. 'No gentleman can be a
Socialist', he said; and then, with a thoughtful look, 'He might be an
Anarchist.' He had no philosophy, but things distressed his palate,
and two of those things were international propaganda and the
organized State, and Socialism aimed at both, nor could he speak
such words as 'philanthropy', 'humanitarianism', without showing
by his tone of voice that they offended him. The Church pleased
him little better; there was an old Fenian quarrel there, and he
would say, 'My religion is the old Persian, to pull the bow and tell
the truth'. He had no self-consciousness, no visible pride, and
would have hated anything that could have been called a gesture,
was indeed scarce artist enough to invent a gesture; yet he would
never speak of the hardship of his prison life—though abundantly
enough of its humours—and once, when I pressed him, replied, 'I
was in the hands of my enemy, why should I complain?' A few years
ago I heard that the Governor of the prison had asked why he did
not report some unnecessary discomfort, and O'Leary had said, 'I
did not come here to complain'. Now that he is dead, I wish that I
could question him, and perhaps discover whether in early youth he
had come across some teacher who had expounded Roman virtue,
but I doubt if I would have learnt anything, for I think the wax had
long forgotten the seal—if seal there were. The seal was doubtless
made before the eloquent humanitarian 'forties and 'fifties, and was
one kind with whatever moulded the youthful mind of Savage Landor. Stephens, the founder of Fenianism, had discovered him searching the second-hand bookstalls for rare editions, and enrolled him
in his organization. 'You have no chance of success', O'Leary had
said, 'but it will be good for the morale of the country' (morale was
his great word), 'and I will join on the condition that I am never
asked to enrol anybody.' He still searched the second-hand bookstalls, and had great numbers of books, especially of Irish history
and literature, and when I, exhausted over our morning's casuistry,
would sit down to my day's work (I was writing *The Secret Rose*[31])

he would make his tranquil way to the Dublin quays. In the evening, over his coffee, he would write passages for his memoirs upon postcards and odd scraps of paper, taking immense trouble with every word and comma, for the great work must be a master-piece of style. When it was finished, it was unreadable,[32] being dry, abstract, and confused; no picture had ever passed before his mind's eye. He was a victim, I think, of a movement where opinions stick men together, or keep them apart, like a kind of bird-lime, and with-out any relation to their natural likes and tastes, and where men of rich nature must give themselves up to an irritation which they no longer recognize because it is always present. I often wonder why he gave me his friendship, why it was he who found almost all the sub-scribers for my *Wanderings of Oisin,* and why he now supported me in all I did, for how could he like verses that were all picture, all emotion, all association, all mythology? He could not have approved my criticism either, for I exalted Mask and Image above the eighteenth-century logic which he loved, and set experience before observation, emotion before fact. Yet he would say, 'I have only three followers, Taylor, Yeats, and Rolleston', and presently he cast out Rolleston—'Davitt wants to convert thousands, but I want two or three'. I think that perhaps it was because he no more wished to strengthen Irish Nationalism by second-rate literature than by second-rate morality, and was content that we agreed in that. 'There are things a man must not do to save a nation', he had once told me, and when I asked what things, had said, 'To cry in public', and I think it probable that he would have added, if pressed, 'To write oratorical or insincere verse'.

O'Leary's movements and intonations were full of impulse, but John F. Taylor's voice in private discussion had no emotional qual-ity except in the expression of scorn; if he moved an arm it moved from the shoulder or elbow alone, and when he walked he moved from the waist only, and seemed an automaton, a wooden soldier, as if he had no life that was not dry and abstract. Except at moments of public oratory, he lacked all personality, though when one saw him respectful and gentle with O'Leary, as with some charming woman, one saw that he felt its fascination. In letters, or in painting, it repelled him unless it were harsh and obvious, and therefore, though his vast erudition included much art and letters, he lacked artistic feeling, and judged everything by the moral sense.

He had great ambition, and had he joined some established party, or found some practicable policy, he might have been followed, might have produced even some great effect, but he must have known that in defeat no man would follow him as they followed O'Leary, as they followed Parnell. His oratory was noble, strange, even beautiful, at moments the greatest I have ever listened to; but, the speech over, where there had been, as it seemed, so little of himself, all coming from beyond himself, we saw precisely as before an ungainly body in unsuitable, badly fitting clothes, and heard an excited voice speaking ill of this man or that other. We knew that he could never give us that one price we would accept, that he would never find a practicable policy; that no party would admit, no Government negotiate with, a man notorious for a temper[33] that, if it gave him genius, could at times carry him to the edge of insanity.

Born in some country town, the son of some little watchmaker, he had been a shop-assistant, put himself to college and the bar, learned to speak at temperance meetings and Young Ireland Societies, and was now a Queen's Counsel famous for his defence of country criminals, whose cases had seemed hopeless—Taylor's boys, their neighbours called them or they called themselves. He had shaped his style and his imagination from Carlyle, the chief inspirer of self-educated men in the 'eighties and early 'nineties. 'I prefer Emerson's *Oversoul*',[34] the Clondalkin cobbler said to me, 'but I always read Carlyle when I am wild with the neighbours'; but he used his master's style, as Mitchel had done before, to abase what his master loved, to exalt what his master scorned. His historical erudition seemed as vast as that of York Powell, but his interests were not Powell's, for he had no picture before the mind's eye, and had but one object—a plea of not guilty—entered in his country's name before a jury which he believed to be packed. O'Leary cared nothing for his country's glory, its individuality alone seemed important in his eyes; he was like some man who serves a woman all his life without asking whether she be good or bad, wise or foolish; but Taylor cared for nothing else. He was so much O'Leary's disciple that he would say in conversation, 'We are demoralized, what case for change if we are not?' for O'Leary admitted no ground for reform outside the moral life, but when he spoke to the great plea he would make no admission. He spoke to it in the most obscure places, in little halls in back streets where the whitewashed walls are foul with grease from many heads, before some audience of medical students or of shop-assistants, for he was like a man under a curse, compelled to hide his genius, and compelled to show in conspicuous places his ill-judgment and his temper.

His distaste for myself, broken by occasional tolerance, in so far as it was not distaste for an imagination that seemed to him aesthetic rather than ethical, was because I had published Irish folklore in English reviews to the discredit, as he thought, of the Irish peasantry, and because, England within earshot, I found fault with the Young Ireland prose and poetry. He would have hated *The Playboy of the Western World,* and his death a little before its performance was fortunate for Synge and myself. His articles are nothing, and his one historical work, a life of Owen Roe O'Neill, is almost nothing, lacking the living voice; and now, though a most formidable man, he is forgotten but for the fading memory of a few friends, and for what an enemy has written here and elsewhere. Did not Leonardo da Vinci warn the imaginative man against preoccupation with arts that cannot survive his death?[35]

VI

When Carleton was dying in 1869, he said there would be nothing more about Irish literature for twenty years, and his words were fulfilled, for the land war had filled Ireland with its bitterness; but imagination had begun to stir again. I had the same confidence in the future that Lady Gregory and I had eight or nine years later, when we founded an Irish Theatre,[36] though there were neither, as it seemed, plays nor players. There were already a few known men to start my popular series, and to keep it popular until the men whose names I did not know had learnt to express themselves. I had met Dr. Douglas Hyde when I lived in Dublin, and he was still an undergraduate. I have a memory of meeting in college rooms for the first time a very dark young man, who filled me with surprise, partly because he had pushed a snuffbox towards me, and partly because there was something about his vague serious eyes, as in his high cheek-bones, that suggested a different civilization, a different race. I had set him down as a peasant, and wondered what brought him to college, and to a Protestant college, but somebody explained that he belonged to some branch of the Hydes of Castle Hyde, and that he had a Protestant Rector for father. He had much frequented the company of old countrymen, and had so acquired the Irish language, and his taste for snuff, and for moderate quantities of a detestable species of illegal whiskey distilled from the potato by certain of his neighbours. He had already—though intellectual Dublin knew nothing of it—considerable popularity as a Gaelic poet, mowers and reapers singing his songs from Donegal to Kerry. Years afterwards I was to stand at his side and listen to Galway mowers singing his Gaelic words without their knowing whose words they sang.[37] It is so in India, where peasants sing the words of the great poet of Bengal[38] without knowing whose words they sing, and it must often be so where the old imaginative folk-life is undisturbed, and it is so amongst schoolboys who hand their story-books to one another without looking at the title-page to read the author's name. Here and there, however, the peasants had not lost the habit of Gaelic criticism, picked up, perhaps, from the poets who took refuge among them after the ruin of the great Catholic families, from men like that O'Rahilly, who cries in a translation from the Gaelic that is itself a masterpiece of concentrated passion:

> The periwinkle and the tough dog-fish
> Towards evening time have got into my dish.[39]

An old rascal was kept in food and whiskey for a fortnight by some Connacht village under the belief that he was 'Craoibhin Aoibhin', 'the pleasant little branch', as Dr. Hyde signed himself in the newspapers where the villagers had found his songs. The impostor's thirst only strengthened belief in his genius, for the Gaelic song-writers have had the infirmities of Robert Burns; 'It is not the drink but the company', one of the last has sung.[40] Since that first meeting Dr. Hyde and I had corresponded, and he had sent me in manuscript the best tale in my *Fairy and Folk Tales*,[41] and I think I had something to do with the London publication of his *Beside the Fire*,[42] a book written in the beautiful English of Connacht, which is Gaelic in idiom and Tudor in vocabulary, and, indeed, the first book to use it in the expression of emotion and romance, for Carleton and his school had turned it into farce. Henley had praised him, and York Powell had said, 'If he goes on as he has begun, he will be the greatest folklorist who has ever lived'; and I know no first book of verse of our time that is at once so romantic and so concrete as his

Gaelic *Abhla de'n Craoibh;*[43] but in a few years Dublin was to laugh him, or rail him, out of his genius. He had no critical capacity, having indeed for certain years the uncritical folk-genius, as no educated Irishman or Englishman has ever had it, writing out of an imitative sympathy like that of a child catching a tune and leaving it to chance to call the tune; and the failure of our first attempt to create a modern Irish literature permitted the ruin of that genius. He was to create a great popular movement, far more important in its practical results than any movement I could have made, no matter what my luck, but, being neither quarrelsome nor vain, he will not be angry if I say—for the sake of those who come after us—that I mourn for the 'greatest folklorist who ever lived', and for the great poet who died in his youth. The Harps and Pepperpots got him and the Harps and Pepperpots kept him till he wrote in our common English—'It must be either English or Irish', said some patriotic editor, Young Ireland practice in his head—that needs such sifting that he who would write it vigorously must write it like a learned language, and took for his model the newspaper upon his breakfast-table, and became for no base reason beloved by multitudes who should never have heard his name till their schoolmasters showed it upon his tomb. That very incapacity for criticism made him the cajoler of crowds, and of individual men and women; 'He should not be in the world at all', said one admiring elderly woman, 'or doing the world's work'; and for certain years young Irish women were to display his pseudonym, 'Craoibhin Aoibhin', in gilt letters upon their hat-bands.

> Dear Craoibhin Aoibhin, . . . impart to us—
> We'll keep the secret—a new trick to please;
> Is there a bridle for this Proteus
> That turns and changes like his draughty seas,
> Or is there none, most popular of men,
> But when they mock us, that we mock again?[44]

VII

Standish O'Grady, upon the other hand, was at once all passion and all judgment. And yet those who knew him better than I assured me he could find quarrel in a straw; and I did know that he had quarrelled a few years back with Jack Nettleship. Nettleship's account had been: 'My mother cannot endure the God of the Old Testament, but likes Jesus Christ; whereas I like the God of the Old Testament, and cannot endure Jesus Christ; and we have got into the way of quarrelling about it at lunch; and once, when O'Grady lunched with us, he said it was the most disgraceful spectacle he had ever seen, and walked out'. Indeed, I wanted him among my writers because of his quarrels, for, having much passion and little rancour, the more he quarrelled, the nobler, the more patched with metaphor, the more musical his style became, and if he were in his turn attacked, he knew a trick of speech that made us murmur, 'We do it wrong, being so majestical, to offer it the show of violence'.[45] Sometimes he quarrelled most where he loved most. A Unionist in politics, a leader-writer on the *Daily Express,* the most Conservative paper in Ireland, hater of every form of democracy, he had given all his heart to the smaller Irish landowners, to whom he belonged, and with whom his childhood had been spent, and for them he wrote his books, and would soon rage over their failings in certain famous passages[46] that many men would repeat to themselves like poets' rhymes. All round us people talked or wrote for victory's sake, and were hated for their victories—but here was a man whose rage was a swan-song over all that he had held most dear, and to whom for that very reason every Irish imaginative writer owed a portion of his soul. In his unfinished *History of Ireland* he had made the old Irish heroes, Finn, and Oisin, and Cuchulain, alive again, taking them, for I think he knew no Gaelic, from the dry pages of O'Curry and his school, and condensing and arranging, as he thought Homer would have arranged and condensed. Lady Gregory has told the same tales, but keeping closer to the Gaelic text, and with greater powers of arrangement and a more original style, but O'Grady was the first, and we had read him in our teens. I think that, had I succeeded, a popular audience could have changed him little, and that his genius would have stayed as it had been shaped by his youth in some provincial society, and that to the end he would have shown his best in occasional thrusts and parries. But I do think that if, instead of that one admirable little book, *The Bog of Stars,* we had got all his histories and imaginative works into the hands of our young men, he might have brought the imagination of Ireland nearer the Image and the honeycomb.

Lionel Johnson was to be our critic, and above all our theologian, for he had been converted to Catholicism, and his orthodoxy, too learned to question, had accepted all that we did, and most of our plans. Historic Catholicism, with all its councils and its dogmas, stirred his passion like the beauty of a mistress, and the unlearned parish priests who thought good literature or good criticism dangerous were in his eyes 'all heretics'. He belonged to a family that had, he told us, called itself Irish some generations back, and its English generations but enabled him to see as one single sacred tradition Irish nationality and Catholic religion. How should he fail to know the Holy Land? Had he not been in Egypt? He had joined our London Irish Literary Society, attended its committee meetings, and given lectures in London, in Dublin, and in Belfast, on Irish novelists and Irish poetry, reading his lectures always, and yet affecting his audience as I, with my spoken lectures, could not, perhaps because Ireland had still the shape it had received from the eighteenth century, and so felt the dignity, not the artifice, of his elaborate periods. He was very little, and at a first glance he seemed but a schoolboy of fifteen. I remember saying one night at the Rhymers', when he spoke of passing safely, almost nightly, through Seven Dials, then a dangerous neighbourhood, 'Who would expect to find anything in your pockets but a peg-top and a piece of string?' But one never thought of his small stature when he spoke or read. He had the delicate strong features of a certain filleted head of a Greek athlete in the British Museum, an archaistic Graeco-Roman copy of a masterpiece of the fourth century, and that resemblance seemed symbolic of the austere nobility of his verse. He was now in his best years, writing with great ease and power; neither I nor, I think, any other foresaw his tragedy.

He suffered from insomnia, and some doctor, while he was still at the University, had recommended alcohol, and he had, in a vain hope of sleep, increased the amount, as Rossetti had increased his doses of chloral, and now he drank for drinking's sake. He drank a great deal too much, and, though nothing could, it seemed, disturb his calm or unsteady his hand or foot, his doctrine, after a certain number of glasses, would become more ascetic, more contemptuous of all that we call human life. I have heard him, after four or five glasses of wine, praise some Church Father who freed himself from sexual passion by a surgical operation, and deny with scorn, and much historical evidence, that a gelded man lost anything of intellectual power. Even without stimulant his theology conceded nothing to human weakness, and I can remember his saying with energy, 'I wish those people who deny the eternity of punishment could realize their unspeakable vulgarity'.

Now that I know his end, I see him creating, to use a favourite adjective of his, 'marmorean' verse, and believing the most terrible doctrines to keep down his own turbulence. One image of that stay in Dublin[47] is so clear before me that it has blotted out most other images of that time. He is sitting at a lodging-house table, which I have just left at three in the morning, and round him lie or sit in huddled attitudes half a dozen men in various states of intoxication: and he is looking straight before him with head erect, and one hand resting upon the table. As I reach the stairs I hear him say, in a clear, unshaken voice, 'I believe in nothing but the Holy Roman Catholic Church'. He sometimes spoke of drink as something which he could put aside at any moment, and his friends believed, and I think he liked us to believe, that he would shortly enter a monastery. Did he deceive us deliberately? Did he himself already foresee the moment when he would write 'The Dark Angel'?[48] I am almost certain that he did, for he had already written 'Mystic and Cavalier',[49] where the historical setting is, I believe, but masquerade.

> Go from me: I am one of those who fall.
> What! hath no cold wind swept your heart at all,
> In my sad company? Before the end,
>   Go from me, dear my friend!
>
> Yours are the victories of light: your feet
> Rest from good toil, where rest is brave and sweet.
> But after warfare in a morning gloom
>   I rest in clouds of doom.
>
>   .   .   .   .
>
> Seek with thine eyes to pierce this crystal sphere:
> Canst read a fate there, prosperous and clear?
> Only the mists, only the weeping clouds:
>   Dimness, and airy shrouds.
>
>   .   .   .   .

O rich and sounding voices of the air!
Interpreters and prophets of despair:
Priests of a fearful sacrament! I come
    To make with you my home.

VIII

Sir Charles Gavan Duffy arrived.[50] He brought with him much
manuscript, the private letters of a Young Ireland poetess,[51] a dry
but informing unpublished historical essay by Davis,[52] and an
unpublished novel by William Carleton, into the middle of which
he had dropped a hot coal, so that nothing remained but the borders of every page. He hired a young man to read him, after dinner,
Carlyle's *Heroes and Hero-Worship,*[53] and before dinner was gracious to all our men of authority and especially to our Harps and
Pepperpots. Taylor compared him to Odysseus returning to Ithaca,
and every newspaper published his biography. He was a white-
haired old man, who had written the standard history of Young Ireland,[54] had emigrated to Australia, had been the first Australian
Federalist, and later Prime Minister, but, in all his writings, in
which there is so much honesty, so little rancour, there is not one
sentence that has any meaning when separated from its place in
argument or narrative, not one distinguished because of its thought
or music. One imagined his youth in some little gaunt Irish town,
where no building or custom is revered for its antiquity; and there
speaking a language where no word, even in solitude, is ever spoken
slowly and carefully because of emotional implication; and of his
manhood of practical politics, of the dirty piece of orange-peel in
the corner of the stairs as one climbs up to some newspaper office;
of public meetings where it would be treacherous amid so much
geniality to speak or even to think of anything that might cause a
moment's misunderstanding in one's own party. No argument of
mine was intelligible to him, and I would have been powerless, but
that fifty years ago he had made an enemy,[55] and though the enemy
was long dead, the enemy's school remained. He had attacked, why
or with what result I do not remember, the only Young Ireland
politician who had music and personality, though rancorous and
devil-possessed. At some public meeting[56] of ours, where he spoke
amid great applause, in smooth, Gladstonian periods, of his pro-

posed Irish publishing firm, one heard faint hostile murmurs, and at last a voice cried, 'Remember Newry', and a voice answered, 'There is a grave there!' and a part of the audience sang, 'Here's to John Mitchel[57] that is gone, boys, gone; Here's to the friends that are gone'. The meeting over, a group of us, indignant that the meeting we had called for his welcome should have contained those malcontents, gathered about him to apologize. He had written a pamphlet,[58] he explained: he would give us copies. We would see that he was in the right, how badly Mitchel had behaved. But in Ireland personality, if it be but harsh and hard, has lovers, and some of us, I think, may have gone home muttering, 'How dare he be in the right if Mitchel is in the wrong?'

IX

He wanted 'to complete the Young Ireland movement'—to do all that had been left undone because of the Famine, or the death of Davis, or his own emigration; and all the younger men were upon my side in resisting that. They might not want the books I wanted, but they did want books written by their own generation, and we began to struggle[59] with him over the control of the company. Taylor became very angry, and I can understand what I looked like in his eyes, when I remember Edwin Ellis's seriously-intended warning, 'It is bad manners for a man under thirty to permit himself to be in the right'. But John O'Leary supported me throughout.

When Gavan Duffy had gone to London to draw up articles of association for his company, for which he had found many shareholders in Dublin, the dispute became very fierce. One night members of the general public climbed the six flights of stairs to our committee-room, now no longer in the Mansion House, and found seats for themselves just behind our chairs. We were all too angry to send them away, or even to notice their presence, for I was accused of saying at a public meeting in Cork, 'Our books', when I should have said, 'Sir Charles Gavan Duffy's books'. I was not Taylor's match with the spoken word, and barely matched him with the written word. At twenty-seven or twenty-eight I was immature and clumsy, and O'Leary's support was capricious, for, being but a spectator of life, he would desert me if I used a bad argument, and would not return till I found a good one; and our chairman, Dr.

Hyde, 'most popular of men', sat dreaming of his old white cockatoo in far-away Roscommon. Our very success had been a misfortune, for an opposition which had been literary and political brought, now that it had spread to the general public, religious prejudice to its aid. Suddenly, when the company seemed all but established, and a scheme had been thought out which gave some representation on its governing board to contemporary Irish writers, Gavan Duffy produced a letter from Archbishop Walsh, and threw the project up. The letter had warned him that after his death the company would fall under a dangerous influence. At this moment the always benevolent friend[60] to whom I had explained in confidence, when asking his support, my arrangements with my publisher, went to Gavan Duffy and suggested that they should together offer Mr. Fisher Unwin a series of Irish books, and Mr. Fisher Unwin and his reader[61] accepted the series under the belief that it was my project that they accepted. I went to London to find the contract signed, and that all I could do was to get two sub-editors appointed,[62] responsible to the two societies. Two or three good books were published, especially Dr. Hyde's *Short History of Gaelic Literature,* and Standish O'Grady's *Bog of Stars;* but the series was killed by its first volume, Thomas Davis's dry but informing historical essay.[63] So important had our movement seemed that ten thousand copies had been sold before anybody had time to read it, and then the sale came to a dead stop.

Gavan Duffy knew nothing of my plans, and so was guiltless, and my friend had heard me discuss many things that evening. I had perhaps dispraised the humanitarian Stephen Phillips, already in his first vogue, and praised Francis Thompson, but half rescued from his gutter; or flouted his belief in the perpetual marriage of genius and virtue by numbering the vices of famous men; this man's venery, that man's drink. He could not be expected to remember that where I had said so much of no account, I said one thing, and he had made one reply, that I thought of great account. He died a few months ago, and it would have surprised and shocked him if any man had told him that he was unforgiven; had he not forgotten all about it long ago? A German doctor[64] has said that if we leave an umbrella at a friend's house it is because we have a subconscious desire to revisit that house; and he had perhaps a subconscious desire that my too tumultuous generation should not have its say.

X

I was at Sligo when I received a letter from John O'Leary, saying that I could do no more in Dublin, for even the younger men had turned against me, were 'jealous', his letter said, though what they had to be jealous of God knows. He said further that it was all my own fault, that he had warned me what would happen if I lived on terms of intimacy with those I tried to influence. I should have kept myself apart and alone. It was all true; through some influence from an earlier generation, from Walt Whitman, perhaps, I had sat talking in public bars, had talked late into the night at many men's houses, showing all my convictions to men that were but ready for one, and used conversation to explore and discover among men who looked for authority. I did not yet know that intellectual freedom and social equality are incompatible; and yet, if I had, could hardly have lived otherwise, being too young for silence. The trouble came from half a dozen obscure young men, who having nothing to do attended every meeting and were able to overturn a project that seemed my only bridge to other projects, including a travelling theatre. We had planned small libraries of Irish literature in connection with our country branches; we collected books and money, sending a lecturer to every branch and taking half the proceeds of that lecture to buy books. Maud Gonne,[65] whose beauty could draw a great audience in any country town, had been the lecturer. The scheme was very nearly self-supporting, and six or seven bundles of books, chosen after much disputation by John O'Leary, J. F. Taylor, and myself, had been despatched to some six or seven branches. 'The country will support this work', Taylor had said somewhere on some public platform, 'because we are the most inflammable people on God's earth', his harsh voice giving almost a quality of style to Carlylean commonplace; but we are also a very jealous people. The half a dozen young men, if a little jealous of me, were still more jealous of those country branches which were getting so much notice, and where there was so much of that peasant mind their schoolmasters had taught them to despise. One must be English or Irish, they would have said. I returned to find a great box of books appropriated for some Dublin purpose and the whole scheme abandoned.[66] I knew that it was a bitter moment because I remember with gratitude words spoken not to my ear, but for my ear, by a young man who had lately joined our Society, Mr. Stephen MacKenna, now well known amongst scholars for his distinguished translations of Plotinus, and I seem to remember that I lost through anger what gift of persuasion I may possess, and that I was all the more helpless because I felt that even the best of us disagreed about everything at heart. I began to feel that I needed a hostess more than a society, but that I was not to find for years to come. I tried to persuade Maud Gonne to be that hostess, but her social life was in Paris, and she had already formed a new ambition, the turning of French public opinion against England. Without intellectual freedom there can be no agreement, and in Nationalist Dublin there was not—indeed there still is not—any society where a man is heard by the right ears, but never overheard by the wrong, and where he speaks his whole mind gaily, and is not the cautious husband of a part; where fantasy can play before matured into conviction; where life can shine and ring, and lack utility. Mere life lacking the protection of wealth or rank, or some beauty's privilege of caprice, cannot choose its company, taking up and dropping men merely because it likes or dislikes their manners and their looks, and in its stead opinion crushes and rends, and all is hatred and bitterness: wheel biting upon wheel, a roar of steel or iron tackle, a mill of argument grinding all things down to mediocrity.

If, as I think, minds and metals correspond, the goldsmiths of Paris foretold the French Revolution when they substituted steel for that unserviceable gold in the manufacture of the more expensive jewel work, and made those large, flat steel buttons for men of fashion wherein the card-sharpers were able to study the reflections of the cards.

XI

No country could have more natural distaste for equality, for in every circle there was some man ridiculous for posing as the type of some romantic or distinguished trait. One of our friends, a man of talent and of learning, whose ancestors had come, he believed, from Denmark in the ninth century,[67] looked and talked the distinguished foreigner so perfectly that a patriotic newspaper gave particulars of his supposed relations in contemporary Denmark! A half-mad old man[68] who had served for a few months in the Pope's army, many years before, still rode an old white war-horse in all National processions, and, if their enemies were not lying, one city councillor had challenged another to a duel by flinging his glove upon the floor; while a popular Lord Mayor[69] had boasted in a public speech that he never went to bed at night without reading twelve pages of the poet Sappho. Then, too, in those conversations of the small hours, to which O'Leary had so much objected, whenever we did not speak of art and letters, we spoke of Parnell.[70] We told each other that he had admitted no man to his counsel; that when some member of his party found himself in the same hotel by chance, that member would think to stay there a presumption, and move to some other lodging; and, above all, we spoke of his pride, that made him hide all emotion while before his enemy. Once he had seemed callous and indifferent to the House of Commons—Forster had accused him of abetting assassination—but when he came among his followers his hands were full of blood, because he had torn them with his nails. What excitement there would have been, what sense of mystery would have stirred all our hearts, and stirred hearts all through the country, where there was still, and for many years to come, but one overmastering topic, had we known the story Mrs. Parnell tells[71] of that scene on Brighton Pier. He and the woman that he loved stood there upon a night of storm, when his power was at its greatest height, and still unthreatened. He caught her from the ground and held her at arm's length out over the water and she lay there motionless, knowing that, had she moved, he would have drowned himself and her. Perhaps unmotived self-immolation, were that possible, or else at mere suggestion of storm and night, were as great evidence as such a man could give of power over self, and so of the expression of the self.

XII

When I look back upon my Irish propaganda of those years I can see little but its bitterness. I never met with, or but met to quarrel with, my father's old family acquaintance; or with acquaintance I myself might have found, and kept among the prosperous educated class, who had all the great appointments at University or Castle;[72] and this I did by deliberate calculation. If I must attack so much that seemed sacred to Irish Nationalist opinion, I must, I knew, see to it that no man suspect me of doing it to flatter Unionist opinion.[73] Whenever I got the support of some man who belonged by birth and education to University or Castle, I would say, 'Now you must be baptized of the gutter'. I chose Royal visits[74] especially for demonstrations of disloyalty, rolling up with my own hands the red carpet spread by some elderly Nationalist, softened or weakened by time, to welcome Viceroyalty; and threatening, if our London society drank to the King's health, that my friends and I would demonstrate against it by turning our glasses upside-down; and was presently to discover that one can grow impassioned and fanatical about opinions which one has chosen as one might choose a side upon the football field; and I thought many a time of the pleasant Dublin houses that would never ask me to dine; and the still pleasanter houses with trout-streams near at hand, that would never ask me upon a visit. I became absurdly sensitive, glancing about me in certain public places, the private view of our Academy,[75] or the like, to discover imagined enemies; and even now, after twenty or thirty years, I feel at times that I have not recovered my natural manner. Yet it was in those pleasant houses, among the young men and the young girls, that we were to make our converts. When we loathe ourselves or our world, if that loathing but turn to intellect, we see self or world and its anti-self as in one vision; when loathing remains but loathing, world or self consumes itself away, and we turn to its mechanical opposite. Popular Nationalism and Unionism so changed into one another, being each but the other's headache. The Nationalist abstractions were like the fixed ideas of some hysterical woman, a part of the mind turned into stone, the rest a seething and burning; and Unionist Ireland had reacted from that seething and burning to a cynical indifference, and from those fixed ideas to whatever might bring the most easy and obvious success.

I remember Taylor at some public debate, stiff of body and tense of voice; and the contrasting figure of Fitzgibbon, the Lord Justice of Appeal of the moment, and his calm, flowing sentences, satisfactory to hear and impossible to remember. Taylor speaks of a little nation of antiquity, which he does not name, 'set between the great Empire of Persia and the great Empire of Rome'. Into the mouths of those great Empires he puts the arguments of Fitzgibbon and such as he: 'Join with our greatness! What in comparison to that is your little, beggarly nationality?' And then I recall the excitement, the shiver of the nerves, as his voice rose to an ecstatic cry, 'Out of that nation came the salvation of the world'.[76] I remember, too, and grow angry as it were yesterday, a letter from that Lord Justice of Appeal, who had changed his politics for advancement's sake, recommending a correspondent to avoid us, because we dissuaded people from the study of 'Shakespeare and Kingsley'.

Edward Dowden, my father's old friend, with his dark romantic face, the one man of letters Dublin Unionism possessed, was withering in that barren soil. Towards the end of his life he confessed to a near friend that he would have wished before all things to have been the lover of many women; and some careless lecture, upon the youthful Goethe, had in early life drawn down upon him the displeasure of the Protestant Archbishop. And yet he turned Shakespeare into a British Benthamite, flattered Shelley but to hide his own growing lack of sympathy, abandoned for like reason that study of Goethe that should have been his life-work, and at last cared but for Wordsworth, the one great poet who, after brief blossom, was cut and sawn into planks of obvious utility.[77] I called upon him from time to time out of gratitude for old encouragements, and because, among the Dublin houses open to me, his alone was pleasant to the eye, with its many books and its air of scholarship. But when O'Grady had declared, rancorous for once but under substantial provocation, that he had 'a bad head and a worse heart', I found my welcome troubled and called no more.

XIII

The one house where nobody thought or talked politics was a house in Ely Place, where a number of young men lived together, and, for want of a better name, were called Theosophists. Besides the resident members, other members dropped in and out during the day, and the reading-room was a place of much discussion about philosophy and about the arts. The house had been taken in the name of the engineer to the Board of Works, a black-bearded young man,[78] with a passion for Manichaean philosophy, and all accepted him as host; and sometimes the conversation, especially when I was there, became too ghostly for the nerves of his young and delicate wife, and he would be made angry. I remember young men struggling, with inexact terminology and insufficient learning, for some new religious conception, on which they could base their lives; and some few strange or able men.

At the top of the house lived a medical student[79] who read Plato and took hashish, and a young Scotsman[80] who owned a vegetarian restaurant, and had just returned from America, where he had gone as the disciple of the Prophet Harris, and where he would soon return in the train of some new prophet. When one asked what set him on his wanderings, he told of a young Highlander, his friend in boyhood, whose cap was always plucked off at a certain twist in the road, till the fathers of the village fastened it upon his head by recommending drink and women. When he had gone, his room was inherited by an American hypnotist, who had lived among the Zuñi Indians with the explorer Cushing, and told of a Zuñi Indian who, irritated by some white man's praise of telephone and telegraph, cried out, 'Can they do that?' and cast above his head two handfuls of sand that burst into flame, and flamed till his head seemed wrapped in fire. He professed to talk the philosophy of the Zuñi Indians, but it seemed to me the vague Platonism that all there talked, except that he spoke much of men passing in sleep into the heart of mountains; a doctrine that was presently incorporated in the mythology of the house, to send young men and women hither and thither inquiring for sacred places. On a lower floor lived a strange red-haired girl,[81] all whose thoughts were set upon painting and poetry, conceived as abstract images like Love and Penury in the *Symposium;* and to these images she sacrificed herself with Asiatic fanaticism. The engineer had discovered her starving somewhere in an unfurnished or half-furnished room, and that she had lived for many weeks upon bread and shell-cocoa, so that her food never cost her more than a penny a day. Born into a county family, who were so haughty that their neighbours called them the Royal Family, she had quarrelled with a mad father, who had never, his tenants declared, 'unscrewed the top of his flask with any man', because she wished to study art, had run away from home, had lived for a time by selling her watch, and then by occasional stories in an Irish paper. For some weeks she had paid half-a-crown a week to some poor woman to see her to the art schools and back, for she considered it wrong for a woman to show herself in public places unattended; but of late she had been unable to afford the school fees. The engineer engaged her as a companion for his wife, and gave her money enough to begin her studies once more. She had talent and imagination, a gift for style; but, though ready to face death for painting and poetry, conceived as allegorical figures, she hated her own genius, and had not met praise and sympathy early enough to overcome the hatred. Face to face with paint and canvas, pen and paper, she saw nothing of her genius but its cruelty, and would have scarce arrived before she would find some excuse to leave the schools for the day, if indeed she had not invented over her breakfast some occupation so laborious that she could call it a duty, and so not go at all. Most watched her in mockery, but I watched in sympathy; composition strained my nerves and spoiled my sleep; and yet, for generations—and in Ireland we have long memories— my paternal ancestors had worked at some intellectual pursuit, while hers had shot and hunted. She could at any time, had she given up her profession, which her father had raged against, not because it was art, but because it was a profession, have returned to the common comfortable life of women. When, a little later, she had quarrelled with the engineer or his wife, and gone back to bread and shell-cocoa I brought her an offer from some Dublin merchant of fairly well paid advertisement work, which would have been less laborious than artistic creation; but she said that to draw advertisements was to degrade art, thanked me elaborately, and did not disguise her indignation. She had, I believe, returned to starvation with joy, for constant anaemia would shortly give her an argument strong enough to silence her conscience when the allegorical images glared upon her, and, apart from that, starvation and misery had a large share in her ritual of worship.

XIV

At the top of the house, and at the time I remember best in the same room with the young Scotsman, lived Mr. George Russell (A.E.),[82] and the house and the society were divided into his adherents and those of the engineer; and I heard of some quarrelling between the factions. The rivalry was subconscious. Neither had willingly opposed the other in any matter of importance. The engineer had all the financial responsibility, and George Russell was, in the eyes of the community, saint and genius. Had either seen that the question at issue was the leadership of mystical thought in Dublin, he would, I think, have given way, but the dispute seemed trivial. At the weekly meetings, anything might be discussed; no chairman called a speaker to order; an atheistic workman could denounce religion, or a pious Catholic confound theosophy with atheism; and the engineer, precise and practical, disapproved. He had an object. He wished to make converts for a definite form of belief, and here an enemy, if a better speaker, might make all the converts. He wished to confine discussion to members of the society, and had proposed in committee, I was told, a resolution on the subject; while Russell, who had refused to join my National Literary Society, because the party of Harp and Pepperpot had set limits to discussion, resisted, and at last defeated him. In a couple of years some new dispute arose; he resigned, and founded a society which drew doctrine and method from America or London; and Russell became, as he is to-day, the one masterful influence among young Dublin men and women who love religious speculation, but have no historical faith.

When Russell and I had been at the art schools six or seven years before, he had been almost unintelligible. He had seemed incapable of coherent thought, and perhaps was so at certain moments. The idea came upon him, he has told me, that if he spoke he would reveal that he had lost coherence; and for the three days that the idea lasted he spent the hours of daylight wandering upon the Dublin mountains, that he might escape the necessity for speech. I used to listen to him at that time, mostly walking through the streets at night, for the sake of some stray sentence, beautiful and profound, amid many words that seemed without meaning; and there were others, too, who walked and listened, for he had become, I think, to all his fellow-students, sacred, as the fool is sacred in the East. We copied the model laboriously, he would draw without research into the natural form, and call his study *Saint John in the Wilderness*; but I can remember the almost scared look and the half-whisper of a student, now a successful sculptor,[83] who said, pointing to the modelling of a shoulder, 'That is too easy, a great deal too easy!' For with brush and pencil he was too coherent.

We derided each other, told absurd tales to one another's discredit, but we never derided him, or told tales to his discredit. He stood outside the sense of comedy his friend John Eglinton has called 'the social cement' of our civilization; and we would 'gush' when we spoke of him, as men do when they praise something incomprehensible. But when he painted there was no difficulty in comprehending. How could that ease and rapidity of composition, so far beyond anything that we could attain to, belong to a man whose words seemed often without meaning?

A few months before I had come to Ireland he had sent me some verses, which I had liked till Edwin Ellis had laughed me from my liking by proving that no line had a rhythm that agreed with any other, and that, the moment one thought he had settled upon some scheme of rhyme, he would break from it without reason. But now his verse was clear in thought and delicate in form. He wrote without premeditation or labour. It had, as it were, organized itself, and grown as nervous and living as if it had, as Dante said[84] of his own work, paled his cheek. The Society he belonged to published a little magazine,[85] and he had asked the readers to decide whether they preferred his prose or his verse, and it was because they so willed it that he wrote the little transcendental verses afterwards published in *Homeward; Songs by the Way.*[86]

Life was not expensive in that house, where, I think, no meat was eaten; I know that out of the sixty or seventy pounds a year which he earned as accountant in a Dublin shop, he saved a considerable portion for his private charity; and it was, I think, his benevolence that gave him his lucidity of speech, and, perhaps, of writing. If he convinced himself that any particular activity was desirable in the public interest or in that of his friends, he had at once the ardour that came to another from personal ambition. He was always surrounded with a little group of infirm or unlucky persons, whom he explained to themselves and to others, turning cat to griffin, goose to swan. In later years he was to accept the position of organizer of a co-operative banking system,[87] before he had even read a book upon economics or finance, and within a few months to give evidence before a Royal Commission upon the system, as an acknowledged expert, though he had brought to it nothing but his impassioned versatility.

At the time I write of him, he was the religious teacher, and that alone—his painting, his poetry, and his conversation all subservient to that one end. Men watched him with awe or with bewilderment; it was known that he saw visions continually, perhaps more continually than any modern man since Swedenborg; and when he painted and drew in pastel what he had seen, some accepted the record without hesitation, others, like myself, noticing the academic Graeco-Roman forms, and remembering his early admiration for the works of Gustave Moreau, divined a subjective element, but no one doubted his word. One might not think him a good observer, but no one could doubt that he reported with the most scrupulous care what he believed himself to have seen; nor did he lack occasional objective corroboration. Walking with some man in his park—his demesne, as we say in Ireland—he had seen a visionary church at a particular spot, and the man had dug and uncovered its foundations; then some woman had met him with, 'O, Mr. Russell, I am so unhappy', and he had replied, 'You will be perfectly happy this evening at seven o'clock', and left her to her blushes. She had an appointment with a young man for seven o'clock. I had heard of this a day or so after the event, and I asked him about it, and was told it had suddenly come into his head to use those words; but why he did not know. He and I often quarrelled, because I wanted him to examine and question his visions, and write them out as they occurred; and still more because I thought symbolic what he thought real like the men and women that had passed him on the road. Were they so much a part of his subconscious life that they would have vanished had he submitted them to question; were they like those voices that only speak, those strange sights that only show themselves for an instant, when the attention has been withdrawn; that phantasmagoria of which I had learnt something in London: and had his verse and his painting a like origin? And was that why the same hand that painted a certain dreamy, lovely sandy shore,[88] now in the Dublin Municipal Gallery, could with great rapidity fill many canvases with poetical commonplace; and why, after writing *Homeward; Songs by the Way,* where all is skilful and much exquisite, he would never again write a perfect book? Was it precisely because in Swedenborg alone the conscious and the subconscious became one—as in that marriage of the angels, which he has described as a contact of the whole being[89]—so completely one indeed that Coleridge thought Swedenborg both man and woman?[90]

Russell's influence, which was already great, had more to support it than his versatility, or the mystery that surrounded him, for his sense of justice, and the daring that came from his own confi-

dence in it, had made him the general counsellor. He would give
endless time to a case of conscience, and no situation was too difficult for his clarity; and certainly some of the situations were difficult. I remember his being summoned to decide between two ladies
who had quarrelled about a vacillating admirer, and called each
other, to each other's faces, the worst names in our somewhat
anaemic modern vocabulary; and I have heard of his success on an
occasion when I think no other but Dostoievsky's idiot[91] could have
avoided offence. The Society was very young, and, as its members
faced the world's moral complexities as though they were the first
that ever faced them, they drew up very vigorous rules. One rule
was that if any member saw a fault growing upon any other member, it was his duty to point it out to that member. A certain young
man became convinced that a certain young woman had fallen in
love with him; and, as an unwritten rule pronounced love and the
spiritual life incompatible, that was a heavy fault. As the young
man felt the delicacy of the situation, he asked for Russell's help,
and side by side they braved the offender, who, I was told, received
their admonishment with surprised humility, and promised amendment. His voice would often become high, and lose its self-possession during intimate conversation, and I especially could put him in
a rage; but the moment the audience became too large for intimacy,
or some exciting event had given formality to speech, he would be
at the same moment impassioned and impersonal. He had, and has,
the capacity, beyond that of any man I have known, to put with
entire justice not only the thoughts, but the emotions of the most
opposite parties and personalities, as it were dissolving some public
or private uproar into drama by Corneille or by Racine; and men
who have hated each other must sometimes have been reconciled,
because each heard his enemy's argument put into better words
than he himself had found for his own; and this gift was in later
years to give him political influence, and win him respect from Irish
Nationalist and Unionist alike. It is, perhaps, because of it—joined
to a too literal acceptance of those noble images of moral tradition
which are so like late Graeco-Roman statues—that he has come to
see all human life as a mythological system, where, though all cats
are griffins, the more dangerous griffins are only found among
politicians he has not spoken to, or among authors he has but
glanced at; while those men and women who bring him their con-

fessions and listen to his advice carry but the snowiest of swan's plumage. Nor has it failed to make him, as I think, a bad literary critic; demanding plays and poems where the characters must attain a stature of seven feet, and resenting as something perverse and morbid all abatement from that measure. I sometimes wonder what he would have been had he not met in early life the poetry of Emerson and Walt Whitman, writers who have begun to seem superficial precisely because they lack the Vision of Evil; and those translations of the Upanishads, which it is so much harder to study by the sinking flame of Indian tradition than by the serviceable lamp of Emerson and Walt Whitman.

We are never satisfied with the maturity of those whom we have admired in boyhood; and because we have seen their whole circle—even the most successful life is but a segment—we remain to the end their harshest critics. One old school-fellow of mine will never believe that I have fulfilled the promise of some rough unscannable verses that I wrote before I was eighteen. Does any imaginative man find in maturity the admiration that his first half-articulate years aroused in some little circle; and is not the first success the greatest? Certainly, I demanded of Russell some impossible things, and if I had any influence upon him—and I have little doubt that I had, for we were very intimate—it may not have been a good influence, for I thought there could be no aim for poet or artist except expression of a 'Unity of Being' like that of a 'perfectly proportioned human body'—though I would not at the time have used that phrase. I remember that I was ironic and indignant when he left the art schools because his 'will was weak, and must grow weaker if he followed any emotional pursuit'; as, later, when he let the readers of a magazine decide between his prose and his verse. I now know that there are men who cannot possess 'Unity of Being', who must not seek it or express it—and who, so far from seeking an anti-self, a Mask that delineates a being in all things the opposite to their natural state, can but seek the suppression of the anti-self, till the natural state alone remains. These are those who must seek no image of desire, but await that which lies beyond their mind—unities not of the mind, but unities of Nature, unities of God—the man of science, the moralist, the humanitarian, the politician, Saint Simeon Stylites upon his pillar, Saint Anthony in his cavern, all whose preoccupation is to seem nothing; to hollow their hearts till they are void and without form, to summon a creator by revealing chaos, to become the lamp for another's wick and oil; and indeed it may be that it has been for their guidance in a very special sense that the 'perfectly proportioned human body' suffered crucifixion. For them Mask and Image are of necessity morbid, turning their eyes upon themselves, as though they were of those who can be law unto themselves, of whom Chapman has written, 'Neither is it lawful that they should stoop to any other law',[92] whereas they are indeed of those who can but ask, 'Have I behaved as well as So-and-so?' 'Am I a good man according to the commandments?' or, 'Do I realize my own nothingness before God?' 'Have my experiments and observations excluded the personal factor with sufficient rigour?' Such men do not assume wisdom or beauty as Shelley did, when he masked himself as Ahasuerus, or as Prince Athanase, nor do they pursue an Image through a world that had else seemed an uninhabitable wilderness till, amid the privations of that pursuit, the Image is no more named Pandemos, but Urania;[93] for such men must cast all Masks away and fly the Image, till that Image, transfigured because of their cruelties of self-abasement, becomes itself some Image or epitome of the whole natural or supernatural world, and itself pursues. The wholeness of the supernatural world can only express itself in personal form, because it has no epitome but man, nor can the Hound of Heaven[94] fling itself into any but an empty heart. We may know the fugitives from other poets because, like George Herbert, like Francis Thompson, like George Russell, their imaginations grow more vivid in the expression of something which they have not themselves created, some historical religion or cause. But if the fugitive should live, as I think Russell does at times, as it is natural for a Morris or a Henley or a Shelley to live, hunters and pursuers all, his art surrenders itself to moral or poetical commonplace, to a repetition of thoughts and images that have no relation to experience.

I think that Russell would not have disappointed even my hopes had he, instead of meeting as an impressionable youth with our modern subjective romanticism, met with some form of traditional belief, which condemned all that romanticism admires and praises, indeed, all images of desire; for such condemnation would have turned his intellect towards the images of his vision. It might, doubtless, have embittered his life, for his strong intellect would have been driven out into the impersonal deeps where the man shudders; but it would have kept him a religious teacher, and set him, it may be, among the greatest of that species; politics, for a vision-seeking man, can be but half achievement, a choice of an almost easy kind of skill instead of that kind which is, of all those not impossible, the most difficult. Is it not certain that the Creator yawns in earthquake and thunder and other popular displays, but toils in rounding the delicate spiral of a shell?[95]

XV

I heard the other day of a Dublin man recognizing in London an elderly man who had lived in that house in Ely Place in his youth, and of that elderly man, at the sudden memory, bursting into tears. Though I have no such poignant memories, for I was never of it, never anything but a dissatisfied critic, yet certain vivid moments come back to me as I write. . . . Russell has just come in from a long walk on the Two Rock mountain, very full of his conversation with an old religious beggar, who kept repeating, 'God possesses the heavens, but He covets the earth—He covets the earth'.

.   .   .   .   .

I get in talk with a young man who has taken the orthodox side in some debate. He is a stranger, but explains that he has inherited magical art from his father, and asks me to his rooms to see it in operation. He and a friend of his kill a black cock, and burn herbs in a big bowl, but nothing happens except that the friend repeats again and again, 'O, my God', and when I ask him why he has said that, does not know that he has spoken; and I feel that there is something very evil in the room.

.   .   .   .   .

We are sitting round the fire one night, and a member, a woman, tells a dream that she has just had. She dreamed that she saw monks digging in a garden. They dug down till they found a coffin, and when they took off the lid she saw that in the coffin lay a beautiful young man in a dress of gold brocade. The young man railed against the glory of the world, and when he had finished, the monks closed the coffin reverently, and buried it once more. They smoothed the ground, and then went on with their gardening.

.   .   .   .   .

I have a young man with me, an official of the National Literary Society, and I leave him in the reading-room with Russell, while I go upstairs to see the young Scotsman. I return after some minutes to find that the young man has become a Theosophist, but a month later, after an interview with a friar, to whom he gives an incredible account of his new beliefs, he goes to Mass again.

BOOK III

HODOS CHAMELIONTOS[1]

I

When staying with Hyde in Roscommon,[2] I had driven over to Lough Kay, hoping to find some local memory of the old story of Tumaus Costello, which I was turning into a story now called 'Proud Costello, Macdermot's Daughter, and the Bitter Tongue'.[3] I was rowed up the lake that I might find the island where he died; I had to find it from Hyde's account[4] in the *Love Songs of Connacht*, for when I asked the boatman, he told the story of Hero and Leander,[5] putting Hero's house on one island, and Leander's on another. Presently we stopped to eat our sandwiches at the 'Castle Rock', an island all castle. It was not an old castle, being but the invention of some romantic man, seventy or eighty years ago. The last man who had lived there had been Dr. Hyde's father, and he had but stayed a fortnight. The Gaelic-speaking men in the district were accustomed, instead of calling some specially useless thing a 'white elephant', to call it 'The Castle on the Rock'. The roof was, however, still sound, and the windows unbroken. The situation in the centre of the lake, that has little wood-grown islands, and is surrounded by wood-grown hills, is romantic, and at one end, and perhaps at the other too, there is a stone platform where meditative persons might pace to and fro. I planned a mystical Order which should buy or hire the castle, and keep it as a place where its members could retire for a while for contemplation, and where we might establish mysteries like those of Eleusis and Samothrace; and for ten years to come my most impassioned thought was a vain attempt to find philosophy and to create ritual for that Order. I had an unshakable conviction, arising how or whence I cannot tell, that invisible gates would open as they opened for Blake, as they opened for Swedenborg, as they opened for Boehme, and that this philosophy would find its manuals of devotion in all imaginative literature, and set before Irishmen for special manual an Irish literature which, though made by many minds, would seem the work of a single mind, and turn our places of beauty or legendary association into holy symbols. I did not think this philosophy would be altogether pagan, for it was plain that its symbols must be selected from all those things that had moved men most during many, mainly Christian, centuries.

I thought that for a time I could rhyme of love, calling it *The Rose*, because of the Rose's double meaning; of a fisherman who had 'never a crack' in his heart; of an old woman complaining of the idleness of the young, or of some cheerful fiddler, all those things that 'popular poets' write of, but that I must some day—on that day when the gates began to open—become difficult or obscure. With a rhythm that still echoed Morris I prayed to the Red Rose, to Intellectual Beauty:

> Come near, come near, come near—Ah, leave me still
> A little space for the rose-breath to fill!
> Lest I no more hear common things . . .
> But seek alone to hear the strange things said
> By God to the bright hearts of those long dead,
> And learn to chaunt a tongue men do not know.[6]

I do not remember what I meant by 'the bright hearts', but a little later I wrote of spirits 'with mirrors in their hearts'.[7]

My rituals were not to be made deliberately, like a poem, but all got by that method Mathers had explained to me, and with this hope I plunged without a clue into a labyrinth of images, into that labyrinth that we are warned against in those *Oracles* which antiquity has attributed to Zoroaster, but modern scholarship to some Alexandrian poet: 'Stoop not down to the darkly splendid world wherein lieth continually a faithless depth and Hades wrapped in cloud, delighting in unintelligible images'.[8]

II

I found a supporter at Sligo in my elderly uncle,[9] a man of fifty-three or fifty-four, with the habits of a much older man. He had never left the West of Ireland, except for a few days to London every year, and a single fortnight's voyage to Spain on board a trading schooner, in his boyhood. He was in politics a Unionist and Tory of the most obstinate kind, and knew nothing of Irish literature or history. He

was, however, strangely beset by the romance of Ireland, as he discovered it among the people who served him, sailing upon his ships
or attending to his horses, and, though narrow and obstinate of
opinion, and puritanical in his judgment of life, was perhaps the
most tolerant man I have ever known. He never expected anybody
to agree with him, and if you did not upset his habits by cheating
him over a horse, or by offending his taste, he would think as well
of you as he did of other men, and that was not very well; and help
you out of any scrape whatever. I was accustomed to people much
better read than he, much more liberal-minded, but they had no life
but the intellectual life, and if they and I differed, they could not
take it lightly, and were often angry, and so for years now I had gone
to Sligo, sometimes because I could not afford my Dublin lodging,
but most often for freedom and peace. He would receive me with, 'I
have learned that your friend So-and-so has been seen at the Gre-
sham Hotel talking to Mr. William Redmond. What will not people
do for notoriety?' He considered all Irish Nationalist Members of
Parliament as outside the social pale, but after dinner, when conversation grew intimate, would talk sympathetically of the Fenians in
Ballina, where he spent his early manhood, or of the Fenian priva-
teer that landed the wounded man at Sligo in the 'sixties. When Parnell was contesting an election at Sligo a little before his death, other
Unionist magistrates refused or made difficulties when asked for
some assistance, what I do not remember, made necessary under
election law; and so my uncle gave that assistance. He walked up
and down some Town Hall assembly-room or some court-room
with Parnell, but would tell me nothing of that conversation, except
that Parnell spoke of Gladstone with extravagant hatred.[10] He
would not repeat words spoken by a great man in his bitterness, yet
Parnell at the moment was too angry to care who listened. I knew
one other man who kept as firm a silence; he had attended Parnell's
last public meeting, and after it sat alone beside him, and heard him
speak of the followers that had fallen away, or were showing their
faint hearts; but Parnell was the chief devotion of his life.

When I first began my visits, he had lived in the town itself, and
close to a disreputable neighbourhood called the Burrough, till one
evening, while he sat over his dinner, he heard a man and woman
quarrelling under his window. 'I mind the time', shouted the man,
'when I slept with you and your daughter in the one bed.' My uncle

was horrified, and moved to a little house about a quarter of a mile into the country, where he lived with an old second-sighted servant,[11] and a man-servant to look after the racehorse that was browsing in the neighbouring field, with a donkey to keep it company. His furniture had not been changed since he set up house for himself as a very young man, and in a room opposite his dining-room were the saddles of his youth, and though he would soon give up riding, they would be oiled and the stirrups kept clean and bright till the day of his death. Some love affair had gone wrong when he was a very young man; he had now no interest in women; certainly never sought favour of a woman, and yet he took great care of his appearance. He did not let his beard grow, though he had, or believed that he had, for he was hypochondriacal, a sensitiveness of the skin that forced him to spend an hour in shaving, and he would take to club and dumb-bell if his waist thickened by a hair's breadth, and twenty years after, when a very old man, he had the erect shapely figure of his youth. I often wondered why he went through so much labour, for it was not pride, which had seemed histrionic in his eyes—and certainly he had no vanity; and now, looking back, I am convinced that it was from habit, mere habit, a habit formed when he was a young man, and the best rider of his district.

Probably through long association with Mary Battle, the second-sighted servant, he had come to believe much in the supernatural world, and would tell how several times arriving home with an unexpected guest, he had found the table set for three, and that he himself had dreamed of his brother's illness in Liverpool before he had other news of it. He saw me using images learned from Mathers to start reverie, and, though I held out for a long time, thinking him too old and habit-bound, he persuaded me to tell him their use, and from that on we experimented continually, and after a time I began to keep careful record. In summer he always had the same little house at Rosses Point,[12] and it was at Rosses Point that he first became sensitive to the cabbalistic symbols. There are some high sandhills and low cliffs, and I adopted the practice of walking by the seashore while he walked on cliff or sandhill; I, without speaking, would imagine the symbol, and he would notice what passed before his mind's eye, and in a short time he would practically never fail of the appropriate vision. In the symbols which are used certain colours are classified as 'actives', while certain other colours are 'passives', and I had soon discovered that if I used 'actives' George Pollexfen would see nothing. I therefore gave him exercises to make him sensitive to those colours, and gradually we found ourselves well fitted for this work, and he began to take as lively an interest as was possible to a nature given over to habit in my plans for the Castle on the Rock.

I worked with others, sworn to the scheme for the most part, and I made many curious observations. It was the symbol itself, or, at any rate, not my conscious intention that produced the effect, for if I made an error and told some one to gaze at the wrong symbol—they were painted upon cards—the vision would be suggested by the symbol, not by my thought, or two visions would appear side by side, one from the symbol and one from my thought. When two people, between whose minds there was even a casual sympathy, worked together under the same symbolic influence, the dream or reverie would divide itself between them, each half being the complement of the other; and now and again these complementary dreams, or reveries, would arise spontaneously. I find, for instance, in an old notebook: 'I saw quite suddenly a tent with a wooden badly-carved idol, painted dull red; a man looking like a Red Indian was prostrate before it. The idol was seated to the left. I asked X. what he saw. He saw a most august immense being, glowing with a ruddy opalescent colour, sitting on a throne to the left', or, to summarize from a later notebook, . . . I am meditating in one room and my fellow-student in another, when I see a boat full of tumult and movement on a still sea, and my friend sees a boat with motionless sails upon a tumultuous sea. There was nothing in the originating symbol to suggest a boat.

We never began our work until George's old servant was in her bed; and yet, when we went upstairs to our beds, we constantly heard her crying out with nightmare, and in the morning we would find that her dream echoed our vision. One night, started by what symbol I forget, we had seen an allegorical marriage of Heaven and Earth. When Mary Battle brought in the breakfast next morning, I said, 'Well, Mary, did you dream anything last night?' and she replied (I am quoting from an old notebook) 'indeed she had', and that it was 'a dream she would not have liked to have had twice in one night'. She had dreamed that her bishop, the Catholic bishop of Sligo, had gone away 'without telling anybody', and had married 'a very high-up lady, and she not too young, either'. She had thought in her dream, 'Now all the clergy will get married, and it will be no use going to confession'. There were 'layers upon layers of flowers, many roses, all round the church'.

Another time, when George Pollexfen had seen in answer to some evocation of mine a man with his head cut in two, she woke to find that she 'must have cut her face with a pin, as it was all over blood'. When three or four saw together, the dream or vision would divide itself into three or four parts, each seeming complete in itself, and all fitting together, so that each part was an adaptation of the general meaning to a particular personality. A visionary being would give, let us say, a lighted torch to one, an unlighted candle to another, an unripe fruit to a third, and to the fourth a ripe fruit. At times coherent stories were built up, as if a company of actors were to improvise, and play, not only without previous consultation, but without foreseeing at any moment what would be said or done the moment after. Who made the story? Was it the mind of one of the visionaries? Perhaps, for I have endless proof that, where two worked together, the symbolic influence commonly took upon itself, though no word was spoken, the quality of the mind that had first fixed a symbol in the mind's eye. But, if so, what part of the mind? One friend, in whom the symbolic impulse produced actual trance, described an elaborate and very strange story while the trance was upon him, but upon waking told a story that after a certain point was quite different. 'They gave me a cup of wine, and after that I remembered nothing.' While speaking out of trance he had said nothing of the cup of wine, which must have been offered to a portion of his mind quite early in the dream. Then, too, from whence come the images of the dream? Not always, I was soon persuaded, from the memory, perhaps never in trance or sleep. One man,[13] who certainly thought that Eve's apple was the sort that you got from the greengrocer, and as certainly never doubted its story's literal truth, said, when I used some symbol to send him to Eden, that he saw a walled garden on the top of a high mountain, and in the middle of it a tree with great birds in the branches, and fruit out of which, if you held a fruit to your ear, came the sound of fighting. I had not at the time read Dante's *Purgatorio,* and it caused me some trouble to verify the mountain garden, and, from some passage in the *Zohar,* the great birds among the boughs.[14] A young girl, on being sent to the same garden, heard 'the music of Heaven' from a tree, and on listening with her ear against the trunk, found that it was made by the 'continual clashing of swords'.[15] Whence came that fine thought of music-making swords, that image of the garden, and many like images and thoughts? I had as yet no clear answer, but knew myself face to face with the Anima Mundi[16] described by Platonic philosophers, and more especially in modern times by Henry More, which has a memory independent of embodied individual memories, though they constantly enrich[17] it with their images and their thoughts.

III

At Sligo we walked twice every day, once after lunch and once after dinner, to the same gate on the road to Knocknarea; and at Rosses Point, to the same rock upon the shore; and as we walked we exchanged those thoughts that never rise before me now without bringing some sight of mountain or of shore. Considering that Mary Battle received our thoughts in sleep, though coarsened or turned to caricature, do not the thoughts of the scholar or the hermit, though they speak no word, or something of their shape and impulse, pass into the general mind? Does not the emotion of some woman of fashion, caught in the subtle torture of self-analysing passion, pass down, although she speak no word, to Joan with her Pot, Jill with her Pail and, it may be, with one knows not what nightmare melancholy, to Tom the Fool?[18]

Seeing that a vision could divide itself in divers complementary portions, might not the thought of philosopher or poet or mathematician depend at every moment of its progress upon some complementary thought in minds perhaps at a great distance? Is there nation-wide multiform reverie, every mind passing through a stream of suggestion, and all streams acting and reacting upon one another, no matter how distant the minds, how dumb the lips? A man walked, as it were, casting a shadow, and yet one could never say which was man and which was shadow, or how many the shadows that he cast. Was not a nation, as distinguished from a crowd of chance comers, bound together by this interchange among streams or shadows; that Unity of Image, which I sought in national literature, being but an originating symbol?

From the moment when these speculations grew vivid, I had created for myself an intellectual solitude, most arguments that could influence action had lost something of their meaning. How could I judge any scheme of education, or of social reform, when I could not measure what the different classes and occupations contributed to that invisible commerce of reverie and of sleep; and what is luxury and what necessity when a fragment of gold braid or a flower in the wallpaper may be an originating impulse to revolution or to philosophy? I began to feel myself not only solitary but helpless.

IV

I had not taken up these subjects wilfully, nor through love of strangeness, nor love of excitement, nor because I found myself in some experimental circle, but because unaccountable things had happened even in my childhood, and because of an ungovernable craving. When supernatural events begin, a man first doubts his own testimony, but when they repeat themselves again and again, he doubts all human testimony. At least he knows his own bias, and may perhaps allow for it, but how trust historian and psychologist that have for some three hundred years ignored in writing of the history of the world, or of the human mind, so momentous a part of human experience? What else had they ignored and distorted? When mesmerists first travelled about as public entertainers, a favourite trick was to tell a mesmerized man that some letter of the alphabet had ceased to exist, and after that to make him write his name upon the blackboard. Brown, or Jones, or Robinson would become upon the instant, and without any surprise or hesitation, Rown, or Ones, or Obinson.

Was modern civilization a conspiracy of the subconscious? Did we turn away from certain thoughts and things because the Middle Ages lived in terror of the dark, or had some seminal illusion been imposed upon us by beings greater than ourselves for an unknown purpose? Even when no facts of experience were denied, might not what had seemed logical proof be but a mechanism of change, an automatic impulse? Once in London, at a dinner-party, where all the guests were intimate friends, I had written upon a piece of paper, 'In five minutes York Powell will talk of a burning house', thrust the paper under my neighbour's plate, and imagined my fire symbol, and waited in silence. Powell shifted conversation from topic to topic and within the five minutes was describing a fire he had seen as a young man. When Locke's French translator Coste asked him how, if there were no 'innate ideas', he could explain the skill shown by a bird in making its nest, Locke replied, 'I did not write to explain the actions of dumb creatures', and his translator thought the answer 'very good, seeing that he had named his book *A Philosophical Essay upon Human Understanding*'. Henry More, upon the other hand, considered that the bird's instinct proved the existence of the Anima Mundi, with its ideas and memories. Did modern enlightenment think with Coste that Locke had the better logic, because it was not free to think otherwise?

V

I ceased to read modern books that were not books of imagination, and if some philosophic idea interested me, I tried to trace it back to its earliest use, believing that there must be a tradition of belief older than any European Church, and founded upon the experience of the world before the modern bias. It was this search for a tradition that urged George Pollexfen and myself to study the visions and thoughts of the countrypeople, and some country conversation, repeated by one or the other, often gave us a day's discussion. These visions, we soon discovered, were very like those we called up by symbol. Mary Battle, looking out of the window at Rosses Point, saw coming from Knocknarea, where Queen Maeve, according to local folk-lore, is buried under a great heap of stones, 'the finest woman you ever saw, travelling right across from the mountains and straight to here'.—I quote a record written at the time. 'She looked very strong, but not wicked' (that is to say, not cruel). 'I have seen the Irish Giant' (some big man shown at a fair) 'and though he was a fine man he was nothing to her, for he was round and could not have stepped out so soldierly . . . She had no stomach on her but was slight and broad in the shoulders, and was handsomer than any one you ever saw; she looked about thirty.' And when I asked if she had seen others like her, she said, 'Some of them have their hair down, but they look quite different, more like the sleepy-looking ladies one sees in the papers. Those with their hair up are like this one. The others have long white dresses, but those

with their hair up have short dresses, so that you can see their legs
right up to the calf.' And when I questioned her, I found that they
wore what might well be some kind of buskin. 'They are fine and
dashing-looking, like the men one sees riding their horses in twos
and threes on the slopes of the mountains with their swords swinging. There is no such race living now, none so finely proportioned.
. . . When I think of her and the ladies now they are like little children running about not knowing how to put their clothes on
right . . . why, I would not call them women at all.'[19]

Not at this time, but some three or four years later, when the
visions came without any conscious use of symbol for a short time,
and with much greater vividness, I saw two or three forms of this
incredible beauty, one especially that must always haunt my memory. Then, too, the Master Pilot told us of meeting at night close to
the Pilot House a procession of women in what seemed the costume
of another age. Were they really people of the past, revisiting, perhaps, the places where they lived, or must I explain them, as I
explained that vision of Eden as a mountain garden, by some memory of the race, as distinct from living memory? Certainly these
Spirits, as the countrypeople called them, seemed full of personality; were they not capricious, generous, spiteful, anxious, angry,
and yet did that prove them more than images and symbols? When
I used a combined earth and fire and lunar symbol, my seer, a girl of
twenty-five, saw an obvious Diana and her dogs, about a fire in a
cavern. Presently, judging from her closed eyes, and from the tone
of her voice, that she was in trance, not in reverie, I wished to
lighten the trance a little, and made through carelessness or hasty
thinking a symbol of dismissal; and at once she started and cried
out, 'She says you are driving her away too quickly. You have made
her angry.' Then, too, if my visions had a subjective element, so had
Mary Battle's, for her faeries had but one tune, 'The Distant Waterfall', and she never heard anything described in a sermon at the
Cathedral that she did not 'see it after', and spoke of seeing in this
way the gates of Purgatory.

Furthermore, if my images could affect her dreams, the folk-
images could affect mine in turn, for one night I saw between sleeping and waking a strange long-bodied pair of dogs, one black and
one white, that I found presently in some country tale. How, too,
could one separate the dogs of the country tale from those my uncle

heard bay in his pillow? In order to keep myself from nightmare, I had formed the habit of imagining four watch-dogs, one at each corner of my room, and, though I had not told him or anybody, he said, 'Here is a very curious thing; most nights now, when I lay my head upon the pillow, I hear a sound of dogs baying—the sound seems to come up out of the pillow'. A friend of Strindberg's, in delirium tremens, was haunted by mice, and a friend in the next room heard the squealing of the mice.

VI

I have much evidence that these images, or the symbols that call them up, can influence the bodily health. My uncle told me one evening that there were cases of smallpox—it turned out to be untrue—somewhere under Knocknarea, and that the doctor was coming to vaccinate him. Vaccination, probably from some infection in the lymph, brought on a very serious illness, blood-poisoning I heard it called, and presently he was delirious and a second doctor called in consultation. Between eleven and twelve one night when the delirium was at its height, I sat down beside his bed and said, 'What do you see, George?' He said, 'Red dancing figures', and without commenting, I imagined the cabbalistic symbol of water and almost at once he said, 'There is a river running through the room', and a little later, 'I can sleep now'. I told him what I had done and that, if the dancing figures came again, he was to bid them go in the name of the Archangel Gabriel. Gabriel is angel of the Moon in the Cabbala[20] and might, I considered, command the waters at a pinch. The doctor found him much better and heard that I had driven the delirium away and given him such a word of command that when the red men came again in the middle of the night, they looked greatly startled, and fled.

The doctor came, questioned, and said, 'Well, I suppose it is a kind of hypnotism, but it is very strange, very strange'. The delirium did not return.

VII

To that multiplicity of interest and opinion, of arts and sciences, which had driven me to conceive a Unity of Culture defined and evoked by Unity of Image, I had but added a multiplicity of images, and I was the more troubled because, the first excitement over, I had done nothing to rouse George Pollexfen from the gloom and hypochondria always thickening about him. I asked no help of books, for I believed that the truth I sought would come to me like the subject of a poem, from some moment of passionate experience, and that if I filled my exposition with other men's thought, other men's investigation, I would sink into all that multiplicity of interest and opinion. That passionate experience could never come—of that I was certain—until I had found the right image or right images. From what but the image of Apollo, fixed always in memory and passion, did his priesthood get that occasional power a classical historian has described of lifting great stones and snapping great branches; and did not Gemma Galgani, like many others that had gone before, in 1889 cause deep wounds to appear in her body by contemplating her crucifix? In the essay that Wilde read[21] to me one Christmas Day, occurred these words: 'What does not the world owe to the imitation of Christ, what to the imitation of Caesar?' and I had seen MacGregor Mathers paint little pictures combining the forms of men, animals, and birds, according to a rule which provided a combination for every possible mental condition, and I had heard him say, upon what authority I do not remember, that citizens of ancient Egypt assumed, when in contemplation, the images of their gods.

But now image called up image in an endless procession, and I could not always choose among them with any confidence; and when I did choose, the image lost its intensity, or changed into some other image. I had but exchanged the temptation of Flaubert's *Bouvard et Pécuchet* for that of his *Saint Anthony,* and I was lost in that region a cabbalistic manuscript, shown me by MacGregor Mathers, had warned me of; astray upon the Path of the Chameleon, upon Hodos Chameliontos.[22]

VIII

Now that I am a settled man and have many birds—the canaries have just hatched out five nestlings—I have before me the problem that Locke waved aside. As I gave them an artificial nest, a hollow vessel like a saucer, they had no need of that skill the wild bird shows, each species having its own preference among the lichen, or moss; but they could sort out wool and hair and a certain soft white down that I found under a big tree. They would twist a stem of grass till it was limber, and would wind it all about the centre of the nest, and when the five grey eggs were laid, the mother bird knew how to turn them over from time to time, that they might be warmed evenly; and how long she must leave them uncovered that the white might not be dried up, and when to return that the grow-ing bird might not take cold. Then the young birds, even when they had all their feathers, were very still as compared with the older birds, as though any habit of movement would disturb the nest or make them tumble out. One of them would now and again pass on the food that he had received from his mother's beak to some other nestling. The father had often pecked the mother bird before the eggs were laid, but now, until the last nestling was decently feath-ered, he took his share in the feeding, and was very peaceable, and it was only when the young could be left to feed themselves that he grew jealous and had to be put into another cage.

When I watch my child,[23] who is not yet three years old, I can see so many signs of knowledge from beyond her own mind; why else should she be so excited when a little boy passes outside the win-dow, and take so little interest in a girl; why should she put a cloak about her, and look over her shoulder to see it trailing upon the stairs, as she will some day trail a dress; and why, above all, as she lay against her mother's side, and felt the unborn child moving within, did she murmur, 'Baby, baby'?

When a man writes any work of genius, or invents some creative action, is it not because some knowledge or power has come into his mind from beyond his mind? It is called up by an image, as I think; all my birds' adventures started when I hung a little saucer at one side of the cage, and at the other a bundle of hair and grass; but our images must be given to us, we cannot choose them deliberately.

IX

I know now that revelation is from the self, but from that age-long memoried self, that shapes the elaborate shell of the mollusc and the child in the womb, that teaches the birds to make their nest; and that genius is a crisis that joins that buried self for certain moments to our trivial daily mind. There are, indeed, personifying spirits that we had best call but Gates and Gate-keepers, because through their dramatic power they bring our souls to crisis, to Mask and Image, caring not a straw whether we be Juliet going to her wedding,[24] or Cleopatra to her death; for in their eyes nothing has weight but passion. We have dreamed a foolish dream these many centuries in thinking that they value a life of contemplation, for they scorn that more than any possible life, unless it be but a name for the worst crisis of all. They have but one purpose, to bring their chosen man to the greatest obstacle he may confront without despair. They contrived Dante's banishment,[25] and snatched away his Beatrice, and thrust Villon into the arms of harlots, and sent him to gather cronies at the foot of the gallows, that Dante and Villon might through passion become conjoint to their buried selves, turn all to Mask and Image, and so be phantoms in their own eyes. In great lesser writers like Landor and like Keats we are shown that Image and that Mask as something set apart; Andromeda and her Perseus—though not the sea-dragon[26]—but in a few in whom we recognize supreme masters of tragedy, the whole contest is brought into the circle of their beauty. Such masters—Villon and Dante, let us say—would not, when they speak through their art, change their luck; yet they are mirrored in all the suffering of desire. The two halves of their nature are so completely joined that they seem to labour for their objects, and yet to desire whatever happens, being at the same instant predestinate and free, creation's very self. We gaze at such men in awe, because we gaze not at a work of art, but at the re-creation of the man through that art, the birth of a new species of man, and it may even seem that the hairs of our heads stand up, because that birth, that re-creation, is from terror. Had not Dante and Villon understood that their fate wrecked what life could not rebuild, had they lacked their Vision of Evil, had they cherished any species of optimism, they could but have found a false beauty, or some momentary instinctive beauty, and suffered no change at all, or but changed as do the wild creatures, or from Devil well to Devil sick, and so round the clock.

They and their sort alone earn contemplation, for it is only when the intellect has wrought the whole of life to drama, to crisis, that we may live for contemplation, and yet keep our intensity.

And these things are true also of nations, but the Gate-keepers who drive the nation to war or anarchy that it may find its Image are different from those who drive individual men, though I think at times they work together. And as I look backward upon my own writing, I take pleasure alone in those verses where it seems to me I have found something hard and cold, some articulation of the Image which is the opposite of all that I am in my daily life, and all that my country is; yet man or nation can no more make this Mask or Image[27] than the seed can be made by the soil into which it is cast.

ILLE

What portion in the world can the artist have
Who has awakened from the common dream
But dissipation and despair?

HIC

And yet
No one denies to Keats love of the world;
Remember his deliberate happiness.

ILLE

His art is happy, but who knows his mind?
I see a schoolboy when I think of him
With face and nose pressed to a sweet-shop window,
For certainly he sank into his grave
His senses and his heart unsatisfied,
And made—being poor, ailing and ignorant,
Shut out from all the luxury of the world,
The coarse-bred son of a livery-stable keeper—
Luxuriant song.[28]

BOOK IV

THE TRAGIC GENERATION

I

Two or three years after our return to Bedford Park *A Doll's House* had been played at the Royalty Theatre in Dean Street, the first Ibsen play to be played in England,[1] and somebody had given me a seat for the gallery. In the middle of the first act, while the heroine was asking for macaroons, a middle-aged washerwoman who sat in front of me stood up and said to the little boy at her side, 'Tommy, if you promise to go home straight, we will go now'; and at the end of the play, as I wandered through the entrance hall, I heard an elderly critic murmur, 'A series of conversations terminated by an accident'. I was divided in mind, I hated the play; what was it but Carolus Duran, Bastien-Lepage, Huxley and Tyndall all over again? I resented being invited to admire dialogue so close to modern educated speech that music and style were impossible.

'Art is art because it is not nature', I kept repeating to myself, but how could I take the same side with critic and washerwoman? As time passed Ibsen became in my eyes the chosen author of very clever young journalists, who, condemned to their treadmill of abstraction, hated music and style; and yet neither I nor my generation could escape him because, though we and he had not the same friends, we had the same enemies. I bought his collected works in Mr. Archer's translation[2] out of my thirty shillings a week and carried them to and fro upon my journeys to Ireland and Sligo, and Florence Farr, who had but one great gift, the most perfect poetical elocution, became prominent as an Ibsen actress and had almost a success in *Rosmersholm*,[3] where there is symbolism and a stale odour of spilt poetry. She and I and half our friends found ourselves involved in a quarrel with the supporters of old-fashioned melodrama, and conventional romance, in the support of the new dramatists who wrote in what the daily Press chose to consider the manner of Ibsen. In 1894 she became manageress of the Avenue

Theatre with a play of Dr. Todhunter's, called *The Comedy of Sighs,* and Mr. Bernard Shaw's *Arms and the Man.* She asked me to write a one-act play that her niece, Miss Dorothy Paget, a girl of eight or nine, might make her first stage appearance, and I, with my Irish Theatre in mind, wrote *The Land of Heart's Desire,* in some discomfort when the child was theme, for I knew nothing of children, but with an abundant mind when Mary Bruin was, for I knew an Irish woman[4] whose unrest troubled me. When Florence Farr opened her theatre she had to meet a hostile audience, almost as violent as that Synge met in January 1907, and certainly more brutal, for the Abbey audience had no hatred for the players, and I think but little for Synge himself. Nor had she the certainty of final victory to give her courage, for *The Comedy of Sighs* was a rambling story told with a little paradoxical wit. She had brought the trouble upon herself perhaps, for always in revolt against her own poetical gift, which now seemed obsolete, and against her own Demeter-like face in the mirror, she had tried when interviewed by the Press to shock and startle; and yet, unsure of her own judgment, being out of her own trade, had feared to begin with Shaw's athletic wit; and now outraged convention saw its chance. For two hours and a half, pit and gallery drowned the voices of the players with boos and jeers that were meant to be bitter to the author who sat visible to all in his box surrounded by his family, and to the actress struggling bravely through her weary part; and then pit and gallery went home to spread their lying story that the actress had a fit of hysterics in her dressing-room.

Todhunter had sat on to the end, and there were, I think, four acts of it, listening to the howling of his enemies, while his friends slipped out one by one, till one saw everywhere their empty seats, but nothing could arouse the fighting instincts of that melancholy man. Next day I tried to get him to publish his book of words[5] with satirical designs and illustrations by Beardsley, who was just rising into fame, and an introduction attacking the public, but though petulant and irascible he was incapable of any emotion that could give life to a cause. He shared the superstition still current in the theatre, that the public wants sincere drama, but is kept from it by some conspiracy of managers or newspapers, and could not get out of his head that the actors were to blame. Shaw, whose turn came next, had foreseen all months before, and had planned an opening that would confound his enemies. For the first few minutes *Arms and the Man* is crude melodrama and then just when the audience are thinking how crude it is, it turns into excellent farce. At the dress rehearsal, a dramatist who had his own quarrel with the public, was taken in the noose; at the first laugh he stood up, turned his back on the stage, scowled at the audience, and even when everybody else knew what turn the play had taken, continued to scowl, and order those nearest to be silent.

On the first night the whole pit and gallery, except certain members of the Fabian Society, started to laugh at the author, and then, discovering that they themselves were being laughed at, sat there not converted—their hatred was too bitter for that—but dumbfounded, while the rest of the house cheered and laughed. In the silence that greeted the author after the cry for a speech one man did indeed get his courage and boo loudly. 'I assure the gentleman in the gallery', was Shaw's answer, 'that he and I are of exactly the same opinion, but what can we do against a whole house who are of the contrary opinion?'[6] And from that moment Bernard Shaw became the most formidable man in modern letters, and even the most drunken of medical students knew it. My own play, which had been played with *The Comedy of Sighs,* had roused no passions, but had pleased a sufficient minority for Florence Farr to keep it upon the stage with *Arms and the Man,* and I was in the theatre almost every night for some weeks. 'O yes, the people seem to like *Arms and the Man*', said one of Mr. Shaw's players to me, 'but we have just found out that we are all wrong. Mr. Shaw did really mean it quite seriously, for he has written a letter to say so, and we must not play for laughs any more.' Another night I found the manager triumphant and excited, the Prince of Wales and the Duke of Edinburgh had been there, and the Duke of Edinburgh had spoken his dislike out loud so that the whole stalls could hear, but the Prince of Wales had been 'very pleasant' and 'got the Duke of Edinburgh away as soon as possible'. 'They asked for me', he went on, 'and the Duke of Edinburgh kept on repeating, "The man is mad", meaning Mr. Shaw, and the Prince of Wales asked who Mr. Shaw was, and what he meant by it.'[7] I myself was almost as bewildered, for though I came mainly to see how my own play went, and for the first fortnight to vex my most patient actors with new lines, I listened to *Arms and the Man* with admiration and hatred.[8] It seemed to me inorganic, logical straightness and not the crooked road of life, yet I stood aghast before its energy as to-day before that of the *Stone Drill* by Mr. Epstein or of some design by Mr. Wyndham Lewis.[9] Shaw was right to claim Samuel Butler for his master, for Butler was the first Englishman to make the discovery that it is possible to write with great effect without music, without style, either good or bad, to eliminate from the mind all emotional implication and to prefer plain water to every vintage, so much metropolitan lead and solder to any tendril of the vine. Presently I had a nightmare that I was haunted by a sewing-machine, that clicked and shone, but the incredible thing was that the machine smiled, smiled perpetually. Yet I delighted in Shaw, the formidable man. He could hit my enemies and the enemies of all I loved, as I could never hit, as no living author that was dear to me could ever hit.

Florence Farr's way home was mine also for a part of the way, and it was often of this that we talked, and sometimes, though not always, she would share my hesitations, and for years to come I was to wonder, whenever Shaw became my topic, whether the cock crowed for my blame or for my praise.

II

Shaw and Wilde, had no catastrophe come, would have long divided the stage between them, though they were most unlike—for Wilde believed himself to value nothing but words in their emotional associations, and he had turned his style to a parade as though it were his show, and he Lord Mayor.

I was at Sligo again and I saw the announcement of his action against Lord Queensberry,[10] when starting from my uncle's house to walk to Knocknarea to dine with Cochrane of the Glen, as he was called, to distinguish him from others of that name, an able old man. He had a relation, a poor mad girl, who shared our meals, and at whom I shuddered. She would take a flower from the vase in front of her and push it along the tablecloth towards any male guest who sat near. The old man himself had strange opinions, born not from any mental eccentricity, but from the solitude of his life; and a freedom from all prejudices that were not of his own discovery. 'The world is getting more manly,' he would say, 'it has begun to drink port again', or 'Ireland is going to become prosperous.

Divorced couples now choose Ireland for a retreat, just as before Scotland became prosperous they began to go there. There are a divorced wife and her lover living at the other side of the mountain.' I remember that I spoke that night of Wilde's kindness to myself, said I did not believe him guilty, quoted the psychologist Bain, who has attributed to every sensualist 'a voluminous tenderness',[11] and described Wilde's hard brilliance, his dominating self-possession. I considered him essentially a man of action, that he was a writer by perversity and accident, and would have been more important as soldier or politician; and I was certain that, guilty or not guilty, he would prove himself a man. I was probably excited, and did most of the talking, for if Cochrane had talked, I would have remembered an amusing sentence or two; but he was certainly sympathetic. A couple of days later I received a letter from Lionel Johnson, denouncing Wilde with great bitterness. He had 'a cold scientific intellect'; he got a 'sense of triumph and power, at every dinner-table he dominated, from the knowledge that he was guilty of that sin which, more than any other possible to man, would turn all those people against him if they but knew'. He wrote in the mood of his poem, 'To the Destroyer of a Soul', addressed to Wilde,[12] as I have always believed, though I know nothing of the circumstance that made him write it.

I might have known that Wilde's fantasy had taken some tragic turn, and that he was meditating upon possible disaster, but one took all his words for play—had he not called insincerity 'a mere multiplication of the personality' or some such words? I had met a man who had found him in a barber's shop in Venice, and heard him explain, 'I am having my hair curled that I may resemble Nero'; and when, as editor of an Irish anthology, I had asked leave to quote 'Tread lightly, she is near under the snow',[13] he had written that I might do so if I pleased, but his most characteristic poem was that sonnet with the lines—

> Lo! with a little rod
> I did but touch the honey of romance—
> And must I lose a soul's inheritance?[14]

When in London for my play I had asked news from an actor who had seen him constantly. 'He is in deep melancholy', was the answer. 'He says that he tries to sleep away as much of life as possible, only leaving his bed at two or three in the afternoon, and spending the rest of the day at the Café Royal. He has written what he calls the best short story in the world, and will have it that he repeats to himself on getting out of bed and before every meal: "Christ came from a white plain to a purple city, and as He passed through the first street He heard voices overhead, and saw a young man lying drunk upon a window-sill. 'Why do you waste your soul in drunkenness?' He said. 'Lord, I was a leper and You healed me, what else can I do?' A little further through the town He saw a young man following a harlot, and said, 'Why do you dissolve your soul in debauchery?' and the young man answered, 'Lord, I was blind, and You healed me, what else can I do?' At last in the middle of the city He saw an old man crouching, weeping upon the ground, and when He asked why he wept, the old man answered, 'Lord, I was dead, and You raised me into life, what else can I do but weep?' " '

Wilde published that story[15] a little later, but spoiled it with the verbal decoration of his epoch, and I have to repeat it to myself as I first heard it, before I can see its terrible beauty. I no more doubt its sincerity than I doubt that his parade of gloom, all that late rising and sleeping away his life, that elaborate playing with tragedy, was an attempt to escape from an emotion by its exaggeration. He had three successful plays running at once; he had been almost poor, and now, his head full of Flaubert, found himself with ten thousand a year:—'Lord, I was dead, and You raised me into life, what else can I do but weep?' A comedian, he was in the hands of those dramatists who understand nothing but tragedy.

A few days after the first production of my *Land of Heart's Desire*, I had my last conversation with him. He had come into the theatre as the curtain fell upon my play, and I knew that it was to ask my pardon that he overwhelmed me with compliments; and yet I wonder if he would have chosen those precise compliments, or spoken so extravagantly, but for the turn his thoughts had taken: 'Your story in the *National Observer*, 'The Crucifixion of the Outcast', is sublime, wonderful, wonderful'.[16]

Some business or other brought me to London once more and I asked various Irish writers for letters of sympathy, and I was refused by none but Edward Dowden, who gave me what I considered an irrelevant excuse—his dislike for everything that Wilde had written. I heard that Wilde was at his mother's house in Oakley Street,[17] and I called there, but the Irish servant said, her face drawn and tragic as in the presence of death, that he was not there, but that I could see his brother. Willie Wilde received me with, 'Who are you; what do you want?' but became all friendship when I told him that I had brought letters of sympathy. He took the bundle of letters in his hand, but said, 'Do these letters urge him to run away? Every friend he has is urging him to, but we have made up our minds that he must stay and take his chance.' 'No,' I said, 'I certainly do not think that he should run away, nor do those letters advise it.' 'Letters from Ireland', he said. 'Thank you, thank you. He will be glad to get those letters, but I would keep them from him if they advised him to run away.' Then he threw himself back in his chair and began to talk with incoherent emotion, and in phrases that echoed now and again his brother's style at its worst; there were tears in his eyes, and he was, I think, slightly intoxicated. 'He could escape, O yes, he could escape—there is a yacht in the Thames, and five thousand pounds to pay his bail—well, not exactly in the Thames, but there is a yacht—O yes, he could escape, even if I had to inflate a balloon in the back-yard with my own hand, but he has resolved to stay, to face it out, to stand the music like Christ. You must have heard—it is not necessary to go into detail—that he and I have not been friends; but he came to me like a wounded stag, and I took him in.' 'After his release'—after he had been bailed out, I suppose—'Stewart Headlam engaged a room at an hotel and brought him there under another name, but the manager came up and said, "Are you Mr. Wilde?" You know what my brother is, you know how he would answer that. He said, "Yes, I am Oscar Wilde", and the manager said he must not stay. The same thing happened in hotel after hotel, and at last he made up his mind to come here. It is his vanity that has brought all this disgrace upon him; they swung incense before him.' He dwelt upon the rhythm of the words as his brother would have done—'They swung it before his heart'. His first emotion at the thought of the letters over, he became more simple, and explained that his brother considered that his crime was not the vice itself, but that he should have brought such misery upon his wife and children, and that he was bound to accept any chance, however slight, to re-establish his position. 'If he is acquitted', he said, 'he will stay out of England for a few years, and can then gather his friends about him once more—even if he is condemned he will purge his offence—but if he runs away he will lose every friend that he has.' I heard later, from whom I forget now, that Lady Wilde had said, 'If you stay, even if you go to prison, you will always be my son, it will make no difference to my affection, but if you go, I will never speak to you again'. While I was there, some woman who had just seen him—Willie Wilde's wife, I think—came in, and threw herself in a chair, and said in an exhausted voice, 'It is all right now, he has made up his mind to go to prison if necessary'. Before his release, two years later, his brother and mother were dead, and a little later his wife, struck by paralysis during his imprisonment, I think, was dead, too;[18] and he himself, his constitution ruined by prison life, followed quickly; but I have never doubted, even for an instant, that he made the right decision, and that he owes to that decision half of his renown.

Cultivated London, that before the action against Lord Queensberry had mocked his pose and his affected style, and refused to acknowledge his wit, was now full of his advocates, though I did not meet a single man who considered him innocent. One old enemy of his overtook me in the street and began to praise his audacity, his self-possession. 'He has made', he said, 'of infamy a new Thermopylae.' I had written in reply to Lionel Johnson's letter that I regretted Wilde's downfall but not that of his imitators, but Johnson had changed with the rest. 'Why do you not regret the fall of Wilde's imitators?'—I had but tried to share what I thought his opinion—'They were worthless, but should have been left to criticism'. Wilde himself was a martyr in his eyes, and when I said that tragedy might give his art a greater depth, he would not even grant a martyr's enemies that poor merit, and thought Wilde would produce, when it was all over, some comedy exactly like the others, writing from an art where events could leave no trace. Everywhere one met writers and artists who praised his wit and eloquence in the witness-box, or repeated some private saying. Willie Redmond told of finding him, to his astonishment, at the conversazione of some theatrical society, standing amid an infuriated crowd, mocking with more than all his old satirical wit the actors and their country. He had said to a well-known painter during one or other of the trials, 'My poor brother writes to me that he is defending me all over London; my poor, dear brother, he could compromise a steam-engine'.

His brother, too, had suffered a change, for, if rumour did not wrong him, the 'wounded stag' had not been at all graciously received. 'Thank God my vices were decent', had been his comment, and refusing to sit at the same table, he had dined at some neighbouring hotel at his brother's expense. His successful brother who had scorned him for a drunken ne'er-do-well was now at his mercy, and besides, he probably shared, until tragedy awoke another self, the rage and contempt that filled the crowds in the street, and all men and women who had an over-abundant normal sexual instinct. 'Wilde will never lift his head again,' said the art critic, Gleeson White, 'for he has against him all men of infamous life.' When the verdict was announced the harlots in the street outside danced upon the pavement.

III

Somewhere about 1450, though later in some parts of Europe by a hundred years or so, and in some earlier, men attained to personality in great numbers, 'Unity of Being', and became like 'a perfectly proportioned human body', and as men so fashioned held places of power, their nations had it too, prince and ploughman sharing that thought and feeling. What afterwards showed for rifts and cracks were there already, but imperious impulse held all together. Then the scattering came, the seeding of the poppy, bursting of pea-pod, and for a time personality seemed but the stronger for it. Shakespeare's people make all things serve their passion, and that passion is for the moment the whole energy of their being—birds, beasts, men, women, landscape, society, are but symbols and metaphors, nothing is studied in itself, the mind is a dark well, no surface, depth only. The men that Titian painted, the men that Jongsen painted, even the men of Van Dyck seemed at moments like great hawks at rest. In the Dublin National Gallery there hung, perhaps there still hang, upon the same wall, a portrait of some Venetian gentleman by Strozzi, and Mr. Sargent's painting of President Wilson.[19] Whatever thought broods in the dark eyes of that Venetian gentleman has drawn its life from his whole body; it feeds upon it as the flame feeds upon the candle—and should that thought be changed, his pose would change, his very cloak would rustle, for his whole body thinks. President Wilson lives only in the eyes, which are steady and intent; the flesh about the mouth is dead, and the hands are dead, and the clothes suggest no movement of his body, nor any movement but that of the valet, who has brushed and folded in mechanical routine. There all was an energy flowing outward from the nature itself; here all is the anxious study and slight deflection of external force; there man's mind and body were predominantly subjective; here all is objective, using those words not as philosophy uses them, but as we use them in conversation.

The bright part of the moon's disk, to adopt the symbolism of a certain poem,[20] is subjective mind, and the dark, objective mind, and we have eight-and-twenty Phases for our classification of mankind, and of the movement of its thought. At the first Phase— the night where there is no moonlight—all is objective, while when, upon the fifteenth night, the moon comes to the full, there is only subjective mind. The mid-Renaissance could but approximate to the full moon, 'For there's no human life at the full or the dark', but we may attribute to the next three nights of the moon the men of Shakespeare, of Titian, of Strozzi, and of Van Dyck, and watch them grow more reasonable, more orderly, less turbulent, as the nights pass; and it is well to find before the fourth—the nineteenth night counting from the start—a sudden change, as when a cloud becomes rain, or water freezes, for the great transitions are sudden; popular, typical men have grown more ugly and more argumentative; the face that Van Dyck called a fatal face[21] has faded before Cromwell's[22] warty opinionated head. Henceforth no mind made like 'a perfectly proportioned human body' shall sway the public, for great men must live in a portion of themselves, become professional and abstract; but seeing that the moon's third quarter is scarce passed; that abstraction has attained but not passed its climax; that a half, as I affirm it, of the twenty-second night still lingers, they may subdue and conquer, cherish even some Utopian dream, spread abstraction ever further till thought is but a film, and there is no dark depth any more, surface only. But men who belong by nature to the nights near to the full are still born, a tragic minority, and how shall they do their work when too ambitious for a private station, except as Wilde of the nineteenth Phase,[23] as my symbolism has it, did his work? He understood his weakness, true personality was impossible, for that is born in solitude, and at his moon one is not solitary; he must project himself before the eyes of others, and, having great ambition, before some great crowd of eyes; but there is no longer any great crowd that cares for his true thought. He must humour and cajole and pose, take worn-out stage situations, for he knows that he may be as romantic as he please, so long as he does not believe in his romance, and all that he may get their ears for a few strokes of contemptuous wit in which he does believe.

We Rhymers did not humour and cajole; but it was not wholly from demerit, it was in part because of different merit, that he refused our exile. Shaw, as I understand him, has no true quarrel with his time, its moon and his almost exactly coincide. He is quite content to exchange Narcissus and his Pool for the signal-box at a railway junction, where goods and travellers pass perpetually upon their logical glittering road. Wilde was a monarchist, though content that monarchy should turn demagogue for its own safety, and he held a theatre by the means whereby he held a London dinner-table. 'He who can dominate a London dinner-table', he had boasted, 'can dominate the world.' While Shaw has but carried his street-corner Socialist eloquence on to the stage, and in him one discovers, in his writing and his public speech, as once—before their outline had been softened by prosperity or the passage of the years—in his clothes and in his stiff joints, the civilization that Sargent's picture has explored. Neither his crowd nor he have yet made a discovery that brought President Wilson so near his death, that the moon draws to its fourth quarter. But what happens to the individual man whose moon has come to that fourth quarter, and what to the civilization . . . ?

I can but remember pipe music to-night, though I can half-hear beyond it in the memory a weightier music, but this much at any rate is certain—the dream of my early manhood, that a modern nation can return to Unity of Culture, is false; though it may be we can achieve it for some small circle of men and women, and there leave it till the moon bring round its century.

> The cat went here and there
> And the moon spun round like a top,
> And the nearest kin of the moon,
> The creeping cat, looked up.

.   .   .   .   .

Minnaloushe creeps through the grass
From moonlit place to place,
The sacred moon overhead
Has taken a new phase.
Does Minnaloushe know that his pupils
Will pass from change to change,
And that from round to crescent,
From crescent to round they range?
Minnaloushe creeps through the grass
Alone, important and wise,
And lifts to the changing moon
His changing eyes.[24]

IV

Henley's troubles and infirmities were growing upon him. He, too, an ambitious, formidable man, who showed alike in his practice and in his theory—in his lack of sympathy for Rossetti and Landor, for instance—that he never understood how small a fragment of our own nature can be brought to perfect expression, nor that even but with great toil, in a much divided civilization; though, doubtless, if our own Phase be right, a fragment may be an image of the whole, the moon's still scarce-crumbled image, as it were, in a glass of wine. He would be, and have all poets be, a true epitome of the whole mass, a Herrick and Dr. Johnson in the same body, and because this—not so difficult before the Mermaid closed its door—is no longer possible, his work lacks music, is abstract, as even an actor's movement can be when the thought of doing is plainer to his mind than the doing itself: the straight line from cup to lip, let us say, more plain than the hand's own sensation weighed down by that heavy spillable cup. I think he was content when he had called before our eyes—before the too understanding eyes of his chosen crowd the violent burly man that he had dreamed, content with the mere suggestion, and so did not work long enough at his verses. He disliked Victor Hugo as much as he did Rossetti, and yet Rossetti's translation from *Les Burgraves*, because of its mere technical mastery, out-sings Henley in his own song:

My mother is dead; God's patience wears;
It seems my Chaplain will not have done.
Love on: who cares?
Who cares? Love on.[25]

I can read his poetry with emotion, but I read it for some glimpse of what he might have been as Border balladist, or Cavalier,[26] or of what he actually was, not as poet but as man. He had what Wilde lacked, even in his ruin, passion, was maybe as passionate as some great man of action, as Parnell, let us say. When he and Stevenson quarrelled,[27] he cried over it with some woman or other, and his notorious article was but for vengeance upon Mrs. Stevenson, who had arranged for the public eye what he considered an imaginary figure, with no resemblance to the gay companion who had founded his life, to that life's injury, upon 'the august, the immortal Musketeers'. She had caused the quarrel, as he believed, and now she had robbed him over again by blotting from the world's memory the friend of his youth; and because he believed in the robbery I read those angry exaggerated paragraphs with deep sympathy; and I think that the man who has left them out of Henley's collected writings has wronged his memory, as Mrs. Stevenson may have wronged that of Stevenson.

He was no contemplative man, no pleased possessor of wooden models, and paper patterns, but a great passionate man, and no friend of his would have him pictured otherwise. I saw little of him in later years, but I doubt if he was ever the same after the death of his six-year-old daughter.[28] Few passages of his verse touch me as do those few mentions of her though they lack precision of word and sound. When she is but a hope, he prays that she may have his 'gift of life' and his wife's 'gift of love', and when she is but a few months old he murmurs over her sleep:

When you wake in your crib,
You, an inch of experience—
Vaulted about
With the wonder of darkness;
Wailing and striving
To reach from your feebleness
Something you feel
Will be good to and cherish you.[29]

And now he commends some friend 'boyish and kind, and shy', who greeted him, and greeted his wife, 'that day we brought our Beautiful One to lie in the green peace', and who is now dead himself; and after that he speaks of love 'turned of death to longing'[30] and so to an enemy.

When I spoke to him of his child's death he said, 'She was a person of genius; she had the genius of the mind, and the genius of the body'. And later I heard him talk of her as a man talks of something he cannot keep silence over because it is in all his thoughts. I can remember, too, his talking of some book of natural history he had read, that he might be able to answer her questions.

He had a house now at Mortlake on the Thames with a great ivy-tod shadowing door and window, and one night there he shocked and startled a roomful of men by showing that he could be swept beyond our reach in reveries of affection. The dull man, who had tried to put Wilde out of countenance, suddenly said to the whole room, roused by I cannot remember what incautious remark meant for the man at my side, 'Yeats believes in magic; what nonsense!' Henley said, 'No, it may not be nonsense; black magic is all the go in Paris now'. And then turning towards me with a changed sound in his voice, 'It is just a game, isn't it?' I replied, not noticing till too late his serious tone, and wishing to avoid discussion in the dull man's company, 'One has had a vision; one wants to have another, that is all'. Then Henley said, speaking in a very low voice, 'I want to know how I am to get to my daughter. I was sitting here the other night when she came into the room and played round the table and went out again. Then I saw that the door was shut and I knew that I had seen a vision.' There was an embarrassed silence, and then somebody spoke of something else and we began to discuss it hurriedly and eagerly.

V

I came now to be more in London, never missing the meetings of the Rhymers' Club, nor those of the council of the Irish Literary Society, where I constantly fought out our Irish quarrels and pressed upon the unwilling Gavan Duffy the books of our new movement. The Irish members of Parliament looked upon us with some hostility because we had made it a matter of principle never to put a politician in the chair, and upon other grounds. One day, some old Irish member of Parliament made perhaps his only appearance at a gathering of members. He recited with great emotion a ballad of his own composition in the manner of Young Ireland, repeating over his sacred names, Wolfe Tone, Emmet, and Owen Roe,[31] and mourning that new poets and new movements should have taken something of their sacredness away. The ballad had no literary merit, but I went home with a troubled conscience; and for a dozen years perhaps, till I began to see the result of our work in a deepened perception of all those things that strengthen race, that trouble remained. I had in mind that old politician as I wrote but the other day—

> Our part
> To murmur name upon name
> As a mother names her child.[32]

The Rhymers had begun to break up in tragedy, though we did not know that till the play had finished. I have never found a full explanation of that tragedy; sometimes I have remembered that, unlike the Victorian poets, almost all were poor men, and had made it a matter of conscience to turn from every kind of money-making that prevented good writing, and that poverty meant strain, and, for the most part, a refusal of domestic life. Then I have remembered that Johnson had private means, and that others who came to tragic ends had wives and families. Another day I think that perhaps our form of lyric, our insistence upon emotion which has no relation to any public interest, gathered together overwrought, unstable men; and remember, the moment after, that the first to go out of his mind had no lyrical gift, and that we valued him mainly because he seemed a witty man of the world; and that a little later another who seemed, alike as man and writer, dull and formless, went out of his mind, first burning poems which I cannot believe would have proved him, as the one man who saw them claims, a man of genius. The meetings were always decorous and often dull; some one would read out a poem and we would comment, too politely for the criticism to have great value; and yet that we read out our poems, and thought that they could be so tested, was a definition of our aims. 'Love's Nocturne' is one of the most beautiful poems in the world, but no one can find out its beauty, so intricate its thought and metaphor, till he has read it over several times, or stopped several times to re-read a passage; and the 'Faustine' of Swinburne, where much is powerful and musical, could not, were it read out, be understood with pleasure, however clearly it were read, because it has no more logical structure than a bag of shot. I shall, however, remember all my life that evening when Lionel Johnson read or spoke aloud in his musical monotone, where meaning and cadence found the most precise elocution, his poem suggested 'by the Statue of King Charles at Charing Cross'. It was as though I listened to a great speech. Nor will that poem be to me again what it was that first night. For long I only knew Dowson's 'O Mors', to quote but the first words of its long title, and his 'Villanelle of Sunset' from his reading, and it was because of the desire to hold them in my hand that I suggested the first *Book of The Rhymers' Club*.[33] They were not speech but perfect song, though song for the speaking voice. It was perhaps our delight in poetry that was, before all else, speech or song, and could hold the attention of a fitting audience like a good play or good conversation, that made Francis Thompson, whom we admired so much—before the publication of his first poem I had brought to the Cheshire Cheese the proof-sheets of his 'Ode to the Setting Sun',[34] his first published poem—come but once and refuse to contribute to our book. Preoccupied with his elaborate verse, he may have seen only that which we renounced, and thought what seemed to us simplicity, mere emptiness. To some members this simplicity was perhaps created by their tumultuous lives, they praised a desired woman and hoped that she would find amid their praise her very self, or at worst their very passion; and knew that she, ignoramus that she was, would have slept in the middle of 'Love's Nocturne',[35] lofty and tender though it be. Woman herself was still in our eyes, for all that, romantic and mysterious, still the priestess of her shrine, our emotions remembering the *Lilith* and the *Sibylla Palmifera* of Rossetti;[36] for as yet that sense of comedy which was soon to mould the very fashion-plates, and, in the eyes of men of my generation, to destroy at last the sense of beauty itself, had scarce begun to show here and there, in slight subordinate touches, among the designs of great painters and craftsmen. It could not be otherwise, for Johnson's favourite phrase, that life is ritual, expressed something that was in some degree in all our thoughts, and how could life be ritual if woman had not her symbolical place?

If Rossetti was a subconscious influence, and perhaps the most powerful of all, we looked consciously to Pater for our philosophy. Three or four years ago I re-read *Marius the Epicurean*, expecting to find I cared for it no longer, but it still seemed to me, as I think it seemed to us all, the only great prose in modern English, and yet I began to wonder if it, or the attitude of mind of which it was the noblest expression, had not caused the disaster of my friends. It taught us to walk upon a rope tightly stretched through serene air, and we were left to keep our feet upon a swaying rope in a storm. Pater had made us learned; and, whatever we might be elsewhere, ceremonious and polite, and distant in our relations to one another, and I think none knew as yet that Dowson, who seemed to drink so little and had so much dignity and reserve, was breaking his heart for the daughter of the keeper of an Italian eating-house,[37] in dissipation and drink; and that he might that very night sleep upon a sixpenny bed in a doss-house. It seems to me that even yet, and I am speaking of 1894 and 1895, we knew nothing of one another but the poems that we read and criticized; perhaps I have forgotten or was too much in Ireland for knowledge, but of this I am certain, we shared nothing but the artistic life. Sometimes Johnson and Symons would visit our sage at Oxford, and I remember Johnson, whose reports, however, were not always to be trusted, returning with a sentence that long ran in my head. He had noticed books on political economy among Pater's books, and Pater had said, 'Everything that has occupied man, for any length of time, is worthy of our study'. Perhaps it was because of Pater's influence that we, with an affectation of learning, claimed the whole past of literature for our authority, instead of finding it, like the young men in the age of comedy that followed us, in some new, and so still unrefuted authority; that we preferred what seemed still uncrumbled rock to the still unspotted foam; that we were traditional alike in our dress, in our manner, in our opinions, and in our style.

Why should men who spoke their opinions in low voices, as though they feared to disturb the readers in some ancient library, and timidly as though they knew that all subjects had long since been explored, all questions long since decided in books whereon the dust settled, live lives of such disorder and seek to rediscover in verse the syntax of impulsive common life? Was it that we lived in what is called 'an age of transition' and so lacked coherence, or did we but pursue antithesis?

VI

All things, apart from love and melancholy, were a study to us: Horne, already learned in Botticelli, had begun to boast that when he wrote of him there would be no literature, all would be but learning; Symons, as I wrote when I first met him, studied the music-halls as he might have studied the age of Chaucer; while I gave much time to what is called the Christian Cabbala;[38] nor was there any branch of knowledge Johnson[39] did not claim for his own. When I had first gone to see him in 1888 or 1889, at the Charlotte Street house, I had called about five in the afternoon, but the man-servant that he shared with Horne and Image told me that he was not yet up, adding with effusion, 'He is always up for dinner at seven'. This habit of breakfasting when others dined had been started by insomnia, but he came to defend it for its own sake. When I asked if it did not separate him from men and women he replied, 'In my library I have all the knowledge of the world that I need'. He had certainly a considerable library, far larger than that of any young man of my acquaintance, so large that he wondered if it might not be possible to find some way of hanging new shelves from the ceiling like chandeliers. That room was always a pleasure to me, with its curtains of grey corduroy over door and window and book-case, and its walls covered with brown paper, a fashion invented, I think, by Horne, that was soon to spread. There was a portrait of Cardinal Newman, looking a little like Johnson himself, some religious picture by Simeon Solomon, and works upon theology in Greek and Latin and a general air of neatness and severity; and talking there by candlelight it never seemed very difficult to murmur Villiers de l'Isle-Adam's proud words, 'As for living, our servants will do that for us'.[40] Yet I can now see that Johnson himself in some half-conscious part of him desired the world he had renounced. I was often puzzled as to when and where he could have met the famous men or beautiful women whose conversation, often wise, and always appropriate, he quoted so often, and it was not till a little before his death that I discovered that these conversations were imaginary. He never altered a detail of speech, and would quote what he had invented for Gladstone or Newman for years without amplification or amendment, with what seemed a scholar's accuracy. His favourite quotations were from Newman, whom, I believe, he had never met, though I can remember nothing now but Newman's greeting to Johnson, 'I have always considered the profession of a man of letters a third order of the priesthood!' and these quotations became so well known that, at Newman's death, the editor of the *Nineteenth Century* asked them for publication. Because of his delight in all that was formal and arranged he objected to the public quotation of private conversation even after death, and this scruple helped his refusal. Perhaps this dreaming was made a necessity by his artificial life, yet before that life began he wrote from Oxford to his Tory but flattered family, that as he stood mounted upon a library ladder in his rooms taking a book from a shelf, Gladstone, about to pass the open door on his way upstairs to some college authority, had stopped, hesitated, come into the room and there spent an hour of talk. Presently it was discovered that Gladstone had not been near Oxford on the date given; yet he quoted that conversation without variation of a word until the end of his life, and, I think, believed in it as firmly as did his friends. These conversations were always admirable in their drama, but never too dramatic or even too polished to lose their casual accidental character; they were the phantasmagoria through which his philosophy of life found its expression. If he made his knowledge of the world out of his fantasy, his knowledge of tongues and books was certainly very great; and yet was that knowledge as great as he would have us believe? Did he really know Welsh, for instance, had he really, as he told me, made his only love-song, his incomparable 'Morfydd', out of three lines in Welsh, heard sung by a woman at her door on a walking tour in Wales, or did he but wish to hide that he shared in their emotion?

> O, what are the winds?
> And what are the waters?
> Mine are your eyes.[41]

He wanted us to believe that all things, his poetry with its Latin weight, his religion with its constant reference to the Fathers of the Church, or to the philosophers of the Church, almost his very courtesy, were a study and achievement of the intellect. Arthur Symons' poetry made him angry, because it would substitute for that achievement Parisian impressionism, 'a London fog, the blurred tawny lamplight, the red omnibus, the dreary rain, the depressing mud, the glaring gin-shop, the slatternly shivering women, three dexterous stanzas telling you that and nothing more'. I, on the other hand, angered him by talking as if art existed for emotion only, and for refutation he would quote the close of the Aeschylean Trilogy,[42] the trial of Orestes on the Acropolis. Yet at moments the thought came to him that intellect, as he conceived it, was too much a thing of many books, that it lacked lively experience. 'Yeats,' he said to me, 'you need ten years in a library, but I have need of ten years in the wilderness.' When he said 'wilderness' I am certain, however, that he thought of some historical, some bookish desert, the Thebaid,[43] or the lands about the Mareotic Sea.[44] Though his best poetry is natural and impassioned, he spoke little of it, but much about his prose, and would contend that I had no right to consider words made to read less natural than words made to be spoken; and he delighted in a sentence in his book on Thomas Hardy, that kept its vitality, as he contended, though two pages long. He punctuated after the manner of the seventeenth century and was always ready to spend an hour discussing the exact use of the colon. 'One should use a colon where other people use a semi-colon, a semi-colon where other people use a comma', was, I think, but a condescension to my ignorance, for the matter was plainly beset with many subtleties.

VII

Not till some time in 1895 did I think he could ever drink too much for his sobriety—though what he drank would certainly be too much for that of most of the men whom I knew—I no more doubted his self-control, though we were very intimate friends, than I doubted his memories of Cardinal Newman. The discovery that he did was a great shock to me, and, I think, altered my general view of the world. I had, by my friendship with O'Leary, by my fight against Gavan Duffy, drawn the attention of a group of men who at that time controlled what remained of the old Fenian movement in England and Scotland; and at a moment when an attempt, that came to nothing, was being made to combine once more our constitutional and unconstitutional politics, I had been asked to represent this group at some convention in the United States.[45] I went to consult Johnson, whom I found sitting at a table with books about him. I was greatly tempted, because I was promised complete freedom of speech; and I was at the time enraged by some wild articles published by some Irish-American newspaper, suggesting the burning down of the houses of Irish landlords. Nine years later I was lecturing in America,[46] and a charming old Irishman came to see me with an interview to write, and we spent, and as I think in entire neglect of his interview, one of the happiest hours I have ever spent, comparing our tales of the Irish faeries, in which he very firmly believed. When he had gone I looked at his card, to discover that he was the writer of that criminal incitement. I told Johnson that if I had a week to decide in I would probably decide to go, but as they had only given me three days, I had refused. He would not hear of my refusal with so much awaiting my condemnation; and that condemnation would be effective with Catholics, for he would find me passages in the Fathers condemning every kind of political crime, that of the dynamiter and the incendiary especially. I asked how could the Fathers have condemned weapons they had never heard of, but those weapons, he contended, were merely developments on old methods and weapons; they had decided all in principle; but I need not trouble myself about the matter, for he would put into my hands before I sailed the typewritten statement of their doctrine, dealing with the present situation in the utmost detail. He seemed perfectly logical, though a little more confident and impassioned than usual, and I had, I think, promised to accept—when he rose from his chair, took a step towards me in his eagerness, and fell on to the floor; and I saw that he was drunk. From that on, he began to lose control of his life; he shifted from Charlotte Street, where, I think, there was fear that he would overset lamp or candle and burn the house, to Gray's Inn, and from Gray's Inn to old rambling rooms in Lincoln's Inn Fields, and at last one called to find his outer door shut, the milk on the doorstep sour. Sometimes I would urge him to put himself, as Jack Nettleship had done, into an Institute. One day when I had been very urgent, he spoke of 'a craving that made every atom of his body cry out' and said the moment after, 'I do not want to be cured', and a moment after that, 'In ten years I shall be penniless and shabby, and borrow half-crowns from friends'. He seemed to contemplate a vision that gave him pleasure, and now that I look back, I remember that he once said to me that Wilde's pleasure and excitement were perhaps increased by the degradation of that group of beggars and black-mailers where he sought his pathics, and I remember, too, his smile at my surprise, as though he spoke of psychological depths I could never enter. Did the austerity, the melancholy of his thoughts, that spiritual ecstasy which he touched at times, heighten, as comple-mentary colours heighten one another, not only the Vision of Evil, but its fascination? Was it only Villon, or did Dante also feel the fas-cination of evil, when shown in its horror, and, as it were, judged and lost; and what proud man does not feel temptation strength-ened from the certainty that his intellect is not deceived?

VIII

I began now to hear stories of Dowson,[47] whom I knew only at the Rhymers', or through some chance meeting at Johnson's. I was indolent and procrastinating, and when I thought of asking him to dine, or taking some other step towards better knowledge, he seemed to be in Paris, or at Dieppe. He was drinking, but, unlike Johnson, who, at the autopsy after his death, was discovered never to have grown, except in the brain, after his fifteenth year, he was full of sexual desire. Johnson and he were close friends, and John-son lectured him out of the Fathers upon chastity, and boasted of the great good done him thereby. But the rest of us counted the glasses emptied in their talk. I began to hear now in some detail of the restaurant-keeper's daughter,[48] and of her marriage to the waiter, and of that weekly game of cards with her that filled so great a share of Dowson's emotional life. Sober, he would look at no other woman, it was said, but, drunk, desired whatever woman chance brought, clean or dirty.

Johnson was stern by nature, strong by intellect, and always, I think, deliberately picked his company, but Dowson seemed gentle, affectionate, drifting. His poetry shows how sincerely he felt the fascination of religion, but his religion had certainly no dogmatic outline, being but a desire for a condition of virginal ecstasy. If it is true, as Arthur Symons, his very close friend, has written, that he loved the restaurant-keeper's daughter for her youth, one may be almost certain that he sought from religion some similar quality, something of that which the angels find who move perpetually, as Swedenborg has said, towards 'the day-spring of their youth'.[49] Johnson's poetry, like Johnson himself before his last decay, conveys an emotion of joy, of intellectual clearness, of hard energy; he gave us of his triumph: while Dowson's poetry is sad, as he himself seemed, and pictures his life of temptation and defeat:

> Unto us they belong,
> Us the bitter and gay,
> Wine and women and song.[50]

Their way of looking at their intoxication showed their characters. Johnson, who could not have written 'The Dark Angel'[51] if he did not suffer from remorse, showed to his friends an impenitent face, and defeated me when I tried to prevent the foundation of an Irish convivial club—it was brought to an end after one meeting by the indignation of the members' wives—whereas the last time I saw Dowson he was pouring out a glass of whiskey for himself in an empty corner of my room and murmuring over and over in what seemed automatic apology, 'The first to-day'.

IX

Two men are always at my side, Lionel Johnson and John Synge whom I was to meet a little later; but Johnson is to me the more vivid in memory, possibly because of the external finish, the clearly-marked lineaments of his body, which seemed but to express the clarity of his mind. I think Dowson's best verse immortal, bound, that is, to outlive famous novels and plays and learned histories and other discursive things, but he was too vague and gentle for my affections. I understood him too well, for I had been like him but for the appetite that made me search out strong condiments. Though I cannot explain what brought others of my generation to such misfortune, I think that (falling backward upon my parable of the moon) I can explain some part of Dowson's and Johnson's dissipation:

> What portion in the world can the artist have
> Who has awakened from the common dream
> But dissipation and despair?[52]

When Edmund Spenser described the islands of Phaedria and of Acrasia[53] he aroused the indignation of Lord Burleigh, that 'rugged forehead', and Lord Burleigh was in the right if morality were our only object.

In those islands certain qualities of beauty, certain forms of sensuous loveliness were separated from all the general purposes of life, as they had not been hitherto in European literature—and would not be again, for even the historical process has its ebb and flow, till Keats wrote his 'Endymion'. I think that the movement of our thought has more and more so separated certain images and regions of the mind, and that these images grow in beauty as they grow in sterility. Shakespeare leaned, as it were, even as craftsman, upon the general fate of men and nations, had about him the excitement of the playhouse; and all poets, including Spenser in all but a few pages, until our age came, and when it came almost all, have had some propaganda or traditional doctrine to give companionship with their fellows. Had not Matthew Arnold his faith in what he described as the best thought of his generation,[54] Browning his psychological curiosity, Tennyson, as before him Shelley and Wordsworth, moral values that were not aesthetic values? But Coleridge of the 'Ancient Mariner', and 'Kubla Khan', and Rossetti in all his writings, made what Arnold has called that 'morbid effort', that search for 'perfection of thought and feeling, and to unite this to perfection of form',[55] sought this new, pure beauty, and suffered in their lives because of it. The typical men of the classical age (I think of Commodus, with his half-animal beauty, his cruelty, and his caprice) lived public lives, pursuing curiosities of appetite, and so found in Christianity, with its Thebaid and its Mareotic Sea, the needed curb. But what can the Christian confessor say to those who more and more must make all out of the privacy of their thought, calling up perpetual images of desire, for he cannot say, 'Cease to be artist, cease to be poet', where the whole life is art and poetry, nor can he bid men leave the world, who suffer from the terrors that pass before shut eyes. Coleridge, and Rossetti, though his dull brother[56] did once persuade him that he was an agnostic, were devout Christians, and Stenbock and Beardsley were so towards their lives' end, and Dowson and Johnson always, and yet I think it but deepened despair and multiplied temptation.

Dark Angel, with thine aching lust
To rid the world of penitence:
Malicious angel, who still dost
My soul such subtil violence!

When music sounds, then changest thou
A silvery to a sultry fire:
Nor will thine envious heart allow
Delight untortured by desire.

Through thee, the gracious Muses turn
To Furies, O mine Enemy!
And all the things of beauty burn
With flames of evil ecstasy.

Because of thee, the land of dreams
Becomes a gathering-place of fears:
Until tormented slumber seems
One vehemence of useless tears.[57]

Why are these strange souls born everywhere to-day, with hearts that Christianity, as shaped by history, cannot satisfy? Our love-letters wear out our love; no school of painting outlasts its founders, every stroke of the brush exhausts the impulse, Pre-Raphaelitism had some twenty years; Impressionism thirty perhaps. Why should we believe that religion can never bring round its antithesis? Is it true that our air is disturbed, as Mallarmé said, by 'the trembling of the veil of the Temple',[58] or that 'our whole age is seeking to bring forth a sacred book'?[59] Some of us thought that book near towards the end of last century, but the tide sank again.

X

I do not know whether John Davidson,[60] whose life also was tragic, made that 'morbid effort', that search for 'perfection of thought and feeling', for he is hidden behind failure to unite it 'to perfection of form'. At eleven one morning I met him in the British Museum Reading-Room, probably in 1894, when I was in London for the production of *The Land of Heart's Desire*, but certainly after some long absence from London. 'Are you working here?' I said. 'No,' he said, 'I am loafing, for I have finished my day's work.' 'What, already?' 'I work an hour a day—I cannot work longer without exhaustion, and even as it is, if I meet anybody and get into talk, I cannot write the next day; that is why I loaf when my work is finished.' No one had ever doubted his industry; he had supported his wife and family for years by 'devilling' many hours a day for some popular novelist. 'What work is it?' I said. 'I am writing verse', he answered. 'I had been writing prose for a long time, and then one day I thought I might just as well write what I liked, as I must starve in any case. It was the luckiest thought I ever had, for my agent now gets me forty pounds for a ballad, and I made three hundred out of my last book of verse.'

He was older by ten years than his fellow Rhymers; a National schoolmaster from Scotland, he had been dismissed, he told us, for asking for a rise in his salary, and had come to London with his wife and children. He looked older than his years. 'Ellis,' he had said, 'how old are you?' 'Fifty', Edwin Ellis replied, or whatever his age was. 'Then I will take off my wig. I never take off my wig when there is a man under thirty in the room.' He had endured, and was to endure again, a life of tragic penury, which was made much harder by the conviction that the world was against him, that he was refused for some reason his rightful position. Ellis thought that he pined even for social success, and I that his Scots jealousy kept him provincial and but half articulate.

During the quarrel over Parnell's grave a quotation from Goethe ran through the papers, describing our Irish jealousy: 'The Irish seem to me like a pack of hounds, always dragging down some noble stag'.[61] But I do not think we object to distinction for its own sake; if we kill the stag, it is that we may carry off his head and antlers. 'The Irish people', O'Leary used to say, 'do not know good from bad in any art, but they do not hate the good once it is pointed out to them because it is good.' An infallible Church, with its Mass in Latin and its mediaeval philosophy, and our Protestant social prejudice, have kept our ablest men from levelling passions; but Davidson with a jealousy which may be Scottish, seeing that Carlyle had it, was quick to discover sour grapes. He saw in delicate, laborious, discriminating taste an effeminate pedantry, and would, when that mood was on him, delight in all that seemed healthy, popular, and bustling. Once when I had praised Herbert Horne for his knowledge and his taste, he burst out, 'If a man must be a connoisseur, let him be a connoisseur in women'. He, indeed, was accustomed, in the most characteristic phrase of his type, to describe the Rhymers as lacking in 'blood and guts', and very nearly brought us to an end by attempting to supply the deficiency by the addition of four Scotsmen. He brought all four upon the same evening, and one read out a poem upon the Life-boat, evidently intended for a recitation; another described how, when gold-digging in Australia, he had fought and knocked down another miner for doubting the rotundity of the earth; while of the remainder I can remember nothing except that they excelled in argument. He insisted upon their immediate election, and the Rhymers, through that complacency of good manners whereby educated Englishmen so often surprise me, obeyed, though secretly resolved never to meet again; and it cost me seven hours' work to get another meeting, and vote the Scotsmen out. A few days later I chanced upon Davidson at some restaurant; he was full of amiability, and when we parted shook my hand, and proclaimed enthusiastically that I had 'blood and guts'. I think he might have grown to be a successful man had he been enthusiastic instead about Dowson or Johnson, or Horne or Symons, for they had what I still lacked, conscious deliberate craft, and what I must lack always, scholarship. They had taught me that violent energy, which is like a fire of straw, consumes in a few minutes the nervous vitality, and is useless in the arts. Our fire must burn slowly, and we must constantly turn away to think, constantly analyse what we have done, be content even to have little life outside our work, to show, perhaps, to other men, as little as the watch-mender shows, his magnifying-glass caught in his screwed-up eye. Only then do we learn to conserve our vitality, to keep our mind enough under control and to make our technique sufficiently flexible for expression of the emotions of life as they arise. A few months after our meeting in the Museum, Davidson had spent his inspiration. 'The fires are out', he said, 'and I must hammer the cold iron.' When I heard a few years ago that he had drowned himself, I knew that I had always expected some such end. With enough passion to make a great poet, through meeting no man of culture in early life, he lacked intellectual receptivity, and, anarchic and indefinite, lacked pose and gesture, and now no verse of his clings to my memory.

XI

Gradually Arthur Symons[62] came to replace in my intimate friendship Lionel Johnson, from whom I was slowly separated by a scruple of conscience. If he came to see me he sat tongue-tied unless I gave him the drink that seemed necessary to bring his vitality to but its normal pitch, and if I called upon him he drank so much that I became his confederate. Once, when a friend and I had sat long after our proper bedtime at his constantly repeated and most earnest entreaty, knowing what black melancholy would descend upon him at our departure, and with the unexpressed hope of getting him to his bed, he fixed upon us a laughing and whimsical look, and said, 'I want you two men to understand that you are merely two men that I am drinking with'. That was the only time that I was to hear from him an imaginary conversation that had not an air of the most scrupulous accuracy. He gave two accounts of a conversation with Wilde in prison; in one Wilde wore his hair long, and in the other it had been cropped by the prison barber. He was gradually losing, too, the faculty of experience, and in his prose and verse repeated the old ideas and emotions, but faintly, as though with fading interest. I am certain that he prayed much, and on those rare days that I came upon him dressed and active before mid-day or but little after, I concluded that he had been to morning Mass at Farm Street.

When with Johnson I had tuned myself to his mood, but Arthur Symons, more than any man I have ever known, could slip as it were into the mind of another, and my thoughts gained in richness and in clearness from his sympathy, nor shall I ever know how much my practice and my theory owe to the passages that he read me from Catullus and from Verlaine and Mallarmé. I had read *Axël*[63] to myself or was still reading it, so slowly, and with so much difficulty, that certain passages had an exaggerated importance, while all remained so obscure that I could without much effort imagine that here at last was the Sacred Book I longed for. An Irish friend of mine lives in a house[64] where beside a little old tower rises a great new Gothic hall and stair, and I have sometimes got him to extinguish all light but a little Roman lamp, and in that faint light and among great vague shadows, blotting away the unmeaning ornament, have imagined myself partaking in some incredible romance. Half a dozen times, beginning in boyhood with Shelley's *Prometheus Unbound,* I have in that mood possessed for certain hours or months the book that I long for; and Symons, without ever being false to his own impressionist view of art and of life, deepened, as I think, my longing.

It seems to me, looking backward, that we always discussed life at its most intense moment, that moment which gives a common sacredness to the Song of Songs and to the Sermon on the Mount,[65] and in which one discovers something supernatural, a stirring as it were of the roots of the hair. He was making those translations from Mallarmé and from Verlaine, from Calderón, from Saint John of the Cross, which are the most accomplished metrical translations of our time, and I think that those from Mallarmé may have given elaborate form to my verses of those years, to the latter poems of *The Wind Among the Reeds,* to *The Shadowy Waters,* while Villiers de l'Isle-Adam had shaped whatever in my *Rosa Alchemica* Pater had not shaped. I can remember the day in Fountain Court when Symons first read me Herodiade's address to some Sibyl who is her nurse and, it may be, the moon also:

> The horror of my virginity
> Delights me, and I would envelop me
> In the terror of my tresses, that, by night,
> Inviolate reptile, I might feel the white
> And glimmering radiance of thy frozen fire,
> Thou that art chaste and diest of desire,
> White night of ice and of the cruel snow!
> Eternal sister, my lone sister, lo
> My dreams uplifted before thee! now, apart,
> So rare a crystal is my dreaming heart,
> And all about me lives but in mine own
> Image, the idolatrous mirror of my pride,
> Mirroring this Herodiade diamond-eyed.[66]

Yet I am certain that there was something in myself compelling me to attempt creation of an art as separate from everything heterogeneous and casual, from all character and circumstance, as some Herodiade of our theatre, dancing seemingly alone in her narrow moving luminous circle. Certainly I had gone a great distance from my first poems, from all that I had copied from the folk-art of

Ireland, as from the statue of Mausolus and his Queen, where the luminous circle is motionless and contains the entire popular life; and yet why am I so certain? I can imagine an Aran Islander who had strayed into the Luxembourg Gallery turning bewildered from Impressionist or Post-Impressionist, but lingering at Moreau's *Jason*,[67] to study in mute astonishment the elaborate background, where there are so many jewels, so much wrought stone and moulded bronze. Had not lover promised mistress in his own island song, 'A ship with a gold and silver mast, gloves of the skin of a fish, and shoes of the skin of a bird, and a suit of the dearest silk in Ireland'?[68]

XII

Hitherto when in London I had stayed with my family in Bedford Park, but now I was to live for some twelve months in chambers in the Temple that opened through a little passage into those of Arthur Symons. If anybody rang at either door, one or other would look through a window in the connecting passage, and report. We would then decide whether one or both should receive the visitor, whether his door or mine should be opened, or whether both doors were to remain closed. I have never liked London, but London seemed less disagreeable when one could walk in quiet, empty places after dark, and upon a Sunday morning sit upon the margin of a fountain almost as alone as if in the country. I was already settled there, I imagine, when a publisher called and proposed that Symons should edit a review or magazine,[69] and Symons consented on the condition that Beardsley[70] were Art Editor—and I was delighted at his condition, as I think were all his other proposed contributors. Aubrey Beardsley had been dismissed from the art-editorship of the *Yellow Book* under circumstances that had made us indignant. He had illustrated Wilde's *Salomé*, his strange satiric art had raised the popular Press to fury, and at the height of the excitement aroused by Wilde's condemnation, a popular novelist,[71] a woman who had great influence among the most conventional part of the British public, had written demanding his dismissal. She owed it to her position before the British people, she had said. Beardsley was not even a friend of Wilde's—they even disliked each other—he had no sexual abnormality, but he was certainly unpopular, and the moment had come to get rid of unpopular persons. The public at once concluded—they could hardly conclude otherwise, he was dismissed by telegram—that there was evidence against him, and Beardsley, who was some twenty-three years old, being embittered and miserable, plunged into dissipation. We knew that we must face an infuriated Press and public, but being all young we delighted in enemies and in everything that had an heroic air.

XIII

We might have survived but for our association with Beardsley; perhaps but for his *Under the Hill*, a Rabelaisian fragment promising a literary genius as great maybe as his artistic genius; and for the refusal of the bookseller who controlled the railway bookstalls to display our wares. The bookseller's manager, no doubt looking for a design of Beardsley's, pitched upon Blake's *Antaeus setting Virgil and Dante upon the verge of Cocytus*[72] as the ground of refusal, and when Arthur Symons pointed out that Blake was considered 'a very spiritual artist', replied, 'O, Mr. Symons, you must remember that we have an audience of young ladies as well as an audience of agnostics'. However, he called Arthur Symons back from the door to say, 'If contrary to our expectations the *Savoy* should have a large sale, we should be very glad to see you again'. As Blake's design illustrated an article of mine, I wrote a letter upon that remarkable saying to a principal daily newspaper. But I had mentioned Beardsley, and I was told that the editor had made it a rule that his paper was never to mention Beardsley's name. I said upon meeting him later, 'Would you have made the same rule in the case of Hogarth?' against whom much the same objection could be taken, and he replied with what seemed to me a dreamy look, as though suddenly reminded of a lost opportunity, 'Ah, there was no popular Press in Hogarth's day'. We were not allowed to forget that in our own day there was a popular Press, and its opinions began to affect our casual acquaintance, and even our comfort in public places. At some well-known house, an elderly man to whom I had just been introduced got up from my side and walked to the other end of the room; but it was as much my reputation as an Irish rebel as the evil company that I was supposed to keep that excited some young men in a railway carriage to comment upon my general career in voices raised that they might catch my attention. I discovered, however, one evening that we were perhaps envied as well as despised. I was in the pit at some theatre, and had just noticed Arthur Symons a little in front of me, when I heard a young man, who looked like a shop-assistant or clerk, say, 'There is Arthur Symons. If he can't get an order, why can't he pay for a stall?' Clearly we were supposed to prosper upon iniquity, and to go to the pit added a sordid parsimony. At another theatre I caught sight of a woman that I once liked, the widow of some friend of my father's youth, and tried to attract her attention, but she had no eyes for anything but the stage curtain; and at some house where I met no hostility to myself, a popular novelist snatched out of my hand a copy of the *Savoy*, and opening it at Beardsley's drawing, called *The Barber*,[73] expounded what he called its bad drawing and wound up with, 'Now if you want to admire really great black-and-white art, admire the *Punch* cartoons of Mr. Linley Sambourne'. Our hostess, after making peace between us, said, 'O, Mr. Yeats, why do you not send your poems to the *Spectator* instead of to the *Savoy?*' The answer, 'My friends read the *Savoy* and they do not read the *Spectator*', called up a puzzled, disapproving look.[74]

Yet, even apart from Beardsley, we were a sufficiently distinguished body: Max Beerbohm, Bernard Shaw, Ernest Dowson, Lionel Johnson, Arthur Symons, Charles Conder, Charles Shannon, Havelock Ellis, Selwyn Image, Joseph Conrad; but nothing counted but the one hated name. I think that had we been challenged we might have argued something after this fashion: 'Science through much ridicule and some persecution has won its right to explore whatever passes before its corporeal eye, and merely because it passes, to set as it were upon an equality the beetle and the whale, though Ben Jonson could find no justification for the entomologist in *The New Inn*, but that he had been crossed in love.[75] Literature now demands the same right of exploration of all that passes before the mind's eye, and merely because it passes.' Not a complete defence, for it substitutes a spiritual for a physical objectivity, but sufficient, it may be, for the moment, and to settle our place in the historical process.

The critic might well reply that certain of my generation delighted in writing with an unscientific partiality for subjects long forbidden. Yet is it not most important to explore especially what has been long forbidden, and to do this not only 'with the highest moral purpose', like the followers of Ibsen, but gaily, out of sheer mischief, or sheer delight in that play of the mind? Donne could be as metaphysical as he pleased, and yet never seemed unhuman and hysterical as Shelley often does, because he could be as physical as he pleased; and besides, who will thirst for the metaphysical, who have a parched tongue, if we cannot recover the Vision of Evil?

I have felt in certain early works of my own which I have long abandoned, and here and there in the work of others of my generation, a slight, sentimental sensuality which is disagreeable, and does not exist in the work of Donne, let us say, because he, being permitted to say what he pleased, was never tempted to linger, or rather to pretend that we can linger, between spirit and sense. How often had I heard men of my time talk of the meeting of spirit and sense, yet there is no meeting but only change upon the instant, and it is by the perception of a change, like the sudden 'blacking out' of the lights of the stage, that passion creates its most violent sensation.

XIV

Dowson was now at Dieppe, now at a Normandy village. Wilde, too, was at Dieppe; and Symons, Beardsley, and others would cross and recross, returning with many tales, and there were letters and telegrams. Dowson wrote a protest against some friend's too vivid essay upon the disorder of his life, and explained that in reality he was living a life of industry in a little country village; but before the letter arrived that friend received a wire, 'Arrested, sell watch and send proceeds'—Dowson's watch had been left in London—and then another wire, 'Am free'. Dowson, or so ran the tale as I heard it ten years after, had got drunk and fought the baker, and a deputation of villagers had gone to the magistrate and pointed out that Monsieur Dowson was one of the most illustrious of English poets. 'Quite right to remind me', said the magistrate; 'I will imprison the baker.'

A Rhymer had seen Dowson at some café in Dieppe with a particularly common harlot, and as he passed, Dowson, who was half drunk, caught him by the sleeve and whispered, 'She writes poetry—it is like Browning and Mrs. Browning'. Then there came a

wonderful tale repeated by Dowson himself, whether by word of
mouth or by letter I do not remember. Wilde had arrived in Dieppe,
and Dowson pressed upon him the necessity of acquiring 'a more
wholesome taste'. They emptied their pockets on to the café table,
and though there was not much, there was enough if both heaps
were put into one. Meanwhile the news had spread, and they set
out accompanied by a cheering crowd. Arrived at their destination,
Dowson and the crowd remained outside, and presently Wilde
returned. He said in a low voice to Dowson, 'The first these ten
years, and it will be the last. It was like cold mutton'—always, as
Henley had said, 'a scholar and a gentleman', he now remembered
that the Elizabethan dramatists used the words 'cold mutton'—and
then aloud so that the crowd might hear him, 'But tell it in England,
for it will entirely restore my character'.

XV

When the first few numbers of the *Savoy* had been published, the
contributors and the publisher gave themselves a supper, and
Symons explained that certain among us were invited afterwards to
the publisher's house, and if I went there that once I need never go
again. I considered the publisher a scandalous person,[76] and had
refused to meet him; we were all agreed as to his character, and only
differed as to the distance that should lie between him and us. I had
just received two letters, one from T. W. Rolleston protesting with
all the conventional moral earnestness of an article in the *Spectator*
newspaper, against my writing for such a magazine; and one from
A.E., denouncing with the intensity of a personal conviction that
magazine, which he called the 'Organ of the Incubi and the Suc-
cubi'. I had forgotten that Arthur Symons had borrowed the letters
until, as we stood about the supper-table waiting for the signal to be
seated, I heard the infuriated voice of the publisher shouting, 'Give
me the letter, give me the letter, I will prosecute that man', and I saw
Symons waving Rolleston's letter just out of reach. Then Symons
folded it up and put it in his pocket, and began to read out A.E.,
and the publisher was silent, and I saw Beardsley listening.
Presently Beardsley came to me and said, 'Yeats, I am going to surprise you very much. I think your friend is right. All my life I have
been fascinated by the spiritual life—when a child I saw a vision of

a Bleeding Christ over the mantelpiece—but after all, to do one's work when there are other things one wants to do so much more is a kind of religion.'[77]

Something, I forget what, delayed me a few minutes after the supper was over, and when I arrived at our publisher's I found Beardsley propped up on a chair in the middle of the room, grey and exhausted, and as I came in he left the chair and went into another room to spit blood, but returned immediately. Our publisher, perspiration pouring from his face, was turning the handle of a hurdy-gurdy piano—it worked by electricity, I was told, when the company did not cut off the supply—and very plainly had had enough of it, but Beardsley pressed him to labour on, 'The tone is so beautiful', 'It gives me such deep pleasure', etc., etc. It was his method of keeping our publisher at a distance.

Another image competes with that image in my memory. Beardsley has arrived at Fountain Court a little after breakfast with a young woman who belongs to our publisher's circle and certainly not to ours, and is called 'twopence coloured', or is it 'penny plain'? He is a little drunk and his mind has been running upon his dismissal from the *Yellow Book,* for he puts his hand upon the wall and stares into a mirror. He mutters, 'Yes, yes. I look like a Sodomite', which he certainly did not. 'But no, I am not that', and then begins railing against his ancestors, accusing them of that and this, back to and including the great Pitt,[78] from whom he declares himself descended.

XVI

I can no more justify my convictions in these brief chapters than Shakespeare could justify within the limits of a sonnet his conviction that the soul of the wide world dreams of things to come; and yet as I have set out to describe nature as I see it, I must not only describe events but those patterns into which they fall, when I am the looker-on. A French miracle-working priest[79] once said to Maud Gonne and myself and to an English Catholic who had come with us, that a certain holy woman had been the 'victim' for his village, and that another holy woman, who had been 'victim' for all France, had given him her crucifix, because he, too, was doomed to become a 'victim'.

French psychical research has offered evidence to support the historical proofs that such saints as Lydwine of Schiedam, whose life suggested to Paul Claudel his *L'Annonce faite à Marie,* did really cure disease by taking it upon themselves. As disease was considered the consequence of sin, to take it upon themselves was to copy Christ. All my proof that mind flows into mind, and that we cannot separate mind and body, drives me to accept the thought of victimage in many complex forms, and I ask myself if I cannot so explain the strange, precocious genius of Beardsley. He was in my Lunar metaphor a man of the thirteenth Phase,[80] his nature on the edge of Unity of Being, the understanding of that Unity by the intellect his one overmastering purpose; whereas Lydwine of Schiedam and her like, being of the saints, are at the seven-and-twentieth Phase, and seek a unity with a life beyond individual being; and so being all subjective he would take upon himself not the consequences but the knowledge of sin. I surrender myself to the wild thought that by so doing he enabled persons who had never heard his name to recover innocence. I have so often, too, practised meditations, or experienced dreams, where the meditations or dreams of two or three persons contrast with and complement one another, in so far as those persons are in themselves complementary or contrasting, that I cannot but see him gathering his knowledge from the saint or potential saint. I see in his fat women and shadowy, pathetic girls, his horrible children, half child, half embryo, in all the lascivious monstrous imagery of the privately published designs, the phantasms that from the beginning have defied the scourge and the hair shirt. I once said to him half seriously, 'Beardsley, I was defending you last night in the only way in which it is possible to defend you, by saying that all you draw is inspired by rage against iniquity', and he answered, 'If it were so inspired the work would be in no way different', meaning, as I think, that he drew with such sincerity that no change of motive could change the image.

I know that some turn of disease had begun to parade erotic images before his eyes, and I do not doubt that he drew these images. 'I make a blot upon the paper', he said to me, 'and I begin to shove the ink about and something comes.' But I was wrong to say that he drew these things in rage against iniquity, for to know that rage he must needs be objective, concerned with other people, with the Church or the Divinity, with something outside his own head, and responsible not for the knowledge but for the consequence of sin. His preparation had been the exhaustion of sin in act, while the preparation of the saint is the exhaustion of his pride, and instead of the saint's humility, he had come to see the images of the mind in a kind of frozen passion, the virginity of the intellect.

Does not all art come when a nature, that never ceases to judge itself, exhausts personal emotion in action or desire so completely that something impersonal, something that has nothing to do with action or desire, suddenly starts into its place, something which is as unforeseen, as completely organized, even as unique, as the images that pass before the mind between sleeping and waking?

But all art is not victimage; and much of the hatred of the art of Beardsley came from the fact that victimage, though familiar under another name to French criticism since the time of Baudelaire, was not known in England. He pictures almost always disillusion, and apart from those privately published drawings[81] which he tried upon his death-bed to have destroyed, there is no representation of desire. Even the beautiful women are exaggerated into doll-like prettiness by a spirit of irony, or are poignant with a thwarted or corrupted innocence. I see his art with more understanding now than when he lived, for in 1895 or 1896 I was in despair at the new breath of comedy that had begun to wither the beauty that I loved, just when that beauty seemed to have united itself to mystery. I said to him once, 'You have never done anything to equal your Salomé with the head of John the Baptist'.[82] I think that for the moment he was sincere when he replied, 'Yes, yes; but beauty is so difficult'. It was for the moment only, for as the popular rage increased and his own disease increased, he became more and more violent in his satire, or created out of a spirit of mockery a form of beauty where his powerful logical intellect eliminated every outline that suggested meditation or even satisfied passion.

The distinction between the Image, between the apparition, as it were, and the personal action and desire, took a new form at the approach of death. He made two or three charming and blasphemous designs; I think especially of a Madonna and Child, where the Child has a foolish, doll-like face, and an elaborate modern baby's dress; and of a Saint Rose of Lima[83] in an expensive gown decorated with roses, ascending to Heaven upon the bosom of the Madonna, her face enraptured with love, but with that form of it which is least associated with sanctity. I think that his conversion to Catholicism was sincere, but that so much of impulse as could exhaust itself in prayer and ceremony, in formal action and desire, found itself mocked by the antithetical image; and yet I am perhaps mistaken, perhaps it was merely his recognition that historical Christianity had dwindled to a box of toys, and that it might be amusing to empty the whole box on to the counterpane.

XVII

I had been a good deal in Paris, though never very long at any time, my later visits with a member of the Rhymers' Club[84] whose curiosity or emotion was roused by every pretty girl. He treated me with a now admiring, now mocking wonder, because being in love, and in no way lucky in that love, I had grown exceedingly puritanical so far as my immediate neighbourhood was concerned. One night, close to the Luxembourg, a strange young woman in bicycling costume came out of a side street, threw one arm about his neck, walked beside us in perfect silence for a hundred yards or so, and then darted up another side street. He had a red and white complexion and fair hair, but how she discovered that in the dark I could not understand. I became angry and reproachful, but he defended himself by saying, 'You never meet a stray cat without caressing it: I have similar instincts'. Presently we found ourselves at some café—the Café d'Harcourt, I think—and when I looked up from my English newspaper, I found myself surrounded with painted ladies and saw that he was taking vengeance. I could not have carried on a conversation in French, but I was able to say, 'That gentleman over there has never refused wine or coffee to any lady', and in a little they had all settled about him like greedy pigeons.

I had put my ideal of those years, an ideal that passed away with youth, into my description of Proud Costello:[85] 'He was of those ascetics of passion who keep their hearts pure for love or for hatred, as other men for God, for Mary and for the Saints.'[86] My friend was not interested in passion. A woman drew him to her by some romantic singularity in her beauty or her circumstance, and drew him the more if the curiosity she aroused were half intellectual. A little after the time I write of, throwing himself into my chair after some visit to a music-hall or hippodrome, he began, 'O, Yeats, I was never in love with a serpent-charmer before'. He was objective. For him 'the visible world existed', as he was fond of quoting, and I suspect him of a Moon that had entered its fourth quarter.[87]

XVIII

At first I used to stay with MacGregor Mathers and his gracious young wife near the Champ de Mars, or in the Rue Mozart,[88] but later by myself, in a students' hotel in the Latin Quarter, and I cannot remember always where I stayed when this or that event took place. MacGregor Mathers, or MacGregor, for he had now shed the 'Mathers', would come down to breakfast one day with his Horace, the next day with his Macpherson's Ossian, and read out fragments during breakfast, considering both books of equal authenticity. Once when I questioned that of Ossian, he got into a rage—what right had I to take sides with the English enemy?—and I found that for him the eighteenth-century controversy still raged.[89] At night he would dress himself in Highland dress, and dance the sword dance, and his mind brooded upon the ramifications of clans and tartans. Yet I have at moments doubted whether he had seen the Highlands, or even, until invited there by some White Rose Society, Scotland itself. Every Sunday he gave to the evocation of spirits, and I noted that upon that day he would spit blood. That did not matter, he said, because it came from his head, not his lungs; what ailed him I do not know, but I think that he lived under some great strain, and presently I noted that he was drinking too much neat brandy, though not to drunkenness. It was in some measure a Scottish pose and whether he carried it into later life like his Jacobite[90] opinions I do not know.

He began to foresee changes in the world, announcing in 1893 or 1894 the imminence of immense wars, and was it in 1895 or 1896 that he learned ambulance work, and made others learn it? He had a sabre wound on his wrist—or perhaps his forehead, for my memory is not clear—got in some student riot that he had mistaken for the beginning of war. It may have been some talk of his that made me write the poem that begins:

The dews drop slowly and dreams gather: unknown spears
Suddenly hurtle before my dream-awakened eyes,
And then the clash of fallen horsemen and the cries
Of unknown perishing armies beat about my ears.[91]

Was this prophecy of his, which would shortly be repeated by mediums and clairvoyants all over the world, an unconscious inference taken up into an imagination brooding upon war, or was it prevision? An often-repeated statement that anarchy would follow and accompany war suggests prevision, and so too does that unreasoning confidence in his own words. His dream whether prevision or inference was doubtless vague in outline, and as he attempted to make it definite nations and individuals seemed to change into the arbitrary symbols of his desires and fears. He imagined a Napoleonic rôle for himself, a Europe transformed according to his fancy, Egypt restored, a Highland Principality, and even offered subordinate posts to unlikely people. I was soon to quarrel with him, but up to his death in the middle of the Great War heard of him from time to time. Somewhere in 1914 or 1915 he turned his house into a recruiting office and raised six hundred volunteers for the Foreign Legion—they were used in some other way—from Englishmen or Americans born in France, or from Frenchmen born in England, and had some part in their training. He had lost the small income he had lived on when I first knew him, and had sunk into great poverty, but to set the balance right remembered a title Louis XV. had conferred upon a Jacobite ancestor who had fought at Pondicherry and called himself Comte de Glenstrae, and gathered about him Frenchmen and Spaniards whose titles were more shadowy perhaps, an obscure claimant to the French throne among the rest, the most as poor as he and some less honest, and in that dream-Court cracked innumerable mechanical jokes—to hide discouragement—and yet remained to the end courageous in thought and kind in act. He had tried to prolong his youthful dream, had mounted into Hodos Chameliontos, and I have known none mount there and come to good that lacked philosophy. All that he knew of that was a vague affirmation, a medicinal phrase that he would repeat and have friends repeat in all moments of adversity: 'There is no part of me that is not of the gods'.

Once, when Mathers had told me that he met his Teachers in some great crowd, and only knew that they were phantoms by a shock that was like an electric shock to his heart, I asked him how he knew that he was not deceived or hallucinated. He said, 'I had been visited by one of them the other night, and I followed him out, and followed him down that little lane to the right. Presently I fell over the milk-boy, and the milk-boy got in a rage because he said that not only I but the man in front had fallen over him.' He, like all that I have known who have given themselves up to images, and to the speech of images, thought that when he had proved that an image could act independently of his mind, he had proved also that neither it, nor what it had spoken, had originated there. Yet had I need of proof to the contrary, I had it while under his roof. I was eager for news of the Spanish-American war, and went to the Rue Mozart before breakfast to buy a *New York Herald*. As I went out past the young Normandy servant who was laying breakfast, I was telling myself some schoolboy romance, and had just reached a place where I carried my arm in a sling after some remarkable escape. I bought my paper and returned, to find Mathers on the doorstep. 'Why, you are all right', he said. 'What did the *bonne* mean by telling me that you had hurt your arm and carried it in a sling?'

Once when I met him in the street in his Highland clothes, with several knives in his stocking, he said, 'When I am dressed like this I feel like a walking flame', and I think that everything he did was but an attempt to feel like a walking flame. Yet at heart he was, I think, gentle, and perhaps even a little timid. He had some impediment in his nose that gave him a great deal of trouble, and it could have been removed had he not shrunk from the slight operation; and once when he was left in a mouse-infested flat with some live traps, he collected his captives into a large birdcage, and, to avoid the necessity of their drowning, fed them there for a couple of weeks. Being an unscholarly, though learned man, he was bound to express the fundamental antithesis in the most crude form, and being arrogant, to prevent as far as possible that alternation between the two natures which is, it may be, necessary to sanity. When the nature turns to its spiritual opposite alone there can be no alternation, but what nature is pure enough for that?

I see Paris in the Eighteen-nineties as a number of events separated from one another, and without cause or consequence, without lot or part in the logical structure of my life; I can often as little find their dates as I can those of events in my early childhood. William Sharp, who came to see me there, may have come in 1895, or on some visit four or five years later, but certainly I was in an hotel in the Boulevard Raspail. When he stood up to go he said, 'What is that?' pointing to a geometrical form painted upon a little piece of cardboard that lay upon my window-sill. And then before I could answer, looked out of the window, saying, 'There is a funeral passing'. I said, 'That is curious, as the Death symbol is painted upon the card'. I did not look, but I am sure there was no funeral. A few days later he came back and said, 'I have been very ill; you must never allow me to see that symbol again'. He did not seem anxious to be questioned, but years later he said: 'I will now tell you what happened in Paris. I had two rooms at my hotel, a front sitting-room and a bedroom leading out of it. As I passed the threshold of the sitting-room, I saw a woman standing at the bureau, writing, and presently she went into my bedroom. I thought somebody had got into the wrong room by mistake, but when I went to the bureau I saw the sheet of paper she had seemed to write upon, and there was no writing upon it. I went into my bedroom and I found nobody, but as there was a door from the bedroom on to the stairs I went down the stairs to see if she had gone that way. When I got out into the street I saw her just turning a corner, but when I turned the corner there was nobody there, and then I saw her at another corner. Constantly seeing her and losing her like that I followed till I came to the Seine, and there I saw her standing at an opening in the wall, looking down into the river. Then she vanished, and I cannot tell why, but I went to the opening in the wall and stood there, just as she had stood, taking just the same attitude. Then I thought I was in Scotland, and that I heard a sheep-bell. After that I must have lost consciousness, for I knew nothing till I found myself lying on my back, dripping wet, and people standing all round. I had thrown myself into the Seine.'

I did not believe him, and not because I thought the story impossible, for I knew he had a susceptibility beyond that of any one I had ever known, to symbolic or telepathic influence, but because he never told one anything that was true; the facts of life disturbed him and were forgotten. The story had been created by the influence but it had remained a reverie, though he may in the course of years have come to believe that it happened as an event. The affectionate husband of his admiring and devoted wife, he had created an imaginary beloved, had attributed to her the authorship of all his books that had any talent, and though habitually a sober man, I have known him to get drunk, and at the height of his intoxication when most men speak the truth, to attribute his state to remorse for having been unfaithful to Fiona Macleod.

Paul Verlaine[92] alternated between the two halves of his nature with so little apparent resistance that he seemed like a bad child, though to read his sacred poems is to remember perhaps that the Holy Infant shared His first home with the beasts. In what month was it that I received a note inviting me to 'coffee and cigarettes plentifully', and signed 'Yours quite cheerfully, Paul Verlaine'? I found him at the top of a tenement house in the Rue St. Jacques, sitting in an easy chair, his bad leg swaddled in many bandages. He asked me, speaking in English, if I knew Paris well, and added, pointing to his leg, that it had scorched his leg, for he knew it 'well, too well' and 'lived in it like a fly in a pot of marmalade'. He took up an English dictionary, one of the few books in the room, and began searching for the name of his disease, selecting after a long search and with, as I understood, only comparative accuracy 'Erysipelas'. Meanwhile his homely middle-aged mistress made the coffee and found the cigarettes; it was obviously she who had given the room its character; her canaries in several cages hanging in the window, and her sentimental lithographs nailed here and there among the nude drawings and newspaper caricatures of her lover as various kinds of monkey, which he had pinned upon the wall. A slovenly, ragged man came in, his trousers belted with a piece of rope and an opera-hat upon his head. She drew a box over to the fire, and he sat down, now holding the opera-hat upon his knees, and I think he must have acquired it very lately, for he kept constantly closing and opening it. Verlaine introduced him by saying, 'He is a poor man, but a good fellow, and is so like Louis XI. to look at that we call him Louis XI.' I remember that Verlaine talked of Victor Hugo, who was 'a supreme poet, but a volcano of mud as well as of flame', and of Villiers de l'Isle-Adam, who was 'exalté' and wrote excellent French; and of *In Memoriam,* which he had tried to translate and could not. 'Tennyson is too noble, too *anglais;* when he should have been broken-hearted, he had many reminiscences.'

At Verlaine's burial, but a few months after, his mistress quarrelled with a publisher at the graveside as to who owned the sheet
by which the body had been covered, and Louis XI. stole fourteen
umbrellas that he found leaning against a tree in the cemetery.

XIX

I am certain of one date, for I have gone to much trouble to get it
right. I met John Synge[93] for the first time in the autumn of 1896,
when I was one-and-thirty, and he four-and-twenty. I was at the
Hôtel Corneille instead of my usual lodging, and why I cannot
remember, for I thought it expensive. Synge's biographer says that
you boarded there for a pound a week, but I was accustomed to
cook my own breakfast, and dine at an Anarchist restaurant in the
Boulevard St. Jacques for little over a shilling. Some one, whose
name I forget, told me there was a poor Irishman at the top of the
house, and presently introduced us.[94] Synge had come lately from
Italy, and had played his fiddle to peasants in the Black Forest—six
months of travel upon fifty pounds—and was now reading French
literature and writing morbid and melancholy verse. He told me
that he had learned Irish at Trinity College, so I urged him to go to
the Aran Islands and find a life that had never been expressed in literature, instead of a life where all had been expressed. I did not
divine his genius, but I felt he needed something to take him out of
his morbidity and melancholy. Perhaps I would have given the same
advice to any young Irish writer who knew Irish, for I had been that
summer upon Inishmaan and Inishmore,[95] and was full of the subject. My friends and I had landed from a fishing-boat to find ourselves among a group of islanders, one of whom said he would
bring us to the oldest man upon Inishmaan. This old man, speaking
very slowly, but with laughing eyes, had said, 'If any gentleman has
done a crime, we'll hide him. There was a gentleman that killed his
father, and I had him in my own house six months till he got away
to America.'[96]
      From that on I saw much of Synge, and brought him to Maud
Gonne's, under whose persuasion, perhaps, he joined the 'Young
Ireland Society of Paris',[97] the name we gave to half a dozen Parisian
Irish, but resigned after a few months because 'it wanted to stir up
Continental nations against England, and England will never give

us freedom until she feels she is safe', the one political sentence I ever heard him speak. Over a year was to pass before he took my advice and settled for a while in an Aran cottage, and became happy, having escaped at last, as he wrote, 'from the squalor of the poor and the nullity of the rich'.[98] I almost forget the prose and verse he showed me in Paris, though I read it all through again when after his death I decided, at his written request, what was to be published and what not. Indeed, I have but a vague impression, as of a man trying to look out of a window and blurring all that he sees by breathing upon the window. According to my Lunar parable, he was a man of the twenty-third Phase;[99] a man whose subjective lives—for a constant return to our life is a part of my dream—were over; who must not pursue an image, but fly from it, all that subjective dreaming, that had once been power and joy, now corrupting within him. He had to take the first plunge into the world beyond himself, the first plunge away from himself that is always pure technique, the delight in doing, not because one would or should, but merely because one can do.

He once said to me, 'A man has to bring up his family and be as virtuous as is compatible with so doing, and if he does more than that he is a puritan; a dramatist has to express his subject and to find as much beauty as is compatible with that, and if he does more he is an aesthete', that is to say, he was consciously objective. Whenever he tried to write drama without dialect he wrote badly, and he made several attempts, because only through dialect could he escape self-expression, see all that he did from without, allow his intellect to judge the images of his mind as if they had been created by some other mind. His objectivity was, however, technical only, for in those images paraded all the desires of his heart. He was timid, too shy for general conversation, an invalid and full of moral scruple, and he was to create now some ranting braggadocio, now some tipsy hag full of poetical speech, and now some young man or girl full of the most abounding health. He never spoke an unkind word, had admirable manners, and yet his art was to fill the streets with rioters, and to bring upon his dearest friends enemies that may last their lifetime.

No mind can engender till divided into two, but that of a Keats or a Shelley falls into an intellectual part that follows, and a hidden emotional flying image, whereas in a mind like that of Synge the emotional part is deadened and stagnant, while the intellectual part is a clear mirror-like technical achievement.

But in writing of Synge I have run far ahead, for in 1896 he was but one picture among many. I am often astonished when I think that we can meet unmoved some person, or pass some house, that in later years is to bear a chief part in our life. Should there not be some flutter of the nerve or stopping of the heart like that MacGregor Mathers experienced at the first meeting with a phantom?

XX

Many pictures come before me without date or order. I am walking somewhere near the Luxembourg Gardens when Synge, who seldom generalizes and only after much thought, says, 'There are three things any two of which have often come together but never all three: ecstasy, asceticism, austerity; I wish to bring all three together'.

.   .   .   .   .   .

I notice that MacGregor Mathers considers William Sharp vague and sentimental, while Sharp is repelled by Mathers' hardness and arrogance. William Sharp met Mathers in the Louvre, and said, 'No doubt considering your studies you live upon milk and fruit'. And Mathers replied, 'No, not exactly milk and fruit, but very nearly so'; and now Sharp has lunched with Mathers and been given nothing but brandy and radishes.

.   .   .   .   .   .

Mathers is much troubled by ladies who seek spiritual advice, and one has called to ask his help against phantoms who have the appearance of decayed corpses, and try to get into bed with her at night. He has driven her away with one furious sentence, 'Very bad taste on both sides'.

.   .   .   .   .   .

I take hashish with some followers of the eighteenth-century mystic Saint-Martin.[100] At one in the morning, while we are talking wildly, and some are dancing, there is a tap at the shuttered window; we open it and three ladies enter, the wife of a man of letters who thought to find no one but a confederate, and her husband's two young sisters whom she has brought secretly to some disreputable dance. She is very confused at seeing us, but as she looks from one to another understands that we have taken some drug and laughs; caught in our dream we know vaguely that she is scandalous according to our code and to all codes, but smile at her benevolently and laugh.

. . . . .

I am at Stuart Merrill's, and I meet there a young Jewish Persian scholar. He has a large gold ring, seemingly very rough, made by some amateur, and he shows me that it has shaped itself to his finger, and says, 'That is because it contains no alloy—it is alchemical gold'.[101] I ask who made the gold, and he says a certain Rabbi, and begins to talk of the Rabbi's miracles. We do not question him—perhaps it is true—perhaps he has imagined it all—we are inclined to accept every historical belief once more.

. . . . .

I am sitting in a café with two French-Americans, a German poet, Dauthendey, and a silent man whom I discover to be Strindberg, and who is looking for the Philosophers' Stone.[102] One French-American reads out a manifesto he is about to issue to the Latin Quarter; it proposes to establish a communistic colony of artists in Virginia, and there is a footnote to explain why he selects Virginia: 'Art has never flourished twice in the same place. Art has never flourished in Virginia.'

Dauthendey, who has some reputation as a poet, explains that his poems are without verbs, as the verb is the root of all evil in the world. He wishes for an art where all things are immovable, as though the clouds should be made of marble. I turn over the page of one of his books which he shows me, and find there a poem in dramatic form, but when I ask if he hopes to have it played he says: 'It could only be played by actors before a black marble wall, with masks in their hands. They must not wear the masks, for that would not express my scorn for reality.'

. . . . .

I go to the first performance of Alfred Jarry's *Ubu Roi*, at the Théâtre de L'Oeuvre, with the Rhymer who had been so attractive to the girl in the bicycling costume.[103] The audience shake their fists at one another, and the Rhymer whispers to me, 'There are often duels after these performances', and he explains to me what is happening on the stage. The players are supposed to be dolls, toys, marionettes, and now they are all hopping like wooden frogs, and I can see for myself that the chief personage, who is some kind of King, carries for sceptre a brush of the kind that we use to clean a closet. Feeling bound to support the most spirited party, we have shouted for the play, but that night at the Hôtel Corneille I am very sad, for comedy, objectivity, has displayed its growing power once more. I say: 'After Stéphane Mallarmé, after Paul Verlaine, after Gustave Moreau, after Puvis de Chavannes, after our own verse, after all our subtle colour and nervous rhythm, after the faint mixed tints of Conder, what more is possible? After us the Savage God.'

BOOK V

THE STIRRING OF
THE BONES

I

It may have been in the spring of 1897 that Maud Gonne, who was
passing through London, told me that for some reason unknown to
her she had failed to get a Dublin authorization for an American
lecturing tour.[1] The young Dublin Nationalists planned a monument to Wolfe Tone which, it was hoped, might exceed in bulk and
in height that of the too compromised and compromising Daniel
O'Connell,[2] and she proposed to raise money for it by these lectures. I had left the Temple and taken two rooms in Bloomsbury,[3]
and in Bloomsbury lived important London Nationalists, elderly
doctors, who had been medical students during the Fenian movement. So I was able to gather a sufficient committee to pass the necessary resolution. She had no sooner sailed than I found out why
the Dublin committee had refused it, or rather put it off by delay
and vague promises. A prominent Irish-American had been murdered for political reasons, and another Irish-American had been
tried and acquitted, but was still accused by his political opponents,
and the dispute had spread to London and to Ireland,[4] and had
there intermixed itself with current politics and gathered new bitterness. My committee and the majority of the Nationalist Irish
societies throughout England were upon one side, and the Dublin
committee and the majority of the Nationalist societies in Ireland
upon the other, and feeling ran high. Maud Gonne had the same
political friends that I had, and the Dublin committee could not be
made to understand that whatever money she collected would go to
the movement,[5] not to her friends. It seemed to me that if I accepted
the Presidency of the '98 Commemoration Association of Great
Britain,[6] I might be able to prevent a public quarrel, and so make a
great central council possible; and a public quarrel I did prevent,
though with little gain perhaps to anybody, for at least one active

man assured me that I had taken the heart out of his work, and no gain at all perhaps to the movement, for our central council had commonly to send two organizers or to print two pamphlets, that both parties might be represented when one pamphlet or one organizer had served.

II

It was no business of mine, and that was precisely why I could not keep out of it. Every enterprise that offered, allured just in so far as it was not my business.[7] I still think that in a species of man, wherein I count myself, nothing so much matters as Unity of Being, but if I seek it as Goethe sought, who was not of that species, I but combine in myself, and perhaps as it now seems, looking backward, in others also, incompatibles. Goethe, in whom objectivity and subjectivity were intermixed, I hold, as the dark is mixed with the light at the eighteenth Lunar Phase,[8] could but seek it as Wilhelm Meister seeks it, intellectually, critically, and through a multitude of deliberately chosen experiences; events and forms of skill gathered as if for a collector's cabinet; whereas true Unity of Being, where all the nature murmurs in response if but a single note be touched, is found emotionally, instinctively, by the rejection of all experience not of the right quality, and by the limitation of its quantity. Of all this I knew nothing, for I saw the world by the light of what my father had said, speaking about some Frenchman who frequented the dissecting-rooms to overcome his dread in the interest of that Unity. My father had mocked, but had not explained why he had mocked, and I for my unhappiness had felt a shuddering fascination. Nor did I understand as yet how little that Unity, however wisely sought, is possible without a Unity of Culture in class or people that is no longer possible at all.

> The fascination of what's difficult
> Has dried the sap out of my veins, and rent
> Spontaneous joy and natural content
> Out of my heart.[9]

III

I went hither and thither speaking at meetings in England and Scotland and occasionally at tumultuous Dublin conventions, and endured some of the worst months of my life. I had felt years before that I had made a great achievement when the man who trained my uncle's horses invited me to share his Christmas dinner, which we roasted in front of his harness-room fire; and now I took an almost equal pride in an evening spent with some small organizer into whose spittoon I secretly poured my third glass of whiskey.[10] I constantly hoped for some gain in self-possession, in rapidity of decision, in capacity for disguise, and am at this moment, I daresay, no different for it all, having but burgeoned and withered like a tree.

When Maud Gonne returned she became our directing mind both in England and in Ireland, and it was mainly at her bidding that our movement became a protest against the dissensions, the lack of dignity, of the Parnellite and Anti-Parnellite parties, who had fought one another for seven or eight years, till busy men passed them by, as they did those performing cats that in my childhood I used to see, pretending to spit at one another, on a table outside Charing Cross station. Both parliamentary parties, seeing that all young Ireland, and a good part of old, were in the movement, tried to join us, the Anti-Parnellite without abandoning its separate identity. They were admitted, I think, but upon what terms I do not remember. I and two or three others had to meet Michael Davitt and a member of Parliament called F. X. O'Brien, to talk out the question of separate identity, and I remember nothing of what passed but the manner and image of Michael Davitt. He seemed hardly less unfitted for such negotiation, perhaps even for any possible present politics, than I myself, and I watched him with sympathy. One knows by the way a man sits in his chair if he have emotional intensity, and Davitt's suggested to me a writer, a painter, an artist of some kind, rather than a man of action. Then, too, F. X. O'Brien did not care whether he used a good or a bad argument, whether he seemed a fool or a clever man, so that he carried his point, but if he used a bad argument Davitt would bring our thought back to it though he had to wait several minutes and re-state it. One felt that he had lived always with small, unimaginative, ineffective men whom he despised; and that perhaps through some lack of early education, perhaps because nine years' imprisonment at the most plastic period of his life had jarred or broken his contact with reality, he had failed, except during the first months of the Land League, to dominate those men. He told me that if the split in the Irish Party had not come he would have carried the Land League into the Highlands, and recovered for Ireland as much of Scotland as was still Gaelic in blood or in language. Our negotiations, which interested so much F. X. O'Brien and my two negotiators, a barrister and a doctor, bored him, I thought, even more than they did me, to whom they were a novelty; but the Highland plan with its historical foundation and its vague possibilities excited him, and it seemed to me that what we said or did stirred him, at other moments also, to some similar remote thought and emotion. I think he returned my sympathy, for a little before his death he replied to some words of congratulation I sent him after the speech in which he resigned his seat in the House of Commons, with an account of some project of his for improving the quality of the Irish representation there.[11]

IV

I think that he shared with poet and philosopher the necessity of speaking the whole mind or remaining silent or ineffective, and he had been for years in a movement where, to adapt certain words of a friend of mine, it was as essential to carry the heart upon the sleeve as the tongue in the cheek. The founders of the Irish Agrarian movement had acted upon the doctrine, contradicted by religious history, that ignorant men will not work for an idea, or feel a political passion for its own sake, and that you must find 'a lever' as it was called, some practical grievance; and I do not think that I am fantastic in believing that this faith in 'levers', universal among revolutionaries, is but a result of that mechanical philosophy of the eighteenth century, which has, as Coleridge said, turned the human mind into the quicksilver at the back of a mirror,[12] though it still permits a work of art to seem 'a mirror dawdling along a road'.[13]

O'Leary had told me the story, not, I think, hitherto published.[14] A prominent Irish-American, not long released from the prison where Fenianism had sent him, cabled to Parnell: 'Take up Land Reform side by side with the National Question and we will support you. See Kickham.' What had Parnell, a landowner and a haughty man, to do with the peasant or the peasant's grievance? And he was indeed so ignorant of both that he asked Kickham, novelist and Fenian leader, if he thought the people would take up a land agitation, and Kickham answered, 'I am only afraid they would go to the Gates of Hell for it'; and O'Leary's comment was, 'And so they have'.

And so was founded an agitation where some men pretended to national passion for the land's sake; some men to agrarian passion for the nation's sake; some men to both for their own advancement, and this agitation at the time I write of had but old men to serve it, who found themselves after years of labour, some after years of imprisonment, derided for unscrupulous rascals. Unscrupulous they certainly were, for they had grown up amid make-believe, and now because their practical grievance was too near settlement to blind and to excite, their make-believe was visible to all. They were as eloquent as ever, they had never indeed shared anything in common but the sentimental imagery, the poetical allusions inherited from a still earlier generation, but were faced by a generation that had turned against all oratory. I recall to my memory a member of Parliament[15] who had fought for Parnell's policy after Parnell's death, and much against his own interest, who refused to attend a meeting my friends had summoned at the declaration of the Boer War, because he thought 'England was in the right', and yet a week later, when the Dublin mob had taken the matter up, advised Irish soldiers to shoot their officers and join President Kruger. I recall another and more distinguished politician[16] who supported the Anti-Parnellite party in his declining years, and in his vigorous years had raked up some scandal about some Colonial Governor. A friend of mine, after advising that Governor's son to write his father's life, had remembered the scandal and called in her alarm upon the politician; 'I do beseech you', he had said, and with the greatest earnestness, 'to pay no attention whatever to anything I may have said during an election'.

Certain of these men, public prepossessions laid aside, were excellent talkers, genial and friendly men, with memories enriched by country humour, much half sentimental, half practical philosophy, and at moments by a poetical feeling not all an affection—found moving by English sympathizers—of the tear and the smile in

Erin's eye. They may even have had more sincerity than their sort elsewhere, but they had inherited a cause men had died for, and they themselves had gone to jail for it, and so worn their hereditary martyrdom that they had seemed for a time no common men, and now must pay the penalty. 'I have just told Mahaffy', Wilde had said to me, 'that it is a party of men of genius', and now John O'Leary, Taylor, and many obscure sincere men had pulled them down; and yet, should what followed, judged by an eye that thinks most of the individual soul, be counted as more clearly out of the common? A movement first of poetry, then of sentimentality, and land hunger, had struggled with, and as the nation passed into the second period of all revolutions given way before a movement of abstraction and hatred; and after some twenty years of the second period, though abstraction and hatred have won their victory, there is no clear sign of a third, a *tertium quid,* and a reasonable frame of mind.

Seeing that only the individual soul can attain to its spiritual opposite, a nation in tumult must needs pass to and fro between mechanical opposites, but one hopes always that those opposites may acquire sex and engender. At moments when I have thought of the results of political subjection upon Ireland I have remembered a story told me by Oscar Wilde, who professed to have found it in a book of magic. 'If you carve a Cerberus upon an emerald', he said, 'and put it in the oil of a lamp and carry it into a room where your enemy is, two new heads will come upon his shoulders and all three devour one another.'

Instead of sharing our traditional sentimental rhetoric with every man who had found a practical grievance, whether one cared a button for the grievance or not, most of us were persecuting heretics. Nationality was like religion, few could be saved, and meditation had but one theme—the perfect nation and its perfect service. 'Public opinion', said an anonymous postcard sent to a friend of mine, 'will compel you to learn Irish', and it certainly did compel many persons of settled habits to change tailor and cloth. I believed myself dressed according to public opinion, until a letter of apology from my tailor informed me that 'It takes such a long time getting Connemara cloth as it has to come all the way from Scotland'.

The Ireland of men's affections must be, as it were, self-moving, self-creating, though as yet (avoiding a conclusion that seemed hopeless) but few added altogether separate from England politically. Men for the moment were less concerned with the final achievement than with independence from English parties and influence during the struggle for it. We had no longer any leaders, abstractions were in their place; and our Conventions, where O'Leary presided, interrupting discussion when the moment came for his cup of coffee, without the least consideration for rules of procedure, were dominated by little groups, the Gaelic propagandists being the most impassioned, which had the intensity and narrowness of theological sects.

I had in my head a project to reconcile old and new that gave Maud Gonne and myself many stirring conversations upon journeys by rail to meetings in Scotland, in Dublin, or in the Midlands. Should we not persuade the organizations in Dublin and in London, when the time drew near for the unveiling of our statue, or even perhaps for the laying of its foundation-stone, to invite the leaders of Parnellite or Anti-Parnellite, of the new group of Unionists who had almost changed sides in their indignation at the overtaxation of Ireland, to lay their policy before our Convention—could we not then propose and carry that the Convention sit permanently, or appoint some Executive Committee to direct Irish policy and report from time to time? The total withdrawal from Westminster had been proposed in the 'seventies, before the two devouring heads were of equal strength—for our Cerberus had but two—and now that the abstract head seemed the stronger, would be proposed again, but the Convention could send them thither, not as an independent power, but as its delegation, and only when and for what purpose the Convention might decide. I dreaded some wild Fenian movement, and with literature perhaps more in my mind than politics, dreamed of that Unity of Culture which might begin with some few men controlling some form of administration. I began to talk my project over with various organizers, who often interrupted their attention, which was perhaps only politeness, with some new jibe at Mr. Dillon or Mr. Redmond.[17] I thought I had Maud Gonne's support, but when I overheard her conversation, she commonly urged the entire withdrawal of the Irish Members, or if she did refer to my scheme, it was to suggest the sending to England of eighty ragged and drunken Dublin beggars or eighty pugilists 'to be paid by results'.

She was the first who spoke publicly or semi-publicly of the with-drawal of the Irish Members as a practical policy for our time, so far as I know, but others may have been considering it. A nation in crisis becomes almost like a single mind, or rather like those minds I have described that become channels for parallel streams of thought, each stream taking the colour of the mind it flows through. These streams are not set moving, as I think, through conversation or publication, but through 'telepathic contact' at some depth below that of normal consciousness; and it is only years afterwards, when future events have shown the theme's importance, that we discover that they are different expressions of a common theme. That self-moving, self-creating nation necessitated an Irish centre of policy, and I planned a premature impossible peace between those two devouring heads because I was sedentary and thoughtful; but Maud Gonne was not sedentary, and I noticed that before some great event she did not think but became exceedingly superstitious. Are not such as she aware, at moments of great crisis, of some power beyond their own minds; or are they like some good portrait-painter of my father's generation and only think when the model is under their eye? Once upon the eve of some demonstration, I found her with many caged larks and finches which she was about to set free for the luck's sake.

I abandoned my plans on discovering that our young men, not yet educated by Mr. Birrell's University,[18] would certainly shout down every one they disagreed with, and that their finance was so extravagant that we must content ourselves with a foundation-stone and an iron rail to protect it, for there could never be a statue; while she carried out every plan she made.

Her power over crowds was at its height, and some portion of the power came because she could still, even when pushing an abstract principle to what seemed to me an absurdity, keep her own mind free, and so when men and women did her bidding they did it not only because she was beautiful, but because that beauty suggested joy and freedom. Besides, there was an element in her beauty that moved minds full of old Gaelic stories and poems, for she looked as though she lived in an ancient civilization where all superiorities whether of the mind or the body were a part of public ceremonial, were in some way the crowd's creation, as the entrance of the Pope into Saint Peter's is the crowd's creation. Her beauty, backed by her great stature, could instantly affect an assembly, and not, as often with our stage beauties, because obvious and florid, for it was incredibly distinguished, and if—as must be that it might seem that assembly's very self, fused, unified, and solitary—her face, like the face of some Greek statue, showed little thought, her whole body seemed a master-work of long labouring thought, as though a Scopas had measured and calculated, consorted with Egyptian sages, and mathematicians out of Babylon, that he might outface even Artemisia's sepulchral image[19] with a living norm.

But in that ancient civilization abstract thought scarce existed, while she but rose partially and for a moment out of raging abstraction; and for that reason, as I have known another woman do, she hated her own beauty, not its effect upon others, but its image in the mirror. Beauty is from the antithetical self,[20] and a woman can scarce but hate it, for not only does it demand a painful daily service, but it calls for the denial or the dissolution of the self.

> How many centuries spent
> The sedentary soul
> In toils of measurement
> Beyond eagle or mole,
> Beyond hearing or seeing
> Or Archimedes' guess,
> To raise into being
> That loveliness?[21]

V

On the morning of the great procession,[22] the greatest in living memory, the Parnellite and Anti-Parnellite members of Parliament, huddled together like cows in a storm, gather behind our carriage, and I hear John Redmond say to certain of his late enemies, 'I went up nearer the head of the procession, but one of the marshals said, "This is not your place, Mr. Redmond; your place is further back". "No," I said, "I will stay here." "In that case", he said, "I will lead you back." ' Later on I can see by the pushing and shouldering of a delegate from South Africa how important place and precedence is; and noticing that Maud Gonne is cheered everywhere, and that the Irish Members march through street after street without welcome, I wonder if their enemies have not intended their humiliation.

.   .   .   .   .   .

We are at the Mansion House Banquet, and John Dillon is making the first speech he has made before a popular Dublin audience since the death of Parnell; and I have several times to keep my London delegates from interrupting. Dillon is very nervous, and as I watch him the abstract passion begins to rise within me, and I am almost overpowered by an instinct of cruelty; I long to cry out, 'Had Zimri peace who slew his master?'[23]

.   .   .   .   .   .

Is our Foundation Stone still unlaid when the more important streets are decorated for Queen Victoria's Jubilee?[24]

I find Maud Gonne at her hotel talking to a young working-man who looks very melancholy. She had offered to speak at one of the regular meetings of his Socialist society about Queen Victoria, and he has summoned what will be a great meeting in the open air. She has refused to speak, and he says that her refusal means his ruin, as nobody will ever believe that he had any promise at all. When he has left without complaint or anger, she gives me very cogent reasons against the open-air meeting, but I can think of nothing but the young man and his look of melancholy. He has left his address, and presently, at my persuasion, she drives to his tenement, where she finds him and his wife and children crowded into a very small space—perhaps there was only one room—and, moved by the sight, promises to speak. The young man is James Connolly[25] who, with Padraic Pearse,[26] is to make the Insurrection of 1916 and to be executed.

.   .   .   .   .   .

The meeting is held in College Green and is very crowded, and Maud Gonne speaks, I think, standing upon a chair. In front of her is an old woman with a miniature of Lord Edward Fitzgerald, which she waves in her excitement, crying out, 'I was in it before she was born'. Maud Gonne tells how that morning she had gone to lay a wreath upon a martyr's tomb at Saint Michael's Church,[27] for it is the one day in the year when such wreaths are laid, but had been refused admission because it is the Jubilee. Then she pauses, and after that her voice rises to a cry, 'Must the graves of our dead go undecorated because Victoria has her Jubilee?'

.   .   .   .   .   .

It is eight or nine at night, and she and I have come from the City Hall, where the Convention has been sitting, that we may walk to the National Club in Rutland Square,[28] and we find a great crowd in the street, who surround us and accompany us. Presently I hear a sound of breaking glass, the crowd has begun to stone the windows of decorated houses, and when I try to speak that I may restore order, I discover that I have lost my voice through much speaking at the Convention. I can only whisper and gesticulate, and as I am thus freed from responsibility, I share the emotion of the crowd, and perhaps even feel as they feel when the glass crashes. Maud Gonne has a look of exultation as she walks with her laughing head thrown back.

Later that night Connolly carries in procession a coffin with the words 'British Empire' upon it, and police and mob fight for its ownership, and at last, that the police may not capture it, it is thrown into the Liffey. And there are fights between police and window-breakers, and I read in the morning papers that many have been wounded; some two hundred heads have been dressed at the hospitals; an old woman killed by baton blows, or perhaps trampled under the feet of the crowd; and that two thousand pounds' worth of decorated plate-glass windows have been broken. I count the links in the chain of responsibility, run them across my fingers, and wonder if any link there is from my workshop.

.   .   .   .   .   .

Queen Victoria visits the city, and Dublin Unionists have gathered together from all Ireland some twelve thousand children and built for them a grandstand, and bought them sweets and buns that they may cheer. A week later Maud Gonne marches forty thousand children through the streets of Dublin, and in a field beyond Drumcondra, and in the presence of a priest of their Church, they swear to cherish towards England, until the freedom of Ireland has been won, an undying enmity.[29]

How many of these children will carry bomb or rifle when a little under or a little over thirty?

.   .   .   .   .   .

Feeling is still running high between the Dublin and London organizations, for a London doctor, my fellow-delegate, has called a little after breakfast to say he was condemned to death by a certain secret society the night before. He is very angry, though it does not seem that his life is in danger, for the insult is beyond endurance.

       .   .   .   .   .   .

We arrive at Chancery Lane for our Committee meeting, but it is Derby Day,[30] and certain men who have arranged a boxing match are in possession of our rooms. We adjourn to a neighbouring pub-lic-house where there are little panelled cubicles as in an old-fash-ioned eating-house, that we may direct the secretary how to answer that week's letters. We are much interrupted by a committee-man who has been to the Derby, and now, half lying on the table, keeps repeating, 'I know what you all think. Let us hand on the torch, you think; let us hand it on to our children; but I say no! I say, let us order an immediate rising.'

Presently one of the boxers arrives, sent up to apologize, it seems, and to explain that we had not been recognized. He begins his apology but stops, and for a moment fixes upon us a meditative critical eye. 'No, I will not', he cries. 'What do I care for any one now but Venus and Adonis and the other planets of Heaven?'

       .   .   .   .   .   .

French sympathizers have been brought to see the old buildings in Galway, and, with the towns of Southern France in their mind's eye, are not in the least moved. The greater number are in a small crowded hotel. Presently an acquaintance of mine, peeping, while it is still broad day, from his bedroom window, sees the proprietress of the hotel near the hall door, and in the road a serious-minded, quixotic Dublin barrister, with a little boy who carries from a stick over his shoulder twelve chamber-pots. He hears one angry, and one soft pleading explanatory voice, 'But, Madam, I feel certain that at the unexpected arrival of so many guests—so many guests of the Nation,[31] I may say—you must have found yourself unpre-pared.' 'Never have I been so insulted.' 'Madam, I am thinking of the honour of my country.'

       .   .   .   .   .   .

I am at Maud Gonne's hotel, and an Italian sympathizer, Cipriani,[32] the friend of Garibaldi, is there, and though an old man now, he is the handsomest man I have ever seen. I am telling a ghost story in

English at one end of the room, and he is talking politics in French at the other. Somebody says, 'Yeats believes in ghosts', and Cipriani interrupts for a moment his impassioned declamation to say in English, and with a magnificent movement and intonation, 'As for me, I believe in nothing but cannon'.

· · · · · ·

I call at the office of the Dublin organisation in Westmoreland Street,[33] and find the front door open, and the office door open, and though the office is empty the cupboard door open and eighteen pounds in gold upon the shelf.

· · · · · ·

At a London Committee meeting I notice a middle-aged man who slips into the room for a moment, whispers something to the secretary, lays three or four shillings on a table, and slips out. I am told that he is an Irish board-school teacher who, in early life, took an oath neither to drink nor smoke, but to contribute the amount so saved weekly to the Irish Cause.

· · · · · ·

VI

When in my twenty-second year I had finished *The Wanderings of Oisin,* my style seemed too elaborate, too ornamental, and I thought for some weeks of sleeping upon a board. Had I been anywhere but at Sligo, where I was afraid of my grandfather and grandmother, I would have made the attempt. When I had finished 'Rosa Alchemica' for the *Savoy,* I had a return of the old trouble and went to consult a friend[34] who, under the influence of my cabbalistic symbols, could pass into a condition between meditation and trance. A certain symbolic personality who called herself, if I remember rightly, Megarithma, said that I must 'live near water and avoid woods because they concentrate the solar ray'. I believed that this enigmatic sentence came from my own Daimon,[35] my own buried self speaking through my friend's mind. 'Solar', according to all that I learnt from Mathers, meant elaborate, full of artifice, rich, all that resembles the work of a goldsmith, whereas 'water' meant 'lunar', and 'lunar' all that is simple, popular, traditional, emotional. But why should woods concentrate the solar ray? I did not understand why, nor do I now, and I decided to reject that part of the message as an error. I accepted the rest without difficulty, for after *The Wanderings of Oisin*, I had simplified my style by filling my imagination with country stories. My friends believed that the dark portion of the mind—the subconscious—had an incalculable power, and even over events. To influence events or one's own mind, one had to draw the attention of that dark portion, to turn it, as it were, into a new direction. Mathers described how as a boy he had drawn over and over again some event that he longed for; and called those drawings an instinctive magic. But for the most part one repeated certain names and drew or imagined certain symbolic forms which had acquired a precise meaning, and not only to the dark portion of one's own mind, but to the mind of the race. I decided to repeat the names associated with the moon in the cabbalistic tree of life,[36] the divine name, the name of the angelic order, the name of the planetary sphere, and so on, and probably, though my memory is not clear upon the point, to draw certain geometrical forms. As Arthur Symons and I were about to stay with Mr. Edward Martyn at Tulira Castle, in Galway, I decided that it was there I must make my invocation of the moon. I made it night after night just before I went to bed, and after many nights—eight or nine perhaps—I saw between sleeping and waking, as in a kinematograph,[37] a galloping centaur, and a moment later a naked woman of incredible beauty, standing upon a pedestal and shooting an arrow at a star.[38] I still remember the tint of that marvellous flesh which makes all human flesh seem unhealthy, and remember that others who have seen such forms have remembered the same characteristic. Next morning before breakfast Arthur Symons took me out on to the lawn to recite a scrap of verse, the only verse he had ever written to a dream.[39] He had dreamt the night before of a woman of great beauty, but she was clothed and had not a bow and arrow. When he got back to London, he found awaiting him a story sent to the *Savoy* by Fiona Macleod and called, I think, 'The Archer'.[40] Some one in the story had a vision of a woman shooting an arrow into the sky and later of an arrow shot at a faun that pierced the faun's body and remained, the faun's heart torn out and clinging to it, embedded in a tree. Some weeks later I, too, was in London, and found among Mathers' pupils a woman whose little child[41]—perhaps at the time of my vision, perhaps a little later—had come running in from the garden calling out, 'O, mother, I have seen a woman shooting an arrow into the sky and I am afraid that she has killed God'. I have somewhere among my papers a letter from a very old friend[42] describing how her little cousin—perhaps a few months later—dreamed of a man who shot at a star with a gun and that the star fell down, but, 'I do not think', the child said, 'it minded dying because it was so very old', and how presently the child saw the star lying in a cradle. Had some great event taken place in some world where myth is reality and had we seen some portion of it? One of my fellow-students quoted a Greek saying, 'Myths are the activities of the Daimons',[43] or had we but seen in the memory of the race something believed thousands of years ago, or had somebody—I myself perhaps—but dreamed a fantastic dream which had come to those others by transference of thought? I came to no conclusion, but I was sure there was some symbolic meaning could I but find it. I went to my friend[44] who had spoken to Megarithma, and she went once more into her trance-like meditation and heard but a single unexplained sentence: 'There were three that saw; three will attain a wisdom older than the serpent, but the child will die.' Did this refer to myself, to Arthur Symons, to Fiona Macleod, to the child who feared that the archer had killed God? I thought not, for Symons had no deep interest in the subject, and there was the second child to account for. It was probably some new detail of the myth or an interpretation of its meaning. There was a London coroner[45] in those days, learned in the Cabbala, whom I had once known though we had not met for some years. I called upon him and told all that I have set down here. He opened a drawer and took out of it two water-colour paintings, made by a clumsy painter who had no object but a symbolical record: one was of a centaur, the other of a woman standing upon a stone pedestal and shooting her arrow at what seemed a star. He asked me to look carefully at the star, and I saw that it was a little golden heart. He said: 'You have hit upon things that you can never have read of in any book; these symbols belong to a part of the Christian Cabbala'—perhaps this was not his exact term—'that you know nothing of. The centaur is the elemental spirit and the woman the divine spirit of the path Samekh, and the golden heart is the central point upon the cabbalistic Tree of Life[46] and corresponds to the Sephiroth

Tiphareth.' I was full of excitement, for now at last I began to understand. The Tree of Life is a geometrical figure made up of ten circles or spheres called Sephiroth joined by straight lines. Once men must have thought of it as like some great tree covered with its fruit and its foliage, but at some period, in the thirteenth century perhaps, touched by the mathematical genius of Arabia in all likelihood, it had lost its natural form. The Sephiroth Tiphareth, attributed to the sun, is joined to the Sephiroth Yesod, attributed to the moon, by a straight line called the path Samekh, and this line is attributed to the constellation Sagittarius. He would not or could not tell me more, but when I repeated what I had heard to one of my fellow-students, a yachtsman and yacht-designer and cabbalist, he said, 'Now you know what was meant by a wisdom older than the serpent'. He reminded me that the cabbalistic tree has a green serpent winding through it which represents the winding path of nature or of instinct, and that the path Samekh is part of the long straight line that goes up through the centre of the tree, and that it was interpreted as the path of 'deliberate effort'. The three who saw must, he said, be those who could attain to wisdom by the study of magic, for that was 'deliberate effort'. I remember that I quoted Balzac's description[47] of the straight line as the line of man, but he could not throw light on the other symbols except that the shot arrow must symbolise effort, nor did I get any further light.

.   .   .   .   .   .

A couple of weeks after my vision, Lady Gregory,[48] whom I had met once in London for a few minutes, drove over to Tulira, and after Symons' return to London I stayed at her house.[49] When I saw her great woods on the edge of a lake, I remembered the saying about avoiding woods and living near the water. Had this new friend come because of my invocation, or had the saying been but prevision and my invocation no act of will, but prevision also? Were those unintelligible words—'avoid woods because they concentrate the solar ray'—but a dream-confusion, an attempt to explain symbolically an actual juxtaposition of wood and water? I could not say nor can I now. I was in poor health, the strain of youth had been greater than it commonly is, even with imaginative men, who must always, I think, find youth bitter, and I had lost myself besides, as I had done periodically for years, upon Hodos Chameliontos.[50] The first time was in my eighteenth or nineteenth year, when I tried to create a more multitudinous dramatic form, and now I had got there through a novel[51] that I could neither write nor cease to write which had Hodos Chameliontos for its theme. My chief person was to see all the modern visionary sects pass before his bewildered eyes, as Flaubert's Saint Anthony saw the Christian sects,[52] and I was as helpless to create artistic, as my chief person to create philosophic, order. It was not that I do not love order, or that I lack capacity for it, but that—and not in the arts and in thought only— I outrun my strength. It is not so much that I choose too many elements, as that the possible unities themselves seem without number, like those angels that, in Henry More's paraphrase of the schoolman's problem, dance spurred and booted upon the point of a needle.[53] Perhaps fifty years ago I had been in less trouble, but what can one do when the age itself has come to Hodos Chameliontos?

Lady Gregory, seeing that I was ill, brought me from cottage to cottage to gather folk-belief, tales of the faeries, and the like, and wrote down herself what we had gathered, considering that this work, in which one let others talk, and walked about the fields so much, would lie, to use a country phrase, 'very light upon the mind'. She asked me to return there the next year, and for years to come I was to spend my summers at her house. When I was in good health again, I found myself indolent, partly perhaps because I was affrighted by that impossible novel, and asked her to send me to my work every day at eleven, and at some other hour to my letters, rating me with idleness if need be, and I doubt if I should have done much with my life but for her firmness and her care. After a time, though not very quickly, I recovered tolerable industry, though it has only been of late years that I have found it possible to face an hour's verse without a preliminary struggle and much putting off.

Certain woods at Sligo, the woods above Dooney Rock and those above the waterfall at Ben Bulben, though I shall never perhaps walk there again, are so deep in my affections that I dream about them at night; and yet the woods at Coole, though they do not come into my dream, are so much more knitted to my thought that when I am dead they will have, I am persuaded, my longest visit. When we are dead, according to my belief, we live our lives backward for a certain number of years, treading the paths that we have trodden, growing young again, even childish again, till some attain an innocence that is no longer a mere accident of nature, but the human intellect's crowning achievement.[54] It was at Coole that the first few simple thoughts that now, grown complex through their contact with other thoughts, explain the world, came to me from beyond my own mind. I practised meditations, and these, as I think, so affected my sleep that I began to have dreams that differed from ordinary dreams in seeming to take place amid brilliant light, and by their invariable coherence, and certain half-dreams, if I can call them so, between sleep and waking. I have noticed that such experiences come to me most often amid distraction, at some time that seems of all times the least fitting, as though it were necessary for the exterior mind to be engaged elsewhere, and it was during 1897 and 1898, when I was always just arriving from or just setting out to some political meeting, that the first dreams came. I was crossing a little stream near Inchy Wood and actually in the middle of a stride from bank to bank, when an emotion never experienced before swept down upon me. I said, 'That is what the devout Christian feels, that is how he surrenders his will to the will of God'. I felt an extreme surprise, for my whole imagination was preoccupied with the pagan mythology of ancient Ireland, I was marking in red ink, upon a large map, every sacred mountain. The next morning I awoke near dawn, to hear a voice saying, 'The love of God is infinite for every human soul because every human soul is unique; no other can satisfy the same need in God'.[55]

Lady Gregory and I had heard many tales of changelings, grown men and women as well as children, who, as the people believe, are taken by the faeries, some spirit or inanimate object bewitched into their likeness remaining in their stead, and I constantly asked myself what reality there could be in these tales, often supported by so much testimony. I woke one night to find myself lying upon my back with all my limbs rigid, and to hear a ceremonial measured voice, which did not seem to be mine, speaking through my lips. 'We make an image of him who sleeps', it said, 'and it is not he who sleeps, and we call it Emmanuel.'[56] After many years that thought, others often found as strangely being added to it, became the thought of the Mask, which I have used in these memoirs to explain men's characters. A few months ago at Oxford I was asking myself why it should be 'an image of him who sleeps', and took down from the shelf, not knowing what I did, Burkitt's *Early Eastern Chris-*

tianity,[57] and opened it at random. I had opened it at a Gnostic Hymn that told of a certain King's son who, being exiled, slept in Egypt—a symbol of the natural state—and how an Angel while he slept brought him a royal mantle; and at the bottom of the page I found a footnote saying that the word mantle did not represent the meaning properly, for that which the Angel gave had the exile's own form and likeness. I did not, however, find in the Gnostic Hymn my other conviction that Egypt and that which the Mask represents are antithetical. That, I think, became clear when a countryman told Lady Gregory and myself that he had heard the crying of new-dropped lambs in November—spring in the world of Faery being November with us.

.　　.　　.　　.　　.　　.

On the sea-coast at Duras, a few miles from Coole, an old French Count, Florimond de Basterot, lived for certain months in every year. Lady Gregory and I talked over my project of an Irish Theatre,[58] looking out upon the lawn of his house, watching a large flock of ducks that was always gathered for his arrival from Paris, and that would be a very small flock, if indeed it were a flock at all, when he set out for Rome in the autumn. I told her that I had given up my project because it was impossible to get the few pounds necessary for a start in little halls, and she promised to collect or give the money necessary. That was her first great service to the Irish intellectual movement. She reminded me the other day that when she first asked me what she could do to help our movement I suggested nothing; and, certainly, I no more foresaw her genius than I foresaw that of John Synge, nor had she herself foreseen it. Our theatre had been established before she wrote or had any ambition to write, and yet her little comedies have merriment and beauty, an unusual combination, and those two volumes where the Irish heroic tales are arranged and translated in an English so simple and so noble may do more than other books to deepen Irish imagination.[59] They contain our ancient literature, are something better than our *Mabinogion,*[60] are almost our *Morte d'Arthur.* It is more fitting, however, that in a book of memoirs I should speak of her personal influence, and especially as no witness is likely to arise better qualified to speak. If that influence were lacking, Ireland would be greatly impoverished, so much has been planned out in the library or among the woods at Coole; for it was there that John Shawe-Taylor found the independence from class and family that made him summon the conference between landlord and tenant that brought Land Purchase,[61] and it was there that Hugh Lane formed those Irish ambitions that led to his scattering many thousands, and gathering much ingratitude;[62] and where, but for that conversation at Florimond de Basterot's, had been the genius of Synge?

I have written these words instead of leaving all to posterity, and though my friend's ear seems indifferent to praise or blame, that young men, to whom recent events are often more obscure than those long past, may learn what debts they owe and to what creditor.

THE END

DRAMATIS
PERSONAE

1896–1902

DRAMATIS PERSONAE

I

When I was thirty years old the three great demesnes of three Galway houses, Coole House, Tulira Castle, Roxborough House, lay within a half-hour or two hours' walk of each other. They were so old they seemed unchanging; now all have been divided among small farmers, their great ancient trees cut down. Roxborough House was burnt down during the Civil War;[1] Coole House has passed to the Forestry Department;[2] but Tulira Castle is inhabited by blood relatives of those who built it. I went there for the first time with Arthur Symons,[3] then editor of the *Savoy* magazine. I was taking him here and there through Ireland. We had just been sightseeing in Sligo. Edward Martyn,[4] met in London, perhaps with George Moore, had seemed so heavy, uncouth, countrified that I said as we turned in at the gate: 'We shall be waited on by a barefooted servant'. I was recalling a house seen at Sligo when a child. Then I saw the great trees, then the grey wall of the Castle.

Edward Martyn brought us up the wide stairs of his Gothic hall decorated by Crace and showed us our rooms. 'You can take your choice', he said. I took out a penny to toss, shocking Symons, who was perhaps all the more impressed by his surroundings because of what I had said about bare feet. I think the man of letters has powers of make-believe denied to the painter or the architect. We both knew that those pillars, that stair and varnished roof with their mechanical ornament, were among the worst inventions of the Gothic revival, but upon several evenings we asked Edward Martyn to extinguish all light except that of a little Roman lamp, sat there in the shadows, as though upon a stage set for *Parsifal*. Edward Martyn sat at his harmonium, so placed among the pillars that it seemed some ancient instrument, and played Palestrina. He hated that house in all its detail—it had been built by his mother when he was a very young man to replace some plain eighteenth-century house—all except an ancient tower where he had his study. A fire had destroyed the old house, and whatever old furniture or pictures the family possessed, as though fate had deliberately prepared for an abstract mind that would see nothing in life but its vulgarity and temptations. In the tower room, in a light filtered through small stained-glass windows, without any quality of design, made before Whall rediscovered the methods of mediaeval glass-workers, he had read Saint Chrysostom, Ibsen, Swift,[5] because they made abstinence easy by making life hateful in his eyes. He drank little, ate enormously, but thought himself an ascetic because he had but one meal a day, and suffered, though a courteous man, from a subconscious hatred of women. His father had been extravagantly amorous; I was later to collect folk-lore from one of his father's peasant mistresses, then an old woman. I have heard of his getting from his horse to chase a girl for a kiss. Edward's mother, who still lived, and is a frail, pinched figure in my memory, had tried to marry him to women who did not share or even understand his tastes and were perhaps chosen for that reason. Edward, who admired Beardsley for his saturnine genius, had commissioned from him a great stained-glass window for the hall. And had Beardsley lived another year, his fat women, his effeminate men, his children drawn so as to suggest the foetus, would have fed Edward's hatred of life. I can remember his mother's current selection, a pretty somewhat ruddy girl, saying: 'I never could stand those Beardsleys', fixing her eye on an incomparable Utamaro. The drawing-room furniture was vulgar and pretentious, because he thought himself bound to satisfy what he believed to be the taste of women. Only his monk-like bedroom, built over the stables and opening into the tower on the opposite side to the house, his study in the tower, and the pictures, showed his own improving taste. His first purchase, a large coffee-coloured sea picture by Edwin Ellis—not my friend the Blake scholar, but the Academician—had been a mistake; then, perhaps under the influence of George Moore, a relative on his father's side, came Degas, Monet, Corot, Utamaro, and of these pictures he talked with more intelligence, more feeling than when he talked of literature. His Degas showed the strongly marked shoulder-blades of a dancing-girl, robbing her of voluptuous charm. Degas had said to him: 'Cynicism is the only sublimity'. It hung somewhere near the Utamaro, which pleased him because of its almost abstract pattern, or because the beautiful women portrayed do not stir our Western senses.

II

When Symons and I paid our visit, Martyn had just finished *The Heather Field*. Alexander had praised it and refused it, and he talked of having it produced in Germany. He sat down daily to some task, perhaps *Maeve,* but I was certain even then, I think, that though he would find subjects, construct plots, he would never learn to write; his mind was a fleshless skeleton. I used to think that two traditions met and destroyed each other in his blood, creating the sterility of a mule. His father's family was old and honoured; his mother but one generation from the peasant. Her father, an estate steward, earned money in some way that I have forgotten. His religion was a peasant religion; he knew nothing of those interpretations, casuistries, whereby my Catholic acquaintance adapt their ancient rules to modern necessities. What drove him to those long prayers, those long meditations, that stern Church music? What secret torture?

III

Presently, perhaps after Arthur Symons had gone, Lady Gregory called, reminded me that we had met in London though but for a few minutes at some fashionable house. A glimpse of a long vista of trees, over an undergrowth of clipped laurels, seen for a moment as the outside car approached her house on my first visit, is a vivid memory. Coole House, though it has lost the great park full of ancient trees, is still set in the midst of a thick wood, which spreads out behind the house in two directions, in one along the edges of a lake which, as there is no escape for its water except a narrow subterranean passage, doubles or trebles its size in winter. In later years I was to know the edges of that lake better than any spot on earth, to know it in all the changes of the seasons, to find there always some new beauty. Wondering at myself, I remember that when I first saw that house I was so full of the mediaevalism of William Morris that I did not like the gold frames, some deep and full of ornament, round the pictures in the drawing-room; years were to pass before I came to understand the earlier nineteenth and later eighteenth century, and to love that house more than all other houses. Every generation had left its memorial; every generation had been highly educated; eldest sons had gone the grand tour, returning with statues or pictures; Mogul or Persian paintings had been brought from the Far East by a Gregory chairman of the East India Company,[6] great earthenware ewers and basins, great silver bowls, by Lady Gregory's husband, a famous Governor of Ceylon,[7] who had married in old age, and was now some seven years dead; but of all those Gregorys, the least distinguished, judged by accepted standards, most roused my interest—a Richard[8] who at the close of the eighteenth century was a popular brilliant officer in the Guards. He was accused of pleading ill-health to escape active service, and though exonerated by some official inquiry, resigned his commission, gave up London and his friends. He made the acquaintance of a schoolgirl, carried her off, put her into a little house in Coole demesne, afterwards the steward's house, where she lived disguised as a boy until his father died. They married, and at the end of last century the people still kept the memory of her kindness and her charity. One of the latest planted of the woods bore her name, and is, I hope, still called, now that the Government Foresters are in possession, 'The Isabella Wood'. While compelled to live in boy's clothes she had called herself 'Jack the Sailor' from a song of Dibdin's. Richard had brought in bullock-carts through Italy the marble copy of the Venus de' Medici in the drawing-room, added to the library the Greek and Roman Classics bound by famous French and English binders, substituted for the old straight avenue two great sweeping avenues each a mile or a little more in length. Was it he or his father who had possessed the Arab horses, painted by Stubbs? It was perhaps Lady Gregory's husband, a Trustee of the English National Gallery, who had bought the greater number of the pictures. Those that I keep most in memory are a Canaletto, a Guardi, a Zurbarán. Two or three that once hung there had, before I saw those great rooms, gone to the National Gallery, and the fine portraits by Augustus John and Charles Shannon were still to come. The mezzotints and engravings of the masters and friends of the old Gregorys that hung round the small downstairs breakfast-room, Pitt, Fox, Lord Wellesley, Palmerston, Gladstone, many that I have forgotten, had increased generation by generation, and amongst them Lady Gregory had hung a letter from Burke[9] to the Gregory that was chairman of the East India Company saying that he committed to his care, now that he himself had grown old, the people of India. In the hall, or at one's right hand as one ascended the stairs, hung Persian helmets, Indian shields, Indian swords in elaborate sheaths, stuffed birds from various parts of the world, shot by whom nobody could remember, portraits of the members of Grillion's Club, illuminated addresses presented in Ceylon or Galway, signed photographs or engravings of Tennyson, Mark Twain, Browning, Thackeray, at a later date paintings of Galway scenery by Sir Richard Burton, bequeathed at his death, and etchings by Augustus John. I can remember somebody saying: 'Balzac would have given twenty pages to the stairs'. The house itself was plain and box-like, except on the side towards the lake where somebody, probably Richard Gregory, had enlarged the drawing-room and dining-room with great bow windows. Edward Martyn's burnt house had been like it doubtless, for it was into such houses men moved, when it was safe to leave their castles, or the thatched cottages under castle walls; architecture did not return until the cut stone Georgian houses of a later date.

IV

Lady Gregory, as I first knew her, was a plainly dressed woman of forty-five, without obvious good looks, except the charm that comes from strength, intelligence and kindness. One who knew her at an earlier date speaks of dark skin, of an extreme vitality, and a portrait by Mrs. Jopling that may have flattered shows considerable beauty. When her husband died, she had given up her London house, had devoted herself to the estate and to her son, spending little that mortgages might be paid off. The house had become her passion. That passion grew greater still when the house took its place in the public life of Ireland. She was a type that only the superficial observer could identify with Victorian earnestness, for her point of view was founded, not on any narrow modern habit, but upon her sense of great literature, upon her own strange feudal, almost mediaeval youth. She was a Persse—a form of the name Shakespeare calls Percy—descended from some Duke of Northumberland; her family had settled in the seventeenth century somewhere in the midlands, but finding, the legend declares, the visits of Lord Clanricarde, going and returning between his estate and Dublin, expensive, they had moved that they might be no longer near the high road and bought vast tracts of Galway land. Roxborough House, small and plain, but interesting for its high-pitched roof—the first slate roof built in Galway—was beside the road from Gort to Loughrea, a few yards from the bounding wall of a demesne that was nine miles round. Three or four masons were, during Lady Gregory's girlhood, continually busy upon the wall. On the other side of the road rose the Slievoughter range,[10] feeding grouse and wild deer. The house contained neither pictures nor furniture of historic interest. The Persses had been soldiers, farmers, riders to hounds and, in the time of the Irish Parliament, politicians; a bridge within the wall commemorated the victory of the Irish Volunteers[11] in 1782, but all had lacked intellectual curiosity until the downfall of their class had all but come. In the latter half of the nineteenth century Lady Gregory was born, an older and a younger sister gave birth to Sir Hugh Lane and to that John Shawe-Taylor who, by an act of daring I must presently describe, made the settlement of the Land Question possible.[12]

Popular legend attributes to all the sons of the house daring and physical strength; some years ago, Free State Ministers were fond of recounting the adventures of Lady Gregory's 'Seven Brothers',[13] who, no matter who objected to their rents, or coveted their possessions, were safe 'because had one been killed, the others would have run down and shot the assassin'; how the wildest of the brothers, excluded by some misdemeanour from a Hunt Ball, had turned a hose on the guests; how, a famous shot, he had walked into a public-house in a time of disturbance and put a bullet through every number on the clock. They had all the necessities of life on the mountain, or within the walls of their demesne, exporting great quantities of game, ruling their tenants, as had their fathers before, with a despotic benevolence, were admired, and perhaps loved, for the Irish people, however lawless, respect a rule founded upon some visible supremacy. I heard an old man say once to Lady Gregory: 'There was never a man that could hold a bow with your brothers'. Those brothers were figures from the eighteenth century. Sir Jonah Barrington[14] might have celebrated their lives, but their mother and the mother of John Shawe-Taylor were of the nineteenth in one of their characteristics. Like so many Irish women of the upper classes, who reacted against the licence, the religious lassitude of the immediate past, they were evangelical Protestants,[15] and set out to con-

vert their neighbourhood. Few remember how much of this movement was a genuine enthusiasm; that one of its missionaries[16] who
travelled Ireland has written her life, has described meetings in
peasant cottages where everybody engaged in religious discussion,
has said that she was everywhere opposed and slandered by the
powerful and the wealthy because upon the side of the poor. I can
turn from the pages of her book with sympathy. Were I a better man
and a more ignorant I had liked just such a life. But that missionary
would have met with no sympathy at Roxborough, except, it may
be, amongst those boisterous brothers or from one studious girl, for
Roxborough Protestantism was on the side of wealth and power.
All there had an instinctive love for their country or their neighbourhood, the mail-boat had not yet drawn the thoughts of the
wealthy classes elsewhere. My great-grandmother Corbet, the mistress of Sandymount Castle, had been out of Ireland but once. She
had visited her son, afterwards Governor of Penang,[17] at his English
school, carrying a fortnight's provisions, so great were the hazards
of the crossing; but that was some two generations earlier. Their
proselytism expressed their love, they gave what they thought best.
But the born student of the great literature of the world cannot
proselytize, and Augusta Persse, as Lady Gregory was then named,
walked and discussed Shakespeare with a man but little steadier
than her brothers, a scholar of Trinity,[18] in later years a famous
botanist, a friendship ended by her alarmed mother. Was it earlier
or later that she established a little shop upon the estate and herself
sold there that she might compel the shopkeepers to bring down
their exorbitant prices? Other well-born women of that time,
Ruskin's Rose[19] amongst them, did the same. Born in 1852, she had
passed her formative years in comparative peace, Fenianism a far-
off threat; and her marriage with Sir William Gregory[20] in her
twenty-ninth year, visits to Ceylon, India, London, Rome, set her
beyond the reach of the bitter struggle between landlord and tenant
of the late 'seventies and early 'eighties. She knew Ireland always in
its permanent relationships, associations—violence but a brief
interruption—, never lost her sense of feudal responsibility, not of
duty as the word is generally understood, but of burdens laid upon
her by her station and her character, a choice constantly renewed in
solitude. 'She has been', said an old man to me, 'like a serving-maid
among us. She is plain and simple, like the Mother of God, and that

was the greatest lady that ever lived.' When in later years her literary style became in my ears the best written by woman, she had
made the people a part of her soul; a phrase of Aristotle's had
become her motto: 'To think like a wise man, but to express oneself
like the common people'.[21]

V

When I went to Coole the curtain had fallen upon the first act of my
drama. In 1891 I had founded in London the Irish Literary Society,
joined by most London journalists of Irish birth, a couple of years
later in Dublin, the National Literary Society; these societies had
given, as I intended, opportunity to a new generation of critics and
writers to denounce the propagandist verse and prose that had
gone by the name of Irish literature, and to substitute for it certain
neglected writers: Sir Samuel Ferguson, a writer of ballads dry in
their eighteenth-century sincerity; Standish O'Grady, whose *History
of Ireland* retold the Irish heroic tales in romantic Carlylean prose;
the Clarence Mangan of the 'Dark Rosaleen' and 'O'Hussey's Ode
to The Maguire', our one poet raised to the first rank by intensity,
and only that in these or perhaps in the second of these poems. No
political purpose informed our meetings; no Lord Mayor, no Member of Parliament, was elected to the chair. John O'Leary, the old Fenian, since his return from his Parisian exile more scholar than
politician, first president of the National Literary Society, was succeeded by Dr. Douglas Hyde. His famous presidential lecture upon
what he called 'The De-Anglicisation of Ireland'[22] led to the foundation of the Gaelic League, which, though not yet the great movement it became, was soon stronger than the movement in English.
Irishmen who wrote in the English language were read by the Irish
in England, by the general public there, nothing was read in Ireland
except newspapers, prayer-books, popular novels; but if Ireland
would not read literature it might listen to it, for politics and the
Church had created listeners. I wanted a Theatre—I had wanted it
for years, but knowing no way of getting money for a start in Ireland, had talked to Florence Farr, that accomplished speaker of
verse, less accomplished actress, of some little London hall, where
I could produce plays. I first spoke to Lady Gregory of my abandoned plan for an Irish Theatre, if I can call anything so hopeless a

plan, in the grounds of a little country house at Duras, on the sea-coast, where Galway ends and Clare begins. She had brought me to see the only person in Galway, perhaps I should say in Ireland, who was in any real sense her friend. His romantic name is written on the frame of a picture by Stott of Oldham in the Dublin Municipal Gallery: 'Given by A. Gregory and W. R. Gregory'—Lady Gregory's son, at the time of my first visit a boy of seventeen—'in memory of Count Florimond de Basterot'. He was a Catholic, an old man crippled by the sins of his youth, much devoted to his prayers, but an accomplished man of the world. He had flats in Paris and in Rome and divided his year between them and his little Galway house, passing through Dublin as quickly as possible because he thought it 'a shabby England'. Ancestors had fled from the French Revolution, bought a considerable Galway estate long since sold to some other landlord or divided among the tenants. In a few years, seven or eight, he was to speak to Lady Gregory and to myself, and for the first time, of estate and house, to drive us through what had once been park, show where the walls had stood, what had been garden, an aviary in the midst of it, where the avenue had wound, where upon that avenue he, a boy in his teens, and his father's men-servants had thrown a barricade across it and stood with guns in their hands. His father had died in debt, and at that time a creditor could seize a body and prevent its burial until paid. The creditor arrived, but at the sight of armed men fled. De Basterot fulfilled a saying I have heard some-where: 'Things reveal themselves passing away'.[23] We never saw him again. In five or six weeks, several men and women with old French titles announced upon a black-edged card the death of 'Florimond, Alfred Jacques, Comte de Basterot, Chevalier de l'Ordre du Saint Sépulcre, leur Cousin Germain et Cousin'. In his garden under his friendly eyes, the Irish National Theatre, though not under that name, was born. I may then have used for the first time the comparison which in later years I turned into a proverb. Except during certain summer months, when they roost in the fields, crows at nightfall return to the vast rookeries round Tulira Castle, whirling, counter-whirling, clamorous; excited, as it seems, by the sublime dance. It was the one unforgettable event of my first visit as of other visits there. And I was accustomed to say to Lady Gregory when it seemed that some play of mine must be first performed outside Ireland, or when it seemed, as it did once or twice, that I myself might find it impossible to live in Ireland: 'The crows of Tulira return to their trees in winter' or 'The crows return at nightfall', meaning that, after my death, my books would be a part of Irish literature. She, however, with her feeling for immediate action, for the present moment, disapproved of my London project. She offered to collect or give the money for the first Irish performances. My *Countess Cathleen* was ready, and either I or Lady Gregory spoke to Edward Martyn, who gave up a proposed German performance and became enthusiastic. Then came an unexpected difficulty. Dublin had two theatres, the Royal and the Gaiety, that had been granted patents, a system obsolete everywhere else. No performance, except for charity, could be given but at these two theatres; they were booked for the best months of the year by English travelling companies and in the worst months were expensive. We had to change the law,[24] which we did with the assistance of an old friend of Lady Gregory's husband, Lecky the historian, representative in Parliament of Trinity College. The writing of letters, talks in the Lobby of the House of Commons, seemed to take up all our time.

VI

I must have spent the summer of 1897 at Coole. I was involved in a miserable love affair,[25] that had but for one brief interruption absorbed my thoughts for years past, and would for some years yet. My devotion might as well have been offered to an image in a milliner's window, or to a statue in a museum, but romantic doctrine had reached its extreme development. Dowson was in love with a girl[26] in an Italian restaurant, courted her for two years; at first she was too young, then he too disreputable; she married the waiter and Dowson's life went to wreck. Sober, he looked on no woman; drunk, he picked the cheapest whore. 'He did not even want them clean', said a friend. 'I have been faithful to thee, Cynara, in my fashion.' My health was giving way, my nerves had been wrecked. Finding that I could not work, and thinking the open air salutary, Lady Gregory brought me from cottage to cottage collecting folk-lore. Every night she wrote out what we had heard in the dialect of the cottages. She wrote, if my memory does not deceive me, two hundred thousand words, discovering that vivid English she was the first to use upon the stage. My object was to find actual experience of the supernatural, for I did not believe, nor do I now, that it is possible to discover in the text-books of the schools, in the manuals sold by religious booksellers, even in the subtle reverie of saints, the most violent force in history. I have described elsewhere our discovery that when we passed the door of some peasant's cottage, we passed out of Europe as that word is understood. 'I have longed', she said once, 'to turn Catholic, that I might be nearer to the people, but you have taught me that paganism brings me nearer still.' Yet neither she nor those peasants were pagans. Christianity begins to recognize the validity of experiences that preceded its birth and were, in some sense, shared by its founders. When later she asked me to annotate and introduce her book, *Visions and Beliefs*,[27] I began a study of 'Spiritualism' not only in its scientific form but as it is found among the London poor, and discovered that there was little difference except that the experience of the cottagers was the richer. Requiring no proof that we survive the grave, they could turn to what was dramatic or exciting and, though more ignorant than the townsmen, lacked vulgarity. Do the cottagers still live that mysterious life? Has it been driven away by exciting tales of ambush and assassination or has it become more inaccessible? When I was yet a very young man Sligo people told me whatever I asked, because all knew my mother's father, and some still remembered my father's grandfather. The people of South Galway did the same because Lady Gregory was my friend; an old witch-doctor in Clare said to us both: 'I have told you now what I have not told my own wife'; but if a stranger, or a neighbour that might mock, questioned them, they would say that all such things had long disappeared through the influence of the school. Once when I heard an old shepherd at Doneraile, where I spent a few days, give Lord Castletown such an answer, I said: 'Has anybody ever gone from here to consult Biddy Early?'—a famous Clare witch—and in a moment the man's face became excited; he himself had stood at the roadside, watching spirits playing hurley in a field, until one came and pulled the cap over his eyes. What he saw, what he did not see but thought he saw, does not concern me here, being but a part of that traditional experience which I have discussed only too much elsewhere. That experience is my obsession, as Coole and its history, her hope that her son or her grandson might live there, were Lady Gregory's.

VII

It was now that George Moore[28] came into our affairs, brought by
Edward Martyn, who invited him to find a cast for *The Heather Field*.
They were cousins and inseparable friends, bound one to the other
by mutual contempt. When I told Martyn that Moore had good
points, he replied: 'I know Moore a great deal longer than you do.
He has no good points.' And a week or two later Moore said: 'That
man Martyn is the most selfish man alive. He thinks that I am
damned and he doesn't care.' I have described their friendship in a
little play called *The Cat and the Moon;* the speaker is a blind beg-
gar-man, and Laban is a townland where Edward Martyn went to
chapel: . . . 'Did you ever know a holy man but had a wicked man
for his comrade and his heart's darling? There is not a more holy man
in the barony than the man who has the big house at Laban, and he
goes knocking about the roads day and night with that old lecher
from the county of Mayo, and he a woman-hater from the day of his
birth. And well you know and all the neighbours know what they talk
of by daylight and candlelight. The old lecher does be telling over all
the sins he committed, or maybe never committed at all, and the man
of Laban does be trying to head him off and quiet him down that he
may quit telling them.'[29] Moore and Martyn were indeed in certain
characteristics typical peasants, the peasant sinner, the peasant
saint. Moore's grandfather or great-grandfather had been a convert,
but there were Catholic marriages. Catholic families, beaten down
by the Penal Laws,[30] despised by Irish Protestants, by the few English Catholics they met, had but little choice as to where they picked
their brides; boys, on one side of old family, grew up squireens, half-
sirs, peasants who had lost their tradition, gentlemen who had lost
theirs. Lady Gregory once told me what marriage coarsened the
Moore blood, but I have forgotten.

George Moore had a ceaseless preoccupation with painting and
the theatre, within certain limits a technical understanding of both;
whatever idea possessed him, courage and explosive power; but
sacrificed all that seemed to other men good breeding, honour,
friendship, in pursuit of what he considered the root facts of life. I
had seen him once in the Cheshire Cheese. I had with me some
proof-sheets of the Ellis and Yeats study of Blake's philosophy,[31]
and the drooping tree on the second page of *The Book of Thel*[32]

stirred him to eloquence. His 'How beautiful, how beautiful!' is all I can remember. Then one evening, in a narrow empty street between Fleet Street and the river, I heard a voice resounding as if in a funnel, someone in a hansom cab was denouncing its driver, and Moore drove by. Then I met him in Arthur Symons' flat in the Temple. He threw himself into a chair with the remark: 'I wish that woman would wash'. He had just returned from an assignation with his mistress, a woman known to Symons personally, to me by repute, an accomplished, witty, somewhat fashionable woman. All his friends suffered in some way; good behaviour was no protection, for it was all chance whether the facts he pursued were in actual life or in some story that amused him. Had 'that woman' prided herself upon her cleanliness, he would, had he decided upon a quarrel, have said with greater publicity: 'I wish that woman would wash'. His pursuit had now and then unfortunate results. 'What has depressed you, Moore?' said an acquaintance. 'I have been paying attention to a certain woman. I had every reason to think she liked me. I came to the point to-day and was turned down completely.' 'You must have said something wrong.' 'No, what I said was all right.' 'What was it?' 'I said I was clean and healthy and she could not do better.' Upon occasion it made him brutal and witty. He and I went to the town of Galway for a Gaelic festival that coincided with some assembly of priests. When we lunched at the Railway Hotel the room was full of priests. A Father Moloney, supposed to know all about Greek Art, caught sight of Moore and introduced himself. He probably knew nothing about Moore, except that he was some kind of critic, for he set out upon his favourite topic with: 'I have always considered it a proof of Greek purity that though they left the male form uncovered, they invariably draped the female'. 'Do you consider, Father Moloney,' said Moore in a voice that rang through the whole room, 'that the female form is inherently more indecent than the male?' Every priest turned a stern and horrified eye upon Father Moloney, who sat hunched up and quivering.

I have twice known Moore alarmed and conscience-struck, when told that he had injured somebody's financial prospects—a financial prospect is a root fact—but he attacked with indifference so long as nothing suffered but his victim's dignity or feelings. To injure a famous scholar in a quarrel[33] not his he had printed all the scandalous stories he could rake together, or invent, in a frenzy of political hatred. I had remonstrated in vain, except that he cut out a passage describing his victim as 'a long pink pig', yet when he thought he might have deprived that scholar of a post he was miserable.

He had gone to Paris straight from his father's racing stables, from a house where there was no culture, as Symons and I understood that word, acquired copious inaccurate French, sat among art students, young writers about to become famous, in some café; a man carved out of a turnip, looking out of astonished eyes. I see him as that circle saw him, for I have in memory Manet's caricature.[34] He spoke badly and much in a foreign tongue, read nothing, and was never to attain the discipline of style. 'I wrote a play in French', he said, 'before I had seen dialogue on paper.' I doubt if he had read a play of Shakespeare's even at the end of his life. He did not know that style existed until he returned to Ireland in middle life; what he learned, he learned from conversation, from acted plays, from pictures. A revolutionary in revolt against the ignorant Catholicism of Mayo, he chose for master Zola as another might have chosen Karl Marx. Even to conversation and acted plays, he gave an inattentive ear, instincts incapable of clear expression deafened him and blinded him; he was Milton's lion[35] rising up, pawing out of the earth, but unlike that lion, stuck half-way. He reached to middle life ignorant even of small practical details. He said to a friend: 'How do you keep your pants from falling about your knees?' 'O', said the friend, 'I put my braces through the little tapes that are sewn there for the purpose.' A few days later, he thanked the friend with emotion. Upon a long country bicycle ride with another friend, he had stopped because his pants were about his knees, had gone behind a hedge, had taken them off, and exchanged them at a cottage for a tumbler of milk. Only at pictures did he look undeafened and unblinded, for they impose their silence upon us. His *Modern Painting* has colloquial animation and surprise that might have grown into a roundness and ripeness of speech that is a part of style had not ambition made him in later life prefer sentences a Dublin critic has compared to ribbons of tooth-paste squeezed out of a tube. When the Irish Theatre was founded, he had published *A Mummer's Wife*, which had made a considerable sensation, for it was the first realistic novel in the language, the first novel where every incident was there not because the author thought it beautiful, exciting or amusing, but because certain people who were neither beautiful, exciting, nor amusing must have acted in that way: the root facts of life, as they are known to the greatest number of people, that and nothing else. Balzac would have added his wisdom. Moore had but his blind ambition. *Esther Waters* should have been a greater novel, for the scene is more varied. Esther is tempted to steal a half-crown; Balzac might have made her steal it and keep our sympathy, but Moore must create a personification of motherly goodness, almost an abstraction. Five years later he begged a number of his friends to read it. 'I have just read it', he said. 'It has done me good, it radiates goodness.' He had wanted to be good as the mass of men understand goodness. In later life he wrote a long preface to prove that he had a mistress in Mayfair.

VIII

I knew nothing of Moore at the time I write of except what Symons or Martyn told me, or I had learnt from his occasional articles. I had read no book of his, nor would I, had he not insisted, for my sympathies were narrow. I cared for nothing but poetry or prose that shared its intensity. Florence Farr and I had just begun that attempt described in 'Speaking to the Psaltery'[36] to revive the ancient art of minstrelsy. Florence Farr had ruined her career by premature success. For ten years she had played a series of parts, which had through their association with controversial movements attained great publicity. I remember most vividly her performance in *Arms and the Man* and in *Rosmersholm,* but most of all her first success in Dr. Todhunter's *Sicilian Idyll.*[37] Because she could not accept less than twenty pounds a week without loss of status and got it but rarely, she was doomed to remain an amateur. Yet her voice was among the most beautiful of her time, her elocution, her mastery of poetical rhythm incomparable.

IX

To remind myself of these and other events I have been looking through the letters I wrote to Lady Gregory during those first years of our friendship.[38] She was now at Coole, now at Queen Anne's

Mansions, now in Paris, I at 18 Woburn Buildings, London, or with an uncle at Sligo. On the ground floor at Woburn Buildings lived a shoemaker; on the first floor a workman and his family; I on the second floor; in the attic an old pedlar, who painted a little in water-colours. I wrote in one of the earliest letters: 'I have measured the window' (Lady Gregory must have given me the great blue curtain that was a principal feature there for twenty years). 'Ought I to let you do all these kind things for me? . . . I have reasoned myself out of the instincts and rules by which one mostly surrounds oneself. I have nothing but reason to trust to, and so am in continual doubt about simple things.'

Presently she gave me a great leather arm-chair which is before my eyes at this moment. From her came the great collection of folk-lore that, turned into essays for the monthly reviews, brought ten or fifteen pounds at a time.[39] Then one night when she and the other guests had gone I found twenty pounds behind my clock. I went to see her and tried to return it. 'You must take this money', she said. 'You should give up journalism. The only wrong act that matters is not doing one's best work.' She had that test for everyone. We were all like packets of herbs, each with its special quality. From time to time from that on she gave me money. I was not to consider it a loan, though I might return it some day if well off. When I finished my first lecture tour in the United States, the winter of 1903–04, I tried to return it, but she said: 'Not until I think you have enough money to feel independent'. I inherited a little money from a relative,[40] but she still refused. Four or five years later she consented. I asked how much; she said, 'Five hundred'. It was a shock to find I owed so much. I wrote to an American lecture agent, earned the money and paid it back. That I am ashamed of that long debt to so dear a friend, that I have told it after a struggle with myself, puts me to shame. Of still greater service were those summers at Coole. For twenty years I spent two or three months there in every year. Because of those summers, because of that money, I was able through the greater part of my working life to write without thought of anything but the beauty or the utility of what I wrote. Until I was nearly fifty, my writing never brought me more than two hundred a year, and most often less, and I am not by nature economical.

I wrote from Sligo of my uncle George Pollexfen (I have described him in *The Trembling of the Veil*): 'He is just at this moment in one of his bad fits owing to the fact that the inhabitants attack him as they cannot get at me. He brought me to a Masonic concert on Thursday. Somebody sang a stage Irishman's song—the usual whiskey, shillelagh kind of thing—and I hissed him, and lest my hiss might be lost in the general applause, waited until the applause had died down and hissed again. That gave somebody also courage, and we both hissed. My uncle defends me, but says that he makes a poor hand of it and gets beaten.'[41]

Then I wrote about 'A great battle[42] with George Armstrong' (Professor of Literature at Cork; author of a trilogy, *Saul, David, Solomon*). 'He lectured on *The Two Irelands, or Ireland in Literature,* and his whole lecture was an attack on the "Celtic Movement", full of insinuations about conspiracies to prevent his success as a poet, to keep him out of anthologies, etc. I replied with a great deal of fierceness, described the barrenness of the so-called intellect of Ireland, told him that all the cleverest of the young men were leaving him and coming to us. I then attacked his scholarship and showed that his knowledge of Irish things was of the most obsolete kind. I believe I was unanswerable. At any rate Armstrong made no attempt to reply, but excused himself because of the lateness of the hour, which was weak as he had brought the contest upon himself, and made the hour late by speaking for two hours. Father Barry, who was in the chair, said afterwards: "Thank you for your speech. I agree with almost every word of it." I was glad of this, as it was probably the fiercest the Society had ever heard.'

Then I told how I had taken the chair at some public meeting in London where speakers talked open sedition: 'A principal speaker was the Vicar of Plumpton, who advised everybody to buy a breechloader and prepare for the day of battle and wound up by singing a patriotic song, apparently of his own making. . . . I was in such a rage that I forgot to put the Resolutions.'[43] Then I described old Cipriani, who spoke as though he stood 'on a battlefield, and he has stood on fifty'. A magnificent-looking old man, a friend of Garibaldi, he had gone all over the world fighting for liberty, and Maud Gonne had brought him to Ireland[44] to work out a scheme for insurrection, then to some London Irish to make his report. In one letter I used a phrase Lady Gregory was often to chaff me about, though never to repudiate: 'In a battle like Ireland's, which is one of poverty against wealth, we must prove our sincerity by making ourselves unpopular to wealth. We must accept the baptism of the gutter.[45] Have not all the leaders done that?'

Then an adventure: 'Yesterday I was in a tea-shop', I wrote from London, 'when a woman with an obvious look of the country introduced herself to me as a Gaelic Leaguer, and straightway introduced me to two friends, a man and a woman who had an equally country look. They told me with wonderful brogues that they were on their way to the Paris Exhibition, and wanted to shake hands with me. They had a great deal to say about the Movement and talked very fast for fear I might go before they had said it. What they said was chiefly about a play in Irish to be acted in Macroom next Monday. It is by one Father Peter O'Leary, and is about a man who lived in Macroom and arranged his own funeral to escape the bailiff. There was immense local enthusiasm over it, and deep indignation among the descendants of the bailiff.'[46]

There is an allusion to the Cabbalistic Society, which had taught me methods of meditation that had greatly affected my thought. A talented girl[47] I had tried to find work for had after years of victorious prudery become the mistress of a drunken scoundrel, and advertised the fact everywhere, even pouring out tea with his arm round her waist. 'Because she has enough genius', I wrote, 'to make her thirst for reality, and not enough intellect to understand the temporal use of unreal things, she is throwing off every remnant of respectability.'[48] Presently, from excitability, shock, bewilderment at her private circle, which had no objection to lovers but much to that particular lover, her health broke down. Then the Cabbalistic Society took her affairs in hand, a rich member had 'collected all her unpaid bills . . . another mystic sees her to-day and will give her whatever help may be wanted. These mystics will not bemoralize her, which her other friends have been doing, especially Lady ——.'[49] (She had denounced the crime of picking the wrong man. Her own entanglement was notorious but exalted.) 'For their faith makes them look on everything in the world as so wrong that the conventional errors seem to them trivial, and all defiance meritorious. They keep their morality for each other, and are firmly divided just now into the compassionate who lack idealism, and the idealists who lack compassion—Moore's "Idle Devout"; and —— has been handed over to the compassionate, to the joy of the "Idle Devout" who are anxious to be forgotten by their enemies.'[50] A year or two later I was to describe her crying over Wilde's death: ' "He was so kind, nobody ever lived who was so kind". As she said it I thought of Homer's description of the captive women: "Weeping in seeming for Patroclus, yet each weeping for her own sorrow, because he was ever kind".'[51] I wrote to Lady Gregory about this girl, because I was certain of her sympathy, yet those who did not know her thought her stern. A beautiful woman, whose love affairs were notorious, once said to me: 'When I got into the train at Broadstone, there were only two vacant places, one next Lady Gregory and one next the Bishop of Tuam. I thought "I am in for a lecture from somebody" and took the place next the Bishop, and all he said was: "Well, my child, you know a great deal more of the world than when I confirmed you".'

X

I invited Florence Farr to find players for my *Countess Cathleen*.[52] I do not remember whether it was Florence Farr or I or Edward Martyn who asked a Dublin amateur actor to play a principal part in both plays, but it was certainly Edward Martyn who invited George Moore to a rehearsal of *The Heather Field*. I wrote to Lady Gregory in March or April 1899: 'Moore first got rid of practically the whole cast', putting X (the Dublin amateur actor) out of the part of Usher. 'He ran at the chairs, kicked them and called Moore names, upon which the prompter threatened him with personal violence if he used such language in the presence of ladies.'[53]

Then Moore descended upon my rehearsals. I was relieved, for I was rehearsing in the part of Countess Cathleen a young girl who had made a great success some years before as the Faery Child in my *Land of Heart's Desire*. She had a beautiful speaking voice but lacked experience. I describe the result: 'Moore has put a Miss Whitty to act Countess Cathleen. She acts admirably, and has no sense of rhythm whatever. . . . She enrages me every moment, but will make the part a success. I am getting the others to speak with a little, a very little music. Mrs. Emery (Florence Farr) alone satisfies my ear.'[54] Perhaps I should have insisted upon the young girl, for after Miss Whitty's dress rehearsal somebody said: 'Miss Whitty brought tears into my eyes because she had them in her voice, but that young girl brought them into my eyes with beauty'.[55]

When 'The Antient Concert Rooms' had been taken, the rehearsals almost begun, Edward Martyn wrote to Lady Gregory and myself withdrawing financial support. Some monk, I never learned the name, had called *The Countess Cathleen* heretical. She sells her soul to certain demons for money that the people may not be compelled by starvation to sell theirs. She dies. The demons had deceived themselves, had trusted to bond and signature, but God sees 'the motive, not the deed'. My error was doubly dangerous, for I had put the thought into the mouth of an angel. A political enemy[56] wrote a pamphlet against the play, quoting the opinions of the demons as if they were the author's, sold it in the shops, in the streets, dropped copies into every doctor's letter-box, but Edward Martyn was not disturbed. No popular agitation disturbed him. Somebody had read or shown the pamphlet to old Cardinal Logue, and he had written to the newspapers that if the play was as represented, no Catholic should go to it. And that, too, did not disturb him, because Cardinal Logue had not seen the play.[57] Lady Gregory and I thought that two ecclesiastics might be got to outvote one; Martyn agreed to accept the verdict, and Lady Gregory made Moore promise silence for a fortnight. I have lost Father Finlay's letter, it approved the play, but I have Father Barry's. He was the author of *The New Antigone,* a famous book in those days, and what is more, a learned, accomplished man.[58] 'From the literal point of view', he wrote, 'theologians, Catholic or other, could object that no one is free to sell his soul in order to buy bread even for the starving, but Saint Paul says: "I wish to be anathema for my people", which is another way for expressing what you have put into the story. I would give the play and the explanation afterwards.' Edward Martyn was quite content, but not Moore. 'Martyn', I wrote to Lady Gregory, 'is in excellent spirits, but says that if any person in authority were to speak, he would withdraw again.' (The votes would be equal.) Moore, upon the other hand, lamented his lost row. He had meant to write an article called 'Edward Martyn and his Soul'. He said: 'It was the best opportunity I ever had. What a sensation it would have made! Nobody has ever written that way about his most intimate friend. What a chance! It would have been heard of everywhere.'[59] As Florence Farr and I sat at breakfast in a Dublin hotel, having just arrived by the mail-boat to make some final arrangements, Martyn came wiping the perspiration from his face in great excitement. His first sentence was: 'I withdraw again'. He had just received by post 'Edward Martyn and his Soul' in the form of a letter. We comforted him all we could, and before twelve o'clock all was well. Before the first performance, to the charge of heresy was added that of representing Irish men and women as selling their souls, whereas 'their refusal to change their religion, even when starving, proved that they would not'. On the night of the performance, there was a friendly house drawn from the general public, but many interrupters in the gallery. I had asked for police protection and found twenty or thirty police awaiting my arrival. A sergeant explained that they could not act unless called upon. I turned to a friend, once Secretary to the Land League,[60] and said: 'Stay with me, I have no experience'. All the police smiled, and I remembered a lying rumour that I had organized the Jubilee riots;[61] people had even told each other what sum I paid for every rioter. The selling of the souls; the lines—

> The Light of Lights
> Looks always on the motive, not the deed;[62]

and

> Sign with this quill.
> It was a feather growing on the cock
> That crowed when Peter dared deny his Master,
> And all who use it have great honour in Hell;[63]

the last four considered an attack on the Pope, caused disturbances. Every disturbance was drowned by cheers. Arthur Griffith, afterwards slanderer of Lane and Synge, founder of the Sinn Fein Movement, first President of the Irish Free State, and at that time an enthusiastic anti-cleric, claimed to have brought 'a lot of men from the Quays and told them to applaud everything the Church would not like'. I did not want my play turned into an anti-clerical demonstration, and decided from the general feeling of discomfort when an evil peasant in my first act trampled upon a Catholic shrine that the disturbances were in part my own fault. In using what I considered traditional symbols I forgot that in Ireland they are not symbols but realities. But the attacks in the main, like those upon Synge and O'Casey,[64] came from the public ignorance of literary method. The play itself was ill-constructed, the dialogue turning aside at the lure of word or metaphor, very different, I hope, from the play as it is to-day after many alterations, every alteration tested by performance. It was not, nor is it now, more than a piece of tapestry. The Countess sells her soul, but she is not transformed. If I were to think out that scene to-day, she would, the moment her hand has signed, burst into loud laughter, mock at all she has held holy, horrify the peasants in the midst of their temptations. Nothing satisfied me but Florence Farr's performance in the part of Aleel. Dublin talked of it for years, and after five-and-thirty years I keep among my unforgettable memories the sense of coming disaster she put into the words:

> . . . but now
> Two grey horned owls hooted above our heads.[65]

I telegraphed to Moore: 'Play a success'; he arrived in time for *The Heather Field*. He says in *Ave* that Martyn telegraphed: 'The sceptre of intellect has passed from England to Ireland',[66] but that sounds more like Moore than the economical, tongue-tied Martyn, and suggests the state of exaltation he arrived in. *The Heather Field* was a much greater success than *The Countess Cathleen,* being in the manner of Ibsen, the manner of the moment. The construction seemed masterly. I tried to believe that a great new dramatist had appeared. Miss Whitty, who in *The Countess Cathleen* had been effective and commonplace, moving us to tears by the tears in her own voice, was now acrid, powerful, original; an actor who played the hero[67] driven to madness by his too practical wife (Mrs. Martyn's attempts to find a wife for her son came into my head) was perhaps even better. At the end of the performance, Moore forced his way through the crowded lobby triumphant (I did not know until months afterwards that the masterly construction had been his), and catching sight of a tall friend near the street door shouted: 'I see by the morning paper that . . . has provided Lord . . . with an heir', thereby starting a scandal that ran for months from village to village, disturbing several circles, private and official.

XI

A couple of years before, it had seemed for a few months that the old political groupings were about to break up, everywhere people had looked forward, expecting, speculating. A Royal Commission, its members drawn from all parties, appointed by a Conservative Government, presided over by Gladstone's Lord Chancellor, had reported that the over-taxation of Ireland for the last fifty years amounted to some three hundred millions. The Irish Landlord Party, which based its politics upon the conviction that Ireland had gained by the Union, had a revulsion of conscience. Lord Castletown made a famous speech declaring that Ireland must imitate the colonists who flung the tea into Boston Harbour. Landlord committees were appointed in every county. Then Lord Salisbury appointed a second Royal Commission to consider the wrongs of landlords, and not one of those committees met again.[68] There was deep disappointment. Protestant Ireland had immense prestige, Burke, Swift, Grattan, Emmet, Fitzgerald, Parnell, almost every name sung in modern song, had been Protestant; Dublin's dignity depended upon the gaunt magnificence of buildings founded under the old Parliament; but wherever it attempted some corporate action, wherein Ireland stood against England, the show, however gallant it seemed, was soon over. It sold its Parliament for solid money, and now it sold this cause for a phantom. Nobody was the better or worse for Lord Salisbury's new Commission. Protestant Ireland could not have done otherwise; it lacked hereditary passion. Parnell, its last great figure, finding that this lack had made the party of my father's old friend Isaac Butt powerless, called in the peasants' tenacity and violence, but for months now the peasants had stood aside and waited, hoping that their old masters might take the leadership again. Standish O'Grady,[69] a man past middle life, was now principal leader-writer of the *Daily Express*, the most uncompromising of the Dublin Unionist newspapers. He was of landlord stock, based all his hopes for Ireland upon that stock. He resigned his position in despair, bought a provincial newspaper, hoped, having made it a success, to buy up other provincial newspapers till he had all the provincial newspapers in Ireland. They would keep their local news, but all would contain his articles, all would rouse the gentry to their duty. He wrote pamphlets, published a weekly review, the same theme recurring. A famous passage[70] described the downfall and flight of the Catholic aristocracy, lamented by the poor, sung by poets, but their successors, he cried out, would pass unlamented, unsung. In another, fixing his thought upon the poorer gentry, he compared them to the lean hounds that are the best hunters: 'O, lean hounds, when will you begin to hunt?' His plans brought him misfortune. A certain man had, in his opinion, wronged and slandered a county family. He denounced him, and because the county took no notice wrote lofty essays upon its lack of public spirit. He wrote for his equals, wrote as Grattan spoke, not for the mob that he scorned. Hearing a great noise under his window, he looked out; men were marching to take ship for South Africa, cheering for Kruger, at their head the man he had denounced. His words had destroyed that man's influence among those O'Grady scorned without affecting it anywhere else. He lost his head and in fierce melancholy wrote that he no longer condemned 'the poor wretch himself, but the three bad men who supported him', naming the Master of the Foxhounds, the Bishop and the principal nobleman of that district. After that an action for libel and financial disaster. The Bishop—or was it the Master of Foxhounds?—never heard of the essays, never knew that there was a charge against 'the poor wretch himself', and as O'Grady was unable to prove the contrary, friends arranged for his apology and mitigated his bankruptcy. All that, however, was yet to come.

Horace Plunkett had bought the *Daily Express*. Under T. P. Gill, an ex-Parnellite Member and London journalist, it expounded Plunkett's agricultural policy, avoiding all that might excite passion. Gill had spent his life manipulating incompatibles; at the Parnellite split he took neither side. I think of him as making toy houses with little bits of pasteboard, gummed together with stamp-paper. 'So-and-so is flat-footed', he would say, characterizing some person whose heavy step might shake the table, and the flat-footed abounded at the moment. The relations of England and France were disturbed, a French officer, batoned in the Dublin streets, reported to the French War Office that Ireland was ready for insurrection. Maud Gonne had persuaded that Office to take from a pigeon-hole a scheme for an invasion of Ireland. A man I met in Sligo dreamed that he was entrenched in a swamp, fighting against invaders. 'What will you do', somebody asked the *Express* Editor, 'if the French land at Killala?' 'I will write the best article of my life', was the answer. 'I will call upon my readers to remember their great traditions, to remember their own ancestors, to make up their minds with the utmost resolution, without a moment's hesitation, which side they are going to take.'

The *Daily Express* was almost as unsuccessful financially as Standish O'Grady's paper. When it wrote of a Protestant and of a Catholic Archbishop, old subscribers withdrew because the first, being the only true Archbishop, required no prefix. New subscribers bought little but the Friday number, which reviewed books, avoided contemporary politics, but contained articles that made people say: 'Something is going to happen'. In its correspondence column, controversies were fought out that are still remembered.

Then Horace Plunkett told Gill to give a public dinner to Edward Martyn and myself. I do not remember who took the chair, or the names of more than half a dozen of the guests. Moore has described it in *Ave*,[71] but our memories differ. I doubt even his first sentence: 'Not an opera hat amongst them, and no one should be seen without one . . . perhaps they have not even changed their socks'. He was thinking of taking up politics, wanted to go into Parliament as an Irish patriot, had suggested, with that ingenuous way of his, that I should do the same, he would even accept me as his leader, and when I would not, wrote—or did that come later?— to John Redmond, then in control of the reunited Party, and offered himself as a candidate. He came to the dinner carrying in his hand the only political speech he was ever to deliver, an attack on William O'Brien, then about to return to public life at the head of his Mayo peasants. A little before he stood up, J. F. Taylor came, late for the dinner, but in time for his main interest, the speeches. He was Moore's opposite, a great orator, the greatest I have heard, doomed by the violence of his temper to speak before Law Students' Debating Societies, obscure Young Ireland Societies, Workmen's Clubs. His body was angular, often rigid with suppressed rage, his gaze fixed upon some object, his clothes badly made, his erect attitude suggesting a firm base. Moore's body was insinuating, upflowing, circulative, curvicular, pop-eyed. What brought Taylor, I do not know. He hated me, partly because his mind, trained in Catholic schools, where formal logic had importance, was dry and abstract, except in the great flights of his rhetoric, mine romantic, but mainly because jealous of my influence with the old Fenian John O'Leary. O'Leary used to say: 'I have three followers—Taylor, Yeats, and Rolleston'.[72] But now that Rolleston had taken office under the Crown, he had but Taylor and me. He came perhaps because *The Heather Field*'s lack of sensuous form, or its logical structure, attracted him. Moore seemed timid, and was certainly all but inaudible. Taylor alone seemed to listen, but he listened stiffening. William O'Brien was his special private butt, he had denounced him for ten years as the type of an unscrupulous, reckless demagogue. How dared anybody touch his pheasant, his partridge, his snipe? What Moore said, I do not remember. I remember Taylor, though lacking the crowd of young men, the instrument on which he had learned to play, he was not at his best. 'When William O'Brien was making the sacrifice of Mr. Yeats' *Countess Cathleen,* damning his soul for his country, where was Mr. Moore? In London, in Paris?' Thereon he described Moore's life, in phrases that were perhaps influenced by Carlyle's description at the opening of his *French Revolution,* of the 'Scarlet Woman' Dubarry. Moore has written[73] that I tried to make him answer, but I was at the other side of the table, and had learnt from defeats of my own not to rouse that formidable man. Moore with *Esther Waters* and *A Mummer's Wife* to his account, one or other in the mind of every man there, had no need to answer. Towards the end of the evening, when everybody was more or less drunk, O'Grady spoke. He was very drunk, but neither his voice nor his manner showed it. I had never heard him speak, and at first he reminded me of Cardinal Manning. There was the same simplicity, the same gentleness. He stood between two tables, touching one or the other for support, and said in a low penetrating voice: 'We have now a literary movement, it is not very important; it will be followed by a political movement, that will not be very important; then must come a military movement, that will be important indeed'. Tyrrell, Professor of Greek in Trinity College, known to scholars for his share in the Tyrrell-Purser edition of Cicero's Letters, a Unionist, but very drunk, led the applause. Then O'Grady described the Boy Scout Act, which had just passed, urged the landlords of Ireland to avail themselves of that Act and drill the sons of their tenants—'paying but little attention to the age limit'—then, pointing to where he supposed England to be, they must bid them 'march to the conquest of that decadent nation'. I knew what was in his mind. England was decadent because, democratic and so without fixed principles, it had used Irish landlords, his own ancestors or living relatives, as its garrison, and later left them deserted among their enemies. Tyrrell, understanding nothing but the sweetness of that voice, the nobility of that gesture, continued to lead the applause. Moore for all his toil had never style. Taylor had it in flights of oratorical frenzy, but drunk or sober, idle or toiling, this man had it; their torch smoked, their wine had dregs, his element burned or ran pure. When in later years compelled to answer some bitter personal attack, he showed that alone among our public men he could rise above bitterness, use words that, for all their convincing logic, made his reader murmur:

> Ye do it wrong, being so majestical,
> To offer it the show of violence.[74]

When I try to recall his physical appearance, my father's picture in the Municipal Gallery[75] blots out my own memory. He comes before me with a normal robust body, dim obsessed eyes, upon the wall above his head the title of a forgotten novel: *Ye Loste Lande*.[76]

XII

The Countess Cathleen and *The Heather Field* were performed in the week commencing May 8th, 1899, and such was our faith in the author of *The Heather Field* that, though we had not seen his unfinished play, we engaged the Gaiety Theatre for a week in 1900. His play, understood to be satirical and topical, was to be the main event. *Maeve*,[77] originally published with *The Heather Field*, would accompany it, but was, we thought, too poetical, too remote from normal life to draw the crowd. I spent the summer at Coole; George Moore was at Tulira, but on Sunday mornings Edward Martyn's old coachman would drive up by the Gort Avenue, George Moore behind him on the old outside car: Moore had been to Mass. As Moore had been brought up a Catholic, Martyn insisted upon Mass; how they avoided the Ardrahan church and Martyn's company I cannot remember; perhaps Martyn went to early Mass; but Gort suited them both. Moore would listen for a minute, would slip out, meet his coachman at the side door of a public-house which ignored the Act of Parliament for its more valuable customers, find the outside car in some yard. Coole was but two miles off, one mile of road, one mile of demesne under great trees. Devotion to Parnell had made the coachman an anti-cleric. A couple of years later I saw him for the last time, he wanted an introduction to somebody he knew of that lacked a coachman. When Lady Gregory asked about his dismissal he said: 'I think Mr. Martyn thought I must soon die because I am an old man, and that he might see my ghost'. Lady Gregory remembered that Mrs. Martyn had died the year before, that Martyn, whose conscience tortured him because he had opposed her plans, perhaps because he had refused to marry, had seen some sight or heard some sound that terrified him. Sometimes Moore drove over in the afternoon. One afternoon he asked to see me alone. I brought him to the path by the lakeside. He had constructed *The Heather Field,* he said, telling Martyn what was to go into every speech but writing nothing, had partly constructed *Maeve*—I heard only the other day that Arthur Symons had revised the style for a fee, setting it high above Martyn's level—but that Martyn now refused his help. 'He can find subjects', Moore said, 'and I cannot, but he will never write a play alone; I am ready to collaborate all my life and say nothing about it. You must go to Tulira and persuade Martyn.' This was a Moore I had known nothing of; he had certainly kept silent; it was improbable he could do so now that the play was a success, but it did not seem so at the moment. Moore in his moments of self-abnegation was convinced and convincing. I do not remember whether he had brought the new play as Martyn had written it or whether Martyn sent it later, but I know that my interview with Martyn was postponed until Lady Gregory and I had read it. It seemed to us crude throughout, childish in parts, a play to make our movement and ourselves ridiculous. I was now Moore's advocate and, unlike Lady Gregory, unable to see with Martyn's eyes. I went to Tulira and there denounced the play. I seem to remember Moore as anxious and subdued. Later when he described the scene he compared me to Torquemada.[78] Martyn told us to do what we liked with the play. Moore asked for my collaboration as it was a satire upon contemporary Irish politics and of these he knew nothing. I moved from Coole to Tulira. The finished work was Moore's in its construction and characterization, but most of the political epigrams and certain bitter sentences put into the mouth of Deane,[79] a dramatization of Standish O'Grady, were mine. A rhetorical, undramatic second act about the Celtic Movement, which I had begun to outlive, was all Moore's; as convert he was embarrassing, unsubduable, preposterous.

Lady Gregory thought that no man could endure the sight of others altering all that he had done and discussing the alterations within earshot. She was doubtless right, for Martyn suddenly took the play back. If he could not write his own plays he was no use, he said; but when the position of the theatre was put before him, my determination and Lady Gregory's to refuse his play, his loss of money, for he was to pay for all, if we had only *Maeve,* he gave way once more. Moore, however, must sign the play; he would not sign with him 'because Moore would put in what he liked'. Moore was unwilling, he thought little could be made of such material; but being for the moment all self-abnegation, agreed, and was soon convinced that he had written a masterpiece.

There were continual quarrels, sometimes because both were woman-mad, Martyn with contempt, sometimes because Moore did not want to go to Mass, once because he had over-slept himself 'on purpose.' Yet Moore was at this time neither anti-clerical nor anti-Catholic. He had written not only *Evelyn Innes* but *Sister Teresa,* a sympathetic study of a convent; nor was he ever to lose an understanding of emotions and beliefs remembered from childhood. He did not want to go to Mass, because his flesh was unwilling, as it was a year later when the teacher, engaged to teach him Gaelic, was told that he was out.

He had exhausted his England in *A Mummer's Wife* and *Esther Waters,* and had turned to us, seeking his new task with an ungovernable childlike passion. In later years he attributed his distaste for England to his work upon *The Bending of the Bough,* his name for Martyn's rewritten play, and it is possible that it made him aware of change. Violent and coarse of temper, he was bound to follow his pendulum's utmost swing; hatred of Queen Victoria, admiration of Catholicism, hatred of the English language, love of everything Gaelic, were bound to follow one upon another till he had found his new limit. His relations to men and women ran through like alternations, in his relations to women he touched madness. On a visit to Coole, during some revising of *The Bending of the Bough,* or to begin *Diarmuid and Grania,*[80] its successor, he behaved well till there came a long pause in the conversation one night after dinner. 'I wonder', said Moore, 'why Mrs. —— threw me over; was it because she wanted to marry ——'—he named a famous woman and a famous peer—'or was it conscience?' I followed Moore to his room and said, 'You have broken the understanding?' 'What understanding?' 'That your conversation would be fit for Robert.' Robert, Lady Gregory's son, was on holiday there from Harrow. 'The word conscience can have only one meaning.' 'But it's true.' 'There is a social rule that bars such indiscretions.' 'It has gone out.' 'Not here.' 'But it is the only thing I can say about her that she would mind.' Mrs.——had been much taken with Moore, I had heard her talk of him all evening, but was of strict morals: I knew from the friend who had listened to Moore's daily complaints and later to his contradictory inventions, that he had courted her in vain. Two or three years after his Coole transgression, he was accustomed to say: 'Once she and I were walking in the Green Park. "There is nothing more cruel than lust", she said. "There is", I said. "What is that?" "Vanity", and I let her go a step or two ahead and gave her a kick behind.'

XIII

On February 19th, *The Bending of the Bough* and a narrative undramatic play by Alice Milligan, *The Last Feast of the Fianna;* on February 20th, *Maeve,* were performed at the Gaiety Theatre. The actors had been collected by Moore in London. Our audiences, which seemed to us very large, did not fill the house, but were enthusiastic; we worked, perhaps I still work, for a small fanatical sect. *The Bending of the Bough* was badly constructed, had never become a single thought or passion, but was the first dramatization of an Irish problem. Lady Gregory wrote in her diary: 'M. is in great enthusiasm over it, says it will cause a revolution' (whoever M. was he was not Martyn, who hated the play). 'H. says no young man who sees that play will leave the house as he came into it. . . . The Gaelic League, in great force, sang "Fainne geal an lae" between the acts, and "The Wearing of the Green" in Irish. . . . The play hits so impartially all round that no one is really offended.'[81] Edward Martyn had shaped Peg Inerny, a principal character in *Maeve,* under the influence of stories gathered by Lady Gregory and myself. She is one of those women who in sleep pass into another state, are 'away' as the people say, seem to live among people long dead, in the midst of another civilization. We had thought the play dim and metaphysical, but it did not seem so in performance. *Maeve*, Lady Gregory wrote, 'which we did not think a nationalist play at all, has turned out to be one, the audience understanding and applauding the allegory. There is such applause at "I am only an old woman, but I tell you that Erin will never be subdued", Lady —— reported to the Castle that they had better boycott it, which they have done.'[82]

XIV

I disliked Moore's now sentimental, now promiscuous amours, the main matter of his talk. A romantic, when romanticism was in its final extravagance, I thought one woman, whether wife, mistress, or incitement to platonic love, enough for a lifetime: a Parsifal, Tristram, Don Quixote, without the intellectual prepossessions that gave them solidity. I disliked almost as much the manner of his talk, I told him that he was more mob than man, always an enthusiastic listener or noisy interrupter. Yet I admired him and found myself his advocate. I wrote to Lady Gregory: 'He is constantly so likeable that one can believe no evil of him, and then in a moment a kind of devil takes hold of him, his voice changes, his look changes, and he becomes hateful. . . . It is so hard not to trust him, yet he is quite untrustworthy. He has what Talleyrand calls "the terrible gift familiarity".'[83] One must look upon him as a mind that can be of service to one's cause.'[84] Moore, driven to frenzy by the Boer War, had some project of lecturing in America against an Anglo-American alliance, much talked of at the time. 'I shall be glad', I wrote, 'if he himself goes.' (I had refused to go with him.) 'Less because of any harm he may do the Anglo-American alliance than because it will help to make our extremists think about the foundations of life and letters, which they certainly do not at present. To transmute the anti-English passion into a passion of hatred against the vulgarity and materialism whereon England has founded her worst life and the whole life that she sends us, has always been a dream of mine, and Moore may help in that transmutation.'[85] Moore, accustomed by his journalism to an immediate sensational contact with public opinion, was always urging Lady Gregory and me to do this or do that, that we might be more notorious, more popular. 'How Moore lives in the present', I wrote. 'If the National Theatre is ever started' (the company of players that was to succeed to the annual dramatic event with English players) 'what he is and what I am will be weighed, and very little what we have said or done. A phrase more or less matters little. . . . Yet I suppose we would both be more popular if I could keep from saying what I think, and Moore from saying what he does not think. You may tell him that the wisest of men does not know what is expedient, but that we can all know what is our particular truth, cajolery never lit the fire.'[86] Yet to friends who complained by letter or word of mouth against my bringing such a man into the movement, I defended him and attacked his enemies. George Russell (A.E.), afterwards Moore's chief Dublin friend, had complained much, and I wrote—too much aware of what I thought my own quality—'He and I are the opposite of one another. I think I understand people easily, easily sympathise with all kinds of character, easily forgive all kinds of defects. Apart from opinions which I judge too sternly, I scarcely judge people at all, am altogether lax in my attitude towards conduct. He understands nobody but himself, so must be always condemning or worshipping. He is a good judge of right and wrong so long as they can be judged apart from people, so long as they are merely action to be weighed by the moral sense. His moral enthusiasm is an inspiration, but it makes him understand ideas and not human nature. One pays a price for everything.'[87] My advocacy had threatened to disrupt the Irish Literary Society which I had founded and still thought a useful instrument. Early in the year its treasurer, Charles Russell, the famous lawyer, invited Moore to become a member, forgot he had done so, proposed that the Committee should blackball him—there was some anti-Catholic passage in A Drama in Muslin—and was supported by Barry O'Brien, who could not abide Parnell and his Island. I got rid of Charles Russell by producing his letter of invitation, but Barry O'Brien remained, and after a long fight I withdrew Moore's name and resigned rather than force his resignation.[88] He and I had given the Society what energy it had, keeping it out of the commonplace that was bound to overtake it in the end.

It was Moore's own fault that everybody hated him except a few London painters. In one of Dostoievsky's novels[89] there is a man who proposes that everybody present should tell his worst action. Nobody takes the proposal seriously; everybody is witty or amusing until his turn comes. He confesses that he once stole half-a-crown and left a servant-girl to bear the blame. Moore might have so confessed, but his confession would have been a plagiarism or a whole lie. I met a man who hated Moore because Moore told some audience that he had selected a Parisian street-boy, for one day dressed him in good clothes, housed him in an expensive hotel, gave him all that he wanted, then put him back into rags and turned him out to discover what would happen: a plagiarism from a well-known French author.[90] 'Yeats,' he said to me once, 'I was sitting here in my room the other night when there was a ring. My servant was out; when I opened the door a woman ran in and threw her arms round my neck. "At last I have found you. There were thirteen George Moores in the *London Directory.* You're the ninth I have called on. What? Not recollect me—not recollect the woman you raped in Paris twenty years ago?" ' She had called about her daughter's musical education, he said. Had I been more sympathetic I would have heard of a new Evelyn Innes. He was jealous of his own Sir Owen Asher.[91] He was all self and yet had so little self that he would destroy his reputation, or that of some friend, to make his audience believe that the story running in his head at the moment had happened, had only just happened.

XV

I saw Moore daily, we were at work on *Diarmuid and Grania.* Lady Gregory thought such collaboration would injure my own art, and was perhaps right. Because his mind was argumentative, abstract, diagrammatic, mine sensuous, concrete, rhythmical, we argued about words. In later years, through much knowledge of the stage, through the exfoliation of my own style, I learnt that occasional prosaic words gave the impression of an active man speaking. In dream poetry, in 'Kubla Khan', in 'The Stream's Secret', every line, every word, can carry its unanalysable, rich associations; but if we dramatize some possible singer or speaker we remember that he is moved by one thing at a time, certain words must be dull and numb. Here and there in correcting my early poems I have introduced such numbness and dullness, turned, for instance, 'the curd-pale moon' into the 'brilliant moon',[92] that all might seem, as it were, remembered with indifference, except some one vivid image. When I began to rehearse a play I had the defects of my early poetry; I insisted upon obvious all-pervading rhythm. Later on I found myself saying that only in those lines or words where the beauty of the passage came to its climax, must rhythm be obvious. Because Moore thought all drama should be about possible people set in their appropriate surroundings, because he was fundamentally a realist ('Who are his people?' he said after a performance of George Russell's *Deirdre*. 'Ours were cattle merchants') he required many dull, numb words. But he put them in more often than not because he had no feeling for words in themselves, none for their historical associations. He insisted for days upon calling the Fianna 'soldiers'. In *A Story-teller's Holiday* he makes a young man in the thirteenth century go to the 'salons' of 'the fashionable ladies' in Paris, in his last story men and women of the Homeric age read books.[93] Our worst quarrels, however, were when he tried to be poetical, to write in what he considered my style. He made the dying Diarmuid say to Finn: 'I will kick you down the stairway of the stars'.[94] My letters to Lady Gregory show that we made peace at last, Moore accepting my judgment upon words, I his upon construction.[95] To that he would sacrifice what he had thought the day before not only his best scene but 'the best scene in any modern play', and without regret: all must receive its being from the central idea; nothing be in itself anything. He would have been a master of construction, but that his practice as a novelist made him long for descriptions and reminiscences. If *Diarmuid and Grania* failed in performance, and I am not sure that it did, it failed because the second act, instead of moving swiftly from incident to incident, was reminiscent and descriptive; almost a new first act. I had written enough poetical drama to know this and to point it out to Moore. After the performance and just before our final quarrel the letters speak of an agreement to rewrite this act. I had sent Moore a scenario.

XVI

When in later years some play after months of work grew more and more incoherent, I blamed those two years' collaboration. My father began life a Pre-Raphaelite painter; when past thirty he fell under the influence of contemporary French painting. Instead of finishing a picture one square inch at a time, he kept all fluid, every detail dependent upon every other, and remained a poor man to the end of his life, because the more anxious he was to succeed, the more did his pictures sink through innumerable sittings into final confusion. Only when he was compelled to finish in eight or nine sittings were his pictures the work of a great painter. *Deirdre* and *On Baile's Strand*, unified after I had torn up many manuscripts, are more profound than the sentimental *Land of Heart's Desire*, than the tapestry-like *Countess Cathleen*, finished scene by scene, but that first manner might have found its own profundity. It is not far from popular songs and stories with their traditional subject-matter and treatment, it travels a narrow path. A painter or poet can from the first carry the complete work in his head and so finish scene by scene, but when the puppet-play becomes Goethe's *Faust*, Parts I and II, when *Gil Blas* is transformed into *Wilhelm Meister*, the *Waverley Novels* into the *Comédie Humaine*, he must, unhelped by tradition, all nature there to tempt him, try, fail perhaps, to impose his own limits. Hodos Chameliontos had no terrors for Moore; he was more simple, more naïve, more one-idea'd than a Bank-holiday schoolboy. Yet whatever effect that collaboration had on me, it was unmixed misfortune for Moore, it set him upon a pursuit of style that made barren his later years. I no longer underrate him, I know that he had written, or was about to write, five great novels. But *A Mummer's Wife, Esther Waters, Sister Teresa* (everything is there of the convent, a priest said to me, except the religious life), *Muslin, The Lake*, gained nothing from their style. I may speak later of the books he was to write under what seems to me a misunderstanding of his powers.

England had turned from style, as it has been understood from the translators of the Bible to Walter Pater, sought mere clarity in statement and debate, a journalistic effectiveness, at the moment when Irish men of letters began to quote the saying of Sainte-Beuve: 'There is nothing immortal in literature except style'.[96] Style was his growing obsession, he would point out all the errors of some silly experiment of mine, then copy it. It was from some such experiment that he learnt those long, flaccid, structureless sentences, 'and, and and, and and'; there is one of twenty-eight lines in *Muslin*. Sometimes he rebelled: 'Yeats, I have a deep distrust of any man who has a style', but it was generally I who tried to stop the obsession. 'Moore, if you ever get a style', I would say, 'it will ruin you.

It is coloured glass and you need a plate-glass window.' When he formed his own circle he found no escape; the difficulties of modern Irish literature, from the loose, romantic, legendary stories of Standish O'Grady to James Joyce[97] and Synge, had been in the formation of a style. He heard those difficulties discussed. All his life he had learnt from conversation, not from books. His nature, bitter, violent, discordant, did not fit him to write the sentences men murmur again and again for years. Charm and rhythm had been denied him. Improvement makes straight roads; he pumice-stoned every surface because will had to do the work for nature. I said once: 'You work so hard that, like the Lancelot of Tennyson, you will almost see the Grail'. But now, his finished work before me, I am convinced that he was denied even that 'almost'.

XVII

Douglas Hyde[98] was at Coole in the summer of 1899. Lady Gregory, who had learnt Gaelic to satisfy her son's passing desire for a teacher, had founded a branch of the Gaelic League; men began to know the name of the poet whose songs they had sung for years. Lady Gregory and I wanted a Gaelic drama, and I made a scenario for a one-act play founded upon an episode in my *Stories of Red Hanrahan;* I had some hope that my invention, if Hyde would but accept it, might pass into legend as though he were a historical character.[99] In later years Lady Gregory and I gave Hyde other scenarios and I always watched him with astonishment. His ordinary English style is without charm; he explores facts without explaining them, and in the language of the newspapers—Moore compared one of his speeches to frothing porter. His Gaelic, like the dialect of his *Love Songs of Connacht,* written a couple of years earlier, had charm, seemed all spontaneous, all joyous, every speech born out of itself. Had he shared our modern preoccupation with the mystery of life, learnt our modern construction, he might have grown into another and happier Synge. But emotion and imagery came as they would, not as he would; somebody else had to put them together. He had the folk mind as no modern man has had it, its qualities and its defects, and for a few days in the year Lady Gregory and I shared his absorption in that mind. When I wrote verse, five or six lines in two or three laborious hours were a day's work, and I longed for somebody to interrupt me; but he wrote all day, whether in verse or prose, and without apparent effort. Effort was there, but in the unconscious. He had given up verse writing because it affected his lungs or his heart. Lady Gregory kept watch, to draw him from his table after so many hours; the game-keeper had the boat and the guns ready; there were ducks upon the lake. He wrote in joy and at great speed because emotion brought the appropriate word. Nothing in that language of his was abstract, nothing worn-out; he need not, as must the writer of some language exhausted by modern civilization, reject word after word, cadence after cadence; he had escaped our perpetual, painful, purification. I read him, translated by Lady Gregory or by himself into that dialect which gets from Gaelic its syntax and keeps its still partly Tudor vocabulary; little was, I think, lost.

> I was myself one time a poor barnacle goose;
> The night was not plain to me more than the day
> Till I got sight of her.[100]

That does not impress me to-day; it is too easy to copy, too many have copied it; when I first read it, I was fresh from my struggle with Victorian rhetoric. I began to test my poetical inventions by translating them into like speech. Lady Gregory had already, I think, without knowing it, begun a transformation of her whole mind into the mind of the people, begun 'to think like a wise man' but to express herself like 'the common people'. I proposed that *Diarmuid and Grania* should be turned or half turned into dialect, the rough, peasant-like characters using much, the others using little or none. But Moore was impatient and would not listen. Later on this method was more clearly defined by Lady Gregory. The more educated characters should use as much dialect as would seem natural in the mouth of some country gentleman who had spent all his life on his estate. It was first tested in *The White Cockade*. *Deirdre of the Sorrows*,[101] had Synge lived to weave, as he had intended, a grotesque peasant element through the entire play, would have justified it by a world-famous masterpiece. It should have been obvious from the first; Shakespeare made his old man with the ass talk 'Somerset'.[102] The distant in time and space live only in the near and present. Lady Gregory's successful translations from Molière are in dialect.[103] The Indian yogi sinks into a trance, his thought, like his eye, fixed upon the point of his tongue, symbolical of all the senses. He must not meditate upon abstractions, nor, because unseen, upon eye and ear. Yet when I made my suggestion to Moore I was not sure, I was easily put off it. A movement develops in darkness and timidity, nor does it follow that Lady Gregory remembered my suggestion when she began *The White Cockade;* a movement is like an animal, its shape is from the seed.

XVIII

Diarmuid and Grania was read to famous actors and actresses, was greatly admired; a famous actress[104] offered some hundreds as a first payment; but there was always the difficulty; there must be a simultaneous or first performance in Dublin. The actress said: 'If you make a failure there, it will be no use coming to me'. I was in negotiation with her, but took to my bed with influenza. After a fortnight Moore came: 'I have withdrawn the play. She asked me to call upon her manager. I said that her manager should call upon me. Am I not right?' I said: 'The naturalist Waterton climbed to the top of Saint Peter's at Rome and put his glove on the lightning-conductor; such feats make me dizzy'. 'But don't you see it?' he replied. 'I thought her manager was going to refuse the play; now instead of that refusal getting into the papers there will be weeks of controversy as to whether a manager should call upon an author or an author upon a manager.' 'And now,' I said, 'in spite of all that, you want me to call upon her, repudiate you, and give the play back.' Yes, that was what he wanted. He was repudiated, and all seemed well. I cannot remember, and my letters to Lady Gregory do not record, what arrangements were made or unmade except that Benson undertook the Dublin performance, with Mrs. Benson as Grania. 'She will be all right', said Moore. 'She will play her body.' Moore had behaved well, although convinced that the play was worth 'two thousand pounds'—I learnt later that always when writing a play he valued it at that sum—he risked it for the sake of the Irish Literary Theatre. On October 2nd, 1901, *Diarmuid and Grania,* preceded by *The Twisting of the Rope,*[105] was produced for a week by the Benson Company at the Gaiety Theatre, Dublin. Theatre managers must have thought it failed, or that the newspapers' comments had taken freshness from it, for the London managers

who had admired it in MS. were silent. Yet it did not seem to fail;
when Maud Gonne and I got into our cab to go to some supper
party after the performance, the crowd from the gallery wanted to
take the horse out of the cab and drag us there, but Maud Gonne,
weary of public demonstrations, refused. What was it like? York
Powell, Scandinavian scholar, historian, an impressionable man,
preferred it to Ibsen's *Vikings at Helgeland*.[106] I do not know. I have
but a draft of some unfinished scenes, and of the performance I can
but recall Benson's athletic dignity in one scene and the notes of the
horn in Elgar's dirge[107] over the dead Diarmuid. *The Twisting of the
Rope*, Hyde as the chief character—he had always acted his
speeches—, the enthusiasm of his Gaelic Leaguers for the first
Gaelic play ever acted in a theatre, are still vivid. But then Lady
Gregory's translation of the Gaelic text has renewed my memory.

XIX

Moore had inherited a large Mayo estate, and no Mayo country
gentleman had ever dressed the part so well. He lacked manners,
but had manner; he could enter a room so as to draw your attention
without seeming to, his French, his knowledge of painting, suggested travel and leisure. Yet nature had denied to him the final
touch: he had a coarse palate. Edward Martyn alone suspected it.
When Moore abused the waiter or the cook, he had thought, 'I
know what he is hiding'. In a London restaurant on a night when
the soup was particularly good, just when Moore had the spoon at
his lip, he said: 'Do you mean to say you are going to drink that?'
Moore tasted the soup, then called the waiter, and ran through the
usual performance. Martyn did not undeceive him, content to
chuckle in solitude. Moore had taken a house in Upper Ely Place; he
spent a week at our principal hotel while his furniture was moving
in: he denounced the food to the waiter, to the manager, went down
to the kitchen and denounced it to the cook. 'He has written to the
proprietress', said the manager, 'that the steak is like brown paper.
How can you believe a word such a man would say, a steak cannot
be like brown paper.' He had his own bread sent in from the baker
and said on the day he left: 'How can these people endure it?'
'Because', said the admiring head-waiter, 'they are not *comme il
faut*.'[108] A little later I stayed with him and wrote to Lady Gregory:

'He is boisterously enduring the sixth cook'. Then from Sligo a few days later:[109] 'Moore dismissed the sixth cook the day I left—six in three weeks. One brought in a policeman, Moore had made so much noise. He dragged the policeman into the dining-room and said: "Is there a law in this country to compel me to eat this abominable omelette?" '

Sometimes Moore, instead of asking us to accept for true some monstrous invention, would press a spontaneous action into deliberate comedy; starting in bad blood or blind passion, he would all in a moment see himself as others saw him. When he arrived in Dublin, all the doors in Upper Ely Place had been painted white by an agreement between the landlord and the tenants. Moore had his door painted green, and three Miss Beams—no, I have not got the name quite right—who lived next door protested to the landlord. Then began a correspondence between Moore and the landlord wherein Moore insisted on his position as an art critic, that the whole decoration of his house required a green door—I imagine that he had but wrapped the green flag around him—then the indignant young women bought a copy of *Esther Waters,* tore it up, put the fragments into a large envelope, wrote thereon: 'Too filthy to keep in the house', dropped it into his letter-box. I was staying with Moore, I let myself in with a latch-key some night after twelve, and found a note on the hall table asking me to put the door on the chain. As I was undressing, I heard Moore trying to get in; when I had opened the door and pointed to the note he said: 'Oh, I forgot. Every night I go out at eleven, at twelve, at one, and rattle my stick on the railing to make the Miss Beams' dogs bark.' Then I saw in the newspapers that the Miss Beams had hired organ-grinders to play under Moore's window when he was writing, that he had prosecuted the organ-grinders. Moore had a large garden on the other side of the street, a blackbird sang there; he received his friends upon Saturday evening and made a moving speech upon the bird. 'I enjoy its song. If I were the bad man people say I am, could I enjoy its song?' He wrote every morning at an open window on the ground floor, and one morning saw the Miss Beams' cat cross the street, and thought, 'That cat will get my bird'. He went out and filled his pocket with stones, and whenever he saw the cat, threw a stone. Somebody, perhaps the typist, must have laughed, for the rest of the tale fills me with doubt. I was passing through Dublin just on my way to Coole; he came to my hotel. 'I remembered how early that cat got up. I thought it might get the blackbird if I was not there to protect it, so I set a trap. The Miss Beams wrote to the Society for the Prevention of Cruelty to Animals, and I am carrying on a correspondence with its secretary, cat versus bird.' (Perhaps after all, the archives of the Society do contain that correspondence. The tale is not yet incredible.) I passed through Dublin again, perhaps on my way back. Moore came to see me in seeming great depression. 'Remember that trap?' 'Yes.' 'Remember that bird?' 'Yes.' 'I have caught the bird.'

Moore gave a garden party during the annual festival of the Gaelic League; there was a Gaelic play by Douglas Hyde[110] based upon a scenario of Moore's, and to this garden party he invited the Catholic Archbishop, beginning the letter with: 'Cher confrère'. The Archbishop did not answer. He had already in a letter to the Press invited the Archbishop to institute a stage censorship. 'But, my dear Yeats, Archbishops are educated men. If there is some difficulty about a play, I will call upon him. I will explain. He will approve the play. No more mob rule. No more such trouble as we had about *The Countess Cathleen*. No more letters to the Press signed "Father of a Family".'

XX

I was depressed; we had promised, seeing no other way, to bring over English actors for a week in every year for three years, and now the three years were up. Moore wanted to negotiate with Benson for a stock company, taught by English actors, or made up of actors chosen by Benson, or with such actors in the principal parts. At first it seemed probable that Martyn would find the money; I urged him to employ Gordon Craig,[111] a young unknown man who had staged a Purcell opera at his own or his friends' expense. But Martyn said with characteristic decision: 'Henceforth I will pay for nobody's plays but my own'. Perhaps somebody, or some committee, would take his place, negotiation dragged on; perhaps Moore's unpopularity, or mine, made Benson hesitate. We had attacked Queen Victoria, said that she came to Ireland recruiting, that she had, in Moore's words, driven through the city 'a shilling between her finger and thumb, a bag of shillings under the seat'. William Fay and his brother,[112] whose company of amateurs played in a Lock-hart's coffee-house,[113] were putting their case, and all my National-ist friends backing it. I summarized their arguments in *Samhain*,[114] a little annual published in the interests of the movement. Any pro-ject that needed much money would have to promise good behav-iour, and Ireland was turning towards revolution, but I did not give my own opinion. As yet I had none, and if I had I would have held it back.

I felt that Moore wanted the professional stage that he had known all his life. I wanted to keep him in good humour till *Diar-muid and Grania* was finished; we had learnt from the performance, and he had just accepted my sketch of a new second act. Then I wanted to write; I had been organizing for ten years and if I joined Fay I saw no end to it. I felt acutely my unpopularity and told my publisher not to send my books for review in Ireland, a decision kept for many years. A. H. Bullen, Elizabethan scholar, a handsome man with a great mass of curly grey hair, at that time my publisher, came to Dublin. 'He told me', I wrote to Lady Gregory 'that he was amazed to find the hostility of the booksellers. A——,[115] he declared, seemed hardly to like to speak my name. I am looked upon as het-erodox. *The Secret Rose* was particularly disapproved of, but they spoke with hostility, too, of *The Shadowy Waters*. . . . Memory of the *Countess Cathleen* dispute accounts for a great deal. Bullen found the Protestant booksellers little better, asked if T.C.D. disliked me. B——, the College bookseller, said, "What is he doing here? Why doesn't he go away and leave us in peace?" Bullen was rather drunk, but his travellers gave the same account. He had tried to sell a book of Carleton's, too, and said that Carleton and I were received with the same suspicion. This was, of course, because of Carleton's early stories. I imagine that as I withdraw from politics my friends among the Nationalists grow less and my foes more numerous. What I have heard confirms the idea that I had at the time of the *Countess Cathleen* row, that it would make a serious difference in my position.' I had withdrawn from politics because I could not bear perplexing, by what I said about books, the simple patriotic men whose confidence I had gained by what I said about nationality.

Some work connected with our theatrical project brought Lady Gregory to Dublin. Bullen asked to be introduced, and until we arrived at her hotel I did not notice how drunk he was. When he sat down he was on the verge of tears. 'Yeats is an astrologer. He knows the moment of my death. No, no, it is no use denying it, he knows the moment of my death.' Presently I wrote from Sligo that my uncle, the High Sheriff, had been warned that I must keep away from a certain Club.[116] Moore was constantly attacked in the English Press, and every attack reached Dublin. I found that certain of our enemies were passing round some article in a monthly review, pointing out the plagiarisms in his *Modern Painting*,[117] and I, not knowing how well-founded the attack was, had suggested a reply. 'The man I object to', said Moore, 'is the man who plagiarizes without knowing it; I always know; I took ten pages.' To Lady Gregory he said, 'We both quote well, but you always put inverted commas, I never do'.

XXI

I saw William Fay's amateur company play Miss Milligan's *Red Hugh*, an historical play in two scenes in the style of Walter Scott. 'Yonder battlements', all the old rattle-traps acquired modernity, reality, spoken by those voices. I came away with my head on fire. I wanted to hear my own unfinished *On Baile's Strand*, to hear Greek tragedy, spoken with a Dublin accent. After consulting with Lady Gregory I gave William Fay my *Cathleen ni Houlihan*, the first play where dialect was not used with an exclusively comic intention, to be produced in April 1902, in a hall attached to a church in a back street. A.E. gave his *Deirdre*, a protest against *Diarmuid and Grania* because the play had made mere men out of heroes. It was well constructed (A.E. in later years gave plots, or incidents that suggested plots, to several dramatists), but all its male characters resembled Lord Tennyson's King Arthur. Five or six years earlier he had published his lovely *Homeward; Songs by the Way*, and because of those poems and what he was in himself, writers or would-be writers, among them James Stephens, who has all my admiration to-day, gathered at his house upon Sunday nights, making it a chief centre of literary life in Dublin. I was not friendly with that centre, considering it made up for the most part of 'barren rascals'—critics as Balzac saw critics. For the next few years it seemed to lead the opposition, not the violent attacks, but the sapping and mining. A.E. himself, then as always, I loved and hated, and when I read or saw his play, I distrusted my judgment, fearing it mere jealousy, or some sort of party dislike. It was admired by everybody, hurt no national susceptibility, but in a few years A.E. himself abandoned it as Moore and I abandoned *Diarmuid and Grania*. I wrote to Lady Gregory,[118] who was then in Italy: 'They took to *Deirdre* from the first. The hall was crowded and great numbers could not get in. I hated *Deirdre*. In fact I did not remain in the theatre because I was nervous about it. I still hate it, but I suppose Moore is the only person who shares my opinion. When I saw it in rehearsal I thought it superficial and sentimental as I thought when it came out in the *All Ireland Review*.[119] *Cathleen ni Houlihan* was also enthusiastically received. The one defect was that the mild humour of the part before Cathleen came in kept them in such delighted laughter that it took them some little while to realize the tragic meaning of Cathleen's part though Maud Gonne played it magnificently and with weird power. I should have struck a tragic note at the start.' Then two days later: 'The plays are over. Last night was the most enthusiastic of all. The audience now understands *Cathleen ni Houlihan* and there is no difficulty in getting from humour to tragedy. There is continual applause, and strange to say I like *Deirdre*. The absence of character is like the absence of individual expression in wall decoration. It was acted with great simplicity; the actors kept very quiet, often merely posing and speaking. The result was curiously dream-like and gentle. Russell is planning a play on the Children of Tuireann[120] and will, I imagine, do quite a number of plays. The costumes and scenery from designs of his were beautiful; there was a thin gauze veil in front. It was really a wonderful sight to see crowds of people standing up at the back of the hall where they could hardly see because there were people in front, yet patient, and enthusiastic.' I gave Fay a little farce, *The Pot of Broth*, written with Lady Gregory's help but showing that neither Lady Gregory nor I could yet distinguish between the swift-moving town dialect—the dialect of the Irish novelists no matter what part of Ireland they wrote of—and the slow-moving country dialect. In *Cathleen ni Houlihan,* written too with Lady Gregory's help, the dialect is as it were neutral, neither predominantly town nor country; my stage technique, swifter than Lady Gregory's when a tragic crisis is the theme, had pared it to the bone. It was, I think, this spareness, or barrenness, that made

Arthur Symons tell me after he had seen Synge's first play[121] to write no more peasant plays.

I had joined Fay's dramatic society but had as yet no authority. I wrote to Lady Gregory that I had not marked my scornful analysis of one of Fay's dramatists 'private' because 'the sooner I have that man for an enemy the better'.[122] When *The Pot of Broth* was played in the Antient Concert Rooms in October, that trivial, unambitious retelling of an old folk-tale showed William Fay for the first time as a most lovable comedian. He could play dirty tramp, stupid countryman, legendary fool, insist on dirt and imbecility, yet play— paradox of the stage—with indescribable personal distinction.

XXII

In the early autumn Zola died, asphyxiated by a charcoal stove. Innumerable paragraphs and leading articles made Moore jealous and angry; he hated his own past in Zola. He talked much to his friends on Saturday nights. 'Anybody can get himself asphyxiated.' Then after some six weeks announced that he himself had awakened that very morning to smell gas, a few minutes more and he would have been dead; the obsession was over. But there had been another torture earlier in the year. A brother of his, Augustus Moore, a London journalist, had taken an action about a scenario, whether against an actor, a writer or a manager, I cannot remember; he would appear in the witness-box, be examined, cross-examined, re-examined, and would not, could not, rise to the occasion, whereas he, George Moore, could have been amusing, profound, all the world looking on. When it seemed likely that Benson, or some company brought together by Martyn, would continue the Irish Literary Theatre, I had told Moore a fantastic plot for a play, suggested collaboration, and for twenty minutes or half an hour walked up and down a path in his garden discussing it. He proposed that my hero's brother should seduce the housemaid. When I had decided to work with Fay, Moore had withdrawn from the movement. I had written him regretting that I must write that play without his help. He did not answer, the letter required no answer. Weeks or months passed, then at some Gaelic festival in the town of Galway we met. I saw that he had something on his mind, he was gloomy and silent. I pointed out the number of young women with

Douglas Hyde's pseudonym in gilt letters round their hats: 'No woman, Moore, has ever done that for you', I said. He took my banter well, threw off his gloom; had I not started his favourite theme? But on his return to Dublin he telegraphed: 'I have written a novel on that scenario we composed together. Will get an injunction if you use it.' Had I known about his brother's law-case I would have known that Moore had not written a line and that his telegram was drama; knowing nothing, I wrote or telegraphed that I would use nothing of his but would certainly use my own plot. I went to Coole, asked the assistance of Lady Gregory and of a certain cautious friend,[123] whose name must be left out of this narrative, and in a fortnight they and I dictated or wrote a five-act tragedy. I called it *Where there is Nothing* and published it as a supplement to *United Ireland*,[124] afterwards the organ of the Sinn Fein movement. Moore had been talking and his talk had reached me, he was expecting a London trial, and this was checkmate. Boys were shouting the supplement in the streets as he came out of the Antient Concert Rooms, where he had seen Fay's company. He bought a copy, spoke to nobody about it, always declared that he never read it, nor any other edition of the play. 'Has Yeats's hero got a brother?' he said to somebody. 'Yes.' 'Then Yeats has stolen the spoons.' But my hero's brother was in a monastery. Some months later an American friend, John Quinn,[125] a strong supporter and helper of our movement, brought us together, but we were never cordial again; on my side distrust remained, on his disgust. I look back with some remorse. 'Yeats,' Moore had said, 'a man can only have one conscience, mine is artistic.' Had I abandoned my plot and made him write the novel, he might have put beside *Muslin* and *The Lake* a third masterpiece, but I was young, vain, self-righteous, and bent on proving myself a man of action. *Where there is Nothing* is a bad play; I had caught sight of Tolstoy's essay[126] about the Sermon on the Mount lying on a chair and made the most important act pivot upon pacificist commonplace. I soon came to my senses, refused a distinguished Frenchman[127] permission to translate it, and in later years with Lady Gregory's help turned it into *The Unicorn from the Stars*. For the moment it was successful; it could not be played in Ireland for religious reasons, but the Stage Society[128] found an approving audience and it set the tinkers of Mayo rioting. My anonymous collaborator, when asked to name a tinker in the play, had named him after a real tinker. A farmer who had read the *United Ireland* supplement reproached that tinker for letting his daughter marry a man with no visible means of subsistence and permitting her to solemnize the marriage by jumping over a bucket. The angry parent called God to witness that he had done no such thing, other farmers and tinkers joined what grew into a considerable fight, and all were brought up before the magistrate.

XXIII

During these first years Lady Gregory was friend and hostess, a centre of peace, an adviser who never overestimated or underestimated trouble, but neither she nor we thought her a possible creator. And now all in a moment, as it seemed, she became the founder of modern Irish dialect literature.[129] When her husband died she had sold her London house, hiring instead a small flat in Queen Anne's Mansions, lived most of the year at Coole, cutting down expenses that her son might inherit an unencumbered estate. In early life she had written two or three articles,[130] such as many clever fashionable women write, more recently had edited her husband, Sir William Gregory's, *Autobiography* and *Mr. Gregory's Letter-Box,* a volume of letters to Richard Gregory,[131] Irish Under-Secretary at the beginning of the nineteenth century, from Palmerston, Wellesley, many famous men, drawn from the Coole archives. Some slight desire to create had been put aside until her son reached manhood; but now he had left the university and she was fifty. I told her that Alfred Nutt had offered to supply me with translations of the Irish heroic cycles if I would pick the best versions and put my English upon them, attempting what Malory had done for the old French narratives. I told her that I was too busy with my own work. Some days later she asked if I would object to her attempting it, making or finding the translations herself. An eminent Trinity College professor[132] had described ancient Irish literature as 'silly, religious, or indecent', and she thought such work necessary for the dignity of Ireland. 'We work to add dignity to Ireland' was a favourite phrase of hers. I hesitated, I saw nothing in her past to fit her for that work; but in a week or two she brought a translation of some heroic tale, what tale I cannot now remember, in the dialect of the neighbourhood, where one discovers the unemphatic cadence, the occasional poignancy of Tudor English. Looking back, *Cuchulain of Muirthemne* and *Gods and Fighting Men*[133] at my side, I can see that they were made possible by her past; semi-feudal Roxborough, her inherited sense of caste, her knowledge of that top of the world where men and women are valued for their manhood and their charm, not for their opinions, her long study of Scottish Ballads, of Percy's *Reliques,* of the *Morte d'Arthur.* If she had not found those tales, or finding them had not found the dialect of Kiltartan, that past could not, as it were, have drawn itself together, come to birth as present personality. Sometimes in her letters, in her books when she wrote ordinary English, she was the late-Victorian woman turning aside from reality to what seems pleasing, or to a slightly sentimental persiflage as a form of politeness—in society, to discover 'eternity glaring', as Carlyle did when he met Charles Lamb for the first time,[134] is scarcely in good taste—but in her last years, when speaking in her own character, she seemed always her greater self. A writer must die every day he lives, be reborn, as it is said in the Burial Service, an incorruptible self, that self opposite of all that he has named 'himself'. George Moore, dreading the annihilation of an impersonal bleak realism, used life like a mediaeval ghost making a body for itself out of drifting dust and vapour; and have I not sung in describing guests at Coole—'There one that ruffled in a manly pose, For all his timid heart'[135]—that one myself? Synge was a sick man picturing energy, a doomed man picturing gaiety; Lady Gregory, in her life much artifice, in her nature much pride, was born to see the glory of the world in a peasant mirror. 'I saw the household of Finn; it was not the household of a soft race; I had a vision of that man yesterday. . . . A King of heavy blows; my law; my adviser, my sense and my wisdom, prince and poet, braver than kings, King of the Fianna, brave in all countries; golden salmon of the sea, clean hawk of the air . . . a high messenger in bravery and in music. His skin lime-white, his hair golden; ready to work, gentle to women. His great green vessels full of rough sharp wine, it is rich the king was, the head of his people.'[136] And then Grania's song over the sleeping Diarmuid:

' "Sleep a little, sleep a little, for there is nothing at all to fear, Diarmuid, grandson of Duibhne; sleep here soundly, soundly, Diarmuid, to whom I have given my love. It is I will keep watch for you, grandchild of shapely Duibhne; sleep a little, a blessing on you, beside the well of the strong field; my lamb from above the lake, from the banks of the strong streams. Let your sleep be like the sleep in the North of fair comely Fionnchadh of Ess Ruadh, the time he took Slaine with bravery as we think, in spite of Failbhe of the Hard Head.

"Let your sleep be like the sleep in the West of Aine, daughter of Gailian, the time she went on a journey in the night with Dubhthach from Dorinis, by the light of torches.

"Let your sleep be like the sleep in the East of Deaghadh the proud, the brave fighter, the time he took Coincheann, daughter of Binn, in spite of fierce Decheall of Duibhreann.

"O heart of the valour of the world to the west of Greece, my heart will go near to breaking if I do not see you every day. The parting of us two will be the parting of two children of the one house; it will be the parting of life from the body."

'And then to rouse him she would make another song, and it is what she would say: "Caoinche will be loosed on your track; it is not slow the running of Caoilte will be; do not let death reach to you, do not give yourself to sleep forever.

"The stag to the East is not asleep, he does not cease from bellowing; the bog lark is not asleep to-night on the high stormy bogs; the sound of her clear voice is sweet; she is not sleeping between the streams." '[137]

THE END

ESTRANGEMENT

EXTRACTS FROM A DIARY
KEPT IN 1909[1]

ESTRANGEMENT

I

[undated 'Journal' no. 5]

To keep these notes natural and useful to me I must keep one note from leading on to another, that I may not surrender myself to literature. Every note must come as a casual thought, then it will be my life. Neither Christ nor Buddha nor Socrates wrote a book, for to do that is to exchange life for a logical process.

2

[14 January (1909) 'Journal' no. 4]

Last night there was a debate in the Arts Club[2] on a political question. I was for a moment tempted to use arguments merely to answer something said, but did not do so, and noticed that every argument I had been tempted to use was used by somebody or other. Logic is a machine, one can leave it to itself; unhelped it will force those present to exhaust the subject, the fool is as likely as the sage to speak the appropriate answer to any statement, and if an answer is forgotten somebody will go home miserable. You throw your money on the table and you receive so much change.

Style, personality—deliberately adopted and therefore a mask— is the only escape from the hot-faced bargainers and the money-changers.

3

[22 January (1909) 'Journal' no. 6]

I have been talking to a man[3] typical of a class common elsewhere but new in Ireland: often not ill-bred in manner and therefore the more manifestly with the ill-breeding of the mind, every thought made in some manufactory and with the mark upon it of its whole-sale origin—thoughts never really thought out in their current form in any individual mind, but the creation of impersonal mechanism—of schools, of text-books, of newspapers, these above all. He had that confidence which the first thinker of anything never has, for all thinkers are alike in that they approach the truth full of hesitation and doubt. Confidence comes from repetition, from the breath of many mouths. This ill-breeding of the mind is a far worse thing than the mere bad manners that spit on the floor. Is not all charm inherited, whether of the intellect, of the manners, of the character, or of literature? A great lady is as simple as a good poet. Neither possesses anything that is not ancient and their own, and both are full of uncertainty about everything but themselves, about everything that can be changed, about all that they merely think. They assume convictions as if they were a fashion in clothes and remould all slightly.

4
[(21 January 1909) 'Journal' no. 9]

The articles upon *The Miser* in to-day's paper[4] show the old dislike of farce and dialect; written by men who are essentially parvenus in intellectual things, they shudder at all that is not obviously and notoriously refined—the objection to the word 'shift'[5] over again. Our Abbey secretary[6] has a deep hatred of Molière. None of these people can get it out of their heads that we are exaggerating the farce of Molière. We reduce it. Years ago Dr. Sigerson said of the last verse of my 'Moll Magee',[7] 'Why candles? Surely tapers?'

5
[undated 'Journal' no. 11]

To oppose the new ill-breeding of Ireland, which may in a few years destroy all that has given Ireland a distinguished name in the world—'Mother of the bravest soldiers and the most beautiful women', cried Borrow, or some such words, remembering the hospitality shown to him, a distributor of Bibles, by the Irish Monks of Spain[8]—I can only set up a secondary or interior personality created out of the tradition of myself, and this personality (alas, only possible to me in my writings) must be always gracious and simple. It must have that slight separation from interests which makes charm possible, while remaining near enough for passion. Is not charm what it is because an escape from mechanism? So much of the world as is dominated by the contest of interests is a mechanism. The newspaper is the roar of the machine. Argument, the moment acknowledged victory is sought, becomes a clash of interests. One should not—above all in books, which sigh for immortality—argue at all if not ready to leave to another apparent victory. In daily life one becomes rude the moment one grudges to the clown his perpetual triumph.

6
[undated 'Journal' no. 14]

My father says, 'A man does not love a woman because he thinks her clever or because he admires her, but because he likes the way she has of scratching her head'.

7
[(23 or 24 January 1909) 'Journal' no. 16]

It seems to me that true love is a discipline, and it needs so much wisdom that the love of Solomon and Sheba[9] must have lasted, for all the silence of the Scriptures. Each divines the secret self of the other, and refusing to believe in the mere daily self, creates a mirror where the lover or the beloved sees an image to copy in daily life; for love also creates the Mask.

8
[24 January (1909) 'Journal' no. 18]

Our modern poetry is imaginative. It is the poetry of the young. The poetry of the greatest periods is a sustained expression of the appetites and habits. Hence we select where they exhausted.

9
[undated 'Journal' no. 19]

I have remembered to-day that the Brahmin Mohini said to me, 'When I was young I was happy. I thought truth was something that could be conveyed from one man's mind to another. I now know that it is a state of mind.'

10
[undated 'Journal' no. 20]

Last night I met A——.[10] There was some rich man there, and some person spoke of the great power that wealth might have for good. The rich man was talking of starting a deer forest in Connacht. A—— said, 'Wealth has very little power, it can really do very little'. I said, 'Yet every now and then one meets some charming person

who likes all fine things and is quite delightful and who would not
have had these qualities if some great-grandfather had not sold his
country for gold'. A—— answered, 'I admit that wealth occasionally—Darwin is an example—enables someone to write a great
book'. I answered, 'O, I was not thinking of that. I meant that it
creates the fine life which we look at with affectionate eyes out of
our garret windows. We must not leave our garrets, but we could
not write well but for what we see from their windows.' A——
answered, 'Then writers are parasites'. I noticed that most of the
guests seemed, besides A—— and the rich man, too sympathetic
and anxious to please; I myself among the rest. We talked, they
were talked to. Dean B——[11] was there too, a charming and intelligent man with an ingratiating manner like that of certain well-edu-
cated Catholic priests, a manner one does not think compatible
with deep spiritual experience. We discussed self-realization and
self-sacrifice. He said the classic self-realization had failed and yet
the victory of Christian self-sacrifice had plunged the world into the
Dark Ages. I reminded him of some Norse God, who was hung over
an abyss for three days, 'a sacrifice to himself', to show that the two
were not incompatible, but he answered, 'Von Hartmann[12] discusses the question whether the soul may not sacrifice itself, even to
the losing of itself, for some good end'. I said, 'That is the problem
of my *Countess Cathleen*', and he said, 'It is a further problem
whether a nation may make this sacrifice'. He must have been
thinking of Ireland.

II

[undated 'Journal' no. 22]

I see clearly that when I rewrite 'The Adoration of the Magi'[13] the
message given to the old men must be a series of seemingly arbitrary
commands: A year of silence, certain rules of diet, and so on.
Without the arbitrary there cannot be religion, because there
cannot be the last sacrifice, that of the spirit. The old men should
refuse to record the message on hearing that it contains not wisdom
but the supernaturally sanctioned arbitrary, the commanded pose
that makes all definite. The tree has to die before it can be made
into a cross.

12

[undated 'Journal' no. 24]

I have noticed that when these men (certain disciples of A.E.) take to any kind of action it is to some kind of extreme politics. Partly, I think, because they have never learned the discipline which enables the most ardent nature to accept obtainable things, even if a little sadly; but still more because they cannot believe in any success that is not in the unconditioned future, and because, like an artist described by Balzac,[14] they long for popularity that they may believe in themselves.

13

[25 January (1909) 'Journal' no. 25]

A.E. endures them because he has the religious genius, for to the religious genius all souls are of equal value: the queen is not more than an old apple-woman. His poetical genius does not affect his mind as a whole, and probably he puts aside as unworthy every suggestion of his poetical genius which would separate man from man. The most fundamental of divisions is that between the intellect, which can only do its work by saying continually 'thou fool', and the religious genius which makes all equal. That is why we have discovered that the mountain-top and the monastery are necessary to civilization. Civilization dies of all those things that feed the soul, and both die if the Remnant refuse the wilderness.

14

[undated 'Journal' no. 26 excerpt]

One of their errors is to continually mistake a philosophical idea for a spiritual experience. The very pre-occupation of the intellect with the soul destroys that experience, for everywhere impressions are checked by opinion.

15

[undated 'Journal' no. 27]

The real life being despised is only prized when sentimentalized over, and so the soul is shut off alike from earth and Heaven.

16
[undated 'Journal' no. 28]

I heard Miss A—— B——[15] speak this the other day: 'We have such a wonderful cat and it is so full of dignity that if the kitten goes to take its food it leaves the dish. It will not struggle. It will not assert itself. And what's more, our cat won't eat at all if there is not a perfectly clean napkin spread under the plate. I assure you it is quite true. I have often noticed it. It will not eat if there is even a spot on the napkin.'

17
[undated 'Journal' no. (29) (as '28')]

When A.E. and I were fellow-students at the art-schools there was a strange mad pious student[16] who used to come sometimes with a daisy chain round his neck. A.E. lent him a little theosophical book, *Light on the Path*. He stayed away for several days and then came one day looking very troubled. He gave the book back saying, 'You will drift into a penumbra'.

18
[undated 'Journal' no. 30]

In Christianity what was philosophy in Eastern Asia became life, biography and drama. A play passes through the same process in being written. At first, if it has psychological depth, there is a bundle of ideas, something that can be stated in philosophical terms; my *Countess Cathleen,* for instance, was once the moral question, may a soul sacrifice itself for a good end? but gradually philosophy is eliminated until at last the only philosophy audible, if there is even that, is the mere expression of one character or another. When it is completely life it seems to the hasty reader a mere story. Was the *Bhagavad Gita* the 'scenario' from which the Gospels were made?

19
[26 January (1909) 'Journal' no. 31]

One reason for the tendency of the A.E. group to extreme political opinion is that a taste fed for long on milk diet thirsts for strong flavours. In England the reaction would be vice, in Ireland it is politics.

20

[undated 'Journal' no. 32]

I have once more met Miss A—— B——. 'O, it is not because of the pictures that I said I liked Mr. Lane's Gallery. I like it because it has such a beautiful atmosphere, because of the muffed glass.'[17]

21

[undated 'Journal' no. 33]

All empty souls tend to extreme opinion. It is only in those who have built up a rich world of memories and habits of thought that extreme opinions affront the sense of probability. Propositions, for instance, which set all the truth upon one side can only enter rich minds to dislocate and strain, if they can enter at all, and sooner or later the mind expels them by instinct.

22

[undated 'Journal' no. 34]

There is a relation between discipline and the theatrical sense. If we cannot imagine ourselves as different from what we are and assume that second self, we cannot impose a discipline upon ourselves, though we may accept one from others. Active virtue as distinguished from the passive acceptance of a current code is therefore theatrical, consciously dramatic, the wearing of a mask. It is the condition of arduous full life. One constantly notices in very active natures a tendency to pose, or if the pose has become a second self a preoccupation with the effect they are producing. One notices this in Plutarch's *Lives,* and every now and then in some modern who has tried to live by classical ideas, in Oscar Wilde, for instance, and less obviously in men like Walt Whitman. Wordsworth is often flat and heavy, partly because his moral sense has no theatrical element, it is an obedience to a discipline which he has not created. This increases his popularity with the better sort of journalists, writers in the *Spectator,*[18] for instance, with all who are part of the machine and yet care for poetry.

23
[undated 'Journal' no. 35]

All my life I have been haunted with the idea that the poet should know all classes of men as one of themselves, that he should combine the greatest possible personal realization with the greatest possible knowledge of the speech and circumstances of the world. Fifteen or twenty years ago I remember longing, with this purpose, to disguise myself as a peasant and wander through the West, and then to ship as sailor. But when one shrinks from all business with a stranger, and is unnatural with all who are not intimate friends, because one underrates or overrates unknown people, one cannot adventure forth. The artist grows more and more distinct, more and more a being in his own right as it were, but more and more loses grasp of the always more complex world. Some day setting out to find knowledge, like some pilgrim to the Holy Land, he will become the most romantic of characters. He will play with all masks.

24
[undated 'Journal' no. 36]

Tragedy is passion alone, and rejecting character, it gets form from motives, from the wandering of passion; while comedy is the clash of character. Eliminate character from comedy and you get farce. Farce is bound together by incident alone. In practice most works are mixed: Shakespeare being tragi-comedy. Comedy is joyous because all assumption of a part, of a personal mask, whether of the individualized face of comedy or of the grotesque face of farce, is a display of energy, and all energy is joyous. A poet creates tragedy from his own soul, that soul which is alike in all men. It has not joy, as we understand that word, but ecstasy, which is from the contemplation of things vaster than the individual and imperfectly seen, perhaps, by all those that still live. The masks of tragedy contain neither character nor personal energy. They are allied to decoration and to the abstract figures of Egyptian temples. Before the mind can look out of their eyes the active will perishes, hence their sorrowful calm. Joy is of the will which labours, which overcomes obstacles, which knows triumph. The soul knows its changes of state alone, and I think the motives of tragedy are not related to action but to changes of state. I feel this but do not see clearly, for I am hunting truth into its thicket and it is my business to keep close to the impressions of sense, to common daily life. Yet is not ecstasy some fulfilment of the soul in itself, some slow or sudden expansion of it like an overflowing well? Is not this what is meant by beauty?

25
[undated 'Journal' no. 38; 31 January (1909) 'Journal' no. 39; undated 'Journal' no. 42]

Allingham and Davis[19] have two different kinds of love of Ireland. In Allingham I find the entire emotion for the place one grew up in which I felt as a child. Davis on the other hand was concerned with ideas of Ireland, with conscious patriotism. His Ireland was artificial, an idea built up in a couple of generations by a few commonplace men. This artificial idea has done me as much harm as the other has helped me. I tried to free myself from it, and all my enemies come from my fighting it in others. The beauty of peasant thought is partly from a spontaneity unspoiled by the artificial town-made thought. One cannot sum up a nation intellectually, and when the summing up is made by half-educated men the idea fills one with alarm. I remember when I was nine or ten years old walking along Kensington High Street so full of love for the fields and roads of Sligo that I longed—a strange sentiment for a child—for earth from a road there that I might kiss it. I had no politics; a couple of years before, I had read with delight a volume of Orange verses belonging to my grandmother's stable-boy,[20] and my mother, who loved Sligo where she had been born and bred with the same passion, was, if she had any politics, Unionist. This love was instinctive and left the soul free. If I could have kept it and yet never felt the influence of Young Ireland I had given a more profound picture of Ireland in my work. Synge's purity of genius comes in part from having kept this instinct and this alone. Emotion is always justified by time, thought hardly ever. It can only bring us back to emotion. I went to see Synge yesterday and found him ill:[21] if he dies it will set me wondering if he could have lived had he not had his long misunderstanding with the wreckage of Young Ireland. Even a successful performance of one of his plays seems to have made him ill. My sister[22] reminded me of this the other day and urged me not to revive the *Playboy* while he is ill. In one thing he and Lady Gregory are the strongest souls I have ever known. He and she alike have never for an instant spoken to me the thoughts of their inferiors as their own thoughts. I have never known them to lose the self-possession of their intellects. The others here—even Moore for all his defiance—possess their own thoughts above the general flood only for a season, and Moore has in addition an automatic combativeness that makes even his original thought a reaction not a creation. Both Synge and Lady Gregory isolate themselves, Synge instinctively and Lady Gregory consciously, from all contagious opinions of poorer minds: Synge so instinctively and naturally—helped certainly by the habits of an invalid—that no one is conscious of rejection. Lady Gregory's life is too energetic and complex for her rejections to be other than deliberate. I do neither the one nor the other, being too talkative, too full of belief in whatever thought lays hold on me to reject people from my company, and so keep by angry outbreaks which are pure folly, from these invasions of the soul. One must agree with the clown or be silent, for he has in him the strength and confidence of the multitudes.

Lady Gregory is planting trees; for a year they have taken up much of her time. Her grandson[23] will be fifty years old before they can be cut. We artists, do not we also plant trees and it is only after some fifty years that we are of much value? Every day I notice some new analogy between the long-established life of the well-born and the artists' life. We come from the permanent things and create them, and instead of old blood we have old emotions and we carry in our heads always that form of society aristocracies create now and again for some brief moment at Urbino or Versailles.[24] We too despise the mob and suffer at its hands, and when we are happiest we have some little post in the house of Duke Frederick where we watch the proud dreamless world with humility, knowing that our knowledge is invisible and that at the first breath of ambition our dreams vanish. If we do not see daily beautiful life at which we look as old men and women do at young children, we become theorists—thinkers as it is called,—or else give ourselves to strained emotions, to some overflow of sentiment 'sighing after Jerusalem in the regions of the grave'.[25] How can we sing without our bush of whins, our clump of heather, and does not Blake say that it takes a thousand years to create a flower?[26]

26
[3 February (1909) 'Journal' no. 46]

Blake talking to Crabb Robinson said once that he preferred to any man of intellect a happy thoughtless person, or some such phrase. It followed, I suppose, from his praise of life—'all that lives is holy'[27]—and from his dislike of abstract things. Balzac, though when he is praising some beautiful high-bred woman he makes one think he had the same preference, is too much taken up with his worship of the will, which cannot be thoughtless even if it can be happy, to be aware of the preference if he has it. Nietzsche had it doubtless at the moment when he imagined the 'Superman'[28] as a child. We artists suffer in our art if we do not love most of all life at peace with itself and doing without forethought what its humanity bids it and therefore happily. We are, as seen from life, an artifice, an emphasis, an uncompleted arc perhaps. Those whom it is our business to cherish and celebrate are complete arcs. Because the life man sees is not the final end of things, the moment we attain to greatness of any kind by personal labour and will we become fragmentary, and find no task in active life which can use our finest faculties. We are compelled to think and express and not to do. Faust in the end was only able to reclaim land like some official of the Agricultural Board. It is right that Romeo should not be a man of intellect or learning, it is enough for us that there is nature in him. We see all his arc, for in literature we need completed things. Men of action, our celebrators of life and passion, should be in all men's eyes, but it is not well that we should be too much talked of. Plutarch was right when he said the artist should not be too prominent in the State because no young man, born for war and love, desires to be like Phidias.[29] Life confesses to the Priest and honours him, but we confess to Life and tell it all that we would do if we were young, beautiful and rich, and Life answers, 'I could never have thought of all that for myself, I have so little time'. And it is our praise that it goes upon its way with shining eyes forgetting us.

27
[undated 'Journal' no. 47]

I have to speak to-night at the Arts Club[30] and have no time for much preparation. I will speak, I think, of the life of a young Irishman, his gradual absorption in some propaganda. How the very nature of youth makes this come readily. Youth is always giving itself, expending itself. It is only after years that we begin the supreme work, the adapting of our energies to a chosen end, the disciplining of ourselves. A young man in Ireland meets only crude, impersonal things, things that make him like others. One cannot discuss his ideas or ideals, for he has none. He has not the beginning of aesthetic culture. He never tries to make his rooms charming, for instance. The slow perfecting of the senses which we call taste has not even begun. When he throws himself into the work of some league he succeeds just in so far as he puts aside all delicate and personal gifts. I myself know the sense of strain that comes when one speaks to ignorant or, still worse, half-ignorant men. There is a perpetual temptation not merely to over-simplification but to exaggeration, for all ignorant thought is exaggerated thought. I can only wish that a young Irishman of talent and culture may spend his life, from eighteen to twenty-five, outside Ireland. Can one prescribe duties to a developed soul?—and I suppose him to grow conscious of himself in those years. If one can, I would wish him to return. I will then describe the idea of modern culture as I see it in some young Oxford man: to have perfect taste; to have felt all the finest emotions that art can give. The young Dublin man who sticks to his books becomes a pedant because he only believes in external things. I will then describe a debate at Oxford a few years ago when I felt so much pity for that young brilliant man full of feminine sensitiveness. Surely the ideal of culture expressed by Pater can only create feminine souls. The soul becomes a mirror not a brazier. This culture is self-knowledge in so far as the self is a calm, deliberating, discriminating thing, for when we have awakened our tastes, and criticized the world in tasting it, we have come to know ourselves; ourselves, not as misers, or spendthrifts, or magistrates, or pleaders, but as men, face to face with what is permanent in the world. Newman defines culture as wise receptivity, though I do not think he uses these words. Culture of this kind produces the most perfect flowers in a few high-bred women. It gives to its sons an exquisite delicacy. I will then compare the culture of the Renaissance, which seems to me founded not on self-knowledge but on knowledge of some other self, Christ or Caesar, not on delicate sincerity but on imitative energy.

28
[4 February (1909) 'Journal' no. 50]

This morning I got a letter telling me of A—— C——'s[31] illness. I did not recognize her son's writing at first, and my mind wandered, I suppose because I was not well. I thought my mother was ill and that my sister was asking me to come at once: then I remembered that my mother died years ago and that more than kin was at stake. She has been to me mother, friend, sister and brother. I cannot realize the world without her—she brought to my wavering thoughts steadfast nobility. All the day the thought of losing her is like a conflagration in the rafters. Friendship is all the house I have.

29
[6 February (1909) 'Journal' no. 51 excerpt;
undated 'Journal' no. 54 (refers to Wednesday, 7 February 1909);
undated 'Journal' no. 53 excerpt (poem)]

A—— C—— is better but writes in pencil that she 'very nearly slipped away'. All Wednesday I heard Castiglione's phrase ringing in my memory, 'Never be it spoken without tears, the Duchess, too, is dead',[32] and that phrase, which—coming where it did among the numbering of his dead—often moved me till my eyes dimmed, brought before me now all his sorrow and my own, as though one saw the worth of life fade for ever.

> Sickness brought me this
> Thought, in that scale of his:
> Why should I be dismayed
> Though flame had burned the whole
> World, as it were a coal,
> Now I have seen it weighed
> Against a soul?[33]

30
[7 February (1909) 'Journal' no. 56; undated 'Journal' no. 57; undated
'Journal' no. 58]

I went for a walk in the woods with little E——[34] and we talked of religion. He said, 'There is no longer belief, nobody with belief ever comes to my Bible Class but you yourself. If people believed, they would talk of God and Christ. They think it good taste not to talk of such things, and yet people always talk of what they care for. Belief makes a mind abundant'. I thought of the perpetual desire of all lovers to talk of their love and how many lovers' quarrels have come from it. I said, 'What of the Dublin theosophists?' He said fiercely, 'They are thieves. They pick up names and thoughts all over the world and these never become being in their minds, never become their own, because they have no worship'. He is not easy to understand, but I gradually drew from him these thoughts. 'They are all self, all presumption. They do not know what it is to abase themselves before Christ, or their own Gods, or anything. If one does that, one is filled with life. Christ is so full of life that it flows into us. The whole world is vivid to us. They are all self, and so they despise the foundation'. He means by the foundation, life, nature. I said, 'But what are the forms they see?' He answered, 'They can only be lesser spirits—part of what they call the Astral—creatures that live on them and draw away their life.' I said, 'Must one therefore either feed or be fed?' He said, 'Yes, surely. Have you not noticed that they are all fluid, tenuous, flimsy-minded? You know Miss A—— B——?[35] They are all like that. It is the astral fluid. There is no life, the life has been sucked out. They despise the foundation, and that no one can do till after the resurrection. They are all self, and so they live on stolen goods. Of course there are a few chosen spirits who need not enter into life, but they are very few. Ah! if only one could see all boys and girls after nineteen married.' He told me earlier in the day that once when mountaineering he was in great danger. Someone had slipped and dragged another with him, and he had the weight of two men hanging from the rope—but he felt a great being descending into him and strengthening him. Even when the danger was over he felt no loss of nerve as he looked back on the danger. He had been filled with life. On the way back E—— said, 'There is so little life now. Look at the modern soldier—he is nothing—and the ancient soldier was something—he had to be strong and skilful, they fought man to man.' I said, 'There are some books like that—ideas as wonderful as a campaign by Moltke, but no man. The plan of campaign was not so impressive in the old books, but all was human!' He answered, 'When races cease to believe in Christ, God takes the life out of them, at last they cease to procreate.' E—— himself, all muscular force and ardour, makes me think of that line written, as one believes, of Shakespeare by Ben Jonson—'So rammed with life that he can but grow in life with being.'[36] The irregular line of his thought which makes him obscure is itself a sign of this. He is as full of twists and turns as a tree.

31
[8 February (1909) 'Journal' no. 59]

The other day when I was speaking at the Arts Club[37] someone asked me what life I would recommend to young Irishmen, the thought my whole speech if it were logical should have led up to. I was glad to be able to reply, 'I do not know, though I have thought much about it'. Who does not distrust complete ideas?

32
[9 February (1909) 'Journal' no. 60]

There is an astrological sense in which a man's wife or sweetheart is always an Eve made from a rib of his body.[38] She is drawn to him because she represents a group of stellar influences in the radical horoscope.[39] These influences also create an element in his character, and his destiny, in things apart from love or marriage. Whether this element be good or evil she is therefore its external expression. The happiest have such horoscopes that they find what they have of good in their wives, others must find what they have of evil, or a man may have both affinities. Sometimes a man may find the evil of his horoscope in a woman, and in rescuing her from her own self may conquer his own evil, as with Simon Magus who married a harlot. Others may find in a woman the good that conquers them and shapes them. All external events of life are of course an externalization of character in the same way, but not to the same degree as the wife, who may represent the gathering up of an entire web of influences. A friend represented by a powerful star in the eleventh house may be the same, especially if the sun apply to the star. We are mirrors of the stellar light and we cast this light outward as incidents, magnetic attractions, characterizations, desires. This casting outward of the light is that fall into the circumference the mystics talk of.

33
[12 February (1909) 'Journal' no. 61]

By implication the philosophy of Irish faery lore declares that all
power is from the body, all intelligence from the spirit. Western civilization, religion and magic insist on power and therefore on body,
and hence these three doctrines—efficient rule—the Incarnation—
thaumaturgy. Eastern thoughts answer to these with indifference to
rule, scorn of the flesh, contemplation of the formless. Western
minds who follow the Eastern way become weak and vapoury,
because unfit for the work forced upon them by Western life. Every
symbol is an invocation which produces its equivalent expression in
all worlds. The Incarnation invoked modern science and modern
efficiency, and individualized emotion. It produced a solidification
of all those things that grow from individual will. The historical
truth of the Incarnation is indifferent, though the belief in that truth
was essential to the power of the invocation. All civilization is held
together by the suggestions of an invisible hypnotist—by artificially
created illusions. The knowledge of reality is always in some measure a secret knowledge. It is a kind of death.

34
[6 February (1909) 'Journal' no. 51 excerpt]

While Lady Gregory has brought herself to death's door with over-
work, to give us, while neglecting no other duty, enough plays,
translated or original, to keep the Theatre alive, our base half-men
of letters, or rather half-journalists, that coterie of patriots who
have never been bought because no one ever thought them worth
a price, have been whispering everywhere that she takes advantage
of her position as director to put her own plays upon the stage.
When I think, too, of Synge dying at this moment of their bitterness
and ignorance, as I believe, I wonder if I have been right to shape
my style to sweetness and serenity, and there comes into my mind
that verse that Fergus spoke, 'No man seeks my help because I be
not of the things I dream'.[40] On the night of the 'Playboy debate'[41]
they were all there, silent and craven, but not in the stalls for fear
they might be asked to speak and face the mob. A—— D——[42] even
refused by a subterfuge and joined the others in the gallery. No man
of all literary Dublin dared show his face but my own father,[43]

who spoke to, or rather in the presence of, that howling mob with sweetness and simplicity. I fought them, he did a finer thing—forgot them.

35
[undated 'Journal' no. 55]

Those who accuse Synge of some base motive are the great-grand-children of those Dublin men who accused Smith O'Brien of being paid by the Government to fail. It is of such as these Goethe thought when he said, 'The Irish always seem to me like a pack of hounds dragging down some noble stag'.[44]

36
[undated 'Journal' no. 65 excerpt]

Last night, Miss Allgood, who has been bad hitherto, gave a good performance in *Kincora*.[45] This play in its new form gives me the greatest joy—colour, speech, all has its music, and the scenes with the servants make one feel intimate and friendly with those great people who otherwise would be far off—mere figures of speech. The joy that this play gives makes me understand how much I dislike plays like —— and —— and ——.[46] If at all possible I will now keep at the Theatre till I have seen produced a mass of fine work. If we can create a taste for translated work—which we have not yet done—we can carry on the Theatre without vulgarity. If not, the mere growth of the audience will make all useless, for the Irish town mind will by many channels, public and private, press its vulgarity upon us. If we should feel that happening, if the Theatre is not to continue as we have shaped it, it must, for the sake of our future influence, for the sake of our example, be allowed to pass out of our hands, or cease. We must not be responsible for a compromise.

37
[23 February (1909) 'Journal' no. 68]

Last night I read E——[47] a passage in which Coventry Patmore says we cannot teach another religious truth; we can only point out to him a way whereby he may find it for himself. E—— said, 'If one could show another religious experience, which is of the whole being, one would have to give one's whole being, one would be Christ. He alone can give Himself.'

38

[25 February (1909) 'Journal' no. 71]

I often wonder if my talent will ever recover from the heterogeneous labour of these last few years. The younger Hallam says that vice does not destroy genius but that the heterogeneous does. I cry out vainly for liberty and have ever less and less inner life. Evil comes to us men of imagination wearing as its mask all the virtues. I have certainly known more men destroyed by the desire to have wife and child and to keep them in comfort than I have seen destroyed by drink and harlots. L—— E——[48] at the Rhymers' Club used to say that he meant to have a butler and that he thought it his duty to his wife to keep a house on that scale. Harlots in his case finished what the virtues began, but it was the virtues and not the harlots that killed his knack of verse. I thought myself loving neither vice nor virtue; but virtue has come upon me and given me a nation instead of a home. Has it left me any lyrical faculty? Whatever happens I must go on that there may be a man behind the lines already written; I cast the die long ago and must be true to the cast.

39

[2 March (1909) 'Journal' no. 74 excerpt]

Two hours' idleness—because I have no excuse but to begin creative work, an intolerable toil. Little D—— F—— of Hyderabad[49] told me that in her father's garden one met an opium-eater who made poems in his dreams and wrote the title-pages when he awoke but forgot the rest. He was the only happy poet.

40

[3 March (1909) 'Journal' no. 75 excerpt]

A couple of days ago I went to see Dr. F—— F——.[50] He spoke of the attacks on both him and myself in *Sinn Fein* and of their untruthfulness. He said, 'I congratulated Edward Martyn some time ago on being leader of an important political party,[51] and he answered, "I don't want to be, I want to do my own work". Says I, "I want to do my own work also", and then says he, "The worst of it is that those fellows would not leave either of us there for five minutes if they thought we liked it".'

41

[undated 'Journal' no. 78]

The root of it all is that the political class in Ireland—the lower-middle class from whom the patriotic associations have drawn their journalists and their leaders for the last ten years—have suffered through the cultivation of hatred as the one energy of their movement, a deprivation which is the intellectual equivalent to a certain surgical operation. Hence the shrillness of their voices. They contemplate all creative power as the eunuchs contemplate Don Juan as he passes through Hell on the white horse.[52]

42

[undated 'Journal' no. 78]

To-night G——[53] said that he has always thought that the bad luck of Ireland comes from hatred being the foundation of our politics. It is possible that emotion is an evocation and in ways beyond the senses alters events—creating good and evil luck. Certain individuals who hate much seem to be followed by violent events outside their control. B—— G——[54] has been so followed always. It is possible to explain it by saying that hatred awakens hatred in others and in oneself a tendency to violent action; but there are times when there seems more than this—an actual stream of ill-luck. Certainly evocation with symbol has taught me that much that we think limited to certain obvious effects influences the whole being. A meditation on sunlight, for instance, affects the nature throughout, producing all the effects which follow from the symbolical nature of the sun. Hate must, in the same way, create sterility, producing many effects which would follow from meditation on a symbol. Such a symbol would produce not merely hate but associated effects. An emotion produces a symbol—sensual emotion dreams of water, for instance—just as a symbol produces emotion. The symbol without emotion is more precise and, perhaps, more powerful than an emotion without symbol. Hatred as a basis of imagination, in ways which one could explain even without magic, helps to dry up the nature and make the sexual abstinence, so common among young men and women in Ireland, possible. This abstinence reacts in its turn on the imagination, so that we get at last that strange eunuch-like tone and temper. For the last ten or twenty years there has been a perpetual drying of the Irish mind with the resultant dust-cloud.

43
[5 March (1909) 'Journal' no. 79]

I saw Synge to-day and asked how much of his *Deirdre* was done. He said the third act was right, that he had put a grotesque character, a new character, into the second act and intended to weave him into Act One.[55] He was to come in with Conchubar, carrying some of his belongings, and afterwards at the end of the act to return for a forgotten knife—just enough to make it possible to use him in Act Two. He spoke of his work this winter doubtfully, thought it not very good, seemed only certain of the third act. I did not like to ask more questions lest he should understand that I wished to know if another could complete the work if he died. He is certainly too ill to work himself, and will be for a long time.

44
[6 March (1909) 'Journal' no. 80]

Met MacDonagh[56] yesterday—a man with some literary faculty which will probably come to nothing through lack of culture and encouragement. He had just written an article for the *Leader*, and spoke much as I do myself of the destructiveness of journalism here in Ireland, and was apologetic about his article. He is managing a school on Irish and Gaelic League principles but says he is losing faith in the League. Its writers are infecting Irish not only with the English idiom but with the habits of thought of current Irish journalism, a most un-Celtic thing. 'The League', he said, 'is killing Celtic civilization.' I told him that Synge about ten years ago foretold this in an article in the *Academy*.[57] He thought the National Movement practically dead, that the language would be revived but without all that he loved it for. In England this man would have become remarkable in some way, here he is being crushed by the mechanical logic and commonplace eloquence which give power to the most empty mind, because, being 'something other than human life',[58] they have no use for distinguished feeling or individual thought. I mean that within his own mind this mechanical thought is crushing as with an iron roller all that is organic.

45
[undated 'Journal' no. 81]

The soul of Ireland has become a vapour and her body a stone.

46
[7 March (1909) 'Journal' no. 82]

Ireland has grown sterile, because power has passed to men who lack the training which requires a certain amount of wealth to ensure continuity from generation to generation, and to free the mind in part from other tasks. A gentleman is a man whose principal ideas are not connected with his personal needs and his personal success. In old days he was a clerk or a noble, that is to say, he had freedom because of inherited wealth and position, or because of a personal renunciation. The names are different to-day, and I would put the artist and the scholar in the category of the clerk, yet personal renunciation is not now sufficient or the *hysterica passio*[59] of Ireland would be inspiration, or perhaps it is sufficient but is impossible without inherited culture. For without culture or holiness, which are always the gift of a very few, a man may renounce wealth or any other external thing, but he cannot renounce hatred, envy, jealousy, revenge. Culture is the sanctity of the intellect.[60]

47
[9 March (1909) 'Journal' no. 83]

I have been talking of the literary element in painting with Miss E—— G——[61] and turning over the leaves of Binyon's book[62] on Eastern Painting, in which he shows how traditional, how literary that is. The revolt against the literary element in painting was accompanied by a similar revolt in poetry. The doctrine of what the younger Hallam called the Aesthetic School was expounded in his essay on Tennyson,[63] and when I was a boy the unimportance of subject was a canon. A French poet[64] had written of girls taking lice out of a child's hair. Henley was supposed to have founded a new modern art in the 'hospital poems',[65] though he would not have claimed this. Hallam argued that poetry was the impression on the senses of certain very sensitive men. It was such with the pure artists, Keats and Shelley, but not so with the impure artists who, like Wordsworth, mixed up popular morality with their work. I now see that the literary element in painting, the moral element in poetry, are the means whereby the two arts are accepted into the social order and become a part of life and not things of the study and the exhibition. Supreme art is a traditional statement of certain heroic and religious truths, passed on from age to age, modified by individual genius, but never abandoned. The revolt of individualism came because the tradition had become degraded, or rather because a spurious copy had been accepted in its stead. Classical morality—not quite natural in Christianized Europe—dominated this tradition at the Renaissance, and passed from Milton to Wordsworth and to Arnold, always growing more formal and empty until it became a vulgarity in our time—just as classical forms passed on from Raphael to the Academicians. But Anarchic revolt is coming to an end, and the arts are about to restate the traditional morality. A great work of art, the 'Ode to a Nightingale' not less than the 'Ode to Duty', is as rooted in the early ages as the Mass which goes back to savage folk-lore. In what temple garden did the nightingale first sing?

48
[undated 'Journal' no. 84]

No art can conquer the people alone—the people are conquered by an ideal of life upheld by authority. As this ideal is rediscovered, the arts, music and poetry, painting and literature, will draw closer together.

49
[undated 'Journal' no. 85]

The Abbey Theatre will fail to do its full work because there is no accepted authority to explain why the more difficult pleasure is the nobler pleasure. The fascination of the National Movement for me in my youth was, I think, that it seemed to promise such authority. One cannot love a nation struggling to realize itself without an idea of that nation as a whole being present in our mind. One could always appeal to that idea in the mind of others. National spirit is, for the present, dying, because the influence of the *Nation* newspaper, which first gave popular expression to that idea in English, has passed away. *Kincora,* which should have certain poems and traditions to help it, and at its first production caused so much excitement, rouses now but slight interest, while H——'s[66] plays grow more and more popular. H—— alone requires nothing but his own thought.

50
[undated 'Journal' no. 87]

I cry continually against my life. I have sleepless nights, thinking of the time that I must take from poetry—last night I could not sleep—and yet, perhaps, I must do all these things that I may set myself into a life of action and express not the traditional poet but that forgotten thing, the normal active man.

51
[undated 'Journal' no. 81]

We require a new statement of moral doctrine, which shall be accepted by the average man, but be at the same time beyond his power in practice. Classical morality in its decay became an instrument in the hands of commonplace energy to overthrow distinguished men. A true system of morals is from the first a weapon in the hands of the most distinguished. The Catholic Church created a system only possible for saints, hence its prolonged power. Its definition of the good was narrow, but it did not set out to make shopkeepers. A lofty morality should be tolerant, for none declare its laws but those worn out with its warfare, and they must pity sinners. Besides, it must needs take a personal form in their minds and give to those minds the timidity of discoverers, not less than the courtesy of soldiers.

52
[12 March (1909) 'Journal' no. 93 excerpt summary]

A few days ago my sister Lolly[67] dreamed that she saw three dead bodies on a bed. One had its face to the wall, one had a pink mask like a child's toy mask, and before she could look at the third, somebody put a mask on that too. While she was looking at them the body with its face to the wall suddenly moved. The same night J——[68] dreamed that she saw three very long funerals and that she saw what she thought a body on a bed. She thought it the body of a brother of hers who had died lately. She lay down on the bed by it, and it suddenly moved. The same night my sister Lily dreamed that she had received three telegrams.

53
[12 March (1909) 'Journal' no. 94]

There is a dying-out of national feeling very simple in its origin. You
cannot keep the idea of a nation alive where there are no national
institutions to reverence, no national success to admire, without a
model of it in the mind of the people. You can call it 'Cathleen ni
Houlihan' or the 'Shan van Voght' in a mood of simple feeling, and
love that image, but for the general purposes of life you must have
a complex mass of images, something like an architect's model. The
Young Ireland poets created a mass of obvious images that filled the
minds of the young—Wolfe Tone, King Brian, Emmet, Owen Roe,
Sarsfield, the Fisherman of Kinsale[69]—answered the traditional slan-
ders on Irish character and entered so into the affections that it followed men on to the scaffold. The ethical ideas implied were of
necessity very simple, needing neither study nor unusual gifts for their
understanding. Our own movement thought to do the same thing in
a more profound and therefore more enduring way. When I was
twenty-five or twenty-six I planned a *Légende des Siècles*[70] of Ireland
that was to set out with my *Wanderings of Oisin,* and show something of every century. Lionel Johnson's work and, later, Lady Gregory's, carried on the dream in a different form; and I did not see,
until Synge began to write, that we must renounce the deliberate creation of a kind of Holy City in the imagination, and express the individual. The Irish people were not educated enough to accept images
more profound, more true to human nature, than the schoolboy
thoughts of Young Ireland. You can only create a model of a race to
inspire the action of that race as a whole, apart from exceptional individuals, when you and it share the same simple moral understanding of life. Milton and Shakespeare inspire the active life of England,
but they do it through exceptional individuals. Having no understanding of life that we can teach to others, we must not seek to create a school. Could we create a vision of the race as noble as that of
Sophocles and of Aeschylus, it would be attacked upon some trivial
ground by minds that prefer Young Ireland rhetoric, or the obvious
sentiment of popular English literature, a few Irish thoughts and feelings added for conscience' sake.

Meanwhile, the need of a model of the nation, of some moral
diagram, is as great as in the early nineteenth century, when

national feeling was losing itself in a religious feud over tithes and emancipation. Neither the grammars of the Gaelic League nor the industrialism of the *Leader,* nor the *Sinn Fein* attacks upon the Irish Party, give sensible images to the affections. Yet in the work of Lady Gregory, of Synge, of O'Grady, of Lionel Johnson, in my own work, a school of journalists with simple moral ideas could find right building material to create a historical and literary national-ism as powerful as the old and nobler. That done, they could bid the people love and not hate.

54

[13 February (1909) 'Journal' no. 64 excerpt]

Nobody running at full speed has either a head or a heart.

55

[undated 'Journal' no. 95]

I told my sister that I was to spend the night in the K—— Street haunted house.[71] She said, 'O, I know about that house. I saw a fur-niture-van there one day and furniture going in, and ten days after, the house was empty again; and somebody I know was passing by in the early morning and saw an old woman on a window-sill, clinging to the sash. She was the caretaker. The ghost had driven her out and there was a policeman trying to get her down. But the pious Protestants say that there is no ghost or anything but the young novices in the Convent opposite "screaming in the night-time".'

THE END

THE DEATH OF SYNGE

OF SYNGE

EXTRACTS FROM A DIARY
KEPT IN 1909[1]

THE DEATH OF SYNGE

I

[undated 'Journal' no. 97]

Why does the struggle to come at truth take away our pity, and the struggle to overcome our passions restore it again?

2

[14 March (1909) 'Journal' no. 98 excerpt]

National feeling could be roused again if some man of good education—if a Catholic, he should have been educated outside Ireland—gathered about him a few men like himself, and founded a new *Nation* newspaper, forbidding it all personal attacks, all arguments that assume a base motive in an opponent, and choosing for its national policy, not what seems most desirable in the abstract, but such policy as may stir the imagination and yet gather to its support the greatest possible number of educated men. Ireland is ruined by abstractions, and should prefer what may seem a worse policy if it gathers better men. So long as all is ordered for attack, and that alone, leaders will instinctively increase the number of enemies that they may give their followers something to do, and Irish enemies rather than English because they are the more easily injured. The greater the enemy, the greater the hatred, and therefore the greater seems the power. They would give a nation the frenzy of a sect. A sign that this method, powerful in the time of Parnell, no longer satisfies the nation is that parties are drifting into the hands of feebler and more ignorant men.

3

[undated 'Journal' no. 99]

The education of our Irish secondary schools, especially the Catholic schools, substitutes pedantry for taste. Men learn the dates of writers, the external facts of masterpieces, and not sense of style or feeling for life. I have met no young man out of these schools who has not been injured by the literature and the literary history learned there. The arts have nothing to give but that joy of theirs which is the other side of sorrow, that exhausting contemplation: and in youth before habits have been formed—unless our teachers be wise men—we turn from it to pedantry, which opens to the mind a kind of sensual ease. The young Catholic men and women who have not been through the secondary schools are upon the other hand more imaginative than Protestant boys and girls of the same age. Catholic secondary education destroys, I think, much that the Catholic religion gives. Provincialism destroys the nobility of the Middle Ages.

4
[17 March (1909) 'Journal' no. 100;
undated (cancelled dating: 18 March [1909]) 'Journal' no. 101;
undated 102]

March 17

As I go to and from my bedroom, here at Coole, I pass a wall covered with Augustus John's etchings and drawings.[2] I notice a woman with strongly marked shoulder-blades and a big nose, and a pencil drawing called *Epithalamium*. In the *Epithalamium* an ungainly, ill-grown boy holds out his arms to a tall woman with thin shoulders and a large stomach. Near them is a vivid etching of a woman with the same large stomach and thin shoulders. There is not one of these fifty or sixty clerks and seamstresses and students that has not been broken by labour or wasted by sedentary life. A gymnast would find in all something to amend; and the better he mended the more would those bodies, as with the voice of Dürer, declare that ancient canon discovered in the Greek gymnasium, which, whenever present in painting or sculpture, shows a compact between the artist and society. John is not interested in the social need, in the perpetual thirst for greater health, but in character, in the revolt from all that makes one man like another. The old art, if carried to its logical conclusion, would have led to the creation of one single type of man, one single type of woman; gathering up by a kind of deification a capacity for all energy and all passion, into a Krishna, a Christ, a Dionysus; and at all times a poetical painter, a Botticelli, a Rossetti, creates as his supreme achievement one type of face, known afterwards by his name. The new art can create innumerable personalities, but in each of these the capacity for passion has been sacrificed to some habit of body or of mind. That woman with the big shoulder-blades has, for instance, a nature too keen, too clever for any passion, with the cleverness of people who cannot rest, and that young lad with his arms spread out will sink back into disillusionment and exhaustion after the brief pleasure of a passion which is in part curiosity. Some limiting environment or idiosyncrasy is displayed; man is studied as an individual fact, and not as that energy which seems measureless and hates all that is not itself. It is a powerful but prosaic art, celebrating the 'fall into division' not the 'resurrection into unity'.[3] Did not even Balzac, who looked at the world so often with similar eyes, find it necessary to deny character to his great ladies and young lovers that he might give them passion? What beautiful woman delights us by her look of character? That shows itself when beauty is gone, being the creation of habit, the bare stalk when the flower of spring has withered. Beauty consumes character with what Patmore calls 'the integrity of fire'.[4]

It is this lack of the capacity for passion which makes women dislike the schools of characterization, and makes the modern artist despise woman's judgment. Women, for the same reason, dislike pure comedy. How few women like Molière!

Here at Coole my room is hung with Arundel prints[5] from Botticelli, Benozzo Gozzoli, Giorgione, Mantegna and the Van Eycks. Here everywhere is the expression of desire, though in the Van Eycks the new interest has begun. All display bodies to please an amorous woman's eyes or the eyes of a great King. The martyrs and saints even must show the capacity for all they have renounced.

5

[18 March (1909) 'Journal' no. 105]

These notes are morbid, but I heard a man of science say that all progress is at the outset pathological, and I write for my own good.

The pain others give passes away in their later kindness, but that of our own blunders, especially when they hurt our vanity, never passes away. Our own acts are isolated and one act does not buy absolution for another. They are always present before a strangely abstract judgment. We are never a unity, a personality to ourselves. Small acts of years ago are so painful in the memory that often we start at the presence a little below 'the threshold of consciousness' of a thought that remains unknown. It sheds a vague light like that

of the moon before it rises, or after its setting. Vanity is so intimately associated with our spiritual identity that whatever hurts it,
above all if it came from it, is more painful in the memory than serious sin, and yet I do not think it follows that we are very vain. The
harm we do to others is lost in changing events and passes away
and so is healed by time, unless it was very great. Looking back, I
find only one offence[6] which is as painful to me as a hurt to vanity.
It was done to a man who died shortly after. Because of his death,
it has not been touched by the transforming hand—tolerant Nature
has not rescued it from Justice.

6
[undated 'Journal' no. 107]

I think that all happiness depends on the energy to assume the mask
of some other self;[7] that all joyous or creative life is a rebirth as
something not oneself, something which has no memory and is created in a moment and perpetually renewed. We put on a grotesque
or solemn painted face to hide us from the terrors of judgment,
invent an imaginative Saturnalia where one forgets reality, a game
like that of a child, where one loses the infinite pain of self-realization. Perhaps all the sins and energies of the world are but its flight
from an infinite blinding beam.

7
[20 March (1909) 'Journal' no. 108]

F——[8] is learning Gaelic. I would sooner see her in the Gaelic movement than in any Irish movement I can think of. I fear some new
absorption in political opinion. Women, because the main event of
their lives has been a giving themselves and giving birth, give all to
an opinion as if it were some terrible stone doll. Men take up an
opinion lightly and are easily false to it, and when faithful keep the
habit of many interests. We still see the world, if we are of strong mind
and body, with considerate eyes, but to women opinions become as
their children or their sweethearts, and the greater their emotional
capacity the more do they forget all other things. They grow cruel,
as if in defence of lover or child, and all this is done for 'something
other than human life'.[9] At last the opinion is so much identified
with their nature that it seems a part of their flesh becomes stone
and passes out of life. It was a part of F——'s power in the past that

though she made this surrender with her mind, she kept the sweetness of her voice and much humour, and yet I am afraid. Women should have their play with dolls finished in childish happiness, for if they play with them again it is amid hatred and malice.

8
[undated 'Journal' no. 109]

Women should find in the mask enough joy to forget the doll without regret. There is always a living face behind the mask.

9
[undated 'Journal' no. 114]

Last night at 'The Theatre of Ireland'[10] I talked to the man next to me. 'I have been to your theatre also', he said. 'I like your popular plays, *The Suburban Groove*[11] and those plays by the Frenchman, I do not remember his name' (evidently Molière), 'but I don't like your mysteries.' I thought he meant something of mine, as the word 'mystery' is a popular reproach since *The Shadowy Waters,* but I found he meant *Kincora.* I said, 'Why do you find that mysterious?' He said, 'O, I know nothing about all that history'. I replied, 'When I was young every Irish Nationalist young man knew as much about King Brian as about Saint Patrick'. He thought I was talking of the peasants and said he was afraid that sort of knowledge was dying out amongst them. He evidently thought it their business alone, like the rath and the blessed well.

10
[23 March (1909) 'Journal' no. 116]

March 23

MacDonagh called to-day.[12] Very sad about Ireland. Says that he finds a barrier between himself and the Irish-speaking peasantry, who are 'cold, dark and reticent' and 'too polite'. He watches the Irish-speaking boys at his school, and when nobody is looking, or when they are alone with the Irish-speaking gardener, they are merry, clever and talkative. When they meet an English speaker or one who has learned Gaelic, they are stupid. They are in a different world. Presently he spoke of his nine years in a monastery and I asked what it was like. 'O,' he said, 'everybody is very simple and happy enough. There is a little jealousy sometimes. If one brother goes into a town with a Superior, another brother is jealous.' He then told me that the Bishop of Raphoe[13] had forbidden anybody in his See to contribute to the Gaelic League because its Secretary 'has blasphemed against the holy Adamnan'. The Secretary had said, 'The Bishop is an enemy, like the founder of his See, Saint Adamnan, who tried to injure the Gaelic language by writing in Latin'. MacDonagh says, 'Two old countrymen fell out and one said, "I have a brother who will make you behave", meaning the Bishop of Raphoe, and the other said, "I have a son who will put sense into you", meaning Cardinal Logue.'

II
[undated 'Journal' no. 117]

Molly Allgood[14] came to-day to ask where I would be to-morrow, as Synge wishes to send for me if strong enough. He wants 'to make arrangements'. He is dying. They have ceased to give him food. Should we close the Abbey or keep it open while he still lives? Poor Molly is going through her work as always. Perhaps that is best for her. I feel Synge's coming death less now than when he first became ill. I am used to the thought of it and I do not find that I pity him, I pity her. He is fading out of life. I felt the same when I saw M——[15] in the madhouse. I pitied his wife. He seemed already dead. One does not feel that death is evil when one meets it,—evil, I mean, for the one who dies. Our Daimon is silent as was that other before the death of Socrates.[16] The wildest sorrow that comes at the thought of death is, I think, 'Ages will pass over and no one ever again look on that nobleness or that beauty'. What is this but to pity the living and to praise the dead?

I2
[24 March (1909) 'Journal' no. 118]

March 24

Synge is dead. In the early morning he said to the nurse, 'It is no use fighting death any longer' and he turned over and died. I called at the hospital this afternoon and asked the assistant matron if he knew he was dying. She answered, 'He may have known it for weeks, but he would not have said so to anyone. He would have no fuss. He was like that.' She added, with emotion in her voice, 'We were devoted to him'.

13

[28 March (1909) 'Journal' no. 119]

March 28

Mr. Stephens, Synge's brother-in-law, said he suffered no pain but only great weakness. On Sunday he questioned the doctor and convinced himself that he was dying. He told his brother-in-law next day and was quite cheerful, even making jokes. In the evening he saw Molly and told her to be brave and sent her to me that I might arrange about his writings. On the morning when I heard of his death a heavy storm was blowing and I doubt not when he died that it had well begun. That morning Lady Gregory felt a very great depression and was certain that some evil was coming, but feared for her grandchild, feared it was going to be ill. On the other hand, my sister Lolly said at breakfast, 'I think it will be all right with Synge, for last night I saw a galley struggling with a storm and then it shot into calm and bright sunlight and I heard the keel grate on the shore'. One remembers the voyages to Tir-nan-oge, certainly the voyages of souls after death to their place of peace.

14

[undated 'Journal' no. 120]

I have been looking through his poems and have read once more that on page 21, 'I asked if I got sick and died'.[17] Certainly they were there at the funeral, his 'idiot' enemies: A——[18] who against all regulations rushed up to the dressing-rooms during the *Playboy* riot to tell the actors they should not have played in so disgraceful a play; B——[19] who has always used his considerable influence with the company against Synge, and has spoken against him in public; there, too, were the feeble friends who pretended to believe but gave no help. And there was C——[20] whose obituary notice speaks of Synge's work as only important in promise, of the exaggeration of those who praise it, and then claims that its writer spent many hours a day with Synge in Paris (getting the date wrong by two years, however), with Synge who was proud and lonely, almost as proud of his old blood as of his genius, and had few friends. There was D——,[21] the Secretary of the Society— it had sent a wreath—whose animosity had much to do with the attacks in *Sinn Fein*. It was, to quote E——,[22] a funeral 'small but select'. A good friend of Synge's quoted to me:

> How shall the ritual then be read,
> The requiem how be sung
> By you, by yours the evil eye,
> By yours the slanderous tongue,
> That did to death the innocence
> That died, and died so young?[23]

Yet these men came, though but in remorse; they saw his plays, though but to dislike; they spoke his name, though but to slander. Well-to-do Ireland never saw his plays nor spoke his name. Was he ever asked to any country house but Coole? Was he ever asked to a dinner-party? How often I have wished that he might live long enough to enjoy that communion with idle, charming and culti-vated women which Balzac in one of his dedications calls 'the chief consolation of genius'![24]

15
[undated 'Journal' no. 122]

In Paris Synge once said to me, 'We should unite stoicism, asceti-cism and ecstasy. Two of them have often come together, but the three never.'

16
[undated 'Journal' no. 123; undated 'Journal' no. 126;
undated 'Journal' no. 127 excerpt]

I believe that some thing I said may have suggested 'I asked if I got sick and died'.[25] S——[26] had frequently attacked his work while admitting him a man of genius. He attacked it that he might remain on good terms with the people about him. When Synge was in hos-pital to be operated upon, S—— was there too as a patient, and I told Synge that whenever I spoke of his illness to any man that man said, 'And isn't it sad about S——?' until I could stand it no longer and burst out with 'I hope he will die', and now, as someone said, I was 'being abused all over the town as without heart'. I had learned that people were calling continually to inquire how S—— was, but hardly anybody called to ask for Synge. Two or three weeks later Synge wrote this poem. Had my words set his mind running on the thought that fools flourish, more especially as I had prophesied that

S—— would flourish, and in my mood at the moment it seemed that for S—— to be operated on at the same time with Synge was a kind of insolence? S——'s illness did, indeed, win for him so much sympathy that he came out to lucrative and honourable employment, and now when playing golf he says with the English accent he has acquired of late, to some player who needs a great man's favour, 'I know him well, I will say a word in that quarter'.

The Irish weekly papers notice Synge's death with short and for the most part grudging notices. There was an obscure Gaelic League singer who was a leader of the demonstration against the *Playboy*. He died on the same day. *Sinn Fein*[27] notices both deaths in the same article and gives three-fourths of it to the rioter. For Synge it has but grudging words, as was to be expected.

Molly tells me that Synge went to see Stephen MacKenna and his wife before going into hospital and said good-bye with 'You will never see me again'.

17
[undated 'Journal' no. 128]
CELEBRATIONS

1. He was one of those unmoved souls in whom there is a perpetual 'Last Day', a perpetual trumpeting and coming up for judgment.

2. He did not speak to men and women, asking judgment, as lesser writers do; but knowing himself part of judgment he was silent.

3. We pity the living and not such dead as he. He has gone upward out of his ailing body into the heroical fountains. We are parched by time.

4. He had the knowledge of his coming death and was cheerful to the end, even joking a little when that end had all but come. He had no need of our sympathies. It was as though we and the things about us died away from him and not he from us.

18

[2 April (1909) 'Journal' no. 129; undated 'Journal' no. 130]

DETRACTIONS

He had that egotism of the man of genius which Nietzsche com-
pares to the egotism of a woman with child. Neither I nor Lady
Gregory had ever a compliment from him. After *Hyacinth*[28] Lady
Gregory went home the moment the curtain fell, not waiting for the
congratulation of friends, to get his supper ready. He was always
ailing and weakly. All he said of the triumphant *Hyacinth* was, 'I
expected to like it better'. He had under charming and modest manners, in almost all things of life, a complete absorption in his own
dream. I have never heard him praise any writer, living or dead, but
some old French farce-writer.[29] For him nothing existed but his
thought. He claimed nothing for it aloud. He never said any of
those self-confident things I am enraged into saying, but one knew
that he valued nothing else. He was too confident for self-assertion.
I once said to George Moore, 'Synge has always the better of you,
for you have brief but ghastly moments during which you admit the
existence of other writers; Synge never has'. I do not think he disliked other writers—they did not exist. One did not think of him as
an egotist. He was too sympathetic in the ordinary affairs of life
and too simple. In the arts he knew no language but his own.

I have often envied him his absorption as I have envied Verlaine
his vice. Can a man of genius make that complete renunciation of
the world necessary to the full expression of himself without some
vice or some deficiency? You were happy or at least blessed, 'blind
old man of Scio's rocky isle'.[30]

19

[undated 'Journal' no. 131]

Two plays last night, *Time,* a play of suggestion, *Cross-roads,* a logical play.[31] We accepted this last play because of its central idea, a
seeming superstition of its creator, a promise of a new attitude
towards life, of something beyond logic. In the four morning papers
Time is cursed or ignored and *Cross-roads* given great praise, but
praise that is never for the central idea, and the only critic who
speaks of that idea misunderstands it completely. State a logical

proposition and the most commonplace mind can complete it. Suggestion is richest to the richest and so grows unpopular with a democracy like this. They misunderstood Robinson's idea,[32] luckily for his popularity, and so turned all into commonplace. They allow their minds to dwell so completely on the logic that they do not notice what, as it were, swims upon it or juts up from its river-bed. That is how they combine religion with a journalism which accepts all the implications of materialism. A thought that stirs me in *Time* is that 'only women and great artists love time, others sell it', but what is Blake's 'naked beauty displayed',[33] visible audible wisdom, to the shopkeeping logicians? How can they love time or anything but the day's end?

20

[undated 'Journal' no. 134; 3 April (1909) 'Journal' no. 137]

To-day Molly told me that Synge often spoke of his coming death, indeed constantly for a year past, and tried hard to finish *Deirdre*.[34] Sometimes he would get very despondent, thinking he could not finish it, and then she would act it for him and he would write a little more, and then he would despond again, and so the acting would begin again.

My sister Lily says that the ship Lolly saw on the night of Synge's death was not like a real ship, but like the *Shadowy Waters* ship on the Abbey stage,[35] a sort of allegorical thing. There was also a girl in a bright dress, but she seemed to vanish as the ship ran ashore; all about the girl, and indeed everything, was broken and confused until the bow touched the shore in bright sunlight.

21

[undated 'Journal' no. 138; undated 'Journal' no. 140]

I see that between *Time,* suggestion, and *Cross-roads,*[36] logic, lies a difference of civilization. The literature of suggestion belongs to a social order when life conquered by being itself and the most living was the most powerful, and not to a social order founded upon argument. Leisure, wealth, privilege were created to be a soil for the most living. The literature of logic, the most powerful and the most empty, conquering all in the service of one metallic premise, is for those who have forgotten everything but books and yet have only just learnt to read. They fill their minds with deductions, as they fill their empty houses, where there is nothing of the past, with machine-made furniture. I used to think that the French and Irish democracies follow, as John O'Leary used to say, a logical deduction to its end, no matter what suffering it brings, from a resemblance in the blood. I now believe that they do this because they have broken from the past, from the self-evident truths, from 'naked beauty displayed'.[37] The English logicians may be as ignorant but they are timid.

Robinson should become a celebrated dramatist[38] if this theatre lasts long enough. He does not argue like the imitators of Ibsen, though his expression of life is as logical, hence his grasp on active passion. Passion is logical when bent on action. In the drama of suggestion there must be sufficient loosening and slackening for meditation and the seemingly irrelevant, or else a Greek chorus, and neither is possible without rich leisurely minds in the audience, lovers of Father Time, men who understand Faust's last cry to the passing moment.[39]

Florence Farr once said to me, 'If we could say to ourselves, with sincerity, "This passing moment is as good as any I shall ever know", we would die upon the instant, or be united to God'. Desire would have ceased, and logic the feet of desire.

22
[5 April (1909) 'Journal' no. 141]

April 5

Walked home from Gurteen Dhas with D——[40] and walked through the brick-kilns of Egypt.[41] He states everything in a slightly argumentative form and the soul is starved by the absence of self-evident truth. Good conversation unrolls itself like the spring or like the dawn; whereas effective argument, mere logical statement, founds itself on the set of facts or of experiences common to two or more. Each hides what is new or rich.

23
[undated 'Journal' no. 143; undated 'Journal' no. 144]

The element which in men of action corresponds to style in literature is the moral element. Books live almost entirely because of their style, and the men of action who inspire movements after they are dead are those whose hold upon impersonal emotion and law lifts them out of immediate circumstance. Mitchel wrote better prose than Davis, Mangan better poetry, D'Arcy Magee better popular verse, Fintan Lalor saw deeper into a political event, O'Connell had more power and Meagher more eloquence, but Davis alone has influenced generations of young men, though Mitchel's narrower and more faulty nature has now and again competed with him. Davis showed this moral element not merely in his verse—I doubt if that could have had great effect alone—but in his action, in his defence, for instance, of the rights of his political opponents of the Royal Irish Academy.[42] His verses were but an illustration of principles shown in action. Men are dominated by self-conquest; thought that is a little obvious or platitudinous if merely written, becomes persuasive, immortal even, if held to amid the hurry of events. The self-conquest of the writer who is not a man of action is style.

Mitchel's influence comes mainly, though not altogether, from style, that also a form of power, an energy of life. It is curious that Mitchel's long martyred life, supported by style, has had less force than that of a man who died at thirty, was never in the hulks,[43] did not write very well, and achieved no change of the law.

The act of appreciation of any great thing is an act of self-conquest. This is one reason why we distrust the serene moralist who has not approved his principles in some crisis. He would be troubled, broken even, if he had made that conquest. Yet the man who has proved himself in a crisis may be serene in words, for his battle was not in contemplation where words are combatants.

24
[undated 'Journal' no. 145]

Last night my sister told me that this book of Synge's (his poems)[44] was the only book they began to print on a Friday. They tried to avoid this but could not, and it is not at all well printed. Do all they could, it would not come right.

25
[undated 'Journal' no. 147]

Molly Allgood has just told me of three pre-visions. Some years ago, when the company were in England on that six weeks' tour,[45] she, Synge and D——[46] were sitting in a tea-shop, she was looking at Synge, and suddenly the flesh seemed to fall from his face and she saw but a skull. She told him this and it gave him a great shock, and since then she had not allowed images to form before her eyes of themselves, as they often used to do. Synge was well at the time. Again last year, but before the operation and at a time when she had no fear, she dreamed that she saw him in a coffin being lowered into a grave, and a 'strange sort of cross' was laid over the coffin. (The company sent a cross of flowers to his funeral and it was laid upon the grave.) She told this also to Synge and he was troubled by it. Then some time after the operation she dreamed that she saw him in a boat. She was on the shore, and he waved his hand to her and the boat went away. She longed to go to him but could not.

26

[April 11 (1909) 'Journal' no. 150]

March 11[47]

   Stratford-on-Avon

   Some weeks ago C——[48] wrote to me that it was a phase of M——'s madness to believe himself in heaven. All the great poets of other times were there, and he was helping to prepare for the reception of Swinburne. The angels were to stand in groups of three. And now I have just heard that Swinburne is dead.[49]

27

[undated 'Journal' no. 152]

Dined with Ricketts and Shannon. Ricketts spoke of the grief Synge's death gave him—the ending of all that work. We talked of the disordered and broken lives of modern men of genius and the so different lives of the Italian painters. He said in those days men of genius were cared for, but now the strain of life is too heavy, no one thinks of them till some misfortune comes—madness or death. He then spoke, as he often does, of the lack of any necessary place for the arts in modern life and said, 'After all, the ceiling of the Sistine Chapel was the Pope's ceiling'. Later he said in comment upon some irascible act of Hugh Lane's, 'Everybody who is doing anything for the world is very disagreeable, the agreeable people are those for whom the world is doing something'.

28
[undated 'Journal' no. 153 excerpt]

Our modern public arts, architecture, plays, large decorations, have too many different tastes to please. Some taste is sure to dislike and to speak its dislike everywhere, and then because of the silence of the rest—partly from apathy, partly from dislike of controversy, partly from the difficulty of defence, as compared with the ease of attack—there is general timidity. All creation requires one mind to make and one mind of enjoyment. The theatre can at rare moments create this one mind of enjoyment, and once created, it is like the mind of an individual in solitude, immeasurably bold— all is possible to it. The only building received with enthusiasm during my time has been the Catholic Cathedral of Westminster— religion or the politics of religion created that one mind.

29
[15 April (1909) 'Journal' no. 156]

I asked Molly if any words of hers made Synge write 'I asked if I got sick and died'[50] and she said, 'He used often to joke about death with me and one day he said, "Will you go to my funeral?" and I said, "No, for I could not bear to see you dead and the others living".'

30
[undated 'Journal' no. 173 excerpt]

Went to S——'s[51] the other night—everybody either too tall or too short, crooked or lop-sided. One woman had an excited voice, an intellect without self-possession, and there was a man with a look of a wood-kern, who kept bringing the conversation back and back to Synge's wrongdoing in having made a girl in the *Playboy* admire a man who had hamstrung 'mountain ewes'.[52] He saw nothing else to object to but that one thing. He declared that the English would not give Home Rule because they thought Ireland cruel, and no Irishman should write a sentence to make them go on thinking that. There arose before my mind an image of this man arguing about Ireland with an endless procession of second-rate men. At last I said, 'When a country produces a man of genius he never is what it wants or believes it wants; he is always unlike its idea of itself. In the eighteenth century Scotland believed itself religious, moral and gloomy, and its national poet Burns[53] came not to speak of these things but to speak of lust and drink and drunken gaiety. Ireland, since the Young Irelanders, has given itself up to apologetics. Every impression of life or impulse of imagination has been examined to see if it helped or hurt the glory of Ireland or the political claim of Ireland. A sincere impression of life became at last impossible, all was apologetics. There was no longer an impartial imagination, delighting in whatever is naturally exciting. Synge was the rushing up of the buried fire, an explosion of all that had been denied or refused, a furious impartiality, an indifferent turbulent sorrow. His work, like that of Burns, was to say all the people did not want to have said. He was able to do this because Nature had made him incapable of a political idea.' The wood-kern made no answer, did not understand a word I said, perhaps; but for the rest of the evening he kept saying to this person or to that person that he objected to nothing but the passage about the 'mountain ewes'.

31
[8 July (1909) 'Journal' no. 178]

July 8

I dreamed this thought two nights ago: 'Why should we complain if men ill-treat our Muses, when all that they gave to Helen while she still lived was a song and a jest?'

32
[20 September (1909) 'Journal' no. 191]

September 20

An idle man has no thought, a man's work thinks through him. On the other hand a woman gets her thought through the influence of a man. A man is to her what work is to a man. Man is a woman to his work and it begets his thoughts.

33
[undated 'Journal' no. 192]

The old playwrights took old subjects, did not even arrange the subject in a new way. They were absorbed in expression, that is to say in what is most near and delicate. The new playwrights invent their subjects and dislike anything customary in the arrangement of the fable, but their expression is as common as the newspapers where they first learned to write.

34
[October (1909) 'Journal' no. 194 excerpt]

October

I saw *Hamlet* on Saturday night,[54] except for the chief 'Ophelia' scenes, and missed these (for I had to be in the Abbey) without regret. Their pathos, as they are played, has always left me cold. I came back for Hamlet at the graveside: there my delight always begins anew. I feel in *Hamlet*, as so often in Shakespeare, that I am in the presence of a soul lingering on the storm-beaten threshold of sanctity. Has not that threshold always been terrible, even crime-haunted? Surely Shakespeare, in those last seeming idle years, was no quiet country gentleman, enjoying, as men like Dowden think,[55] the temporal reward of an unvalued toil. Perhaps he sought for wisdom in itself at last, and not in its passionate shadows. Maybe he had passed the threshold, and none the less for Jonson's drinking bout. Certainly one finds here and there in his work praise of country leisure sweetened by wisdom.

35
[October (1909) 'Journal' no. 194 excerpt]

Am I going against nature in my constant attempt to fill my life with work? Is my mind as rich as in idle days? Is not perhaps the poet's labour a mere rejection? If he seek purity—the ridding of his life of all but poetry—will not inspiration come? Can one reach God by toil? He gives Himself to the pure in heart. He asks nothing but attention.

36
[27 October (1909) 'Journal' no. 195]

I have been looking at Venetian costumes of the sixteenth century as pictured in *The Mask*[56]—all fantastic; bodily form hidden or disguised; the women with long bodices, the men in stuffed doublets. Life had become so learned and courtly that men and women dressed with no thought of bodily activity. If they still fought and hunted, their imagination was not with these things. Does not the same happen to our passions when we grow contemplative and so liberate them from use? They also become fantastic and create the strange lives of poets and artists.

37

[15 (January) (as 'December') (1910)] 'Journal' no. 203]

December 15[57]

Deirdre of the Sorrows (first performances). I was anxious about this play and on Thursday both Lady Gregory and I felt the strain of our doubts and fears. Would it seem mere disjointed monotony? Would the second act be intelligible? The audience seemed to like it, and I was greatly moved by certain passages in the last act. I thought the quarrel at the graveside with its last phrase, 'And isn't it a poor thing we should miss the safety of the grave, and we trampling its edge?' and Deirdre's cry to the quarrelling Kings, 'Draw a little back with the squabbling of fools', as noble and profound drama as any man has written. On the first night the thought that it was Synge's reverie over death, his own death, made all poignant. 'The filth of the grave', 'death is a poor, untidy thing, though it's a queen that dies', and the like, brought him dying before me. I remembered his extreme gentleness in the last weeks, that air of being done with ambition and conflict. Last night the audience was small—under ten pounds—and less alive than the first night. No one spoke of the great passages. Someone thought the quarrel in the last act too harsh. Others picked out those rough peasant words that give salt to his speech, as 'of course adding nothing to the dialogue, and very ugly'. Others objected to the little things in the costuming of the play which were intended to echo these words, to vary the heroic convention with something homely or of the fields. Then as I watched the acting I saw that O'Donovan and Molly (Maire O'Neill) were as passionless as the rest. Molly had personal charm, pathos, distinction even, fancy, beauty, but never passion—never intensity; nothing out of a brooding mind. All was but observation, curiosity, desire to please. Her foot never touched the unchanging rock, the secret place beyond life; her talent showed like that of the others, social, modern, a faculty of comedy. Pathos she has, the nearest to tragedy the comedian can come, for that is conscious of our presence and would have our pity. Passion she has not, for that looks beyond mankind and asks no pity, not even of God. It realizes, substantiates, attains, scorns, governs, and is most mighty when it passes from our sight.

38
[16 (January) (as 'December') (1910) 'Journal' no. 204]

December 16

Last night Molly had so much improved that I thought she may have tragic power. The lack of power and of clarity which I still find amid great charm and distinction, comes more from lack of construction, through lack of reflection and experience, than from mere lack of emotion. There are passages where she attempts nothing, or where she allows herself little external comedy impulses, more, I now think, because they are habitual than because she could not bring emotion out of herself. The chief failure is towards the end. She does not show immediately after the death of Naoise enough sense of what has happened, enough normal despair to permit of a gradual development into the wild unearthly feeling of the last speeches, though these last speeches are exquisitely spoken. My unfavourable impression of Friday came in part from the audience, which was heavy and, I thought, bored. Yesterday the audience— the pit entirely full—was enthusiastic and moved, raising once again my hope for the theatre and for the movement.

39
[25 May (1911) 'Journal' no. 231]

May 25

At Stratford-on-Avon the *Playboy* shocked a good many people,[58] because it was a self-improving, self-educating audience, and that means a perverted and commonplace audience. If you set out to educate yourself you are compelled to have an ideal, a model of what you would be; and if you are not a man of genius, your model will be commonplace and prevent the natural impulses of the mind, its natural reverence, desire, hope, admiration, always half unconscious, almost bodily. That is why a simple round of religious duties, things that escape the intellect, is often so much better than its substitute, self-improvement.

40

[18 September (1911) 'Journal' no. 233]

September 18
    S.S. Zeeland

I noticed in the train, as I came to Queenstown,[59] a silent, fairly well-dressed man, who struck me as vulgar. It was not his face, which was quite normal, but his movements. He moved from his head only. His arm and hand, let us say, moved in direct obedience to the head, had not the instinctive motion that comes from a feeling of weight, of the shape of an object to be touched or grasped. There were too many straight lines in gesture and in pose. The result was an impression of vulgar smartness, a defiance of what is profound and old and simple. I have noticed that beginners sometimes move this way on the stage. They, if told to pick up something, show by the movement of their body that their idea of doing it is more vivid than the doing of it. One gets an impression of thinness in the nature. I am watching Miss V——[60] to find out if her inanimate movements when on the stage come from lack of experience or if she has them in life. I watched her sinking into a chair the other day to see if her body felt the size and shape of the chair before she reached it. If her body does not so feel she will never be able to act, just as she will never have grace of movement in ordinary life. As I write I see through the cabin door a woman feeding a child with a spoon. She thinks of nothing but the child, and every movement is full of expression. It would be beautiful acting. Upon the other hand her talk—she is talking to someone next her—in which she is not interested, is monotonous and thin in cadence. It is a mere purpose in the brain, made necessary by politeness.

41

[October (1914) 'Journal' no. 246]

October

A good writer should be so simple that he has no faults, only sins.

THE END

THE BOUNTY
OF SWEDEN

THE BOUNTY OF SWEDEN[1]

I

Thirty years ago I visited Paris for the first time.[2] The Cabbalist MacGregor Mathers said, 'Write your impressions at once, for you will never see Paris clearly again'. I can remember that I had pleased him by certain deductions from the way a woman at the other end of the café moved her hands over the dominoes. I might have seen that woman in London or in Dublin, but it would not have occurred to me to discover in her every kind of rapacity, the substance of the legendary harpy. 'Is not style', as Synge once said to me, 'born out of the shock of new material?'

I am about to write, as in a kind of diary, impressions of Stockholm which must get whatever value they have from excitement, from the presence before the eyes of what is strange, mobile and disconnected.

II

Early in November [1923] a journalist called to show me a printed paragraph saying that the Nobel Prize would probably be conferred upon Herr Mann, the distinguished novelist, or upon myself. I did not know that the Swedish Academy had ever heard my name; tried to escape an interview by talking of Rabindranath Tagore, of his gift to his School of the seven thousand pounds awarded him;[3] almost succeeded in dismissing the whole Reuter paragraph from my memory. Herr Mann has many readers, is a famous novelist with his fixed place in the world, and, said I to myself, well fitted for such an honour; whereas I am but a writer of plays which are acted by players with a literary mind for a few evenings, and I have altered them so many times that I doubt the value of every passage. I am more confident of my lyrics, or of some few amongst them, but then I have got into the habit of recommending or commending myself to general company for anything rather than my gift of lyric writing, which concerns such a meagre troop.

* * *

Every now and then, when something has stirred my imagination, I begin talking to myself. I speak in my own person and dramatize myself, very much as I have seen a mad old woman do upon the Dublin quays, and sometimes detect myself speaking and moving as if I were still young, or walking perhaps like an old man with fumbling steps. Occasionally, I write out what I have said in verse, and generally for no better reason than because I remember that I have written no verse for a long time. I do not think of my soliloquies as having different literary qualities. They stir my interest, by their appropriateness to the men I imagine myself to be, or by their accurate description of some emotional circumstance, more than by any aesthetic value. When I begin to write I have no object but to find for them some natural speech, rhythm and syntax, and to set it out in some pattern, so seeming old that it may seem all men's speech, and though the labour is very great, I seem to have used no faculty peculiar to myself, certainly no special gift. I print the poem and never hear about it again, until I find the book years after with a page dog-eared by some young man, or marked by some young girl with a violet, and when I have seen that, I am a little ashamed, as though somebody were to attribute to me a delicacy of feeling I should but do not possess. What came so easily at first, and amidst so much drama, and was written so laboriously at the last, cannot be counted among my possessions.

On the other hand, if I give a successful lecture, or write a vigorous, critical essay, there is immediate effect; I am confident that on some one point, which seems to me of great importance, I know more than other men, and I covet honour.

III

Then some eight days later, between ten and eleven at night, comes a telephone message from the *Irish Times* saying that the prize has indeed been conferred upon me; and some ten minutes after that comes a telegram from the Swedish Ambassador; then journalists come for interviews. At half past twelve my wife[4] and I are alone, and search the cellar for a bottle of wine, but it is empty, and as a celebration is necessary we cook sausages. A couple of days pass and a letter from the Ambassador invites me to receive the prize at Stockholm, but a letter from the Swedish Academy offers to send medal, money, and diploma to Dublin.[5]

I question booksellers in vain for some history of Sweden, or of Swedish literature. Even Gosse's *Studies in the Literature of Northern Europe,* which I read twenty years ago, is out of print, and among my own books there is nothing but the Life of Swedenborg,[6] which contains photographs of Swedenborg's garden and garden-house, and of the Stockholm House of Nobles,[7] built in Dutch style, and beautiful, with an ornament that never insists upon itself, and a dignity that has no pomp. It had housed in Swedenborg's day that Upper Chamber of the Swedish Parliament where he had voted and spoken upon finance, after the ennoblement of his family.

IV

My wife and I leave Harwich for Esbjerg in Denmark, on the night of December 6, and find our alarms were needless, for the sea is still and the air warm. The Danish steamboat is about the size of the Dublin-Holyhead mail-boat, but the cabins are panelled in pale birchwood, and when we sit down to supper, the table is covered by an astonishing variety of cold food, most of which we refuse because we do not recognize it, and some, such as eels in jelly, because we do. Our companions are commercial travellers and presently we are recognized, for somebody has a newspaper with my portrait, and a man who has travelled in Ireland for an exporter of Danish agricultural machinery talks to us at dinner. He was in Munster for the first part of our Civil War,[8] and when the trains were stopped had found himself in great difficulties, and during parts of his journey had moved at breakneck speed, that his motor might escape capture by the Insurgents, but our Civil War was no part of his business, and had not stirred his imagination. He had, however, discovered a defect in Irish agriculture that was very much a part. Through lack of warm winter sheds and proper winter food for cattle, the Irish farmers had no winter butter, and so Ireland must import butter from his country. Though, as he said, against Danish interests, he had pointed this out to Irish farmers. 'But you have a Government', they said, 'which looks after these things', and this time he became really excited—'Put that idea out of your head', I told them. 'It was we ourselves who looked after these things, our Government has nothing to do with it.'

He asks why the Irish have so little self-reliance, and want the Government to do everything, and I say, 'Were the Danes always self-reliant?' and after a moment's thought, he answers, 'Not till the Bishop established his Schools; we owe everything to his High Schools'. I know something of Bishop Grundtvig and his Schools, for I often hear A.E. or some other at Plunkett House[9] tell how he educated Denmark, by making examinations almost nothing and the personality of the teacher almost everything, and rousing the imagination with Danish literature and history. 'What our peasants need', he had said, 'is not technical training, but mental.'[10]

As we draw near our journey's end, an elderly Swede comes to say 'good-bye', and kisses my wife's hand, bending very low, and the moment he is out of ear-shot, the Danish commercial traveller says with a disgusted voice, 'No Dane would do that. The Swedes are always imitating the French.'

I see that he does not like Swedes, and I ask what he thinks of Norwegians. 'Rough,' he says, 'and they want everything, they want Greenland now.'

V

At Esbjerg I find a young man, a distinguished Danish poet sent by a Copenhagen newspaper, and he and I and my wife dine together. At Copenhagen journalists meet us at the railway station, and others at the hotel, and when I am asked about Ireland I answer always that if the British Empire becomes a voluntary Federation of Free Nations, all will be well, but if it remains as in the past, a domination of one, the Irish question is not settled. That done with, I can talk of the work of my generation in Ireland, the creation of a literature to express national character and feeling but with no deliberate political aim. A journalist who has lived in Finland says, 'Finland has had to struggle with Russian influence to preserve its national culture.' I ask many questions and one journalist says, 'O—Denmark is well educated, and education can reach everybody, as education cannot in big nations like England and America', and he goes on to say that in Denmark 'you may dine at some professor's house, and find that you are sitting next your housemaid, who is among his favourite pupils, and next morning she will be your housemaid again, and too well educated to presume, or step out of her place'. Another, however, a very distinguished man, will have it that it is 'all wrong, for people who should hardly know what a book is now read books, and even write them. The High Schools have made the intellect of Denmark sentimental.' A little later on he says, 'We may have a Socialist Government one of these days', and I begin to wonder what Denmark will make of that mechanical eighteenth-century dream; we know what half-mediaeval Russia has made of it. Another Dane speaks of the Danish Royal Family as 'bourgeois and sporting, like the English'; but says, when I ask about the Royal Family of Sweden, 'O—such educated and intelligent people.' It is he, I think, who first tells me of Prince Eugene, friend and patron of Swedish artists, and himself an accomplished painter who has helped to decorate the Stockholm Town Hall,[11] 'beginning every day at nine o'clock, and working all day like the rest, and for two years', and how at the opening ceremony he had not stood among the Royal Family, 'but among the artists and workmen', and that it was he who saw to it 'that every artist was given freedom to create as he would'. Another spoke much of Strindberg, and though he called him the 'Shakespeare of Sweden', seemed to approve the Swedish Academy's refusal of recognition; 'they could not endure his quarrels with his friends nor the book about his first wife'.

A train-ferry brings us across some eighteen miles of sea, and so into Sweden, and while we are waiting for the train to start again, I see through a carriage window many faces, but it is only just as the train starts, when a Swedish interviewer says—for there are interviewers here also—'Did you not see all those people gazing at the Nobel Prize winner?', that I connect those faces with myself.

Away from the lights of the station it is too dark to see anything, but when the dawn breaks, we are passing through a forest.

VI

At the Stockholm station a man[12] introduces himself, and reminds me that I met him in Paris thirty years ago, and asks me to read a pamphlet which he has written in English upon Strindberg, and especially a chapter called 'Strindberg and the Wolves'. The pamphlet comes to the hotel a couple of hours later, and turns out to be an attack upon the Swedish Academy, and an ardent defence of Strindberg. That outrageous, powerful book about his first wife is excused on the ground that it was not written for publication, and was published by an accident.[13] And somebody once met Strindberg in a museum, dressed up according to the taste of one or other of his wives, 'with cuffs upon his pantaloons', by which the pamphlet meant, I imagine, that like 'Mr. Prufrock' he wore 'the bottoms of his trousers rolled'.[14] I had met its writer in the rooms of an American artist, who was of Strindberg's Paris circle, and it was probably there that I had heard for the first time of stage scenery that might decorate a stage and suggest a scene, while attempting nothing that an easel painting can do better. I am pleased to imagine that the news of it may have come from Strindberg, whom I seem to remember as big and silent. I have always felt a sympathy for that tortured, self-torturing man who offered himself to his own soul as Buddha offered himself to the famished tiger. He and his circle were preoccupied with the deepest problems of mankind. He himself, at the time I speak of, was seeking with furnace and athanor for the philosophers' stone.[15]

At my hotel, I find a letter from another of that circle, whom I remember as a fair girl like a willow,[16] beginning with this sentence—'God's blessing be upon your wife and upon yourself through the many holy men and women of this land'.

VII

The diplomas and medals are to be given us by the King at five in the afternoon of December 10th.

The American Ambassador, who is to receive those for an American man of science, unable to be present,[17] and half a dozen men of various nations sit upon the platform. In the body of the Hall every seat is full, and all there are in evening dress, and in the front row are the King, Princess Ingeborg, wife of the King's brother, Prince Wilhelm, Princess Margaretha, and I think another Royalty.[18] The President of the Swedish Academy speaks in English, and I see from the way he stands, from his self-possession, and from his rhythmical utterance, that he is an experienced orator. I study the face of the old King, intelligent and friendly, like some country gentleman who can quote Horace and Catullus, and the face of the Princess Margaretha, full of subtle beauty, emotional and precise, and impassive with a still intensity suggesting that final consummate strength which rounds the spiral of a shell. One finds a similar beauty in wooden busts taken from Egyptian tombs of the Eighteenth Dynasty, and not again till Gainsborough paints.[19] Is it very ancient and very modern alone or did painters and sculptors cease to notice it until our day?

The Ambassador goes towards the King, descends from the platform by some five or six steps, which end a yard from the King's feet, and having received the diploma and medal, ascends those five or six steps walking backward. He does not go completely backward, but sideways, and seems to show great practice. Then there is music, and a man of science repeats the movement, imitating the Ambassador exactly and easily, for he is young and agile, and then more music, and two men of science go down the steps, side by side, for they have made discoveries that are related to one another, and the prize is divided between them. As it would be impossible for two men to go up backward, side by side, without much practice, one repeats the slanting movement, and the other turns his back on Royalty. Then the British Ambassador receives diploma and medal for two Canadians,[20] but as he came from the body of the hall he has no steps to go up and down. Then more music and my turn comes. When the King has given me my diploma and medal and said, 'I thank you for coming yourself', and I have bowed my thanks, I glance for a moment at the face of the Princess Margaretha, and move backward towards the stair. As I am about to step sideways like the others, I notice that the carpet is not nailed down, and this suddenly concentrates my attention upon the parallel lines made by the two edges of the carpet, and, as though I were hypnotized, I feel that I must move between them, and so straight up backward without any sidelong movement. It seems to me that I am a long time reaching the top, and as the cheering grows much louder when I get there, I must have roused the sympathy of the audience. All is over, and I am able to examine my medal, its charming, decorative, academic design, French in manner, a work of the 'nineties.[21] It shows a young man listening to a Muse, who stands young and beautiful with a great lyre in her hand, and I think as I examine it, 'I was good-looking once like that young man, but my unpractised verse was full of infirmity, my Muse old as it were; and now I am old and rheumatic, and nothing to look at, but my Muse is young. I am even persuaded that she is like those Angels in Swedenborg's vision,[22] and moves perpetually "towards the day-spring of her youth".' At night there is a banquet, and when my turn comes, I speak of Swedenborg, Strindberg, and Ibsen.[23] Then a very beautiful, stately woman introduces herself with this sentence, spoken slowly as though English were unfamiliar, 'What is this new religion they are making up in Paris that is all about the dead?' I wonder who has told her that I know anything of psychical research, for it must be of that she speaks, and I tell her of my own studies. We are going to change the thought of the world, I say, to bring it back to all its old truths, but I dread the future. Think what the people have made of the political thought of the eighteenth century, and now we must offer them a new fanaticism. Then I stop ashamed, for I am talking habitual thoughts, and not adapting them to her ear, forgetting beauty in the pursuit of truth, and I wonder if age has made my mind rigid and heavy. I deliberately falter as though I could think of nothing more to say, that she may pass upon her smiling road.

VIII

Next day is the entrance of the new Crown Princess,[24] and my wife and I watch it, now from the hotel window, now from the quayside. Stockholm is almost as much channelled by the sea as Venice; and with an architecture as impressive as that of Paris, or of London, it has the better even of Paris in situation. It seems to shelter itself under the walls of a great Palace,[25] begun at the end of the seventeenth century. We come very slowly to realize that this building may deserve its great architectural reputation. The windows, the details of the ornaments, are in a style that has spread everywhere, and I cannot escape from memories of houses at Queen's Gate, and even, it may be, from that of the Ulster Bank at Sligo,[26] which I have hardly seen since my childhood. Was it not indeed a glory and shame of that architecture that we have been able to combine its elements in all sorts of ways and for all sorts of purposes, as if they had come out of a child's box of wooden bricks? Among all these irrelevant associations, however, I discover at last a vast, dominating, unconfused outline, a masterful simplicity. The Palace is at the other side of the river, and away towards our left runs the river bordered by tall buildings, and above the roofs of the houses, towards our right, rises the tower of the new Town Hall, the glittering pole upon its top sustaining the three crowns of the Swedish Arms. Copenhagen is an anarchy of commercial streets, with fine buildings here and there, but here all seems premeditated and arranged.

Everywhere there are poles with flags, and at the moment when the Crown Prince and Princess leave the railway station for the Palace, the salvoes of artillery begin. After every salvo there are echoes, and I feel a quickening of the pulse, an instinctive alarm. I remember firing in Dublin last winter, the sudden noise that drew like echoes from the streets. I have to remind myself that these cannon are fired out of gaiety and good-will. There are great crowds, and I get the impression of a family surrounded by loyalty and affection.

IX

The next night there is a reception at the Palace, and the Nobel Prize winners are among the guests. We wait in a long gallery for our turn to enter the throne-room, and upon the black coats of the civilians, as upon the grey and silver of the Guards, lie the chains of the three Swedish Orders. Among the black-coated men are men of learning, men of letters, men of science, much of the intellect of Sweden. What model has made all this, one wonders: Goethe's Weimar, or Sweden's own eighteenth-century Courts? There may be, must be, faults of commission or omission, but where else could a like assembly be gathered? I who have never seen a Court, find myself before the evening is ended moved as if by some religious ceremony, though to a different end, for here it is Life herself that is praised.

Presently we walk through lines of sentries, in the costume of Charles XII., the last of Sweden's great military Kings, and then bow as we pass rapidly before the tall seated figures of the Royal Family. They seem to be like stage royalties. Just such handsome men and women would have been chosen by a London manager staging, let us say, some dramatized version of *The Prisoner of Zenda*. One has a general impression of youthful distinction, even the tall, slight figure of the old King seems young. Then we pass from the throne-room into a vast hall hung with Gobelins tapestries, which seem in the distance to represent scenes like those in a Watteau or in a Fragonard. Their green colour by contrast turns the marble pillars above into a dusky silver. At the end of the hall musicians are sitting in a high marble gallery, and in the side galleries are women in white dresses, many very young and handsome. Others upon the level of the floor sit grouped together, making patches of white among the brilliant uniforms and the black coats. We are shepherded to our places, and the musicians play much Swedish music, which I cannot describe, for I know nothing of music. During our first long wait all kinds of pictures had passed before me in reverie and now my imagination renews its excitement. I had thought how we Irish had served famous men and famous families, and had been, so long as our nation had intellect enough to shape anything of itself, good lovers of women, but had never served any abstract cause, except the one, and that we personified by a woman,[27] and I wondered if the service of woman could be so different from that of a Court. I had thought how, before the emigration of our poor began, our gentlemen had gone all over Europe, offering their swords at every Court, and that many had stood, just as I, but with an anxiety I could but imagine, for their future hung upon a frown or a smile.[28] I had run through old family fables and histories, to find if any man of my blood had so stood, and had thought that there were men living, meant by nature for that vicissitude, who had served a woman through all folly, because they had found no Court to serve. Then my memory had gone back twenty years to that summer when a friend[29] read out to me at the end of each day's work Castiglione's commendations and descriptions of that Court of Urbino where youth for certain brief years imposed upon drowsy learning the discipline of its joy, and I remembered a cry of Bembo's made years after, 'Would that I were a shepherd that I might look down daily upon Urbino'.[30] I had repeated to myself what I could remember of Ben Jonson's address to the Court of his time, 'Thou art a beautiful and brave spring and waterest all the noble plants of this Island. In thee the whole Kingdom dresseth itself and is ambitious to use thee as her glass. Beware then thou render men's figures truly and teach them no less to hate their deformities, than to love their forms. . . . Thy servant but not slave, Ben Jonson.'[31]

And now I begin to imagine some equivalent gathering to that about me, called together by the heads of some State where every democratic dream had been fulfilled, and where all men had started level and only merit, acknowledged by all the people, ruled. The majority so gathered, certainly all who had supreme authority, would have reached that age when an English novelist becomes eligible for the Order of Merit.[32] Times of disturbance might indeed carry into power some man of comparative youth, of fifty or sixty years perhaps, but I think of normal times. Here and there one would notice sons and daughters, perhaps even the more dutiful grandsons and granddaughters, but in the eyes of those, though not in their conversation, an acute observer might discover disquiet and a restless longing for the moment when they could slip away to some night-club's compensating anarchy. In the conversation of old and young there would be much sarcasm, great numbers of those tales which we all tell to one another's disadvantage. For all men would display to others' envy the trophies won in their life of struggle.

Then suddenly my thought runs off to that old Gaelic poem made by the nuns of Iona. A Swedish or Danish ship had been cast upon the rocks, and all royalties on board had perished, but one baby. The nuns mothered the baby, and their cradle-song, famous for generations after, repeated over and over, praising in symbol every great man's child—every tested long-enduring stock— 'Daughter of a Queen, granddaughter of a Queen, great-grand-daughter of a Queen, great-great-granddaughter of a Queen'.[33] Nature, always extravagant, scattering much to find a little, has found no means but hereditary honour to sustain the courage of those who stand waiting for the signal, cowed by the honour and authority of those who lie wearily at the goal. Perhaps, indeed, she created the family with no other object, and may even now mock in her secret way our new ideals—the equality of man, equality of rights—meditating some wholly different end. Certainly her old arrangements, in all pursuits that gain from youth's recurring sway, or from its training in earliest childhood, surpassed what begins to be a world of old men. The politic Tudor kings and the masterful descendants of Gustavus Vasa were as able as the American presidents, and better educated, and the artistic genius of old Japan continually renewed itself through dynasties of painters. The descendants of Kanoka made all that was greatest in the art of their country from the ninth to the eleventh century, and then it but passed to other dynasties, in whom, as Mr. Binyon says, 'the flower of genius was being continually renewed and revived in the course of many generations'.[34] How serene their art, no exasperation, no academic tyranny, its tradition as naturally observed as the laws of a game or dance. Nor has our individualistic age wholly triumphed in Japan even yet, for it is a few years since a famous player published in his programme his genealogy, running back through famous players to some player of the Middle Ages; and one day in the British Museum Print-Room, I saw a Japanese at a great table judging Chinese and Japanese pictures. 'He is one of the greatest living authorities,' I was told, 'the Mikado's hereditary connoisseur, the fourteenth of his family to hold the post.'[35] May it not have been possible that the use of the mask in acting, and the omission from painting of the cast shadow, by making observation and experience of life less important, and imagination and tradition more, made the arts transmittable and teachable? But my thoughts have carried me far away.

X

Near me stands a man[36] who is moved also by the spectacle of the Court, but to a Jacobin frenzy, Swede, Englishman, American, German, what does it matter, seeing that his frenzy is international. I had spoken to him earlier in the day and found him a friendly, even perhaps a cultivated man, and certainly not the kind of man who is deliberately rude; but now, he imagines that an attempt has been made to impose upon him. He speaks his thoughts aloud, silenced occasionally by the music, but persistent in the intervals. While waiting to enter the throne-room, he had been anxious to demonstrate that he was there by accident, drifting irresponsibly, no way implicated, as it were, and having accomplished this demonstration by singing a little catch, 'I'm here because I'm here', had commented abundantly upon all he saw: 'The smaller the nation the grander the uniform'. 'Well—they never got those decorations in war', and so on. He was certain that the breastplates of the sentries were made of tin, but added with a meditative voice, as though anxious to be fair, 'The breastplates of the English Horse Guards are also made of tin'.

As we came through the throne-room, I had heard him say, 'One of the royalties smiled, they consider us as ridiculous', and I had commented, entangled in my dream, 'We are ridiculous, we are the learned at whom the little boys laugh in the streets'. And now when, at a pause in the music, the Queen passes down the great hall, pages holding her train, he says in the same loud voice as before, 'Well, a man has not to suffer that indignity', and then upbraids all forms of ceremony, and repeats an incident of his school life to demonstrate his distaste for Bishops.

As I leave the Palace, a man wearing orders stops for a moment to say, 'I am the Headmaster of a big school, I was the Prince's tutor, and I am his friend'.

XI

For the next two or three days we visit picture galleries, the gallery of the National Museum, that of Prince Eugene, that of Baron Thiel.[37] At the National Museum pictures have been taken down and lean against the wall, that they may be sent to London for an exhibition of Swedish art. Someone, exaggerating the influence in London of the Nobel Prize winner, asks me to write something to get people to go and see it, and I half promise, but feel that I have not the necessary knowledge. I know something of the French Impressionism[38] that gave their painters their first impulse, but almost nothing of German or Austrian, and I have seen that of Sweden for the first time. At a first glance Impressionism seems everywhere the same, with differences of power but not of sight or mind, and one has to live with it and make many comparisons, I think, to write more than a few sentences. The great myth-makers and mask-makers, the men of aristocratic mind, Blake, Ingres in the *Perseus,* Puvis de Chavannes, Rossetti before 1870, Watts when least a moralist, Gustave Moreau at all times, Calvert in the woodcuts, the Charles Ricketts of *The Danaides,* and of the earlier illustrations of *The Sphinx,*[39] have imitators, but create no universal language. Administrators of tradition, they seem to copy everything, but in reality copy nothing, and not one of them can be mistaken for another, but Impressionism's gift to the world was precisely that it gave, at a moment when all seemed sunk in convention, a method as adaptable as that box of architectural Renaissance bricks. It has suddenly taught us to see and feel, as everybody that wills can see and feel, all those things that are as wholesome as rain and sunlight, to take into our hearts with an almost mystical emotion whatsoever happens without forethought or premeditation. It is not, I think, any accident that their art has coincided everywhere with a new sympathy for crowds, for the poor and the unfortunate. Certainly it arrived in these Scandinavian countries just at the moment when an intellectual awaking of the whole people was beginning, for I always read, or am told, that whatever I inquire about began with the 'eighties, or was the outcome of some movement of that time.

When I try to define what separates Swedish Impressionism from French, I notice that it has a stronger feeling for particular places. Monet will paint a group of trees by a pond in every possible light,[40] changing his canvas every twenty minutes, and only returning to a canvas when the next day's clock brings up the same light,[41] but then it is precisely the light that interests him, and interests the buyers of those almost scientific studies. Nobody will buy because it is a pond under his window, or that he passed in his boyhood on his way to school. I noticed in some house where I lunched two pictures of the Stockholm river, painted in different lights by Eugene Janson, and in the National Museum yet another with a third effect of light, but much as the light pleased his imagination, one feels that he cared very much for the fact before him, that he was never able to forget for long that he painted a well-loved, familiar scene. I am constantly reminded of my brother, who continually paints from memory the people and houses of the village where he lived as a child;[42] but the people of Rosses will never care about his pictures, and these painters paint for all educated Stockholm. They have found an emotion held in common, and are no longer, like the rest of us, solitary spectators. I get the impression that their work rouses a more general interest than that of other painters, is less confined to small groups of connoisseurs; I notice in the booksellers' shops that there seems to be some little paper-covered pamphlet, full of illustrations, for every notable painter of the school, dead or living, and the people I meet ask constantly what I think of this painter or that other, or somebody will say, 'This is the golden age of painting'. When I myself try to recall what I have seen, I remember most clearly a picture of a white horse on the seashore, with its tints separated by little lines, that give it a general effect of mosaic, and certain portraits by Ernst Josephson,[43] which prove that their painter was entirely preoccupied with the personality of the sitter, light, colour, design, all subordinate to that. An English portrait-painter is sometimes so pre-occupied with the light that one feels he would have had equal pleasure in painting a bottle and an apple. But a preference after so brief a visit may be capricious, having some accidental origin.

XII

On Thursday I give my official lecture to the Swedish Royal Academy. I have chosen 'The Irish Theatre' for my subject, that I may commend all those workers, obscure or well-known, to whom I owe much of whatever fame in the world I may possess. If I had been a lyric poet only, if I had not become through this Theatre the representative of a public movement, I doubt if the English committees would have placed my name upon that list from which the Swedish Academy selects its prize-winner. They would not have acknowledged a thought so irrelevant, but those dog-eared pages, those pressed violets, upon which the fame of a lyric poet depends at the last, might without it have found no strong voice. I have seen so much beautiful lyric poetry pass unnoticed for years, and indeed at this very moment a little book of exquisite verse[44] lies upon my table, by an author who died a few years ago, whom I knew slightly, and whose work I ignored, for chance had shown me only that part of it for which I could not care.

On my way to the lecture hall I ask an Academician what kind of audience I will have, and he replies, 'An audience of women, a fit audience for a poet'; but there are men as well as women. I had thought it would be difficult to speak to an audience in a language they had learnt at school, but it is exceedingly easy. All I say seems to be understood, and I am conscious of that sympathy which makes a speaker forget all but his own thoughts, and soliloquize aloud. I am speaking without notes and the image of old fellow-workers comes upon me as if they were present, above all of the embittered life and death of one, and of another's laborious, solitary age, and I say,[45] 'When your King gave me medal and diploma, two forms should have stood, one at either side of me, an old woman sinking into the infirmity of age and a young man's ghost. I think when Lady Gregory's name and John Synge's name are spoken by future generations, my name, if remembered, will come up in the talk, and that if my name is spoken first their names will come in their turn because of the years we worked together. I think that both had been well pleased to have stood beside me at the great reception at your Palace, for their work and mine has delighted in history and tradition.' I think as I speak these words of how deep down we have gone, below all that is individual, modern and restless, seeking foundations for an Ireland that can only come into existence in a Europe that is still but a dream.

XIII

On Friday we visit the great Town Hall, which is the greatest work of Swedish art, a master-work of the Romantic movement. The Royal Palace[46] had taken ninety years to build, and been the organizing centre of the art of its time, and this new magnificence, its narrow windows opening out upon a formal garden, its tall tower rising from the quayside, has taken ten years. It, too, has been an organizing centre, but for an art more imaginative and amazing. Here there is no important French influence, for all that has not come out of the necessities of site and material, no matter in what school the artist studied, carries the mind backward to Byzantium.[47] I think of but two comparable buildings, the Pennsylvania terminus in New York, and the Catholic Cathedral at Westminster,[48] but the Pennsylvania terminus, noble in austerity, is the work of a single mind, elaborating a suggestion from a Roman Bath, a mind that—supported by the American deference to authority—has been permitted to refuse everything not relevant to a single dominating idea. The starting-hours of the trains are upon specially designed boards, of a colour that makes them harmonize with the general design, and all other advertisements are forbidden, even in the stations that the trains pass immediately after leaving or before entering the terminus. The mood of severity must be prolonged or prepared for. The Catholic Cathedral is of a greater magnificence in general design, but being planted in a country where public opinion rules and the subscribers to every fund expect to have their way, is half ruined by ignoble decoration, the most ignoble of all planned and paid for by my countrymen. The Town Hall of Stockholm, upon the other hand, is decorated by many artists, working in harmony with one another and with the design of the building as a whole, and yet all in seeming perfect freedom. In England and Ireland public opinion compels the employment of the worst artists, while here the authority of a Prince and the wisdom of a Socialist Minister of culture, and the approval of the most educated of all nations, have made possible the employment of the best. These myth-makers and mask-makers worked as if they belonged to one family, and the great walls where the roughened surface of the bricks, their carefully varied size and tint, takes away all sense of mechanical finish; the mosaic-covered walls of the 'Golden Room';[49] the paintings hung upon the walls of the committee-rooms; the fresco paintings upon the greater surfaces with their subjects from Swedish mythology; the wrought iron and the furniture, where all suggests history, and yet is full of invention; the statuary in marble and in bronze, now mythological in subject, now representations of great Swedes, modelled naked as if they had come down from some Roman heaven; all that suggestion of novelty and of an immeasurable past; all that multitude and unity, could hardly have been possible, had not love of Stockholm and belief in its future so filled men of different minds, classes, and occupations that they almost attained the supreme miracle, the dream that has haunted all religions, and loved one another. No work comparable in method or achievement has been accomplished since the Italian cities felt the excitement of the Renaissance, for in the midst of our individualistic anarchy, growing always, as it seemed, more violent, have arisen once more subordination, design, a sense of human need.

XIV

On Saturday I see at the Royal Theatre a performance of my *Cathleen ni Houlihan*. The old father and mother are excellent and each performance differs but little from an exceedingly good Abbey performance, except for certain details of scene, and for differences of interpretation, made necessary by the change of audience. Lines spoken by Cathleen ni Houlihan just before she leaves the cottage always move an Irish audience powerfully for historical reasons, and so the actress begins at much the same emotional level as those about her, and then works up to a climax upon these lines. But here they could have no special appeal, so she strikes a note of tragedy at once, and does not try for a strong climax. The management had sent to the West of Ireland for photographs of scenery, and the land-scape, seen through the open door, has an appropriateness and grandeur our poverty-stricken Abbey has never attained. Upon the other hand the cottage and costume of the peasants suggest a richer peasantry than ours. The management has, I think, been misled by that one-hundred-pound dowry, for in Sweden, where the standard of living is high, a farmer would probably have thought it more necessary to feed his family and himself, and to look after his daughter's education, than to save one hundred pounds for her dowry. This affects the acting. The peasants are permitted to wear a light buckle-shoe indoors, whereas they would in reality have gone barefooted, or worn heavy working boots. Almost the first thing a new actor at the Abbey has to learn is to walk as if he wore those heavy boots, and this gives awkwardness and slowness to his movements. I do not point this out as an error in the Swedish pro-duction, for a symbolic play like *Cathleen* should, in most cases, copy whatever environment is most familiar to the audience. It is followed by *She Stoops to Conquer,* and by comparison our Abbey performance of that play seems too slow. Goldsmith's play is not in Sweden, I should think, the established classic that it is with us, and so a Swedish producer is less reverent. He discovers quickly that there are dull places and unrealities, that it is technically infe-rior to Molière, and that we may not discover this also, prefers a rattling pace.

XV

Everybody has told us that we have not seen Stockholm at its best because we have not seen it with the trees all white and the streets deep in snow. When snow has fallen it has melted immediately, and there is central heating everywhere. While we are packing for our journey a young American poet comes to our room, and introduces himself. 'I was in the South of France', he says, 'and I could not get a room warm enough to work in, and if I cannot get a warm room here I will go to Lapland.'

THE IRISH DRAMATIC
MOVEMENT

A Lecture delivered to the Royal Academy of Sweden

Your Royal Highness,[1] ladies and gentlemen, I have chosen as my theme the Irish Dramatic Movement, because when I remember the great honour that you have conferred upon me, I cannot forget many known and unknown persons. Perhaps the English committees would never have sent you my name if I had written no plays, no dramatic criticism, if my lyric poetry had not a quality of speech practised upon the stage, perhaps even—though this could be no portion of their deliberate thought—if it were not in some degree the symbol of a movement. I wish to tell the Royal Academy of Sweden of the labours, triumphs and troubles of my fellow-workers.

The modern literature of Ireland, and indeed all that stir of thought which prepared for the Anglo-Irish war, began when Parnell fell from power in 1891. A disillusioned and embittered Ireland turned from parliamentary politics; an event was conceived; and the race began, as I think, to be troubled by that event's long gestation. Dr. Hyde founded the Gaelic League,[2] which was for many years to substitute for political argument a Gaelic grammar, and for political meetings village gatherings, where songs were sung and stories told in the Gaelic language. Meanwhile I had begun a movement in English,[3] in the language in which modern Ireland thinks and does its business; founded certain societies where clerks, working men, men of all classes, could study the Irish poets, novelists and historians who had written in English, and as much of Gaelic literature as had been translated into English. But the great mass of our people, accustomed to interminable political speeches, read little, and so from the very start we felt that we must have a theatre of our own. The theatres of Dublin had nothing about them that we could call our own. They were empty buildings hired by the English travelling companies, and we wanted Irish plays and Irish players. When we thought of these plays we thought of everything that was romantic and poetical, because the nationalism we had called up— the nationalism every generation had called up in moments of discouragement—was romantic and poetical. It was not, however, until I met in 1896 Lady Gregory, a member of an old Galway family, who had spent her life between two Galway houses, the house where she was born, the house into which she married,[4] that such a theatre became possible. All about her lived a peasantry who told stories in a form of English which has much of its syntax from Gaelic, much of its vocabulary from Tudor English, but it was very slowly that we discovered in that speech of theirs our most powerful dramatic instrument, not indeed until she herself began to write. Though my plays were written without dialect and in English blank verse, I think she was attracted to our movement because their subject-matter differed but little from the subject-matter of the country stories. Her own house has been protected by her presence, but the house where she was born was burned down by incendiaries some few months ago, and there has been like disorder over the greater part of Ireland. A trumpery dispute about an acre of land can rouse our people to monstrous savagery, and if in their war with the English auxiliary police they were shown no mercy, they showed none: murder answered murder. Yet their ignorance and violence can remember the noblest beauty. I have in Galway a little old tower,[5] and when I climb to the top of it I can see at no great distance a green field where stood once the thatched cottage of a famous country beauty, the mistress of a small local landed proprietor. I have spoken to old men and women who remembered her, though all are dead now, and they spoke of her as the old men upon the wall of Troy spoke of Helen, nor did man and woman differ in their praise. One old woman of whose youth the neighbours cherished a scandalous tale said of her, 'I tremble all over when I think of her'; and there was another on the neighbouring mountain who said, 'The sun and the moon never shone on anybody so handsome, and her skin was so white that it looked blue, and she had two little blushes on her cheeks'.[6] And there were men that told of the crowds that gathered to look at her upon a fair day, and of a man 'who got his death swimming a river', that he might look at her. It was a song written by the Gaelic poet Raftery that brought her such great fame, and the cottages still sing it, though there are not so many to sing it as when I was young:

> O star of light and O sun in harvest,
> O amber hair, O my share of the world,
> It is Mary Hynes, the calm and easy woman,
> Has beauty in her body and in her mind.[7]

It seemed as if the ancient world lay all about us with its freedom of imagination, its delight in good stories, in man's force and woman's beauty, and that all we had to do was to make the town think as the country felt; yet we soon discovered that the town would only think town thoughts.

In the country you are alone with your own violence, your own ignorance and heaviness, and with the common tragedy of life, and if you have any artistic capacity you desire beautiful emotion; and, certain that the seasons will be the same always, care not how fantastic its expression.[8] In the town, where everybody crowds upon you, it is your neighbour not yourself that you hate, and if you are not to embitter his life and your own life, perhaps even if you are not to murder him in some kind of revolutionary frenzy, somebody must teach reality and justice. You will hate that teacher for a while, calling his books and plays ugly, misdirected, morbid, or something of that kind, but you must agree with him in the end. We were to find ourselves in a quarrel with public opinion that compelled us against our own will and the will of our players to become always more realistic, substituting dialect for verse, common speech for dialect.

I had told Lady Gregory that I saw no likelihood of getting money for a theatre and so must put away that hope, and she promised to find the money among her friends. Her neighbour, Mr. Edward Martyn,[9] paid for our first performances; and our first players came from England; but presently we began our real work with a company of Irish amateurs.[10] Somebody had asked me at a lecture, 'Where will you get your actors?' and I had said, 'I will go into some crowded room, put the name of everybody in it on a different piece of paper, put all those pieces of paper into a hat and draw the first twelve'. I have often wondered at that prophecy, for though it was spoken probably to confound and confuse a questioner it was very nearly fulfilled. Our two best men actors were not indeed chosen by chance, for one was a stage-struck solicitors' clerk and the other a working man who had toured Ireland in a theatrical company managed by a Negro.[11] I doubt if he had learned much in it, for its methods were rough and noisy, the Negro whitening his face when he played a white man, but, so strong is stage convention, blackening it when he played a black man. If a player had to open a letter on the stage I have no doubt that he struck it with the flat of his hand, as I have seen players do in my youth, a gesture that lost its meaning generations ago when blotting-paper was substituted for sand. We got our women, however, from a little political society[12] which described its object as educating the children of the poor, or, according to its enemies, teaching them a catechism that began with this question, 'What is the origin of evil?' and the answer, 'England'.

And they came to us for patriotic reasons and acted from precisely the same impulse that had made them teach, and yet two of them proved players of genius, Miss Allgood and Miss Maire O'Neill. They were sisters, one all simplicity, her mind shaped by folk-song and folk-story; the other sophisticated, lyrical and subtle. I do not know what their thoughts were as that strange new power awoke within them, but I think they must have suffered from a bad conscience, a feeling that the patriotic impulse had gone, that they had given themselves up to vanity or ambition. Yet I think it was that first misunderstanding of themselves made their peculiar genius possible, for had they come to us with theatrical ambitions they would have imitated some well-known English player and sighed for well-known English plays. Nor would they have found their genius if we had not remained for a long time obscure like the bird within its shell, playing in little halls, generally in some shabby out-of-the-way street. We could experiment and wait, with nothing to fear but political misunderstanding. We had little money and at first needed little, twenty-five pounds given by Lady Gregory and twenty pounds by myself and a few pounds picked up here and there. And our theatrical organization was preposterous, players and authors all sitting together and settling by vote what play should be performed and who should play it. It took a series of disturbances, weeks of argument during which no performance could be given, before Lady Gregory and John Synge and I were put in control. And our relations with the public were even more disturbed. One play was violently attacked[13] by the patriotic Press because it described a married peasant woman who had a lover, and when we published the old Aran folk-tale upon which it was founded the Press said the tale had reached Aran from some decadent author of pagan Rome.[14] Presently Lady Gregory wrote her first comedy. My verse plays were not long enough to fill an evening and so she wrote a little play on a country love story in the dialect of her neighbourhood.[15] A countryman returns from America with a hundred pounds and discovers his old sweetheart married to a bankrupt farmer. He plays cards with the farmer, and by cheating against himself gives him the hundred pounds. The company refused to perform it because they said to admit an emigrant's return with a hundred pounds would encourage emigration. We produced evidence of returned emigrants with much larger sums, but were told that only made the matter worse. Then after interminable argument had worn us all out Lady Gregory agreed to reduce the sum to twenty, and the actors gave way. That little play was sentimental and conventional, but her next discovered her genius.[16] She too had desired to serve, and that genius must have seemed miraculous to herself. She was in middle life, and had written nothing but a volume of political memoirs and had no interest in the theatre.

Nobody reading to-day her *Seven Short Plays* can understand why one of them, now an Irish classic, *The Rising of the Moon*, could not be performed for two years because of political hostility. A policeman discovers an escaped Fenian prisoner and lets him free, because the prisoner has aroused with some old songs the half-forgotten patriotism of his youth. The players would not perform it because they said it was an unpatriotic act to admit that a policeman was capable of patriotism. One well-known leader of the mob wrote to me, 'How can the Dublin mob be expected to fight the police if it looks upon them as capable of patriotism?' When performed at last the play was received with enthusiasm, but only to get us into new trouble. The chief Unionist Dublin newspaper[17] denounced us for slandering His Majesty's forces, and Dublin Castle[18] denied to us a privilege which we had shared with the other Dublin theatres of buying, for stage purposes, the cast-off clothes of the police. Castle and Press alike knew that the police had frequently let off political prisoners, but 'that only made the matter worse'. Every political party had the same desire to substitute for life, which never does the same thing twice, a bundle of reliable principles and assertions.[19] Nor did religious orthodoxy like us any better than political; my *Countess Cathleen* was denounced by Cardinal Logue as an heretical play, and when I wrote that we would like to perform 'foreign masterpieces' a Nationalist newspaper declared that 'a foreign masterpiece is a very dangerous thing'. The little halls where we performed could hold a couple of hundred people at the utmost and our audience was often not more than twenty or thirty, and we performed but two or three times a month, and during our periods of quarrelling not even that. But there was no lack of leading articles, we were from the first a recognized public danger. Two events brought us victory: a friend gave us a theatre, and we found a strange man of genius, John Synge. After a particularly angry leading article I had come in front of the curtain and appealed to the hundred people of the audience for their support. When I came down from the stage an old friend, Miss Horniman, from whom I had been expecting a contribution of twenty pounds, said, 'I will find you a theatre'. She found and altered for our purpose what is now the Abbey Theatre, Dublin, and gave us a small subsidy for a few years.[20]

I had met John Synge in Paris in 1896. Somebody had said, 'There is an Irishman living on the top floor of your hotel; I will introduce you'.[21] I was very poor, but he was much poorer. He belonged to a very old Irish family and, though a simple courteous man, remembered it and was haughty and lonely. With just enough to keep him from starvation and not always from half-starvation, he had wandered about Europe, travelling third-class or upon foot, playing his fiddle to poor men on the road or in their cottages. He was the man that we needed, because he was the only man I have ever known incapable of a political thought or of a humanitarian purpose. He could walk the roadside all day with some poor man without any desire to do him good or for any reason except that he liked him. He was to do for Ireland, though more by his influence on other dramatists than by his direct influence, what Robert Burns did for Scotland. When Scotland thought herself gloomy and religious, Providence restored her imaginative spontaneity by raising up Robert Burns to commend drink and the Devil. I did not, how-

ever, see what was to come when I advised John Synge to go to a
wild island off the Galway coast and study its life because that life
'had never been expressed in literature'. He had learned Gaelic at
College and I told him that, as I would have told it to any young
man who had learned Gaelic and wanted to write. When he found
that wild island he became happy for the first time, escaping, as he
said, 'from the nullity of the rich and the squalor of the poor'.[22] He
had bad health, he could not stand the island hardship long, but he
would go to and fro between there and Dublin.

Burns himself could not have more shocked a gathering of Scots
clergy than did he our players. Some of the women got about him
and begged him to write a play about the rebellion of '98, and
pointed out very truthfully that a play on such a patriotic theme
would be a great success. He returned at the end of a fortnight with
a scenario upon which he had toiled in his laborious way. Two
women take refuge in a cave, a Protestant woman and a Catholic,
and carry on an interminable argument about the merits of their
respective religions. The Catholic woman denounces Henry VIII.
and Queen Elizabeth, and the Protestant woman the Inquisition
and the Pope. They argue in low voices, because one is afraid of
being ravished by the rebels and the other by the loyal soldiers. But
at last either the Protestant or the Catholic says that she prefers any
fate to remaining any longer in such wicked company and climbs
out. The play was neither written nor performed, and neither then
nor at any later time could I discover whether Synge understood the
shock that he was giving. He certainly did not foresee in any way
the trouble that his greatest play brought on us all.

When I had landed from a fishing yawl on the middle of the
island of Aran,[23] a few months before my first meeting with Synge,
a little group of islanders, who had gathered to watch a stranger's
arrival, brought me to 'the oldest man upon the island'. He spoke
but two sentences, speaking them very slowly: 'If any gentleman
has done a crime we'll hide him. There was a gentleman that killed
his father, and I had him in my house six months till he got away to
America.' It was a play[24] founded on that old man's story Synge
brought back with him. A young man arrives at a little public-house
and tells the publican's daughter that he has murdered his father.
He so tells it that he has all her sympathy, and every time he retells
it, with new exaggerations and additions, he wins the sympathy of

somebody or other, for it is the countryman's habit to be against the law. The countryman thinks the more terrible the crime, the greater must the provocation have been. The young man himself, under the excitement of his own story, becomes gay, energetic and lucky. He prospers in love, comes in first at the local races, and bankrupts the roulette tables afterwards. Then the father arrives with his head bandaged but very lively, and the people turn upon the impostor. To win back their esteem he takes up a spade to kill his father in earnest, but, horrified at the threat of what had sounded so well in the story, they bind him to hand over to the police. The father releases him and father and son walk off together, the son, still buoyed up by his imagination, announcing that he will be master henceforth. Picturesque, poetical, fantastical, a masterpiece of style and of music, the supreme work of our dialect theatre, his *Playboy* roused the populace to fury. We played it under police protection, seventy police in the theatre the last night, and five hundred, some newspaper said, keeping order in the streets outside. It is never played before any Irish audience for the first time without something or other being flung at the players. In New York a currant cake and a watch were flung, the owner of the watch claiming it at the stage door afterwards. The Dublin audience has, however, long since accepted the play. It has noticed, I think, that everyone upon the stage is somehow lovable and companionable, and that Synge has described, through an exaggerated symbolism, a reality which he loved precisely because he loved all reality. So far from being, as they had thought, a politician working in the interests of England, he was so little a politician that the world merely amused him and touched his pity. Yet when Synge died in 1909 opinion had hardly changed, we were playing to an almost empty theatre and were continually denounced. Our victory was won by those who had learned from him courage and sincerity but belonged to a different school. Synge's work, the work of Lady Gregory, my own *Cathleen ni Houlihan* and my *Hour-Glass* in its prose form,[25] are characteristic of our first ambition. They bring the imagination and speech of the country, all that poetical tradition descended from the Middle Ages, to the people of the town. Those who learned from Synge had often little knowledge of the country and always little interest in its dialect. Their plays are frequently attacks upon obvious abuses, the bribery at the appointment of a dispensary Doctor, the attempts of some local politician to remain friends with all parties. Indeed the young Ministers and party politicians of the Free State have had, I think, some of their education from our plays. Then, too, there are many comedies which are not political satires though they are concerned with the life of the politics-ridden people of the town. Of these Mr. Lennox Robinson's are the best known; his *White-headed Boy*[26] has been played in England and America. Of late it has seemed as if this school were coming to an end, for the old plots are repeated with slight variations and the characterization grows mechanical. It is too soon yet to say what will come to us from the melodrama and tragedy of the last four years, but if we can pay our players and keep our theatre open something will come.[27] We are burdened with debt, for we have come through war and civil war and audiences grow thin when there is firing in the streets. We have, however, survived so much that I believe in our luck, and think that I have a right to say my lecture ends in the middle or even, perhaps, at the beginning of the story. But certainly I have said enough[28] to make you understand why, when I received from the hands of your King the great honour your Academy has conferred upon me, I felt that a young man's ghost should have stood upon one side of me and at the other a living woman sinking into the infirmity of age. Indeed I have seen little in this last week that would not have been memorable and exciting to Synge and to Lady Gregory, for Sweden has achieved more than we have hoped for our own country. I think most of all, perhaps, of that splendid spectacle of your Court, a family beloved and able that has gathered about it not the rank only but the intellect of its country. No like spectacle will in Ireland show its work of discipline and of taste, though it might satisfy a need of the race no institution created under the influence of English or American democracy can satisfy.

THE END

NOTES

1. JBY leased an attached three-story house at 23 Fitzroy Road, near Regent's Park, London, 1867–73.
2. JBY married Susan Mary Pollexfen (1841–1900) in 1863. Her parents were William Pollexfen (1811–92) and Elizabeth Middleton Pollexfen (1819–92). Susan Yeats and the children were often at Merville, their home in Sligo, 1867–70, and there continually, 1870–74.
3. Middleton, William (great uncle) (1820–82). Brother of Elizabeth Middleton Pollexfen and partner in the firm with William Pollexfen.
4. Pollexfen, William (grandfather) (1811–92). Born at Berry Head, near the port of Brixham, Devonshire, son of Anthony Pollexfen (1781–1833) and Mary Stephens (1771–1830) of Co. Wexford. He ran away to sea at the age of twelve and, at twenty-six, owned his own ship, the 'Dasher'. He came to Sligo to see if he could help Elizabeth Pollexfen Middleton, then widowed, and married her daughter, Elizabeth Middleton (1819–92), in 1837. He became a partner in his brother-in-law William Middleton's firm. See 'Introductory Rhymes,' 'Under Saturn,' and 'In Memory of Alfred Pollexfen' P 101, 179, 156.
5. Great-uncle William's father was also William Middleton of Sligo (c. 1770–1832).
6. 'The great famine' refers to the potato crop failures of 1845–49, which catastrophically reduced the population of Ireland by starvation, disease, and emigration.
7. Frederick H. Pollexfen (1852–1929) (LY note).
8. A Middleton (LY note).
9. William Pollexfen kept a picture of Kitley Manor, Yealmpton, Devon, on his bedroom wall all his life, regarding himself as the rightful heir to the estate. The Pollexfens were a Cornish and Devonshire family who claimed they were descended from the Phoenicians.
10. Anthony Pollexfen (c. 1781–1833), Barrack Master and Keeper of the forts on Berry Head, Torquay (LY scrapbook).

11. Kitley Manor, Yealmpton, Devon (Murphy, *Yeats Family* 10, 25).
12. Mary Stephens (1771–1830), who married Anthony Pollexfen in Co. Wexford in 1809 or 1810.
13. Elizabeth Middleton Pollexfen (1819–92). Married 1837.
14. Alfred Pollexfen (1854–1916) worked as a clerk in Liverpool. See 'In Memory of Alfred Pollexfen' (w. 1916, publ. 1917) P 156.
15. William Middleton Pollexfen (1847–1913), an engineer. He went mad and was in a mental institution in Northampton, England, until his death in 1913.
16. Susan Mary ('Lily') Yeats (1866–1949).
17. George Pollexfen (uncle) (1839–1910). JBY met him while studying at the Atholl Academy on the Isle of Man and married his sister, Susan Mary, in 1863. He became close to WBY in the early 1890s because of their shared interest in the occult. See 'In Memory of Major Robert Gregory' P 132.
18. Frederick H. Pollexfen (1852–1929) (LY note).
19. WBY's Pollexfen aunts included Elizabeth Anne (Mrs. Alexander Barrington Orr; 1843–1933), Isabella (Mrs. John Varley; 1849–1938), Alice Jane (Mrs. Arthur Jackson; 1857–1932), and Agnes Middleton (Mrs. Robert Gorman; 1855–1926).
20. Acts: 27
21. Johnny Healy.
22. In 1795, the Protestant Peep o'Day boys founded an 'Orange Society', later called the Orange Order. Its declared purpose was to support the Protestant Ascendancy and the laws and government benefiting it, by violence if necessary. The order was broken up in 1837, but reborn in 1845, and was a force against Home Rule in the 1880s.
23. The Fenian Brotherhood was established by James Stephens in Dublin in 1858. The name came from the 'Fianna', legendary fighting force led by Finn MacCool, also known as the Irish Republican Brotherhood (IRB); members were determined to free Ireland of English rule as soon as possible by any means necessary, including violence.
24. A mill where weaver's bobbins are manufactured (O.E.D.).
25. Mountain (elev. 1730 ft.), six miles north of Sligo, rising above WBY's grave in Drumcliff churchyard.
26. Middleton, George (b. 1847). A son of great-uncle William Middleton (LY scrapbook).
27. Lily Yeats (LY note).
28. Great-uncle John Middleton (d. 1892), merchant in Glasgow (LY note).
29. Susan Mary Pollexfen (1841–1900). Susan was the daughter of William and Elizabeth Middleton Pollexfen and married John

Butler Yeats on 10 September 1863. She led a life of disappointment after her marriage, for she had thought she was marrying a
barrister and an Irish landlord, but JBY proved to be a struggling,
landless artist. She never fully accepted his bohemian life, and she
enjoyed only her visits to her parents' home in Sligo and a period
of living at Howth (1881–3). Susan Yeats suffered a stroke while
the family was living at Eardley Crescent, Earls Court, London,
in 1887, and a second stroke and a fall down a staircase while at
her sister's (Elizabeth Orr) in Denby, near Huddersfield. She
never regained her health and died on 3 January 1900, after
twelve years of illness and mental deterioration. Lily Yeats wrote:
'She was prim and austere, suffered all in silence. She asked no
sympathy and gave none . . . When we were children and were ill
she always said, "Grin and bear it," and so she did. She endured
and made no moan' (LY scrapbook in Murphy, *Yeats Family* 53).

30. Possibly Henry Middleton (1862–1932).
31. Lucy Middleton, a cousin (*E&I* 44–45, Hone, *Yeats* 112).
32. Yeats, Mary (1821–91). Great-aunt Micky's house was Seaview.
33. John Yeats (Rector of Drumcliff) (1774–1846 [not 1847]).
34. Benjamin Yeats (1750–95).
35. Mary Butler (1751–1834). Daughter of John Butler of Dublin
    Castle, married Benjamin Yeats (great-great-grandfather) 22
    August 1773. Through her, the family has a claim to a connection
    with the old Irish Ormondes, the Butler family who settled in Ire-
    land in the twelfth century. Because of an inheritance that stems
    from Mary Butler, Parson John Yeats became landlord of Co. Kil-
    dare property and a house in Dorset Street, Dublin. These prop-
    erties remained in the family until the 1880s.
36. Great-aunt Ellen (née Terry) Yeats, widow of John Yeats (b. 1808),
    lived near Great-aunt Micky's home. John had been a county
    surveyor for Kildare.
37. Mat Yeats (great-uncle) (1819–85) was a land agent involved in
    the 'striping' [dividing land into strips or plots] of the Rosses in
    1860 and not liked by the tenants. He also handled the Kildare
    property for JBY after the death of Robert Corbet until his own
    death. His home was Fort Louis, Rathbroughan (or Rathbraug-
    han) (not Rathbrochen), near Sligo (LY note). See McGarry 76.
38. Through JBY's mother, Jane Grace Corbet (1811–76), the Yeats
    children were descended from John Armstrong (d. 1742), who
    was one of Marlborough's generals and is buried in the Tower of
    London (LY note). The general's great-great-granddaughter, Grace
    Armstrong, married William Corbet in 1791, their daughter
    being Jane Grace, who married the Reverend William Butler
    Yeats in 1835 (LY scrapbook in Murphy, *Yeats Family* 20–21).

39. Colonel Arthur Young of the 12th Dragoons, Lahard, Co. Cavan, brother of WBY's great-great-grandmother (LY note).

40. WBY sailed from New York 2 April 1914; on the previous trips he had sailed 18 October 1911 and 9 March 1904.

41. Lily Yeats identifies this picture as a posthumously dated 'engraving of portrait of Sir John Armstrong in breast plate 1745'. Armstrong (1674–1742) was an officer under the Duke of Marlborough and became Major-General and Colonel of the royal regiment of foot in Ireland, and was chief engineer of England.

42. Untraced.

43. Untraced.

44. Patrick Sarsfield, Earl of Lucan (d. 1693), Irish Jacobite and soldier, descendant of an Anglo-Norman family. He served against Monmouth at Sedgemoor (1685), assisted in James II's reorganization of Irish forces into a Roman Catholic army, fled with James II to France, returned with him to Ireland (1689), and was present at the battle of the Boyne (1690). After the capitulation of Limerick, he joined the French service with his troops and was mortally wounded at Landen in August 1693.

45. Rev. Thomas Butler, who was killed in 1793.

46. A Jacquerie is a rebellion of local peasants.

47. Lily Yeats identified him only as 'one of the Butlers' (LY note).

48. Founded as the Society of United Irishmen in 1791 by Wolfe Tone (1763–98), Thomas Russell (1767–1803), and Napper Tandy (1740–1803). Its aim was to unite Irishmen against English domination, and it was responsible for several unsuccessful invasions and uprisings in which its leaders perished. The quotation, which until 1925 was printed without quotation marks, is untraced.

49. Great-grandfather Rev. John Yeats (1774–1846) of Drumcliff. He knew Emmet while they were both at Trinity College, Dublin (see 'Introductory Rhymes' P 101). Robert Emmet (1778–1803) was a member of the United Irishmen and led his own rising, the Dublin rebellion of 1803. The disorganized and ineffective rioters were dispersed; Emmet fled, was arrested by Major Sirr, and condemned to death. His oratory in court and on the scaffold became central to Irish patriotic rhetoric.

50. Alexander (Uncle Sandy) Armstrong, killed at the siege of New Orleans in 1813 during the War of 1812.

51. Major Patrick Corbet (d. 1840), brother of Jane Grace Yeats (1811–76).

52. Great-uncle Robert Corbet (1795–1870) was in the army during the Peninsular Wars and later appointed stockbroker to the Court of Chancery. He made enough money to buy Sandymount

Castle, Dublin, where JBY lived when a student from 1857 to 1862. Both JBY's maternal grandmother, Grace Armstrong Corbet (1774–1861), and her sister, Mrs. Jane Armstrong Clendenin, lived with uncle Robert. He apparently had financial troubles and suffered creeping paralysis, which may have been why he committed suicide during a mail-boat crossing by jumping into the Irish Sea.

53. Walpole, Horace (1717–97). English writer. The home that was responsible for the influence was bought by him in 1747, a villa at Strawberry Hill, Twickenham, England, which Walpole enthusiastically remodelled into a small Gothic castle. It inspired a trend and stands today.

54. Lily Yeats's note reads 'Armstrong I think?'

55. Dublin Castle, center of British administration in Ireland.

56. Lily Yeats's note corrects this to 'great-uncle'.

57. The family had oval, monochrome miniatures of William Corbet (c. 1790; 7.2 cm. x 5.5 cm.) and Col. Arthur Young (6.7 cm. x 5.1 cm.), mounted with five others in a frame made in London sometime after 1898 (collection of Anne Yeats).

58. Perhaps Benjamin Yeats (1750–95), who married Mary Butler in 1773; Lily Yeats's note reads 'Patrick Corbet (d. 1791)'.

59. In *Early Memories* (1928), JBY recalled: 'I myself am eagerly communicative and when my son first revealed to me his gift of verse "Ah!" I said, "Behold I have given a tongue to the sea-cliffs" ' (20).

60. Rev. Thomas Beatty married Letitia Armstrong on 14 May 1797. She was the daughter of Robert and Dorothea Young Armstrong, who were also the parents of Grace Armstrong Corbet (1774–1861), who lived in Sandymount Castle with her husband, Robert Corbet, and her sister. Their daughter, Jane Grace Corbet, married Rev. W. B. Yeats in 1835. Rev. Beatty was thus an uncle by marriage to grandmother Jane Grace Corbet Yeats. In 1937, WBY described the drawing as a 'portrait by some forgotten master' and that it 'hangs upon my bedroom wall' (LE 206). The drawing is now lost.

61. Lily Yeats remembers that Uncle Beattie's father was Goldsmith's friend (LY note). For Oliver Goldsmith, see Background Notes on Writers, p. 533.

62. The Pollexfen aunts were concerned about WBY's education and the fact that he could not read at age seven: 'irritated and wearied out of patience' by young Willie (JBY's unpublished memoirs, quoted Murphy, *Prodigal Father* 82).

63. John Butler Yeats (1839–1922). Painter. JBY was born in his father's parish of Tullylish, County Down, on 16 March 1839,

and educated at the Atholl Academy, Isle of Man, and Trinity College, Dublin. He graduated in 1862, enrolled at the King's Inns to study law, inherited property in Kildare, and married Susan Pollexfen of Sligo on 10 September 1863. To the dismay of his wife and her family, he decided to give up law and, in 1867, went to London to study painting at Heatherley's Art School. The Yeats children spent much of their youth in Sligo with relatives. In 1870, JBY left Heatherley's for the Slade Art School, was accepted as a student by Edward Poynter, studied landscape painting on his own in 1876, exhibited at the Royal Hibernian Academy (Dublin) and the Royal Academy (London) and was elected to the Royal Hibernian Academy in 1892. Hugh Lane got commissions for him to paint portraits, and these became a group of portraits of Irish literary and intellectual figures. JBY accompanied Lily Yeats to New York in 1907—Lily left for home in June 1908, but he stayed for the rest of his life, moving to his last residence on West 29th Street in September. W. B. supported his father by selling his manuscripts to John Quinn, one of which was *Reveries. Passages from the Letters of John Butler Yeats* was published in 1917; *Essays* followed in 1918, and *Further Letters of John B. Yeats* in 1920. He died in New York on 3 February 1922. *Early Memories* appeared in 1928, and *J. B. Yeats: Letters to his Son W. B. Yeats and Others* in 1946.

64. JBY was not pleased with this revelation or with some others in *Reveries*. He wrote to Mrs. Edward Caughey on 8 April 1916: 'Did you ever throw a book at your daughter or your husband? If so be careful. They may write their memoirs' (quoted in Murphy, *Prodigal Father* 446).

65. Sligo, probably 1873. A dame school is a private school for early education, usually run by one woman. Lily Yeats's note points out that Mrs. Armstrong had been their mother's bridesmaid, so 'she can't have been old.'

66. Susan Mary ('Lily') Yeats (1866–1949). WBY's other sister was Elizabeth Corbet ('Lollie') Yeats (1868–1940). A third sister, Jane Grace Yeats, was born in 1875, but died less than a year later.

67. Bought in India by great-grandfather Middleton on his wedding trip, about 1817 or 1818 (LY note).

68. pathic: 'man or boy upon whom sodomy is practiced' (O.E.D.).

69. Robert Corbet Yeats (Bobbie) (1870–3). He died at Merville of croup, which had begun as a simple cold a few days earlier, on 3 March 1873.

70. In Irish folklore, 'an attendant fairy that follows old families, and none but them, and wails before a death' (WBY note to *FFT* [1888], P&I 16).

71. Agnes Middleton Pollexfen (1855–1926) (LY scrapbook in Murphy, *Prodigal Father* 102).

72. At Beech Villa, Farnham Royal, near Slough (Murphy, *Prodigal Father* 110).

73. On the Yeats family's return to London in 1874, they settled at 14 Edith Villas, North End, now West Kensington.

74. Bedford Park. Near the Turnham Green Station of the suburban railway. The estate of John Lindley (1799–1864), Professor of Botany and Fellow of the Royal Society, was developed into the housing settlement of Bedford Park, designed by Jonathan Carr (1845–1915) in 1876. Norman Shaw designed several houses and the church, and William Morris designed wallpaper (see p. 66 below). Bedford Park was meant to be a community of artists and those who appreciated the arts. In the spring of 1879, JBY moved his family into Bedford Park, 8 Woodstock Road, off the avenue.

75. The Great Potato Famine of 1845–49 resulted in a population decline of more than two million people through disease, starvation, and emigration. The ships that carried the emigrants to North America were called coffin ships.

76. Lloyd's of London, the great insurance company.

77. Lily Yeats (LY note).

78. WBY was in San Francisco 21 January–3 February 1904.

79. WBY attended the Godolphin School, Hammersmith, January 1877–summer 1880.

80. Edward Bulwer-Lytton's *Godolphin* (1833).

81. Untraced.

82. The beginning of the Irish Parliament, essentially Protestant, dates from 1297. The last was 'Grattan's parliament', 1782–1800.

83. Reverend William Butler Yeats (1806–62).

84. From the refrain of 'The British Grenadiers': 'With a tow, row, row, row, row, row, / For the British Grenadiers'.

85. Scenes of famous English military victories, 1346 and 1415.

86. City located at the mouth of the Shannon River, Co. Limerick. Limerick withstood a siege by William of Orange in 1690, but fell in a second siege in 1691, after which the English signed the Treaty of Limerick, which they later repudiated.

87. In 1598, the English were defeated by Hugh O'Neill in the Battle of the Yellow Ford, on the river Callan, Co. Armagh.

88. Irish political organization active 1879–1882, designed to support the peasantry and stop evictions; it demanded fair rent, fixity of tenure, and the right of the tenant to sell occupancy at the highest price. The demands were not met; evictions continued

and rents were withheld; the league was suppressed and agrarian violence followed.

89. Cyril Veasey, who later went to India (LY note).

90. Rupert H. Morris, Headmaster, Godolphin School, Hammersmith.

91. Boys at Eton, one of the most prestigious English public schools, wore black formal clothing, including top hats.

92. Untraced.

93. Alexander Middleton (LY note). This event happened a decade later, in 1888 (CL 1 48; Foster 1 62).

94. Untraced.

95. Thomas Matthews Rooke (1842–1942), English artist (LY note).

96. Pre-Raphaelite. Nineteenth-century aesthetic movement which called for a return to the style of art before the High Renaissance and aimed at an art that reflected nature more accurately in color and shades of light. It emphasized detail, a personal and sometimes sentimentalized feeling for the subject, and a moral tone in regard to the ills of the industrial revolution. It represented the first major challenge to the Royal Academy of Art, London, and was helped into this position by the support of John Ruskin.

97. Rossetti's letter is untraced. JBY reported it in a letter to Dowden, 1868, and frequently referred to it thereafter (Murphy, *Prodigal Father* 60, 556).

98. Frank Huddlestone Potter (1845–77), *Little Dormouse*, oil on canvas, 57 cm. x 47 cm., Tate Gallery, London (no. 2214), gift of Lady Tate, 1908. It is one of the eight works by Potter in the Tate.

99. Sally Whelan, who had an Italian mother and an Irish father; she sent a telegram to WBY on his seventieth birthday (LY note).

100. Untraced.

101. George Wilson (1848–90), a Scottish artist, was a close friend of JBY and probably gave him two paintings—the Arno with Florence in the background (gouache, 14 cm. x 24 cm.) and a forest scene (watercolor, 34 cm. x 24 cm.)—sometime between 1908 and 1922. They were in the custody of Lily and Lollie Yeats while JBY was in New York (1907–22), and at JBY's death in 1922 were inherited by WBY; they are now in the collection of Anne Yeats. Seventy-three of Wilson's works were exhibited at the Spring 1983 Aberdeen Artists' Society Exhibition; relatives in and near Abdereen own 'a considerable number' (*Ten Phototypes of the Works of George Wilson Exhibited at the Aberdeen Artists' Exhibition 1983* [Aberdeen: Geo. W. Wilson & Co. (photographers). November1983]); the Aberdeen Art Gallery owns three landscapes and one watercolor and pencil study for 'Alastor'.

102. Sir Walter Scott, *Ivanhoe* (1820); Gurth is in ch. 1, Friar Tuck in ch. 40.
103. Geoffrey Chaucer (c. 1340–1400), *Prioress's Tale* and *The Tale of Sir Thopas.*
104. Balzac's *Illusions Perdues* was published in three parts, 1837–43. The scene recalled here is at the end of *A Distinguished Provincial in Paris (Un Grand homme de province à Paris).*
105. Captain Keebles, afterwards Harbour Master at Sligo (LY note).
106. 'An omen that sometimes accompanies the banshee is the *coach-a- bower* (cóiste-bodhar)—an immense black coach, mounted by a coffin, and drawn by headless horses driven by a *Dullahan*', a headless phantom (WBY note to FFT [1888]; P&I 16).
107. See note 32 above.
108. Jack B. Yeats (1871–1957). Painter and writer. He was born at 23 Fitzroy Road, London, on 29 August 1871, and spent most of his childhood with his Pollexfen grandparents in Sligo. He studied at the Westminster, South Kensington, and Chiswick Schools of Art in the late 1880s, and married Mary Cottenham White in 1894. His first exhibition of watercolours was held in the Clifford Gallery, London, in 1897, and he began painting in oil in 1902. He lived in England from 1897 to 1910. He illustrated books of his close friend John Synge, *The Aran Islands* (1907) and *Wicklow, West Kerry and Connemara* (1911). Jack Yeats also wrote *Sligo* (1930), *Apparitions* (1933, three plays), *Sailing, Sailing Swiftly* (1933), *The Careless Flower* (1947), *La La Noo* (1943, a play). He joined the Victor Waddington Galleries in Dublin in 1940 and had a series of retrospective exhibitions at the National Gallery, London, in 1942. He exhibited at the Tate Gallery in 1948, and retrospectives of his work toured the United States and Canada in 1951 and 1952. See Hilary Pyle Carey, *Jack B. Yeats: A Biography* (London: Routledge & Kegan Paul, 1970).
109. *Memory Harbour* (1900). Watercolour on board, 32 cm. x 47 cm. A gift of the artist to WBY, c. 1901; 1940s or 1950s, mislaid in the attic of Mrs. W. B. Yeats's house in Palmerston Road, Dublin, and presumed to have been lost; in 1969, Michael B. Yeats found it, damaged, after his mother's death. *Memory Harbour,* which was to have been the title for *Reveries over Childhood and Youth* (see Textual Introduction, p. 16), was used as the frontispiece or illustration to each edition up through *Auto* 1926, with the following note by WBY (1915; publ. only in *Reveries* Cuala 1916, *Reveries* 1916, and *Auto* 1926): 'The picture "Memory Harbour" is the village of Rosses Point, but with the distances shortened and the houses run together as in an old-fashioned panoramic map. The man on the pedestal in the mid-

dle of the river is the "metal man", and he points to where the water is deep enough for ships. The coffin, crossbones, skull, and loaf at the point of the headland are to remind one of the sailor who was buried there by a ship's crew in a hurry not to miss the tide. As they were not sure if he was really dead they buried with him a loaf, as the story runs. W.B.Y.' In *Reveries* 1916 (and *Auto* 1926 only) WBY added: 'My brother painted the picture many years ago.'

110. Michael Gillen (LY note).

111. Reverend William Butler Yeats.

112. LY scrapbook in Murphy, *Prodigal Father* 549 n. 15.

113. Great-uncle William Middleton's daughter Mary. The 'brawling squireen' is John Robert Ormbsy (LY note), whose family owned Castle Dargan, near Ballygawley, Co. Sligo, and whose daughter eloped with a groom and so provided the germ of WBY's play *Purgatory* (prod. 1938) CPlays 681–89. See McGarry 27–28.

114. Castle Fury. On Castle Dargan Lake, near Ardnabrack, Co. Sligo. It is at the end of the lake and does not face Castle Dargan (McGarry 28).

115. WBY bought his own tower with a winding stair, Thoor Ballylee, in 1917; see note 2, p. 439.

116. A rifle used in the British Army, 1871–91, combining a breech mechanism invented by Friedrich von Martini with a .45 calibre barrel devised by Benjamin T. Henry.

117. See note 88 above.

118. The family first lived in Balscadden Cottage at Howth, but moved to Island View, which overlooked the harbor, in 1881, until moving to Rathgar in 1883.

119. Mary Butler inherited these lands, which then passed to Parson John Yeats, his son William, and finally to JBY in 1846. By 1886, JBY was ready to sell the land to his tenants, and thus his son never became an Irish landlord. All the land was sold under the Ashbourne Act in 1887. The declining economy, not the land war or mismanagement, caused the estate to yield little income (Murphy, *Prodigal Father* 131, 568). See note 35 above.

120. John Doran, the Bailiff (LY note; Foster 1 18).

121. Harcourt Street (Erasmus Smith) High School, 40 Harcourt Street, Dublin. The headmaster was William Wilkins (Foster 1 32).

122. *Hamlet*, I.iii.78–80. For Shakespeare, see Background Notes on Writers, p. 536.

123. Cyril Veasey; see note 89 above.

124. Untraced.

125. James Ussher (1581–1656), Archbishop of Armagh. His chronology placed the date of creation at 4004 B.C.

126. The family left Bedford Park in 1881 and moved to Balscadden Cottage, Kilrock Rd., Howth, and soon to Island View, which faces Howth Harbour and which Lily Yeats described as 'a horrible little house' (LY notes). They moved to Rathgar in 1883.

127. Small structure for changing clothes at the seaside.

128. WBY had first published the 'Village Ghosts' section (*Myth* 15–21) of *The Celtic Twilight* (1893, 1902) in Henley's *The Scots Observer*, 11 May 1889.

129. WBY gave another version of this awakening in the first draft of his autobiography:

> I was tortured by sexual desire and had been for many years. . . . It began when I was fifteen years old. I had been bathing, and lay down in the sun on the sand on the Third Rosses and covered my body with sand. Presently the weight of the sand began to affect the organ of sex, though at first I did not know what the strange growing sensation was. It was only at the orgasm that I knew, remembering some boy's description or the description in my grandfather's encyclopaedia. It was many days before I discovered how to renew that wonderful sensation. From then on it was a continual struggle against an experience that almost invariably left me with exhausted nerves (*Mem* 71).

130. The sense here is that country girls, pretending to be poltergeists (mischievous ghosts held to be responsible for unexplained disturbances), use long hairs to move plates.

131. Song of Solomon 2:3.

132. The title character in Byron's dramatic poem *Manfred* (1817) is a remorseful, archly romantic young man. Prince Athanase—in 'Prince Athanase: A Fragment' (1817)—roams the world searching for perfect love, with thoughts driven 'like lights & sounds, from haunted tower to tower' (l. 69). Alastor drifts away in Shelley's *Alastor; or The Spirit of Solitude* (1815), ll. 369–419.

133. Cythna in Shelley's *The Revolt of Islam* (1817).

134. 44 York Street, west of St. Stephen's Green, Dublin.

135. *Coriolanus*, IV.v.

136. WBY'S NOTE (first publ. in *Auto* 1955; it is not in the 1932/1936 page proofs):

> 'I hear
> Your voices, sweet and melancholy sounds' . . .
> *Manfred*, Act I, Scene I.

137. For Keats and Shelley, see Background Notes on Writers, p. 535 and p. 537, respectively.

138. Reverend Stopford Brooke (1832–1916). For Wordsworth, see Background Notes on Writers, p. 539.

139. Pre-Raphaelitism was the first real challenge to the authority of the Royal Academy of Art, London, but its influence was more extensive in literature than in the visual arts.

140. For Spenser, see Background Notes on Writers, p. 537.

141. WBY's early attempts at writing plays include *The Island of Statues, Love and Death, Mosada,* and *Time and the Witch Vivien,* all four written in 1884; P 453–84, 491–502, 514–17.

142. George Pollexfen (1839–1910) returned to take the place of uncle William Middleton, who died in 1882, not the place of WBY's grandfather William Pollexfen (1811–92). The firm, Middleton and Pollexfen, became the W. and G. T. Pollexfen Company.

143. Charlemont; Lily Yeats notes that in the 1930s it had become a high school.

144. Saint John's. Church of Ireland, Sligo, where WBY's parents were married, 10 September 1863. Grandfather Pollexfen designed his own tomb and was buried with his wife in the churchyard.

145. National Library of Ireland, Kildare Street, Dublin.

146. Untraced.

147. He rode under the name of Paul Hamilton; his racing colors were primrose and violet (LY note).

148. William Gregory Wood-Martin, *History of Sligo* (Dublin, 1882), pp. 63–64.

149. Possibly George Pollexfen's housekeeper, Kate.

150. Charles Middleton (LY note).

151. 'Love and Death: A Tragedy' (c. April 1884; NLI Ms. 30,356) never published, except for one song titled 'Love and Death' (1885) P 483–84.

152. Ballina, Co. Mayo (named in the typescript NLI Ms. 30,868, fol. 70).

153. Laura Armstrong (b. 1862), daughter of barrister Sergeant Richard Armstrong, WBY's distant cousin through the Corbet family and, as Foster observes, the model for the 'belles dames sans merci in his early work: the witch Vivian, Margaret Leland in *John Sherman* and the enchantress in *The Island of Statues'* (34). She married Henry Morgan Byrne, a solicitor, in 1884, and later—allegedly—' "a Welsh gardener" who fled from her eccentricities' (Foster 1 550 n. 34; Murphy 569 n. 43 & n. 44).

154. Lucy Middleton.

155. For persons 'taken' by the fairies, see, e.g., FFT, CT, 'Away' (1902) in UP2 267–82.

156. Raths are prehistoric hill-forts, associated in folklore with the fairies.

157. John 20:19–29.
158. Passage graves are megalithic tombs dating from the Stone Age.
159. 10 Ashfield Terrace, now 418 Harolds Cross Road (LY note), in the Dublin suburb Terenure.
160. In 1884–86, WBY attended first the Dublin Municipal School of Art, adjoining the National Library of Ireland, and then drawing classes at the Royal Hibernian Academy.
161. Trinity College, Dublin, conferred an honorary D.Litt. on WBY in 1922. The three previous generations of Yeatses had received degrees at Trinity College. These included great-grandfather Reverend John Yeats (B.A., 1797), grandfather Reverend W. B. Yeats (B.A., 1833; M.A., 1840), great-uncle Thomas Yeats (B.A., 1836), father JBY (B.A., 1862), and uncle Isaac Butt Yeats (B.A., 1876).
162. Untraced.
163. Philip Francis Little.
164. The monument to Léon Gambetta (1838–82), French lawyer and politician, was in the Tuileries.
165. J.M.W. Turner, *The Golden Bough* (1834), oil, 1.04 m. x 1.64 m., National Gallery, London, from 1847, transferred to the Tate Gallery in 1929 (no. 371); illus. Martin Butlin and Evelyn Joll, *The Paintings of J.M.W. Turner* (New Haven and London: Yale University Press, 1977), plate 334. That catalogue raisonné has no listing of any exhibition of any Turner painting in Dublin, so perhaps WBY, who could easily have seen *The Golden Bough* at the National Gallery, London, is wrong about having seen it in Dublin.
166. In this untitled and undated watercolour (17 cm. x 25 cm.), which proably dates from the nineteenth (or perhaps eighteenth) century, a girl in white night clothes slightly raises herself from a bed to kiss the right hand of an old, grey-haired man who is wearing a long plain brown coat. The man's left hand is tucked inside the coat, like Napoleon's. The action is viewed by six other children, all in white night clothes and sitting on two large beds, one at left and one at right. Stairs ascend from the center background, lit by a shallow oil lamp which hangs from the ceiling. WBY acquired it 1917–26, probably at his father's death in 1922. Anne Yeats recalls that her father displayed this framed picture on his desk for years. It is now is her collection. WBY'S NOTE (first publ. in Auto 1926):
    This little picture has been found and hangs in my house. 1926.
167. The biblical reference and the JBY painting are untraced.
168. By the late 1880s, JBY's oil portraits included Lord Justice

Fitzgibbon, Sir Andrew Hart, D. H. Madden, John O'Leary, and Katharine Tynan.

169. Probably JBY's painting *Going to Their Work*, exhibited at the Royal Hibernian Academy, Dublin, 1885, and the Royal Academy, London, 1887; present location unknown.

170. Ronald Schuchard, 'Yeats, Titian and the New French Painting' in *Yeats the European*, pp. 143 and 305 n. 3, suggests a pastel by Édouard Manet, *Les Bockeuses* (Women Drinking Beer) (1878; Burrell Collection, Glasgow Museums and Art Galleries), illus. (in color) Hollis Clayson, *Painted Love: Prostitution in French Art of the Impressionist Era* (New Haven: Yale University Press, 1991), plate 60; and *Yeats the European*, plates between pp. 142–43. For a similar instance of these café pictures, see Pierre-Auguste Renoir, *At the Café (Le Petit Café)* (1876–77, oil on canvas, 35 cm. x 28 cm., Rijksmuseum Kröller-Müller, Otterlo, Netherlands), illus. (in color) *Painted Love*, plate 61 (color).

171. James McNeill Whistler, *Arrangement in Grey and Black: Portrait of the Painter's Mother* (1871), oil, 1.44 m. x 1.63 m., Musée d'Orsay, Paris; illus. Richard Dorment and Margaret F. MacDonald, *James McNeill Whistler* (New York: Abrams, 1995), plate 60. It was exhibited in Dublin in 1884; the Dublin Sketching Club Annual Exhibition of Sketches, Pictures, & Photography (no. 244), Leinster Hall, 35 Molesworth Street, which opened 1 December 1884; it was organized by Logan Pearsal Smith. Whistler's mother was sixty-seven years old when the painting was made. WBY had a framed reproduction of this painting at 18 Woburn Buildings (CL2 729), and he praised Whistler's preference for 'patterns and rhythms of colour' rather than realism ('A Symbolic Artist [Althea Gyles] and the Coming of Symbolic Art', 1898, UP2 133–34). JBY later wrote an introduction for the catalogue of a Whistler exhibition in New York in 1914 (Murphy, *Prodigal Father* 427).

172. For JBY having taken WBY in boyhood to see Henry Irving as Hamlet, see p. 69 above.

173. Probably *Byron Landing from a Boat*, a miniature (1807) by the Scottish painter George Sanders (1774–1846).

174. See note 159 above.

175. At the end of 1883, JBY moved to a studio at 7 Stephen's Green, Dublin, owned by a grocer, Mr. Smyth, who had a store below the studio (Murphy, *Prodigal Father* 135).

176. Edward Dowden (1843–1913) was a friend of JBY from student days at Trinity College, Dublin. At the age of twenty-four, he was made the first Professor of English Literature at Trinity. He had poetic ambitions, but published only one volume, *Poems* (1876),

and was otherwise a literary critic. Works include *Shakespeare, His Mind and Art* (1875), *Shakespeare Primer* (1877), and the *Life of Shelley* (1886).

177. Edward Dowden, 'Renunciants', *Poems* (London: Henry S. King, 1876), p. 176: a short poem about the burden of gentlemanly repression.

178. A characteristic remark, but not in the published letters of JBY.

179. In *The Nineteenth Century* (January 1888), reprinted in *The Complete Works of Matthew Arnold*, ed. R. H. Super (Ann Arbor: University of Michigan Press, 1977), XI, 305–27. For Arnold, see Background Notes on Writers, p. 531.

180. In the first published version, WBY had been even harsher on Dowden, continuing with this passage, deleted in the revisions for *Auto 1926*: 'He had abandoned too, or was about to abandon, what was to have been his master-work, "The Life of Goethe," though in his youth a lecture course at Alexandra College that spoke too openly of Goethe's loves had brought him the displeasure of our Protestant Archbishop of Dublin. Only Wordsworth, he said, kept more than all, his early love' (*Reveries* Cuala 1916 100–01).

181. *The Letters of Edward Dowden and His Correspondents* (London: J. M. Dent, 1914). JBY wrote from Regent's Park in the autumn of 1869 and on 31 December 1869; Dowden's reply is dated 6 December 1869. *The Letters of Edward Dowden and His Correspondents* (London: J. M. Dent, 1914), pp. 43–48. JBY's letters are reprinted in Hone, *JBY Letters* 47–48.

182. The Cuala Press, under Lollie Yeats's direction, did print a posthumous collection of Edward Dowden's verse, *A Woman's Reliquary* (1913). Lollie made the decision without consulting her brother. WBY had her print a note to the Cuala Press Prospectus in 1914: 'This book is not a part of the Cuala series arranged by W. B. Yeats' (Murphy, *Prodigal Father* 407–9; Liam Miller, *The Dun Emer Press, Later the Cuala Press* [Dublin: Dolmen, 1973], 67, 108).

183. William Wilkins (1852–1912), poet and Headmaster of the Erasmus Smith High School, Harcourt Street, Dublin, 1879–1908.

184. Charles Johnston (1867–1931).

185. Baron Karl von Reichenbach (1788–1869), a German physicist who conducted a scientific study of several hundred 'sensitives', persons who could see emanations from crystals and magnets in total darkness and could see an aura surround the human body. See his *Od Force; Letters On A Newly Discovered Power In Nature, And Its Relation To Magnetism, Electricity, Heat And Light* (1852), tr. J. George Guenther (Boston: Mussey, 1854).

186. In 1875, Helena Petrovna Blavatsky and Colonel H. S. Olcott (1832–1907) founded the Theosophical Society, New York City. The London counterpart was founded in 1878, and Madame Blavatsky came to London in 1884. WBY probably joined in 1887, becoming a member of the Esoteric Section in 1888, a group for particularly serious students that studied tables of Oriental symbolism.

187. Founded 16 June 1885 by WBY and Charles Johnston. Other members were W. K. Magee, Claude Falls Wright, Charles Weekes, and George Russell.

188. Ernest Renan's *Life of Christ* (1863) applies the historian's method to the narrative of the Bible and was widely influential. *Esoteric Buddhism* (1883) is a tract by Alfred Percy Sinnett (1840–1921).

189. William Johnston of Ballykilbeg, Co. Down (LY note, Foster 1 46).

190. Untraced.

191. Mir Aland Ali, Professor of Persian, Arabic, and Hindustani, Trinity College, Dublin (Foster 1 47).

192. In 1885, Mohini M. Chatterjee visited the Dublin Hermetic Society. See 'Mohini Chatterjee' (P 247).

193. The *Dublin University Review* published 'Song of the Faeries' and 'Voices' in March 1885. The two poems were included in *The Island of Statues,* Act II, scene iii, in its appearance in the *Dublin University Review* (July 1885). They were again used in *The Wanderings of Oisin* (1889). 'Voices' appeared in a revised form under the title 'The Cloak, the Boat, and the Shoes' in Poems (1895). See P 9.

194. The Contemporary Club, which met for discussion on Saturday evenings; WBY began attending in 1885 (Foster 1 41–42).

195. Unionists supported the constitutional and legislative connection between England and Ireland established by the Act of Union in 1800. For 'Orange', see note 22 above. Nationalists were determined to abolish the union and establish an independent Ireland. Their tactics ranged from the moderate parliamentary nationalism of Home Rule to the revolutionary, physical-force separatism of the Fenians and the Irish Republican Brotherhood.

196. The Metal Bridge, a pedestrian bridge three hundred yards west of the O'Connell Street Bridge.

197. John O'Leary (1830–1907), Fenian leader and man of letters. Before he was twenty, O'Leary had joined the Young Ireland movement and been jailed, released, and gone into exile in France. He returned, became involved in the Fenian movement, and edited its journal, *The Irish People,* from 1863 until it was

siezed in 1865. O'Leary was arrested, spent nine years in English prisons, was released under the Amnesty Act in 1874, lived in exile in Paris, and was permitted to return to Ireland in 1885. He and his sister, the poet Ellen O'Leary (1831–89), became the center of a nationalist literary circle that included JBY, WBY, Maud Gonne, Arthur Griffith, and J. F. Taylor. He represented for WBY both romantic, literary nationalism, and 'a kind of free-thinking Catholic intelligentsia' (Foster 1 42–43). O'Leary's works include *Young Ireland* (1885), *What Irishmen Should Read* (1889), and *Recollections of Fenians and Fenianism* (1896). See 'September, 1913', 'Beautiful Lofty Things' P 108, 303.

198. Plutarch is the first-century biographer of famous Greek and Roman figures, frequently translated in Europe and England, most notably by Sir Thomas North (1579), whose versions provide some of the plots for Elizabethan drama. Hence, WBY asserts, both John and Ellen O'Leary are larger than life, figures of national consequence.

199. Thomas Osborne Davis (1814–45). Poet and politician who joined Daniel O'Connell's Repeal Association in 1839 and led the rise of the militant separatist Young Ireland party within its ranks. In 1842, he founded the *Nation* with John Dillon and Charles Gavan Duffy and it became the voice of Young Ireland. In 1847, John Mitchel started the *United Irishmen* and was arrested in May 1848. Smith O'Brien led a rising in July, but it was ineffective, and O'Brien, Duffy, Thomas Francis Meagher (1823–67), Terence Bellew MacManus (1823–60), and others were jailed. Davis's works, all nationalist and posthumously published, include *Literary and Historical Essays* (1846), *The Poems of Thomas Davis* (1846), *Collected Prose Writings of Thomas Davis* (1891).

200. In a typescript draft, WBY continued:

His room was full of books, always second hand copies that had often been ugly and badly printed when new and had not grown to my unhistoric mind more pleasing from the dirt of some old Dublin bookshop. Great numbers were Irish and for the first time I began to read histories and verses that a Catholic Irishman knows from boyhood. He seemed to consider politics almost wholly as a moral discipline, and seldom said of any proposed course of action that it was practical or otherwise. When he spoke to me of his prison life he spoke of all with seeming freedom but presently one noticed that he never spoke of hardship, and if one asked him why, he would say 'I was in the hands of my enemies, why should I complain?' I have heard since that the governor of his jail found out that he had endured some unnecessary discomfort for months and had asked why he did not speak of it. 'I did not come here to complain' was the answer (NLI Ms. 30,868, fol. 93–94).

201. Katharine Tynan Hinkson (1861–1931). Poet and novelist. Minor but assiduously productive member of the Literary Revival who lived and wrote in England and Ireland and completed over one hundred novels, eighteen volumes of poetry, twelve collections of short stories, three plays, several anthologies, innumerable articles, and four volumes of memoirs. WBY first met her at her father's farm at Clondalkin, near Maynooth, in the summer of 1885. She was 'attracted to him, nurtured his talent, helped publicize his early work, possibly received a nervous proposal from him, and then seen him outstrip her' (Foster 1 54–55, 72–73).

202. Douglas Hyde (1860–1949) studied divinity and law at Trinity College, Dublin, and earned an LL.D in 1888, but his real interests were Irish language and literature. He was from Frenchpark, Co. Roscommon, two miles from Co. Mayo and two miles from Co. Sligo. See also Background Notes on Writers, p. 534.

203. John F. Taylor (1850–1902). Barrister and orator. Taylor delivered the Inaugural Address of 1886, the 'Parliaments of Ireland', to the Young Ireland Society and wrote a book on *Owen Roe O'Neill* (London: Unwin, 1896). He was an opponent in WBY's attempt to secure the editorship of the New Irish Library series, which went to Sir Charles Gavan Duffy in 1892. See UP1 239–44, and CL1 310–4, for WBY's commentary on Taylor's involvement. WBY reviewed *Owen Roe O'Neill,* which was part of the New Irish Library series, in the *Bookman* (June 1896) (UP1 406–8) and wrote more of Taylor in *Reveries* Cuala 1916 113.

204. Gerald Fitzgibbon (1837–1909), the Lord Justice of Appeal.

205. From a pamphlet of Taylor's speech, 'The Language of the Outlaw', published in Dublin, c. 1903. Taylor appeared before the Law Students' Debating Society, 24 October 1901. An account of the speech also appeared in the *Freeman's Journal* (25 October 1901). Joyce used the speech in the 'Aeolus' episode of *Ulysses;* see also WBY's note 76, p. 464.

206. From John Stuart Mill's essay 'What is Poetry?' (1833): 'Poetry and eloquence are both alike the expression or utterance of feeling. But if we may be excused the antithesis, we should say that eloquence is heard, poetry is overheard.'

207. Terence Bellew MacManus (1823–60), Young Ireland revolutionary, died in poverty in San Francisco after escaping from Van

Diemen's Land to which he had been transported. WBY had used this ancedote about the dying brother and the hawk-like bird in FFT (1888) (P&I 235).

208. See note 199.

209. John O'Leary delivered the Inaugural Address of this society, drawing its name from the Young Irelanders of the 1840s, on 19 January 1885. WBY joined the society in 1886. The aim was to promote the idea and feeling of Irish nationalism through literature. As O'Leary made clear in his address, this meant original writings for inspiration, reading books pertaining to Ireland and urging others to do the same, spreading the societies throughout the United Kingdom, publishing presentations made at meetings of the society, and fine public speaking. All ideas should be tolerated if they were for the sake of Ireland, and the 'localization of patriotism' should be pursued. Above all, their mission was one of education, or, as O'Leary quoted from Duffy: 'Educate, that you may be free.' O'Leary's address was published as 'Young Ireland: The Old and the New' (Dublin: Dollard, 1885).

210. Charles McCarthy Teeling, a vice president of the Young Ireland Society.

211. Between 1883 and 1885, several dynamite explosions occurred, mainly in London, which were planned by a group of Irish-American terrorists, also known as the 'Dynamitards'.

212. Bartholomew Teeling (1774–98), United Irishman. He left for France with Wolfe Tone in 1796 to arrange for a French invasion of Ireland. In 1798, Teeling was Aide-de-camp to the French General Humbert and landed at Killala. He was captured after the surrender of Ballinamuck and subsequently sentenced to death.

213. Jeremiah Joseph Callanan (1795–1829), Irish poet and translator, 'The Recluse of Inchydoney' (1830); Inchedony (variously spelled Inchydoney, Inchidoney, Inchdoney) Island, connected to the mainland by causeways, is in Clonakilty Bay, Co. Cork.

214. The first published version continued with a lengthy passage (Reveries Cuala 1916 120–22), given below, which WBY deleted before 1926:

> It was because of this dream when we returned to London that I made with pastels upon the ceiling of my study a map of Sligo decorated like some old map with a ship and an elaborate compass and wrote, a little against the grain, a couple of Sligo stories, one a vague echo of "Grettir the Strong,"[a] which my father had read to me in childhood, and finished with better heart my "Wanderings of Oisin," and began after ridding

my style of romantic colour "The Countess Cathleen."[b] I saw
that our people did not read, but that they listened patiently
(how many long political speeches have they listened to?) and
saw that there must be a theatre, and if I could find the right
musicians, words set to music. I foresaw a great deal that we
are doing now, though never the appetite of our new middle-
class for "realism," nor the greatness of the opposition, nor
the slowness of the victory. Davis had done so much in the
four years of his working life, I had thought all needful pam-
phleteering and speech-making could be run through at the
day's end, not knowing that taste is so much more deeply
rooted than opinion that even if one had school and newspaper to help, one could scarcely stir it under two generations.
Then too, bred up in a studio where all things are discussed
and where I had even been told that indiscretion and energy
are inseparable, I knew nothing of the conservatism or of the
suspicions of piety. I had planned a drama like that of Greece,
and romances that were, it may be half Hugo and half de la
Motte Fouqué, to bring into the town the memories and
visions of the country and to spread everywhere the history
and legends of mediaeval Ireland and to fill Ireland once more
with sacred places. I even planned out, and in some detail, (for
those mysterious lights and voices were never long forgotten,)
another Samothrace, a new Eleusis.[c] I believed, so great was
my faith, or so deceptive the precedent of Young Ireland, that
I should find men of genius everywhere. I had not the conviction as it may seem, that a people can be compelled to write
what one pleases, for that could but end in rhetoric or in some
educational movement but believed I had divined the soul of
the people and had set my shoes upon a road that would be
crowded presently.

[a]The 'Sligo stories' are the novella *John Sherman* (w. 1888) and
short story 'Dhoya' (w. 1887), which were published together in
1891. For Grettir the Strong (996–1031), an Icelandic outlaw,
in the Grettir saga, see *The Story of Grettir the Strong*, tr.
William Morris and Eirikr Magnusson (1869), repr. in *The
Collected Works of William Morris*, vol. VII (London: Longmans,
Green, 1911) (O'Shea no. 1389).
[b]*The Wanderings of Oisin and Other Poems* (1889) and *The
Countess Cathleen* (1892).
[c]For a detailed account of WBY's scheme for establishing Celtic
Mysteries, analogous to the Eleusinian Mysteries, see CL2 663–69.
215. Untraced.

216. In the revisions for *Auto* 1926, WBY softened the first published version: 'My father was indignant, almost violent, and would hear of nothing but drama'. (*Reveries* Cuala 1916 122).

217. Katharine Tynan. She recalled the séance in *Twenty-five Years: Reminiscences:* 'Willie Yeats was banging his head on the table. . . . He explained to me afterwards that the spirits were evil. To keep them off he had been saying the nearest approach to a prayer he could remember, which was the opening lines of Paradise Lost' ([London: Smith, Elder, 1913], 209).

218. Milton, *Paradise Lost* (1667), I, 1–6.

219. *The Wanderings of Oisin* (1889). The 'book of stories' was *John Sherman and Dhoya* (1891). WBY had edited *Fairy and Folk Tales of The Irish Peasantry* (1888) and *Stories from Carleton* (1889).

220. Maud Gonne. WBY's grandmother Elizabeth Pollexfen died on 2 October 1892. WBY had proposed to Maud Gonne for the first time in 1891.

221. William Pollexfen died on 12 November 1892.

THE TREMBLING OF THE VEIL.
BOOK I. FOUR YEARS 1887–1891

1. Arthur Symons may have told WBY of this comment by Mallarmé, which first appeared in 'Vers et Musique en France', *National Observer,* 26 March 1892: '. . . une inquiétude du voile dans le temple, avec des plis significatifs et un peu sa déchirure' (p. 484; '. . . a fluttering in the temple's veil—meaningful folds and even a little tearing;' see 'Crisis in Poetry,' tr. Bradford Cook, *Mallarme: Selected Prose Poems, Essays, & Letters* [Baltimore: Johns Hopkins, 1956], p. 34). WBY also recalled it in 'The Adoration of the Magi' (1897) and *Per Amica Silentia Lunae* (1917) (Myth 309, LE 367). The biblical allusion is Matthew 27:51.

2. Tower three miles northeast of Gort, Co. Galway. WBY bought Thoor Ballylee in 1917, had it restored as his home and stayed there periodically, 1918–27. See Mary Hanley and Liam Miller, *Thoor Ballylee—Home of William Butler Yeats* (Dublin: Dolmen Press, 1965; rev. edn. 1977).

3. For Bedford Park, see note 74, p. 425. After a year at 58 Eardley Crescent, South Kensington, the family returned to Bedford Park in 1888 and moved into a house at 3 Blenheim Road. WBY lived there until 1895, his father and sisters until 1902. His mother had suffered a stroke at Eardley Crescent and died in 1900; see note 29, p. 420.

4. St. Michael and All Angels, Church of England, Bath Road.

5. Dante Gabriel Rossetti's *Dante's Dream at the Time of the Death of Beatrice* depicts an incident from Dante's *Vita Nuova* in which Dante dreams he sees the dead Beatrice laid upon a bier. The Walker Art Gallery has a large replica (1871; oil, 211 cm. x 318 cm., no. 3091) of the original 1856 watercolour (47 cm. x 65.3 cm., Tate Gallery, London, no. 5229). Illustrated in Virginia Surtess, *The Paintings and Drawings of Dante Gabriel Rossetti (1828-1882): A Catalogue Raisonné* (Oxford: Clarendon Press, 1981), II, plate 95 (catalogue no. 81, replica 1).

6. In the revision for *Auto* 1926, WBY deleted a comment here that JBY 'now painted portraits of the first comer, children selling newspapers, or a consumptive girl with a basket of fish upon her head' (*Trembling* 1922 5).

7. Charles Émile Auguste Carlous Duran (1837–1917), a French realist artist and portrait painter, known especially for naturalistic portraits of fashionable women who reigned over the Paris salons. Jules Bastien-Lepage (1848–84), French realist painter known for portraits and for ancedotal, often sentimental, scenes of peasant life, such as *Les Foins;* see notes 8 and 24 below.

8. Thomas Henry Huxley (1825–95), English physician, writer, controversialist, who defined and defended the new scientific attitudes of the mid-nineteenth century; he coined the word 'agnostic' to describe his own philosophical stance. John Tyndall (1820–93) English scientist, who was Professor of Natural Philosophy (1853–87) and Superintendent (1867–87) of the Royal Institution. He advanced science by his investigations and popularized it by his lectures and writings. WBY frequently combines Carolus-Duran, Bastien-Lepage, Huxley, and Tyndall into a unified image of nineteenth-century realism and materialism.

9. This portrait by Titian (Tiziano Vecellio; 1488–1576) sometimes has been called *Arisoto,* but now is known as *Portrait of a Man* (c. 1508), and might be a self-portrait. It is in the National Gallery, London (oil, 81 cm. x 66 cm.; no. 1944) and shows the man dressed in purple and crimson, with a rose and gloves, facing forward with an open expression. Titian did paint a portrait of the Italian poet Ludovico Ariosto (1474–1533), now in the Casa Oriani, Ferrara (c. 1532; oil, 60 cm. x 50 cm.), but which was earlier (by 1877) in the private collection of the eighth Earl of Darnley, Cobham Hall, Cobham, Kent, England. Both portraits are illustrated in *Titian Paintings and Drawings* (Vienna: Phaidon Press; London: Allen & Unwin, 1937), figs. 3 and 94, respectively.

10. Titian (now regarded as School of Titian), *Supper at Emmaus* (c. 1540; oil, 1.63 m. x 2 m.), National Gallery of Ireland, no. 84, purchased 1870, illus. Harold E. Wethey, *The Paintings of Titian* (London: Phaidon, 1969), I, plate 228. In addition, in 1885 the NGI had purchased Titian's *Ecco Homo* (c. 1560), illus. *The Paintings of Titian*, I, plate 100, and already owned *St. Peter, Martyr* and *Male Portrait* by followers of Titian.

11. John Todhunter (1839–1916). Irish physician and writer. Friend of JBY. Todhunter was educated at Trinity College, Dublin, studied medicine in Paris and Vienna, and returned to Dublin to practise. He was physician to Cork Street Fever Hospital and became Professor of English Literature, Alexandria College, Dublin. An essay, 'A Theory of the Beautiful', made his reputation in 1872, and in 1874 he moved to London to pursue a literary career and there helped found the Irish Literary Society. WBY encouraged Todhunter, and his play *A Sicilian Idyll* was first performed at the Bradford Park Theatre on 5 May 1890. Other plays are a version of Euripides' *Helena in Troas* (1886) and *A Comedy of Sighs,* unsuccessfully produced in London with WBY's *Land of Heart's Desire* in 1894. See *Images of a Poet,* 56–58, and its Catalogue numbers 118–26.

12. Frederick York Powell (1850–1904). English historian and Icelandic scholar, Regius Professor of Modern History, Oxford (1894-1904). JBY and Powell were members of the Calumet Talking Club at Bedford Park.

13. Henry Marriott Paget (1856–1936), painter and illustrator.

14. Possibly Dr. George C. Haite.

15. The club opened on 3 May 1879 and was the first public meeting place in Bedford Park; designed by Norman Shaw in 1878, later enlarged and altered by E. J. May (1853–1941). It had a billiards room, a library, and an assembly room used as a small theatre.

16. 'Fragment of an Ode to Maia, Written on May Day, 1818'. For *A Sicilian Idyll,* see note 11 above.

17. Milton, 'Lycidas' (1637), l. 192.

18. Florence Farr (1860–1917), English actress, also known as Mrs. Emery. WBY saw her act in Todhunter's *A Sicilian Idyll* at the Bedford Park Clubhouse in June 1890 and considered her essential to the theatre productions of the verse plays he planned to write. She played Aleel in the first production of *The Countess Cathleen* in 1892 and Louka in Shaw's *Arms and the Man* at the Avenue Theatre, London, 1894. She was a member of MacGregor Mathers's Order of the Golden Dawn and was also involved with WBY's musical experiments with the psaltery in 1902. She later went to Ceylon where she taught in a Buddhist school and

died there in 1917. WBY remembers her in 'All Souls' Night' (P 227). Brook Green is a district of London north of Hammersmith. See note 3, p. 469.

19. The British Museum's life-size marble statue of the seated figure of Demeter (c. 330 B.C., height 1.47 m., sculpture 1300), excavated at Cnidus in 1858, is one of the finest examples of Hellenistic sculpture. It is now in the Hellenistic Room (13). Demeter, the Greek goddess of corn, is shown mourning for her daughter Persephone. Illus. B. F. Cook, *Greek and Roman Art in the British Museum* (London: British Museum, 1976), plate 113.

20. Edith Maud Gonne MacBride (1866–1953). WBY met Maud Gonne on 30 January 1889. His lengthy romantic pursuit is reflected in many of his love poems, and he made his first proposal of marriage to her in 1891. For a more frank account of her and of their relationship, see Mem 40–43, 45–50, 131–34.

21. *Aeneid,* I, 405. Aeneas has come ashore after a storm and his mother, Venus, appears to him disguised as a huntress. Only when she turns to leave does he recognize her: 'and from her gait it was clear that she was truly a goddess.'

22. In a manuscript draft, WBY wrote at greater length and less guardedly about Maud Gonne:

> I was twenty-three years old when Maud Gonne got out of the hansom at our door at Bedford Park with an introduction to my father from John O'Leary the old Fenian leader. . . . I had never thought to see in living woman so great beauty, a beauty belonging to great poets, and famous pictures of[?] some legendary past. A complexion like the blossom of an apple and yet a form that had the beauty of linaments which Blake called the highest beauty because it is changeless from youth to age, and a stature so great she seemed to have walked down from Olympus. Her movements matched her form and I understood at last why the poets of antiquity, where we would praise smile and eyes say rather she walked like a goddess. . . .
>
> Then as she was now returning to Paris where she had made her home to be near Millevoye her lover as I found years afterward. I think I dined with her every night for the eight or nine days of her stay in London and it seemed natural that she should give her attention, her friendship in overflowing measure. There was no flirtation in our talk unless it is flirtation to expound every secret ambition and to exchange with wordless approval philosophies of life. . . . From then on and for many years, before I fell deeply in love, and even after love had

changed into friendship, I was some kind of father confessor talking of art and peace to the whirlwind; and I made 'The Countess Cathleen' to tell the tale in allegory . . . and often day after day would find her and leave her in absorbed discourse. And then of a sudden, she would be . . . hurried into some form of political activity that seemed to my mind without direction, like the movement of a squirrel on a wheel (NLI Ms. 30,471, pp. 56a, 56c, 56d–e).

23. Henley, William Ernest (1849–1903). English editor, who lived at 1 Merton Road, Chiswick. The portrait by WBY's friend William Rothenstein (1872–1945) is a lithograph (1897; 28 cm. x 18 cm.) in his English Portraits series (750 copies; many destroyed by a fire in 1899). WBY purchased his copy in October 1916; it is no longer extant. For an illustration, see William Rothenstein, *Men and Memories: Recollections of William Rothenstein: 1872–1900,* [I] (London: Faber, 1931), I, facing p. 298.

24. Poems Henley called 'Bric-a-brac' (1877–88). *Vers libre,* or free verse, is verse in irregular metre, usually without rhyme.

25. J. Bastien-Lepage, *Les Foins* (The Hay-Makers) (La Réunion des Musées Nationaux, Paris), illus. in Ronald Schuchard, 'Yeats, Titian and the New French Painting,' in *Yeats the European,* plates between pp. 142–43; see also WBY's comment on p. 146, l. 21.

26. Henley's hospital poems appeared in *A Book of Verses* (1888) and *In Hospital* (1903). Tubercular arthritis had initially caused him to lose a foot to amputation, which was followed by amputation of his leg at the Royal Edinburgh Infirmary in 1875.

27. Tommaso Salvini (1829–1915). Italian tragic actor, who played the title roles in *Othello, Hamlet, Macbeth,* and *King Lear.*

28. John Ruskin (1819–1900) dominated the English art world from about 1843 when the first volume of *Modern Painters* was published in London. Four more volumes followed by 1860. Other influential works include *The Seven Lamps of Architecture* (1849), *Pre-Raphaelitism* (1851), *The Stones of Venice* (3 vols., 1851–53), *Fors Clavigera* (1871–84), and *Unto This Last* (1862). Ruskin was an early and ardent advocate of Turner, the Pre-Raphaelites, landscape and painterly detail, and of a vital connection between the spiritual and the aesthetic. He later turned to the social and political conditions for the production of art and attacked what he saw as the mechanistic materialism of his age. Whether the impulse came from Romanticism or medievalism or evangelical Christianity, there was a strongly didactic element in his art criticism. WBY's sense of Ruskinism would have been

mediated through his father's commitment to portraiture and Blake's to visionary, symbolic landscapes.

29. The year is probably 1888, the year WBY met Henley. In early 1889, Henley left London for Edinburgh to become editor of the *Scots Observer*, later the *National Observer*. The Gaelic League was founded in 1893.

30. Max Beerbohm called Henley's young men 'the Henley Regatta.' They met at Solferino's Restaurant, Rupert Street, and then at Henley's home, Addiscombe Anna, in Chiswick, west of Hammersmith.

31. Probably James N. Dunn (1856–1919), a Scottish journalist, who was just nine years older than WBY and seven years younger than Henley.

32. Manuscripts circulating in the twelfth century that drew on the oral tradition. These constitute an important body of references to the King Arthur of Celtic tradition.

33. Large meetings called to discuss and support some aspect of the arts.

34. Leslie Cope Cornford (1867–1927), later a biographer of Henley.

35. Henley began editing the *Scots Observer* in 1889. In December 1890, it became the *National Observer* and moved from Edinburgh to London. Its writers included J. M. Barrie, Leslie Cornford, Hardy, Kipling, Andrew Lang, Alice Meynell, R. L. Stevenson, Swinburne, Francis Watt, H. G. Wells, and WBY. The paper ceased publication in 1894 and Henley became editor of the *New Review*.

36. WBY published a total of twenty poems, twelve essays, and eight stories in Henley's journals, *The Scots Observer/The National Observer* (1889–94), and then the *New Review* (1895–97).

37. Henley received Kipling's *Barrack Room Ballads* in manuscript form in 1890 and many of these were published in the *Scots Observer* that year. Shaw decided not to contribute further because of Henley's habit of making revisions. The two poems for which there is evidence of Henley's revisions are limited to spelling and punctuation except for one likely emendation of word order ('Tell us it then' for 'Tell it us then' ('A Faery Song', l. 12), but WBY probably saw proofs and he let the changes stand in book publication. See: 'A Faery Song' *VPoems* 115–16 and George Bornstein, ed., *The Early Poetry. Volume II . . . Manuscript Materials* (Ithaca: Cornell University Press, 1994), pp. xxxiii, 290, and 'Into the Twilight' *VPoems* 147–48, and Carolyn Holdsworth, ed., *The Wind Among the Reeds: Manuscript Materials* (Ithaca: Cornell University Press, 1993), pp. xix, 54–55.

38. For Wilde, see Background Notes on Writers, p. 538.
39. For Pater, see Background Notes on Writers, p. 536.
40. The firm was Cassell & Company (Richard Ellmann, *Oscar Wilde* [1988], pp. 291–93). JBY's publisher friend, C. Elkin Mathews, was not with Cassell & Company but might have heard and retold the story.
41. Velásquez, Diego (1599–1660). Naturalistic painter of the Spanish court. Stevenson's book is *The Art of Velásquez* (London: G. Bell and Sons, 1895), revised as *Velásquez* (London: Bell, 1899).
42. *The Wanderings of Oisin* was finished 18 November 1887 and published January 1889. 'The Decay of Lying: A Dialogue' was first published in *The Nineteenth Century,* January 1889. Wilde reviewed *The Wanderings of Oisin* in *Woman's World* (March 1889) and in the *Pall Mall Gazette* (July 1889). WBY met Wilde at Henley's in September 1888 and spent Christmas 1888 with Wilde, his wife, Constance Lloyd, a Dubliner whom he had married in 1884, and their two sons, Cyril (b. 1885) and Vyvyan (b. 1886), at their home, 16 Tite Street, Chelsea.
43. WBY is quoting accurately. 'The Decay of Lying', *The Nineteenth Century* 25 (January 1889): 48.
44. WBY published poems and essays in two American papers, the *Boston Pilot* and the *Providence Sunday Journal,* 1887–92. See *Letters to the New Island,* ed. George Bornstein and Hugh Witemeyer, vol. 7 of the *Collected Works* of W. B. Yeats (New York: Macmillan, 1989). The *Boston Pilot* paid from £1 3s. to £4 per article.
45. Sir William Robert Wills Wilde (1815–76), Irish physician, who developed a reputation as an oculist and ear specialist in Dublin. He founded a hospital in 1844, and was made editor of the *Dublin Journal of Medical Science* in 1845. He was knighted for his work as Medical Commissioner for the Irish census (1841) in 1864 and was also the author of books on Irish antiquities.
46. Lady Jane Francesca Wilde (1826–96), Irish writer of poetry and prose under the pseudonym of 'Speranza' for the *Nation* from 1845 until its suppression in 1848. She admitted to writing 'Jacta alea est', an article considered seditious because it advocated the taking up of arms by young Irishmen. She married Sir William Wilde in 1851 and moved to London with her sons, William and Oscar, after his death in 1876. Lady Wilde continued to hold salons in London, as she had in Dublin, which the Yeatses attended. She died during her son's imprisonment. Among her books are *Poems* (1864), *Ancient Legends of Ireland* (1887), and *Ancient Cures* (1890). The last was reviewed by WBY in the *Scots Observer* (1 March 1890) (UP1 169–73).

47. Wilde's *A House of Pomegranates* (London: Osgood, 1891) is dedicated to Constance Mary Wilde, his wife; 'The Young King' to 'Margaret Lady Brooke' (the Ranee of Sarawak); 'The Birthday of the Infanta' to 'Mrs. William H. Grenfell of Taplow Court' (Lady Desborough); 'The Fisherman and His Soul' to 'H.S.H. Alice, Princess of Monaco'; 'The Star-Child' to 'Miss Margot Tennant' (Mrs. Asquith).

48. WBY probably knew of Cellini's dedication to Michelangelo, and of his boisterous and combative life, through the translation (1888) of his autobiography by John Addington Symonds. WBY later owned a copy of *The Life of Benvenuto Cellini* (London: Macmillan, 1923).

49. For Morris, see Background Notes on Writers, p. 535.

50. Dante Gabriel Rossetti, *Proserpine* (1872), for which Mrs. Morris, neé Jane Burden, was the model. Proserpine is shown as Empress of Hades, holding the pomegranate of which she has eaten one grain. Rossetti made eight versions and replicas, including those in the Tate Gallery, London (1877; oil, 125 cm. x 61 cm., no. 5064) and the Birmingham City Museum and Art Gallery (no. 7'27). At Morris's home, WBY could have seen a pastel and black chalk study (97 cm. x 46 cm., titled *Proserpina Imperatrix*) and/or a small early replica in ink (22 cm. x 11 cm., titled *Proserpine*), both of which Mrs. Morris received from Rossetti. See Virginia Surtess, *The Paintings and Drawings of Dante Gabriel Rossetti (1828–1882): A Catalogue Raisonné* (Oxford: Clarendon Press, 1981), catalogue no. 233 (plate 331), replicas 1–3 and no. 233A.

51. William Pollexfen.

52. George Frederick Watts, *Portrait of William Morris* (1870; oil, 65 cm. x 52 cm., National Portrait Gallery, London, no. 078). Illustrated in *National Portrait Gallery, G. F. Watts: The Hall of Fame: Portraits of his Famous Contemporaries* (London: HMSO, 1975), plate 45. Elizabeth Bergmann Loizeaux has pointed out, in her *Yeats and the Visual Arts* (New Brunswick: Rutgers University Press, 1986), p. 213 n. 5, that this comparison of Titian and Watts echoes that in Charles Ricketts's *The Prado and Its Masterpieces* (New York: Dutton, 1903), p. 147, a book WBY and Charles Shannon had discussed over dinner in 1904.

53. See 'Irish Witch Doctors' (essay, 1900), UP2 227–28 and 'The Queen and the Fool' (first published as 'The Fool of Faery', 1901), *The Celtic Twilight* (1902), Myth 112–16.

54. *Hamlet*, V.ii.298.

55. Morris, *The Earthly Paradise* (1868–70), 'An Apology', l. 7.

56. May Morris. Morris's daughter Mary (1862–1938). Lily Yeats

learned embroidery from May Morris, who had been taught by her father, and worked for her, 1888–94. The family welcomed the money, but May was a demanding employer and it was a difficult time for Lily who, with Ellen Wright, did the bedspread and hanging designed by May for the 1893 Exhibition. See Murphy, *Family Secrets,* 65–77. For a photograph of the elaborate embroidery, see Peter Davey, *Arts and Crafts Architecture* (London: Phaidon, 1995), p. 35.

57. Morris's praise of the *Wanderings of Oisin* never did manifest itself in *Commonweal,* the paper of the Socialist League.

58. D—— is George Bernard Shaw; WBY wrote 'G' in a manuscript version. Shaw joined the Fabian Society (of non-revolutionary socialists) when it was founded in 1884. Hyndman's Social Democratic Federation was founded in 1881, formed largely from London radical clubs, the first important socialist body in England. See Shaw's *Fabian Essays in Socialism* (London, New York: W. Scott, 1889).

59. 'Light on the goal and darkness, on the way,/Light all through night and darkness all through day', Swinburne's 'Tiresias' in *Songs Before Sunrise, the Complete Works of Algernon Charles Swinburne,* ed. Edmund Gosse and T. J. Wise (London: Heinemann, 1925), II 240.

60. The uncle is William Bernard Shaw (Uncle Barney). Michael Holroyd, *Bernard Shaw, v I: 1856–98, The Search for Love* (London: Chatto & Windus, 1988), pp. 7–8.

61. James Tochatti, a tailoring worker and an active propagandist in the Hammersmith Branch of the Socialist League.

62. Untraced.

63. Great Russell Street, Bloomsbury, London. It housed the British Library until 1997.

64. *Fairy and Folk Tales of the Irish Peasantry* (London: Walter Scott, 1888), a volume in the Camelot series, edited by Ernest Rhys, who is mentioned just below as 'Mr. E.'

65. *Representative Irish Tales* (New York: G. P. Putnam's Sons, 1891), a two-volume edition published in the Knickerbocker Nuggets series.

66. Ernest Rhys.

67. From the tomb of Mausolus, ruler of Caria, c. 353 B.C. Sir C. Newton excavated it in 1857 and was responsible for bringing to the British Museum the statues of Mausolus and Artemisia, who was his sister, wife, widow, and successor. See also p. 133, ll. 20–22 for mention of the tomb's bas-relief figures of a battle of Greeks and Amazons, also in the British Museum. For illustrations, see Salomon Reinach, *Apollo: An Illustrated Manual of the History of*

Art throughout the Ages, tr. Florence Simmonds (1904; rpt. London: Heinemann, 1907), O'Shea no. 1734, figs. 88 and 89.

68. In *Parzival,* a Middle High German epic poem of the first decade of the thirteenth century, Wolfram von Eschenbach (c. 1170–c. 1220) reveals indirectly what little is known of his life, including the fact that he was a poor nobleman dependent on patronage.

69. Untraced.

70. Hesiod, 'Hymn to Delian Apollo', verses 168–73, *The Homeric Hymns and Homerica* (London: Heinemann, Loeb Classical Library, rev. edn., 1936), 337. The Greek island Chios has associations with Homer as one of the seven places that claimed to be his birthplace; it was famed for its school of epic poets known as the Homeridae. See note 30, p. 512 and Mem 206 n. 2.

71. Untraced.

72. To wander endlessly, alienated from the land. Genesis 4: 11–12.

73. Romance by Morris (1896). See WBY's review (1896; UP1 418–20) and also his essay on Morris, 'The Happiest of the Poets' (1903; E&I 53–64).

74. Leader of a band of mercenaries common in Europe between the fourteenth and sixteenth centuries.

75. Jacques-Louis David, *The Coronation (Le Sacre)* (also known as *The Coronation of Josephine* and *The Coronation of Josephine and Napoleon*) (1805–07), oil, 6.10 m. x 9.31 m., Louvre, Paris; illus. Anita Brookner, *Jacques-Louis David* (London: Chatto & Windus, 1980), plate 95. It shows Napoleon wearing a crimson velvet imperial mantle with a wreath of gold laurel leaves on his head, although in fact he had already placed the crown of Charlemagne on his own head. Ronald Schuchard quotes WBY telling Mabel Dickinson in June 1908: 'I find the things that delight me this year at the Louvre are the big classic pictures by David. . . .' ('Yeats, Titian and the New French Paintings' in *Yeats the European,* p. 152).

76. 'The Lake Isle of Innisfree' (1890) P 39.

77. The Royal Courts of Justice (built 1874–82), Strand, London WC2, designed by George Edmund Street (1823–81); it has been described as 'the last great Gothic public building in London, known by its detractors as "the grave of modern Gothic", although the Great Hall and the Strand façade are triumphs' (Edward Jones and Christopher Woodward, *A Guide to the Architecture of London* [London: Weidenfeld and Nicolson, 1983], p. 227; illus. plate K106d).

78. The London publisher Alfred Nutt paid WBY to copy, at the Bodleian Library, Oxford, in August 1889, a 1592 English translation of a fifteenth-century Italian prose allegory by Francesco

Colonna, *Hypnerotomachia,* Book I, which WBY described in a letter to John O'Leary as 'dull old allegory about love' (CL1 180; with standard spelling). In August 1888, also at the Bodleian Library, WBY had transcribed part of Caxton's 1484 edition of Aesop's *Fables,* with those of Avian, Alfonso, and Poggio, for the same publisher.

79. Shakespeare, *Coriolanus,* IV.v.41–45.

80. Only a few of John Trivett Nettleship's early drawings (c. 1870) are extant. Five sketch drawings in a manner generally reminiscent of Blake are in the collection of the University of Reading (*W. B. Yeats: Images of a Poet,* ed. D. J. Gordon [Manchester: Manchester University Press, 1961], catalogue nos. 202–206, plates 27 and 28). WBY owned a reproduction of a small, highly detailed allegorical drawing, 'Madness' (Summer 1870) with elaborate commentary added later (24 April 1890) by the artist. For another early design, 'God creating Evil', see note 79 below.

81. In *Reveries* (p. 67 above), WBY attributed the praise to Dante Gabriel Rossetti, but in a copy of *The Countess Cathleen* (1892) given to John Quinn in 1904 (for which Nettleship designed the frontispiece of Cuchulain fighting the waves), he wrote, 'Nettleship who made this rather disappointing picture might have been a great imaginative artist. Browning once in a fit of enthusiasm said a design of his of "God creating Evil" was "the most sublime conception of ancient or modern art" ' (Wade 25). William M. Murphy, citing JBY's unpublished letters and memoirs, notes that the design was admired by JBY, Rossetti, 'and many others' and that Edward Burne-Jones thought well of Nettleship (*Prodigal Father* 60, 69). 'God Creating Evil' is not extant, but D. J. Gordon has suggested (*Images of a Poet,* p. 93, and catalogue no. 213) that it is identical with 'God with eyes turned inward upon his own glory', reproduced in Thomas Wright, *Life of John Payne* (London: Unwin, 1919), plate facing p. 30.

82. In April 1890, WBY was actively planning (and perhaps writing) an illustrated article on Nettleship's designs for the *Art Review,* edited by a Scottish political economist, James Mavor (1854–1925), but that journal ceased publication two months later (CL1 211, 215 and nn. 1–2). No manuscript is extant.

83. See note 7 above.

84. In the manuscript version, WBY had continued Nettleship's remarks: 'and on another day "My lion pictures are my raison d'être" ' (NLI Ms. 30,471, fol. 68).

85. Edwin John Ellis (1848–1916). English poet, painter, and critic; JBY's friend, who later collaborated with WBY on the three-

volume annotated and illustrated edition *The Works of Blake, Poetic, Symbolic and Critical* (1893).

86. Alexander John Ellis (1814–90). English philologist and mathematician, father of the poet Edwin.

87. From 'To Earth, Mother of All', in Ellis's *Fate in Arcadia and Other Poems* (London: Ward and Downey, 1892), 105.

88. WBY may have been thinking of 'Fate in Arcadia', the dramatic title poem of *Fate in Arcadia and Other Poems* (see CL1 133–36).

89. From 'Himself', *Fate in Arcadia and Other Poems*, 158–63. See also WBY's review of *Fate in Arcadia* (1892; UP1 234–37).

90. Blake, 'To the Jews' (ll. 1–4), preface to ch. 2 of *Jerusalem* (1804–1820).

91. Blake belonged to the Great Eastcheap Swedenborgian Society, and, about 1789, annotated Swedenborg's *Wisdom of Angels Concerning Divine Love and Divine Wisdom,* and, in 1790, *Wisdom of Angels Concerning Divine Providence.* For WBY's views of Blake's relationship to Swedenborg, see the 'Introduction' (1893, rev. 1905) to his edition of the *Poems of William Blake* P&I 90.

92. John Linnell (1821–1906), son of Blake's patron. See CL1 201–2.

93. WBY's complete set of Blake's seven unfinished engravings for Dante's *Inferno* (1827; approx. 24 cm. x 34 cm.) was probably from the second commercial printing of fifty copies. The set was a gift, c. 1892, from John Linnell Jr. or the Linnell family and is now in the collection of Anne Yeats. For illustrations, see Albert S. Roe, *Blake's Illustrations to the Divine Comedy* (Princeton: Princeton University Press, 1953) (10E, 41E, 42E, 51E, 53E, 58E, 65E); David Bindman, *The Complete Graphic Works of William Blake* (London: Thames and Hudson, 1978), (647–53); and Robert N. Essick, *William Blake: Printmaker* (Princeton: Princeton University Press, 1980), pp. 250–54 and plates 230–34.

94. A bible associated with a martyr, whose faith has been tested by suffering, is assumed to have special potency. The cardinal virtues are the four upon which all the moral virtues turn: wisdom, temperance, courage, justice. The clergyman and jockey are untraced.

95. Rhymers' Club. A club formed by WBY, Ernest Rhys, and T. W. Rolleston, an open forum with no officers or rules. Karl Beckson ('Yeats and the Rhymers' Club', *Yeats Studies* 1 [1971], 22, 41) says the club was founded in early 1890 and last met in 1896. WBY mentions most of the membership; George Arthur Greene and Aubrey Beardsley are possible additions. The Rhymers published two books collectively: *The Book of the Rhymers'*

Club (London: Mathews, 1892) and *The Second Book of the Rhymers' Club* (London: Mathews and Lane, 1894). See WBY, 'Modern Poetry: A Broadcast' (1936) LE 89–92.

96. James Joyce.
97. Lionel Johnson, Herbert Horne, Selwyn Image, and Arthur Mackmurdo lived at 20 Fitzroy Street, Bloomsbury, London.
98. Herbert Horne, *Alessandro Filipepi, commonly called Sandro Botticelli, painter of Florence* (London: G. Bell and Sons, 1908).
99. Keats, 'Sleep and Poetry' (1817), 196–99.
100. See note 24 above.
101. WBY wrote in *Per Amica Silentia Lunae* (1918): 'The other self, the anti-self or the antithetical self, as one may choose to name it, comes but to those who are no longer deceived, whose passion is reality' (*LE* 8).
102. For the sexton's daughter who gave writing lessons, see note 65, p. 424. Aristophanes, *The Birds* (414 B.C.).
103. Shelley, 'Prince Athanase' (1817).
104. Shelley, *Hellas* (1822), ll. 152–85.
105. Madame Helena Petrovna Blavatsky (1831–91). She co-founded the Theosophical Society in New York in 1875 with Colonel H. S. Olcott (1832–1907). She wrote *Isis Unveiled* (1877) and *The Secret Doctrine* (1888), came to London in 1884 and founded a Blavatsky lodge there in 1887. WBY called on her with a letter of introduction from his old friend Charles Johnston, who married her niece in 1888. She claimed that she was given secret knowledge from her masters in Tibet, especially Koot-Hoomi and Morya. This secret doctrine was to be passed on from the Theosophical Society to the world so that all would come closer to a more total spirituality.
106. Founded in 1882 to investigate the phenonema that most of science rejected. It investigated Madame Blavatsky's claims and, in its *Proceedings* 3 (December 1885), recorded the evidence found against her, which did not diminish her popularity. WBY was a member of the Theosophical Society from 1887–1890; see note 11 below.
107. Sarah Purser (1848–1943), whose brother Louis Purser was a professor at the Medical School, Trinity College, Dublin.
108. Mabel Collins (1851–1927), author of the occult book *Light on the Path* (London: Reeves and Turner, 1885). In February 1889, Madame Blavatsky expelled her, along with T. B. Harbottle, President of the lodge, for flirtation. She was married to Keningale Robert Cook at the time. See WBY's letter to Katharine Tynan, 21 April 1889 (CL1 162).
109. Untraced.

110. See the interview with WBY in the *Irish Theosophist*, 15 October 1893 (UP1 298–302). WBY recalls there many of the same stories about Madame Blavatsky that he used in 'Four Years'.

111. Shelley, *Hellas* (1822), ll. 162–65.

112. In *Trembling* 1922, WBY had here identified the source as 'that essay on magic, which Sibley, the eighteenth-century astrologer, had bound up with his big book upon astrology' (68; rev. in 1926 to the present reading). The book by Ebenezer Sibly (not Sibley) (1751–1800) is *A New and Complete Illustration of the Celestial Science of Astrology; or, The Art of Foretelling Future Events and Contingencies, by the Aspects, Positions, and Influences of the Heavenly Bodies* (London, 1784–88) (O'Shea no. 1912; without title-page). One seventeenth-century source might be Joseph Glanvill (or Glanvil) (1636–80), English neo-Platonist philosopher and divine, who attacked scholastic philosophy and defended the belief in the pre-existence of souls and in witchcraft and apparitions, in his *Saducismus Triumphatus* (1681; 4th ed., 1726, O'Shea no. 750).

113. In November 1890, WBY was asked to resign from the Esoteric Section of the Theosophical Society. See his letter to John O'Leary, November 1890, CL1 234–35.

114. The Celtic Movement, broadly considered, begins in the mid-eighteenth century and includes the interest in and promotion of Irish history, language, sports, folklore, myth, and literature—all under the aspect of various forms of nationalism. The Irish Literary Revival of the last quarter of the nineteenth century into the 1920s is an expression of the same impulses and at the core of much of what WBY relates here.

115. Samuel Liddell (MacGregor) Mathers (1854–1918). English occultist, who took the name of MacGregor in honor of an ancestor who fought for James IV of Scotland. WBY met him in London sometime before 1890. Mathers had become a Mason in 1877 and was admitted to the Societas Rosicruciana in Anglia, where he met William K. Woodman and Dr. Wynn Westcott with whom he founded the Isis-Urania Temple of the Hermetic Order of the Golden Dawn in 1888. Woodman died in 1890, and Mathers soon had control of the Golden Dawn. He married Moina Bergson and received the support of her friend Miss Annie Horniman, a member of the Golden Dawn, who convinced her father to employ Mathers as curator of his museum at Forest Hill. Mathers lost this position in 1891, but received an allowance from Annie Horniman until 1896. Mathers moved with his wife to Paris on 21 May 1892 and opened the Ahathoor Temple. His behavior became increasingly eccentric, as WBY makes clear on

pp. 257–59 below. In April 1900, Mathers was expelled from the Golden Dawn. The break in WBY's friendship with Mathers occurred because of the controversy that resulted in Mathers's expulsion. They were never really reconciled. WBY remembered him in the character of Maclagan in *The Speckled Bird* (1896–c. 1902), aspects of the character or mask of Michael Robartes, and as Mathers himself in the poem 'All Souls' Night' (P 227).

116. Knorr von Rosenroth, *Kabbala Denudata* (1677), translated by MacGregor Mathers in 1887 (London: G. Redway), was the basis for some rituals of the Golden Dawn.

117. WBY was initiated into the Hermetic Students of the Golden Dawn on 7 March 1890 (not 'May or June 1887'). The Isis-Urania Temple No. 3 of the Order of the Golden Dawn was founded in London in 1888, using a system of grades with progressive initiations, and secrecy. WBY became a member of the inner order in 1893, and his order name was *Demon Est Deus Inversus,* or 'a demon is an inverted god.' Other members of the Golden Dawn included Florence Farr, Annie Horniman, WBY's uncle George Pollexfen, and Maud Gonne for a short time. For more information on the founding of the Golden Dawn and WBY's membership, see Harper, *Yeats's Golden Dawn;* Ellic Howe, *The Magicians of the Golden Dawn: A Documentary History of a Magical Order, 1887–1923* (London: Routledge & Kegan Paul, 1972); John Kelly, CL1 appendix 'The Order of the Golden Dawn', 486–88; and Francis King, *Ritual Magic in England: 1887 to the Present Day* (London: Spearman, 1970).
WBY'S NOTE
(first publ. July 1923 in the *Criterion* and the *Dial;* this note is printed at the end of the book in *Auto* 1926, the 1937–36 page proofs, and *Auto* 1955 [575–76]; *Auto* 1955 [183] adds a cross-reference note ['See Note, p. 575.'] at the end of the sentence):

'The Hermetic Students' was founded by MacGregor Mathers, a Dr. Woodman, and Dr. Wynn Westcott, the London Coroner. Notes and general instructions were given to MacGregor Mathers by a man whose name I am unable to discover,ᵃ and of whom the only survivor from that time, Mrs. MacGregor Mathers, can tell me nothing except that he was probably introduced to her husband by Kenneth Mackenzie, the reputed instructor in magic of Bulwer Lytton, that he lived in France and was of Scottish descent, that he was associated with others of like studies, that he was known to her by a Latin motto, that he had supernormal powers. She adds, 'I was an enthusiastic beginner and certainly greatly impressed'.

Upon this link with an unknown past, she says, and upon her husband's and her own clairvoyance, sought at hours and upon days chosen by the unknown man, the rituals and teachings of the society were established. Dr. Wynn Westcott did receive certain letters which showed knowledge of or interest in the society, but the writers did not, she considers, belong to it, nor were they among its founders, but were connected, she believes, with Continental Freemasonry. Dr. Wynn Westcott and MacGregor Mathers had, however, a bitter quarrel arising out of these things, and Dr. Wynn Westcott claimed an authority based upon the letters. The foundation of this society, which took place some forty years ago, remains almost as obscure as that of some ancient religion. I am sorry to have shed so little light upon a matter which has importance, because in several countries men who have come into possession of its rituals claim, without offering proof, authority from German or Austrian Rosicrucians. I add, however, that I am confident from internal evidence that the rituals, as I knew them, were in substance ancient though never so in language unless some ancient text was incorporated. There was a little that I thought obvious and melodramatic, and it was precisely in this little, I am told, that they resembled Masonic rituals, but much that I thought beautiful and profound. I do not know what I would think if I were to hear them now for the first time, for I cannot judge what moved me in my youth.

I give these few facts about the origin of 'The Hermetic Students' with Mrs. Mathers' permission, but I have not submitted to her my account of her husband because I did not think it right to ask her either to condemn or to accept my statements. She was shocked at the account in the first edition,[b] and apart from one or two errors of fact I have omitted nothing of it, though I have added new passages. Though he did not show me the truth, he did what he professed, and showed me a way to it, and I am grateful, but I think that I must describe notable faults of temper and of mind, that fables may not grow. If I found myself a director of men's consciences, or becoming any kind of idealized figure in their minds, I would, or I fancy that I would, display or even exaggerate my frailties. All creation is from conflict, whether with our own mind or with that of others, and the historian who dreams of bloodless victory wrongs the wounded veterans. My connection with 'The Hermetic Students' ended amid quarrels[c] caused by men, otherwise worthy, who claimed a Rosicrucian sanction for their own fantasies, and I add, to prevent needless correspondence, that I am not now a member of a Cabbalistic society.

[a]The Golden Dawn started with mystical rituals translated by Westcott from an ancient cypher manuscript found by Reverend A. F. A. Woodford in 1884, although much controversy has surrounded Westcott's claims.

[b]Mina, later Moina, Bergson Mathers (1865–1928) wrote WBY three letters (dated 5 January, 12 January, and 4 February 1924) on her negative reaction to the account of her husband, MacGregor Mathers, in the first edition of *The Trembling of the Veil* (1922). (LTWBY 446–49, 451)

[c]Westcott claimed to have been authorized by Fräulein Sprengel, a German Rosicrucian whose name and address were in the cypher manuscript, to found the English section of 'Die Goldene Dämmerung', a German occult order. Mathers increasingly controlled the society, that is, the London Temple, even after his departure to Paris in 1892. Westcott resigned in March 1897 after his employers were informed of his membership, probably through Mathers. Mathers claimed that the original letters between Fräulein Sprengel and Westcott were forgeries; an inquiry proceeded, and Mathers refused to cooperate, sending Aleister Crowley to seize the ceremonial Vault of the Second Order (which he had created in 1891). WBY opposed this effort and Mathers was expelled on 21 April 1900. WBY had further difficulties with the society's structure (Florence Farr had run the Isis-Urania Temple on Mathers's instruction after Westcott's resignation), and, siding with Annie Horniman on this issue, lost in a vote held at a meeting in February 1901. In 1903, he seceded with other members with Dr. R. W. Felkin to create the Amoun Temple of the Stella Matutina, but Dr. Felkin immigrated to New Zealand in 1916 and the Stella Matutina fell apart.

118. Rev. W. A. Ayton.

119. WBY, in a note to FFT (1888), refers to salamanders as elemental fire spirits, citing Paracelsus (*P&I* 233 nn.35, 35b).

120. 24 October 1889, transcribed in Mem 281 ('Occult Notes and Diary, Etc.' NLI Ms. 13,570).

121. The Royal Irish Academy is a Dublin intellectual society founded in 1785.

122. Untraced. Laurence Binyon gives an analogous fable in Chinese art: 'A great artist painted a dragon upon a temple wall, and as he put the final touch to it, the dragon, too instinct with life, soared crashing through the roof and left an empty space' (*Painting in the Far East: An Introduction to the History of Pictorial*

Art in Asia especially China and Japan [London: Edward Arnold, 1908], p. 9).

123. The title character of Goethe's drama (1808–1832), a magician who makes a pact with Satan.

124. See p. 372 below and PASL (1918) LE 10.

125. Anglo-Irish conservative association. Its aims were the opposite of the Irish republican Fenian Brotherhood.

126. WBY first recorded the phrase 'Unity of Being' in an automatic writing session, 3 September 1918. The next year he used the phrase in 'If I were Four-and-Twenty' (LE 46), and then, on 13 October 1919, his wife and he were instructed in an automatic writing session to read Dante's *Il Convito* (*Il Convivio*) (see Harper, *Making of* A Vision, II, 78, 73, 329). Subsequently, he linked 'Unity of Being' with *Il Convito*, beginning in November 1919 with 'A People's Theatre' (Ex 250) and then, in 1921, here and pp. 200 and 227 below.

George Bornstein suggests that WBY conflated two passages from Dante's *Convito* (treatise III, chs. viii and xv); George M. Harper and Walter K. Hood in V(1925)CE (note to p. 18, ll. 12–13) add a third passage (treatise IV, ch. xxv). *The Convivio of Dante Alighieri*, tr. Philip H. Wicksteed, Temple Classics (1903; repr. London: Dent, 1909) (O'Shea no. 467; Mrs. Yeats's copy), pp. 178, 219–20, 358. See Bornstein, 'Yeats's Romantic Dante', *Colby Library Quarterly*, 15 (1979), 107; collected in his *Poetic Remaking: The Art of Browning, Yeats, and Pound* (University Park: Pennsylvania State University Press, 1988), p. 89. See also the Background Notes on Writers, p. 533.

127. Yeats, 'The Hawk' (1916), ll. 1–6 P 149.

128. For the tombs of Mausolus and Artemisia, see page 447 note 67 above.

129. Untraced.

130. William Congreve (1670–1729), 'Mr. Congreve to Mr. Dennis. Concerning Humour in Comedy. A Letter' (1695), *Complete Works*, ed. Montague Summer (London: Nonesuch Press, 1923), III, 166.

131. Yeats, 'The Second Coming' (1920), ll. 1–8 P 187.

THE TREMBLING OF THE VEIL.
BOOK II. IRELAND AFTER PARNELL

1. For Charles Stewart Parnell, Irish Home Rule parliamentary leader, see note 70 below. 'After Parnell' means after his fall from power and premature death in October 1891. For most historians, it means after the virtual end of any realistic possibility for a

constitutional, non-violent settlement of 'The Irish Question', the status of Ireland in relation to English power. For WBY, it also means after the exhaustion of political energy and rhetoric, making room for cultural nationalism.

2. Introduction to *Representative Irish Tales* (1891): 'Meanwhile a true literary consciousness—national to the centre—seems gradually forming out of all this—disguising and prettifying, this penumbra of half-culture. We are preparing likely enough for a new Irish literary movement—like that of '48—that will show itself at the first lull in this storm of politics' (P&I 15–16).

3. Robert Welch suggests that this image, which also is found on p. 104:36 above, is an echo of Standish James O'Grady's *Toryism and Tory Democracy* (1886) (*Oxford Companion to Irish Literature* [Oxford: Clarendon Press, 1996], p. 434).

4. The preliminary meeting of the Irish Literary Society / National Literary Society was held at the Yeats home, 3 Blenheim Road, Bedford Park, on 28 December 1891, and the Irish Literary Society, London, was founded with Sir Charles Gavan Duffy as President, at the Caledonian Hotel, Adelphi, 12 May 1892. WBY had written to Rolleston to express his regrets: 'I am going to Dublin to do my best to found there a society of like purpose and nature' (dated 10 May 1892, CL1 294). A first meeting was held in Dublin on 24 May 1892 to discuss setting up a National Literary Society. Douglas Hyde became its first president on 18 August 1892; WBY was one of its vice presidents, and O'Leary served on the council. The New Irish Library, as it came to be known, was undertaken by both societies in 1892.

5. William Patrick Ryan, *The Irish Literary Revival: Its History, Pioneers and Possibilities* (London: privately published, 1894). Ryan had attended the preliminary meeting at WBY's home on 28 December 1891.

6. The initial meeting discussing the formation of the National Literary Society, Dublin, occurred quickly, at the Wicklow Hotel, Dublin, on 24 May 1892. On 9 June 1892, a public meeting was held in the Small Concert Room, the Rotunda, Dublin, at which WBY introduced a resolution 'to found a National Literary Society'.

7. T. Fisher Unwin (1848–1935) published WBY's *John Sherman and Dhoya* (1891) as part of the 'Pseudonym Library', *Irish Fairy Tales* (1892, edited by WBY), as part of the 'Children's Library', *The Countess Cathleen and Various Legends and Lyrics* (September 1892), as part of the 'Cameo Series', *The Wanderings of Oisin* (re-issued May 1892), *The Land of Heart's Desire* (April 1894), and *Poems* (1895). Later, after WBY had shifted,

first to Lawrence and Bullen for *The Secret Rose* (1897) and then to Elkin Matthews for *The Tables of the Law* and *The Adoration of the Magi* (1897) and *The Wind Among the Reeds* (1899), Unwin published *Literary Ideals in Ireland* (1899, by WBY, John Eglinton, A.E., and W. Larminie), and *Samhain* (1901–8, edited by WBY, nos. 1–4, 7).

8. In 1892, WBY had arranged with Fisher Unwin, through Garnett, for the English publication of the projected New Irish Library series. Sir Charles Gavan Duffy became interested in the project, and, despite vigorous efforts, as well as appeals to Garnett, WBY lost the editorship of the series to Duffy. The man that he had told about the plan was T. W. Rolleston, and he thought that Rolleston 'betrayed me' (Mem 81–82).

9. *Red Hugh's Captivity* (London: Ward and Downey, 1889), re-issued as *The Flight of the Eagle* (London: Lawrence and Bullen, 1897). WBY reviewed it for the *Bookman* (August 1897) as 'a book rather wild, rather too speculative, but forestalling later research' (UP2 47–51).

10. For the Irish nationalist poet Thomas Davis see note 199, p. 435 above.

11. Shelley's active and informed interest in contemporary science included fascination with hot-air balloons and the possibilities of air travel and exploration. In August 1812, he wrote a sonnet, 'To a Balloon laden with *Knowledge*': 'Bright ball of flame that through the gloom of even / silently takest thine aethereal way. . . .' See *The Complete Poetical Works of Percy Bysshe Shelley*, ed. Neville Rogers (Oxford: Clarendon, 1972), I, 118.

12. In the earlier published version, WBY had commented, 'Dr. Sigerson who has picked a quarrel with me and of whom I shall say nothing that he may not pick another' (Trembling 1922 86).

13. In 1867, the franchise had been extended to all urban adult male householders, rescinding the requirement in the Municipal Corporations (Ireland) Act of 1840 for paying taxes on property worth at least £10 per annum.

14. WBY's friend and artistic mentor, Charles Ricketts, admired *The Lady with the Fan* by Velásquez (1599–1660) (Wallace Collection, London), illus. Joseph Darracott, *The World of Charles Ricketts* (London: Eyre Methuen, 1980), p. 97; another example is *Philip IV* ('*The Silver Philip*') in the National Gallery, London (no. 1129), illus. Maurice Sérullaz, *Velázquez* (New York: Abrams, 1978), color plate 19. For an example of El Greco (1548?–1614?; Greek born), the leading exponent of Spanish mysticism in painting, see *St. Jerome as a Cardinal* (1571–79) in the National Gallery, London (no. 1122), illus. Leo Bronstein,

El Greco (New York: Abrams, 1950), p. 47.

15. Ben Jonson, *The Forest* (1616), ix, 'To Celia,' l. 1.

16. Collection of poems and ballads originally published in the *Nation,* printed by James Duffy in 1843, with a second part in 1844, and an enlarged edition in 1845.

17. *The Nation* (1842–48; 2nd series, 1849–96).

18. The Danish Viking raids on Ireland date from 795 to 1014.

19. Presumably John Synge, but James Joyce could be added.

20. The biblical parable of bees and honey in the carcase of a lion; sweetness and light coming from terror and destruction. Judges 14: 5–18.

21. The last stanza of 'Another song of a Fool' (1919) P 170.

22. Thomas Moore began to publish his *Irish Melodies* in 1807. The music for them was arranged by Sir John Stevenson from what were supposed to be old Irish tunes. These songs made both Moore's reputation and his fortune, although the latter was not to last. WBY would have preferred the same to be true of the former, but he did once suggest that the *Melodies* be included as a necessary book in small local libraries (*United Ireland* [3 October 1891] UP1 208).

23. Thomas Moore's popular 'Indian' verse narratives, *Lalla Rookh: An Oriental Romance* (1817).

24. *The Poets of Ireland: A Biographical Dictionary* (1892–93; enlarged 2nd ed., 1912) by David James O'Donoghue (not O'Donohue) (1866–1917), London-born Irish literary historian.

25. In late 1892, WBY briefly shared rooms with John O'Leary at Lonsdale House, St. Lawrence Road, Clontarf, Dublin. At the end of the year, he returned to London, where he was still living at home in Bedford Park.

26. John O'Leary served on the twenty-member council of the National Literary Society, Dublin, but Douglas Hyde was elected its president; WBY had thought O'Leary would be elected (CL1 305).

27. JBY painted two oil portraits of O'Leary, the first in 1892 and the second in 1904, which is in the National Gallery of Ireland, Dublin.

28. With the strength and rectitude of a stoic; WBY may be thinking of Shakespeare's *Julius Caesar* (1599).

29. The change explored in *The Possessed* (1870–72) by the Russian novelist Feodor Dostoievsky (1821–81) is from the politics of 'the highest motive' to various kinds of opportunism.

30. Gladstone was converted to the concept of Home Rule for Ireland after 1882 and came into office in 1886 committed to it, but the bill was defeated. Gladstone then took the issue to the

country in the form of a general election and lost. In July 1892, the Liberals again won a majority. In February 1893, Gladstone introduced a second Home Rule bill, which was passed by the Commons, September 1893, but was rejected by the House of Lords a week later. Gladstone resigned in March 1894, and 'The Union of Hearts' was over.

31. *The Secret Rose,* published after some delay in 1897, contained seventeen stories that WBY wrote 1892–96.

32. John O'Leary's memoirs were published as *Recollections of Fenians and Fenianism* in 1896 (London: Downey). WBY reviewed it for the *Bookman* (February 1897), where, as Colton Johnson points out, 'his approach was to praise the author and ignore the work' (UP2 35–37).

33. In a passage deleted in 1926 from the first published version of *Reveries,* WBY had illustrated Taylor's ill temper by reporting a quip that 'in the words of one of his Dublin enemies, "he had never joined any party and as soon as one joined him he seceded" ' (Reveries Cuala 1916 115).

34. In 'The Oversoul', an essay of 1841, Ralph Waldo Emerson (1803–82) defines this central concept of American transcendentalism as 'that unity within which every man's particular being is contained and made one with all other.' WBY had visited Katharine Tynan at her father's farm at Clondalkin, near Maynooth, Co. Meath, in 1885.

35. 'Shun those studies in which the work that results dies with the worker' (Victoria and Albert Museum, London, Foster Bequest MSS. III, 55r, in *The Notebooks of Leonardo da Vinci,* ed. and tr. Edward MacCurdy [London: Reynal & Hitchcock, 1939; New York: Braziller, 1954], p. 80).

36. WBY, Lady Gregory, and Edward Martyn first began planning the Irish Literary Theatre in 1897; the first production was in 1899, and in 1904 the company moved into the Abbey Theatre.

37. Dominic Daly suggests this was Hyde's song *'Féach tá sinn-ne Clann na hÉireann'* (English version 'We the numerous men'), which gained wide popularity by 1889 (*The Young Douglas Hyde: The Dawn of the Irish Revolution and Renaissance 1874–1893* [Dublin: Irish University Press, 1974], pp. 97, 210 n.38).

38. Rabindranath Tagore (1861–1941); see WBY's enthusiastic introduction to Tagore's *Gitanjali (Song Offerings)* (1912) (LE 165–70).

39. Egan O'Rahilly (Aodhagán Ó Rathaille), *'Is fada liom oíche'* (c.1708), translated from the Irish by James Stephens, 'Egan O Rahilly' (after O'Rahilly), ll. 6–7, in *Reincarnations* (London: Macmillan, 1918), (O'Shea nos. 2004, 2004a), p. 35. WBY

quoted this again in his introduction to the *Oxford Book of Modern Verse* (1936) (LE 186).

40. Perhaps the blind Irish harper Turlough Carolan (1670–1738), known as 'the last of the bards'; see James Hardiman, 'Memoir of Carolan', in *Ancient Irish Minstrelsy* (1831; rpt. New York: Barnes and Noble, 1971), I, xlvii: 'He always delighted in cheerful society, and never refused the circling glass.'

41. 'Teig O'Kane (*Tadhg O Cathan*) and the Corpse' (literally translated from the Irish by Douglas Hyde), FFT (1888) 16–31.

42. For WBY's help in arranging for publication of Hyde's *Beside the Fire: A Collection of Irish Gaelic Folk Stories* (London: David Nutt [title page 1890], 1891), see CL1 112–13, 144, 185.

43. A collection of thirty-three of Hyde's poems in Irish, under his pseudonym *Craoibhín Aoibhinn: Úbhla de'n Craoibh* [Apples from the Branch] (Dublin: Gill, 1900); Lady Gregory translated eleven of them in her *Poets and Dreamers* (1903).

44. Yeats, 'At the Abbey Theatre' (1912), ll. 1, 9–14 P 96.

45. *Hamlet* I.i.143.

46. Standish James O'Grady's address 'To the Landlords of Ireland' (1886), in *Selected Essays and Passages* (Dublin: Talbot, n.d.); see notes 3 above and 70, p. 497.

47. WBY came to Dublin with Lionel Johnson in September 1893. They were planning to found a national magazine, *The Irish Review,* and lived at Florinda Place, near the Mater Misericordia Hospital. See his letters, 26 and c. 27 September 1893, CL1 362–3.

48. Lionel Johnson's poem 'The Dark Angel' (1893).

49. Lionel Johnson, 'Mystic and Cavalier' (1889), ll. 1–8, 21–24, 33–36.

50. Sir Charles Gavan Duffy (1816–1903) founded the *Nation* in 1842 with John Blake Dillon and Thomas Davis. The Young Irelanders, originally part of O'Connell's Repeal Association, broke with O'Connell and planned a rising for August 1848. Duffy was arrested on 9 July and the *Nation* was suppressed on 28 July. He started the journal again after his release in 1849, joined the Irish Tenant League, and was elected M.P. for New Ross in 1852. Duffy immigrated to Australia in 1855, became Prime Minister of Victoria in 1871, and retired in 1880 to France, whence he returned to Ireland.

51. Ellen Mary Patrick Downing (pseudonym: 'Mary of the Nation'), Irish poet (1828–69). *The New Spirit of the Nation,* ed. with an introduction by Martin MacDermott. London: Unwin / Dublin: Sealy / New York: Kennedy, 1894, xix, note.

52. *The Patriot Parliament of 1689* (London: T. Fisher Unwin, 1893), by Thomas Davis, edited by Sir Charles Gavan Duffy, was

the first volume of the New Irish Library series. It was a series of essays that had first appeared in 1843 in the *Dublin Monthly Magazine;* see WBY's August 1894 review for the *Bookman* (UP1 332–35).

53. *Heroes and Hero-Worship,* Thomas Carlyle's popular lectures of 1840, published 1841.

54. *Young Ireland: A Fragment of Irish History 1840–50* (London, New York: Cassell, Petter, Galpin, 1880) and *Four Years of Irish History 1845–1849* (London, New York: Cassell, Petter, Galpin, 1883).

55. The enemy was John Mitchel (see note 57 below). The Irish Confederation split in 1847 because Duffy wanted all classes in Ireland united against English rule and Mitchel wanted to utilize only the farmers and peasants and did not exclude the use of violence. Duffy prevailed, and Mitchel left the confederation, began the *United Irishman,* was transported on sedition charges, and later attacked Duffy in *Jail Journal.*

56. In July or August 1892. See CL1 308, 310–14, for the plans for the National Publishing Company and the New Irish Library.

57. John Mitchel (1815–75), Irish writer and nationalist. Mitchel wrote first for the *Nation,* the Young Ireland journal, after meeting Davis and Duffy in Dublin. He founded *United Irishman* in 1848, was arrested that year, tried for treason-felony, and sent to Bermuda, South Africa, and Van Diemen's Land (Tasmania). He escaped to America in 1853, where he published his famous *Jail Journal, or Five Years in British Prisons* (1854), in which he attacked Sir Charles Gavan Duffy. He founded several papers in the United states and promoted pro-slavery views, for which he was imprisoned. He returned to Ireland in 1875, having been elected M.P. for Tipperary in February (an election that was declared invalid), and was re-elected in March. He died that same month at Newry.

58. Mitchel relentlessly attacked Duffy in *Jail Journal,* originally published (January–August 1854) as a serial in the *Citizen,* the paper Mitchel established in New York. Duffy quickly published the *Journal* in the *Nation* and replied in a pamphlet issued as a supplement to the paper.

59. For WBY's struggle for editorial control of the New Irish Library series, see CL1 329–36. Taylor attacked WBY in letters to the *Freeman's Journal,* 7 and 9 September 1892. WBY wrote to the *Freeman's Journal* 6, 8, and 10 September 1892 (UP1 240–44, CL1 310–14).

60. T. W. Rolleston.

61. Unwin's reader was Edward Garnett.

62. T. W. Rolleston and Douglas Hyde, but Duffy retained full control.

63. Thomas Davis's *The Patriot Parliament 1689* (1893). O'Grady's *The Bog of Stars and Other Stories and Sketches* (1895) was the second volume of the New Irish Library series. Hyde's *The Story of Early Gaelic Literature* appeared in 1895.

64. Sigmund Freud (1856–1939), Austrian neurologist, founder of psychoanalysis.

65. Maud Gonne served on the founding committee of the National Literary Society and, in the winter of 1903, lectured on behalf of the small libraries project. She established three of the seven libraries the National Literary Society succeeded in organizing.

66. WBY submitted a requested written report (CL1 357–58) to the National Literary Society; it was presented on 29 June 1893 by Count George Noble Plunkett. The 'young men', including P. J. McCall who made a motion on this topic, were dissatisfied with the subcommittee's conduct; books were sent to county societies as planned.

67. Dr. George Sigerson.

68. Charles McCarthy Teeling (d. 1922), a vice president of the Young Ireland Society; for details, see CL2 87 n.2.

69. The Rt. Hon. Joseph Michael Meade (1839–1900), who had allowed the National Literary Society to meet in the Mansion House, Dublin, in August 1892.

70. Parnell, Charles Stuart (1846–91). Irish political leader and landowner. Parnell met Isaac Butt, founder of the Home Rule Association, in 1874, and became drawn into Irish politics. He was elected M.P. for County Meath in 1875. In 1877, Parnell made the Irish Party a force within Westminster. He unofficially joined forces with the Fenians and became President of the Land League in 1879. He was M.P. for Cork and Chairman of the Home Rule Party by 1880 and worked toward the goal of home rule for ten years. Just when it seemed possible to achieve it, Captain O'Shea sued his wife for divorce and named Parnell co-respondent. The scandal meant his loss of support at home, as well as the support of Gladstone. The Irish Party split into Parnellites and anti-Parnellites. Parnell died in October 1891 trying to regain his position. See 'Mourn–And Then Onward' (1891), 'Parnell's Funeral' (1934), and 'Parnell' (1938) P 528, 279, 312.

71. Katharine O'Shea (née Wood, 1845–1921) had married Captain O'Shea in 1867, finally divorced him in 1890, and married Parnell, to whom she had been mistress for much of their acquaintance since 1880. She published *Charles Stewart Parnell: His Love Story and Political Life* in 1914.

72. Center of British administration in Ireland.
73. See note 195, p. 434.
74. When the Queen paid a state visit to Ireland, 3–26 April 1900, during the Boer War, WBY wrote a letter to the editor of the *Freeman's Journal,* 20 March 1900, urging that it was 'the duty of Irishmen, who believed that Ireland has an individual national life, to protest with as much courtesy as is compatible with vigour' (L 336).
75. Exhibitions at the Royal Hibernian Academy, Dublin.
76. WBY'S NOTE
(Added by WBY in the 1932/1936 page proofs; first publ. in Auto 1955):

> In the attack upon Fitzgibbon quoted on pages 96 and 97 Taylor made an even more imaginative use of Egypt, but I did not hear that speech. Joyce quotes a slightly different version in *Ulysses,*[a] and one of his characters calls it the greatest extempore speech ever spoken.

[a]Taylor's speech in 'Aeolus' is quoted by the character Professor MacHugh, who calls it 'the finest display of oratory I ever heard'. These speeches occurred at the Law Students' Debating Society on 24 October 1901. See also note 205, p. 436.
77. For Edward Dowden, see note 176, p. 432. A Benthamite is a utilitarian, a follower of Jeremy Bentham (1748–1832).
78. Frederick John Dick (1856–1927), who established the house in April 1891. It served as the headquarters of the Theosophical Society in Dublin until about 1897.
79. Edmund J. King.
80. Arthur Dwyer.
81. Althea Gyles (1868–1949) from Kilmurry, Co. Waterford, came to Dublin in 1889 to attend art school. By 1892, she was in London and attended the Slade School. She was a member of the Golden Dawn and WBY welcomed her designs for the covers of *The Secret Rose* (1897), *Poems* (1899 edition), and *The Wind Among the Reeds* (1899). WBY disapproved of her affair with the publisher Leonard Smithers (1861–1907). In 1900, WBY chose her poem 'Sympathy' for *A Treasury of Irish Poetry,* edited by T. W. Rolleston and Stopford Brooke. She continued to write poetry, but steadily lapsed into ill health and poverty, and died in a nursing home in 1949. See WBY's article on Althea Gyles, 'A Symbolic Artist and the Coming of Symbolic Art', *The Dome* (December 1898), repr. UP2 132–7; and Ian Fletcher, 'Poet and Designer: W. B. Yeats and Althea Gyles', *Yeats Studies,* 1 (1971) 42–79.

82. George Russell (1867–1935) and WBY met in 1884 at the Metropolitan School of Art, Dublin, and became close friends, sharing an interest in theosophy and mysticism. Russell became known as A.E., a shorthand version of an earlier pen name, Aeon, and was a major figure in the Irish Literary Renaissance, as well as a supporter of new, young writers. Russell's play *Deirdre* was produced by the Irish Literary Society in 1902. From November 1897, he was also part of the Irish Agricultural Organisation under Sir Horace Plunkett, and from 1906 until 1930, A.E. edited the group's journal, the *Irish Homestead* (retitled in 1923, *Irish Statesman*). His writings include *Homeward: Songs by the Way* (1894), *The Earth Breath and Other Poems* (1897), *The Divine Vision and Other Poems* (1904), *The Mask of Apollo and Other Stories* (1905), *Collected Poems* (1913), *The National Being: Some Thoughts on Irish Polity* (essays; 1916), *The Candle of Vision* (autobiographical essays on mysticism; 1918), and *The Avatars* (novel; 1933).

83. John Hughes (1865–1941) or Oliver Sheppard (1864–1941).

84. *Inferno,* V, 130–31, where the color drains from the cheeks of Paola and Francesca as they read the story of Lancelot's love for Guinevere, a story which WBY transposes into Dante's 'own work'.

85. *The Irish Theosophist,* first published in October 1892.

86. George Russell's first book of poems (Dublin: Whaley, 1894). WBY reviewed it for the *Bookman* (August 1894), and again on the publication of the American edition, the *Bookman* (May 1895). See UP1 336–39 and 356–58.

87. Russell joined the Irish Agricultural Organisation in 1897.

88. George Russell, *The Waders,* oil on paper, 24 cm. x 47 cm., Hugh Lane Municipal Gallery of Modern Art, Dublin (presented by the artist in 1904).

89. In *Per Amica Silentia Lunae* (1917), WBY had mentioned that, according to Swedenborg, when angels make love in that union which 'is of the whole body' it 'seems from far off an incandescence' (*LE* 25). See Emanuel Swedenborg, *The Delights of Wisdom Pertaining to Conjugial Love; After which follow the Pleasures of Insanity relating to Scortatory Love* (1768) (especially no. 75, sections V–IX, and no. 359), tr. A. H. Searle (1876), rev. R. L. Tafel (1891) (London: Swedenborg Society, 1891), pp. 73–75, 320–21. See also nos. 50, 56, 69, 188–89, 358 (pp. 53–54, 59–60, 69, 178–79, 320), and *Heaven and its Wonders and Hell: from Things Heard and Seen* (1758, in Latin) (no. 382), tr. rev. F. Bayley (1909; repr. London: Dent, 1911), pp. 190–91.

90. This opinion is untraced. Coleridge wrote numerous, largely favorable notes about Emanuel Swedenborg (1688–1772),

Swedish scientist whose religious writings of 1749–56 led his followers to found the New Jerusalem Church. For Coleridge, see Background Notes on Writers, p. 533.

91. Title character of Dostoievsky's novel *The Idiot* (1868–69). Gabriel Fallon recalls that in 1924, two years after publication of *The Trembling of the Veil*, WBY said that Sean O'Casey's play *Juno and the Peacock* 'particularly in its final scene, reminded him of a Dostoievsky novel. Lady Gregory turned to him and said, "You know, Willie, you never read a novel by Dostoievsky." And promised to amend this deficiency by sending him a copy of *The Idiot*' (*Sean O'Casey: The Man I Knew* [London: Routledge, 1965], pp. 21–22).

92. George Chapman, *Byron's Conspiracy* (or *The Conspiracie and Tragedie of Charles, Duke of Byron, Marshall of France*), III, i (London: G. Eld for T. Thorppe, 1608).

93. Pandemos, or Pandemus, in Greek myth a figure of worldly or profane love, an aspect of Aphrodite or Venus. Urania is the other aspect, heavenly or sacred love.

94. In Celtic mythology, a companion of Garbh Ogh and Lugh. It is a white hound with red ears that are the wind, and the hound leaps across the sky in pursuit of stags that represent souls. There are Gabriel's hounds in British folklore, and these, too, are a symbol of death. Greek mythology depicts them as companions of Artemis. There are Orion's hounds or the constellation of Canis Major. The Hound of Heaven is also a reference to a savior or Christ. Francis Thompson's most famous poem is 'The Hound of Heaven', *Poems* (London: Elkin Mathews and John Lane, 1893).

95. Untraced; when WBY used this same notion in the poem 'Crazy Jane Reproved' (w. 1929; publ. 1930), ll.1–4, 8–11, he described it as 'what the sailors say' l. 1 P 256–57.

THE TREMBLING OF THE VEIL.
BOOK III. HODOS CHAMELIONTOS

1. WBY translates 'Hodos Chameliontos' as 'The Path of the Chameleon'; i.e., multiplicity, changeableness, confusion, unpredictability. The non-standard spelling 'Chameliontos' is from the occult document. See WBY's note 22 below.

2. WBY visited Ratra House, Frenchpark, Co. Roscommon, 13 April–1 May 1895.

3. The story was first titled 'Costello the Proud' (*Pageant*, December 1896) and then 'Of Costello the Proud, of Oona the Daughter of Dermott and of the Bitter Tongue' (*The Secret Rose*,

1897) (Myth 196–210).

4. *Abhráin Grádh Chúige Connacht or Love Songs of Connacht* (London: Unwin, 1893), pp. 47–59; reprinted, with minor revisions and an introduction by WBY, in Hyde's *Love Songs of Connacht* (Dundrum, Co. Dublin: Dun Emer, 1904), pp. 33–47.

5. After seeing Hero, a priestess of Aphrodite, at a festival, Leander swam the Hellespont each night to be with her. Finally, a storm put out the light she used to guide Leander across, and he drowned. Hero then committed suicide by throwing herself into the sea after him. See Ovid, *Heroides,* 18–9, and Virgil, *Georgics,* 3.258 ff.

6. Yeats, 'To the Rose upon the Rood of Time' (1892), ll. 13–15, 19–21 P 31.

7. Yeats, 'Hanrahan's Vision' (1896), Myth 250–1.

8. Nicephorus, Michael Constantine Psellus (eleventh-century Byzantine philosopher), no. 7, in *The Chaldaean Oracles of Zoroaster,* ed. Sapere Aude (William Wynn Westcott), vol. vi of Collectanea Hermetica series (London: Theosophical Publishing Society, 1895), p. 47, no. 155: 'Change not the barbarous Names of Evocation for there are sacred Names in every language which are given by God, having in the Sacred Rites a Power Ineffable.' WBY had used this earlier in 'Swedenborg, Mediums, and the Desolate Places' (1914), LE 64. For Mathers's method of invoking symbols, see pp. 161–62 above.

9. George Pollexfen. WBY stayed six months at his home, Thornhill, Sligo, from November 1894 to the summer of 1895.

10. For Gladstone and Home Rule, see note 3 above.

11. For Mary Battle, the second-sighted servant, see page 84 above and 207:22 below.

12. Moyle Lodge.

13. WBY here slightly condenses a paragraph from his 1901 essay 'Magic' (E&I 45), which further identifies him as 'a young Church of Ireland man, a bank-clerk in the West of Ireland'. Hone (Yeats 112) adds that this was in Sligo during the winter of 1894–95 and that the young bank clerk came occasionally for séances with WBY's cousin Lucy Middleton. WBY gives another version of this vision in his note to 'The Poet Pleads with the Elemental Powers' in *The Wind Among the Reeds* (VP 811).

14. Dante's Purgatory is a great mountain rising from the sea into the sunshine and having at its summit a garden (*Purgatorio,* XXVIII ff.) with a huge tree (Canto XXXII). This passage closely parallels WBY's earlier account in 'Magic' (1901) E&I 44–45, from which the *Zohar* passage can be identified as Macgregor Mathers's translation, *The Kabbalah Unveiled* (London: Red-

way, 1887), pp. 103–04 (*The Book of Concealed Mystery,* section 31). For the *Zohar* and Cabbalism, see note 36, p. 473. Jon Lanham has pointed out that the Golden Dawn Adeptus Minor ritual mentions the mystical mountain Abiegnus, 'the Symbolic Mountain of God in the centre of the Universe, the sacred Rosicrucian Mountain of Initiation' ('A Critical Edition of *Ideas of Good and Evil* by W. B. Yeats'; Ph.D. thesis, University of Toronto, 1976, p. 217 note to line 3, quoting Israel Regardie, *The Golden Dawn,* II, 237).

15. WBY had used this in 'To Some I Have Talked with by the Fire' (1895), ll. 10–14 P 49.

16. The 'soul of the world', which presupposes belief in a collective consciousness or divinity that unifies all nature. It serves as the basis for the constant expansion of the pool of unconscious images. See the 'Anima Mundi' section of *Per Amica Silentia Lunae,* LE 16–32, especially pp. 22–23, where WBY refers to Henry More's (1614–87; English philosopher of the Cambridge Platonist school) *The Immortality of the Soul* (1659; rev. 1662) (book III, ch. xii, sect. I), in *A Collection of Several Philosophical Writings,* 2nd ed. (London: William Morden, 1662) (O'Shea no. 1377), p. 193.

17. WBY's NOTE
    (first publ. in Auto 1926):

    'Constantly enrich' must not be taken to mean that you can, as some suggest, separate a soul from its memory like a cockle from its shell. 1926.

18. Polly and Jill of the nursery rhymes 'Polly put the kettle on' and 'Jack and Jill went up the hill, /To fetch a pail of water'; Tom the Fool, as in 'tomfoolery', a traditional character as early as the fourteenth century (O.E.D.) and echoed in WBY's poems 'Tom O'Roughley' (1918), 'Tom the Lunatic' (1932), 'Tom at Cruachan' (1932), and 'Old Tom Again' (1932) P 141, 268–269.

19. Adapted from ' "And Fair, Fierce Women," ' *The Celtic Twilight* (1902), *Myth* 57–58; the first quotation mistakenly ends 'straight to here' in all versions of *The Trembling of the Veil,* rather than 'straight to her' as in all versions of *The Celtic Twilight* chapter.

20. In the Cabbala's arrangement of ten levels, the Moon, which Gabriel controls, is the ninth lowest, just above the Earth.

21. 'Think of what we owe to the imitation of Christ, of what we owe to the imitation of Caesar', 'The Decay of Lying', *The Nineteenth Century* 25 (January 1889): 50.

22. WBY's NOTE
    (first publ. in Auto 1926):

Hodos Camelionis, not Hodos Chameliontos, were the words, a mixture of Greek and Latin typical of such documents.[a]

[a] See note 1 above.

23. Anne Butler Yeats, born 26 February 1919.

24. Shakespeare, *Romeo and Juliet* (c. 1595).

25. Dante Alighieri was banished from Florence c. 1302 until his death in 1321.

26. In Greek mythology, Perseus rescued Andromeda from a sea-monster.

27. WBY'S NOTE
(first publ. in Auto 1926):

There is a form of Mask or Image that comes from life and is feted, but there is a form that is chosen.

28. Yeats, 'Ego Dominus Tuus' (w. 1915, publ. 1917), ll. 49–62 P 161-62.

THE TREMBLING OF THE VEIL
BOOK IV. THE TRAGIC GENERATION

1. William Archer's English translation of *A Doll's House* (1879, in Norwegian) was first produced at the Novelty Theatre (later renamed the Kingsway Theatre), Great Queen Street, London, 7 June 1889, but his translation of *The Pillars of Society* (1877, in Norgewian) had been produced 15 December 1880 at the Gaiety Theatre, Strand, London.

2. *Ibsen's Prose Dramas,* ed. William Archer, 5 vols. (London: Scott, 1890); WBY's library still contains three of them: *Lady Inger of Ostrat, Love's Comedy, and The League of Youth* (O'Shea no. 947), *Peer Gynt* (O'Shea no. 949), and *The Pillars of Society and Other Plays* (includes *Ghosts* and *An Enemy of Society*) (O'Shea no. 950; signed by WBY on 5 September 1888); Archer gave WBY an additional copy of *An Enemy of the People* in 1904 (CL3 648).

3. For Florence Farr, see note 18, p. 441 and p. 303 below. In the 1890s, she was close to Shaw, under whose guidance she acted in a number of plays, including Ibsen's *Rosmersholm*.

4. Maud Gonne.

5. For Todhunter, see note 11, p. 441. The 'book of words' was probably his unpublished 'The Comedy of Sighs'.

6. The line, according to Holroyd, Shaw's biographer, is 'My dear fellow, I quite agree with you but what are we against so many?'

(Michael Holroyd, *Bernard Shaw: Vol. I, 1856–1898* [London: Chatto and Windus, 1988], p. 298). Stanley Weintraub has identified the 'gentleman in the gallery' as Reginald Golding Bright (1874–1941), a young man eager to become a drama critic and who later would become Shaw's London theatrical agent (*Bernard Shaw: The Diaries 1885–1897,* ed. Stanley Weintraub [University Park: Pennsylvania State University, 1986], II, 1025–26 [21 April 1894]).

7. See Holroyd, *Bernard Shaw,* p. 303.

8. Compare the blunter early version, which WBY revised to its present form in 1926: '. . . listened with excitement to see how the audience would like certain passages of *Arms and the Man*. I hated it' (Trembling 1922 161).

9. Jacob Epstein (1880–1959) and Wyndham Lewis (1882–1957), London avant-garde artists, a sculptor and a painter/writer, respectively, whose works use images of the machine to critique a mechanistic age. Epstein's famous sculpture *The Rock Drill* (not *The Stone Drill*) (1913–14) was first exhibited in 1915 in a plaster version with an actual mining drill (height 300 cm.; now dismantled) and then in 1916 as a bronze cast of the torso and left arm (71 cm., Tate Gallery, London, no. T340). Both versions are illustrated in Charles Harrison, *English Art and Modernism 1900–1939* (London: Allen Lane, 1981), plates 38 and 39.

10. The Marquess of Queensbury (1844–1900), father of Lord Alfred Douglas, objected to the sexual relationship between Wilde and his son and carried on an extensive attack against Wilde, who sued him for libel in March 1895. Queensbury was acquitted. Wilde was quickly arrested on evidence brought to light during the trial; his trial for indecency began 20 May 1895; he was sentenced to two years hard labor on 27 May.

11. Alexander Bain (1818–1903) was a Scottish psychologist. WBY used a fuller version of this quotation in his essay 'Verlaine in 1894' (1896), citing 'the "voluminous tenderness" which Mr. Bain has called, I believe, "the basis of all immorality" ' (UP1 399).

12. 'To the Destroyer of a Soul' (1892) is inscribed 'To ——'. The dedication is generally assumed to be to Wilde and the soul that of Lord Alfred Douglas (*The Complete Poems of Lionel Johnson,* ed. Ian Fletcher [London: Unicorn Press, 1953], p. 94 and note p. 353). In Ezra Pound's edition of the *Poetical Works of Lionel Johnson* (London: Elkin Mathews, 1915), the poem is re-titled 'The Destroyer of a Soul' and has no dedication.

13. Wilde, 'Requiescat' (1881), ll. 11–12.

14. Wilde, 'Hélas!' (1881), ll. 12–14. No poem by Wilde is included

in WBY's *A Book of Irish Verse Selected from Modern Writers* (London: Methuen, March 1895), introduction dated 5 August 1894.

15. Wilde, 'Poems in Prose': 'The Doer of Good', published July 1894 in the *Fortnightly Review* (*The Complete Works of Oscar Wilde* [London: Collins, 1948], pp. 863–64).

16. 'The Crucifixion of the Outcast' (*Myth* 147–56) was first published as 'A Crucifixion' in the 24 March 1894 issue of the *National Observer*.

17. 146 Oakley Street, Chelsea. Wilde had already left Oakley Street to stay with his friends, Ernest and Ada Leverson, at 2 Courtfield Gardens.

18. Wilde was released from Reading Gaol on 19 May 1897. Wilde's mother had died on 3 February 1896 and his wife, Constance Wilde, died on 7 April 1898; his brother, Willie Wilde, died on 13 March 1899.

19. The National Gallery of Ireland's portrait gallery includes Bernardo Strozzi's (Genoese, 1581–1644) *Portrait of a Venetian Gentleman* (oil, 1.38 m. x 1.07 m., no. 781, Hugh Lane bequest, 1917), John Singer Sargent's (American, 1856–1925) *Portrait of President Wilson* (1917) (oil, 1.53 cm. x 1.09 m., no. 817, Hugh Lane bequest, 1917), and two male portraits by Cornelius Van Ceulen Jonson (or Janssen) (Anglo–Dutch, 1593–1664): *Portrait of an Officer in Armour* (oil, 75 cm. x 65 cm., no. 532, purchased 1903) and *Male Portrait* (1628) (oil, 76 cm. x 63 cm., no. 584, purchased 1907). As Denis Donoghue and Frank Kermode have suggested, 'Jongsen' is presumably an error for 'Janssen' (or 'Jongsen') (TLS 71:3650, 11 February 1972, 157a). Sargent undertook the portrait of President Wilson as a charity project for the Red Cross during World War I, and it is lifeless by comparison with the intense, arresting portrait by Strozzi (illus. Luisa Mortari, *Bernardo Strozzi* [Rome: De Luca (1966)], fig. 439).

20. Yeats, 'The Phases of the Moon' (w. 1918, publ. 1919) P 163.

21. When Sir Anthony van Dyck (1599–1641), Flemish painter working in England, sent his *Head of Charles I in Three Positions* (1635–36) to the Italian sculptor Bernini (1598–1680) as a guide for a marble bust, Bernini reportedly called it a 'fatal face' (*visage funeste*) (*Dictionary of Art*, IX, 482; for an illustration of van Dyck's oil painting, 85 cm. x 97 cm., Royal Collection, Windsor Castle, see *Dictionary of Art*, XXIX, 802).

22. Cromwell, Oliver (1599–1658). Lord Lieutenant and General for the Parliament of England and, from 1653 until his death, Lord Protector of England and hence of Ireland. A Protestant zealot, English nationalist, and able and ruthless soldier and politician,

Cromwell virtually conquered Ireland, drove the Gaelic and Catholic leadership into the Western counties or exile, confiscated church and private property to pay for the wars in England and Ireland, attempted to colonize the country permanently with his soldiers and other settlers, and so fixed English power in Ireland for the next 150 years.

23. From the system of *A Vision* (V1937 147–50).
24. Yeats, 'The Cat and the Moon' (w. 1917, publ. 1918), ll. 1–4, 17–28 P 167–68.
25. D. G. Rossetti's translation from *Les Burgraves,* a song of Victor Hugo's (1847), ll. 11–12.
26. The border region between England and Scotland was wild country described in the Border ballads, narrative poetry meant to be sung. Cavaliers were part of the court of Charles I of England and were known for their lyrics on love and beauty.
27. W. E. Henley and Robert Louis Stevenson (1850–94) became friends in 1875 and collaborated on several plays. In 1887, Stevenson left for the United States. In March 1888, Henley wrote to him suggesting that there was plagiarism in one of his wife's [Fanny Osbourne Stevenson] short stories. The hostility between Henley and Mrs. Stevenson—she thought him a bad influence; he believed that she had caused his friend to sell out to the genteel tradition—intensified and the estrangement between R. L. S. and Henley was irreparable. The 'notorious article' appeared in *Pall Mall Magazine,* XXV (1901), 505–14. 'The immortal Musketeers' is from the 'Envoy' to Stevenson that Henley had written for *In Hospital* (London: David Nutt, 1888). The *Works* were published in seven volumes (London: David Nutt) in 1908, with anonymous editing.
28. Margaret Emma Henley, born in 1888, died 11 February 1894.
29. The opening lines of an untitled poem 'dedicated to Margaret Emma Henley', published in *The Song of the Sword and Other Verses* (London: David Nutt, 1892), pp. 80–82.
30. From Henley's poem 'Two Days' (15 February and 28 September 1894), *Hawthorne and Lavender—With Other Verses* (London: Harper and Brothers, 1901), pp. xcix–c.
31. Theobald Wolfe Tone (1763–98), Robert Emmet (1778–1803), Eoghan Ruodh Ó Néill [Owen Roe O'Neill] (?1584–1694). Revolutionary nationalist martyrs.
32. Yeats, 'Easter, 1916' (1916), ll. 60–62 P 180–81.
33. D. G. Rossetti, 'Love's Nocturn' (1870); A. C. Swinburne, 'Faustine' (1862); Lionel Johnson, 'By the Statue of King Charles at Charing Cross' (1889); Earnest Dowson, 'O Mors! Quam amara est memorio tua homini pacem habenti in substantiis suis' ('You

would have understood me had you waited') (1896), 'Villanelle of Sunset' (1896). *The Book of the Rhymers Club* (London: Mathews, 1892) included the Johnson and Dowson poems.

34. Francis Thompson, 'Ode to the Setting Sun' (1889).

35. Dante Gabriel Rossetti's poem 'Love's Nocturn' [not 'Love's Nocturne'] (1870).

36. D. G. Rossetti's sonnets 'Lilith' (1868; titled 'Body's Beauty' in 1881) and 'Sibylla Palmifera' (1886; titled 'Soul's Beauty' in 1881), describing his pair of contrasting paintings (each oil, 94 cm. x 83 cm.): *Lady Lilith* (1868; Wilmington Society of Fine Arts, Delaware) and *Sibylla Palmifera* (also known as *Venus Palmifera*) (1866–70; Lady Lever Art Gallery, Port Sunlight); illus. Virginia Surtees, *The Paintings and Drawings of Dante Gabriel Rossetti (1828–1882): A Catalogue Raisonné* (Oxford: Clarendon Press, 1971), plates 293 and 285, respectively.

37. Adelaide Foltinowicz, the daughter of the proprietor of a modest resturant in Soho known as 'Poland'. She was twelve when Dowson met her in 1891; she married the waiter in her father's restaurant in 1897 (see p. 240 below).

38. The Cabbala, a collection of medieval Hebrew manuscripts, describes an involved symbolism in which an aspiring adept seeks to ascend through ten stations (Sephiroth) in the Tree of Life. WBY probably first encountered those ideas in a translated compilation, *The Kabbalah Unveiled* (*Kabbala Denudata*) (London: Redway, 1887), which contains the following three books of the *Zohar: The Book of Concealed Mystery, The Greater Holy Assembly,* and *The Lesser Holy Assembly.* It was translated by MacGregor Mathers from the Latin version by Knorr von Rosenroth of the original Chaldee and Hebrew. Mathers was a founder and leader of the Golden Dawn, which used that symbolism in the Christian cabbalism of John Dee (English, 1527–1608) and Cornelius Agrippa (German, 1486?–1535).

39. Lionel Johnson (1867–1902), English poet and critic, who reviewed for the *Academy, Anti-Jacobin, National Observer, Daily Chronicle,* and the *Pall Mall Gazette,* and contributed to the first and second *Book of the Rhymers' Club* (1892, 1894). He was converted to Catholicism in 1891 and became an Irish patriot, joined the London Irish Literary Society, and became involved in the literary movement. He visited Ireland in September 1893, April 1894, and May 1898. His *Poems* (1895) and *Ireland, with Other Poems* (1897) include nationalistic poems, which WBY subordinated in his review of the 1897 volume (UP2 88–91). He also published *The Art of Thomas Hardy* (1894).

40. From Villiers de l'Isle-Adam's *Axel* (1890), part IV, scene 2. WBY

takes this translation from Arthur Symons, 'Villiers de L'Isle-Adam', *The Symbolist Movement in Literature* (London: Heinemann, 1899), p. 56, and quotes it frequently (UP2 117, P&I 112 and 156, LE 33 and 153).

41. Lionel Johnson, 'To Morfydd' (1891), refrain.

42. The Oresteia: *Agamemnon, Choephoroe,* and *Eumenides.*

43. Area near Thebes, Egypt, a center of Christian monasticism in the fourth century.

44. Fourth-century Christian desert monastic hermits are associated with the Thebaid, the district of Thebes (25–45N / 032–50E), ancient capital of Upper Egypt, and with Lake Mariotis (Mariut), just south of Alexandria. James O. Hannay, in a book WBY knew, *The Wisdom of the Desert* (London: Methuen, 1904), described the barren regions (pp. 5–10) and made extensive use of military imagery in recounting the spiritual battles with the devil of the early Christian monks (pp. 19–20; see also pp. 133, 140, 214, 216).

45. Untraced.

46. WBY's first lecture tour of the United States and Canada, 11 November 1903–9 March 1904.

47. Ernest Dowson (1867–1900), English poet. He, like Lionel Johnson, joined the Roman Catholic Church in 1891, but did not alter his dissipation. He worked as a translator and contributed to both the *Savoy* and the *Critic.*

48. See note 35 above.

49. Emanuel Swedenborg, *The Delights of Wisdom Pertaining to Conjugial Love; After which follow the Pleasures of Insanity relating to Scortatory Love* (1768), tr. A. H. Searle (1876), rev. R. L. Tafel (1891) (London: Swedenborg Society, 1891) (O'Shea no. 2038), no. 44, sect. IX. The wording ('dayspring of their youth') that WBY uses here, on p. 347 below, and four other times (LE *53, 92, 280* and LTSM 114), is closer to the translation by Samuel M. Warren, rev. Louis H. Tafel in 1910 ('the springtime of their youth') than to the Searle / Tafel translation that WBY owned, p. 48 ('their vernal youth'). For publication details and for parallel statements in Swedenborg's writings, see LE 455n59.

50. Dowson, 'Villanelle of the Poet's Road' (1899), ll. 10–12.

51. Lionel Johnson's poem (1893), quoted p. 243 below.

52. Yeats, 'Ego Dominus Tuus' (w. 1915, publ. 1917), ll. 49–51 P 160.

53. Both beautiful, seductive characters. Phaedria appears in *Faerie Queene,* II. vi, the Lady of the Idle Lake, immodest mirth. Acrasia appears in *Faerie Queene,* II. xii, intemperance. Robert Cecil, Lord Burleigh of the 'rugged forehead' [*Faerie Queene,*

Book IV, Poem 1, l. 1] is a typical man of action, suspicious of the consequences of both love and poetry.

54. Matthew Arnold, 'The Function of Criticism at the Present Time' (1864), *The Complete Works of Matthew Arnold*, ed. R. H. Super (Ann Arbor: University of Michigan, 1962), III, 268, 283: 'the best that is known and thought in the world'.

55. Untraced as quoted. 'Perfection' is one of Arnold's preoccupations; see especially 'Sweetness and Light' in *Culture and Anarchy* (1869), *The Complete Works* (1965), V, 90–114.

56. William Michael Rossetti (1829-1919), art critic and editor.

57. Lionel Johnson, 'The Dark Angel' (1893), ll. 1–20. In l. 4, 'subtil' should read 'subtile'.

58. See note 1, p. 439.

59. In his essay 'The Celtic Element in Literature' (1898; E&I 187), WBY attributed this idea to the Belgian symbolist poet and dramatist Émile Verhaeren (1855–1916).

60. John Davidson (1857–1909), Scottish poet and playwright. Davidson came to London in 1890, reviewed for the *Speaker,* the *Star,* the *Academy* and contributed to the *Yellow Book.* WBY characterized him in 1897 as 'Mr. Davidson, with his passionate insistence on a few simple ideas, whose main value is in his passionate insistence' (UP2 38–42). Davidson committed suicide in 1909. The popular novelist, mentioned just below, is Charles James Wills (1842–1912), for whom Davidson ghosted most of several novels, although listed as co-author only for *Laura Ruthven's Widowhood* (1892); Davidson also read manuscripts for the publishers John Lane and Grover Richards.

61. See J. P. Eckermann, '7 April 1829', *Conversations with Goethe,* rev. edn. (London and New York: G. Bell and Sons, 1892). Parnell's body was brought back to Ireland, 11 October 1891, and buried at Glasnevin, Dublin.

62. Arthur Symons (1865–1945). Welsh poet, critic, editor, and translator. WBY and Symons shared a flat together at 2 Fountain Court, Middle Temple, London, from early October 1895 until late February 1896. They also went on a journey together through the west of Ireland in 1896. Symons did much to educate WBY in French symbolist literature. He published his own first collection of poems, *Days and Nights,* in 1889. His two volumes of *London Nights* (1895, 1897) were not well received. See WBY's defence of his friend in the *Bookman* (August 1895) (repr. UP1 373–5). Symons almost devoutly represented the 'Decadent' movement in literature. He was involved with the *Yellow Book* for its first three issues and was editor of the *Savoy* (1896). He is best remembered for *The Symbolist Movement in Literature*

(1900), a volume introducing the French symbolists to Britain. Stricken by a mental illness in Italy in 1908, Symons spent two years in mental hospitals, gradually regaining his health. He was back to writing by 1919. See his *Confessions: A Study in Pathology* (New York: J. Cape and H. Smith, 1930).

63. *Axël* (1890). Play by Villiers de l'Isle-Adam. WBY and Maud Gonne saw it performed in Paris at the Théâtre de la Gaité on 26 February 1894. He reviewed it for the *Bookman* (April 1894) (UP1 320–25), and wrote the preface for H. P. R. Finberg's translation in 1925.

64. Edward Martyn's Tulira Castle, Co. Galway.

65. The Song of Solomon 1:1: 'The song of songs, which is Solomon's.' Jesus' Sermon on the Mount is Matthew: 5–7.

66. Symons's translation of Mallarmé's poem 'Hérodiade' (w.1864–67, publ. 1893), II. Scène, ll. 103–16, published in the *Savoy*, December 1896.

67. Gustave Moreau, *Jason and Medea* (1865) (oil, 2.03 m. x 1.14 m., Louvre, Paris); illus. Julius Kaplan, *Gustave Moreau* (Los Angeles: Los Angeles County Museum of Art, 1974), plate 16.

68. Possibly an Aran Islands love song. Beara made a coat for Eoghan from a salmon; see P&I 131 and 280 n. 51.

69. *The Savoy*, January–December 1896.

70. Aubrey Beardsley (1872–98), English artist. His first major project, with the encouragement of Edward Burne-Jones, had been the illustrations and decorations for the *Morte d'Arthur* edition published by Dent and Company in 1891–92. In 1894, he worked on the *Yellow Book* and became its art editor, but in April 1895, a mob, which mistakenly associated Beardsley with Oscar Wilde, smashed windows of the Bodley Head Press where the *Yellow Book* was published. Beardsley was dismissed when the poet William Watson—at the instigation of the popular novelist Mrs. Humphry Ward, and on behalf of a group of Bodley Head authors—telegraphed the publisher, John Lane, threatening to withdraw all his books unless Beardsley's designs were withdrawn. Later that year, Arthur Symons invited Beardsley as Art Editor of the *Savoy,* to be published by Leonard Smithers. Its first two issues, January and February 1896, included a bowdlerised version of his erotic, illustrated, unfinished novel *Venus and Tannhäuser,* re-titled in the *Savoy* as *Under the Hill* and collected posthumously in *Under the Hill and other Essays in Prose and Verse* (London: John Lane, 1904); Smithers privately published an unexpurgated version in 1907, *The Story of Venus and Tannhäuser.* Other notable works by Beardsley include the poster for the Avenue Theatre production of plays by Shaw and WBY

(1894) and illustrations for Wilde's Salomé (1894) and *The Rape of the Lock* (1896). Beardsley's subject matter and sophisticated technique were thought to epitomize the decadence of the '90s. He became a Roman Catholic one year before he died, from consumption, on 16 March 1898. His sister, Mabel, was WBY's inspiration for 'Upon a Dying Lady' (w. 1912–14, publ. 1917) P 157–60. The first draft (Mem 90–92) supplements the description of Beardsley.

71. In his first draft (Mem 90), WBY identifies the novelist as Mrs. Humphry Ward (Mary Augusta, 1851–1920).

72. William Blake, 'Antaeus setting Virgil and Dante upon the verge of Cocytus' (also known as 'Antaeus setting down Dante and Virgil in the Last Circle of Hell' [*Inferno*, Canto 31, ll. 112–43]) (1824–7), (pen and watercolour, 53 cm. x 37 cm., National Gallery of Victoria, Melbourne); illus. W. B. Yeats, 'William Blake and his Illustrations to the *Divine Comedy*', the *Savoy*, no. 3, July 1896, p. 55. It had been exhibited at the Royal Academy, London, in 1893. The bookseller firm was W. H. Smith. Illus. Albert S. Roe, *Blake's Illustrations to the Divine Comedy* (Princeton: Princeton University Press, 1953), no. 63; Martin Butlin, *William Blake* (London: Tate Gallery, 1978), p. 151. (no. 328).

73. Aubrey Beardsley, 'The Coiffing' (1896, ink drawing), illus. to Beardsley's poem 'The Ballad of a Barber' in the *Savoy*, no. 3, July 1896, p. [90]; illus. in Weintraub, p. 187. Edward Linley Sambourne (1844–1910), a cartoonist for *Punch* from 1867 to 1909; for a sample, see his cartoon of President Roosevelt as a medieval crusader riding a hobby-horse, 11 December 1907, illus. in Charles Press, *The Political Cartoon* (Rutherford, NJ: Fairleigh Dickinson University Press, 1981), plate 224. Sambourne was admired for his one hundred illustrations in 1885 for an edition of Charles Kingsley's *The Water-babies* (London: Macmillan).

74. WBY wrote one letter to the editor of the conservative London weekly the *Spectator* in 1916 about Hugh Lane's collection of paintings. Twelve years later, in 1928, he published there an essay on Irish censorship. From 1932 onwards he regularly published poems and prose in the *Spectator*.

75. *The New Inne* (perf. 1629).

76. Leonard Charles Smithers (1861–1907).

77. WBY's account here and in Memoirs (91) corresponds closely with that of Max Beerbohm in an essay written in 1914 and broadcast in 1954, 'First Meetings with W. B. Yeats' (*Mainly on the Air* [New York, 1958]), pp. 107–9; see Weintraub, pp.

159–60. WBY published George Russell's letter in *Some Passages from the Letters of A.E. to W.B. Yeats* (Dundrum: Cuala Press, 1936), p. 4.

78. Beardsley's maternal grandfather was named William Pitt, but there is no evidence to support the family's claim that he was descended from William Pitt (1708–78), first Earl of Chatham (created 1766), English statesman, called 'the Great Commoner' and 'the Elder Pitt'.

79. The Abbé Vachère. WBY arrived at Mirebeau, France, on 11 May 1914 with Maud Gonne and Everard Feilding (Honorary Secretary to the Society for Psychical Research). They had come to investigate the miracle of bleeding oleographs of the sacred heart. WBY wrote an essay on the bleeding oleograph, but chose not to publish it. George Mills Harper has edited and published the essay with an introduction, 'A Subject of Investigation: Miracle at Mirebeau', in *Yeats and the Occult* (London: Macmillan, 1976), pp. 172–89. Feilding's report, 'The Case of the Abbé Vachère', in *Transaction of the Fourth International Congress for Psychical Research*, ed. Theodore Besterman (London: Society for Psychical Research, 1930), p. 142, identifies the two holy women 'victims' as 'the stigmatised German religious seeress Rosalie Putt' and Benedetta of Viterbo, a paralysed Benedictine nun (died 1915).

80. In the extended 'lunar metaphor' WBY uses in *A Vision* (1925, rev. 1937), the Thirteenth Phase is 'the only phase where entire sensuality is possible, that is to say, sensuality without the intermixture of any other element' (V 129). Unity of being is possible in the 'unmixed' phase fourteen; and the saints in phase twenty-seven are adjacent to the other and opposite, unmixed phase, twenty eight, a unity with a life beyond individual being.

81. For example, *The Lysistrata of Aristophanes,* tr. Samuel Smith, illus. Aubrey Beardsley (privately published, London: Leonard Smithers, 1896) and, as mentioned in note 68 above, *The Story of Venus and Tannhäuser* (1907). Beardsley's death-bed letter to Leonard Smithers, postmarked 7 March 1898, asked that he destroy '*all* copies of *Lysistrata* & . . . *all* obscene drawings' (Brophy 110).

82. The reference, which echoes a passage in WBY's 1898 essay on Althea Gyles, 'A Symbolic Artist and the Coming of Symbolic Art' (UP1 134), is almost certainly to Aubrey Beardsley's ink drawing 'The Climax' (1894), an illustration to Oscar Wilde's *Salomé* (London: Elkin Mathews and John Lane; Boston: Copeland and Day, 1894). Beardsley called this a 'redrawn and immensely improved' version of his earlier *Salomé* illustration

lettered 'J'ai baisé ta bouche Iokanaan, j'ai baisé ta bouche', published in the *Studio*, I (April 1893); see Brophy 66 (1893 version) and 73 (1894 version), and Reade (286) and plate 286. Salomé is also shown with the severed head in another of the illustrations, 'The Dancer's Reward' (1894); WBY owned a framed reproduction of 'The Climax' and an unframed reproduction of 'The Dancer's Reward'. Arthur Symons, *Aubrey Beardsley*, 2nd ed. (London: Dent, 1905), p. 87, shows 'The Climax', although the first edition (London: Unicorn, 1898) has 'The Dancer's Reward' (no. 6). For 'The Dancer's Reward', see Reade (282) and plate 282; Kenneth Clark, *The Best of Aubrey Beardsley* (New York: Doubleday, 1978), p. 88 and plate 22; and Weintraub, p. 67.

83. The ink drawing of Madonna and Child is 'A Large Christmas Card', published as an unpaged, loose sheet in the *Savoy*, no. 1 (January 1896); it is reproduced in *The Later Work of Aubrey Beardsley*, 5th ed. (New York: De Capo Press, 1967), plate 113. The other drawing, 'The Ascension of Saint Rose of Lima', is an illustration to Beardsley's *Under the Hill* and was published in the *Savoy*, no. 2 (April 1896), p. 189; see Reade (429) and plate 426; Clark, *Best of Beardsley*, p. 146 and plate 51; and Weintraub, p. 225. WBY owned a reproduction of 'The Ascension of Saint Rose of Lima'.

84. Arthur Symons.

85. 'Proud Costello, Macdermot's Daughter, and the Bitter Tongue.' *The Secret Rose* (London: Lawrence and Bullen, 1897).

86. In 1925, WBY deleted this passage from his short story now titled 'Proud Costello, MacDermot's Daughter, and the Bitter Tongue' (1896); see SRV 73–74, notes to ll. 216–17, and Myth 196–210.

87. WBY placed Symons in phase eighteen; see V(1925)CE note (p. 23) to p. 81, ll. 7–8.

88. WBY stayed with Mathers and his wife, Moina, at 1, Avenue Duquesne, near the Champ de Mars, and later at 87, Rue Mozart, Auteuil.

89. Between 1760 and 1763, James Macpherson (1736–96) published books purporting to be translations from the Gaelic of the Scots Highland poet Ossian. They were much admired but their authenticity was challenged, most notably by Dr. Johnson, and they proved to be liberally edited traditional Gaelic poems and passages of Macpherson's own.

90. Supporter of the exiled Catholic House of Stuart, which originated from and was intertwined with the Kings of Scotland. After the revolution of 1688, James II was deposed, and the Jacobites wanted to restore him to the throne. Two unsuccessful risings

occurred in the eighteenth century, but the Jacobites continued to press the claims of James II's descendants until the end of the Stuart line in 1807.

91. Yeats, 'The Valley of the Black Pig' (1896), ll. 1–4 P 65; see also WBY's note to that poem P 593–94.

92. WBY met Paul Verlaine in Paris in February 1894. Three months earlier, the French poet had stayed with Arthur Symons, in rooms later occupied by WBY. Verlaine's erysipelas, mentioned just below, is an inflammatory disease, generally in the face, marked by a bright redness of the skin. He died in January 1896 in Paris. Verlaine's biographers do not corroborate the account of the funeral, p. 262 below. The mistress was Eugénie Krantz and the publisher, Léon Vanier.

93. For Synge, see Background Notes on Writers, p. 538.

94. WBY was introduced to Synge by Dr. James Cree, who also introduced Synge to Lady Gregory.

95. On the excursion to the Aran Islands in August 1896, WBY was accompanied by Arthur Symons, Edward Martin, and George Moore. Symons's report of the trip, 'A Causerie: From a Castle in Ireland,' is in the *Savoy*, no. 6 (October 1896).

96. This Aran Islands anecdote could have contributed to Synge's *The Playboy of the Western World* (1907).

97. Synge was invited into the society as an Associate. He joined Maud Gonne's Association Irlandaise, begun on New Year's Day 1897, but resigned soon after.

98. *The Aran Islands* (Dublin: Maunsel, 1907) (O'Shea no. 2071), p. 76.

99. For Phase Twenty-three, to which WBY assigned Rembrandt and Synge, see V 163–69.

100. Louis Claude de Saint-Martin (1743–1803), French writer on occultism and mysticism. Martinism combined influences from Rosicrucianism, Swedenborg, Boehme, and, to some extent, a purely spiritual version of Roman Catholicism; it enjoyed a significant following in the nineteenth century. In the earlier published version, WBY had described this as having happened when 'sitting in a Café with two French Americans' (Trembling 1922 220).

101. In the account of these incidents in *Per Amica Silentia Lunae* (1917), the untraced Jewish Persian scholar is described as 'a young Arabic scholar' (LE 32). For the softness of alchemical gold, see SB 60.

102. A miraculous stone in alchemy that was thought to have the power to transmute base metals into gold and to grant eternal youth. August Strindberg (1849–1912), Swedish playwright,

sought to make alchemical gold in Paris during 1894 and 1895; WBY's only trip to Paris during those years was in February 1894. During the next two years, Strindberg maintained occult and Swedenborgian interests in Paris; WBY's next trip was December 1896 to January 1897. The French Canadian with plans for a colony of artists in Virginia is untraced.

103. WBY and Arthur Symons attended the first performance of Alfred Jarry's *Ubu roi*, December 1896.

THE TREMBLING OF THE VEIL.
BOOK V. THE STIRRING OF THE BONES

1. Maud Gonne lectured in America, October through December 1897, to raise money for a Wolfe Tone memorial and the Irish Amnesty Association. For details of WBY's involvement in the Wolfe Tone memorial and the centenary of the 1798 rebellion, see Mem 108–11; CL2 appendix 'The '98 Centennial Association', 695–707; G–YL 63–94, 463–71; and Foster 1 189–93.

2. Daniel O'Connell (1775–1847), popularly known as the 'Liberator'. The dominant nineteenth-century political figure before Parnell, most successfully as the leader of the campaign for Catholic emancipation achieved in 1829. The monument, more than life-size, is at the foot of O'Connell Street facing south to the river.

3. WBY moved to 18 Woburn Buildings in March 1896. For details, see CL2 appendix '18 Woburn Buildings', 725–32.

4. The dispute in Clan na Gael, the American Fenian organization, was bitter and extended to Ireland even after the events had long passed. Alexander Sullivan, a 'Dynamitard' accused of murdering Dr. Patrick Cronin in 1889, was acquitted by a Chicago jury, but that only furthered the split between his followers, the 'Triangle', and the followers of John Devoy (1842–1928).

5. The manuscript reads 'monument' rather than 'movement'; this likely misreading by the typist was never corrected. See Textual Introduction, p. 14 above.

6. In a cancelled passage of reminiscence, WBY stated that the Irish National Alliance (INA, one of several nationalist factions) 'made me President of the '98', behind the scenes, in the spring of 1897 (Foster 1 189). There were many opportunities for quarrels among the factions. The idea of a 'great central council' of Irish opinion to which the elected representatives to Westminster would be responsible came to nothing. See Mem 108–11.

7. The typescript skips an addition to the end of this sentence in the manuscript, where the ending reads: 'business, and in all proba-

bility because of an anecdote and certain words about Unity of Being overheard in childhood.' That likely error was never corrected; see Textual Introduction, p. 14 above.

8. For Unity of Being, see note 124, p. 456. For WBY's assignment of Goethe to phase eighteen, 'The Emotional Man', see V 145–47. WBY thought Wilhelm Meister, the title character of Goethe's novel, emblematic of Romantic biography.

9. Yeats, 'The Fascination of What's Difficult' (1910), ll. 1–4 P 93.

10. Perhaps 20 February 1898, in Liverpool (CL2 701).

11. Michael Davitt, who lived until 1906, retired from the House of Commons on 25 October 1899 with a speech in opposition to the Boer War. He responded to WBY's 2 November (1899) letter (CL2 464–66) on 4 November and expressed relief at regaining his 'freedom from Party restraints' and 'craven expediency', preferring instead to base 'Ireland's right and claim to freedom upon this Justice as Right which we should advocate for every people defending their independence' (NLI microfilm P7529).

12. *Biographia Literaria*, ch. 7 (*The Collected Works of Samuel Taylor Coleridge,* ed. James Engell and W. J. Bate [London: Routledge; Princeton, 1983], vol. 7, part 1, p. 119).

13. Stendhal (Henri Beyle), epigraph to ch. 13, *The Red and the Black* (*Le Rouge et le noir,* 1831).

14. WBY had previously told the story in an anonymously published review for the *Scots Observer,* 19 October 1889 (UP1 146) of William Carleton's *The Red-Haired Man's Wife* (1889) and his own *Stories from Carleton* (1889).

15. Untraced.

16. Probably William O'Brien (1852–1928), Irish nationalist politician.

17. John Blake Dillon (1851–1927) was an organizer of the Land League, nationalist Member of Parliament, and follower of Parnell who, after Parnell's fall in 1890, supported the anti-Parnellite faction. John Redmond (1856–1918) was a nationalist M.P. and leader of the Parnellite faction after 1891, finally re-uniting the Irish Parliamentary Party in 1900.

18. Augustine Birrell (1850–1933). English politician, Chief Secretary for Ireland, 1907–16. He was responsible for the Universities Act of 1908, a re-alignment resulting in the National University of Ireland, consisting of University College, Dublin; University College, Cork; University College, Galway; St. Patrick's College, Maynooth; and Queens University, Belfast, as a separate university. Trinity College, Dublin, became the University of Dublin.

19. Statues of both Artemisia and her husband and brother, Mausolus (King of Caria, c. 353–350 B.C.), were in the British Museum.
20. See V 71–74 and 'The Statues' (w. 1938, publ. 1939) P 336–37.
21. Yeats, 'A Woman's Beauty is like a white frail Bird' (1919), ll. 7–14 P 559; *The Only Jealousy of Emer,* CPlays 281–82.
22. The procession in honor of the Wolfe Tone Centenary was held in Dublin on 15 August 1898. WBY spoke on the platform with John Dillon and John Redmond at the unveiling of a foundation stone.
23. I Kings 16:8–20 and perhaps John Dryden (1631–1700), *Absalom and Achitophel* (1681–82), ll. 544–68; an archetype of political betrayal. For John Dillon, see note 17 above.
24. The celebration in Dublin of Queen Victoria's (reigned, 1837–1901) Jubilee had been on 21 June 1897. It occasioned some demonstrations in which Maud Gonne was active.
25. James Connolly (1868–1916), Irish trade union leader and a leader of the 1916 rising. Connolly founded the socialist paper *The Worker's Republic* and the Irish Socialist Republican Party, as well as the Irish Socialist Federation and a magazine, *The Harp,* in the United States. He became the trade union organizer of the Transport Workers in Belfast, 1911–13, and supported James Larkin (1876–1947) during the lockout in Dublin. Connolly organized the Citizen Army at Liberty Hall in 1914 and was military commander of the Republican forces in Dublin in the 1916 rising. He commanded the General Post Office and was one of seven to sign the Proclamation of the Irish Republic. He was executed by firing squad at Kilmainham Jail, 12 May 1916. See 'Easter, 1916' and 'The Rose Tree' P 180, 183.
26. Padraic Pearse (1879–1916), Irish leader of the 1916 rising, poet, and educator. Pearse edited the Gaelic League's *An Claidheamh Soluis* and founded St. Enda's (Scoil Eanna), a bilingual school, in 1908. He joined the Irish Republican Brotherhood in 1913 and was on the Provisional Committee of the Irish Volunteers. He helped plan the 1916 rising, was Commander-in-Chief of the Irish Republican forces, signed the Proclamation of the Irish Republic, and was President of the Provisional government. Pearse was shot after court-martial at Kilmainham on 3 May 1916. His *Collected Works* appeared in 1917. 'Easter, 1916', 'Sixteen Dead Men', 'The Rose Tree' P 180, 182, 183.
27. St. Michan's Church (not St. Michael's Church), Church Street, near the Four Courts. The tombs of the Sheares brothers—John (1776–98) and Henry (1753–98), executed for their association with the United Irishmen—are there, and the grave of Robert Emmet may be. For the mystery of Emmet's grave, see Leon Ó

Broin, *TheUnfortunate Mr. Robert Emmet* (Dublin: Clonmare & Reynolds, 1958), pp. 173–78.

28. The Convention that had gone on that Jubilee day, 21 June 1897, was that of the '98 Centenary Commemoration Committee. WBY was President of the Centenary Executive Council. Rutland Square is now Parnell Square.

29. On 9 April 1900, the last full day of Queen Victoria's six-day visit to Dublin, Unionists gathered five thousand children in Phoenix Park for 'Children's Day'. On Easter Sunday 1900, Maud Gonne helped to found and became the first President of Inghindhe na hEireann, Daughters of Erin. The 'Patriotic Children's Treat' was held in Clonturk Park, Drumcondra, on 1 July 1900, with thirty thousand children.

30. If the year is 1900, then the reference is to the Derby, Ascot Racecourse, Epsom, Surrey, 5 June 1900, when WBY was in London.

31. Slang for 'jailed prisoners', as in the title story of Frank O'Connor's collection (1931).

32. Amilcare Cipriani (1844–1918), Italian revolutionary, visited Dublin with Maud Gonne and WBY in August 1898; see p. 305 below and CL2 206 nn. 5 and 6.

33. Headquarters of the Wolfe Tone Centenary (or '98 Commemoration) Association.

34. WBY's story 'Rosa Alchemica' was published in the April 1896 issue of the *Savoy*. The friend was Olivia Shakespear (1863–1938), a novelist and a cousin of Lionel Johnson; WBY had met her in 1894. See Mem 85–89 for an account of their love affair, which began in 1896.

35. Greek 'divine spirit', an aspect of divine power, giving good or bad fortune; alter ego; see *Per Amica Silentia Lunae*, 'Anima Hominis', sect. VII (LE 11).

36. See note 36, p. 473.

37. Kinematograph: cinema

38. WBY assembled this note from materials sent to him by Dr. Vacher Burch, an Oxford theologian and scholar, in a letter dated 1 February 1923. As George M. Harper reports, WBY intended to name Burch in the note, but mislaid the letter (*Making of A Vision*, I, 281–82 n. 63). For details, see CL2 appendix 'The Vision of the Archer', 658–63; George M. Harper, I, 130–35 and 280–81 nn. 60–75; and William F. Halloran, 'W. B. Yeats and William Sharp: The Archer Vision', *Engish Language Notes* 6: 4 (June 1969), 273–80. See also Mem 100–4 and Myth 340.

WBY'S NOTE

(first publ. July 1923 in the *Criterion* and the *Dial;* this note is printed at the end of the book in Auto 1926, the (1932/36) page proofs, and Auto 1955 [576–79]; the 1932–36 page proofs add a cross-reference note ['See, however, Note II.'] at the end of the section ['further light.']; in Auto 1955 [375] the cross-reference note adds the page numbers):

The Vision of an Archer

The description of the vision was not in the first edition of this book, and I add it now on the advice of a man learned in East Mediterranean antiquities, met on a lecturing tour in England, who thought it important, and promised annotation. I would like to give his name, or at any rate to write and ask if I might, but though I have spent several hours in the search I cannot find his letter, nor can I trace him at the house where I thought we met. He was no phantom, though a correspondent seems to think so, and I can only offer an apology for my seeming discourtesy. He sent me several pages of notes which I will comment upon and summarize.

(a) The Child and the Tree

On a certain night in Devonshire, farmers and farm-labourers and their wives and children perform a ceremony at the finest apple-tree in the orchard. Punch is poured out at the roots and bread put among the branches, and a boy set among the branches 'who is either the tree in boy-form, or the tree in bird-form', and the men fire blank charges at him. All dance round the tree, singing some such rhyme as this:

'Here's to thee, good apple-tree,
To bear and blow apples enow', etc.*

*(Transactions of the Devonshire Association, 1867. Whitcombe, Bygone Days in Devonshire and Cornwall.)

'This rhyme calls to mind its ancient prototype, the Hymn of the Kowetes, found at Palaikastro in Crete. The Kowetes "leap" the "full jars and rich fruit crops". Moreover, in a previous stanza is celebrated the baby made immortal for Rhea.'

'This boy finds his analogue in Balder, "who is shot to death that is life by means of a sprig or arrow of mistletoe".'

In my vision, the star is shot by an arrow from a bow, and in one of the children's dreams which I have described, God is shot with an arrow, while in another child's dream, a star is shot with a gun. 'Balder is the tree embodied. His name tells us that. Recent philology has said that the name means, or is related to, apple-tree, Abble, Apfel, etc. But that is not true enough. When the first decipherment of Cretan pictographs is published, it will be seen that his name goes back to the

Cretan Apollo who in old Cretan belief was a tree-god.' It is plain too that he is the 'Child hidden in the scented Dikton near Mount Ida' (*Phaen.* 32 ff.) of Aratus' lines, and that part of his significance is solar. 'He was believed to be born and grow up in a year (Aratus; Callimachus, *Zeus,* 55 ff., etc.) and to die once more. Orpheus made much use of these facts (Lobeck, *Aglaophamus,* i. 552 ff.).'

I had used Hebrew names connected with the symbolic tree, and the star at which the arrow was shot seems to have symbolized Kether, a Sephiroth attributed to the sun, and my invocation had for its object the killing or overcoming in some way of a 'solar influence'.[a]

(b) The Woman who shot the Arrow

She was, it seems, the Mother-Goddess, whose representative priestess shot the arrow at the child, whose sacrificial death symbolized the death and resurrection of the Tree-spirit, or Apollo. 'She is pictured upon certain Cretan coins of the fifth century B.C. as a slightly draped, beautiful woman, sitting in the heart of a branching tree. (G. F. Hill, *A Handbook of Greek and Roman Coins,* p. 163.) She goes back to the very earliest form of the religion of Crete, and is, it seems probable, the Tree as Mother, killing the Tree as Son. But she is also Artemis, and there is a beautiful vase at Naples (Reinach, *Répertoire des vases peints grecs,* i.379.1), which shows her archaic image upon a tall pillar with a strung bow in her left hand and a *patera* in her right.'[b]

(c) The Heart torn out

A Father of the Church, Firmicus Maternus, in his book, *On the Errors of the Profane Religions,* turns the Myth of the Child Slain and Reborn into a story of murder and adultery. The Cretan Jupiter 'made an image of his son in gypsum and placed the boy's heart . . . in that part of the figure where the curve of the chest was to be seen'. It had been kept by his sister, Minerva, and a temple was made to contain the image. There were festivals and noisy processions that followed 'a basket in which the sister had hidden the heart'. 'It may be conjectured, perhaps,' writes my learned man, 'that images were made with a chest cavity to contain the heart of the sacrificed.'[c]

(d) The Star

The Star goes right back to the Cretan Mother-Goddess. The later Greek form of it was Asterios or Asterion. The latter, for example, is said to be Jupiter's son by Idaia (Pausanias, ii.31.1). 'This Star name did not mean in its primary use any particular star. It appears to have meant the Starry Heavens . . . Zeus-Asterios is a late Gortynian (Cretan) collocation (Johannes Malala, *Chronicum*, 5). In the earlier thought of Crete, her deified kings bore the same name, Asterion or Asterios (*e.g.* Bacchylides, frag. 47, and Diodorus, iv.60).'[d]

(e) The Centaur

'There is a fragment of a very early Greek pot showing two roughly drawn centaurs with long thin legs, one of the centaurs touching with his hand a tree which has long leaves and what seems to be a round fruit. Above the centaurs, but apparently separate from the tree, a bird perches on a twig (Salzmann, *Nécropole de Camires,* plate XXXIX).'[e]

(f) Sagitta

'About the third century B.C. we find Apollo is closely linked with the constellation Sagitta.' I find in a book upon astrology published this year: 'Sagittarius. The symbol is an arrow shot into the unknown. It is a sign of Initiation and Rebirth.' (*A Student's Textbook of Astrology,* by Vivian E. Robson, p. 178.)[f]

[a]Mary E. J. (Mrs. Henry Pennell Whitcombe, d. 1887) Whitcombe, *Bygone Days in Devonshire and Cornwall, with Notes of Existing Superstitions and Customs* (London: R. Bentley and Son, 1874).

The nine Kouretes (Curetes or WBY's 'Kowetes') were sons of Earth and attendants of the young Zeus in Crete. A fragmentary inscription of about 200 B.C. containing a hymn invoking Zeus in the name of the Kouretes was discovered at Palaikastro. Rhea, mother of Zeus, taught them a wild, leaping dance.

Balder: The Scandinavian god of light and day, the beautiful and blameless god, son of Odin and Frigg, was slain inadvertently by his brother, the blind god Hodur.

Aratus, *Phaenomena,* ll. 32 ff. refer specifically to Zeus, and Callimachus, 'Hymn I. To Zeus', ll. 55 ff., in *Callimachus and Lycophron,* tr. A. W. Mair; *Aratus,* tr. G. R. Mair (London: Heinemann, 1921), pp. 209 and 43, respectively.

For Orpheus, see 'Carminum orphicorum reliquiae' in Christian August Lobeck, *Aglaophamus,* 2 vols. (Konigsberg, Prussia, 1829), I, 552 ff.

In Cabbalism, the highest of the ten emanations (Sephiroth) of god is Kether, the Crown. Its depiction sometimes includes a sun, as in the Golden Dawn diagrams illustrated in Kathleen Raine,

Yeats, the Tarot and the Golden Dawn, 2nd ed., New Yeats Papers no. 2 (Dublin: Dolmen Press, 1976), plates 6 and 7. Kether, however, is specifically associated with the Primum Mobile, not the sun, which is associated with the sixth Sephiroth, Tiphereth, the beauty and splendor of god, as WBY mentions on page 282 below and as Macgregor Mathers lists them in his preface to *The Kabbalah Unveiled* (London: G. Redway, 1887), plates III and IV.

ᵇGeorge F. Hill, *A Handbook of Greek and Roman Coins* (London and New York: Macmillan, 1899), p. 163 and plate IV, no. 2 (as Europa); for this silver coin showing Europa seated in a tree, and for similar silver and bronze coins, see Warwick Wroth, *Catalogue of the Greek Coins of Crete and the Aegean Islands,* ed. R. S. Poole (Bologna: Forni, 1963), p. 38, Gortyna, no. 6 and plate IX, no. 5, and pp. 38–40, 42, nos. 6–30, 40–46.

Salomon Reinach, *Répertoire des vases peints grecs et étrusques,* 2 vols. (Paris, 1899, 1900), I, 379.1. Patera: ancient saucer for drinking or libations.

See 'Parnell's Funeral' (w. 1933, publ. 1934), ll. 1–15 P 285.

ᶜJulius Firmicus Maternus, fourth-century Sicilian pagan astronomer and then Christian polemicist, in his *De errore profanarum religionum* (c. 346), ch. 6.4–5; see *Firmicus Maternus: The Error of the Pagan Religions,* tr. and annotated Clarence A. Forbes, 'Ancient Christian Writers,' no. 37 (New York: Newman Press, 1970), pp. 55–56.

ᵈPausanias, *Description of Greece,* II. xxxi.§1; this passage is in the one volume that WBY owned of the six-volume Loeb Classical Library edition, tr. W. H. S. Jones (London: Heinemann, 1918) (O'Shea no. 1545), I, 415. Johannes Malala, *Historia Chronica* in J.-P. Migne, *Patrologiae Graeca,* XCVII, cols. 679–80 (Book V, 94c and note 10). Bacchylides, fragment 47, in *Greek Lyric,* ed. and tr. David A. Campbell, Loeb Classical Library (Cambridge, MA and London: Harvard University Press, 1992), IV, 296–97. Diodorus of Sicily, *The Library of History,* IV.60 ('Asterius'), tr. C. H. Oldfather (London: Heinemann, 1939), III, 7.

ᵉAuguste Salzmann, *Nécropole de Camiros* (not Camires) *(Île de Rhodes). Journal des fouilles exécutées dans cette nécropole pendant les années 1858 à 1865* (Paris: Detaille, 1875), plate XXXIX.

ᶠVivian E. Robson, *A Student's Textbook of Astrology* (London: Cecil Palmer, 1922) (O'Shea no. 1773), p. 178.

39. Symons, 'To a Woman Seen in Sleep' (dated 15 August 1896), *Love's Cruelty* (London: Secker, 1923), p. 75.

40. William Sharp's story 'The Archer', written under his female pseudonym Fiona Macleod, was not published by the *Savoy*. The CL2 appendix 'The Vision of the Archer' provides a coherent hypothesis for how Sharp added the passage describing a vision similar to WBY's (659), and Donoghue's note at the relevant section of Mem (102–03, 103 n.1) quotes the passage from the story as published in *Tragic Romances* (Edinburgh: Geddes, 1897), pp. 253–54.

41. An untraced member of the Golden Dawn (Mem 103).

42. Maud Gonne and her daughter, Iseult.

43. Untraced.

44. Olivia Shakespear; see note 34 above.

45. Dr. William Wynn Westcott (1848–1925), who founded the Isis-Urania Temple of the Hermetic Order of the Golden Dawn with MacGregor Mathers and William K. Woodman.

46. For the Sephiroth of the Cabbalistic Tree of Life, see notes 38, p. 473 and 38ª above. Tipareth, the beauty and splendour of god, is the sixth lowest of the ten Sephiroth; Yesod, the foundation, is the ninth. For the serpent intertwining the paths that interconnect the Sephiroth, see the Golden Dawn diagrams illustrated in Kathleen Raine, *Yeats, the Tarot and the Golden Dawn*, 2nd ed., New Yeats Papers no. 2 (Dublin: Dolmen Press, 1976), plates 10–13.

47. 'Mark of Man' is not Honoré de Balzac's phrase, but conveys his sense, in *Séraphîta* (1834–35), p. 112: 'Man alone—he alone here on earth having any consciousness of the infinite—can know the straight line' (tr. Clara Bell, *Comédie Humaine*, ed. George Saintsbury [Dent Edition, 1895–98], repr. as vol. XXXIV of the Temple Edition [New York: Macmillan, 1901] [O'Shea n. 106]). In 1926, WBY here added a cross-reference note to see 'however' his note 38 above, which gives the information he received from Dr. Vacher Burch.

48. Lady Isabella Augusta Gregory (1852–1932), Irish writer, patron, co-founder of the Abbey, born at Roxborough, Co. Galway. In 1880, she married Sir William Gregory, who owned the nearby estate of Coole Park. He died in 1892, and, in 1896, Lady Gregory met WBY in London, and he visited Coole Park for the first time. WBY, Lady Gregory, and Edward Martyn founded the Irish Literary Theatre, which became the Abbey Theatre. Lady Gregory's work for the theatre was substantial as a director and as a contributing playwright. Her impact on WBY, as friend, patron, and literary collaborator, is beyond measure. See WBY's own account and tribute in *Personae* and his poems 'Beautiful Lofty Things', 'Coole Park, 1929', and 'Coole and Ballylee, 1931' (P 303, 242, 243).

49. Coole Park, Lady Gregory's estate, near Gort, Co. Galway, had been purchased by Robert Gregory in 1768. The house was pulled down in 1941. See Lady Gregory's *Coole* (Dublin: Cuala Press, 1931; Dolmen Press, 1971).

50. 'The path of the cameleon'; see note 1, p. 466.

51. WBY never finished his autobiographical novel *The Speckled Bird*, on which he worked from 1896 to about 1902. In that novel, the hero attempts to establish a mystical brotherhood that would be a combination of art and magic. This corresponded to WBY's interest in founding his own mystical order of Celtic mysteries. The main characters are based on himself, Maud Gonne, Olivia Shakespear, MacGregor Mathers, and his father. See the annotated edition SB.

52. Gustave Flaubert, *The Temptation of Saint Anthony* (1874), tr. D. F. Hannigan (London: Nichols, 1895) (O'Shea no. 682).

53. Henry More (1614–87, English philosopher of the Cambridge Platonist school), *The Immortality of the Soul* (1659; rev. 1662) (Book III, ch. ii, sec. I) in *A Collection of Several Philosophical Writings,* 2nd ed. (London: William Morden, 1662) (O'Shea no. 1377), p. 151.

54. For a ghost 'dreaming back' through the events of life, see V 220–40.

55. For WBY's other reports of this incident, which occurred in 1898, see Myth 68, SB 32, Mem 126, and LE 19; he recorded it in a two-volume journal titled 'Visions, begun July 11, 1898'.

56. CF. Matthew 1:23.

57. F. Crawford Burkitt, *Early Eastern Christianity* (London: John Murray, 1904), pp. 218–23 for 'The Hymn of the Soul'. There is no footnote.

58. Edward Martyn was also present at this meeting in August 1897 at Duras House.

59. Lady Gregory's plays include: *Spreading the News* (27 December 1904), *Kincora* (25 March 1905), *Hyacinth Halvey* (19 February 1906), *The Goal Gate* (20 October 1906), *The Rising of the Moon* (9 March 1907), *The Poorhouse* (with Douglas Hyde, produced 3 April 1907), and *The Workhouse Ward* (20 April 1908). She created the 'Kiltartan' dialect and translated Celtic legends from the Irish, as collected in *Cuchulain of Muirthemne* (1902) and *Gods and Fighting Men* (1904).

60. *Mabinogion* (1838–49). Lady Charlotte Guest's collection of the first four Welsh tales from the two Welsh manuscripts 'White Book of Rhydderch' (1300–25) and 'Red Book of Hergest' (1375–1425).

61. See note 12, p. 492.

62. Sir Hugh Percy Lane (1875–1915), Irish art dealer and collector, Lady Gregory's nephew, met WBY at Coole Park in 1900. His great collection of modern, mostly French, paintings was disputed between the National Galleries of London and Dublin until 1959, when it was determined to divide the collection and alternate the halves between cities. See Lady Gregory's *Hugh Lane's Life and Achievement* (London: J. Murray, 1921), repr. in *Sir Hugh Lane: His Life and Legacy* (Gerards Cross: Colin Smythe, 1973).

DRAMATIS PERSONAE 1896–1902

1. Roxborough House was Lady Gregory's family home. The Irish Civil War—between the army of the Irish Free State, led by those who had signed and supported the treaty (1921) ending the Anglo-Irish War, and the Republican wing of the IRA—lasted from June 1922 to April 1923.
2. The Ministry of Lands and Agriculture purchased Coole in 1927 and pulled it down in 1941.
3. WBY and Symons went on their tour of Ireland from August to September 1896. Symons wrote his impressions of the visit and published them in the *Savoy*, October and November 1896.
4. Edward Martyn (1859–1924), Irish dramatist, founded the Irish Literary Theatre in 1899 with WBY and Lady Gregory and financed the first season. His play *The Heather Field* was produced in the group's first season, May 1899, and *Maeve* was produced in 1900. Martyn, a devout Catholic and lifelong bachelor, had differences with the theatre group, which became the Abbey Theatre Company, and eventually withdrew in 1914. He helped to found the short-lived Irish Theatre in Dublin with Joseph Plunkett and Thomas MacDonagh, the annual music festival Feis Ceoil, and the Palestrina Choir in Dublin's Pro-Cathedral. He was President of Sinn Féin from 1904 to 1908.
5. For Swift, see Background Notes on Writers, p. 437.
6. Robert Gregory (1727–1810), the great-grandfather of Lady Gregory's husband, Sir William. He was chairman of the great trading company, served in parliament twice, and was responsible for building Coole Park.
7. Sir William Gregory was the Governor of Ceylon from 1871 to 1877.
8. Richard Gregory (1761–1839), Lieutenant in the Life Guards, owned Coole from 1810, and was responsible for its library. His first wife was Isabella Nimmo.

9. For Edmund Burke, see Background Notes on Writers, p. 532.

10. Slieve Aughty (which WBY variously referred to as Slieve Echtge, Echtge Hills, and Slieve Ochta) is a range of mountains east of Gort and south of Loughrea, Co. Galway.

11. A Protestant nationalist organisation which helped to bring about an independent parliament under Grattan in 1782. William Persse (1727–1802) formed the Roxborough Volunteers in 1777.

12. In 1902, George Wyndham, the Irish Secretary, presented a land purchase bill that was rejected. In 1903, John Shawe-Taylor (1866–1911) helped to organize a conference that led to the Land Purchase Act of 1903, which offered favorable terms for tenants to buy and inducements to landlords to sell, and so led to the redistribution of land in Ireland.

13. The nine (not seven) brothers were known to be wild in their hunting and other pastimes: Dudley (half-brother), Richard Dudley, William Norton, Edward, Algernon, Francis Fitz Adelm, Henry, Gerald Dillon, and Alfred Lovaine.

14. Jonah Barrington (1760–1834), author of *Personal Sketches of his own Times,* 3 vols. (London: Colburn, 1827–30 [vols. I, II]; London: Colburn and Bentley, 1833 [vol. III]).

15. Frances Barry of Castle Cor was Lady Gregory's mother and followed the teachings of the evangelical Reverend John Cuming of Scotland. Along with two stepdaughters, Katerine and Maria, and her eldest daughter, Elizabeth, she undertook converting the local Catholic peasantry.

16. Probably Asenath Nicholson. See *Ireland's Welcome to the Stranger, or An Excursion Through Ireland, in 1844 & 45, For the Purpose of Personally Investigating the Condition of the Poor* (New York: Baker and Scribner, 1847).

17. Patrick Corbet (d. 1840).

18. Henry Hart.

19. Rose la Touche (1849–75). After his failed, unconsummated marriage to his cousin Euphemia Gray, John Ruskin fell in love with Rose, who was not quite ten years old when they met in 1859. When she was seventeen and Ruskin almost fifty, he proposed to her, but they did not marry.

20. Sir William Gregory (1817–92). Conservative M.P. for Dublin from 1842 to 1847 and a Liberal M.P. for County Galway from 1857 to 1871. He served as Governor of Ceylon from 1871 to 1877 and was a trustee of the National Gallery from 1867 to 1892. He came home to Coole in 1877 and married Isabella Augusta Persse (Lady Gregory), his second wife, in 1880.

21. Aristotle, in the *Art of Rhetoric,* Book III, recommends appropri-

ate diction. Lady Gregory may have found this favorite remark in the work of Roger Ascham (1515–68); see Lady Gregory's *Journals,* ed. Daniel J. Murphy (Gerrards Cross: Colin Smythe, 1978), I, 450.

22. Douglas Hyde gave a presidential address, 'The Necessity for De-Anglicising Ireland', to the National Literary Society, Dublin, on 25 November 1892; it was published in *The Revival of Irish Literature* (London: T. Fisher Unwin, 1894), pp. 115–61. In 1893, he helped to found the Gaelic League whose purpose was to revive both Gaelic culture and Irish as a spoken language.

23. Untraced as quoted. Likely candidates include Heraclitus, Blake, Hegel, Nietzsche.

24. The amendment to the Ireland Local Government Bill that allowed the granting of licences for theatres in approved buildings was accepted on 11 July 1898.

25. With Maud Gonne. See Mem 125: 'It was a time of great personal strain and sorrow. Since my mistress [Olivia Shakespear] had left me, no other woman had come into my life, and for nearly seven years none did. I was tortured by sexual desire and disappointed love. Often as I walked in the woods at Coole it would have been a relief to have screamed aloud. When desire became unendurable torture, I would masturbate, and that, no matter how moderate I was, would make me ill. It never occurred to me to seek another love. I would repeat to myself again and again the last confession of Lancelot, and indeed it was my greatest pride, "I have loved a queen beyond measure and exceeding long".'

26. See note 35, p. 473.

27. In 1912, WBY began writing two essays, 'Witches and Wizards and Irish Folklore' and 'Swedenborg, Mediums, and the Desolate Places', which were finished in 1914, as well as forty-five notes, finished in 1915, for Lady Gregory's *Visions and Beliefs in the West of Ireland* (LE 47–83, 258–90). The book was in press in 1916, but its publication was delayed until 1920 (New York and London: G. P. Putnam's Sons).

28. George Augustus Moore (1852–1933), Irish novelist, playwright, and landowner. Moore was working as a writer in London by 1880. His novels include *A Modern Lover* (1883), *A Mummer's Wife* (1885), *A Drama in Muslin* (1886), *Esther Waters* (1894), *Evelyn Innes* (1898), *Sister Teresa* (1901), and *The Lake* (1905). His collections of essays include *Parnell and his Ireland* (1887; in French, 1886) and *Modern Painting* (1893). Moore's three-volume autobiography, *Hail and Farewell!: Ave* (1911), *Salve* (1912), *Vale* (1914), is an account of his life in Ireland, to which

he had returned from London in the early 1900s. The collaboration with WBY was a series of quarrels, and their relationship further deteriorated over WBY's play *Where There is Nothing*. Moore did no further work for the Irish theatre and returned to London in 1911. The unflattering portraits of WBY and Lady Gregory in *Hail and Farewell!* were resented by WBY, and *Dramatis Personae* includes his revenge.

29. Yeats, *The Cat and the Moon* (1926) CPlays 465.

30. The penal laws, an intricate series of severe restrictions on the education, ownership of property, and political activity of Catholics in Ireland, were instituted 1695–1727. Their enforcement eased during the second half of the eighteenth century, and the laws were rescinded by a series of relief acts in 1782, 1793, and 1829.

31. *The Works of William Blake, Poetic, Symbolic and Critical* (London: Bernard Quaritch, 1893). See pages 144–147 above.

32. WWB, III, 'Reproductions: Thel', p. 2; see pages 144–147 above.

33. John P. Mahaffy (1839–1919), Irish classicist; Professor of Ancient History (1869) and Provost (1914), Trinity College, Dublin. Moore's attack appeared in the *Leader* (Dublin, 20 July 1901).

34. Édouard Manet, *Portrait of George* Moore (1878 or 1879), pastel on canvas, 55 cm. x 35 cm., Metropolitan Museum of Art, New York; illus. François Cachin and Charles S. Moffett, *Manet 1832–1883* (New York: Abrams, 1983), plate 176. WBY hardly exaggerates in his description of this portrait, which was nicknamed *Le noyé repêché* (the drowned man fished out of the water). Undaunted, Moore published it in 1893 as the frontispiece of his essays *Modern Painting*. There are also two unfinished portraits by Manet from this same time: a well-known oil sketch, *George Moore at the Café de le Nouvelle-Athènes*, 65 cm. x 81 cm., Metropolitan Museum of Art, New York; illus. Joseph Hone, *The Life of George Moore* (London: Gollancz, 1936), facing p. 66 and *Manet 1832–1883*, plate 175; and one of Moore seated on a folding chair in the garden next to Manet's studio, oil, 55 cm. x 46 cm.; illus. Paul Jamot and Georges Wildenstein, *Manet* (Paris: Les Beaux-Arts, 1932), fig. 201.

35. Milton, *Paradise Lost,* VII, 463–66.

36. WBY's essay is 'Speaking to the Psaltery' (1902) (E&I 13–27). Florence Farr and others chanted lyrics of WBY and others to the accompaniment of the psaltery, an ancient stringed instrument similar to a harp, built by Arnold Dolmetsch (1858–1940), an authority on medieval music; and WBY then lectured on the new art form.

37. See note 18, p. 441 and note 3, p. 469.

38. WBY quotes here from letters he wrote between 1898 and 1900.

39. WBY's essays and notes for Lady Gregory's two-volume collection of folklore, *Visions and Beliefs in the West of Ireland,* can be traced back to 1897, when Lady Gregory began taking him along while she collected folklore in the vicinity of Coole Park. Between November 1897 and April 1902, he published six lengthy articles that made extensive use of that folklore (UP2 54–70, 74–87, 94–108, 167–83, 219–36, and 267–82).

40. The reference here could be to an inheritance from uncle George Pollexfen in 1910 or from Alfred Pollexfen in 1916 or, less likely, from uncle William Middleton Pollexfen in 1913. WBY's subsequent lecture tours in America were in 1914 and 1920.

41. WBY letter to Lady Gregory, 6 November (1898), CL2 289 (L 304). For the singing by Captain C. K. Greene at this concert, 3 November 1898 at the Sligo Town Hall, see CL2 288 n.6.

42. WBY letter to Lady Gregory (1 June 1898), CL2 231–32 (dated [29 June 1898] in L 300–01). For the lecture by George Francis Savage-Armstrong (1846–1906), Professor of English at Queen's College, Cork (now University College, Cork) and Fellow in English at the Royal University, Dublin (now University College, Dublin), on 27 May 1898 at the Society of Arts, Adelphi, London, see CL2 231 n.4.

43. WBY letter to Lady Gregory (11–12 August 1898), CL2 259 (dated [11 August 1898] in L 303).

44. Amilcare Cipriani (1844–1918), Italian revolutionary who fought in Italy, Greece, Egypt, and France, had been imprisoned, and befriended by Maud Gonne in Paris. He travelled to Dublin with WBY and Maud Gonne for the 15 August 1898 celebrations. See CL2 260 nn. 1 and 2, 261 n.1 and page 278 above.

45. WBY letter to Lady Gregory (10 April 1900), CL2 512 (L 339); for Lady Gregory's reply, see CL2 512 n.12.

46. WBY letter to Lady Gregory (12 May 1900), CL2 525–26. Exposition Universelle, Paris, opened 14 April 1900. WBY had included this ancedote in a speech he gave in New York, 28 February 1904 (UP2 324). The play was *Tadg Saor* (Tadhg the Smith) by Father Peter O'Leary (1839–1920), who had been a parish priest in Macroon, Co. Cork. It was first produced 13 May 1898, in Macroon. See CL2 526 n. 4, which includes a translation of the play's jibes at bailiffs, and *Samhain: 1901* (*Ex* 78).

47. Althea Gyles; the scoundrel is the publisher Leonard Smithers (CL2 473–74 and see note 81, p. 464).

48. WBY letter to Lady Gregory (28–29 November 1898), CL2 473–74 (dated 28 November 1898 in L 330).

49. WBY's letter to Lady Gregory, 20 December (1900), identifies the 'rich member' as Annie E. F. Horniman and 'Lady ——' as Lady Colin Campbell (1858–1911), a successful writer and journalist, whose sensational divorce case in 1886 had included a lengthy list of her romantic affairs (CL2 610, 611, 611 n.9). The editors of CL2 suggest that the reference to 'another mystic', who is left unnamed in the letter, is possibly Althea Gyles's cousin, Mrs. Florence Kennedy (611 n.8).

50. WBY's letter of 20 December (1900) (CL2 611); for 'Idle Devout' as Sister Cecilia in George Moore's novel *Sister Teresa* (w. 1899–1900, publ. 1901), p. 96, see CL2 611 n.11.

51. WBY letter to Lady Gregory (12 December 1900), CL2 603 (L 347). The reference to the Greek warrior Patroclus, killed by Hector and mourned by Briseïs and other women captured by the Trojans, is *Iliad,* XIX, 301–2: 'Thus she spoke, weeping; and the women lamented for Patroclus, as a pretext, but [really] each for her own ills' (*The Iliad of Homer,* tr. Theodore Alois Buckley [1865; rpt. London: Bell and Daldy, 1870] [O'Shea no. 905], p. 364; '[really]' is printed thus).

52. The first productions by the Irish Literary Theatre, forerunner of the Abbey, were WBY's *The Countess Cathleen* (CPlays 1–50), 8 May 1899, and Edward Martyn's *The Heather Field,* 9 May 1899, at the Antient Concert Rooms, Brunswick Street, Dublin, now the Academy Cinema in the renamed Pearse Street.

53. WBY letter to Lady Gregory (21 April 1899), which identifies the 'Dublin amateur actor' as Valentine R. Grace (CL2 397–98, 398 n.1).

54. WBY letter to Lady Gregory (21 April 1899), CL2 398. In the role of Countess Cathleen, May Whitty replaced Florence Farr's neice, Dorothy Paget (1883–1980), who had played the Fairy Child in the 1894 production of WBY's *The Land of Heart's Desire* at the Avenue Theatre, London; see CL2 395 nn. 1–3.

55. WBY letter to Dorothy Paget (19 April 1899), CL2 396, in which WBY tells her 'you brought tears to both Mrs. Emery's eyes & mine not by pathos but by beauty.' The comment about May Whitty's performance in the dress rehearsal is untraced.

56. Frank Hugh O'Donnell (1848–1916), Foreign Editor of the *Morning Post,* and M.P., 1874 and 1877–85. He wrote one letter about the *Countess Cathleen* to the *Freeman's Journal* and published this with another in the pamphlet 'Souls for Gold! Pseudo-Celtic Drama in Dublin' (1899), reprinted in CL2 674–80, see also CL2 379 n. 2, 387 n. 1, and appendix 'The Countess Cathleen Controversy', 669–74.

57. Michael, Cardinal Logue (1839–1924), Primate of All-Ireland,

letter to the editor of the *Daily Nation,* 10 May 1899, reprinted in CL2 410 n. 2; see also CL2 673.

58. Father William Barry (1849–1930), priest, novelist, critic, essayist, and member of the Irish Literary Society in London. His novel, *The New Antigone,* was published in 1887. He was a friend of Lionel Johnson and other writers. See CL2 160, n. 6, 379 n. 2, and 670.

59. WBY letter to Lady Gregory (9 April 1899), CL2 390–91.

60. Joseph Patrick Quinn (1863?–1915); see CL2 9 n. 1.

61. See pp. 277–279 above and note 24, p. 483.

62. From the Angel's speech at the end of scene V, CPlays 50.

63. Scene V, CPlays 44.

64. Synge's *Playboy of the Western World* had occasioned riots in 1907, as did Sean O'Casey's *The Plough and the Stars* in 1926. For O'Casey, see Background Notes on Writers, p. 536.

65. From Aleel's speech in scene I of *The Countess Cathleen,* CPlays 4.

66. Moore, *Hail and Farewell!:* I: *Ave,* 94–95.

67. *The Heather Field* was first produced on 9 May 1899 at the Antient Concert Rooms, Dublin. May Whitty played Mrs. Grace Tyrrell, and Thomas Kingston played Carden Tyrrell.

68. The Royal Commission promised by Gladstone in 1893 was chaired by his Lord Chancellor, H.C.E. Childers (1827–96). It began work in 1894 and in 1896 confirmed that Ireland had been overtaxed by £250,000,000 since the Act of Union (1800). An All-Ireland Committee was formed which called for a conference of Irish parliamentarians to discuss this wrong and organize against it. The unionists and nationalists could not agree on a plan and it became obvious that the English government was not going to act. The short-lived government of Lord Salisbury appointed a second commission in 1897, chaired by Sir Edward Fry (1827–1918).

69. Standish James O'Grady (1846–1928), Irish historian, editor, and novelist. His *History of Ireland: Heroic Period* (1878) and its second volume, *Cuchulain and his Contemporaries* (1880), are among his several books of Irish history and mythology; his political works include *The Crisis in Ireland* (1882), *Toryism and Tory Democracy* (1886), and *Selected Essays and Passages* (1917). O'Grady edited *The Kilkenny Moderator,* the *All-Ireland Review* (1900–6) and contributed articles to the *New Age* and the *Irish Peasant.*

70. O'Grady's political essays are collected in *Selected Essays and Passages* (Dublin: Talbot, n.d.), pp. 151–266; see note 46, p. 461.

71. *Hail and Farewell!:* I: *Ave,* 135–36; see note 23 above.

72. WBY recalls the same remark on p. 178 above. T. W. Rolleston acted as organiser to the Department of Agriculture, 1900–5. He settled in London in 1908.
73. Moore, *Hail and Farewell!*: I: *Ave,* 154.
74. *Hamlet,* I.i. 143.
75. JBY painted an oil portrait of Standish James O'Grady in 1904, commissioned by John Quinn; Hugh Lane purchased a replica (111 cm. x 84 cm.), which he gave to the Dublin Municipal Gallery of Modern Art (no. 89 in 1908, later no. 297); it was transferred in 1970 to the National Gallery of Ireland, where it joined Quinn's copy (NGI no. 870). For an illustration, see the Municipal Gallery's 1958 catalogue, plate 37, or James White, *John Butler Yeats and the Irish Renaissance* (Dublin: Dolmen Press, 1972), plate 10.
76. The novel, of which O'Grady is not the author, is untraced. George Russell mentioned it in his description of this portrait in tribute to O'Grady included in *Standish James O'Grady—The Man and The Writer* (Dublin: Talbot Press, 1929): 'There hangs in the Municipal Gallery of Dublin the portrait of a man with brooding eyes, and scrawled on the canvas is the subject of his bitter meditation, "The Lost Land" . . .' (74).
77. Edward Martyn, *The Heather Field: A Play in Three Acts* and *Maeve: A Psychological Drama,* introduction by George Moore (London: Duckworth, 1899).
78. Moore, *Hail and Farewell!*: I: *Ave,* p. 281: 'Yeats was a sort of monk of literature, an Inquisitor of Journalism who would burn a man for writing that education was proceeding by leaps and bounds.'
79. The character Jasper Dean in Edward Martyn's play *The Tale of a Town,* re-titled *The Bending of the Bough* when revised by George Moore (London: Unwin, 1900).
80. The result of the unsuccessful attempt at collaborative play-writing, 1899–1901, by WBY and Moore. See below pp. 321 ff. and *Hail and Farewell!*: I: *Ave,* 356–78, passim.
81. 'M' is 'Magragh of the *Freeman* ['s *Journal*].' 'H' is Douglas Hyde. *Lady Gregory's Diaries 1892–1902,* ed. James Pethica (New York: Oxford, 1996), 22–24 February 1900; pp. 244–47.
82. Lady Gregory, *Our Irish Theatre* (London: G. P. Putnam, 1913), pp. 27–28.
83. Not the French statesman Talleyrand-Périgord, but Honoré Gabriel Victor Riqueti, Comte de Mirabeau (1749–91), French orator and revolutionary leader. See CL2 537 n. 4 for the quoted phrase in J. S. Smith, *Mirabeau* (1848), II, 50.
84. WBY letter to Lady Gregory (5 June 1900), CL2 536–37.

85. Untraced. WBY letter to Lady Gregory (1900), not extant.
86. Untraced. WBY letter to Lady Gregory (1900), not extant.
87. WBY letter to Lady Gregory (2 June 1900), CL2 534–35.
88. WBY offered to resign from the Irish Literary Society, London, on 16 March 1901. Foster 1 237, 578 n. 53.
89. Perhaps *The Brothers Karamazov* (1880), where the elder Zosima counsels a mysterious night visitor who confesses to a murder years ago in his youth. He left the scene, successfully, and let the guilt fall on the household servants. He now seeks absolution of sorts from Zosima based on his many good deeds throughout his adult life. See note 91, p. 466.
90. Moore did not write but may have repeated this tale, which is representative of much late nineteenth-century French decadance, such as *Contes cruels* (*Cruel Tales*) (1883) of Villiers de l'Isle-Adam (1838–89).
91. In George Moore's novel *Evelyn Innes* (1898; rev. 1901), Sir Owen Asher, a wealthy aristocrat, is the lover of the beautiful young English Catholic opera singer who is the title character.
92. In 'The Sorrow of Love' (P 40), 'The full round moon' (l. 2) becomes 'The brilliant moon' and 'The curd-pale moon' (l. 10) becomes 'The climbing moon' between the manuscript of 1891 and the final form in *Early Poems and Stories* (1925). Stallworthy, *Between the Lines*, 46–53.
93. In the story first published as *Ulick and Soracha* (1926) and then included in the second edition of *A Story-Teller's Holiday* (London: Heinemann, 1928), Ulick de Burgo visits Paris, where he sings 'in salons where all the fashion collected' (II, 34). Moore's late novel with a Homeric setting is *Aphrodite in Aulis* (1931).
94. It was not retained in the only surviving typescript (publ. 1951) of George Moore and WBY, *Diarmuid and Grania,* VPlays 1168–1222.
95. WBY letter to George Moore (?15 November 1900), CL2 585–86 (L 347, dated [? January 1901]).
96. Not in Sainte-Beuve's works. WBY also quotes it in *The Arrow* (Abbey Theatre, Dublin, June 1907); UP2 354.
97. For Joyce, see Background Notes on Writers, p. 534.
98. For Hyde, see Background Notes on Writers, p. 534.
99. The scenario for Hyde's one-act play in Irish, *Casadh an tSugáin* (The Twisting of the Rope), is from WBY's story 'The Twisting of the Rope' (1892) (Myth 225–33). In turn, the central action of that story was based on a song in Irish 'Súisín Ban' (White Coverlet) that Hyde presumably had introduced to WBY; Hyde included it in *Love Songs of Connacht* (1893) and there referred

to a song with the same name in James Hardiman's *Irish Minstrelsy* (1831). For Lady Gregory's English translation of *Casadh an tSugáin*, see note 100 below.

100. From Lady Gregory's translation of Douglas Hyde's *Casadh an tSugáin*, first published in *Samhain* (October 1901), then in Lady Gregory's *Poets and Dreamers* (1903), p. 210.

101. Synge, who died in 1909, had finished the first draft of this play in 1907 and intended to continue. It was edited by WBY, Lady Gregory, and Máire O'Neill (Molly Allgood) and produced at the Abbey, 13 January 1910, with Máire O'Neill as Deirdre.

102. One of Shakespeare's country characters such as Dull in *Love's Labour Lost* or Dogberry in *Much Ado About Nothing*, who wants to be 'set down an ass'.

103. Lady Gregory translated Molière's *The Doctor in Spite of Himself* (Abbey production, 1906), *The Rogueries of Scapin* (1908), *The Miser* (1909), and *The Would-Be Gentleman* (Abbey production, 1926) using her 'Kiltartan' dialect.

104. Mrs. Patrick Campbell (1862–1949), the English actress who had created the title role in Pinero's *The Second Mrs. Tanqueray* (1893). She began 'a long flirtation' with WBY and paid Moore and Yeats £200 for *Diarmuid and Grania*, which helped finance the Dublin performance. Foster 1 236–37.

105. Douglas Hyde's one-act curtain-raiser *Casadh an tSugáin* (*The Twisting of the Rope*) was produced 21 October 1902 in Irish by members of the Gaelic League, with the author as Hanrahan, a wandering poet. It was the first Irish play produced in a theatre. It was published, with an English translation by Lady Gregory, in *Samhain* (October 1901) and in her *Poets and Dreamers* (1903).

106. Henrik Ibsen's *The Vikings at Helgeland* (also translated as *Vikings of Helgeland* or *Warriors at Helgoland*) (1858), the first national Norwegian realistic drama. An undated (1937 or c. 1939) typewritten list of corrections for the never-published Macmillan 'Edition de Luxe' and the Scribner's Sons 'Coole Edition' calls for changing from the reading in the copy-text, *Dramatis Personae 1936*, '*Vikings at Helgeland*' (p. 61) to '*Warriors in Helgeland*' (HRC Texas, Scribner Dublin Edition papers, 'Miscellaneous Case'). That change was not made in the (1932/36) page proofs, in Auto 1955, or in this edition. The play is titled *The Vikings at Helgeland* in WBY's copy (O'Shea no. 947) of the William Archer translation, but *The Warriors at Helgeland* in his copy (O'Shea no. 946) of the R. Farquharson Sharp translation.

107. At George Moore's request, Edward Elgar wrote a horn motif, a song, some incidental music, and a funeral march for *Diarmuid and Grania*.

108. (Fr.) as it should be, proper.
109. WBY letters to Lady Gregory (18 and 21 May 1901), CL3 70, 73.
110. Douglas Hyde, *An Tincéar agus an tSidheóg* (The Tinker and the Fairy), directed by Moore, who made suggestions but did not provide a scenario; it was published in the *New Ireland Review,* May 1902. The garden party was 19 May 1902 at 4 Upper Ely Place for delegates to the *Oireachtas.* See CL3 186 n.10.
111. Gordon Craig produced Purcell's *Dido and Aeneas* and *The Masque of Love* at the Coronet Theatre, London, for the Purcell Society on 26 March 1901.
112. William G. Fay (1872–1947), Irish actor and producer. With his brother, Frank J. Fay (1870–1931), he formed the W. J. Ormonde's Comedy Combination (later, Ormonde Dramatic Society) in 1891. That became the Irish National Dramatic Company (from December 1902, Society), and in 1902, the Fays directed WBY's *Cathleen ni Houlihan* and *The Pot of Broth.* In 1903, they produced *The Hour-Glass, The King's Threshold,* Lady Gregory's *Twenty-Five* and Synge's *In the Shadow of the Glen.* They joined with WBY, Lady Gregory, and Annie Horniman to create the Abbey Theatre in 1904. William Fay directed and acted in Abbey plays until January 1908, creating the part of Christy Mahon in *The Playboy of the Western World.* He resigned from the Abbey in January 1908 when the directors did not make him manager and producer.
113. WBY probably means the Coffee Palace, Townsend Street, Dublin. The Fay brothers had an amateur acting company known as the Ormonde Dramatic Society and also as W. G. Fay's Comedy Combination or W. G. Fay's Celebrated Variety Group. They appeared in and around Dublin, 1891 to 1903, and the Coffee Palace served as their venue five times in 1899 (W. A. Henderson file 1889–1901, NLI Ms. 1729).
114. The arguments for a native, definably Irish, nationalist theatre are incorporated into *Samhain* (1901–8), the Abbey Theatre journal written and edited by WBY and included in 'The Irish Dramatic Movement, 1901–1919', *Plays and Controversies* (1923), Ex 73–243.
115. In WBY's letter to Lady Gregory (21 May 1901), CL3 71–72, 'A——' is identified as Henry Joseph Gill (1836–1903), of the Dublin publisher M. H. Gill & Son; 'B——' is identified as William Magee, a bookseller and publisher adjacent to Trinity College, Dublin.
116. In the same (21 May 1901) letter, the club is identified as the Constitutional Club, Sligo; the High Sheriff of County Sligo was WBY's uncle George J. Pollexfen. CL3 72–73.

117. The article is untraced; *Modern Painting* was published in 1893.
118. WBY letter to Lady Gregory (3 [and 5] April [1902]), CL3 166–68.
119. George Russell's *Deirdre* was produced by W. G. Fay's National Dramatic Company, 2–4 April 1902, in St. Teresa's Hall, Clarendon Street, under the auspices of Indhinde na hEireann; so was WBY's *Cathleen ni Houlihan*, with Maud Gonne in the title role. Act III of *Deirdre* had been published in Standish O'Grady's literary journal, *The All-Ireland Review*, 8 and 15 February 1902.
120. Irish mythological story of the 'Fate of the Children of Tuireann'. A.E. abandoned the project a month later.
121. Synge returned to Aran for four summers from 1899 to 1902, writing the plays *In the Shadow of the Glen* and *Riders to the Sea* in 1902. The first to be produced was *In the Shadow of the Glen*, 8–10 October 1903, by the Irish National Theatre Society at Molesworth Hall, accompanied by public protest. *Riders to the Sea* was published in *Samhain*, September 1903, and was produced 25–27 February 1904.
122. WBY letter to Lady Gregory (26 December 1902), *CL3* 285 (misdated [?26 September 1902] in L 379). For WBY's objections to the play *Sold: A Comedy of Real Life in 2 Acts* by James H. Cousins (1873–1956), see *CL3* 278 n. 2 and 285 n. 3. The first series of productions by the Irish National Dramatic Company, at the Antient Concert Rooms, had included two of his plays, *Connla, or the Sleep of the King* and *The Racing Lug*, on 29 and 31 October, respectively. Just below, WBY praises William G. Fay's performance on 30 October 1902 as the tramp in *The Pot of Broth* by WBY and Lady Gregory.
123. Douglas Hyde.
124. *Where There is Nothing*, supplement to *The United Irishman* (not *Ireland*), 1 November 1902. For that issue having been available a few days earlier, coinciding with the productions of the Irish National Dramatic Company at the Antient Concert Rooms, 28 October–1 November 1902, see Wade, *Bibliography*, pp. 59–60.
125. During John Quinn's first visit to Ireland, in the last week of August 1902, he met WBY and became a peacemaker between WBY and George Moore. He arranged WBY's lecture tour in the United States from November 1903 to March 1904. He also helped with publishing and copyrights in America for WBY, Lady Gregory, and Synge. The friendship between WBY and Quinn ceased for about five years because of WBY's brief affair with Quinn's mistress, Dorothy Coates in 1908 (see Murphy 348–49, 416, for a full account). In early 1914, Quinn arranged for WBY

to sell him some of his manuscripts to pay for the debts of JBY in New York. One was *Reveries* in 1915, now in the Healy Collection, Colby College, Waterville, Maine. WBY dedicated *The Trembling of the Veil* to Quinn in 1922.

126. Tolstoy described his religious beliefs in *What I Believe* (1883).

127. Perhaps Henry D. Davray (1873–1944), who in 1896 and 1898 had translated two of WBY's poems and one story.

128. The Stage Society, London, which gave non-commercial 'private' productions of plays, had first planned to present *Where There is Nothing* by WBY and Lady Gregory in January 1903, but the production was delayed until June 1904.

129. Lady Gregory began to learn Irish two years after Sir William's death in 1892, collecting and translating folklore from the neighborhood about Coole. She borrowed from the local dialect to give her English translations a more authentic feeling, and called it the 'Kiltartan' dialect. She used this dialect in narratives like *Gods and Fighting Men* (1904), *Poets and Dreamers* (1903), and *A Book of Saints and Wonders* (1907), in her plays for the Abbey, and in her translations of Molière. See *The Kiltartan Molière* (Dublin: Maunsel, 1910), or *The Collected Plays of Lady Gregory*, vol. IV (Gerrards Cross: Colin Smythe, 1970).

130. Lady Gregory wrote a pamphlet on Egyptian politics, 'Arabi and His Household' (1882) and one opposing home rule in Ireland, 'A Phantom's Pilgrimage: or Home Ruin' (1893).

131. The Rt. Hon. William Gregory (1762–1840), Sir William Gregory's grandfather was Under-Secretary in Dublin, 1813–30.

132. Dr. Robert Atkinson, Professor of Romance Languages and Sanskrit, responding in February 1900 to the Gaelic League's plan to have Gaelic taught in the schools, made a report on Gaelic literature before the Commission on Intermediate Education: 'It has scarcely been touched by the movements of the great literatures; it is the untrained popular feeling. Therefore it is almost intolerably low in tone.' Lady Gregory, *Gods and Fighting Men*, 461; 1970, 355.

133. WBY wrote a preface for each of these compilations of translated Irish heroic tales. See P&I 119–34, 224–25: 'I think this book is the best that has come out of Ireland in my time' (224).

134. Thomas Carlyle's disparaging opinions of Charles Lamb, recorded after his first meeting with Lamb on 5 July 1824 and a later visit on 2 November 1831, do not include the phrase 'eternity glaring'; see James A. Froude, *Thomas Carlyle: A History of the First Forty Years of his Life 1795–1835* (1882 rpt. New York: Scribner's, 1906), II, 170, and E. V. Lucas, *The Life of Charles Lamb* (London: Methuen, 1905), II, 129, 238–39.

135. Yeats, 'Coole Park, 1929' (w. 1928, publ. 1931), ll. 11–12 P 242.
136. Lady Gregory's *Gods and Fighting Men,* Book XI, 'Oisin and Patrick', part IV, 'Oisin's Laments', 457; 1970, 351–52.
137. Gregory, *Gods and Fighting Men,* Book VII, 'Diarmuid and Grania', part VI, 'The Wanderers', 382–83; 1970, 296–97.

ESTRANGEMENT

1. See the Textual Introduction above, for a discussion of WBY's selection, arrangement, and revisions of the 61 entries in *Estrangement* and the 50 entries in *The Death of Synge,* from among a total of 252 entries in his manuscript 'Journal' published in *Mem* 135–278. The entries are dated 14 January–12 March 1909 for *Estrangement* and 12 March 1909–October 1914 for *The Death of Synge.*
2. The United Arts Club, Lincoln Place, near Trinity College, Dublin (then, from 1910, Stephen's Green), founded in 1907 by Ellen Duncan (1850–1937), Curator of the Municipal Gallery of Modern Art. WBY became a member on 28 May 1908 and was made Vice President in 1910.
3. The man is identified as 'one of the group around George Russell' ('Journal', no. 6, Mem 139). See also p. 344, nos. 12 and 13 below.
4. Lady Gregory's translation of Molière's play opened at the Abbey Theatre on Thursday, 21 January 1909. 'Journal', no. 9, Mem 141, mentions 'an article in Thursday's *Sinn Féin*'.
5. Underwear: 'It's Pegeen I'm seeking only, and what'd I care if you brought me a drift of chosen females, standing in their shifts itself, maybe, from this place to the Eastern World?' (*The Playboy of the Western World,* Act III; first produced at the Abbey, 26 January 1907).
6. W. A. Henderson, with the Abbey, 1906–12.
7. Yeats, 'The Ballad of Moll Magee' (1887), l. 51 P 24.
8. George Borrow was an agent for the Bible Society, 1833–40, and wrote *The Bible in Spain; or, The Journeys, Adventures, and Imprisonments of an Englishman in an Attempt to Circulate the Scriptures in the Penisula* (1843).
9. See 'Solomon to Sheba' (1918) and 'Solomon and the Witch' (1918) P 138–39, 179–80.
10. A—— is Augustine Birrell (1850–1933), Chief Secretaty for Ireland, 1907–16 ('Journal', no. 20, Mem 145).
    WBY's NOTE: The initials used in these extracts are never those of the persons quoted or described. With the exception of A.E.,

George Russell's pseudonym, they are copied from a dictionary of painters, the initials or initial of the first name under A, then of the second under A or the first under B and so on.

11. Dean B—— is John Henry Bernard (1860–1927), Dean of St. Patrick's Cathedral, 1902–1911, Protestant Archbishop of Dublin in 1915 and Provost of Trinity College, Dublin ('Journal', no. 50, Mem 160).

12. Karl Robert Eduard von Hartmann (1842–1906), German philosopher. See 'Vacillation' (1931–32), VIII P 256–57.

13. 'The Adoration of the Magi' (w. 1895–96, publ. 1897; rev. 1904) (SRV 171; Myth 314). WBY did not adopt these ideas in his later, slight revisions of the story for 1914, 1925, and 1932–33.

14. 'Journal', no. 24, Mem 148, specifies the work by Balzac as 'The Unconscious Mummers' ('Les Comédiens sans le savoir') (1845, publ. 1846). Dubourdieu, an artist who has been 'driven crazy by Fourier's notions' of socialism, proudly describes his preposterous painting of an 'allegorical figure of Harmony' with six breasts and, at her feet, 'an enormous Savoy cabbage, the Master's symbol of Concord' (*The Unconscious Mummers*, tr. Ellen Marriage, *Comédie humaine*, ed. George Saintsbury [Dent Edition, 1895–98], repr. as vol. XXXVI of Temple Edition [New York: Macmillan, 1901] [O'Shea no. 108], pp. 46, 44, 45). WBY also mentions this image (although converting the artist into a sculptor) in *Samhain* (Ex 238) and 'If I Were Four-and-Twenty (1919) (LE 40).

15. A—— B—— is Ella Young (1867–1956), poet and mystic, disciple of A.E. and friend of Maud Gonne ('Journal', no. 7, *Mem* 140). See her memoirs, *Flowering Dusk: Things Remembered Accurately and Inaccurately* (New York: Longmans, Green, 1945).

16. Philip Francis Little.

17. 'Mr. Lane's Gallery' is the Municipal Gallery of Modern Art, Clonmell House, 17 Harcourt Street, Dublin, which had opened 20 January 1908. 'Muffed' (or muffled) glass is semi-opaque, crinkled-surface glass made by flattening a cylinder ('muff') of blown glass (O.E.D.).

18. For WBY's relationship with the conservative London weekly the *Spectator,* see p. 250 and note 74, p. 477.

19. For WBY on William Allingham (1824–89) as the poet of Ballyshannon, Co. Donegal, and on the patriot poet Thomas Davis, see his Preface (1894) to *A Book of Irish Verse Selected from Modern Writers* (P&I 104–6).

20. Johnny Healy. See p. 47 above.

21. Synge died two months later, 24 March 1909.

22. Lily Yeats.
23. Richard Gregory (b. 1909), son of Robert Gregory (1881–1918).
24. Versailles was the great center of French court life in the *ancien régime*. WBY visited Urbino, a mountain town in central Italy, with Lady Gregory and Robert Gregory in 1907. Count Baldassare Castiglione (1478–1529), Italian diplomat and writer, was at Urbino, 1504–16, and described in *The Courtier* (1528; Engl. tr. 1561, Thomas Hoby) the ideals of courtly life at Urbino, first under Duke Guidobaldo da Montefeltro and then, from 1508, Francesco Maria della Rovere, Duke of Urbino (1490–1538). WBY owned a 1900 edition of the Hoby translation (O'Shea no. 351) and he used the annotated translation by Leonard E. Opdycke, *The Book of the Courtier* (London: Duckworth, 1902); see V(1925)CE note to p. 42, ll. 9–11.
25. Blake, *Jerusalem,* plate 42, l. 68 (Keynes 671): 'They inquire after Jerusalem in the regions of the dead.'
26. Blake wrote 'To create a little flower is the labor of ages' ('Proverbs of Hell', *The Marriage of Heaven and Hell,* plate 9, l. 17 [Keynes 152]).
27. Blake's wording is 'every thing that lives is holy' in 'A Song of Liberty' (1793), plate 25, of *The Marriage of Heaven and Hell* (1790?–93), last sentence; *Visions of the Daughters of Albion* (1793), plate 8, l. 10; *America a Prophecy* (1793), plate 8, l. 13; and *Vala, or the Four Zoas* (1759–1804), 'Night the Second', plate 34, l. 80 (l. 366) (Keynes 160, 195, 199, 289).
28. Nietzsche's 'Übermensch'. Soon after his first reading of Nietzsche, WBY wrote, in a letter to John Quinn, 6 February (1903): 'I had never read him before, but find that I had come to the same conclusions on several cardinal matters. He is exaggerated and violent but has helped me very greatly to build up in my mind an imagination of the heroic life.' (CL3 313; see also CL3 313 n. 1)
29. *Pericles,* II in *Plutarch's Lives,* tr. Bernadotte Perrin, 10 vols. (London: Heinemann, 1916), III, 5.
30. The title of WBY's speech was 'The Ideas of the Young' ('Journal', no. 47, Mem 159).
31. A—— C—— is Lady Gregory ('Journal', no. 50, Mem 160).
32. *The Book of the Courtier* (1528), Castiglione 10: 'But the thinge that should not be rehersed wythout tears is, that the Dutchesse she is also dead.'.
33. Yeats, 'A Friend's Illness' (w. 1909, publ. 1910) P 97.
34. Little E—— is Edward Evans ('Journal', no. 26, *Mem* 149). He was a member of the United Arts Club and became a lay brother in the Anglican Franciscan Order.
35. Miss A—— B—— is Ella Young ('Journal', no. 56, Mem 164).

See note 15 above.

36. Ben Jonson, *Poetaster* (1601), V.i. 136–37, in which Horace praises Virgil: 'And for his poesie, 'tis so rammed with life, / That it shall gather strength of life, with being . . .' (Ben Jonson, eds. C. H. Herford and Percy Simson [Oxford: Clarendon Press, 1932], [O'Shea no. 1029], IV, 293). Horace is meant to stand for Jonson, and some readers have thought that Virgil is meant to stand for Shakespeare, although, as Jonas A. Barish points out, the relatively early date of Jonson's play could argue against a link with Shakespeare.

37. For his speech, 'The Ideas of the Young', delivered probably 3 February 1909, see p. 351 and note 30 above.

38. The creation of Eve. Genesis 2: 21–25.

39. The radical horoscope is the birth horoscope; Aquarius is the eleventh house of the zodiac, mentioned later in this section.

40. Spoken by the Druid in 'Fergus and the Druid' (1892), l. 26 (1892–1924 versions only), VP 103.

41. At the Abbey Theatre, 4 February 1907; see WBY's 'The Controversy over *The Playboy of the Western World*' (Ex 225–28), which includes an excerpt from his opening speech.

42. A—— D—— is George Russell ('Journal', no. 51, Mem 161).

43. For JBY's own account, see Hone *JBY Letters* 214; see also 'Beautiful Lofty Things' (w. 1937?, publ. 1938), ll. 2–4 P 309.

44. William Smith O'Brien (1803–64) was a leader of the unsuccessful rising of 1848. For the quotation from Goethe, see note 61, p. 475.

45. Molly Allgood played Gormleith in an Abbey Theatre production of Lady Gregory's *Kincora*, 11 February 1909.

46. 'Journal', no. 65, Mem 168, names the three plays, all produced at the Abbey Theatre: *The Man who Missed the Tide* (W. F. Casey, produced 13 February 1908), *The Suburban Groove* (W. F. Casey, 1 October 1908), and *The Country Dressmaker* (George Fitzmaurice, 3 October 1907).

47. E—— is Edward Evans ('Journal', no. 68, Mem 170).

48. L—— E—— is Richard Le Gallienne ('Journal', no. 71, Mem 171). For Le Gallienne and the Rhymers' Club, see also pp. 147–51 above.

49. Little D—— F—— of Hyderabad, India, is Sarojini Naidu (1879–1949; 'Journal', no. 74, Mem 175), a poet and later political activist, who studied in London and Cambridge, 1895–98, and was a friend of Arthur Symons and Edmund Gosse. Her father was an Edinburgh-educated, scientist-philosopher Brahmin, who established a school in Hyderabad in 1878 that pioneered in English and women's education. His house is described

in the Indian *Dictionary of National Biography*, ed. S. P. Sen (Calcutta: Institute of Historical Studies, 1974), as 'attracting intellectuals, poets, philosophers, alchemists and revolutionaries' (III, 194).

50. Dr. F—— F—— is Douglas Hyde ('Journal', no. 75, Mem 175).

51. Sinn Fein.

52. See 'On Those that hated "The Playboy of the Western World," 1907' (w. 1909, publ. 1911) P 110. The poem was based on a painting by Charles Ricketts, *Don Juan* (also known as *Don Juan in Hell*) (1906; oil, 116 cm. x 96 cm., Tate Gallery, London [no. 3221]); illus. Elizabeth Bergmann Loizeuax, *Yeats and the Visual Arts* (New Brunswick: Rutgers University Press, 1986), p. 138, fig. 40.

53. G—— is W. A. Henderson (1863–1927), business manager of the Abbey Theatre ('Journal', no. 78, Mem 176); see CL3 69 n.1.

54. B—— G—— is Maud Gonne ('Journal', no. 78, Mem 176).

55. The character Owen, 'Conchubar's attendant and spy', was not added to the first act.

56. Thomas MacDonagh (1878–1916), Irish poet, essayist, and play-wright, and executed as a leader of the 1916 rising. He had joined the Gaelic League in 1902, and his essay 'The Gaelic League and Politics' was published in the Nationalist paper the *Leader*, 3 April 1909. He had joined the Gaelic League in 1902. MacDonagh was Assistant Head at Padraic Pearse's Sgoil Éanna (St. Edna's School), Dublin, 1908–10. He joined the Irish Republican Brotherhood in 1915 and was part of its military council. WBY'S NOTE: Executed in 1916.

57. Yeats, 'The Old and the New in Ireland', *The Academy and Literature*, 6 September 1902; *Collected Works*, Vol. II, *Prose*, ed. Alan Price (London: Oxford University Press, 1966), pp. 383–86.

58. Blake said of Parliament: 'Houses of Commons & Houses of Lords appear to me to be fools; they seem to me to be something Else besides Human Life' [*Public Address*] from the *Note-Book*, pp. 18–19 (Keynes 600). The phrase from Blake's notebook was first published 1893 in the Ellis and WBY edition WWB, I, 211. D. G. Rossetti's edited transcript of [*Public Address*], which was published in William Gilchrist's *Life of William Blake* in 1863, had omitted it (2nd ed. [London: Macmillan, 1880], II, 164-77).

59. *King Lear* II.iv.57. WBY defined it as 'sheer madness' in 'Rosa Alchemica' (1896) (Myth 278) and later used the term in 'Parnell's Funeral' (1934) and 'A Bronze Head' (1939) (P 279, 340).

60. In a letter to Lady Gregory (8 March 1909 [L 525]), WBY explained that in writing 'culture is the sanctity of the intellect', he was thinking of men like Arthur Griffith (1872–1922), Irish

radical nationalist, and 'how they can renounce external things without it but not envy, revenge, jealousy and so on.'

61. Miss E—— G—— is Beatrice Elvery, née Moss, married 1912 to Charles Henry Gordon Campbell, 2nd Baron Glenavy (1885–1963) ('Journal', no. 78, Mem 176).

62. Laurence Binyon (1869–1943), *Painting in the Far East: An Introduction to the History of Pictorial Art in Asia especially China and Japan* (London: Edward Arnold, 1908).

63. Arthur Henry Hallam (1811–33), 'On Some of the Characteristics of Modern Poetry, and on the Lyrical Poems of Alfred Tennyson', *The Englishman's Magazine*, August 1831.

64. Arthur Rimbaud (1854–91), 'Les Chercheuses de poux' (The Ladies who look for Lice) (1882–83). T. Stuge Moore wrote an English version, 'The Lice-Finders' (*The Poems of T. Sturge Moore: Collected Edition* [London: Macmillan, 1932], II, 195).

65. W. E. Henley, *A Book of Verses* (London: David Nutt, 1888), re-published as *In Hospital* (London, 1903).

66. H—— is William Francis Casey (1884–1957) ('Journal', no. 58, Mem 180); for two of his plays, see note 46 above.

67. Elizabeth (Lollie) Corbet Yeats (1868–1940). Lollie was the manager and publisher of the Cuala Press. She often quarrelled with her brother, who took very seriously his position as editorial advisor of the press.

68. J—— is Ruth Pollexfen (1885–1974) ('Journal', no. 78, Mem 176), a cousin who was living with the Yeats family at Blenheim Road, Bedford Park.

69. Thomas Davis's patriotic ballad 'The Boatman of Kinsale' (c. 1844) (air 'An Cota Caoli'), in his *National and Historical Ballads, Songs, and Poems,* rev. ed (Dublin: Duffy [c. 1870]), pp. 82–83, and in the anthology of patriotic verse *The Spirit of the Nation.* In 1894, WBY had half-praised the ballad as showing Davis's poetic tenderness, except 'for his ideal of a Fisherman defying a foreign soldiery' (P&I 104). Kinsale is a fishing and resort village south of Cork.

70. Literally, 'legends (or inscription) of the centuries'.

71. K—— Street is Baggot Street ('Journal', no. 95, Mem 185). Catholic Sisters of Mercy convent.

THE DEATH OF SYNGE

1. See note 1, p. 504.

2. For an example of that unidealized physical form in the work of the Welsh artist Augustus John (1878–1961), see *Encampment*

on Dartmoor (1906; collection Mrs. E. J. Hesslein) in John Rothenstein, *Augustus John* (London: Phaidon, 1946), plate 6. WBY, in his 1908 diary, published as 'Discoveries: Second Series', in *The Irish Renaissance,* ed. Robin Skelton and David R. Clark (Dublin: Dolmen Press, 1965), comments that John worked 'without even a memory of those traditional forms imagined by artists, who were half men of science, out of a dream of bodily perfection' (p. 87).

3. Blake, *Vala or the Four Zoas* (w. 1795–1804, dated 1797), 'Night the First', l. 21: 'His fall into Division & his Resurrection to Unity' (Keynes 264).

4. Untraced as quoted. WBY had read Coventry Patmore (1823–96) and the idea is compatible with, e.g., 'Poetical Integrity' and other essays in *Principle in Art* (London: Bell, 1889).

5. The Arundel Society issued color reproductions of paintings by the Old Masters.

6. Charging an entrance fee for the Dublin Hermetic Society to a poor student from art school. Mem 33–34.

7. See p. 163 and note 124, p. 456.

8. F—— is Maud Gonne ('Journal', no. 108, Mem 191–92).

9. See note 58, p. 508.

10. This entry can be dated 20–21 March 1909. In a letter to Lady Gregory (21 March 1909), WBY mentioned the Theatre of Ireland production of *The Turn of the Road* (1906) by Rutherford Mayne (pseudonym of Irish playwright and actor Samuel J. Waddell, 1878–1967), at the Rotunda, 20 March 1909, and also mentioned this lengthy journal entry [Berg NYPL]. The Theatre of Ireland was an amateur society founded by Edward Martyn in 1906.

11. The *Suburban Groove* (1908), by William F. Casey (1884–1957), is a popular social satire on the Dublin suburb Rathmines. It had been the Abbey Theatre's first venture into plays not on Irish peasants.

12. For Thomas MacDonagh, see note 56, p. 508.

13. Probably a reference to the Catholic bishop, Patrick O'Donnell (1856–1927).

14. Molly Allgood (stage name: Máire O'Neill) (1887–1952), Abbey actress, 1905–13. She became engaged to Synge in 1906 and created the roles of Maurya in *Riders to the Sea* (1904), Pegeen Mike in *The Playboy of the Western World* (1907), and Deirdre in his posthumous *Deirdre of the Sorrows* (1910). Synge died on 24 March 1909.

15. M—— is Arthur Symons ('Journal', no. 117, Mem 199). He was placed in an asylum at Clapton, London, after having gone mad

in Italy in 1908. He did not recover for some years.

16. In 1909, WBY gave a slightly fuller version of this, in his preface to the first edition of John M. Synge's *Poems and Translations:* 'Our Daimon is as dumb as was that of Socrates when they brought in the hemlock' (E&I 306). See Plutarch, 'On the Sign of Socrates' ('A Discourse Concerning the Daemon of Socrates'), section 24 (593D–94A), in *Plutarch's Moralia,* tr. Phillip H. DeLacy and Benedict Einarson, Loeb Classical Library (London: Heinemann; Cambridge: Harvard University Press, 1959) VII, 481–85.

17. The poem, entitled 'A Question', was published in *Poems and Translations by John M. Synge* (Dublin: Cuala Press, 1909) and reprinted in the *Collected Works of J. M. Synge* (Dublin: Maunsel & Co., 1910):

> . . . I asked if I got sick and died, would you
> With my black funeral go walking too,
> If you'd stand close to hear them talk or pray
> While I'm let down in that steep bank of clay.
>
> And, No, you said, for if you saw a crew,
> Of living idiots pressing round that new
> Oak coffin—they alive, I dead beneath
> That board—you'd rave and rend them with your teeth.

The poem is also mentioned in section 29, p. 383 below.

18. A—— is W. J. Lawrence (1862–1940), Irish theatre historian and drama critic ('Journal', no. 120, Mem 200).

19. B—— is Joseph Holloway (1861–1944), architect, inveterate Dublin theatre-goer, and diarist ('Journal', no. 120, Mem 200). Selections from his lengthy manuscript journal, 'Impressions of a Dublin Playgoer' have been published as *Joseph Holloway's Abbey Theatre,* ed. Robert Hogan and Michael J. O'Neill (Carbondale: Southern Illinois University Press, 1967).

20. C—— is D. J. O'Donoghue ('Journal', no. 120, Mem 201); the obituary notice is 'John Synge: A Personal Appreciation', *Irish Independent,* 26 March 1909; see also p. 475 above.

21. D—— is Seamus O'Connolly ('Journal', no. 120, Mem 201), a member of Sinn Fein, who wrote for *Sinn Féin;* see Mem 201 n. 2.

22. E—— is W. A. Henderson ('Journal', no. 120, Mem 201); see note 6 above.

23. Untraced.

24. Dedication of *Les Employés* (1836) 'to the Contessa Serafina San Severino, née Porcia: Why should I not confess that I am proud

to bear my testimony here and elsewhere to the fact that fair and noble friendships, now as in the sixteenth century, are and have been the solace of men of letters wherever the fashion of the day may rank them? that in those friendships they have ever found consolation for slander, insult, and harsh criticism, while the approval of such an audience enables them to rise above the cares and vexations of the literary life?'

25. For Synge's poem, 'A Question', which begins 'I asked if I got sick and died', see note 17 above.

26. S—— is Maurice Joy (d. 1951), Irish journalist and poet; see Mem 202 n.1 and 203 n.1 ('Journal', no. 123, Mem 202).

27. See Mem 204 n. 2: '*Sinn Féin*, vol. III, no. 152, 3 April 1909, has an obituary essay, "The Dead", on J. M. Synge and John Lawless: "Ireland loses a national musician in Mr. Lawless. . . . Five years hence, the one thing remembered about J. M. Synge will be that he wrote *Riders to the Sea*." ' The front-page article called Synge 'a potentially great dramatist'.

28. The first production of Lady Gregory's one-act comedy *Hyacinth Halvey* was on 19 February 1906 at the Abbey Theatre.

29. Andrieu de la Vigne (d. 1515), author of *Moralité de l'Aveugle et du Boiteux* ('Morality play of the Blind Man and the Cripple'), a source for *The Well of the Saints*. See Nicholas Grene, ed. *The Well of the Saints* (Washington: Catholic University of America, 1982), pp. 6–7.

30. Byron's verse tale *The Bride of Abydos* (1813), II, ii, 27. For the association of Homer with Scio (or Chios), see note 70, p. 448.

31. *Time* by F. Norreys Connell (pseudonym of Conal Holmes O'Connell O'Riordon) (1847–1948) and *The Cross-roads* by Lennox Robinson were first produced at the Abbey Theatre on 1 April 1909. In the original version, WBY described *Time* as 'a fantasy, a little noble, a little profound, and full of suggestion', while *The Cross-roads* was 'a logical work without suggestion or nobility' ('Journal', no. 131, Mem 206–07).

32. The original version here has a sentence about the misinterpretations by the newspaper reviewers: 'Two of them state that the failure of the heroine was her husband's fault and the others imply it' ('Journal', no. 131, Mem 207).

33. *Jerusalem* (1804–20), plate 36, l. 49; *Inscriptions on engraving, The Laocoon* (c. 1820) (Keynes 663, 776).

34. For Synge's unfinished play *Deirdre of the Sorrows,* see note 101, p. 500.

35. For Elizabeth Corbet ('Lollie') Yeats's dream of a ship, see p. 375 above, no. 13, dated 28 March 1909. The 'Acting Version' of WBY's *The Shadowy Waters* was first produced at the Abbey

Theatre on 8 December 1906. It is set on the deck of a mysterious ship, with sea or sky 'represented by a semicircular cloth of which nothing can be seen except a dark abyss' (VPlays 317 [1907 version] *The Shadowy Waters, Acting Version* [London: Bullen, 1907]).

36. See note 31 above.
37. See note 33 above.
38. Lennox Robinson (1886–1958). Irish playwright and theatre manager. His plays include, in addition to *The Cross-Roads* (1909), *Harvest* (1910), *Patriots* (1912), *The Dreamers* (1915), *The Whiteheaded Boy* (1916), and *The Lost Leader* (1918). An autobiographical novel, *A Young Man from the South,* was published in 1917 and the official history of the Abbey, *Ireland's Abbey Theatre, 1899–1951,* in 1951. He was Manager and Producer at the Abbey, 1910–1914 and 1919–1923, then a member of the Board of Directors, and for many years Director of the Abbey School of Acting.
39. Goethe, *Faust,* ll. 11581–82 (Part II, Act V [scene 6; in the great forecourt of the palace]; it echoes Faust's wager with Mephistopheles in Part I). Thomas E. Webb, tr. *The First Part of the Tragedy of Faust,* 2nd ed. (London: Longmans, Green, 1898) (O'Shea no. 753), p. 268: '*Then* to the moment I might say, / O tarry yet! Thou art so fair!' See also LE 229 n. 57.
40. D—— is William Kirkpatrick Magee (1868–1961) ('Journal', no. 114, Mem 210), an Assistant Librarian at the National Library of Ireland and an editor.
41. The reference to oppression and slave labor in the brick kilns (2 Samuel 12:31 and Blake, *Jerusalem,* plate 89, l. 17) is clearer in the original version of this entry: 'Came home cross - had been in Egypt's brick kilns' ('Journal', no. 141, Mem 210).
42. See WBY's lecture, 'Tribute to Thomas Davis', Antient Concert Rooms, Dublin, 20 November 1914: 'The Royal Dublin Society [not the Royal Irish Academy] was in trouble with government and the people. Founded by the Irish Parliament, it had done much to develop the material resources of Ireland, but more and more it became a party club. Nationalists were refused admission, and it was accused of spending its money upon a political newsroom and library for the opponents of the national cause. An English government sympathetic to Ireland, that is to say, sympathetic to the party of O'Connell, was in power and thought to please Ireland by compelling the Royal Dublin Society to put off the partisan, and this it attempted roughly and brusquely, dealing as it believed with a provincial assembly. Davis led a movement in favor of the Society. Mischievous as he thought its political activ-

ities, he would not have its services forgotten nor see it reformed by foreign Law instead of Irish opinion. He asked in letters to the Press and carried public opinion with him. Would England deal so with any of its own institutions or would an Irish government? .. . To affirm national right, he gave up a party advantage. He had taught the like in songs and ballads . . . we struggle for a nation, not for a party' (*Tribute to Thomas Davis* [Cork: Cork University Press; Oxford: B. H. Blackwell, 1947], pp. 15–16).

43. Old ships used as prisons.

44. *Poems and Translations* (Dublin: Cuala Press, 1909).

45. May–June 1906.

46. D—— is Arthur Darley (1873–1929) ('Journal', no. 147, Mem 213), violinist for Abbey Theatre plays until the summer of 1906; he remained associated with the theatre.

47. An error for April 11, the date used in the 'Journal' (no. 150, Mem 214); WBY visited Stratford-on-Avon 10–13 April 1909.

48. C——is Agnes Tobin (1863–1939), American poet. M—— is Arthur Symons; see note 15 above ('Journal', no. 214, Mem 214).

49. The poet A. C. Swinburne died on 10 April 1909. Hone, *Yeats* 230, reports that WBY, upon his return to Ireland a few days later, announced to one of his sisters, 'I am King of the Cats.'

50. For Synge's poem, 'A Question,' which begins 'I asked if I got sick and died', see note 17 above. For Molly Allgood, see note 14 above.

51. S—— is George Russell ('Journal', no. 173, Mem 222); the Sunday evening 'at home' would have been 24 (or perhaps 17) April 1909.

52. Early in Act I of *Playboy of the Western World*, the heroine, Pegeen Mike, speaks admiringly of Marcus Quin, who, 'God rest him, got six months for maiming ewes, and he a great warrant to tell stories of holy Ireland till he'd have the old women shedding down tears about their feet.'

53. For Robert Burns, see Background Notes on Writers, p. 533

54. 23 October 1909, at the Theatre Royal, Dublin.

55. In *Shakespeare, His Mind and Art* (1875), ch. VIII.

56. Illustrations to 'Venetian Costume' (excerpts from *The Book of Cesare Vecellio* [1570], by Cesare Vecellio [or Vecelli] [?1521–1601], Italian painter and cousin of Titian [Tiziano Vecellio], tr. D. Nevile Lees), *The Mask: A Monthly Journal of the Art of the Theatre* (Florence), ed. Edward Craig, vol. 1, no. 12 (February 1909), 226, 229–30; see Mem 230 n. 2.

57. An error for 15 January (1910), here and in the 'Journal' (no. 203, Mem 239); the first production of Synge's *Deirdre of the*

Sorrows was on Thursday, 13 January 1910, at the Abbey Theatre, with Fred O'Donovan as Naisi and Molly Allgood (stage name: Máire O'Neill) as Deirdre.

58. Another British tour of the Abbey took place from May to June of 1911. On 1 May, the company began their tour at Stratford-upon-Avon.

59. WBY and the Abbey company had sailed from Queenstown (Cobh, Co. Cork) on 13 September 1911 for an American tour.

60. Miss V—— is Miss Nic Shiubhliagh ('Journal', no. 233, Mem 262). She replaced the ill Máire O'Neill for the American tour, 1911–12.

THE BOUNTY OF SWEDEN

1. *The Bounty of Sweden* is WBY's tribute and expression of gratitude to Sweden for his Nobel Prize of 1923 and it includes his Nobel Prize lecture, 'The Irish Dramatic Movement', which he delivered to the Swedish Royal Academy in Stockholm on 13 December 1923. His preface, dated 15 June 1924, to the Cuala Press edition of *The Bounty of Sweden: A Meditation, and a Lecture Delivered before the Royal Swedish Academy and Certain Notes* (1925; Wade no. 146) describes 'The Irish Dramatic Movement' lecture, his notes, and 'The Bounty of Sweden': 'Every winner of the Nobel Prize for Literature is invited to deliver a lecture before the Royal Swedish Academy and to send a copy to be printed in the proceedings of that body. I spoke at my own choice about our theatre, and a couple of months ago dictated to a friend as many of my words as I could remember "having failed, pen in hand and sitting at a table to overcome my indolence" and added thereto certain explanatory notes. But immediately upon my return from Stockholm I had written the meditation called "The Bounty of Sweden" which pleases me better, because it has a newer theme; and now I have put both into this little book, adding nothing new but a couple of notes (fol. [A]4ʳ).

2. 7 February 1894.

3. The Bengali poet Rabindranath Tagore (1861–1941) won the Nobel Prize for literature in 1913; he used the award of £8,000 (not £7,000) for the upkeep of the school he had established in 1901 at Santiniketa, Boljur, Bengal, which developed into the international university Visva-Bharati.

4. Mrs. W. B. Yeats (1892–1968). WBY married George Bertha Hyde-Lees on 21 October 1917. A few days after their marriage,

on 24 October, George Yeats experienced the phenomenon of automatic writing, through which WBY received messages from a spirit writer. WBY's fascination with this phenomenon laid the foundation for his mystical, philosophical thoughts that were later expressed in *A Vision* (1925; 1937). George Yeats figures prominently in WBY's poems 'Solomon to Sheba' and 'Solomon and the Witch' (P 138, 176).

5. WBY received a telegram from the Swedish minister notifying him of the prize on 14 November 1923 and a letter from the Swedish Academy dated 15 November. The prize amounted to £7,500. WBY wrote to Lady Gregory, 13 January (1924) (L 701), that he had invested £6,000, 'kept £500 to go to pay off the debt on this house [52 Merrion Square], or pay Lilly's [medical] expenses as the case may be', and £400 for the trip to Stockholm, household furnishings, and books.

6. George Trobridge, *Emanuel Swedenborg, His Life, Teachings and Influence,* 1907; 2nd ed. enlarged and illus. (London: Frederick Warne, 1914).

7. The House of Nobles (*Riddarhuset*), in Stockholm's old town district, was built in the seventeenth century in the Dutch baroque style.

8. June 1922–April 1923; see note 1, p. 491.

9. The Irish Agricultural Organisation Society, founded by Horace Plunkett, and for which A.E. was an organiser, was modelled on Danish dairy cooperatives.

10. The Danish folk high-school movement, founded in 1851 by Kristen Mikkelsen Kold (1816–70), had as its spiritual father the Danish theologian and poet Bishop Nikolai F. S. Grundtvig (1783–1872).

11. For the Stockholm City Hall, which opened in 1923, see note 46 below.

12. Carl Gustaf Uddgren (1865–1927), author of *Strindberg the Man* (tr. from the Swedish by Axel Johan Uppvall [Boston: Four Seas, 1920], 168 pp.); its ch. 7, 'The Poet and the Wolves', contains a version of the story told here.

13. *Confession of a Fool* was completed in 1888 and published without Strindberg's permission in German in 1892, in French (1895), in English (1912; tr. Ellie Schleussner), and in Swedish (1914).

14. T. S. Eliot (1888–1965), 'The Love-Song of J. Alfred Prufrock' (1915), l. 121.

15. In the 'Epilogue' (dated 11 May 1917) to *Per Amica Silentia Lunae,* WBY had reported: 'I met from time to time with the German poet Dauthendey, a grave Swede whom I only discov-

ered after years to have been Strindberg, then looking for the philosophers' stone in a lodging near the Luxembourg' (LE 32). Max Dauthendey (1867–1918) was a painter as well as a poet. August Strindberg (1849–1912), Swedish playwright, sought to make alchemical gold in Paris only during 1894–95, but he maintained occult and Swedenborgian interests during the next two years in Paris. WBY was in Paris during February 1894 and from December 1896 to January 1897. The American artist is unidentified. For the alchemical 'philosphers' stone,' see note 100, p. 480.

16. Untraced.

17. Robert A. Millikan (1868–1953), of the California Institute of Technology, 1923 Nobel laureate in physics.

18. King Gustaf V (1858–1950; reigned 1907–1950), Princess Ingeborg (1878–1958), Prince Wilhelm (1884–1965), and Princess Margaretha (1899–1977).

19. WBY here echoes his linking of Egyptian wooden carved portraits of women and paintings of women's faces by Thomas Gainsborough (English, 1727–88) V(1925) 207 and V 297.

20. Frederick Grant Banting (1891–1941) and John James Richard Macleod (1876–1935), winners of the 1923 Nobel Prize for physiology and medicine, for their discovery of insulin.

21. The Nobel medal in literature (23 kt. gold, 66 mm. diameter) was designed in 1902 by Erik Lindberg. The front has an image of Alfred Nobel; the reverse shows a young man sitting under a laurel tree, who, enchanted, listens to and writes down the song of the Muse. Its inscription, based on the *Aeneid,* VI, 663, reads 'Inventas vitam juvat excoluisse per artes' (Inventions enhance life, which is beautified through art). For an illustration, see Erik Bergengien, *Alfred Nobel: The Man and his Work* (London: Thomas Nelson and Sons, 1962), plate 15.

22. Emanuel Swedenborg, *Conjugial Love* (1768), no. 44, sect. IX; see note 89, p. 465.

23. The inclusion of Ibsen, a Norwegian, led one Stockholm newspaper to wonder whether Yeats had forgotten he was in Sweden (Birgit Bramsbäck, 'Yeats and the "Bounty of Sweden" ', in *Yeats the European,* p. 95). Only in *Prix Nobel en 1923,* p.74, Strindberg was replaced here by the Norwegian writer and politician Björnstjerne Björnson, the 1903 Nobel laureate for literature; Bramsbäck notes that all newspaper reports listed Strindberg (p. 300, n. 8).

24. Louise Mountbatten (1889–1965) married 3 November 1923, in London, to Crown Prince Gustav Adolf (1882–1973), whose first wife had died in 1920. The couple returned to Stockholm 11

December 1923. He reigned as King Gustavus Adolphus VI, 1950–73.

25. For the Royal Palace, see note 26 below.

26. The Royal Palace, Stockholm, designed by Nicodemus Tessin, was constructed 1690–1710, 1728, 1750s, 1770s, and 1850s; for a 1901 photo, see *Dictionary of Art,* XXIX, 689. The Ulster Bank building, designed by Vincent Craig (1869–1925), was built in 1905 as a branch of the Belfast Banking Company; it now houses the Yeats Society of Sligo.

27. Mother Ireland: the 'abstract cause' of nationalism imagined as devotion to a woman; e.g., Cathleen ni Houlihan.

28. Irish emigrés or 'Wild Geese', who offered their services to and became part of seventeenth- and eighteenth-century continental armies.

29. Lady Gregory

30. Pietro Bembo (1470–1547), Italian writer and ecclesiastic, who speaks at length about Platonic love in Book IV of Castiglione's *The Courtier;* see note 24, p. 506. above. The quotation is untraced.

31. Ben Jonson, 'Dedication' to *Cynthia's Revels* (1600); *Ben Johnson,* ed. C. H. Herford and Percy Simpson (Oxford: Clarendon, 1932) (O'Shea no. 1029), V, 33.

32. The Order of Merit (O.M.), a strictly limited English order for eminence in any field, instituted in 1902, was awarded to Thomas Hardy in 1911.

33. The Gaelic poem is untraced. A Benedictine (and later Augustinian) nunnery on Iona (or Hy), Scotland, a small island in southern Inner Hebrides off the southwestern tip of Mull Island, famous as the site of St. Columba's Abbey (founded A.D. 563), was established c. 1200 and continued into the sixteenth century.

34. Laurence Binyon, *Painting in the Far East* (London: Edward Arnold, 1908), p. 93 n.

35. WBY had used this anecdote in his introduction to Rabindranath Tagore's *Gitanjali (Song Offerings)* (1912) (P&I 166), where he identified the speaker as Laurence Binyon (1869–1943), Keeper of Oriental Prints and Drawings in the Department of Prints and Drawings, British Museum.

36. Lily Yeats, in an unpublished letter to Ruth Pollexfen Lane-Poole, 26 December (1923), identifies him as the English physiologist Archibald V. Hill (1886–1977), co-winner of the 1922 Nobel Prize for physiology (awarded 1923)—'an amazing specimen, Willy says'. Her detailed account adds, 'I forget if it was the English Ambassador or one of the ministers who conveyed Willy to and fro in his motor and Mr. Hill, but after his last remark he

collected Willy and went off with him, leaving Mr. Hill to find his own way' (transcription William M. Murphy).

37. The National Museum was built 1846–66 by F. A. Stäler. Prince Eugene's Waldemarsudde overlooking Saltsjön is a house turned into a gallery. For the Thiel Gallery, see note 41 below.

38. The foremost impressionists included Edgar Degas, Claude Monet, Berthe Morisot, Camille Pissarro, Pierre-Auguste Renoir, and Alfred Sisley. WBY probably included Édouard Manet, whose work inspired the impressionist style, but who refused to so label his own work.

39. For William Blake (1757–1827), see notes 91, p. 450 and 72, p. 477, Background Notes on Writers, p. 531, and LE 418 n. 1.

No painting by the French painter Jean Auguste Dominique Ingres (1780–1867) shows Perseus, the Greek mythological hero who rescued Andromeda from a dragon. But Ronald Schuchard, quoting an unpublished letter, WBY to Mabel Dickinson, 20 June 1908, establishes that WBY saw this so-called *Perseus* of Ingres in the Louvre. Schuchard convincingly identifies the *Perseus* as Ingres's *Roger Freeing Angelica* (1819), Louvre, Paris, and notes that it illustrates an episode from Ariosto's *Orlando Furioso* (1532), Canto X, stanzas 92 ff., and was based on the myth of Perseus and Andromeda ('Yeats, Titian and the New French Paintings' in *Yeats the European*, pp. 152, 307 n. 27, and color illustration between pp. 142–43 of a smaller copy by Ingres in the National Gallery, London (no. 3292), *Angelica saved by Ruggiero*.

Puvis de Chavannes (1824–98), French decorative painter, best known for his murals, which WBY praised in 1911 (UP2 398–99), 1916 (E&I 236), and 1938 (LE 249). WBY's friends Charles Ricketts, Charles Shannon, and John Quinn owned a number of Puvis de Chavannes's paintings and drawings.

Dante Gabriel Rossetti (1828–82), English painter and poet, was a founder of the Pre-Raphaelite Brotherhood in 1848. After 1870, he was increasingly afflicted by insomnia and a dependence on chloral and whiskey; he attempted suicide in 1872 and spent most of the last eight years of his life in dejected isolation. For his paintings, see notes 5, p. 440; 50, p. 446; and 36, p. 473. above, and LE 417–18 n. 1.

George Frederick Watts (1817–1904), English painter of portraits, which WBY admired, and allegorical pictures, which WBY disliked. See LE 217, 417 n. 1, Introduction (dated 1937) in E&I vii: 'When I was thirty I thought the best of modern pictures were four or five portraits by Watts (I disliked his allegorical pictures—had not allegory spoiled Edmund Spenser?)'

Gustave Moreau (1826–98), French painter who combined academic style with intensely symbolistic and romantic subjects. See pp. 248 above and WBY's letter to Mabel Dickinson, 20 June 1908 (quoted by Ronald Schuchard, 'Yeats, Titian and the New French Paintings', in *Yeats the European*, p. 152), describing his earlier fascination with all that is mysterious, religious, and gothic in Moreau's paintings. In a diary entry that same year, WBY recalled that in the 1890s 'those pictures would have been to me as mystic gates that would make me long for [an] instant in the shadow of a Pyramid, that I might pause there and meet the gods and speak to them face to face' ('Discoveries: Second Series', in *The Irish Renaissance*, ed. Robin Skelton and David R. Clark [Dublin: Dolmen Press, 1965], p. 85).

In 1917, WBY planned an illustrated lecture and purchased lantern slides of five small wood engravings and two engravings by Edward Calvert (English, 1799–1883), inspired by Blake's pastoral illustrations to Virgil: 'The Ploughman' (also known as 'Christian Ploughing the Last Furrow of Life') (1827), 'The Bride' (1828), 'The Sheep of His Pasture' (1828), 'Ideal Pastoral Life' (1829), 'The Brook' (1829), 'The Return Home' (1830), and 'The Chamber Idyll' (1831); illus. Raymond Lister, *Edward Calvert* (London: Bell, 1962), pp. 100–5 (6, 8, 9A, 11, 12A, 14A, and 15A) and plates XVII, XXIII, XXVII–III, XXX, XXXV–VII, and XL.

Charles Ricketts (1866–1931), English artist, book designer, and collector. For illustrations of his ink drawings reproduced in Oscar Wilde's *The Sphinx* (London: Elkin Mathews and John Lane, 1894), which Ricketts considered his own best drawings, and his wood engravings for T. Sturge Moore's *Danaë: A Poem* (London: Vale Press, 1903), see Stephen Calloway, *Charles Ricketts: Subtle and Fantastic Decorator* (London: Thames and Hudson, 1979), plates 29–40, 64. WBY praised these same examples in V(1925) 208 and V 298.

40. Claude Monet's series of at least fifteen oil paintings entitled *Poplars* (1891); thirteen are illus. in Paul H. Tucker, *Monet in the '90s: The Series Paintings* (New Haven: Yale University Press and Boston Museum of Fine Arts, 1989), plates 33–45.

41. The Swedish painter Eugène Jansson (Janson) (1862–1915) painted dawn and evening twilight landscapes in the 1890s, such as *Riddarfjärden in Stockholm* (1898), oil on canvas, 1.5 m. x 1.35 m., National Museum, Stockholm, illus. *Dictionary of Art*, XVII, 8. Jansson's patron Ernest Thiel (1859–1947), a wealthy Stockholm banker, had established the Thiel Gallery in his private villa in Djurgåden, Stockholm. In 1924, after his bankruptcy, he sold it and his collection to the state; the gallery

opened to the public in 1926.

42. For Jack B. Yeats, see note 108, p. 427.

43. The Swedish painter Ernst Josephson (1851–1906), whose portraits were influenced by Manet, has been described as combining 'a freely executed impressionistic treatment of the background with foreground accessories and facial features executed in sensitive detail to interpret spiritual mood' (*Dictionary of Art,* XVII, 662). The National Museum, Stockholm, has several of his portraits.

44. Untraced.

45. For the difference between the quoted passage here and in the closing sentences of 'The Irish Dramatic Movement' (p. 418 below), see WBY's note below.

46. The Stockholm City Hall (built 1911–23) was designed by Ragnar Östberg (1866–1945); for an illustration, see note 49 below. For the Royal Palace, see note 26 above.

47. In *A Vision* (1925, rev. 1937), WBY described Byzantium during the sixth century and following, as possessing a unity of culture: 'I think that in early Byzantium, maybe never before or since in recorded history, religious, aesthetic and practical life were one, that architect and artificers . . . spoke to the multitude and the few alike' (V[1925] 191 and V 279).

48. Pennsylvania Railroad Station, New York, built 1906–10, was designed by the firm McKim, Mead, and White, headed by Charles F. McKim (1847–1909), William R. Mead (1846–1928), and Howard Judson White (1870–1936). It was designed to be impressive for its colossal scale and extravagant size and materials, and severe decoration; its main waiting room has a 150-foot-high ceiling and no seats. See Carroll L. V. Meeks, *The Railroad Station: An Architectural History* (New Haven: Yale University Press, 1956), figs. 164–66, 173. Westminster Cathedral (Roman Catholic), built 1895–1903, in Victoria Street, near Victoria Station, was designed by John Francis Bentley (1839–1902); it is a unique great example of the revival of Byzantine architecture. The cladding of this brick structure with marble and mosaics has been only half carried out because of the lack of funds, but the Lady Chapel has gold mosaics. Eric Gill designed the Stations of the Cross, mounted on the main piers of the nave, during World War I. See Edward Jones and Christopher Woodward, *A Guide to the Architecture of London* (London: Weidenfeld and Nicolson, 1983), p. 227 and plate K118m.

49. The large Assembly Room, known as the 'Golden Chamber' or 'Golden Room', is richly decorated with mosaic murals; illus. *Sir Banister Fletcher's A History of Architecture,* 18th edition, ed. J. C. Palmes (London: University of London, Atholone Press,

1975), p. 1217. German artisans executed the mosaics from designs by the Swedish artist Einar Forseth (b. 1892) (Birgit Bramsbäck, 'Yeats and the "Bounty of Sweden" ', in *Yeats the European*, p. 96).

'THE IRISH DRAMATIC MOVEMENT'

1. WBY'S NOTE
   (publ. only in *Bounty of Sweden* Cuala 1925, p. 49):

   No man can receive a Nobel prize unless his name has been sent to the Swedish Academy by the committees of the country whose citizen he is. The Swedish Academy need not reward a man so chosen but it cannot reward a man not so chosen. I draw attention to this matter, because now that there is a separate Irish citizenship, there should perhaps be separate Irish committees. I understand that my name was sent to Sweden some years ago.

2. In 1893; see note 22, p. 493.
3. For WBY's accounts of the Irish Literary Society (London) and the National Literary Society (Dublin), both founded in 1892, see pp. 169–191 above.
4. For Lady Gregory, see note 48, p. 489. Her family home was Roxborough House, Co. Galway, ten miles from Coole Park. Roxborough House was looted and burned in 1922 during the Irish Civil War.
5. For Thoor Ballylee, see note 2, p. 439.
6. WBY writes of Mary Hynes in 'Dust Hath Closed Helen's Eye' (1899) Myth 22–30 and 'The Tower' (w. 1925, publ. 1927) P 195. In the (1932/1936) proofs, WBY marked this sentence and the following one for deletion, to be replaced with an ellipsis 'because a similar passage occurs in "The Celtic Twilight",' but the passage was restored in copyediting.
7. Lady Gregory's version, 'Raftery's Praise of Mary Hynes', in her *The Kiltartan Poetry Book* (Dublin: Cuala Press, 1918), pp. 5–6.
8. WBY'S NOTE
   (publ. only in *Bounty of Sweden* Cuala 1925, pp. 50–51 and Auto 1955, pp. 579–80):
   I was in my Galway house during the first months of civil war,[a] the railway bridges blown up and the roads blocked with stones and trees. For the first week there were no newspapers, no reliable news, we did not know who had won nor who had

lost, and even after newspapers came, one never knew what was happening on the other side of the hill or of the line of trees. Ford cars passed the house from time to time with coffins standing upon end between the seats, and sometimes at night we heard an explosion, and once by day saw the smoke made by the burning of a great neighbouring house. Men must have lived so through many tumultuous centuries. One felt an overmastering desire not to grow unhappy or embittered, not to lose all sense of the beauty of nature. A stare (our West of Ireland name for a starling) had built in a hole beside my window and I made these verses out of the feeling of the moment:

The bees build in the crevices
Of loosening masonry, and there
The mother birds bring grubs and flies.
My wall is loosening; honey bees,
Come build in the empty house of the stare.

We are closed in, and the key is turned
On our uncertainty; somewhere
A man is killed, or a house is burned,
Yet no clear fact to be discerned:
Come build in the empty house of the stare.[b]

That is only the beginning but it runs on in the same mood. Presently a strange thing happened. I began to smell honey in places where honey could not be, at the end of a stone passage or at some windy turn of the road, and it came always with certain thoughts. When I got back to Dublin I was with angry people who argued over everything or were eager to know the exact facts: in the midst of the mood that makes realistic drama.

[a]WBY, with his wife and two infant children, lived at Thoor Ballylee, March–September 1922, during the Irish Civil War (June 1922–April 1923); the stone bridge beside Thoor Ballylee was blown up by Republican troops on 19 August 1922

[b]'Meditations in Time of Civil War: VI. The Stare's Nest by My Window' (w. 1922, publ. 1923), ll. 1–10 P 204–05.

9. WBY'S NOTE

(publ. only in *Les Prix Nobel en 1923* [Stockholm, 1924; Wade no. 316]; in *Les Prix Nobel en 1923: The Irish Dramatic Movement* [Stockholm, 1924; Wade no. 144]; and in *Bounty of Sweden* Cuala 1925, pp. 51–52. This note was not published in *Dramatis Personae* 1936 or subsequently):

Our first performances were paid for by Mr. Edward Martyn a Galway land owner with a house part fourteenth century, part a pretentious modern Gothic once dear to Irish Catholic families. He had a great hall, adorned with repeating patterns by that dreary decorator Crace, where he played Palestrina upon an organ, and a study, with pictures of the poets in poor stained glass, where he read Ibsen and the Fathers of the Church and nothing else. A sensible friendly man with intelligence, strength of purpose and a charming manner, he shrank from women like a medieval monk and between him & all experience came one overwhelming terror—'If I do such and such a thing or read such & such a book I may lose my soul.' My 'Countess Cathleen' and a play of his own were our first performances. My play's heroine, having sold her soul to the devil, gets it back again because 'God only sees the motive not the deed' and her motive had been to save a starving people from selling their souls for their bodies' sake. When all our announcements had been made Martyn withdrew his support because a priest told him that the play was heretical. I got two priests to say that it was not, and he was satisfied for we have all democratic ideals. He withdrew permanently however after a few months, foreseeing further peril to his soul. He died a couple of months ago and with him died a family founded in the twelfth century. An unhappy, childless, unfinished, laborious man, typical of an Ireland that is passing away.

10. The Ormonde Dramatic Society, run by W. G. and Frank Fay.
11. W. G. and Frank Fay. Frank was secretary to an accounting firm, and his brother had toured Ireland with a production of *Uncle Tom's Cabin,* headed by the African-American actor R. B. Lewis.
12. The 'little political society' was Inghinidhe na hÉireann, or the Daughters of Erin, formed in 1900 with Maud Gonne as president. This nationalist organization for young women held classes, the most popular of which was the dramatics class. Maire nic Shiubhlaigh (Mary Walker; see note 60, p. 515), Sara Allgood (see note 14, p. 510), and Maire T. Quinn (d. 1947) attended, and all became actresses.
13. Synge's *In the Shadow of the Glen* was first produced at the Molesworth Hall, Dublin, on 8 October 1903 by the Irish National Theatre Society. There ensued a controversy over the play led by Arthur Griffith's attacks in the *United Irishman* and others in the *Irish Independent*. WBY was allowed his say in the *United Irishman* (10, 17, 24 October). He wrote three essays in defence of the play, two of which are reprinted in Ex 114–8, 119–23. His last, 'The Irish National Theatre and Three Sorts of

Ignorance', is reprinted in UP2 306–8. The dispute began all over
again with the revival of the play on 27 December 1904.

14. Synge's source was Aran islander Pat Dirane; the story was
published in Synge's book *The Aran Islands* (1907). For the
press controversy, see WBY's letters to the *United Irishman*
(28 January and 4, 11 February 1905), UP2 331–38.

15. In the 'Kiltartan' dialect, as Lady Gregory fashioned it. Her
Twenty-Five was produced 14 March 1903, along with WBY's
The Hour-Glass.

16. *Spreading the News* was performed for the opening of the Abbey,
27 December 1904.

17. The *Irish Times* attacked Lady Gregory's new play, *The Rising of
the Moon* (first performed 9 March 1907) for impunging the
Royal Irish Constabulary: 'Abbey Theatre', 11 March 1907, p. 7;
quoted in Robert Hogan and James Kilroy, *The Abbey Theatre:
The Years of Synge, 1905–1909,* vol. 3 of *Modern Irish Drama:
A Documentary History* (Dublin: Dolmen, 1978), 173.

18. Dublin Castle, center of British administration in Ireland.

19. WBY'S NOTE
(publ. only in Bounty of Sweden Cuala 1925, pp. 52–53 and
Auto 1955, pp. 580–81):

> Josef Strzygowski in his *Origin of Christian Church Art* (a
> translation of a series of lectures delivered in Uppsala in 1919)
> says that art 'flourished less at courts than anywhere else in
> the world. For at the seat of power everything is subordinated
> to politics; the forces willing to accept this fact are always wel-
> come; those which are not willing must either emigrate or
> remain aloof.'[a] The danger to art and literature comes to-day
> from the tyrannies and persuasions of revolutionary societies
> and from forms of political and religious propaganda. The
> persuasion has corrupted much modern English literature,
> and—during the twenty years that led up to national revolu-
> tion—the tyranny wasted the greater part of the energy of
> Irish dramatists and poets. They had to remain perpetually on
> the watch to defend their creation, and the more natural the
> creation the more difficult the defence.
>
> [a] Josef Strzygowski (1862–1941), Austrian art critic and histo-
> rian, *Origin of Christian Church Art: New Facts and Principles
> of Research. Eight lectures delivered for the Olaus Petri Founda-
> tion at Uppsala (1919), to which is added a chapter on Christian
> Art in Britain,* tr. from the German by O. M. Dalton and
> H. T. Braunholtz (Oxford: Clarendon, 1923) (O'Shea no. 2026),
> p. 48.

20. Annie E. F. Horniman (1860–1937), English patron and member of the Golden Dawn, made the offer after WBY addressed the audience after the curtain of Synge's *In the Shadow of the Glen* on 20 October 1903; she had designed the costumes for WBY's *The King's Threshold*, produced with Synge's play. For the controversy about *In the Shadow of the Glen*, see note 13 above. The Abbey Theatre opened in December 1904 and her subsidies continued until 1910.

21. Dr. James Cree; see note 94, p. 480.

22. J. M. Synge; see note 98, p. 480.

23. August 1896; see note 95, p. 480.

24. *The Playboy of the Western World,* completed in 1904 and produced in January 1907.

25. *Cathleen ni Houlihan* (produced 1902) and *The Hour-Glass* (prose version, produced 1903).

26. Lennox Robinson's three-act comedy *The Whiteheaded Boy* (1916) was his most successful play.

27. WBY'S NOTE
    (w. 1924, publ. in *Les Prix Nobel en 1923* [Stockholm, 1924; Wade no. 316]; in *Les Prix Nobel en 1923: The Irish Dramatic Movement* [Stockholm, 1924; Wade no. 144]; and in Bounty of Sweden Cuala 1925, pp. 53–54. This note was not published in Dramatis Personae 1936 or subsequently):

    > Since I gave my lecture we have produced 'Juno and the Paycock' by Mr. O'Casey, the greatest success we have had for years. In this play, which draws its characters and scenes from the Dublin slums, a mind not unlike that of Dostoevsky looks upon the violence and tragedy of civil war. There is assassination, sudden poverty, and the humour of drunkards and the philosophy of wastrels, and there is little but the out-worn theme of seduction, and perhaps a phrase or two of mechanical humour, to show that its author has not finished his artistic education. He is a working bricklayer who was taken out to be shot by English soldiers in mistake for somebody else, but escaped in a moment of confusion. He knows thoroughly the life which he describes.

28. WBY'S NOTE
    (dated 15 June 1924; publ. only in Bounty of Sweden Cuala 1925, p. 54):
    > I wrote out my lecture from memory, and now that I have read it through I notice that I wrote this passage differently in 'The Bounty of Sweden.'[a] I was excited and spoke on the spur of the moment, and cannot remember accurately what I said.

ᵃThe two versions of the passage mentioned here are the closing four sentences, respectively, of *The Bounty of Sweden,* section XII (pp. 406:08–406:12 above) and of 'The Irish Dramatic Movement' (pp. 418:17–418:31 above).

EMENDATIONS TO THE COPY-TEXT

FORMAT:

Page.Line	Reading in this edition] Reading in copy-text } Authority for emendation
51.26	countrypeople] country people } All 4 other instances
157.25	convictions] eonvictions } *Four Years* Cuala 1921, *Trembling* 1922, *Auto* 1926, 1932–36 page proofs
204.9	*Love Songs*] *Love-Songs* } Book title and 324.31
241.3	day-spring] dayspring } None
290.25	monk-like] monklike } None
295.33	early 'eighties] early' eighties } *Dramatis Personae* 1936
332.24	dream-like] dreamlike } None
334.26	Yeats's] Yeats' } None
386.31	mind. All] mind All } *Dramatis Personae* Cuala 1935, *Dramatis Personae* 1936
388.4	*S.S. Zeeland.*] S.S. 'Zeeland'. } None
401.32	Queen, granddaughter] Queen, grand-/daughter } 13 of 16 instances
401.33–34	great-granddaughter (printed as: great-grand-daughter)] great-grand-daughter } 13 of 16 instances
401.34	great-great-granddaughter] great-great-grand-/daughter } 13 of 16 instances
438.29 (note 214)	divined] devined } *Reveries* 1916
515.28 (note 1)	added thereto certain] added there / to certain } None
524.15 (note 9)	their bodies' sake] their bodies sake } None

END-OF-LINE WORD-DIVISION
IN THE COPY-TEXT

Autobiographies (London: Macmillan, 1955)

I. List of copy-text hyphens that happen to occur at line endings in this edition; each of these is hyphenated in this edition and in the copy-text (*Autobiographies* 1955). The format is: Page.Line in this edition Reading in this edition

43.28 stable- / yard; 50.7 passer- / by; 50.24 oldest- / looking; 50.34 great- / great-grandfather; 52.9 great- / uncle; 54.29 many- / vol-umed; 55.35 bed- / ridden; 56.12 landscape- / painters; 60.38 knee- / breeches; 65.24 school- / fellows; 68.18 stable- / boy's; 71.36 her-ring- / fishing; 74.25 playing- / field; 75.1 natural- / history; 79.4 spirit- / mischief; 81.17 Pre- / Raphaelite; 83.39 foreign- / looking; 85.23 wood- / ranger; 92.19 such-and / -such; 93.25 white- / haired; 113.8 horse- / chestnut; 114.31 well- / drilled; 116.9 broad- / headed; 119.12 Reading- / Room; 121.5 Bastien- / Lepage; 123.32 poppy- / juice; 126.30 Pre- / Raphaelitism; 143.17 window- / sills; 150.23 Bastien- / Lepage; 159.19 thirty- / six; 165.19 subject- / mat-ter; 169.12 shop- / boys; 169.24 London- / Irish; 172.6 wolf- / dog; 172.33 well- / known; 172.34 love- / poetry; 175.12 wine- / mer-chant; 175.19 tombstone- / maker; 177.36 book- / stalls; 180.7 folk- / lore; 182.18 breakfast- / table; 184.25 Graeco- / Roman; 186.15 white- / haired; 191.26 self- / immolation; 204.20 wood- / grown; 207.6 dining- / room; 213.35 folk-images; 223.7 self- / pos-session; 229.16 dinner- / table; 235.14 eating- / house; 236.12 man- / servant; 238.22 semi- / colon; 241.23 clearly- / marked; 245.27 screwed- / up; 259.6 milk- / boy; 260.14 sitting- / room; 265.19 French- / American; 269.36 re- / state; 273.18 over- / taxation; 274.11 self- / creating; 247.25 foundation- / stone; 286.1 Shawe- / Taylor; 289.11 sight- / seeing; 300.27 half- / sirs; 304.3 water- / colours; 312.27 So- / and-so; 321.1 half-a- / crown; 321.8 well- / known; 341.21 money- / changers; 359.3 lower- / middle; 385.12 crime- / haunted; 401.32 great-grand- / daughter; 403.35 mask- / makers

II. End-of-line word-division in the copy-text that could affect hyphen-ation in this edition. The format is: Page.Line in this edition Reading in this edition] Reading in the copy-text Page.Line in copy-text (*Auto-biographies* 1955)

113.6 red-brick] red- / brick 113.6; 120.28 window-sill] window- / sill 124.15; 127.22 terracotta] terra- / cotta 134.27; 129.17 folk-story] folk- / story 137.23; 143.2 barefooted] bare- / footed 158.16;

149.28 public-house] public- / house 168.17; 154.27 dumb-bell] dumb- / bell 175.17; 157.19 overhear] over- / hear 179.26; 158.16 upstairs] up- / stairs 181.7; 160.3 white-haired] white- / haired 184.5; 165.19 subject- / matter] subject- / matter 191.28; 167.10 day-labourer] day- / labourer 194.13; 170.7 publishing-house] publishing- / house 200.18; 171.34 Committee-room] Committee- / room 203.7; 172.35 love-songs] love- / songs 204.23; 175.12 wine-merchant] wine- / merchant 208.9; 177.32 second-hand] second- / hand 212.3; 182.3 folk-genius] folk- / genius 218.23; 187.28 committee-room] committee- / room 227.2; 190.23 goldsmiths] gold- / smiths 231.14; 191.26 self- / immolation] self- / immolation 233.1; 194.23 red-haired] red- / haired 237.19; 208.20 badly-carved] badly- / carved 259.19; 210.21 self-analysing] self- / analysing 262.22; 211.28 subconscious] sub- / conscious 264.19; 213.37 long-bodied] long- / bodied 267.30; 218.1 Gate-keepers] Gate- / keepers 274.4; 220.17 Demeter-like] Demeter- / like 280.30; 226.39 steam-engine] steam- / engine 290.30; 233.18 money-making] money- / making 300.11; 235.14 eating-house] eating- / house 303.6; 238.23 semi-colon] semi- / colon 308.1; 240.26 restaurant-keeper's] restaurant- / keeper's 311.6; 245.27 magnifying-glass] magnifying- / glass 318.12; 275.8 outface] out- / face 365.1; 280.6 subconscious] sub- / conscious 372.6; 290.33 drawing-room] drawing- / room 389.10; 296.25 De-Anglicisation] De- / Anglicisation 396.18; 299.25 witch-doctor] witch- / doctor 401.3; 301.35 conscience-struck] conscience- / struck 404.18; 316.32 Torquemada] Torque- / mada 427.10; 317.13 self-abnegation] self- / abnegation 428.4; 319.27 Anglo-American] Anglo- / American 431.21; 321.35 curd-pale] curd- / pale 435.5; 322.35 Pre-Raphaelite] Pre- / Raphaelite 436.19; 325.5 game-keeper] game- / keeper 439.30; 331.9 well-founded] well- / founded 449.5; 334.29 self-righteous] self- / righteous 454.15; 344.16 self-realization] self- / realization 465.22; 345.27 pre-occupation] pre- / occupation 467.14; 346.12 art-schools] art- / schools 468.3; 378.16 self-assertion] self- / assertion 512.10; 385.11 storm-beaten] storm- / beaten 522.5; 387.23 self-educating] self- / educating 525.19; 399.21 good-will] good- / will 543.19; 399.27 throne-room] throne- / room 543.26; 400.8 throne-room] throne- / room 544.18; 401.18 granddaughters] grand- / daughters 546.16; 401.32 granddaughter] grand- / daughter 547.2; 405.1 booksellers'] book- / sellers' 551.31; 405.2 paper-covered] paper- / covered 552.1; 405.12 pre-occupied] pre- / occupied 552.13; 408.20 barefooted] bare- / footed 557.11; 411.16 sub - / ject-matter] subject- / matter 560.27; 413.20 folk-song] folk- / song 564.2; 418.6 *White-headed*] *White- / headed* 571.11

BACKGROUND NOTES ON WRITERS

Arnold, Matthew (1822–88). British poet and critic, son of Thomas Arnold (the famous headmaster of Rugby), Professor of Poetry at Oxford from 1857 to 1867. In some important matters, WBY defined himself in distinction to Arnold. Arnold's relationship to his father became a type of nineteenth-century Oedipal drama, and WBY inevitably saw his own relationship to JBY against this background. He owned and marked a copy of Arnold's *On the Study of Celtic Literature* (1867) and developed and promoted his own different program. He resisted Arnold's and his era's crisis of religious faith, rationalistic response, and adaptability of Christianity to science, but shared Arnold's inclination to substitute poetry for dogma. As a senator studying education in Ireland, WBY remembered that Arnold had been an inspector of schools from 1851 until 1883 and enjoyed the similarity. Arnold's immensely influential criticism includes *On the Study of Celtic Literature* (1867), *Essays in Criticism* (First Series, 1865; Second Series, 1888), *Culture and Anarchy* (1869).

Blake, William (1757–1827). English artist, poet, visionary. The major works, most of which first appeared as engravings with complex illustrations, include: *Songs of Innocence* (1789), *The Book of Thel* (1789), *The Marriage of Heaven and Hell* (1790), *The French Revolution* (1791), *America* (1793), *Visions of the Daughters of Albion* (1793), *Songs of Experience* (1794), *The Book of Urizen* (1794), *The Book of Los* (1795), *Vala; or The Four Zoas* (1797), *Milton* (1808), *Jerusalem* (1804–20). Blake also designed and engraved illustrations of other texts, e.g. Edward Young's *Night Thoughts* (1795–97), the Book of Job (1826), and the *Divine Comedy* (1825–26).

WBY and Edwin J. Ellis began work on 'The Prophetic Books of William Blake' in 1889 and published *The Works of William Blake, Poetic, Symbolic, and Critical* (London: Bernard Quaritch) in 1893. WBY contributed primarily to volume one, *The System*, including 'William Blake and the Imagination' and 'William Blake and his Illustrations to the Divine Comedy' (E&I 111–45), and edited *The Poems of William Blake* (1893, 1905).

The importance of Blake to WBY is almost beyond exaggeration. WBY learned from Blake the doctrine of correspondence and the elaboration of a symbolic language. He discovered in Blake an attack on destructive rationality and a cosmology that could withstand rationalism, a coherent mythology that went back through Swedenborg and Boehme to Plato, Plotinus, and the Bible. He found a conception of historical cycles and reversals and a symbolism with which to develop them that defined and continued to inform his own ideas. Blake is a presence in and a pressure on WBY from *The Wanderings of Oisin* to 'The Man and the Echo' (CP 355–86, 345).

The lesson of Blake was also moral and psychic as WBY noted when he wrote (E&I 519) that he owed his soul to Spenser, Shakespeare, Blake and to their language. Blake was poet and genius, sage and visionary, revolutionist and national prophet. During the 1890s, he showed WBY what the young poet wanted to know, at a time when he needed to know it: the ethos and authority of the poet. He insisted upon the autonomy and mystery of art and upon the apocalyptic coming of the kingdom of the imagination. He demonstrated the alchemical powers of mind, that it can fasten onto concreteness and particularity and yet, with perseverance and boldness, transform them; that unaccommodated man, when seen with radical severity and strength, is also an adumbration of the divine. He proved by enactment that there are ways to achieve the imaginative coalescence of opposites, the resurrection into unity out of the fragmented, fallen state of time.

Burke, Edmund (1729–97). Anglo-Irish statesman and writer, the father of modern conservatism. In 1765, he became Secretary to Lord Rockingham (the leader of a Whig faction) and a member of Parliament for Wendover. Burke supported a policy of conciliation with the American colonies and opposed English policy and practice in Ireland, urging instead free trade, Catholic emancipation, and legislative independence. His most famous and influential writings are those written at the end of his life to attack the French Revolution and its implications for England, Ireland, and Europe. WBY began reading Burke in the early 1920s, purchased the Bohn's Standard Library edition, read widely and marked many passages, particularly in *An Appeal from the New to the Old Whigs* (1791), which was, according to Mrs. Yeats, his political bible. He also read and marked *Thoughts on the Cause of the Present Discontents* (1770); some of the speeches about Hastings and India; *Reflections on the Revolution in Frocce* (1790); *Reflections on French Affairs* (1791); and *A Letter to a Noble Lord* (1796). He was probably familiar with the *Speech on Conciliation with the Colonies* (1774), the *Letter to the Sheriffs of Bristol* (1777), and the *Letters on a Regicide Peace* (1795–7). He knew many of the Burke anecdotes and said, in a Senate speech of 1924, that Burke's hurling a scalping knife onto the floor of Parliament was 'a fact which has been burning in my imagination' (SS 88). Burke is explicitly invoked in the three Georgian poems—'The Tower', 'Blood and the Moon', and 'The Seven Sages' (P 194, 237, 241); he was included in an early draft of 'The Second Coming'; and he is implied or echoed in several other poems. WBY mentions him in *Autobiographies* and some letters, is preoccupied by him in the *1930 Diary* (Ex 289–340), discusses him in the essays on Swift (Ex 343–69) and Berkeley (LE 103–12), and raises his example in three Senate speeches, a lecture, and *On the Boiler* (LE 220–51).

Burns, Robert (1759–96). Scottish poet, songwriter, and tune collector; he was also a farmer, exciseman, exuberant lover, hard drinker, and sympathetic observer of revolutionary events in France. He was a cultural nationalist whose irreverence toward England and established authority and celebration of verse, song, whiskey, and sex allowed WBY to see him as an antithetical figure. His ballads really did enter popular culture.

Coleridge, Samuel T. (1772–1834). British poet, critic, and philosopher. Friend and collaborator with Wordsworth, especially in the epoch-making *Lyrical Ballads* (1798). His most famous poems are 'The Ancient Mariner', 'Kubla Khan', 'Christabel', and the 'conversation' poems like 'Frost at Midnight'. His influential critical work, *The Biographia Literaria,* was published in 1817. WBY's library included Coleridge's major writings. He embodies for WBY a search for harmony and beauty, balance and synthesis, even at the cost of personal suffering. As an effort against scientific rationalism and naturalism in literature, and for mystery and religious belief, Coleridge's study of the imagination is similar to WBY's researches in the occult, and his symbolic visions of history anticipate *A Vision.* The depth of Coleridge's influence can be seen through a comparison of 'Frost at Midnight' and 'A Prayer for my Daughter' (P 188).

Dante Alighieri (1265–1321). Italian poet whose *Divine Comedy* is the supreme poem of medieval synthesis and harmony and of autobiography set in universal terms. WBY also knew the *Vita Nuova* ('New Life') and *Convivio* ('Banquet'). Dante informs WBY's writing in several thematic ways: the experience and idea of exile; sexual desire and romantic love as a way toward spiritual salvation; a sense of personal harmony, fullness, or 'Unity of Being'; the discovery of self through the encounter with an antithetical or opposite self. See 'Ego Dominus Tuus,' P (160).

Goldsmith, Oliver (1730?–74). English writer, son of a Church of Ireland clergyman born in Longford or Roscommon and educated at Trinity College, Dublin. He wandered about Europe, apparently obtained a medical degree, arrived in London penniless in 1756, and struggled to stay out of debtors' prison for the rest of his life as a physician and writer. His major works include the play *She Stoops to Conquer* (1773), the novel *The Vicar of Wakefield* (1766), and two poems, 'The Traveller' (1764) and 'The Deserted Village' (1770). Goldsmith became part of the 'scheme of intellectual nationalisms' WBY was proposing to his country during the 1920s but did not assume the prominence of his other exemplars: '. . . now I read Swift for months together, Burke and Berkeley less often but always with excitement, and Goldsmith lures and waits' (Ex 344). See *Pages from a Diary Written in Nineteen Hundred and Thirty* and the 'Introduction' to *The Words upon the Window-pane*, Ex 287–369, and 'Blood and the Moon' and 'The Seven Sages' (P 237, 241).

Hyde, Douglas (1860–1949). Gaelic revivalist, poet, and first President of Ireland. He was born at Frenchpark, County Roscommon, where he learned Irish from old native speakers and recorded folktales and poetry from this oral tradition. He received his LL.D. from Trinity College in 1888, was elected President of the Gaelic League when it was founded in 1893, and advocated keeping the language alive and in use. His folk-tales influenced and were used by WBY, Lady Gregory, George Russell, and George Moore. Hyde was Professor of Modern Irish at University College, Dublin, and was appointed a senator of the Irish Free State in 1925 and 1927 and the first President of Ireland in 1937, staying in office until 1945. His works include *Beside the Fire* (1890), *Love Songs of Connacht* (1893), *The Story of Early Gaelic Literature* (1895), *Literary History of Ireland* (1899), *Medieval Tales from the Irish* (1899), a selection of his Irish poems (1900), a collection of Irish plays (1905), and *Religious Songs of Connacht* (1906). WBY reviewed *Beside the Fire, Love Songs of the Connacht,* and *The Story of Early Gaelic Literature* (UP1 186–90, 292–5, 358–9).

Joyce, James (1882–1941). Irish novelist and, with WBY, the preeminent literary imagination of modern Ireland. The major works are *Dubliners* (1914), *A Portrait of the Artist as a Young Man* (1916), *Ulysses* (1922), and *Finnegans Wake* (1939). The drama of WBY and Joyce is most succinctly described by Richard Ellmann in his account of their symbolic meeting of October 1902: 'The defected Protestant confronted the defected Catholic, the landless landlord met the shiftless tenant. WBY, fresh from London, made one in a cluster of writers whom Joyce would never know, while Joyce knew the limbs and bowels of the city of which WBY knew well only the head. The world of the petty bourgeois, which is the world of *Ulysses* and the world in which

Joyce grew up, was for WBY something to be abjured. Joyce had the same contempt for both the ignorant peasantry and the snobbish aristocracy that WBY idealized. The two were divided by upbringing and predilection.' (*James Joyce* [Oxford: New York, 1959]). In spite of his prickly competitiveness and satiric impulse, Joyce genuinely admired WBY and frequently recited his verse from memory. WBY recognized Joyce's genius as well as his arrogance and offered assistance to the younger writer.

Keats, John (1795–1821). English Romantic poet who died of consumption at age twenty-six and left superb letters, a body of imperfect, exciting poetry, and three imperishable Odes of 1819—'On a Grecian Urn', 'To a Nightingale', and 'To Autumn'. WBY's most notorious formulation about Keats, that he made 'luxuriant song' to compensate for poverty, sickness, and ill-breeding ('Ego Dominus Tuus' P 160), reveals more about WBY's dissatisfaction with his early poems than it does about Keats who was a presence in WBY's imagination from the beginning (the language of 'The Wanderings of Oisin') to the end (the movement of 'Lapis Lazuli'). WBY's sense of Keats was filtered through the enthusiasm of his father and William Morris, and three of his doctrines—Unity of Being and poetry as an epiphany and as a perpetual re-creation of the self—are indebted to the earlier poet.

Morris, William (1834–96). British artist, poet, manufacturer, and socialist. At Oxford, he and Edward Burne-Jones were members of 'the Brotherhood', which founded *The Oxford and Cambridge Magazine* in 1856. He met Rossetti in 1857, moving to Red Lion Square, London, with him and Burne-Jones. He married Rossetti's model, Jane Burden, in 1859. About 1860, Morris & Co. was founded, and its products were furniture, embroidery, jewelry, stained glass, metal work, carving, and mural decoration. Morris, sole proprietor by 1874, was also interested in tapestries, textiles, and carpet-weaving. He joined the Democratic Federation in 1883, out of which rose the Socialist League in 1884. *Commonweal* was its paper, and Morris's *A Dream of John Ball* (1888) and *News from Nowhere* (1890) first appeared there. The Kelmscott Press was founded in 1890, and Morris designed the Kelmscott Chaucer from 1893 to 1896. Other major works include: *Defense of Guenevere and Other Poems* (1858), *Earthly Paradise* (poems, 1868–70), *Poems by the Way* (1891), and the prose romances: *The House of Wolfings* (1889), *The Roots of the Mountains* (1890), *The Story of the Glittering Plain* (1891), *The Wood Beyond the World* (1895),*The Well at the World's End* (1896), *The Water of the Wondrous Isles* (1897), *Story of the Sundering Flood* (1898). WBY met Morris in 1885 in Dublin. Later while living at

Bedford Park on 3 Blenheim Road, WBY would visit Morris at nearby
Kelmscott House.

O'Casey, Sean (1884–1964). Irish playwright. O'Casey began submitting plays to the Abbey in 1921 and *The Shadow of a Gunman* was produced in 1923. *Juno and the Paycock* followed in 1924, and *The Plough and the Stars* in 1926, occasioning a riot. O'Casey left for London and submitted *The Silver Tassie* to the Abbey in 1928. The play was rejected, and O'Casey never sought to restore good relations with the Abbey, although the theatre did produce it in 1935. His six-volume autobiography was published between 1939 and 1954.

Pater, Walter (1839–94). English writer. Pater was elected to a fellowship at Brasenose College, Oxford, in 1864 and made his first visit to Italy—and direct encounter with the art of the Italian Renaissance—the following year. The rest of his life is the drama of the ideas of his books; the most influential are *Studies in the History of the Renaissance* (1873), *Marius the Epicurian* (1885), *Imaginary Portraits* (1887), *Appreciations* (1889), and the posthumous *Greek Studies* (1895). His work had an enormous impact on Wilde and other writers of the nineties. His aesthetic philosophy includes a number of ideas that were important to WBY: the sanctity and intensity of the given, particular moment; an emphasis on artistic impression and refining away all that is not essential to it; the conflict or tension inherent in consciousness; the weight of pattern and recurrence.

Shakespeare, William (1564–1616). The plays most frequently mentioned by WBY are *Romeo and Juliet* (1594–5), *Hamlet* (1600–1601), *Othello* (1604–5), *King Lear* (1605–6), and *Antony and Cleopatra* (1606–7). Shakespeare was present in WBY's imagination from boyhood, when his father read passages aloud, to one of his later and most comprehensive poems, 'Lapis Lazuli' (P 294) and one of his last and most personal, 'The Man and the Echo' (P 345). In 1937 he wrote that 'I owe my soul to Shakespeare, to Spenser and to Blake . . .' (E&I 519). Like most original writers, WBY made many things of Shakespeare. He sees him as the end of a medieval and Renaissance synthesis and as the beginning of modern fragmentation. As the two poems mentioned demonstrate, he finds in Shakespeare's plays the fullest and richest embodiment of the tragic—tragic loss, tragic gaiety, and tragic irony: 'Shakespeare's persons, when the last darkness has gathered about them, speak out of an ecstasy that is one-half the self-surrender of sorrow, and one-half the last playing and mockery of the victorious sword before the defeated world' (E&I 254).

Shelley, Percy Bysshe (1792–1822). English romantic poet, visionary, and political radical. The works that most fully reveal Shelley's major influence on WBY include: 'Alastor' (1816), 'The Revolt of Islam' (1818), 'Prince Athanase' (1818), 'Prometheus Unbound' (1819), three lyrics of 1819—'Ode to the West Wind', 'To a Skylark', 'The Cloud',—'Adonais' (1821), 'Epipsychidion' (1821), the prose *Defence of Poetry* (1821), and the lyrical drama *Hellas* (1822). JBY read Shelley aloud as well as Shakespeare; Edward Dowden's failure of sympathy became a measure of Dowden's critical failure; WBY acknowledged his youthful imitations and enjoys the association of his own tower with Shelley's imaginary ones. WBY's interest in the cycles of history and adventures of the soul owes much to Shelley who embodies for WBY both unity of being and the visionary imagination.

Spenser, Edmund (1552?–99). English poet and diplomat. His major poem is the long, complex allegory 'The Faerie Queen' (1589–96); others include 'The Shepheardes Calender' (1579), 'Epithalamion' (1595), and 'Prothalamion' (1596). Spenser was an important and admonitory figure for WBY. He was one of the principal influences on the early poetry (see especially 'The Wanderings of Oisin', P 355–86) and one of the imaginations to whom WBY said he 'owe[d] my soul' (E&I 519). On the other hand, he was secretary to the Lord Deputy of Ireland and an 'undertaker' for the settlement of Munster. His reward was Kilcolman Castle in County Cork, which was burned to the ground in 1598 in one of the insurrections it was his job to suppress. The verse 'Colin Clouts come home againe' (1595) reveals his love of the Irish countryside. The prose *Short View of the Present State of Ireland* (1596) reveals a harsh, almost genocidal assessment of the Irish situation. So Spenser combines the glories of the English language and the burdens of British hegemony in Ireland.

Swift, Jonathan (1667–1745). Dean of St. Patrick's Cathedral, Dublin. Anglo-Irish divine, satirist, and political essayist. His most famous works include *A Tale of a Tub* (1704), *The Drapier's Letters* (1724–5), *Gulliver's Travels* (1726), *A Modest Proposal* (1729), and three volumes of *Poems*. WBY knew some Swift as a schoolboy, read more for essays written or planned in the 1890s and again around 1910. By 1930 his knowledge of Swift and his work was extensive. A substantial portion of the diary he kept in 1930 (Ex 289–340) is devoted to thoughts about Swift and the lessons his writings and example hold for modern Ireland, as are several letters, parts of an essay on Bishop Berkeley (LE 103–12), and a section of his introduction to Brian Merriman's *The Midnight Court* (P&I 159–63). WBY translated Swift's epitaph (P 245) and in 1930 wrote *The Words upon the Win-*

dow-pane (CLP1 595–617), a play about his relationship to Stella and Vanessa, with an 'Introduction' (Ex 343–69) about his philosophy, presence, and importance. Two poems of the period, 'Blood and the Moon' (P 237) and 'The Seven Sages" (P 241) explicitly invoke Swift and his Anglo-Irish contemporaries, and he is a presence behind the outlook and accent of others, most notably 'The Tower' (P 194) and the 'Crazy Jane' series of *Words for Music Perhaps* (P 255–60).

Synge, John Millington (1871–1909). Irish playwright. The memories of Synge's major and controversial career as playwright and as a director of the Abbey, as well as his shortened life, are central to *Autobiographies.* Synge was born in Rathfarnham, County Dublin, educated at Trinity College, Dublin, went to Paris to study at the Sorbonne in 1895, and met WBY and Maud Gonne the following year. He briefly joined L'Association Irlandaise in Paris with Gonne and WBY in 1897, and WBY claims that he was the first to suggest that Synge go to the Aran Islands. Synge returned to Aran for four summers from 1899 to 1902, writing the plays *In the Shadow of the Glen* and *Riders to the Sea* in 1902. The Irish National Theatre Society produced *In the Shadow of the Glen* in 1903, which caused public protest as did *The Playboy of the Western World* in 1907; *Riders to the Sea* was produced in 1904. *The Well of the Saints* was produced at the Abbey in 1905, and Synge travelled with Jack Yeats through the west of Ireland. Synge was engaged to Abbey actress Máire O'Neill (Molly Allgood) in 1906 and died of Hodgkin's disease in Dublin in 1909. Other plays include *The Tinker's Wedding* (1907) and *Deirdre of the Sorrows* (1910). Synge also wrote prose and poetry: *The Aran Islands* (1907), *Poems and Translations* (1909), and *In Wicklow, West Kerry and Connemara* (1910) appearing in the *Collected Works* (1910). See WBY (apart from extended comments on Synge in *Estrangement* and *Synge*): 'J. M. Synge and the Ireland of his Time', E&I 311; 'The Controversy over *The Playboy of the Western World*', Ex 225; 'On those that hated "The Playboy of the Western World," 1907', 'In Memory of Major Robert Gregory', 'The Municipal Gallery Revisited' (P 111, 132, 319.)

Wilde, Oscar (1856–1900). Irish dramatist, poet, and wit. He was educated at Trinity College, Dublin, and Oxford, where he won the Newdigate Prize for poetry in 1879. He arrived in London where he became famous or notorious for his aesthetic philosophy—beauty is the highest good and art the most perfect expression of it—and for his association with the *Savoy* and the *Yellow Book,* journals of *fin de siècle* decadence. His career and social life came to an end in 1895 when he was arrested for sodomy and sentenced to two years' hard labor; he was released in 1897 and lived in Paris until his death. The major works are *Poems* (1881), *The Picture of Dorian Gray* (1891), *Lady Windermere's Fan* (1892), *The Importance of Being Earnest* (1895), *Salomé,* in French (1893), and two long poems written in prison, *The Ballad of Reading Gaol* (1898) and *De Profundis* (1905). Wilde befriended and assisted the young WBY in 1888, and WBY collected letters of sympathy and support during the trials.

Wordsworth, William (1770–1850). English poet whose *Lyrical Ballads* (1798, 1800), written with Coleridge, is frequently seen as the inauguration of the Romantic era in English literature. His most famous and influential poems are the 'Lines: Composed a Few Miles Above Tintern Abbey' (1798) and 'Ode: Intimations of Immortality from Recollections of Early Childhood' (1807), and the long, auto-biographical *The Prelude, or Growth of a Poet's Mind,* written 1799–1805, and posthumously published in 1850. WBY accepted some of his father's antipathy to Wordsworth and reacted similarly to what they both considered Dowden's uncritical praise. He admired the great lyrical moments but thought that Wordsworth, 'after brief blossom' succumbed to imaginative decline, conventional wisdom, and moral rectitude. See section XIII of 'Anima Hominis', *Per Amica Silentia Lunae,* LE 15–16.

INDEX